Photoshop® CS4 Bible

Photoshop® CS4 Bible

Stacy Cates
Simon Abrams
Dan Moughamian

WILEY

Wiley Publishing, Inc.

Photoshop® CS4 Bible

Published by
Wiley Publishing, Inc.
10475 Crosspoint Boulevard
Indianapolis, IN 46256
www.wiley.com

Copyright © 2009 by Wiley Publishing, Inc., Indianapolis, Indiana

Published simultaneously in Canada

ISBN: 978-0-470-34517-7

Manufactured in the United States of America

10 9 8 7 6 5 4 3 2 1

For general information on our other products and services or to obtain technical support, please contact our Customer Care Department within the U.S. at (800) 762-2974, outside the U.S. at (317) 572-3993 or fax (317) 572-4002.

Library of Congress Control Number: 2008941628

Trademarks: Wiley and related trade dress are registered trademarks of Wiley Publishing, Inc., in the United States and other countries, and may not be used without written permission. All other trademarks are the property of their respective owners. Wiley Publishing, Inc., is not associated with any product or vendor mentioned in this book.

Wiley also publishes its books in a variety of electronic formats. Some content that appears in print may not be available in electronic books.

Stacy Cates:

I would like to dedicate this book to my son, Will Cates (a.k.a., the best son in the world), who provided help, love, and support during the writing of this book, and my grandmother, Shirley Boswell (a.k.a., the best grandmother in the world), whose love and prayers never fail.

Simon Abrams:

I would like to dedicate this book to my lovely wife Stephanie — it's a cliché, but I really couldn't have done it without you.

I'd also like to dedicate this book to my father, Donald Abrams, for the opportunities and experiences he made possible for me.

Dan Moughamian:

I'd like to dedicate this book to my colleagues, family, and friends. You have provided opportunity, ideas, and advice throughout my career; I would not be here without you.

About the Authors

Stacy Cates has been in the graphic design and printing industry for more than 20 years. She has been teaching Adobe Photoshop since 2001 and holds Adobe Certified Instructor and Comptia Certified Technical Trainer certifications, as well as a Georgia Institute of Technology Certificate in Web design. Her teaching experience ranges from one-on-one training to teaching college-level computer art courses. Stacy is experienced in a wide variety of practical applications for Photoshop and specializes in preparing images for printing, color correction, and retouching images. Stacy has earned numerous awards for publication design and an award for Web design from the Council for Advancement and Support of Education. Contact Stacey at stacy@stacycates.com

Simon Abrams was smitten with computers ever since the day his dad gave him his first Commodore 64 back in the late '80s. It wasn't until he took a class called *Intro to Microcomputer Graphics* in college that he discovered that the intersection of computers and art was where his true love was to be found. He later attended the Savannah College of Art & Design, where he studied 3D Modeling and Animation. Upon graduating with a BFA in Computer Art, Simon moved to New York City. After a brief stint at Tekserve (New York's premier Mac repair shop), he got a job working as a designer at an interactive advertising agency during the heady dot-com boom of the late '90s. Along the way, he discovered his second love: photography, which he pursues vigorously as a serious amateur around the streets and subways of New York. His photography has been featured on various sites, including Yahoo! News, Gothamist, and Panasonic's Digital Photo Academy.

Simon is an Adobe Certified Photoshop Professional and regularly appears as a guest lecturer teaching Photoshop at New York University's Courant Institute of Mathematical Sciences. He has also led workshops in the theater at Apple's flagship retail location in SoHo, New York. Simon currently lives in Brooklyn, with his wife Stephanie. He recently became a student of karate and works as a Flash developer at an advertising agency in New York City.

Dan Moughamian began exploring Adobe Photoshop in 1993 and never looked back. His passion for digital imaging ultimately led to a career in fine art photography, which continues to present day and has evolved to encompass not only still photography, but video and motion graphics as well. Dan is an accomplished instructor, teaching digital photography and Photoshop classes for Chicago-based venues such as Mac Specialist. Dan is also an Adobe trainer for designProVideo.com, authoring titles such as *Photoshop CS4: Digital Photography Workflows*. Dan lives outside of Chicago with his wife Kathy.

Credits

Senior Acquisitions Editor
Stephanie McComb

Project Editor
Chris Wolfgang

Technical Editor
Robert Barnes

Copy Editor
Lynn Northrup

Editorial Manager
Robyn Siesky

Business Manager
Amy Knies

Senior Marketing Manager
Sandy Smith

Vice President and Executive Group Publisher
Richard Swadley

Vice President and Executive Publisher
Berry Pruett

Project Coordinator
Katherine Key

Graphics and Production Specialists
Ana Carrillo
Nikki Gately
Christin Swinford

Quality Control Technician
John Greenough

Proofreading
Laura L. Bowman

Indexing
Infodex Indexing Services, Inc.

Media Development Project Manager
Laura Moss

Media Development Assistant Project Manager
Jenny Swisher

Media Development Associate Producer
Kit Malone

Contents

Contents

Contents

Part II: Working with Images 153

Chapter 5: Creating New Images, Resizing, and Adjusting Resolution 155

Chapter 6: Undoing Mistakes 175

Chapter 7: Saving Files 189

Part IV: Paths, Shapes, and Text 329

Part V: Enhancing, Correcting, and Retouching   431

Chapter 14: Lightening, Darkening, and Changing Contrast 433

Contents

Contents

Contents

Contents

Contents

Acknowledgments

Stacy Cates: I would like to thank my friends Allison Lemke, Rebecca Garrett, and Shelly Eastman for their loyalty and support during the writing of this book; Berry College, for providing opportunities that helped me expand my knowledge of Adobe Photoshop; and the National Association of Photoshop Professionals (NAPP), for continually providing learning opportunities and creative inspiration.

Special appreciation to the following artists/photographers who donated their work to this book:

Simon Abrams

Brad Barker, 706-766-5158, zero22884@gmail.com

Christopher Angel Alasa, 404-869-6637, chris@sosyes.com

AJ Grier, www.theharleyartist.com, rtist@bellsouth.net

Bobby DeLane Poole, 706-266-8788, poole9005@comcast.net

Rod McClain, www.rodmcclainphotography.net

Will Cates

The Library of Congress and Carol Highsmith, the Carol Highsmith Collection

Simon Abrams: I would like to acknowledge the following people, places and things that provided support, encouragement, and preservation of my sanity for the duration of this project:

Christopher Hayes, you really are the man, and I still want to be like you when I grow up.

Evan Korth, thanks for the opportunities and the opened doors.

Wii nights with the Harfenists.

K-Dog Coffee Shop, for keeping the iced lattés and carrot cake in steady supply.

My work family at Deutsch, Inc., the world's greatest cheerleading squad.

My entire family, thanks for the support. You guys are the best.

Dan Moughamian: I would like to especially thank my wife Kathy for her patience and love; my parents for all the opportunities and support they have provide over the years; Len and Mike for helping a friend keep after his goals; Brian, for the opportunity to learn a lot about this business (and the road trips weren't bad either — pass the carbs!); co-authors Stacy and Simon, as well as Stephanie, Chris, and everyone at Wiley who helped put this project together ... thank you for the opportunity!

Welcome to the *Photoshop CS4 Bible*, the latest edition of the bestselling book on Adobe Photoshop software in publishing history. We are honored to have been given the opportunity to author this edition, and we pay homage to the revered previous *Photoshop Bible* authors: Photoshop-Hall-of-Famer Deke McClelland, the original author, and Photoshop gurus Laurie Ulrich Fuller and Robert C. Fuller.

The *Photoshop Bible* traditionally has been the must-have comprehensive reference for Photoshop users around the world. It is the longest continuously published title on Photoshop, with more than 16 U.S. Editions, dozens of translated editions, and more than a million copies in print worldwide.

Who the Book Is For

This is an exciting time in the evolution of Adobe Photoshop, the world's leading image-editing software, industry standard, and preventer of boredom. I am convinced that you can never run out of new things to do with Photoshop. And if you need to do anything with images, especially on a professional basis, chances are you either already use or would benefit from using Photoshop. It spans the gamut of users, from the home user retouching treasured family photos to the professional user designing logos to the artist creating digital paintings for movies to NASA analyzing space mission photos. And never before has Photoshop had so many features that make working with images easier, more productive, more creative, or more alluring.

With this in mind, the *Photoshop CS4 Bible* is all new and includes information about the Extended version of Photoshop, which has additional features that can help you do more with 3D images; video; and scientific, architectural, or geographic images. We have endeavored to include in this book all the most commonly used features, but unlike the style of Photoshop's Help files, we have incorporated our own experiences and opinions about features (whether positive or not-so-positive), put emphasis on the more important and useful aspects of features, and tried to describe features in a way that can be clear to even less-experienced users. Hopefully, some of our perspectives will be helpful to you in gaining a better understanding of Photoshop and maybe even provide some ideas about new ways to use it. No doubt, you also will discover your own unique ways to use this ground-breaking software.

So, enjoy your trip into the world of Photoshop to learn about ways you can improve your work, hone your skills, and get things done. But above all, take advantage of the creative possibilities of Photoshop, and have fun!

How the Book Is Organized

This book is organized into nine main parts.

- **Part I:** Welcome to Adobe Photoshop CS4
- **Part II:** Working with Images
- **Part III:** Layers, Selections, Channels, and Curves
- **Part IV:** Paths, Shapes, and Text
- **Part V:** Enhancing, Correcting, and Retouching
- **Part VI:** Printing and Special Effects
- **Part VII:** Color Management and Workflow
- **Part VIII:** Video, 3D Images, and Technical Images
- **Part IX:** Appendixes

Each of these parts is broken down into several chapters.

Part I

In Part I, Welcome to Adobe Photoshop CS4, four chapters are ready to introduce you to the fundamentals of the new incarnation of Photoshop:

- **Chapter 1:** Working with Digital Images
- **Chapter 2:** The Photoshop Workspace, Preferences, and Tools
- **Chapter 3:** Finding and Processing Images with Bridge
- **Chapter 4:** Camera Raw Work Area

Part II

Working with Images, as Part II is called, contains three chapters that deal specifically with basic image treatment. To get you started tweaking your images, check these topics out:

- **Chapter 5:** Creating New Images, Resizing, and Adjusting Resolution
- **Chapter 6:** Undoing Mistakes
- **Chapter 7:** Saving Files

Part III

Up the ante a bit with the more-involved information found in Part III: Layers, Selections, Channels, and Curves. Three chapters in this Part will guide you through some essential tools to flesh out your basic knowledge:

- **Chapter 8:** Layers, Layer Masks, Blending Modes, and Smart Objects

- **Chapter 9:** Histograms, Levels, and Curves
- **Chapter 10;** Selections and Chanels

Part IV

Paths, Shapes, and Text are what Part IV is all about. The three chapters here show you how to tweak vector shapes and text to suit the exact needs of your project.

- **Chapter 11:** Working with Paths
- **Chapter 12:** Working with Vector Shapes
- **Chapter 13:** Working with Text

Part V

Part V, Enhancing, Correcting, and Retouching, contains five chapters with the image-editing techniques you need to bring out the best in your photos and even salvage images that you may give up on otherwise.

- **Chapter 14:** Lightening, Darkening, and Changing Contrast
- **Chapter 15:** Color Corrections and Color Changes
- **Chapter 16:** Transparency, Opacity, Silhouettes, and Image Collages
- **Chapter 17:** Noise, Grain, Dust, Pixelization, and Jagged Edges
- **Chapter 18:** Retouching and Restoring Digital Images

Part VI

In the sixth part of this book, Painting and Special Effects are the focus. Four chapters walk you through techniques and effects that will lead you toward creating unique images.

- **Chapter 19:** Painting
- **Chapter 20:** Filters and Layer Styles
- **Chapter 21:** Distortion Effects
- **Chapter 22:** Text Effects

Part VII

Color Management and Workflow, discussed in Part VII, is covered with three chapters. The processes discussed here will help you maximize your efficiency with workflows, and manage color and design appropriately for each project.

- **Chapter 23:** Color Mangement
- **Chapter 24:** Designing for the Web
- **Chapter 25:** Digital Workflow Overview and Automating Processes

Part VIII

Part VIII is appropriately entitled Video, 3-D Images, and Technical Images. The last three chapters of this book cover each of those topics, respectively.

- **Chapter 26**: Working with Video
- **Chapter 27**: Working with 3-D Images
- **Chapter 28**: Working with Technical Images

Part IX

The ninth and final Part contains three appendixes of resources, letting you know what shortcuts and file formats that Photoshop supports, pointing you toward other sources for more specific information if by chance a specific question isn't answered within this book, and a short explanation of what to expect on this book's accompanying CD.

- **Appendix A**: Charts
- **Appendix B**: Professional Resources
- **Appendix C**: What's on the CD?

How to use this book

At over 1000 pages, this book may be intimidating! Don't feel obligated to read it from front to back…it's designed with desktop reference in mind. Simply take a look at the Table of Contents or the Index for the topic you have in mind, and skip right to the chapters, even the sections, you need when you need them.

Of course, if you're brand-new to Photoshop (and CS4 is a wonderful time to begin) and feeling a bit lost, the beginning is a good place to start. This book is written as a desktop reference, but the chapters do escalate in difficulty as their title numbers get higher. The four chapters in Part I serve as an excellent jumping-off point for newcomers, where you can familiarize yourself with Photoshop's workspace, enough tools to get you started, and customizing your own preferences so you can take charge of this robust program on your own terms.

Don't forget that you have access to the original files from some of the image-heavy chapters, such as Chapters 6, 14, and 20 to name a few! The CD that accompanies this book contains digital images used in the book's examples, so you can test out the techniques and experiment on files as soon as you put the CD into your computer and see exactly how we created the images shown in the book.

Part I

Welcome To Adobe Photoshop CS4

Chapter 1

Working with Digital Images

C amera film and photographic prints are not yet things of the past, and hopefully, there will always be a place for these beloved mediums. But humans continue to be endowed with certain irresistible compulsions, not the least of which is the pursuit of convenience. The instant gratification of digital imaging, along with the improvement of its quality, has contributed to making it the standard of today.

On the downside, the convenience of this new technology comes with the inconvenience of having to learn new things. Thankfully, the eye-candy of imagery — and, of course, the anticipation of knowing how to nefariously alter friends' photos — dulls the unpleasantness. Some might even say it makes it fun.

About Digital Images

You can save digital images in many different file formats — for example, JPEG and TIFF — but there are formats and types within the file formats. The characteristics and types of digital images are discussed in this chapter so you can learn how to create the kind of images you need for specific purposes.

First, it is important to know that all digital images contain pixels, usually square in shape, that describe their colors and brightness levels. You can see an image's individual pixels on-screen if you zoom in and look at a magnified version, as shown in Figure 1.1.

FIGURE 1.1

Some of the individual pixels in an image are magnified and shown here.

Color and lightness qualities of digital images

The following terminology is helpful to know when learning about the types of digital images:

- **Tonal range (or dynamic range).** This term refers to the range of dark to light values in an image, usually referred to as shadows, midtones, and highlights. An image that contains all or most of the possible tones, rather than a smaller portion of the possible tones, usually appears more detailed and is said to have a large tonal range, or dynamic range. Tones also may be referred to as levels or intensities.

- **Brightness, lightness, luminosity, luminance.** These terms refer to dark to light tonal characteristics, as opposed to color characteristics. They can be thought of as describing the image as if the colors had been converted to blacks, grays, and whites.

- **Hue.** Hue is identified by the name of the color, such as red, orange, or green. The lightness or darkness of a color is thought of as separate from the hue. Hue can be measured on a location on the standard color wheel and expressed as a degree between 0° and 360°.

- **Color.** In many instances in Photoshop, color refers to the hue, as a separate quality from dark to light tonal qualities. For example, it is common to say, "The color in this image is good and needs to stay the same, but I need to make changes to the luminosity."

  But sometimes color refers to the overall qualities of a color — the hue component together with the lighter or darker components of the color. For example, it is just as correct to say, "I will use a darker blue color fo the type," as it is to say, "I will use the same blue color but one that has a darker luminosity for the type."

- **Saturation.** The strength or purity of the color, or chroma, saturation represents the amount of hue in the color compared to the amount of black, gray, or white in the color. If a color contains some black or gray, it may look darker, and/or muted; if iti contains some white, it may look lighter, muted, and/or pastel. The maximum amount of hue, with no black, gray, or white mixed in, would be fully saturated and look like pure vivid color.

 In Photoshop, color is sometimes, and hue is always, thought of as a separate characteristic from the dark to light characteristics of an image.

Hue, Saturation, and Brightness

The Hue, Saturation, and Brightness (HSB) color model is not a color mode that can be assigned to an image in Photoshop, but it is a useful way of organizing color components. The HSB model is helpful in understanding the meaning of the terms Hue, Saturation, and Brightness. In the HSB model, the hue is specified as an angle from 0° to 360° that corresponds to a location on the color wheel. Saturation is expressed from 0 percent (no hue) to 100 percent (maximum amount of hue). Brightness is expressed from 0 percent (as dark as possible) to 100 percent (as light as possible).

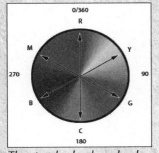

The standard color wheel

Colors and their degrees are shown in the color wheel: R for Red, Y for Yellow, G for Green, C for Cyan, B for Blue, and M for Magenta. Cyan corresponds to 180 degrees, Yellow-Green corresponds to 90 degrees, and Red can be expressed as either 0 degrees or 360 degrees.

The Color Picker is a common tool used to define colors in Photoshop and is shown in the following figure. You can access it by clicking the foreground color box in the Toolbox. In the HSB section of the Color Picker shown, H is set to 180 degrees, which specifies the color Cyan, as shown on the color wheel; S is set to 100 percent, which specifies the maximum amount of hue; and B is set to 100 percent, which specifies the maximum amount of brightness. These values result in a picked color that is a vivid pure version of Cyan. The picked color is shown selected in the top-right corner of the color field box (the large square box on the left side of the Color Picker dialog box).

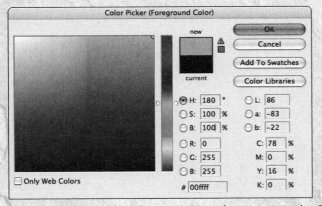

Hue, Saturation, and Brightness (HSB) values are set in the Color Picker.

Overview of the main types and characteristics of digital images

Following are basic descriptions of digital image types and characteristics:

- **Bit depth.** The higher an image's bit depth, the more colors each of its pixels can be; therefore, the more colors and degrees of brightness the image can contain.

- **Bitmap (raster) and vector.** A bitmap, or raster, image gets its detail from the number of pixels it contains. The more pixels a bitmap image has, the more detail the image can contain. A vector image gets its detail from shapes and lines that are mathematically calculated, so its detail does not depend on the number of pixels in the image.

- **Color mode.** The color mode of an image specifies which basic set of colors is used to make up an image. Some common basic sets of colors used to make up full-color images are Red, Green, and Blue (RGB mode) and Cyan, Magenta, Yellow, and Black (CMYK mode; Black is represented by the letter K). Colors within color modes are stored in their own color channels. You can view the channels in the Channels palette.

CROSS-REF See Chapter 10 for more information about the Channels palette.

- **Color space, color profile, gamut.** Within the basic sets of colors used to make up each color mode, such as RGB or CMYK, there are different sets of combinations of these colors. These subordinate sets can be thought of as color palettes chosen for images so they will look better when they reach their final destinations.

- **File format.** Various destinations for an image, such as other software or a computer screen display, require certain file formats because of the software language or properties of the device. Some common file formats are JPEG and GIF, usually used for Web page display, and TIFF, often used for page layout programs and printing.

NOTE The color-mode term Bitmap mode (images that are limited to black and/or white; no gray; no color) is different from the image-type term bitmap, or raster (images that get their detail from the number of pixels they contain). Not all bitmap images are Bitmap mode.

Bit depth

You can see or convert bit depth by choosing Image ➪ Mode ➪ Bits/Channel. At a basic level, all digital images contain components called pixels. Pixels can contain varying amounts of information that describe their color. In this case, color refers to the qualities of hue combined with lightness. The greater an image's bit depth, the more information each of its pixels can contain, and the more colors each of those pixels can potentially be. Therefore, the higher an image's bit depth, the more colors and degrees of brightness the image can contain (see Table 1.1).

Bit depth is measured in bits per channel (bpc):

- **1 bit/channel.** An image with a bit depth of 1 has pixels with only two possible values, black or white. A Bitmap mode image has one channel with pixels that can be either black or white. There is no 1 Bit/Channel option that can be selected in Photoshop, but Bitmap mode images are 1-bpc images.

- **8 bits/channel.** An image with a bit depth of 8 has 2^8, or 256, possible values per channel. An 8-bpc Grayscale mode image's pixels can only be black, white, or shades of gray. Since a Grayscale mode image has only one channel, each 8-bpc Grayscale mode image can have only 256 possible values. An 8-bpc RGB mode image has 256 possible values in each of its three color channels (red, green, and blue). It is possible for each pixel in an RGB image to be any mixture of those three colors. Therefore, each 8-bpc RGB image has 16,777,216 possible values ($256 \times 256 \times 256$).

- **16 bits/channel.** An image with a bit depth of 16 has 2^{16}, or 65,536, possible values per channel.

- **32 bits/channel.** Also known as a high dynamic range (HDR) image, an image with a bit depth of 32 has 2^{32}, or 4,294,967,296, possible values per channel.

TABLE 1.1

Limits of Photoshop's Support for Bit Depths Above 8

16-bpc Images	32-bpc Images
Cannot use Bitmap, Duotone, or Indexed Color mode	Can use only RGB and Grayscale modes
Cannot use Art History Brush tool	Cannot use some blending modes
Cannot use Variations image adjustment	Cannot use some commands from the Image ⇨ Adjustments menu
Cannot use some filters	Cannot use some filters
	Can save these formats only: Photoshop (PSD, PSB) Radiance (HDR) Portable Bit Map (PBM) OpenEXR TIFF
	Cannot fully use a few commands from the Image menu
	Cannot use a few commands from the Layer menu
	Cannot use a few commands from the Select menu
	Cannot use some of the tools in the Toolbox

CAUTION Eight-bpc RGB images are sometimes called 24-bit images (8 bits x 3 channels = 24 bits of data for each pixel). This can be confusing. For example, sometimes 8-bpc RGB images are called 8-bit images and sometimes they are called 24-bit images.

Thirty-two-bpc HDR images can represent the entire dynamic range of the visible world, unlike the lower bit depths, which can represent only a portion of it. Among the advantages of HDR is that adjusting its exposure is like adjusting the exposure when photographing a scene in the real world. Blurs and other real-world lighting effects look realistic in HDR images. Motion pictures, 3-D work, and some high-end photography are mediums that sometimes use HDR images.

HDR images contain brightness levels that a standard monitor cannot display, so Photoshop lets you make choices about the appearance of the on-screen preview of HDR images by choosing View ➪ 32-bit Preview Options.

The Merge to HDR command lets you create HDR images from multiple photographs with different exposures, thereby gaining the larger dynamic range that 32-bpc images can support.

Following are the steps to merge multiple images to HDR format:

1. Choose File ➪ Automate ➪ Merge to HDR.
2. In the Merge to HDR dialog box, click Browse, select the images, and click Open.
3. If you held your camera in your hands when you photographed your multiple images, select the Attempt To Automatically Align Source Images option.
4. Click OK.
5. Set view options by clicking the minus or plus button for zoom in or out, or choose a view percentage or mode from the pop-up menu below the preview image.
6. (Optional) Select or deselect check boxes under the filmstrip thumbnails to specify which images to use in the merge.
7. Choose a bit depth from the Bit Depth menu. Choose 32 Bits/Channel if you want the merged image to store the entire dynamic range of the merged images.
8. Move the slider below the histogram to preview the merged image (this does not remove any image data). This preview adjustment is stored in the HDR image file and applied when the image is open. It can be changed later by choosing View ➪ 32-bit Preview Options.
9. Click OK to create the merged image.

You can convert a 32-bpc HDR image to a 16-bpc or 8-bpc image, but some of the image's information will be lost in the conversion. You will need to make choices about what information to keep and what to throw away based on what you want the converted image to look like.

Following are the steps to convert from 32-bpc HDR to 16- or 8-bpc:

1. Choose Image ➪ Mode ➪ 16 Bits/Channel or 8 Bits/Channel.

2. Make sure the Preview box is checked and choose one of the following four methods for adjusting the brightness and contrast in the image until the image's appearance and tonal range meets your requirements:

   ▪ **Exposure and Gamma.** Move the Exposure slider to adjust the gain, and move the Gamma (midtone) slider to adjust the contrast. If the result is acceptable, click OK to complete the conversion.

   ▪ **Highlight Compression.** This is an automatic method that compresses the highlight values in the HDR image so they fall within the range the lower bit depth can support. If the result is acceptable, click OK to complete the conversion.

   ▪ **Equalize Histogram.** This is an automatic method that compresses the dynamic range of the HDR image while trying to preserve some contrast. If the result is acceptable, click OK to complete the conversion.

   ▪ **Local Adaptation.** Move the radius slider to specify the size of the local brightness regions. Move the threshold slider to specify how far apart two pixels' tonal values must be before they are no longer part of the same brightness region. You can also use the toning curve to make adjustments. It's usually best to uncheck the corner option so the curve will be smooth. (For more about using curves, see Chapter 11.) If the result is acceptable, click OK to complete the conversion.

NOTE   With the HDR dialog box open, you can use the Save or Load button to save or load your custom HDR conversion settings.

Tips for Taking Photos for Merging to HDR

- Use a tripod.
- Take at least five to seven photos to capture the dynamic range of the scene.
- Vary the shutter speed to create different exposures. (Caution: Changing the aperture can produce lower quality, and changing the ISO or aperture may cause noise or vignetting.)
- Keep in mind that auto-bracketing may not provide enough differences in exposures.
- Set exposure differences one or two EV (exposure value) steps apart (equivalent to about one or two f-stops).
- Don't vary the lighting in the images.
- Keep each photo identical except for exposure. The scene must be stationary.

Bitmap (raster) and vector

A bitmap, or *raster*, image gets its detail from the number of pixels it contains, which is called *resolution*. Since they depend on the number of pixels for detail, bitmap images are said to be resolution-dependent. Resolution is commonly expressed in Photoshop as the number of pixels per inch (ppi). Choose Image ➪ Image Size to see the resolution of an image.

CROSS-REF Appendix A includes a chart of required resolutions for different kinds of images.

The more pixels a bitmap image has, the more detail the image can contain. Larger bitmap images need to have more pixels than smaller ones in order to preserve detail. Photos are bitmap images, and paintings or illustrations that donít have well-defined shapes are usually bitmap images.

Very simple images can also be bitmap format (see Figure 1.2). It is necessary for bitmap images to have many pixels if they need to show a lot of detail, and in the case of photos or scanned images, the detail must be captured in the initial creation of the image. It is possible for an image to look deceptively good on-screen but bad in its printed form. If it doesnít have enough pixels, the printed version may lack detail and look blurry or *pixilated* (the undesirable appearance of individual square pixels or their jagged edges).

CROSS-REF Photoshop images can have multiple layers that contain different parts of an image. Having parts on separate layers can make it easier to manipulate the individual parts. You can also create layer masks that can be used to hide and show parts of a layer. Layers are explained in more detail in Chapter 8.

FIGURE 1.2

A bitmap image

A vector image gets its detail from shapes and lines that are mathematically calculated. The shapes and lines in vector images retain their smoothness no matter how much they are resized, regardless of how many pixels are in the image. Although there are pixels in a vector image that display color, a vector imageís detail does not depend on the number of pixels in the image. Therefore, vector images are resolution-independent.

Images that are made up of some combination of solid colors, simple gradations between colors, distinct shapes, and lines can be constructed as vector images. Simple logos and cartoon-type illustrations often have these characteristics, but some complex illustrations do, too. While eliminating the worry about having enough resolution is an advantage, keep in mind that the vector components often have to be created or adjusted by hand, so creating vector images can be more time-consuming than creating bitmap images. Bitmap images can be created by taking a photo with a digital camera or by scanning an image. Vector images must be hand-drawn using vector tools in software such as Photoshop or Illustrato. Note that an image that is a good candidate for the vector format does not necessarily have to be in vector format. It can be a bitmap image.

Since numerous file formats can contain vector information, it is not immediately apparent whether an image is a vector image or contains vector information. If an image contains vector information, you can find it in any of four places in the image:

- On a vector layer mask (right-click [Ctrl-click on a Mac] on a layer mask; if you see vector options, it is a vector mask rather than a standard layer mask).
- On a type layer in the Layers palette. As long as you can still see the T in the layer thumbnail, the type is made up of vectors.
- On a path in the Paths palette. All paths in the Paths palette are vectors.
- In a Smart Object layer. Some have vector information embedded. You can double-click the Smart Object layer to open its linked file and examine it for vector information. The linked file may be a Photoshop or Illustrator file. (Content in Illustrator files is typically vector.)

There can be a combination vector and bitmap image. If an image contains bitmap parts, the image has to have enough resolution to describe the detail in the bitmap parts.

In Figure 1.3, the vector information — the path of the dog — is shown on the vector layer mask.

FIGURE 1.3

A vector-only image in which the active vector information is contained in a vector layer mask

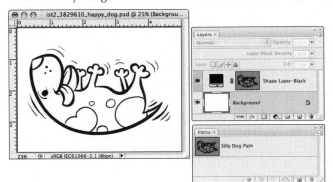

The type of layer shown is a *shape layer*, a layer completely filled with a color (in this case, black) and that has a vector layer mask that hides part of the color on the layer, leaving visible what looks like a shape. White areas on a vector mask allow the color on the layer to be visible; gray on a vector mask hides the layer's color. The layer name is "Shape Layer-Black," and the vector layer mask is immediately to the left of the layer name.

The dog path on the mask allows the corresponding area of black color on the layer to be visible, and the leftover gray part of the vector mask hides all the other black on the layer (makes it invisible, or transparent). The vector mask in Figure 1.3 is small, so it's hard to see that the dog path on the vector mask is filled with white; if you examine the file on the CD, you can see that it is filled with white. The dog path has also been saved in the Paths palette, just for safekeeping. All paths in the Paths palette and on vector layer masks are vector components of the image.

Figure 1.4 shows a vector image in which the vector information is stored in a Smart Object.

FIGURE 1.4

A vector-only image in which the vector information is contained in a Smart Object

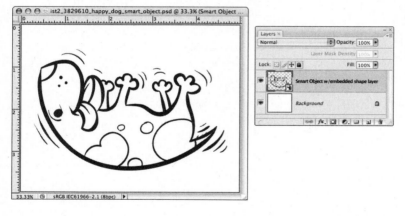

Smart Object layers have a special icon at the lower right of the layer thumbnail and can contain linked Photoshop or Illustrator files. Smart Objects also allow certain Photoshop functions that regular layers may not allow. To confirm that a Smart Object contains vector information, you can double-click the Smart Object, and check the linked file that opens for vector information.

CROSS-REF Smart Objects are discussed in Chapter 8.

Vector-only files can contain color, but in order to take full advantage of the vector format, separate colors must be on separate layers; however, gradients that include more than one color can be on a vector layer. Gradients generally don't contain the kind of detail that requires the bitmap format.

Figure 1.5 shows a vector-only image with four colors. The layers are linked so that they resize together.

Figure 1.6 shows a combination vector and bitmap image. The type layer contains vector information, the Star Shape Layer contains the star shape in the vector layer mask, and the Background layer contains a bitmap image.

FIGURE 1.5

A vector-only image with four colors. Vector information is contained in the vector layer masks.

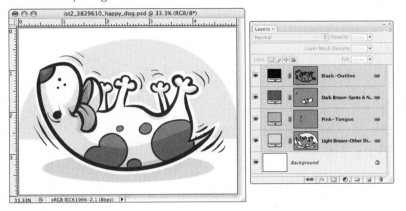

FIGURE 1.6

A combination vector and bitmap image

While the vector parts of the image are still resolution-independent and can be resized with no worries, the image must have enough resolution to describe the detail in the bitmap photo.

Printing an enlarged bitmap image that doesn't have enough resolution to describe the detail in the enlarged size often results in a pixilated look, shown in Figure 1.7.

CROSS-REF **Part IV explains how to create vector paths, type, and shapes.**

FIGURE 1.7

Printing a bitmap image at a size larger than its resolution can result in a pixilated look.

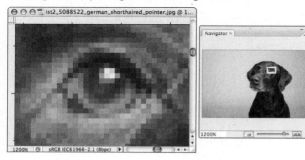

You can print a vector-only image as large as you want without regard to image resolution, and it will still look smooth and not pixilated, as shown in Figure 1.8. A vector-only image will appear pixilated on-screen if you zoom in far enough, but it will print smoothly.

FIGURE 1.8

A vector image will print smoothly without regard to resolution, even if it is enlarged.

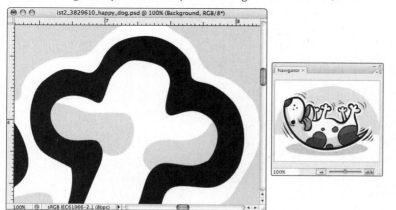

Color mode

The color mode of an image specifies which basic set of colors is used to make up an image. You can specify the color mode in the Image ⇨ Mode menu.

Colors within most color modes are stored in color channels. You can view the channels in the Channels palette.

The color modes available in Photoshop are:

- **RGB color mode.** Red, Green, and Blue are used to make up the image's color. In 8-bpc images, tonal values range from 0 (black) to 255 (white), for each of the three colors. When the values for all three colors are equal, the resulting color is a neutral color — black, white, or a shade of gray with no color hue. RGB mode (see Figure 1.9) is used to display images on-screen because monitors use Red, Green, and Blue light to display color. It is also commonly used when color-correcting images.

FIGURE 1.9

RGB mode channels

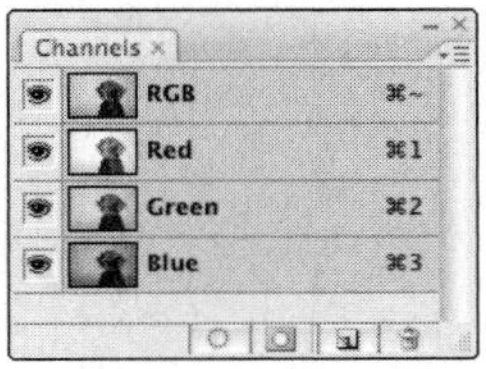

- **CMYK color mode.** Cyan, Magenta, Yellow, and Black are used to make up the image's color. Tonal values range from 0 percent (no color) to 100 percent (maximum amount of color) for each of the four colors. In CMYK-colors that are neutral, Magenta and Yellow have equal values and Cyan has a higher value than either Magenta or Yellow; the amount of Black determines the lightness of the color.

  CMYK mode (see Figure 1.10) is used when printing images with Cyan, Magenta, Yellow, and Black inks. Typically, RGB mode is used to color-correct images in order to preserve the maximum amount of colors and to make assigning neutral color values easier (all three color values are equal in neutral colors in RGB mode), then the image is converted to CMYK mode. But color correction can also take place in CMYK mode.

- **Lab color mode.** The Lab color mode (pronounced *el, ay, bee,* not *lab*) is based on a standardized way to describe color that corresponds to the way a person with normal vision sees it. It is used by color management systems as an intermediate color reference to help accurately convert colors from one color space to another. It is sometimes used in color correction and image manipulation. Lab color (see Figure 1.11) uses the following components to make colors: an **L** (lightness) component, an **a** component that contains green and red, and a **b** component that contains blue and yellow. **L** values range from 0 to 100; **a** and **b** values range from +127 to −128.

15

FIGURE 1.10

CMYK mode channels

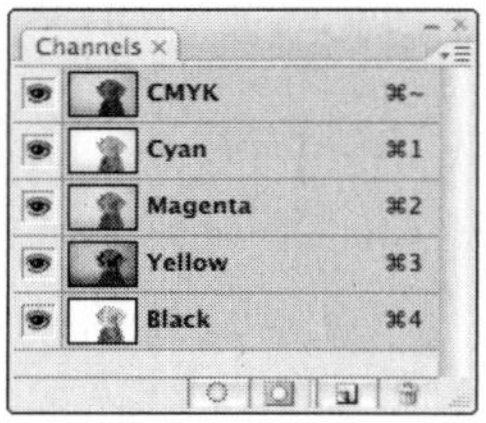

FIGURE 1.11

Lab mode channels

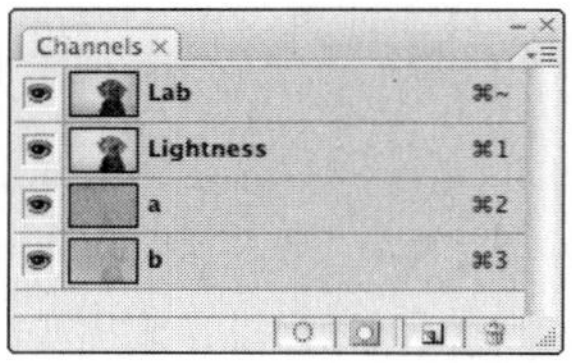

- **Grayscale mode.** Black, white, and shades of gray are used to make up the "colors" in an image (no hue is present). In 8-bpc images, there can be 256 brightness values. Grayscale images' values can be measured in a range from 0 (black) to 255 (white) or with 0 percent–100 percent of black ink coverage.

  Grayscale mode (see Figure 1.12) can be used when preparing images to be printed with one color of ink. Grayscale images can be assigned a color within most page layout software, such as InDesign or Quark Xpress.

FIGURE 1.12

Grayscale mode channels

- **Bitmap mode.** Only black and white pixels are used. Bitmap mode images are 1-bpc images (see Figure 1.13). They are often used for simple artwork that lends itself to reproduction in only black and white pixels, sometimes called *line art*. Bitmap mode images can be assigned a color within most page layout software, such as InDesign or Quark Xpress.

■ **Duotone mode.** In Duotone mode, one to four custom inks can be used to make up the colors in an image. Figure 1.14 shows Duotone-mode channels, options, and curves. A dutone can be used to add a color tint to a black-ink photo printed in a brochure that uses only black ink plus one other color. A quadtone with custom inks can give a rich and uniquely colored look to a photograph. Pantone offers reference books that show sample duotones printed in various inks and their ink percentages.

FIGURE 1.13

Bitmap mode channel

FIGURE 1.14

Duotone mode channels, Duotone options, and Duotone curves

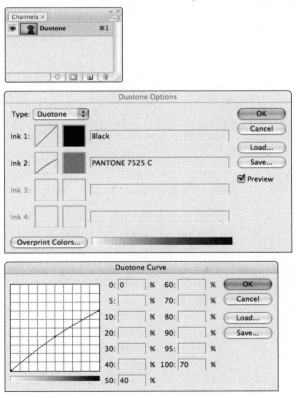

The Duotone-mode images can be referred to as monotones, duotones, tritones, or quadtones. Their values are typically measured with 0%–100% of ink coverage. Duotone mode is used when two, three, or four custom ink colors (other than the typical CMYK combination) are used in printing.

Duotone mode separates the overall image into multiple custom colors, and the Duotone mode curves can be used to adjust the percentage of ink in specific areas of the tonal range of each color.

■ **Indexed color mode.** Up to 256 colors can be used to make up the colors in an image. Colors are stored in a *color lookup table (CLUT)*. Indexed color images are typically used for GIF format images destined for on-screen display (see Figure 1.15). When you save a GIF by choosing File ➪ Save for Web & Devices, the image is automatically converted to Index color mode.

You can generally or selectively reduce the number of colors in an indexed color image to reduce the image's file size, which decreases download time for Web images. In an effort to improve an image's appearance while at the same time using fewer colors, you can also take advantage of *dithering*, the simulation of a third color by generating the appearance of two colors being mixed together.

FIGURE 1.15

Indexed color mode channels and GIF options, including Dither options and Color Table

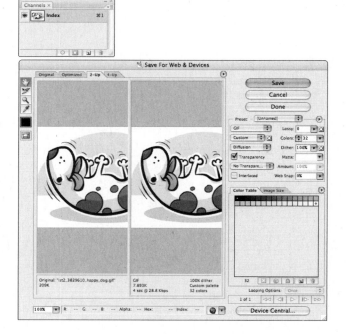

■ **Multichannel mode.** Multichannel mode uses only *spot channels* (see Figure 1.16), channels that store parts of an image that you want to print in custom-selected inks (sometimes called spot colors), such as inks from the Pantone color library. In Multichannel mode, you can put certain parts of an image on each spot channel and assign custom-selected inks to the spot channel.

For example, you can put a custom-red-ink logo on the spot channel for red ink and a custom-blue-ink background on the spot channel for blue ink. You can also put image areas that you want to print in clear varnishes on spot channels.

Spot channels result in inks overprinting each other, so if the logo mentioned previously is to print in red ink only, then the area corresponding to the logo in the blue spot channel must contain no pixels in order to avoid blue ink printing on the red ink logo.

FIGURE 1.16

Multichannel mode spot color channels in a two-color image

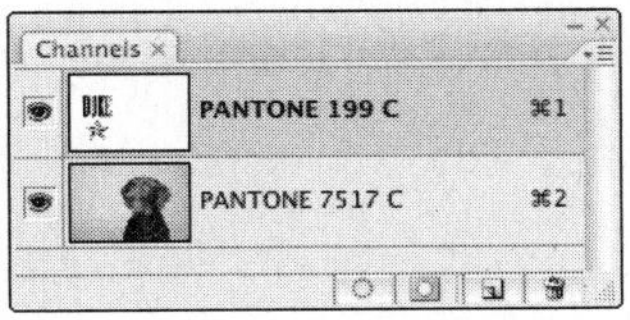

NOTE Spot channels can be added to CMYK images by using the Channel palette menu. A common scenario would be adding a spot channel for a clear varnish to a CMYK image.

Color space

There are many colors that can be formed from combinations of the basic sets of colors that make up each color mode, such as RGB (Red, Green, Blue) or CMYK (Cyan, Magenta, Yellow, Black). But not all devices (monitors, presses, desktop printers) can reproduce all the possible color combinations within each color mode. Therefore, there are sets of color-combinations within each color mode that are customized for different devices and that you can use to make up the colors in your images. You can think of these sets of color-combinations as color palettes. They also can be referred to as color spaces, color *gamuts*, or color profiles.

When you use a set of color-combinations that is specially made for an image's destination device, your image should look better when it is reproduced that device. For example, if you erroneously use a color space that is made for uncoated paper for an image that is going to be printed on glossy paper on a printing press, you are allowing your image to potentially have many more colors than can be reproduced satisfactorily on uncoated paper. There can be unpredictable results in this situation. It's better in this situation to use a color space that is specifically tailored to uncoated paper printed on a printing press.

Before you begin working on an image, you can specify the color spaces (also called *color profiles* or *gamuts*) for various types of images, such as RGB, CMYK, Grayscale, and Spot Color. This enables Photoshop's color management functions, which attempt to keep colors accurate across devices, such as a monitor, a desktop printer, and a printing press.

To specify color spaces, choose Edit ➪ Color Settings (see Figure 1.17). If you are working on images for the Web, the sRGB color space is a good set of RGB colors to work in because it resembles the set of colors available for display on many monitors.

If you are working on images for printing on a sheetfed press on coated paper, you may want to choose the CMYK color space U.S. Sheetfed Coated. Custom color profiles (color spaces) may also be created and loaded.

FIGURE 1.17

The Color Settings dialog box

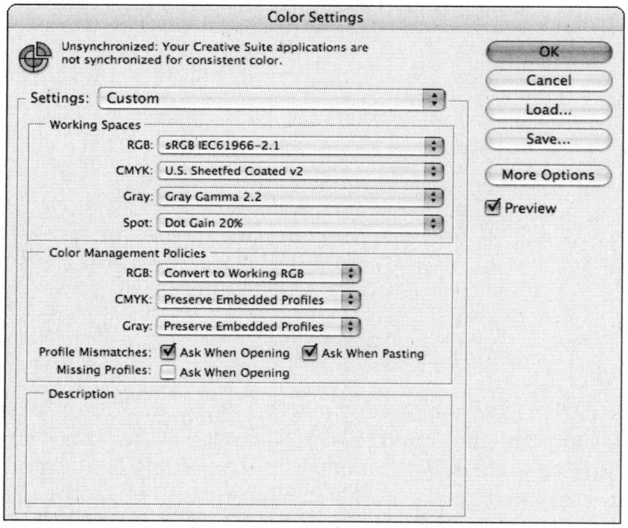

You can change an image's color profile by choosing Edit ➪ Assign Profile or Edit ➪ Convert Profile. Assign Profile uses a conversion method that pays more attention to keeping the color's numeric values the same and does not prioritize keeping the color's appearance consistent from one color space to another. Convert Profile attempts to keep the color's appearance the same from one color space to another and does not prioritize keeping the color's numeric values the same.

Color management is not a perfect system. With that in mind, you may also choose not to use color management by clicking the More Options button in the Color Settings dialog box, then selecting Color Management Off in the Settings menu.

CROSS-REF   More about color management is discussed in Chapter 23.

File format

Various destinations for an image, such as other software or a computer screen display, require certain file formats because of the software language or properties of the device. Some common file formats are JPEG and GIF, usually used for Web page display, and TIFF, often used for page layout programs and printing.

The file formats supported by Photoshop CS4 are listed in Table 1.2.

CROSS-REF   For descriptions and purposes of file formats, see Chapter 7 and Appendix A.

TABLE 1.2

File Formats Supported by Photoshop CS4

Format	Extension
3D Studio Max	.3DS
Adobe Illustrator	.ai
Adobe Illustrator Paths	.ai
Alias PIX	.pix
Alias|Wavefront	.obj
Amiga IFF	.iff, .tdi
AVI	.avi
BMP	.bmp, .rle, .dib
Camera Raw	.tif, .crw, .nef, .raf, .orf, .mrw, .dcr, .mos, .raw, .pef, .srf, .dng, .x3f, .cr2, .erf, .sr2, .kdc, .mfw, .mef, .arw
Cineon	.cin, .spdx, .dpx, .fido
Collada	.dae
CompuServe GIF	.gif
Dicom	.dcm, .dc3, .dic
Digital Negative	.dng
ElectricImage	.img, .ei, .eiz, .eizz
EPS	.eps, .epsf, .epsp
EPS with JPEG Preview	.eps

continued

TABLE 1.2 *(continued)*	
Format	**Extension**
EPS with PICT Preview	.eps
EPS with TIFF Preview	.eps
Filmstrip	.flm
Google Earth 4	.kmz
JPEG	.jpg, .jpeg, .jpe
JPEG 2000	.jpf, .jpx, .jp2, .j2c, .j2k, .jpc
Kodak Photo CD	.pcd
Large Document Format	.psb
MacPaint	.mpt, .mac
OpenEXR	.exr
PCX	.pcx
PDF	.pdf, .pdp
Photoshop	.psd, .pdd
Photoshop DCS 1.0 and 2.0	.eps
Photoshop Raw	.raw
PICT	.pct, .pict
PICT Resource	.rsr
Pixar	.pxr
PixelPaint	.px1
PNG	.png
Portable Bitmap	.pbm, .pgm, .ppm, .pnm, .pfm, .pam
QuickTime Movie	.mov, .avi, .mpg, .mpeg, .mp4, .m4v
Radiance	.hdr, .rgbe, .xyze
Scitex CT	.sct
SGI RGB	.sgi, .rgb, .rgba, .bw
SoftImage	.pic
Targa	.tga, .vda, .icb, .vst
TIFF	.tif
U3D	.u3d
Wavefront RLA	.rla
Wireless Bitmap	.wbm, .wbmp
ZoomView	.mtx

This file format list is taken from Adobe Tech Note: www.adobe.com/go/kb401022

For the most up-to-date comprehensive file format list, search for "Import and export file formats for Photoshop CS4" on the Adobe Support Web site at www.adobe.com/support/photoshop/.

Low versus high resolution

Bitmap images, as opposed to vector-only images, depend on the number of pixels in the image to describe the image's detail. In Photoshop, image resolution is measured in pixels per inch (ppi) and can be seen and changed in the Image Size dialog box (choose Image ➪ Image Size), shown in Figure 1.18. If an image does not have enough resolution for its purpose, it may look blurry or pixilated.

Generally, images destined for print will have enough pixels if the resolution is 300 ppi at the final size in inches. Images destined for on-screen display should be 72 ppi at the final size in pixels.

An adequate number of pixels needed to describe an image's detail should be captured initially, for example, at the time a digital photo is taken or a photographic print is scanned. If the resolution is increased or the size of the image is enlarged after importing it into Photoshop, there may not be enough pixels in the image to adequately describe the image's detail at a larger resolution or size. Even though you can increase the resolution or size in Photoshop, no new pixel information that describes detail is added.

FIGURE 1.18

The Image Size dialog box

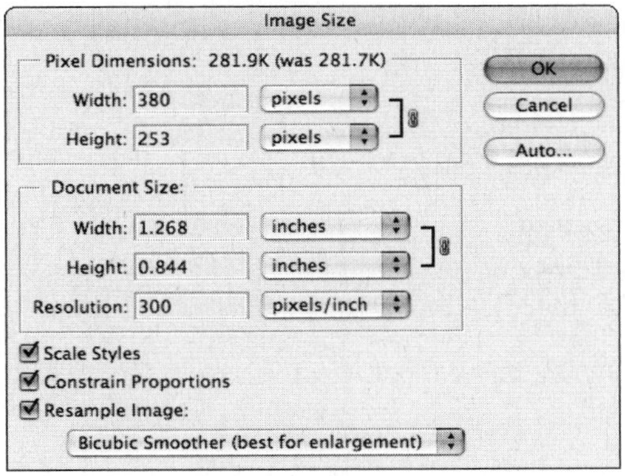

Photoshop may simply guess at what kind of pixels to add, which is called *resampling up* or *interpolation*. This may result in an image that looks blurry or pixilated.

To avoid resampling up, uncheck the Resample Image check box in the Image Size dialog box when you increase size or resolution numbers. You can check the Resample Image check box when you are decreasing an image's size; this will just throw away unneeded pixels by resampling down.

To double-check that there is no resampling up happening, enter the desired numbers in the Image Size dialog box and before you click OK, check the total file size at the top of the dialog box to the right of Pixel Dimensions and make sure it does not display a new larger size, along with a smaller previous size. A new larger size would indicate resampling up.

CROSS-REF For more about image resolution and resizing, see Chapter 5.

Getting Images into Photoshop

It's great to know a lot about Photoshop, and if you've read the previous sections in this chapter, you have already gained knowledge that, believe it or not, many Photoshop users have not taken the time to learn. But to apply that knowledge, you need to know how to get images from their sources onto your computer and ready to open in Photoshop. Next are some tips that will help you get your images from point A to B.

Digital cameras

Digital cameras come with some type of memory card that holds your digital photos, and they usually come with a cable that can connect the camera to your computer, often a USB-type cable.

There are different types of memory cards for digital cameras. Some computers come with memory card slots that may or may not accept your camera's type of memory card. Some desktop printers also come with memory card slots that you can use to transfer photos from the memory card to your computer, assuming that your printer is connected to the computer. If it's not obvious that your type of memory card will fit in your device's memory card slot, check the device's documentation or contact the manufacturer of the device.

If you don't have the device's documentation, you may be able to find a downloadable operation manual on the manufacturer's Web site that will give you the memory card slot information.

Inexpensive card readers that accept virtually all types of memory cards, such as a 35-in-1 card reader, can also be purchased and connected to your computer via a USB- or FireWire-type connection. Check to see which type of connection your computer has before you purchase a card reader.

Transferring images from a memory card slot to your computer doesn't use the camera's battery and can be faster than a USB connection.

Figure 1.19 shows what USB-type connectors look like. Figure 1.20 shows what FireWire connectors look like.

If you want to use a cable connection to transfer images from your camera to your computer, the memory card must be inside the camera. You can purchase a cable that connects your camera to your computer if you don't have one.

One end of the cable will need a smaller USB connector for the camera and the other end will need a larger USB connector for your computer. Look at the ports on your camera and computer to see what type of connector ends the cable needs.

FIGURE 1.19

USB connectors

FIGURE 1.20

FireWire connectors

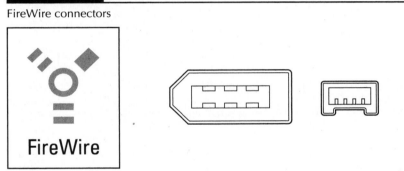

You can also contact the manufacturer to find out what kind of cable you need for your camera model. The major manufacturers, like Canon and Nikon, have Web sites with lots of information, including downloadable camera operation manuals. You can also take the camera to an electronics store, such as Circuit City, for help finding the right cable.

When you either put your camera's memory card into an appropriate card slot or connect your camera to your computer with a cable, an additional drive that represents the memory card should show up on your computer. Figure 1.21 shows a memory card called "NO NAME," listed with the other drives on the computer: Macintosh HD, iDisk, and My Book. The path to the images inside the NO NAME memory card is shown as DCIM ➪ 101CANON ➪ images.

You can use your computer's operating system to copy the images from their location on the memory card to your hard drive, then use Bridge or choose File ➪ Open from within Photoshop to open the files on your hard drive (not directly from the memory card drive) into Photoshop.

CROSS-REF Adobe Bridge provides a useful visual interface to find, open, and process files on your computer. Using Bridge is discussed in Chapter 3.

FIGURE 1.21

An example of a file path from a camera's memory card to the images: NO NAME ⇨ DCIM ⇨ 101CANON ⇨ images

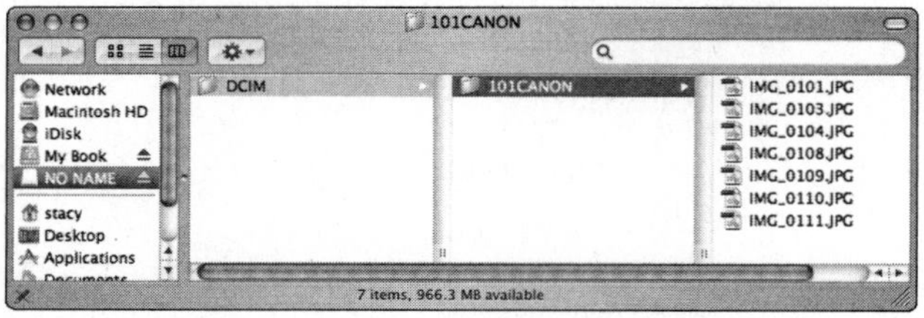

After you connect your camera or memory card to your computer, you can use Adobe Bridge's Photo Downloader by following these steps:

1. **In Photoshop:** Choose File ⇨ Browse (opens Bridge).

2. **In Bridge:** Choose File ⇨ Get Photos from Camera.

Bridge's Photo Downloader (see Figure 1.22) automatically finds the camera's images and allows you to choose a location on your computer to copy the images to and create a new subfolder to put them in. Using Photo Downloader, you can also rename the images with text and a serial number as they are being copied to your computer, preserve the old filename inside the image's file information, and automatically display the images in Adobe Bridge.

Film cameras

A quick, convenient, and inexpensive way to get images from a film camera into digital form is to purchase a photo CD along with your prints when you get your film developed. Simply put the CD into your computer, copy the folder of images to your hard drive, and use Bridge or choose File ⇨ Open from within Photoshop to open the files on your hard drive (not directly from the CD) into Photoshop.

If you have already developed the film without getting a photo CD, you can still purchase a photo CD from many developers if you provide them with your negatives to scan. It is usually more expensive than getting the CD at the time of developing, but still inexpensive at discount developers such as Wal-Mart.

FIGURE 1.22

The Adobe Bridge Photo Downloader

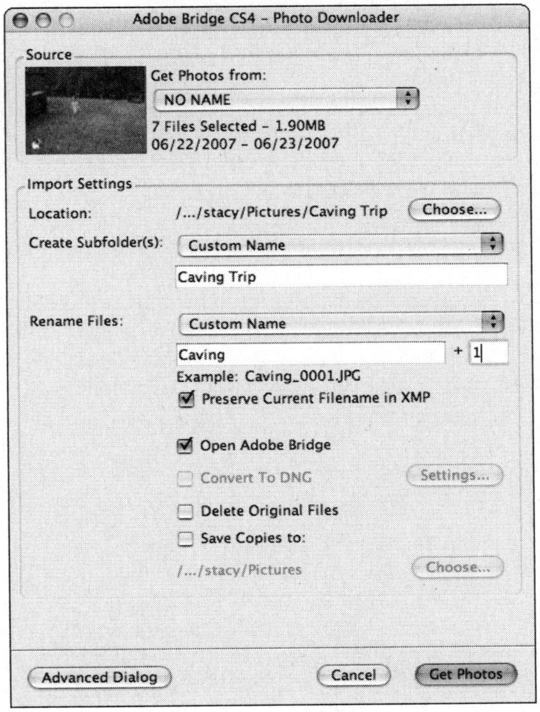

```
●○○          Adobe Bridge CS4 – Photo Downloader

┌─ Source ──────────────────────────────────────────────┐
│          Get Photos from:                              │
│  [img]   [ NO NAME                         ⬍ ]         │
│          7 Files Selected – 1.90MB                     │
│          06/22/2007 – 06/23/2007                       │
└────────────────────────────────────────────────────────┘

┌─ Import Settings ─────────────────────────────────────┐
│  Location:        /.../stacy/Pictures/Caving Trip  ( Choose... )
│  Create Subfolder(s):  [ Custom Name            ⬍ ]   │
│                        [ Caving Trip              ]   │
│                                                        │
│  Rename Files:    [ Custom Name                 ⬍ ]   │
│                   [ Caving          ]  + [ 1 ]        │
│                   Example: Caving_0001.JPG             │
│                   ☑ Preserve Current Filename in XMP   │
│                                                        │
│                   ☑ Open Adobe Bridge                  │
│                   ☐ Convert To DNG      ( Settings... )│
│                   ☐ Delete Original Files             │
│                   ☐ Save Copies to:                   │
│                   /.../stacy/Pictures    ( Choose... ) │
└────────────────────────────────────────────────────────┘

( Advanced Dialog )              ( Cancel )  ( Get Photos )
```

Scanners

You can scan negatives, slides, and other transparencies with a film scanner, or you can scan prints with a flatbed scanner. Some film scanners will do batch scans, which can save loads of scanning time. If you have a lot of slides or negatives, you may also find reasonably priced services on the Web that offer mass film scanning.

Keep in mind that the quality of the scanner, as well as the resolution at which you scan, makes a difference in the quality of the scanned image. Of course, the larger the print, the better. Also keep in mind that a print is a step removed from the original. If your prints are 4 x 6 and you have a good-quality film scanner, you can probably get a better result by scanning the negatives.

Check scanner reviews on the Web to get an idea of scanner quality, or if you have a scanner, do some scans of your own and compare them with scans from other scanners and/or photo CDs to get an idea of the scanner's quality. Pay special attention to shadow and highlight detail. Check the image quality with prints from a good printer rather than on-screen if your scanned images are destined for print.

You can be confident that images for print will have enough resolution if they are scanned at 300ppi resolution or larger than their final printed size in inches. Images for on-screen display need to have 72ppi resolution at their final size in pixels. Web pages are often constrained to an 800 wide x 600 tall pixel area, so that should give you some idea of the pixel dimensions your images for the Web need to be. If in doubt, scan at a larger size. In Photoshop, enlarging image size comes with a much greater risk of loss of detail than reducing it.

If you scan images from printed publications, an undesirable *moiré pattern* will likely be included in the image because images printed in publications are made up of dots rather than continuous tone. You can attempt to avoid or reduce moiré patterns by using a blur option in your scanner software or by raising the image off the scanner bed slightly before you scan it (by mounting it on a firm substrate and placing it on top of coins, for example).

Images that are mostly gray can benefit from being scanned in RGB color mode. You have more initial information to work with in Photoshop, which can be useful even if you plan to convert the image to Grayscale mode. Many scanners also let you choose the color profile. Adobe RGB is a good color profile to use for scanning because it contains a relatively large amount of colors. You can convert the image to another color mode in Photoshop, if necessary.

Be sure to make a note of where you've told your scanner to save the scanned image on your computer. Then use Bridge or choose File ⇨ Open from within Photoshop to open the files on your hard drive into Photoshop.

The Internet

You can save images from Web pages to your computer by right-clicking on the image or image link and choosing Save Image As or Save Linked File As. If you don't have a mouse with a right-click or you are using a Mac, Ctrl+click to get the same context menu.

Images on the Web are low resolution, usually 72 ppi, so keep in mind resolution requirements for the purpose of your image.

If you are using Stock Art services, such as iStockPhoto, or photo collection sites, such as Flickr, there may be different sizes and resolutions available.

E-mail

Like images from Web pages, you can save many images or image attachments in e-mails to your computer by right-clicking on the image or image link and choosing Save Image As or Save Linked File As. If you don't have a mouse with a right-click or you are using a Mac, Ctrl+click to get the same context menu.

There may also be a download button in the e-mail program, which may not give you an opportunity to choose a location on your computer. If you can't choose a location, you will need to know where your computer auto-saves downloaded files or make a note of the image name and search your computer for it after it is downloaded.

JPEG is usually a fail-safe format for easy downloading through e-mail, but if a JPEG doesn't meet your needs, good formats for retrieval from e-mail are those that can be compressed and saved with ZipIt or Stuffit software. Common file extensions are ZIP and SIT files. ZipIt and Stuffit are inexpensive and can create self-extracting files at a reduced size. Once downloaded, either the files automatically decompress when they are saved to your computer, or you can double-click the downloaded files to decompress them. A decompressed version of the file will be saved in the same directory as the compressed version.

Many e-mail servers are set to limit the file size that can be received through e-mail. Often, the limit is 1MB. If the attached files are too large, the e-mail may not reach the recipient. E-mail providers should be able to tell you the file attachment size limitations.

Video

Common types of digital camcorders record to MiniDV tapes, MiniDVDs, or camcorder hard drives. Most use FireWire cables to connect to your computer so you can copy video files to your computer. See Figure 1.20 for FireWire connector types.

If you are shopping for a camcorder and want to edit your video in the video-editing software that comes with your operating system or in Photoshop, be sure to research which camcorder models can be used to transfer video files to your computer.

Transferring video files to your computer is generally easiest from camcorders that use MiniDV tapes. Video-editing software that comes with Windows (Windows Movie Maker) and the Mac OS (iMovie) can import MiniDV video and, if necessary, save it to a format that Photoshop can import. Still frames from videos can also be captured and saved to your computer from Windows Movie Maker and iMovie and opened in Photoshop. Figure 1.23 shows still frames in iMovie on a Mac.

Photoshop can open these Quicktime video file formats: MPEG-1 and -4, MOV, AVI, FLV (if Flash 8 is installed), and MPEG-2 (if an MPEG-2 encoder is installed).

Photoshop can open these image sequence formats: BMP, DICOM, JPEG, OpenEXR, PNG, PSD, Targa, TIFF, Cineon, and JPEG 2000 if the plug-ins are installed.

FIGURE 1.23

iMovie lets you capture and save a still frame by navigating to the frame within the movie clip and choosing Edit⇨Create Still Frame, then File⇨Save Frame.

Typical steps to get video from a digital camcorder onto your computer include:

1. **Make sure any recording media (MiniDV tape, MiniDVD disk) is in the camcorder.**

2. **Open Windows Movie Maker or iMovie.**

3. **Turn on the camcorder and make sure it is set to the video mode rather than the camera mode.** If the camcorder has a camera mode, this means it can also take still photos and save to a memory card.

4. **Connect the camcorder to your computer with an appropriate cable.**

5. **Import the video with Windows Movie Maker or iMovie, then save to a format that Photoshop supports.** For supported video formats, import directly into Photoshop by choosing File⇨Open or File⇨Import⇨Video Frames to Layers. Figure 1.24 shows how you can use iMovie to import video onto a Mac.

FIGURE 1.24

iMovie detects a connected video camera and lets you import the video by clicking the Import button.

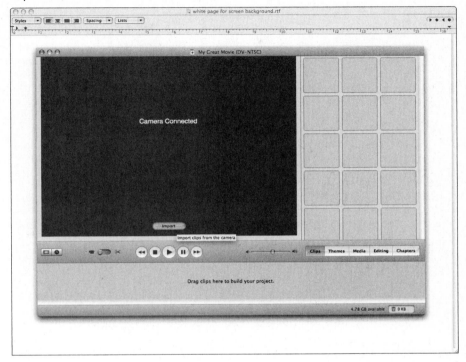

If these steps don't work for your camcorder and media, keep the following tips in mind:

- MiniDVD disks cannot be put into slot-loading DVD drives and require tray-loading DVD drives (which can be purchased inexpensively).

- More advanced video-editing software or video conversion software can be used if other video file conversions are needed to convert the video to a format that Photoshop supports. Quicktime Pro is an inexpensive video-editing software program for Windows and Mac and can be used to convert video formats.

- Some Web sites offer free video conversion for smaller files.

- Video-ripping software, such as MacTheRipper and Alcohol 120%, can extract video from copy-protected DVDs and save it to your computer. This process is subject to copyright laws.

- You may be able to convert VHS tapes to digital video and transfer those files to your computer. Typically, you would need the old camcorder (with the VHS tape inside) connected to a digital camcorder that has an AV to DV chip. An RCA cable may be needed to connect the VHS camcorder to the digital camcorder. The digital camcorder would then need to be connected to the computer, typically with a FireWire cable.

Storing Digital Images

It's easy for digital images to accumulate to an unmanageable number, and storing and backing up images is often a concern.

External hard drives are relatively inexpensive and offer large amounts of storage space. They can be used to regularly back up not only your images but also your entire internal hard drive. These drives are offered in different configurations and amounts of storage space, including those that offer 1TB of space or more, such as Seagate, Maxtor, LaCie, My Book, and Iomega external drives. Archival media include recordable DVD-Rs (which can hold more than 4GB) and CDs (which can hold about 700MB).

Rewritable storage includes DVD-RWs (more expensive than DVD-Rs) and USB Flash drives (very handy when you're on the go).

Summary

This chapter described the characteristics and types of digital images, getting images into Photoshop, and storing digital images. Following are key concepts:

Digital images contain pixels, usually square in shape, that describe their colors and brightness levels. It is important to be familiar with the specific terms Photoshop uses to describe brightness levels and color qualities. Brightness, lightness, luminosity, and luminance describe the dark to light qualities in an image, separate from the color qualities. Tonal range, or dynamic range, is the range of dark to light values in an image, usually referred to as shadows, midtones, and highlights. Hue refers to the color in an image, such as red, orange, or green. Saturation is the strength or purity of a color.

Characteristics of digital images include bit depth, bitmap or vector, color mode, color space, and file format. The images can originate from numerous sources, including digital cameras, film cameras, scanners, the Internet, e-mail, and camcorders. Digital images can be stored on numerous types of media, including internal or external computer hard drives, DVDs, CDs, and USB Flash drives.

Chapter 2

The Photoshop Workspace, Preferences, and Tools

Learning Photoshop is not the quickest or easiest task in the world, but there is something that can make it a lot easier: Start off with a good foundation of knowledge about the workspace and its general functions, including becoming a stickler about knowing the name of each part of the workspace.

I know that may not exactly sound like the fun part of learning Photoshop. But if you are trying to figure out how to accomplish something that *is* fun and you are being directed to the tool options bar, you'll be left behind if you wind up in the Toolbox. If you need to make adjustments to the color space and you wander off to the menu for the workspace, you'll be headed in the wrong direction. You might never find your way to making your friend with a full head of hair look like he's got a toupee flying off in the wind for his 40th birthday card, and in frustration, you might curse Photoshop and sell it on eBay.

So, in the interest of making a smoother ride for yourself on the way to creating utterly useless yet amusing imagery (or an image you actually need to create for your job), you may want to become an expert about the tools of the trade.

Overview of the Photoshop Workspace

With every new version of Photoshop, its work area evolves and improves, sometimes with just a few tweaks here and there.

Is perfection possible? I guess not. But the current workspace provides a powerful set of tools and more conveniences than ever before, as well as a few recently added features that make Photoshop a little more — dare I say — intuitive.

Figure 2.1 shows the Photoshop workspace. Across the very top is the Menu Bar. Under the Menu Bar is the Application Bar, and under that is the Options Bar. The Toolbox is on the far left, Panels are on the far right, and image windows display in the middle.

FIGURE 2.1

The Photoshop workspace with several images open

NOTE   If you don't see the word "Photoshop" in the upper-left corner of your screen, it means Photoshop is not active or is not open. Activate Photoshop by clicking the square blue icon that displays the letters "Ps" in the Taskbar (PC) or Dock (Mac), or open Photoshop by double-clicking the Adobe Photoshop CS4 application in your Programs folder (PC) or Applications folder (Mac). You may also have an application shortcut or favorite you can select to open Photoshop.

Default and custom workspaces

The workspace you see when you open Photoshop includes all of Photoshop's visible components:

- Menu Bar
- Tools panel

- Options Bar
- Image window (or document window)
- Panels

The workspace you see the first time you open Photoshop on your computer or before you change a component of its workspace is called the *default workspace.* It includes panels, bars, and windows that you can rearrange and customize according to which work area parts are convenient for you to have available when you work on various types of images. When you change the initial workspace arrangement, it is called a *custom workspace.*

Note the following ways you can affect the workspace by using the Window menu (found at the top of the screen):

- Save, load, delete, and reset workspaces in the Window ⇨ Workspace menu.
  - Save or delete a custom workspace by choosing Window ⇨ Workspace (Save Workspace or Delete Workspace).
  - Load a saved workspace by selecting its name at the bottom of the Window ⇨ Workspace menu.
  - Reset to the default workspace by choosing Window ⇨ Workspace ⇨ Default Workspace.
- You can activate a missing panel by selecting the panel name in the Window menu (add a check mark).

In addition to changing the arrangement and appearance of the workspace components, you can change the settings and preferences for Photoshop, most of which are in the Preferences menu. The Preferences menu can be found in the Menu Bar under the command Edit (PC) or Photoshop (Mac). Preference settings are saved each time you quit Photoshop so that the next time you open it, your changed preferences will still be active.

Sometimes it's a good idea to reset everything, including the workspace and preferences, to their defaults. For example, many tutorials show the default workspace and settings (or should). If you are doing a tutorial, it would be helpful to reset your workspace and settings to match the tutorial. Also, if unexpected or unexplained things are happening in Photoshop, it might mean the preferences are corrupt; you can try resetting them to their defaults to see if that helps.

To reset the workspace, preferences, and settings, do the following:

1. **Press and hold Alt+Ctrl+Shift (Option+⌘+Shift on a Mac) as you start Photoshop.**
2. **When you see a message about deleting the current settings, click to delete the settings.**
3. **After you delete settings, release the keys.** Photoshop opens with all its defaults active.

CAUTION   If you did not see a delete-settings message, the defaults were not activated. Quit Photoshop and go through the steps again. Sometimes you can press and hold the keys before and during the time you start Photoshop (easier), or you may need to press and hold the keys immediately after you start Photoshop (more difficult). If you have to do the latter, it may take several attempts to get the timing just right so that it brings up the delete-settings message. Yes, this can be frustrating!

Menu Bar

The menu that extends horizontally across the top of the computer screen and gives you access to Photoshop commands is called the Menu Bar. It displays the command set titles: Photoshop, File, Edit, Image, Layer, and so on, as shown in Figure 2.2. Clicking the mouse button on one of the command set titles displays a submenu of commands.

NOTE   *Context menus*, short menus conveniently accessible over some parts of the work area, can be activated by right-clicking (PC or Mac) or Control-clicking (Mac) on parts of the work area, including the image window tabs area, the image, panel tabs, and the rulers.

FIGURE 2.2

The Menu Bar

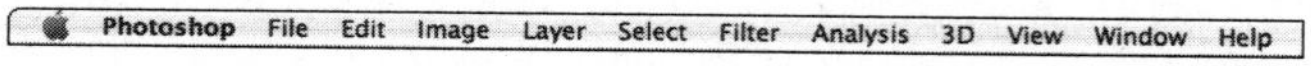

Photoshop   File   Edit   Image   Layer   Select   Filter   Analysis   3D   View   Window   Help

Application Frame

The default organization for the Photoshop workspace includes an Application Frame that is a container for everything in Photoshop except the Menu Bar. Think of it as a frame around Photoshop's work area, or the workspace window.

NEW FEATURE   The Application Frame helps keep Photoshop and its components organized and separate from other items on your computer by functioning like an image window for all your Photoshop "stuff" — it contains the entire workspace. When you minimize the Application Frame "window," all open images and all Photoshop workspace components (except the Menu Bar) minimize along with it. When you close the Application Frame, all open images also close.

The default workspace's Application Frame contains:

- Application Bar
- Options Bar
- Toolbox
- All open images
- Panels

The Application Frame does not contain the Menu Bar.

NOTE You can make one or more of the open images' windows float above and disconnect from the Application Frame by choosing Window ⇨ Arrange ⇨ Float All Windows. You can also turn off the Application Frame by choosing Window ⇨ Application Frame (deselect it), which makes the workspace look similar to the workspace in previous Photoshop versions.

Tabbed image windows, as opposed to floating image windows with title bars, surround open images. Multiple images are opened in side-by-side, overlapping, tabbed areas within an Application Frame (sort of like Web pages opened in separate tabs within one browser window). Clicking on an image's tab brings it to the front and makes it the active image.

Figure 2.3 shows the Application Frame with one open image.

Multiple images are, by default, opened in side-by-side, overlapping, tabbed areas within the Application Frame (see Figure 2.4).

FIGURE 2.3

The Application Frame and its contents, with one open image

FIGURE 2.4

The Application Frame and its contents, with multiple open images

The tabs contain the images' names. In Photoshop's tabbed-image situation, when the Application Frame is closed, any open images automatically close. When the Application Frame is minimized, the open images minimize along with the Application Frame, but the images do not close.

NOTE   You can turn off the Application Frame by choosing Window ➪ Application Frame from the Main Menu (deselect it). This causes any open image windows to become tabbed images within a floating image window, and it makes the Application Frame and its background disappear.

The functions of the Application Frame, which surrounds the workspace and any open images, are similar to the functions of a traditional floating image window in the following ways:

- You can change the size of the Application Frame, just as you can change the size of a floating image window, by dragging its resize box in the lower-right corner. You can also drag any of its edges to resize it (this is new to CS4).

■ Reducing the size of the Application Frame reduces the amount of the work area within view, but the view-percentage size of the work area components and any open images stay the same. This is like the fact that installing a smaller-sized window in your house would not change the appearance of the size of objects outside; it would just change how much of them you could see.

The Application Frame's default size is maximized and fills up the computer screen, so shrinking this frame is one way you can see and access the Desktop area of your computer.

■ You can close, minimize, or maximize the Application Frame by clicking those buttons located in the Application Bar (under the Menu Bar).

▪ **Close button.** Clicking this button closes the Application Frame "window" and its contents, including any open images, but leaves Photoshop and its Menu Bar open. Retrieve a closed Application Frame by choosing Window ➪ Workspace ➪ Default Workspace from the Menu Bar. Open a recently closed image by choosing File ➪ Open Recent ➪ *image name* from the Menu Bar.

▪ **Minimize button.** Clicking this button minimizes the Application Frame, along with any open images it contains, but does not close the images. You can also minimize the Application Frame by double-clicking its Application Bar, just as you can minimize a CS3 image window by double-clicking its title bar. Minimizing the Application Frame is one way you can see and access the Desktop area of your computer. You can retrieve a minimized Application Frame, along with any images it contains, by clicking on it in the Taskbar (PC) or Dock (Mac) area of your computer screen.

▪ **Maximize button.** Clicking this button makes the Application Frame fill the available space on your screen.

■ Move the Application Frame by dragging its Application Bar, which is along the top of the Application Frame (above the Options Bar and below the Menu Bar). This works just like moving a floating image window by dragging its title bar.

It is possible to float image windows above the Application Frame. Floating image windows are not bound to the Application Frame (see Figure 2.5). They do not close or minimize with the Application Frame — they have their own close, minimize, and maximize buttons.

You can float image windows by doing one of the following:

■ Choose Window ➪ Arrange ➪ Float All in Windows from the Menu Bar.

■ Drag a tabbed image window's tab into the section of the window that displays the image, and release the mouse button.

FIGURE 2.5

The Application Frame and its contents, with only floating image windows. Floating windows are not bound to the Application Frame.

You can make floating image windows change to tabbed windows by doing one of the following:

- Choose Window ➪ Arrange ➪ Consolidate All to Tabs from the Menu Bar.
- Drag a floating image window's title bar into the tabs area of a tabbed image window. (Release the mouse button when you see a highlighted drop zone.)

Figure 2.6 shows the work area and images with the Application Frame turned off.

Application Bar

The Application Bar (right below the Menu Bar) offers convenient access to some useful Photoshop features, including some great one-click icons that execute commonly used commands, such as a selection of workspace layout commands.

Figure 2.7 shows the Application Bar.

The Application Bar contains the following buttons (from left to right):

- **Launch Bridge button (symbol with Br):** Click on this button to launch Bridge.

FIGURE 2.6

The workspace with the Application Frame turned off

FIGURE 2.7

The Application Bar

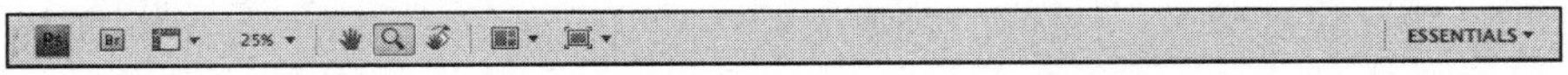

- **View Extras button (rectangle with rulers symbol):** Use this button to access a menu that allows you to choose to show guides, grids, or rulers.
- **Zoom Level button (a percentage number):** You can choose a variety of Zoom levels in this button's menu.
- **Hand tool button (hand symbol):** Click to activate the hand tool, which is used to drag a zoomed-in image to scroll in it.
- **Zoom tool button (magnifying glass symbol):** Click to activate the Zoom tool.
- **Rotate View tool (hand with arrows symbol):** Activate this tool and drag in the image to rotate the image within the image window. This rotates the view of the image only, not the actual image. This action will not work on some systems that don't have a supported graphics card or system version.

- **Arrange Documents button (three rectangles symbol):** You can use this button's menu to choose ways to arrange open documents, such as in a grid pattern in which you can see all open documents. When you choose an arrangement in which you can see multiple images at one time, this is sometimes called an *N-up view*. This buttons menu also features various zoom options.

- **Screen mode button (rectangle with corner borders symbol):** This button has a menu that lets you choose which screen mode you want to apply to the workspace.

Options Bar

The horizontal bar under the Application Bar and above the image window area is called the Options Bar. It is used primarily to set custom options for the active tool in the tools panel. The options you set for a tool determine some of the ways the tool will function. When you select different tools in the tools panel, you can see that the tool options available in the Options Bar change with each selected tool. Photoshop retains the options you set for a tool, so if those options aren't the ones you want the next time you use that tool, you have to change that tool's options.

Three consistent features in the Options Bar include:

- **Preset Picker.** On the far left side of the Options Bar, the Preset Picker offers a menu that you can use to save and load custom tools or sets of tools, along with their custom options. You can also use this menu to reset the active tool or all tools to their default options. Click the circle-and-arrow button inside the picker to see the menu. The Preset Manager can also be accessed in this menu. The Preset Manager can be used to manipulate sets of custom tools, brushes, swatches, and more.

- **Bridge button.** On the right side of the Options Bar, next to the Workspace menu, the Bridge button launches the Bridge application, which offers convenient ways to find and batch-process files (see Chapter 3).

- **Workspace menu.** On the right side of the Options Bar, the Workspace menu is a shorter version of the Menu Bar's Window ➪ Workspace and it allows you to activate the default workspace and save, load, or delete custom workspaces.

Figure 2.8 shows the Options Bar.

FIGURE 2.8

The Options Bar, where you can set the custom options for an active tool. A Workspace menu and a Bridge button (to the left of the Workspace menu) can be seen on the right side of the Options Bar.

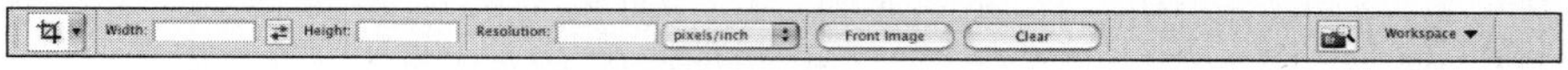

Tools panel

The vertical list of tool icons on the far left side of the work area is the Tools panel. Tools are used on images to move, select, crop, paint, set type, zoom, and more. Tools that have additional hidden tools behind them show a small black triangle to the lower right of the tool icon. Press and hold the mouse button on the tool icon to access one of the hidden tools.

Figure 2.9 shows the Tools panel. Figure 2.10 shows tool tips, which display names and sometimes keyboard shortcuts for a tool or another part of the work area.

FIGURE 2.9

The Tools panel

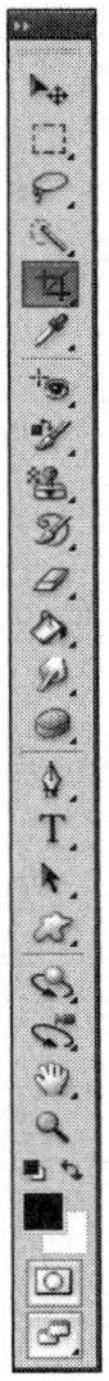

FIGURE 2.10

Tool tips can be displayed for tools and some other parts of the work area by hovering the pointer over an area for about 1 to 3 seconds.

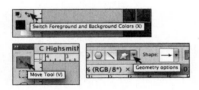

NEW FEATURE Spring-loaded keyboard shortcuts are new to CS4: If one tool is active, you can temporarily make another tool active by holding down its keyboard shortcut. For example: (1) select the Brush tool, (2) hold down the V key while you use the Move tool, and (3) let go of the V key to make the Brush tool active again.

Image windows

The part of the Photoshop work area that displays an image that has been opened in Photoshop is an image window, or document window. Image windows, by default, appear in the center of the workspace between the Tools panel on the left and the other panels on the right. Ah, if only it were that simple, you could stop here!

But, in CS4, multiple images can be open at one time in tabbed format, and by default they are connected to the Application Frame. They can also be open in separate floating image windows (not connected to the Application Frame) or in a combination of tabbed and floating windows. Furthermore, tabbed image windows can be opened in a tiled, or N-up, view so that each open image appears in a different pane (still connected to the Application Frame).

NEW FEATURE Tabbed image windows: Images are, by default, opened in tabbed windows that are within and connected to the Application Frame. Multiple images open in side-by-side, overlapping tabbed areas within the Application Frame, just as Web pages open in separate tabs within one browser window.

Floating windows can be tiled, as in previous Photoshop versions, so you can see part of each open floating window (see Figure 2.11). Multiple tabbed images can also be open within one floating image window. Hm. This may take a little getting used to, but think about the fact that all these choices make the workspace more flexible — even if you don't completely understand why you need so many choices. Read on to find out how you can implement and work with all these new window arrangements. It's actually kind of cool.

NEW FEATURE Multiple open tabbed image windows can be shown in a tiled format, with each image in a separate pane. This is called the N-up view.

You can arrange multiple tabbed image windows in an N-up view by doing one of the following:

- Drag image window tabs up, down, right, or left (release your mouse button when a blue-highlighted line appears in a drop zone). The images' panes can be resized by dragging the pane dividers.

- Choose Window ⇨ Arrange ⇨ Tile from the Menu Bar. You can drag the image window tabs and panes to rearrange.

FIGURE 2.11

Multiple tabbed images shown in a tiled, or N-up, view

You can float image windows by doing one of the following:

- Choose Window ⇨ Arrange ⇨ Float All in Windows (or Float in Window to float only the active image).

- Drag a window's tab on top of the image itself. Release the mouse button. (You will not see a highlight before you release the mouse button in this case.)

You can tile floating image windows by choosing Window ⇨ Arrange ⇨ Tile from the Menu Bar.

> **TIP** You can cycle through open tabbed document windows. Make the next tabbed window active by pressing Ctrl+Tab.

You can change floating windows to tabbed windows by doing one of the following:

- Drag a floating image window's title bar into the tabs area of one or more tabbed image windows. (Release the mouse button when you see a drop zone highlight.)

- Choose Window ⇨ Arrange ⇨ Consolidate All to Tabs from the Menu Bar.

- Right-click (PC or Mac) or Control-click (Mac) in the tabs area of one or more open image windows to get a context menu, and choose Consolidate All to Here.

Figure 2.12 shows an open floating image and two tabbed images. Figure 2.13 shows the Consolidate All to Here context menu.

FIGURE 2.12

This image window arrangement shows one open floating image and two tabbed images.

FIGURE 2.13

The Consolidate All to Here command in the image window tabs context menu changes any floating windows to tabbed windows.

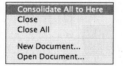

If a floating window is active and you open another image, the image opens as a second tabbed image within the floating image window, resulting in two tabbed images being open in one floating image window.

Tabbed images are normally connected to the Application Frame, but if the tabbed image windows are contained within a floating window, they are not connected to the Application Frame. Figure 2.14 shows a floating image window that contains two tabbed images.

This floating image window contains two tabbed images and one other tabbed image that is still connected to the Application Frame.

Because multiple images can be open in Photoshop at the same time, you can move quickly from image to image because you don't have to wait for each one to open. But only one image can be active at a given time.

The filename of an open image displays at the top of its image window in its tab or in a floating window's title bar. If a floating window contains multiple tabbed windows, the image names display on their tabs, and the active image's name displays on the floating window's title bar.

If multiple images are open in Photoshop, the image with the most visually noticeable image name is the active image. Other open images' names are grayed out or darkened. When an image is active, the panels reflect the characteristics of that image and you can work on that image.

Make an open image the active image by doing one of the following:

■ Click once anywhere on an image or an image's window (such as on its tab, title bar, the image itself, or its scroll bar).

■ If there are so many tabbed images open that you can't see all their tabs, click and hold down the mouse button on the double arrows on the right side of the tabs area to access a menu of all open images. Select the image's name from the open-images menu.

Figures 2.15 through 2.17 show various combinations of multiple open image windows, and their captions describe the active image in each set.

FIGURE 2.15

The tabbed image window in the front with the light-colored tab is active. The two other tabs with image names indicate that there are two other images opened, but they are inactive. Clicking on an inactive image tab brings it to the front and makes it active.

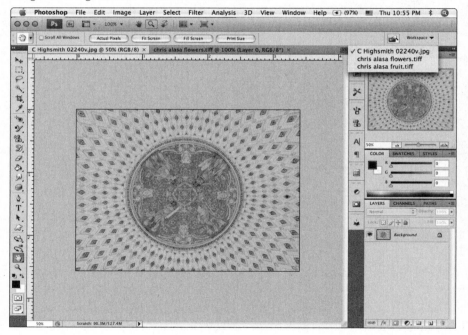

FIGURE 2.16

The image window with the light-colored tab in this N-up arrangement is active. The two other images are open, but inactive. Clicking anywhere on an image or its window brings it to the front and makes it active.

Tabbed image windows (the default) are connected to the Application Frame — they close, minimize, and maximize when you do the same to the Application Frame. A tabbed image can also be closed independently of the Application Frame by clicking the "x" on its tab.

Floating image windows can be closed, minimized, or maximized independently of the Application Frame. Closing a floating image window closes the image — it is no longer open in Photoshop. Minimizing a floating image window stores it on the taskbar or dock until clicked; clicking brings it up again. Maximizing a floating image window makes it fill up all the available space on-screen. The top of a floating image window is called its title bar. You can move a floating image window by dragging its title bar. You can resize it by dragging its resize box in the lower-right corner.

FIGURE 2.17

The floating image window in the front is active. You can see parts of two other open but inactive floating images' windows (see the image names in their title bars). Clicking anywhere on an inactive image or its window brings it to the front and makes it active.

Minimize, maximize, and close buttons look different on PCs and Macs. Figure 2.18 shows the PC and Mac minimize, maximize, and close buttons. You'll find these buttons at the top of floating image windows and at the top of the Application Frame (in the Application Bar, under the Menu Bar).

FIGURE 2.18

Minimize, maximize, and close buttons on a PC (left); the same buttons on a Mac (right)

Figure 2.19 shows a tabbed (the default) and a floating image window.

FIGURE 2.19

Left: a tabbed image window; right: a floating image window

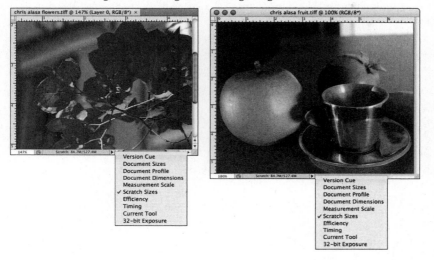

The parts of an image window are as follows:

- **Tab or title bar.** At the top of the image window is a tab that shows the image name (on a tabbed window) or a title bar that shows the image name (on a floating window). The view percentage, color mode, and bit depth are displayed next to the image name. A title bar has close, minimize, and maximize buttons; a tab has a close button.

- **Scroll bars.** If the image is zoomed in far enough that you can't see the entire image, you see scroll bars and scroll arrows on the right and bottom of the image window.

- **Status Bar.** At the bottom left of an image window is the Status Bar, which is made up of the following:

  - **View percentage:** You can enter a specific view percentage size.

  - **File information:** By clicking and holding down the mouse button on the arrow, you can display any information from the remaining bullets.

  - **Version Cue:** Displays the Version Cue workgroup status of your document, such as open, unmanaged, unsaved, and so on. Version Cue is separate software that can help you keep up with different versions of your documents; for example, if multiple people work on the same document at different times.

  - **Document sizes:** The number on the left is the approximate size of the saved, flattened file in Photoshop format (you generally flatten a file's layers before you save a final version). The number on the right is the approximate pre-flattened size of the file with its layers and channels.

- **Document profile:** The name of the color profile used by the image (see Part VII, Color Management and Workflow).

- **Document Dimensions:** The dimensions of the image in the active units, such as inches or pixels.

- **Measurement Scale:** The scale of the document, as used by the Analysis menu, Measurements log panel, and ruler tool (see Part VIII, Video, 3-D Images, and Technical Images).

- **Scratch Sizes:** The total amount of RAM memory plus scratch disk memory that is used to process the image. The number on the left is the amount of memory currently being used to display all open images. The number on the right is the total amount of RAM available on your computer for processing images.

- **Efficiency:** The percentage of time actually spent performing an operation instead of reading or writing to the scratch disk. If the value is below 100 percent, Photoshop is using the scratch disk and is therefore operating more slowly.

- **Timing:** The amount of time it took to complete the last operation.

- **Current tool:** Displays the name of the active tool.

- **32-bit Exposure:** Shows a slider for adjusting the preview image for viewing 32-bits-per-channel high dynamic range (HDR) images on your monitor (see Chapter 1). The slider is available only when 32-bit mode is active.

- **Resize box.** At the lower-right corner of an image window is its resize box. Drag it to resize the image window.

CAUTION   If you make an image window very small, you may not be able to see the Status Bar.

TIP   If there are performance problems in Photoshop, the Scratch Sizes, Efficiency, and Timing information can tell you whether you need to increase RAM memory and hard drive memory (scratch disk space).

TIP   Clicking and holding down the mouse button on the file information display area while clicking and holding the Alt/Option button temporarily displays the active image's width, height, resolution, and number of channels. This is especially useful when you want to double-check that information before releasing your final file.

You can also choose to display rulers and guides in an image window to help you measure, align, or precisely place parts of an image (see Figure 2.20). Following are ways to activate and manipulate rulers and guides:

- To show rulers, choose View ➪ Rulers (to add a check mark).

- To set the ruler's units of measurement, right-click (PC or Mac) or Control-click (Mac) on a ruler to get a context menu, and choose the units.

- To move the zero point of the ruler, drag the cross-hairs at the upper-left corner of the rulers (where they meet) to the area in the image window that you want the zero point to be.

- To add a guide, drag from a ruler into the image window.

- To move a guide, drag it with the Move tool.

- To remove a guide, drag it off the image window.

- To make objects, selection tools, and so on snap to guides, choose View ➪ Snap or View ➪ Snap to ➪ Guides.

- To hide guides, choose View ➪ Extras or press Ctrl+H/⌘+H to toggle the view of the guides. Or you can choose View ➪ Show ➪ Guides or press Ctrl+semicolon/⌘+semicolon to toggle the view of the guides.

FIGURE 2.20

An image window with rulers and guides

There are several new features in the Photoshop workspace, including the much-anticipated Rotate Canvas, shown in Figure 2.21. Also new are the following features:

- Smooth display at odd Zoom levels
- Animated Zoom — Smooth Zoom when clicking and holding down the mouse button
- Animated transitions when doing a one-stop zoom (for example, Ctrl++)
- Flicking or hand-tossing images with the Hand tool
- A pixel grid displays when zoomed to greater than 500 -percent
- Shift+click-hold with the Hand tool selected takes you into Birdseye view

Figure 2.22 shows a Birdseye view. These new features have video card requirements, however. See OpenGL in Performance Preferences for more information.

FIGURE 2.21

A Canvas rotated with the Rotate Canvas tool

FIGURE 2.22

A Birdseye view

Panels

Panels, most of which are found on the right side of the workspace, are used to perform various tasks on images. The Tools panel is on the left side of the workspace. Panels can be displayed individually, as part of a panel group, or they can be collapsed to icons or icons-plus-panel-names. Individual, separate panels appear in their own window. Panel groups contain multiple panels, and their tabs are shown side by side. A panel's tab shows the name of the panel.

The panel icons dock, which initially shows a vertical list of panel icons without panel names, can be seen on the left side of the panel groups in Photoshop's default workspace (choose Window ➪ Workspace ➪ Default Workspace).

 **If you can't find a panel, you can make it appear by choosing Window ➪ *panel name* (to add a check mark) from the Menu Bar.**

Panels, panel icons, panel-icons-plus-names, and panel groups can be moved, separated, rearranged, and combined into different groups. You can reorganize panels by doing any of the following:

- Click on a panel's tab to bring that panel to the front of a group.

- Click on a panel's or panel group's double-arrows icon on its title bar (top bar) to toggle the panel's appearance between a full and an abbreviated view. If it has a title bar, you can also click it (when it highlights slightly after you hover the mouse over it) to toggle the view.

- Move a panel or panel group by doing one of the following:

  - Drag any of the following features that are present in a panel or panel group: icon, title bar, tab, or double-dotted-line gripper (this also applies to the Tools panel, Option Bar, Application Bar, and Application Frame). Drag it to the desired location.

  - If you want to move your panel in between another panel or panel group, release the mouse button when you see a blue-highlighted line or box over a drop zone (a place that Photoshop lets you drop the panel). That highlight is your cue to release the mouse button, placing the panel or panel group in its new location.

  - If you want to move a panel group that doesn't have a title bar, hold down Alt/Option while you drag one of the group's panel tabs.

- Make a panel or panel group dock (or snap) to the edge of another panel by dragging it until you see a blue-highlighted drop zone that is on the edge of another panel.

- Click on a panel icon in the panel icon's dock to temporarily show and use the panel. Clicking on the double arrows in its title bar collapses it back to an icon.

- Resize most panels by dragging their resize box in the lower-right corner or their right, left, or bottom edge. A few panels will not resize. To resize panel groups, drag the black line that separates them up or down.

- Close a panel by dragging its tab out of a group or set, then clicking its close button in the left side of its title bar, or you can deselect the panel's name in the Window menu.

TIP   **If you drag a set of panel groups out of the Application Frame so that the set floats, you can drag the set back into the Application Frame by dragging its title bar to the right edge of the Application Frame until you see a drop zone highlight.**

 When dragging a part of a workspace component or panel to move it, you will see a drop zone highlight appear when your mouse reaches a potential destination that is between or beside other workspace components. The highlight is your cue to release the mouse button. Often the highlight will be a bright blue line or box, or it may be a black line. You can always revert to the original workspace arrangement by choosing Window ⇨ Workspace ⇨ Default Workspace from the Menu Bar.

Figures 2.23 through 2.25 show parts of the workspace you can drag, click on, or move panels to when rearranging the workspace.

FIGURE 2.23

Arrows are shown over some of the panel areas you can drag (to move or resize), circles are shown over some parts of the panels you can click on (to change their view or close them), and squares are shown over some areas of the panels to which you can move other panels.

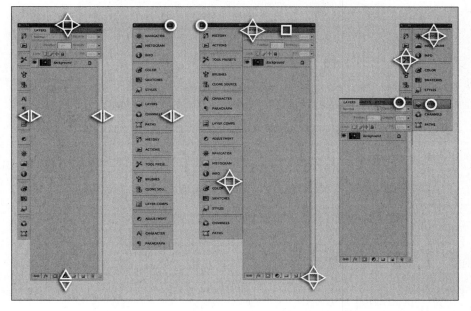

FIGURE 2.24

Arrows are shown over some of the N-up view window areas you can drag (to move or resize), and squares are shown over some areas of the windows to which you can move other windows.

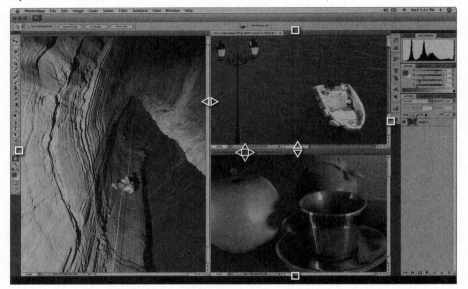

FIGURE 2.25

Arrows are shown over some of the Application Frame areas you can drag (to move or resize).

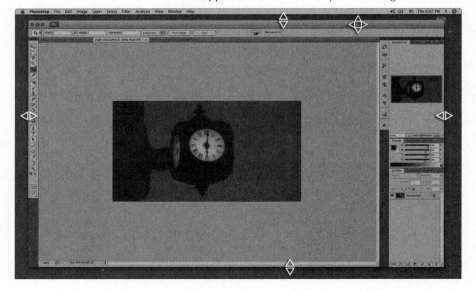

Common Workspace Items

This graphic shows buttons, menu items, and symbols in numerous areas in Photoshop. Each item has the same or a similar function even when it is found in different parts of the workspace. Some items, shown grouped and captioned, have similar uses.

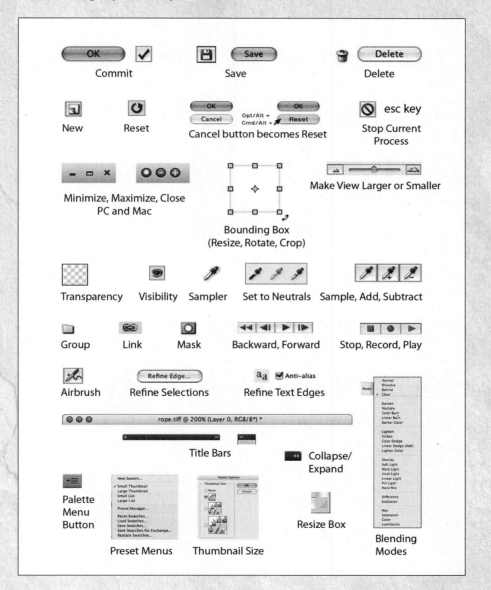

OK ✓
Commit

Save
Save

Delete
Delete

New

Reset

Cancel button becomes Reset

esc key
Stop Current
Process

Minimize, Maximize, Close
PC and Mac

Bounding Box
(Resize, Rotate, Crop)

Make View Larger or Smaller

Transparency   Visibility   Sampler   Set to Neutrals   Sample, Add, Subtract

Group   Link   Mask   Backward, Forward   Stop, Record, Play

Airbrush   Refine Selections   Refine Text Edges

Title Bars

Collapse/
Expand

Palette
Menu
Button

Preset Menus   Thumbnail Size

Resize Box

Blending
Modes

Preferences

The settings in Photoshop's Preferences dialog boxes can have a major effect on Photoshop's performance and your user experience. You can use Preferences to optimize Photoshop's performance, set how some parts of the workspace function, and more. So, it's a good idea to familiarize yourself with them and with what they do. Then you can set them in the way that's best for your computer setup and workflow needs.

On PCs, you can find the Preferences command in the Edit menu, and on Macs, in the Photoshop menu. You can access the various Preferences dialog boxes from the main Preferences window. Figure 2.26 shows the main Preferences dialog box with the General Preferences options active. On the left side of the Preferences menu, the Preferences dialog boxes can be selected and made active so you can change settings.

FIGURE 2.26

The Preferences dialog box, with the General set of preferences active

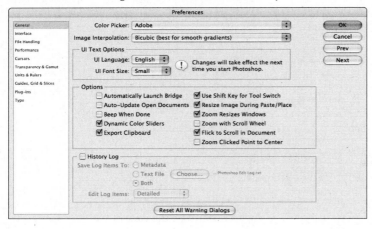

General preferences

Photoshop's Preferences main menu provides access to numerous dialog boxes that can be used to set the way in which some parts of the workspace and the Photoshop application look and function. To access the Preferences menu, choose Edit ➪ Preferences ➪ General/Photoshop ➪ Preferences ➪ General. You can select sets of preferences on the left side of the Preferences menu (except for Camera Raw preferences), and the dialog boxes of those sets are brought to the front. Following are descriptions of the sets of preferences and their options.

Color Picker

The Color Picker is probably the most commonly used dialog box for selecting a color to use in Photoshop. It can be accessed in numerous places in the workspace, including clicking the foreground color box in the Tools panel. The default Color Picker selected in this menu is Adobe, which is a good one to use for photographs and general purposes. I haven't heard of a different Color Picker often being used, but if you want to use a different one, you can select your operating system's Color Picker, or you can install a different Color Picker plug-in and select it.

Image Interpolation

Resizing an entire image (or an object in an image) and causing its total number of pixels to change means that Photoshop must either throw away some of the image's pixels or add pixels that aren't there. This is called *resampling*.

In order to make smooth transitions in the changed areas, Photoshop has to decide what colors to make the newly added, in-between pixels or how to adjust the color of the pixels on the edges of areas where pixels have been thrown away. The way Photoshop resamples image pixels, in an effort to maintain image quality, is called the *interpolation method*. The default interpolation method is set in this preferences menu, and you can also activate an interpolation method for one-time use in the Image Size dialog box.

CROSS-REF Interpolation methods are described in Chapter 5.

UI Text Options

Choose the language and font size for the user interface — including the text in the Options Bar, panels, and tool tips.

- **Automatically Launch Bridge.** This option causes the Bridge application to launch when Photoshop is launched.

- **Auto-Update Open Documents.** This option maintains a link between the open document and the document on disk so that, when a single file that is opened in two applications at the same time or on different computers at the same time, the view of the image updates in both places when it is changed and saved (overwritten) from either place. (Changes can be undone from either place while the image is still open.)

  When this option is off, the view of an image changed and saved from a different application or computer does not update until you close and reopen it.

- **Beep When Done.** This option makes a beeping sound happen when an operation in Photoshop is finished. If you expect an operation to be time-consuming, you could do something else while it is running and be alerted by the beep when it is finished.

- **Dynamic Color Sliders.** The Color panel can be used to mix color modes' individual colors to make a composite color that is assigned to the foreground or background. Each individual color in the Color panel has a slider that can be dragged across a color bar to add or subtract amounts of that color to or from the result color. Turning on this preference makes each slider's color bar show all the possible colors you can make by dragging that particular slider.

If this preference is off, each slider's color bar shows only the values of the slider's single color that can be added to or subtracted from the result color. A result color box in the Color panel previews the new color as you drag the sliders, so this option is just a personal preference.

- **Export Clipboard.** This option automatically saves any Clipboard contents to your operating system's Clipboard when you quit Photoshop. This allows you to paste things that you copied in Photoshop to other applications even after you quit Photoshop (but before you copy something else to the Clipboard, which replaces the Clipboard contents).

- **Use Shift Key for Tool Switch.** If you select a tool that has hidden tools, you can cycle through its tools by pressing the Shift key plus the tool's keyboard shortcut key multiple times. Turning off this option allows you to cycle through hidden tools by pressing only the keyboard shortcut key multiple times. Since it's kind of a pain to have to press the Shift key, too, why not turn this off?

- **Resize Image During Paste/Place.** This option resizes your image during a Place command. If this option is turned on when you are placing an image with larger pixel dimensions into an image with smaller pixel dimensions, the larger image's size is reduced so that you can see the entire image when you place it. A transform box is active around the placed image so you can resize it right away, if necessary.

  If this option is turned off, you can only see part of a larger image that has been placed into the smaller one, and the transform box handles are outside the image window area (zooming out allows you to see the handles).

- **Zoom Resizes Windows.** If you check this option, image windows resize along with images when they are zoomed. You can also activate this feature in the Zoom tool's Options Bar.

- **Zoom with Scroll Wheel.** This option enables you to use the scroll wheel, if your mouse has one, to zoom in or out instead of scrolling in your Photoshop document.

NEW FEATURE You can now flick a document to scroll it *(flick-panning)*. Drag it quickly with the hand tool, let go, and it keeps sliding like a puck on an air-hockey table. This does not work with some video cards.

- **Flick to Scroll in Document.** This option enables flick-panning. When you click the mouse button, drag quickly with the Hand tool, and let go, the image continues to pan or scroll after you let go. Clicking the mouse or using the keyboard during this animation interrupts the panning.

- **Zoom Clicked Point to Center.** This option causes the location that is clicked with the Zoom tool to be in the center of the image window.

History Log

Selecting this option allows you to keep a record of what's been done to a file in Photoshop, either for your or your client's needs, or for legal purposes.

- **Metadata, Text, or Both.** You can choose whether to save the History Log information in an external text file for which you can choose a save location and a name (Choose button), in the metadata of the file itself (which could make the file much larger), or in both an external text file and the metadata inside the file.

  You can view metadata by selecting the image in Adobe Bridge or by choosing File ⇨ File Info while the image is active in Photoshop.

  If you need to prove that the History Log information hasn't been changed by someone, you can save the information in the image's metadata, then use Adobe Acrobat to digitally sign the log file.

- **Edit Log Items.** This option lets you choose how much history information to save:

  - **Sessions Only:** Keeps a record of each time you start or quit Photoshop and each time you open and close files (includes image filenames).

  - **Concise:** Saves the text that appears in the History panel and the Sessions information.

  - **Detailed:** Saves the text that is seen in the Actions, the Concise information, and the Sessions information.

- **Reset All Warning Dialogs.** Clicking this button enables any warning dialog boxes that you have disabled by selecting the warning dialog box's "Don't show again" option.

The History Log does not store what your document looked like after each change. To save a visual record of image changes that coordinates with History Log information, follow these steps:

1. **Make changes to the document.**

2. **Before you close the document, for each state in the History panel, select the state, and then click the Create new document from current state button at the bottom of the History panel.** Each document is named with History States text, which is also saved in the History Log (when Concise or Detailed methods are set in History Log preferences).

3. **In the initial document, choose the last History State again and save the image with all its changes.**

4. **Save each document that was created from each History State (they should still be open).** If you save the History State images in the order the History States were created, it may help you put the documents in order, number them, or match them up to the History Log entries. (Some History States may have the same text; therefore, some of the History State images could have the same names + 1, 2, 3, and so on.)

5. **If you would like to create a presentation of the states of an image, you can use the History State images and Adobe Bridge to create a PDF presentation (choose Tools ⇨ Photoshop ⇨ PDF Presentation).** You can also use the images with other presentation software or animation methods.

Interface preferences

The next tab in the Preferences window is Interface. With the various options shown here, you can easily and precisely adjust what your workspace interface looks like.

General

The options under the General tab for Interface preferences help you configure what shows up in your workspace and how it appears.

- **Use Grayscale Application Icon.** This option makes the "Ps" Photoshop icon in the Application Bar appear in grayscale rather than in color.

- **Show Channels in Color.** This option shows the channels in their respective hues instead of in a grayscale representation. You might want to turn this option on if seeing the channels in color is useful to you for some reason, such as seeing the Cyan channel in Cyan so you can get some idea of what the cyan color separation should look like printed on paper by a printing press (in the absence of a printed proof of the cyan separation).

- **Show Menu Colors.** This option makes visible any colors you have assigned to the background of menu commands, which can be done in the dialog box found by choosing Edit ➪ Menus or Window ➪ Workspace ➪ Keyboard Shortcuts & Menus ➪ Menus. Assigning colors to commands can help you quickly find commonly used commands.

- **Show Tool Tips.** This option enables tool tips, which are names or functions of a part of the workspace that appear when you hover the mouse over the tools and some other parts of the workspace for about 1 to 3 seconds (without pressing the mouse button). Keyboard shortcuts are sometimes shown in the tool tips.

Panels

The Panels preferences in the Interface tab enable you to determine how your panels behave: where they appear when you open them and how they close when you're done with them.

- **Auto-Collapse Icon Panels.** This option causes any panels that have been opened by clicking their icon to automatically close when you click on another part of the workspace.

- **Remember Panel Locations.** When you launch Photoshop, this option makes panels display in the same arrangement as they were the last time Photoshop was open. If it is turned off, the default panel locations are loaded. This is a personal preference; keep in mind you can also save and load custom workspaces. In a computer lab environment, you might want to have this option turned off.

File handling preferences

The third tab in the Preferences window enables you to choose your file saving preferences and your file format preferences.

Image Previews

Choose when and if to save image previews. Image previews determine how your image looks on-screen in operating systems and other applications, as opposed to how it prints. It's a good idea to always save previews, except when saving for the Web if the previews add too much to the file size. If that is an issue, you may want to choose Ask When Saving so you can make decisions about previews in Save dialog boxes.

CROSS-REF   Image Previews options are described in Chapter 7.

Camera Raw Preferences

Click this button to access the Camera Raw Preferences dialog box.

CROSS-REF   See Camera Raw Preferences in Chapter 4.

Prefer Adobe Camera Raw for supported RAW files

This option causes supported RAW files to be opened by Adobe Camera Raw instead of by other software.

Ignore EXIF profile tag

EXIF (Exchangeable Image File) data is information about a photo that is embedded in the photo file by a digital camera. The source color profile of the image — or the set of colors the specific camera used to describe the photo — is among the EXIF information.

If camera color profiles were always accurate, this information would often help Photoshop keep the image colors consistent between the cameras and the view of the photos that you see on your monitor (and further down the chain, as your image is transferred from device to device). Unfortunately, camera color profiles are not always accurate. But since they are sometimes accurate, I like to leave this preference unchecked so Photoshop can use this color information to interpret the colors in the image.

If you don't like the result, no harm done. Try plugging the photo into a different set of colors before you start color-correcting by assigning a color profile to the image after it is in Photoshop or Adobe Camera Raw (as opposed to converting the color profile). Assigning ignores the camera color profile and starts over by plugging the image data into a set of colors of your choice, which is actually what ignoring the EXIF profile would do in the first place.

CROSS-REF   See Chapter 4 for more information about Camera Raw and Chapter 23 for more information about Color Management.

Ask Before Saving Layered TIFF files

I like to keep this preference on. The file size of a layered TIFF can often end up being larger than a layered Photoshop file, and layered TIFFs are not fully compatible with some software. In contrast, flattened (non-layered) TIFFs can be saved with options that make them compatible with most software and are a smaller size.

Since the TIFF format couldn't always support layers, a common workflow has included saving a layered version of an image in Photoshop format and a final flattened version in TIFF format. My preference is to keep this habit in my workflow, partly to help me more quickly recognize my flattened files versus layered files. However, Photoshop can open layered TIFFs as well as layered Photoshop format files, so if layered TIFFs are not causing you a problem, be aware that this is really a personal preference.

Maximize PSD and PSB File Compatibility

This option saves a flattened version of a layered Photoshop or Large Document Format (PSB) file within the file, behind the scenes. This allows very old Photoshop versions, or other software that can't read layers or some of Photoshop's newer features, to open the file. The disadvantage is that a maximized-compatibility file often has a much larger size.

Another thing to consider is that, starting with Photoshop CS3, a little bit of data in addition to the flattened version of the file is included in the file when you choose Maximize Compatibility. This data helps ensure that PSD and PSB files saved in Photoshop CS3 and later will not just open, but will open correctly in earlier versions of Photoshop.

Having this option on causes a warning message to appear if you open a CS3 or later file in a previous version and if it has a feature in it that is not supported by the previous version. This can help you avoid accidentally overlooking something wrong in an opened file that has unsupported features.

This preference is a judgment call, but unless you are often opening CS3 and later files in earlier versions, I recommend selecting Never or Ask When Saving rather than Always, because of the file size issue. If you encounter file compatibility problems or notice differences in a file opened in a previous Photoshop version, you could then save a maximized or flattened version of the file (which will have a smaller size).

Enable Version Cue

Adobe Version Cue is software that manages file versions when multiple people need to work on the same files. It is included in many Adobe software collections. Version Cue can track changes to a file as you or someone else works on it, and it can streamline file sharing and online reviews. If you use Version Cue, of course you'll want to turn this on, but if not, you can leave it off.

Recent file list contains __ files

The number you type in this option determines how many of your recently opened files appear when you choose File ➪ Open Recent menu.

CROSS-REF See Chapter 5 for more information about opening files and Chapter 7 for more information about saving files.

Performance preferences

The fourth tab in the Preferences window is for Performance, where you can tailor Photoshop's operation to your specific needs. Choose how your memory is allocated, set your History options, and choose your graphics production unit (GPU) settings. If you hold your cursor over an option name, a description of it appears in the Description box.

Memory Usage

This dialog box helps you choose memory for Photoshop. It gives you information about the available RAM you have, as well as Photoshop's ideal range, enabling you to configure your memory usage knowledgeably.

Available RAM

This displays the amount of available RAM on your system, minus the amount your operating system is already using. RAM is working-area memory, as opposed to storage memory. The more RAM you have, the more applications you can have open at the same time, the larger files you can work on, and the faster processing speeds you can enjoy.

Ideal Range

This is Photoshop's estimate for the ideal range of the amount of your computer's RAM you should allocate to Photoshop.

Let Photoshop Use

This setting can be used to allocate RAM to Photoshop or limit how much RAM Photoshop can use so that it doesn't gobble up too much. The default percentage is fine for most users. You shouldn't set it to 100 percent unless you have more than 2GB of RAM because other applications that are running at the same time might end up with too little RAM.

If you want to figure out exactly how much RAM you can make available to Photoshop, one way is to start with an amount within the Ideal Range and increase the RAM allocation in 5 percent increments (restart to activate). You can watch Photoshop's Efficiency Indicator in the Status Bar at the bottom of an image window while you work in Photoshop to determine the amount of RAM you need for your open images.

When the Efficiency Indicator goes below 95 to100 percent, you have used up all the RAM and are using the scratch disk (hard disk space) for substitute RAM, which is slower than using real RAM memory. When efficiency gets down to 60 percent, increasing the amount of RAM allocation can greatly improve performance. You may need to purchase more RAM for your computer in order to allocate more RAM to Photoshop. On a Mac, you can also watch the operating systems' Activity Monitor (in Utilities) to view the RAM allocations on your computer (see the System Memory section of the Activity Monitor).

Photoshop CS4 comes with a 64-bit version that you can choose to install on one of the following 64-bit operating systems: Windows XP 64 or Windows Vista 64. No Mac 64-bit OSs are compatible with the 64-bit version of Photoshop at the time of writing. These operating systems run on computers with 64-bit processors. The 64-bit technology makes it possible for a computer to access more RAM than in 32-bit architecture. If you can use the 64-bit version, you can allocate a lot more RAM to Photoshop, which improves performance.

Even running the traditional 32-bit version of Photoshop on a 64-bit system allows you to allocate more RAM to Photoshop than running the 32-bit version on a 32-bit system (if you have ample RAM installed, that is).

NOTE If you want to use plug-ins or other components that are not compatible with 64-bit technology, you will need to install the 32-bit version of Photoshop.

Scratch Disks

When Photoshop runs out of RAM, it uses some hard disk space as a substitute for RAM, which is slower than using RAM memory. A hard disk that is used for this purpose is called a *scratch disk*. It's best to choose a drive other than the startup disk if you have a second internal hard drive. If you have no additional internal drive, you can choose your startup disk as the scratch disk.

CAUTION Don't use a partition on the startup disk as a scratch disk because that slows Photoshop down.

It's okay to use a partition on an internal drive other than the startup disk, or you can use a non-partitioned internal disk as a scratch disk. If you do that, you may want to make the partition around 13GB. If possible, don't use the scratch disk for anything except Photoshop. RAID partitions provide the best performance as Photoshop scratch disks (RAID 0, or an SSD RAID array if you have the budget for one).

In the Scratch Disks preference, you can select which available hard drives are to be used as scratch disks by putting a check mark in the box to the left of the drive names. You can change the order in which Photoshop uses the scratch disks by clicking the arrows to the right of the disk names. Restart to activate.

History and Cache

Here you can choose how far back you can look at changes you've made to your project and how much information to store in its image caching to enable you to pull up a figure again quickly.

History States

This option determines how many History States, or states of the image after each change, are kept in the History panel. You can use the History panel to do multiple undos or to paint on a part of an image from a previous state, so more History States give you more flexibility. If you are cloning or painting, you tend to use up History States quickly because a History State is recorded for each paint stroke. So, set the number of History States higher when painting. The downside is that setting a higher number of History States uses more RAM. If you have performance problems, reduce the number of History States and see if that helps.

Cache Levels

Recently used or often-needed information can be stored in a place on a computer called the *cache* (pronounced "cash"), where it can be accessed quickly. Photoshop can use image caching to store lower-view-size and lower-resolution versions of an image so it can give you the advantage of quicker screen redraws of the less-than-100-percent-view-size versions of an image as you edit the file. Otherwise, Photoshop has to take the time to calculate how a smaller view size at full resolution should look each time you zoom out. The Cache Levels specify how many different lower-view-size versions of the image to save in the cache.

Views at 100-percent-view-size are accurate and give accurate readings whether caching is on or off (the lower-resolution cached versions are all smaller than the 100-percent-view-size, full-resolution version). Files may also take longer to open because during the opening process, they are creating the specified number of cached versions of the files.

To enable the Cache Levels option, specify a number (above 1) of lower-resolution, lower-than-100-percent-view-size versions you want Photoshop to store in the cache.

Setting the Cache Level to 1 turns off caching. Level 1 means only the full-resolution, 100-percent-view-size version is stored in the cache. Turning off caching may make redrawing the screen slower and may interfere with some other functions, such as causing a very slow updating of the Histogram panel, but the image views are more accurate.

If you turn off caching and you notice performance problems, increase the Cache Level number.

If you are working mostly with small files, such as for the Web, you can try setting the cache to 1 or 2 because you'll probably often be working in or close to a 100-percent-view-size and you may not need cached views for faster screen redraws.

If you are working with large files, try leaving the cache setting at its default or try setting it higher if you need faster screen redraws. But keep the disadvantages of caching in mind. If you notice view-quality problems such as banding, or what you think are inaccurate color readings, set the cache lower and see if you can work with the slower screen redraws.

GPU Settings

You can discover the kind of graphics or video card your computer is using and enable or disable OpenGL Drawing.

Detected Video Card

This option detects the kind of graphics processing unit (GPU) or graphics/video card you have in your computer.

Enable OpenGL Drawing

If Photoshop detects a capable GPU or graphics/video card, Enable OpenGL Drawing is automatically checked. If not, it is grayed out.

OpenGL (OGL) is an open specification that makes it possible for an application to work with 2-D and 3-D objects. With OpenGL, it is possible for an application to create the same effects in any operating system by using any graphics processing unit or graphics/video card that adheres to the OpenGL specification.

Some new Photoshop features (see the following list) require OpenGL in order to function, and at the time of writing, these features are only supported on the following systems: Mac OS 10.4.11 and 10.5, and Windows Vista. In addition, these features require a GPU that has Shader Model 3.0 or greater, and you should make sure you are running the latest driver from your card manufacturer.

These features and some 3-D features may also fail to work properly if you don't have enough video memory — 256MB of video memory is recommended for the following OpenGL features, and more if you are using the 3-D painting features. Video memory in the amount of 512MB gives you a little extra memory that may safeguard your system for a while.

Cursors preferences

The fifth tab in the Preferences window allows you to set your preferences for appearance and size of your cursors.

Painting Cursors

You can use this option to select the type of painting cursor you want to see when you use any tools that work like a brush. Standard makes the cursor look like a little picture of the tool you are using; Precise makes it look like cross-hairs; Normal makes it look like 50 percent of the brush's pixel size if there are feathered edges on the brush; Full Size makes it look like the full pixel size of the brush; and Show Crosshair in Brush Tip adds a small cross-hair in the center of the brush. Clicking each option shows you what the cursor looks like in the preview box right above the options.

Other Cursors

This functions like the Painting Cursors preference, except there are fewer options. Standard shows a tool icon cursor, and Precise shows a cross-hair cursor.

Transparency and Gamut preferences

In the sixth tab in the Preferences window, you can choose how you want your transparency grid to appear, and see where your out-of-gamut colors are.

Photoshop Features that Require OpenGL

■ Smooth display at odd Zoom levels

■ Animated Zoom — Smooth Zoom when holding down the mouse button — Animated transitions when doing a one-stop zoom (for example, Ctrl++)

■ Flicking or Hand-tossing Images — like flicking the iPhone

■ Birdseye View — Shift+click-hold with the Hand tool selected takes you into Birdseye View

■ Rotate Canvas

■ Pixel Grid when zoomed to >500 percent

Transparency Settings

When transparency is on a layer in Photoshop, it is represented on the layer thumbnail, and in the image window when only one of the layers is viewed, by a grid pattern of squares that have two alternating colors. When multiple layers that contain transparent areas are viewed at the same time, those areas show as clear in the image window, and pixels on the layers below show through the transparent areas. Erasing part of a background layer actually paints the background color instead of making the erased area transparent. If you change a background layer to a regular layer (double-click the layer name "Background" and then click OK), it behaves like other layers — it shows a transparency grid when there are transparent areas or when some of the layer pixels are erased.

The default pattern that represents transparency is a grid with medium-sized squares of light gray and white. You can change the grid size or grid colors by selecting one of the drop-down lists in this preference, or you can click in the white or gray color boxes to replace either of those colors with another.

Gamut Warning

When colors in an image can be viewed on-screen but not printed, they are *out of gamut*. To see where the out-of-gamut colors are, choose View ➪ Gamut Warning, and Photoshop shows the gamut warning color on top of the out-of-gamut colors. You can then know what areas you might want to change so that their colors are within the printing gamut. You can change the gamut warning color (not the out-of-gamut colors in the image) by clicking the gamut warning color box and choosing a different color. You can also change the gamut color's opacity in this section.

> **TIP** An alternative to viewing the gamut warning is to choose View ➪ Proof Colors to see what the image's colors, including the out-of-gamut colors, will look like when printed, as opposed to showing you an arbitrary gamut warning color on top of the out-of-gamut colors. See Chapter 23 for more information about color management.

Units & Rulers preferences

The seventh tab in the Preferences window enables you to set your ruler units (inches, picas, pixels), the width and height of your columns, and the presets for when you open a new document.

Rulers, Type

Units for rulers and type can be set in the drop-down lists. You can also set the rulers' units by right-clicking a ruler in the image window and choosing a unit. To show rulers in the image window, press Ctrl+R/⌘+R. In print workflows, you may want to set rulers to inches or picas; in a Web workflow, you should set rulers to pixels.

Column Size

When you use the New, Image Size, or Canvas Size command, Columns is available as one of the Width and Height units of measurement in drop-down lists, and you can enter a number of columns in the Width and Height boxes. You can set the sizes of the columns that are used in these commands in this Column Size preference, along with a gutter size.

Using columns can be helpful when you are preparing images for print in a publication that uses columns. In addition, or alternatively, you may want to set the ruler units to be the same as the column-size units you specified in the Column Size preference (such as inches or picas) and drag guides from the rulers into the document window to show where columns begin and end.

New Document Preset Resolutions

The File ⇨ New command allows you to choose Preset document sizes for a new document. Some of these presets use the resolutions you enter in the New Document Preset Resolutions preference. The paper and photo presets use the Print Resolution amount, and the Web and Film & Video presets use the Screen Resolution amount.

Note that in the File ⇨ New command, you can also enter custom sizes and resolutions for a new document, and you can choose File ⇨ New ⇨ Presets ⇨ Custom, enter your custom size information, and click the Save Presets button to save a custom preset with a unique name.

Point/Pica Size

Unfortunately, there is more than one way to define how many points are in an inch. Madness, I know!

The new way

Since picas are almost evenly divisible into inches, the people who came up with the Postscript printing language decided to define them in a way that makes them exactly divisible into inches (instead of almost). Very clever. This definition makes a pica $\frac{1}{6}$ of an inch and a point $\frac{1}{72}$ of an inch. This Postscript setting causes 1 pixel on-screen to translate to 1 point on paper when you print a document at 72 ppi (standard screen resolution), which works out very neatly. You may want to keep the Postscript preference on.

The old way

The old way harks back to when paste-ups were still in use. There are about 6.06 picas and 72.27 points in an inch. If you have some very strange reason to use the old way of measuring points per inch, you can select the Traditional preference.

Guides, Grid & Slices preferences

The options in the eighth tab let you choose a color and line style for Guides; a color for Smart Guides; a color, line style, and size of grid sections for the Grid; and a color for the outline of Slices, as well as whether you want to show Slice numbers. Guides, Smart Guides, Grid, and Slices (which, in this case, refers to the outlines of Slices) can be shown or hidden via the View ⇨ Show menu.

Smart Guides appear temporarily around the pixels on a layer while you move the pixels, and they can help you line up one layer's content with another.

Slices divide an image into sections that can be saved separately with different settings, for optimum display on the Web.

If the colors of any of these guides are hard to see in a particular image, in this preferences section choose colors that contrast with the colors in the image.

> **TIP** **In the View menu, you can set Snap or Snap To options so that image pixels that are being moved and some tools will snap to various guides, layers, slices, and so on. This can help you align image pixels to each other or to precise measurements.**

Plug-Ins preferences

In the ninth tab in the Preferences window, you can specify a new folder to access plug-ins from another application, and, if you need to, you can enter a serial number from an older version of Photoshop.

Additional Plug-Ins Folder

The plug-ins that come with Photoshop are installed in the Photoshop plug-ins folder. In the Additional Plug-Ins Folder preference, you can select an additional plug-ins folder, such as a plug-ins folder stored with another application, so that Photoshop can know where to look for additional compatible plug-ins. Installed plug-ins add many different kinds of functionality to Photoshop, so they are activated in various Photoshop menus.

> **TIP** **If you suspect a plug-in may be causing problems, you can troubleshoot by adding a tilde (~) to the beginning of the plug-in name or plug-in folder name, and Photoshop ignores that plug-in.**

To install a plug-in, use the provided plug-in installer or installation instructions. If none are provided, you can copy an uncompressed plug-in file to the plug-ins folder inside the Photoshop application folder.

If you make changes to plug-ins, you must restart Photoshop to activate the changes.

Legacy Photoshop Serial Number

If you have a serial number from Photoshop version 6 or earlier, enter it here. Photoshop serial numbers changed format after version 6, and some plug-ins won't run unless they can find a serial number in the old format.

Type preferences

In the tenth and final tab for Preferences, you can set your type options: whether or not to use smart quotes, having Asian type options appear in the Character and Paragraph panels, whether or not Photoshop uses font substitutions for missing non-Roman characters, and how you preview fonts.

Use Smart Quotes

When the Smart Quotes option is on, Photoshop can figure out where to put beginning and end quotes. If you are typing text that includes a lot of measurements in feet and inches, which are represented by one or two straight quotes, you may want to uncheck this option so that Photoshop uses straight quotes rather than curved quotes.

Show Asian Text Options

Checking this option allows you to see some Asian language type options in the Character and Paragraph panels.

Enable Missing Glyph Protection

This option causes Photoshop to automatically make font substitutions for any missing glyphs when you type non-Roman text (like Japanese or Cyrillic) after you have selected a Roman font. When you open a document and Photoshop can't find the fonts in the document, you get an alert message to let you know Photoshop is going to substitute the fonts. If this glyph option is on, you don't get an alert message when Photoshop substitutes a font for missing glyphs, specifically. If this option is off and you type a missing glyph, it will likely just show up as an incorrect or unreadable character.

Show Font Names in English

This option causes non-English font names in the font menus to display in English. Of course, the font preview is still shown in its intended language.

Font Preview Size

Select the size you want the font preview to appear in the font menus, which are in the Type tool's Options Bar and the Character panel. If you have your monitor set to a high resolution, the font previews will look smaller, so in that case you may want to set the Font Preview to a larger size.

CROSS-REF   **For more information about using Type, see Chapter 13.**

Presets and the Preset Manager

Presets are preset (or custom) brushes, swatches, gradients, styles, patterns, contours, custom shapes, and tools that come with Photoshop, as well as any that you have created. You can choose individual presets in panels, and you can save, load, replace, or reset to defaults the groups of presets in panels from panel menus. You can use the Preset Manager (see Figure 2.27) to manage groups of individual presets.

FIGURE 2.27

The Preset Manager

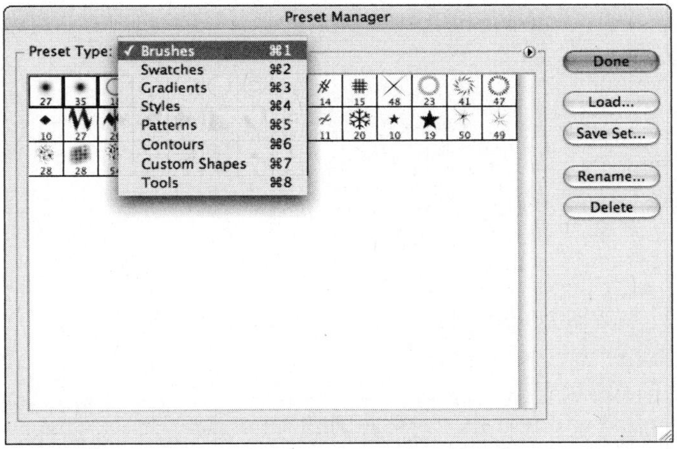

To access the Preset Manager, choose Edit ⇨ Preset Manager. Figure 2.28 shows a panel menu from which you can save or load groups of presets.

The following list details some options to help you work with the Preset Manager:

- To load a group of presets into the Preset Manager, click the Load button or select a set from the Preset Manager panel menu.

- To save a group of presets with the Preset Manager, select multiple individual presets in the main Preset Manager window and click the Save Set button.

- To rename an individual preset in the Preset Manager, select the preset in the main Preset Manager window and click Rename.

- To delete presets in the Preset Manager, select one or more presets in the main Preset Manager window and click Delete. Selecting and deleting all the presets in a group deletes the group.

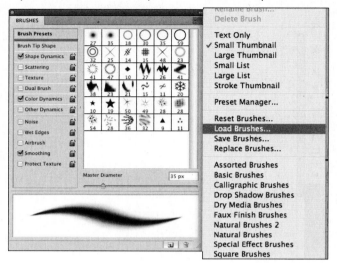

FIGURE 2.28

A panel menu from which you can load and use presets

Selecting and using presets

You can select individual custom brushes from the Brushes panels, and you can select individual color swatch presets from the Swatches panel. You can select tool presets from the Tool Preset Picker in all the tool's Options Bars, and brush presets from the Brush Preset Picker in the Options Bars for all the tools that use a brush (Brush tool, Clone Stamp tool, Eraser tool, and so on).

Custom shapes can be used when the Custom Shapes tool is active and the shapes are selected from the Shapes menu in the Options Bar. Custom patterns can be selected in numerous places: the Fill dialog box, the Pattern Stamp Tool Options Bar, the Layer Style Pattern Overlay dialog box, and more.

You can save or load brush preset groups from the Brushes panel menus, and you can save or load preset groups from the Swatches panel menu. If you want to save a preset group, you first need to make the panel contain only those individual presets you want in the group.

Typically, you can manipulate the presets in a panel so that the panel contains only the individual presets you want in a group, and then choose the Save option from the panel menu and give the group a name. The preset group is then also available in the Preset Manager. To get a panel to contain only certain presets, in many cases you can drag an individual preset to a panel's trashcan to remove it or click the New button at the bottom of a panel to make a new individual preset and add it to a panel.

Create individual presets

To create individual presets, you use various panels, menus, or processes rather than the Preset Manager. In some cases, you can click the New button at the bottom of a panel to create a new preset and add it to a panel.

Following are some additional ways to make individual custom presets.

To make a custom tool preset:

1. **Select a tool and change a setting on its Options Bar.**
2. **Open the Tool Preset Picker on the far left of the Options Bar.**
3. **Click the New button and name the new tool preset.**

To make a custom swatch preset:

1. **Click the Foreground Color box and make a new color in the Color Picker.**
2. **Hover the cursor over the blank area in the Swatches panel until you see a paint bucket, then click to add the new swatch preset and give it a name.**

To make a custom style preset:

1. **Select a layer (other than a background layer).**
2. **Choose one of the options in the Add a Layer Style button at the bottom of the Layers panel.**
3. **Select the options for each effect (Drop Shadow, Outer Glow, and so on) that you want in the Layer Style.**
4. **Click the New Style button and name the style.**

To make a custom brush or pattern preset:

1. **Select the pixels you want to make into a brush or pattern.**
2. **Choose Edit ➪ Define Brush Preset or Edit ➪ Define Pattern.**
3. **You can further refine or create a new brush preset in the Brushes panel by doing the following:**
   a. Select the Brush tool and the Brushes panel.
   b. Select a brush preset in the Brushes panel.
   c. Change some Brushes panel settings.
   d. Click the New button at the bottom of the panel and give the brush preset a new name.

To make a custom shape:

1. **Select a path in the Paths panel.**
   Choose Edit ➪ Define Custom Shape.

CROSS-REF For more information about shapes, see Chapter 12. For more information about brushes, see Chapter 19.

Note that preset names must include their default file extensions so Photoshop will recognize them. Presets are usually located in the Presets folder inside the Photoshop application folder, but may end up in other places on your computer.

If you can't find a preset group on your computer, you can search for its kind; for example, "Custom Shapes." You can also search for the preset type's file extension: Brushes (.abr), Color Swatches (.aco), Contours (.shc), Custom Shapes (.csh), Gradients (.grd), Patterns (.pat), Styles (.asl), or Tools (.tpl).

No matter how you make a new individual preset, it shows up in the appropriate panel. It also shows up in the currently loaded preset group in the Preset Manager (which is whatever the panel contains at that time).

Your newly created individual preset stays in the Preset Manager until you delete it by using the panel or the Preset Manager, even if you close and reopen Photoshop. And if you try to reset or replace a set of presets that has a new preset it in, you get a message from Photoshop asking if you want to save the group, which would save your new preset in the group. This is true whether you try to reset or replace from the panel menu or from the Preset Manager.

You can share copies of presets so other people can use them in Photoshop on their computers. Photoshop can find the presets if they are put in the appropriate folder inside the Presets folder that is in the Photoshop application folder.

Customizing Shortcuts and Menus

You can customize keyboard shortcuts and menus in the Keyboard Shortcuts and Menus dialog box (see Figure 2.29), which you can select from the Edit menu or by choosing Window ➪ Workspace.

You can make your own custom keyboard shortcuts for application menus, panel (panel) menus, or for tools in the Keyboard Shortcuts and Menus dialog box. Be advised that most shortcuts are already in use and if someone else uses Photoshop on your computer, he may want to load the default keyboard shortcuts because he may not be familiar with your custom shortcuts. I usually leave the default keyboard shortcuts loaded to simplify things, but if you have a particular reason to make some custom shortcuts, this could be very useful to you.

To make a new custom keyboard shortcut, click on the Keyboard Shortcuts tab, select the command or tool, click on the existing keyboard shortcut or the blank shortcut area if it doesn't have a shortcut, and type the new shortcut. Photoshop gives you a warning message if another command or tool uses the new shortcut.

FIGURE 2.29

The Keyboard Shortcuts and Menus dialog box with the Keyboard Shortcuts tab active

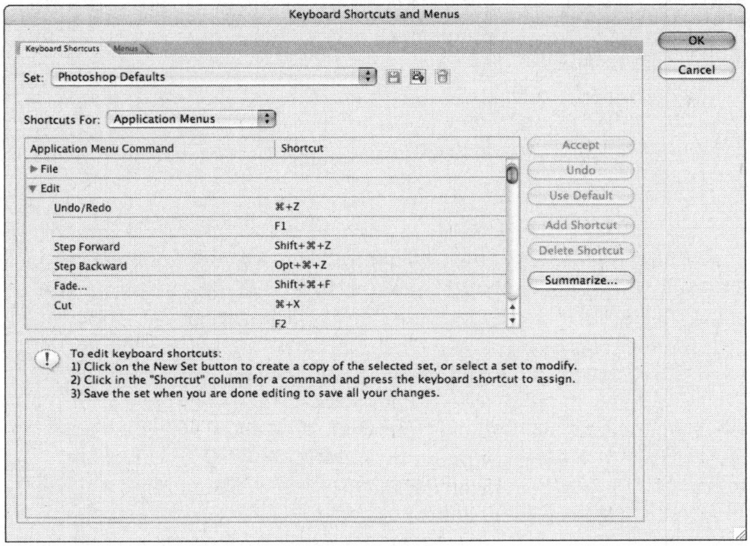

Click the Accept button to accept the new shortcut, the Undo button to undo the new shortcut, the Use Default button to change the shortcut back to the default, the Add Shortcut button to add an additional shortcut to a command or tool, or the Delete Shortcut button to delete a shortcut for a command or tool.

> **TIP**   Clicking the Summarize button in the Keyboard Shortcuts and Menus dialog box creates a Web page that lists all the keyboard shortcuts in the current set and saves the Web page on your computer. You can view it with a Web browser and print it, if you like.

You can load a set of custom keyboard shortcuts in the Set menu (including the Default set), save all changes to the current set of shortcuts by clicking the Save All Changes button, create a new set by clicking the Create a New Set button, or delete the current set by clicking the Delete the Current Set button.

You can use the Menus tab to add colors to the backgrounds of application menus or panel (panel) menu commands or to hide rarely used commands. (You will need to click on the Menu tab if the Keyboard Shortcuts tab is active.) Assigning colors to commands that you use often and hiding commands that you don't use can help you quickly find the commands you need.

To add a color to a command, select the command and choose a color. To hide a command, select the command and click in the visibility box to make the eyeball symbol go away.

CAUTION   **The Show Menu Colors setting in Preferences ⇨ Interface must be checked in order to see menu colors.**

You can load a set of custom menus in the Set menu (including the Default menu set), save all changes to the current set of menus by clicking the Save All Changes button, create a new menu set by clicking the Create a New Set button, or delete the current set by clicking the Delete the Current Set button.

Tools

You can use the tools in the tools panel to work directly on images. The Selection tools select pixels, the Brush tools paint on pixels with the foreground color, the Type tool typesets text, and so on. Most tools have hidden tools behind them, indicated by a small black triangle just below and to the right of the tool. Access hidden tools by clicking the mouse button on a tool and selecting the hidden tool. tool keyboard shortcuts are shown to the right of the tool name.

TIP   **You can cycle through and select hidden tools by pressing a tool's keyboard shortcut multiple times. You must have Use Shift Key for Tool Switch unchecked in Preferences ⇨ General Preferences for this to work. If this preference is checked, you will have to press Shift+*tool shortcut key* to cycle through the hidden tools.**

Following are descriptions of the tools and other buttons in the Tools panel, along with the chapter references of where they are discussed in more detail.

Move tool

Any time you want to move image pixels (not selection borders alone), you need the Move tool, unless you want to nudge pixels a little at a time with the arrow keys. With the Move tool active, click the mouse button and drag the pixels to move them. If a selection is active, the Move tool moves only the selected pixels on the active layer.

CROSS-REF   **See Chapters 8 and 16 for more about the Move tool.**

If there is no selection active, the Move tool (see Figure 2.30) moves all the pixels on the active layer when you drag in the image window, whether the Move tool is directly on the pixels or not. (If the layer is linked to other layers, the linked layers' content also moves.)

FIGURE 2.30

The Move tool

    Move Tool   V

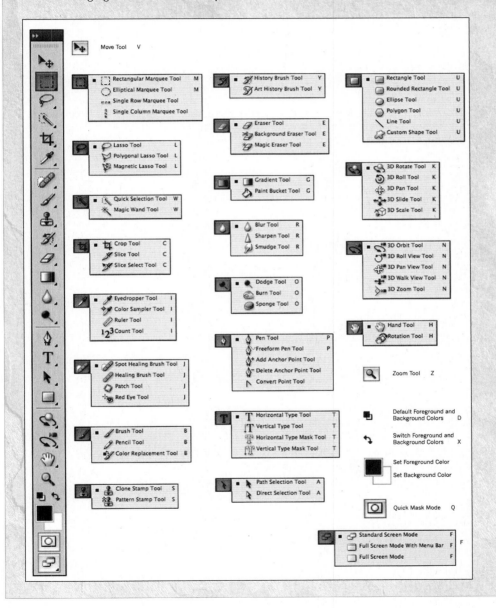

The Tools Panel and All the Tools

The following figure shows the Tools panel as well as all the hidden tools and tool shortcuts.

Marquee selection tools

Use the Marquee selection tools (see Figure 2.31) to select rectangular or oval shapes, or single rows of pixels. Press Shift while you drag with the Rectangular Marquee tool to drag a square, or press Shift while you drag with the Elliptical Marquee tool to drag a circle (release the mouse button first, then release Shift). You can resize these selection borders (not the image pixels) by choosing Select ➪ Transform Selection or by choosing Select ➪ Refine Edge.

CROSS-REF   **See Chapter 10 for more on the Marquee selection tools.**

FIGURE 2.31

The Marquee selection tools

Lasso selection tools

Use these tools (see Figure 2.32) to select pixels by dragging or clicking around objects.

Use the Lasso tool to select rounded, irregular shapes that don't have to be precise (drag around the shape until you get back to the starting point to close the shape). For precise selections, you can make a Pen tool path and load it as a selection (Chapter 11) or manipulate duplicates of channels to help you make a selection (Chapter 10).

The Polygonal Lasso tool is good for selecting objects with straight edges (click on each corner until you click on the first corner again to close the selection). If the edges are really straight, you can be pretty precise with this tool.

The Magnetic Lasso tool finds the edge of an object as you drag near the edge and the selection snaps to the edge as you drag (drag to the starting point to close the shape). The Magnetic Lasso tool works best on objects whose edges have a lot of contrast with the background. If you don't want to complete the Magnetic Lasso selection, press ESC.

FIGURE 2.32

The Lasso selection tools

Quick Selection and the Magic Wand tools

The Quick Selection and Magic Wand tools select pixels by examining their colors. Figure 2.33 shows the Quick Selection and the Magic Wand tools. Use the Quick Selection tool to select multiple different colors that are adjacent to each other but enclosed in a surrounding color that contrasts with all the colors you want to select.

FIGURE 2.33

The Quick Selection and the Magic Wand tools

Drag across the colors you want to select. The Magic Wand tool selects colors that are similar to the color you click on with the Magic Wand. The number of colors it selects depends on the Tolerance setting you enter in its Options Bar.

CROSS-REF See Chapter 10 for more on the Quick Selection and Magic Wand tools.

TIP Add to selections by pressing Shift while you make an additional selection with the same or a different selection tool. Subtract from selections by pressing Alt while making an additional selection. Or choose Select ⇨ Save Selection or Select ⇨ Load Selection) to add to or subtract from selections. Load Selection gives you the option of adding or subtracting the loaded selection from an active selection.

Crop tool

Use the Crop tool to crop an image to its intended size. Drag with the Crop tool, and then move any of its handles to adjust the crop. Press Enter when you're finished. If you don't want to complete the crop, press ESC. You can use the Crop tool's Options Bar to enter the exact dimensions and resolution of your selection, but this can cause undesirable resampling if you are enlarging and don't have enough resolution. (See Chapter 5 for information about resizing images.) If the dimensions and resolution boxes are blank, you don't have to worry about resolution resizing problems.

Slice and Slice Select tools

These tools are used to create and select parts of images that have been sliced up in different sections for better display on the Web. The Slice tool is used to drag through an image to create slices; in other words, to cut the image into grid sections that can be saved with different settings. This way, you may be able to make each section a smaller file. If a large image is left whole and saved for the Web, it might be so large that viewers have to wait for it to load. The Slice Select tool can be used to select slices.

CROSS-REF **See Chapter 24 for more on the Slice tools.**

Figure 2.34 shows the Crop, Slice, and Slice Select tools.

FIGURE 2.34

The Crop, Slice, and Slice Select tools

Eyedropper tool

Use this tool to find out a color's numbers; to do so, hover the Eyedropper tool (see Chapter 16) over a color in the image while you look in the Info panel. This is helpful when color correcting or if you need to share color number information with someone. You can also use the Eyedropper tool to click on a color in the image to make it the foreground color. Drop the foreground color into the Swatches panel by clicking in the gray area inside the Swatches panel.

Color Sampler tool

Click with this tool in your image to set permanent color samplers in your image. The sampler and its color numbers appear in the Info panel until you delete the sampler. To delete a color sampler, Alt-click or right-click on the color sampler with the Color Sampler tool and press Delete.

Figure 2.35 shows the Eyedropper, Color Sampler, Ruler, and Count tools.

FIGURE 2.35

The Eyedropper, Color Sampler, Ruler, and Count tools

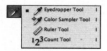

Ruler tool

Use the Ruler tool to measure distances from one object to another or to straighten an image. To measure, drag the Ruler tool across what you want to measure, and check the Info panel for the measurement information. Click the Record Measurements button in the Measurement Log panel to record the data, which you can then Export with the Measurement Log panel menu. You can also set the Measurement Scale in the Measurement Log panel menu. To straighten an image with the Ruler tool, drag with the Ruler tool along the edge of something you want to straighten, then choose Image ⇨ Transform Canvas ⇨ Arbitrary. Photoshop automatically calculates the angle of rotation and straightens the image.

Count tool

Use the Count tool when you need to count objects in an image. Click once on each object, and a serial number, starting with 1, is placed on each object. Click the Record Measurements button in the Measurement Log panel to record the data, which you can then export with the Measurement Log panel menu. Click the Clear button in the Options Bar to start over with a new count or click the Count Group Color button to change the color of the numbers.

> **TIP** You can use the Ruler tool, Count tool, and the Selection tools with the Measurement Log and its panel menu to set the scale in an image and measure distances, count objects, and measure area (such as the area in square feet of a selected pond in an aerial photo).

Healing tools

Use the Healing tools and Patch tool to fill in bad spots, flaws, cracks, or damage with a good nearby texture or a texture in another part of the image, while matching the color that surrounds the flaw. These tools are often good at maintaining texture, but since they pull in some of the surrounding color, it's usually best not to use the Healing tools or Patch tool when there is an undesirable color nearby.

To repair a flaw with the Spot Healing Brush, make this tool at least a little bit bigger than the flaw and either click on the flaw or drag across it. The flaw should magically disappear.

The Healing Brush tool works similar to the Clone Stamp tool, discussed below, in that you Alt-click with the Healing Brush to sample a good place in the image that you want to copy from, then release the mouse button, move the cursor to the flawed area in the image, and start painting over the flaw. The Healing Brush paints from the good area to cover the flawed area.

It's a good idea to make the Healing Brush at least a little bit bigger than the width of the flaw. You may need to resample from different spots often if the good spots are small or if you find you are starting to see repeating patterns in the flaw repair area.

> **TIP** Use the bracket keys to resize a brush.

Use the Patch tool to drag a complete shape around a flawed area, then put the cursor inside the selected area and hold down the mouse button while dragging the selected flawed area on top of a good area (even if the color doesn't match). The flawed area should seem to be magically repaired, with color that matches its surrounding area.

Make sure Source is selected in the Options Bar. This tool comes in handy when there are larger flawed areas and good areas that you can copy from that are about the same size as the flawed area.

Figure 2.36 shows the Spot Healing Brush, Healing Brush, Patch, and Red Eye tools.

FIGURE 2.36

The Spot Healing Brush, Healing Brush, Patch, and Red Eye tools

Red Eye tool

If a person in a photo has red-eye, simply click with the Red Eye tool on the red part of the eye, and it should fill the red part in with black. If it doesn't work quite right the first time, undo and try it again with a different Pupil Size and/or Darken Amount (in the Options Bar). But my favorite thing to do if it makes too large an area of black is to paint out the part of the black you don't want from a previous state of the image with the History Brush (see Chapters 6).

Brush tool

The Brush tool can be used to paint on an image. It uses the foreground color as the paint color.

There are many options you can apply to brushes in the Brushes panel. The Brush tool has to be selected for the options to be available. When you change the options, you can see what a brush stroke looks like with those options in the bottom of the Brushes panel. One exception to the brush using the foreground color exclusively is that if, in the Brushes panel, you choose Color Dynamics and use foreground/background color Jitter, the brush alternately paints with the foreground and background colors when you drag it.

To make a new brush preset, you can choose an existing preset in the Brushes panel, change some options in the Brushes panel, click the New button at the bottom of the panel, and give the new brush a name. You can also drag a rectangular selection around pixels in an image that you want to use for a brush shape, then choose Edit ⇨ Define Brush Preset.

Pencil tool

Use the Pencil tool to paint hard-edged lines. You can't make the Pencil tool have soft edges.

Brush Tool Tips

Use the following tips for tools that use brushes (such as Brush tool, Clone Stamp tool, and Eraser):

- Use bracket keys to resize a brush.
- Press Shift+Bracket Keys to change the hardness or softness of a brush's edges.
- When a brush is active, press the number keys to change the brush's opacity (2 for 20 percent opacity, 3 for 30 percent opacity, and so on).
- Press the X key to switch foreground and background colors.
- To paint a straight line, click once in an image with a brush tool, release the mouse button, and move the mouse to a different part of the image, then Shift-click with the mouse. This should connect the two areas by painting a straight line.

Figure 2.37 shows the Brush, Pencil, and Color Replacement tools.

FIGURE 2.37

The Brush, Pencil, and Color Replacement tools

Color Replacement tool

Use the Color Replacement tool to replace a color in an image with another color. Drag across a color to change it to the foreground color.

The Options Bar settings are critical for this tool:

- **Mode: Color.** Use this setting to change the color of the sampled area (but not the luminosity or lightness).
- **Sampling: Continuous.** This tool continually takes samples of the color to replace as you drag, so you can only let the cross-hairs of the brush go over colors you want to change. It's usually best if you make a large brush in this case.
- **Sampling: Once.** This tool samples the color to change when you first click the mouse button and hold it down to drag across a color.
- **Sampling: Background Swatch.** This tool changes a color in an image if it is the same color as the background color.

Clone Stamp tool

The Clone Stamp tool can be used to fix areas in an image and copy one part of an image over another part. To sample a good part of an image, Alt-click (PC) or Option+click (Mac) with the Clone Stamp tool on a good place in the image that you want to copy from. Then release the mouse button, move the cursor to the flawed area in the image, and start painting over the flaw.

It's good to resample often to avoid repetitive patterns. Use a very soft or semi-soft edge on the brush so that there won't be a hard edge between the cloned areas and original areas. The Clone Stamp tool copies exactly from one area to another, but since you have to use a soft edge, some of the textural detail is lost. The Healing Brush tool maintains texture better, but mixes in colors that surround the flawed area, which may be undesirable. You may need to try both tools to see which one works best.

The Clone Stamp tool can be set to blending modes other than Normal in the Options Bar for very useful retouching techniques.

Figure 2.38 shows the Clone Stamp and Pattern Stamp tools.

Pattern Stamp tool

You can paint patterns onto an image with the Pattern Stamp tool. Choose a pattern preset in the Options Bar.

To make a new pattern preset, make a rectangular selection of image pixels you want to use as a pattern, and choose Edit ➪ Define Pattern.

TIP   You can also fill a layer or selection with a pattern in the Edit ➪ Fill ➪ Use ➪ Pattern menu.

FIGURE 2.38

The Clone Stamp and Pattern Stamp tools

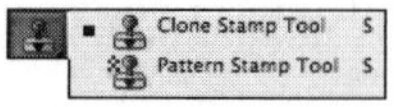

History Brush tool

The History Brush tool (see Figure 2.39) is one of my favorite methods for undoing things, especially just parts of things I don't want. With the History Brush active, click in a box to the left of a previous History State in the History panel that you want to paint from and drag in the image to paint the previous state of the image.

FIGURE 2.39

The History Brush and Art History Brush tools

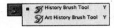

I especially like to use this to paint out halos when I've oversharpened a bit. That way, I can get a lot of extra sharpening in other areas that I might not have been able to if I had stopped before halos appeared. This is useful when sharpening for print, since images tend to soften up on press. You can use reduced opacities with the History Brush, just like other brushes.

The Art History Brush paints from a specified History State just like the History Brush, but it adds a painterly effect.

Eraser tool

The Eraser tool (see Figure 2.40) erases to transparency the pixels you drag over a regular layer. If you use it on a background layer, it paints with the background color instead of transparency. If you use it on a layer that has locked transparency (see the transparency lock button at the top of the Layers panel), it paints with the background color instead of transparency wherever you drag over pixels, but it leaves transparent pixels transparent (because they are locked).

FIGURE 2.40

The Eraser, Background Eraser, and Magic Eraser tools

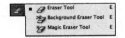

Background Eraser tool

The Background Eraser tool erases sampled colors of pixels on any kind of layer to transparency as you drag over them with the tool. Samples are taken by the cross-hairs in the center of the brush.

Magic Eraser tool

The Magic Eraser tool erases to transparency the sampled colors of pixels on a regular layer when you click on the pixels. If you use it on a background layer, it changes the sampled pixels to the background color instead of transparency. If you use it on a layer that has locked transparency (see the transparency lock button at the top of the Layers panel), it changes sampled pixels to the background color instead of transparency, but it leaves transparent pixels transparent (because they are locked).

 **TIP**   To erase or select objects with intricate or wispy shapes, use the Extract command or another selection method (see Chapter 10).

Gradient tool

Use the Gradient tool to make *gradients* in a layer that contain gradual transitions from one color to another color or between many colors. You can choose different angles of a gradient, such as linear or radial, in the Options Bar.

With the Gradient tool active, click the "Click to edit the gradient" button in the Options Bar to get the Gradient Editor. Click a preset gradient or make a custom gradient by clicking just under the horizontal gradient bar to put a new color in the gradient or click just above the gradient bar to add a different opacity to part of the gradient.

To make the custom gradient into a new gradient preset, enter a name in the Custom box and click the New button. Click OK to set your gradient and close the Gradient Editor.

To apply the gradient to a layer, drag in the layer with the Gradient tool. You can drag different angles and distances to get different results.

Figure 2.41 shows the Gradient and Paint Bucket tools.

FIGURE 2.41

The Gradient and Paint Bucket tools

Paint Bucket tool

When you click to sample a color with the Paint Bucket tool, it fills the sampled color with the foreground color.

The Blur, Sharpen, and Smudge tools

You can paint with the Blur tool to blur portions of an image. The Sharpen tool allows you to sharpen portions of an image. You can drag the Smudge tool to smudge parts of an image, as if you were dabbling in finger paints.

Figure 2.42 shows the Blur, Sharpen, and Smudge tools.

FIGURE 2.42

FIGURE 2.42

The Blur, Sharpen, and Smudge tools

TIP I prefer to use other methods that have more control over blurring and sharpening. Choose Filter ⇨ Blur Filter for other blur options, and Filter ⇨ Unsharp Mask or Filter ⇨ Smart Sharpen) for other sharpening options. You can use masks or the History Brush to blur or sharpen only certain areas. See Chapter 20 for blurring and sharpening techniques.

The Dodge, Burn, and Sponge tools

The Dodge and Burn tools (see Figure 2.43) are used to lighten and darken an image, respectively, by using a brush method of application. They are especially useful when you are manipulating duplicates of channels to help you make selections (see Chapter 10).

The main strength of the Dodge and Burn tools is that in the Options Bar you can set the tools to target mostly highlights, shadows, or midtones. This means you don't have to be as careful when you are using the tools and can usually work more quickly. You can use a larger brush without having to worry as much about affecting areas of a nontargeted lightness that the brush overlaps.

It's generally a good practice to set the Exposure in the Options Bar to a low number and keep painting an area over and over to build up the effect. That way, it's easier to avoid overdoing it.

Paint with the Dodge tool to lighten areas in an image. In the Options Bar, choose whether to affect mostly highlights, shadows, or midtones.

Paint with the Burn tool to darken areas in an image. In the Options Bar, choose whether to affect mostly highlights, shadows, or midtones.

You can drag the Sponge tool (see Figure 2.43) over areas in an image to saturate or desaturate their colors, depending on which option you set in the Options Bar. You may want to set the Flow to a low number and paint over the area multiple times to build up the effect so that you don't overdo it.

FIGURE 2.43

The Dodge, Burn, and Sponge tools

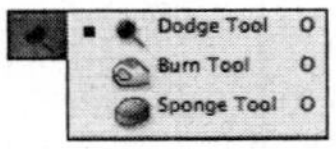

I am a fan of the Sponge tool, but I more often use a Hue/Saturation adjustment layer to saturate or desaturate colors (take color out and make pixels look black and white). To make the effect apply to just part of an image (say, if you want a person in color and the background in black and white), use a mask on an adjustment layer to hide part of the effect. Adjustment layers are very flexible because you can make changes to them any time. See Chapters 8 and 15 for Hue/Saturation adjustment layers and Chapter 8 for masks.

When you need to make a very precise, hard-edged selection, and you haven't found a quicker way to make the selection, the Pen tool is a great tool to use. You can make a path with a Pen tool, then load it as a selection. Figure 2.44 shows the Pen tool, Freeform Pen tool, Add Anchor Point tool, Delete Anchor Point tool, and Convert Point tool.

FIGURE 2.44

The Pen, Freeform Pen, Add Anchor Point, Delete Anchor Point, and Convert Point tools

Paths can be edited very precisely at any time; therefore, they are very flexible. They are stored in the Paths panel with the saved Photoshop file until you delete them. The paths themselves are vector images, meaning resolution-independent — you can enlarge them as much as you want with no loss of quality. (See Chapter 1 for more information about vector images.)

A path may be used to isolate a photograph of a hard-edged object from its background, for example. In that case, the photo would be dependent on resolution for its quality, but the path itself would not. Okay, not all that useful. But the situation in which the vector property of paths becomes really useful is when you use paths to make solid shapes in an image — a logo that contains only solid-color shapes, for example. Then the whole image would be resolution-independent, and you would not have to worry about losing quality when enlarging it.

Another handy thing about paths is that you can easily copy and paste them between Photoshop and Illustrator.

The Pen tool

When you have the time, it's worthwhile to learn how to use the Pen tool, paths, and shapes (see Chapters 11, and 12).

If you're still not convinced — this is gonna be harsh, but I have to tell you — you can't be called a Photoshop Expert until you learn how to use the Pen tool. Seriously, learning to use the Pen tool is for your own good, I promise!

Make a path with the Pen tool by clicking to make corner anchor points and dragging to make curve anchor points (points determine the shape of the path) to outline the object you want to isolate or the shape you want to create. Important: Before you start, click the Paths button in the Pen tool Options panel. When you get all the way around your object by clicking or dragging with the Pen tool, click on the starting point to close the path (a circle pops up next to the Pen tool when you hover it over the starting point). Press Ctrl+Z/⌘+Z to undo. Don't get bogged down making your path perfect when you first create it. That's what the path editing tools are for.

> **NOTE**   The Pen tool can have somewhat of a learning curve for those who haven't used similar tools. See Chapter 11 for more information about using the Pen tool.

You can use the Freeform Pen tool to drag to make a path that does not need to be precise. But why would you want to? Okay, you can check the Magnetic option in the Options Bar to make the Freeform Pen tool snap to the edge of an object while you drag along the edge. (You have to close the shape.) That might give you a pretty good head start on a path, which you could refine later, if Photoshop is able to decipher the location of the edge and if it doesn't put so many points on the path that it will be too time-consuming to edit. You can probably tell I haven't yet found a good use for this tool.

You could use the Add Anchor Point tool to click on a path segment to add an anchor point, but if you have the Pen tool active and you have Auto Add/Delete checked in the Options Bar, the Pen tool becomes the Add Anchor Point tool when you hover it over a path segment.

You could use the Delete Anchor Point tool to click on an anchor point to delete it, but if you have the Pen tool active and you have Auto Add/Delete checked in the Options Bar, the Pen tool becomes the Delete Anchor Point tool when you hover it over an anchor point.

Use the Convert Point tool to click on a curve anchor point to change it to a corner anchor point or drag out from a corner anchor point to change it to a curve point.

> **TIP**   Use the Direct Selection tool to move anchor points or to change path curves by dragging curve anchor point handles (click on the point to see the handles). You can see the Direct Selection and the Path Selection tool set below the Type tool on the Tools panel.

The Type tools

Click in an image with the Horizontal Type tool and start typing to make a horizontal line of text. If you drag a box with the tool and then start typing, the text will be in paragraph form and confined to the box area. Press Enter on the number pad or click the Commit button (check mark) in the Options Bar when you are finished with the text. You can click in the text with the Type tool if you want to edit it later.

Click in an image with the Vertical Type tool and start typing to make a vertical line of text. Press Enter on the number pad or click the Commit button (check mark) in the Options Bar when you are finished with the text.

> **TIP**   Fonts, point sizes, color, and other type options can be accessed in the Options Bar and the Character panel. Drag with a Type tool to highlight the type to which you want to apply options.

When you type with the Horizontal and Vertical Type Mask tools, they make a text-shaped selection. Press Enter on the number pad or click the Commit button (check mark) in the Options Bar when you are finished with the text. You can then save the selection and use it later on a layer or a layer mask, fill or stroke the selection, or anything else you can do to other selections. For best results, make a new layer and select it before you start typing with these tools.

Figure 2.45 shows the Type tools.

FIGURE 2.45

The Type tools

The Path selection tools

Select a path and all its points with the Path Selection tool. Shift-click to select multiple path components on the same path. You can then choose Edit ➪ Free Transform to move the path, nudge it with the arrow keys, or change its size.

Use the Direct Selection tool to select and move anchor points or to change path curves by dragging curve anchor point handles (click on the point to see the handles). Shift-click if you want to select multiple anchor points at the same time.

Figure 2.46 shows the Path Selection and Direct Selection tools.

FIGURE 2.46

The Path Selection and Direct Selection tools. These tools can be used to edit paths made with the Pen tool or Shape tools.

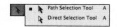

The Shape and Line tools

Use the Shape tools (Rectangle, Rounded Rectangle, Ellipse, and Polygon) to create vector, resolution-independent Shape layers or paths. Click the Shape Layer or Paths button in the Options Bar before you drag in the image with a Shape tool. Press the Shift key while you drag to maintain the shape's proportions.

Use the Line tool (see Figure 2.47) to create vector, resolution-independent lines as Shape layers or paths. Click the Shape Layer or Paths button in the Options Bar before you drag in the image with the Line tool.

FIGURE 2.47

The Shape tools and Line tool

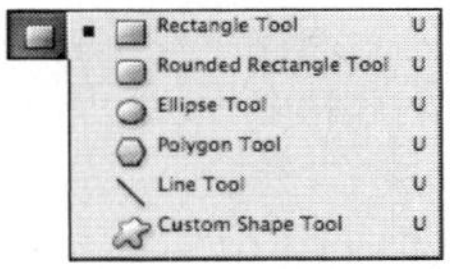
Rectangle Tool U
Rounded Rectangle Tool U
Ellipse Tool U
Polygon Tool U
Line Tool U
Custom Shape Tool U

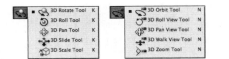

Use the Custom Shape tool to create vector, resolution-independent Shape layers or paths. Choose a custom shape from the Shape menu in the Options Bar. Click the Shape Layer or Paths button in the Options Bar before you drag in the image with the Custom Shape tool. Press the Shift key while you drag to maintain the shape's proportions.

TIP **Create a custom shape by clicking on a path in the Paths panel, then choosing Edit ⇨ Define Custom Shape.**

NEW FEATURE **The 3D Object tools and 3D Camera tools offer convenient ways to manipulate 3-D objects or change the observation point of the view of 3-D objects.**

The 3D tools

Figure 2.48 shows the 3D Object tools and 3D Camera tools. Change the position, orientation, or size of 3-D objects with the 3D Object tools. You can change the observation point or the camera's orientation, position, or distance to the 3-D object with the 3D Camera tools.

FIGURE 2.48

The 3D Object tools and 3D Camera tools

3D Rotate Tool K
3D Roll Tool K
3D Pan Tool K
3D Slide Tool K
3D Scale Tool K
3D Orbit Tool N
3D Roll View Tool N
3D Pan View Tool N
3D Walk View Tool N
3D Zoom Tool N

The Hand, Rotation, and Zoom tools

Scroll in a zoomed-in image window by dragging with the Hand tool (see Figure 2.49).

The Hand and Rotation tools

NEW FEATURE The Rotation tool can rotate the canvas, along with the image, so that the whole canvas looks rotated inside the Photoshop work area. This feature only works if you have certain video cards in your computer — see Performance Preferences for details.

Rotate the image canvas part of the work area with the Rotation tool so that the image and canvas look rotated on-screen. This is like rotating a piece of paper so that it is in a more comfortable position when you are drawing on it. Drag in the image with the Rotation tool to rotate the canvas. Click the Reset View button in the Options Bar to straighten it back out.

Click in the image with the Zoom tool to zoom in or Alt-click with the Zoom tool to zoom out. Double-click the Zoom tool to get a 100 percent view.

Keyboard shortcuts for the Zoom tool:

- **Zoom In.** Ctrl+spacebar+click/⌘+spacebar+click
- **Zoom Out.** Alt+spacebar+click/Option+spacebar+click

Figure 2.50 shows the Zoom tool.

The Zoom tool

       Zoom Tool   Z

Foreground and Background Color tools

Click the Default Foreground and Background Colors button (see Figure 2.51) to make the foreground color black and the background color white (the defaults).

Click the Switch Foreground and Background Colors button (see Figure 2.52) to switch the foreground color and background colors.

The foreground color is the color that is used by the Brush tool to paint. To change the foreground color, click a swatch in the Swatches panel, click the Foreground Color box, and choose a color in the Color Picker, or click on a color in the image with the Eyedropper tool. You can also click the Switch Foreground and Background Colors button.

FIGURE 2.51

The Default Foreground and Background Colors button

   Default Foreground and
Background Colors   D

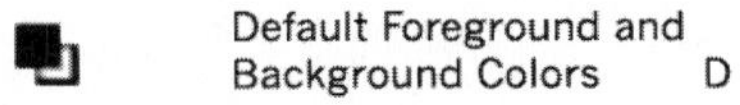

FIGURE 2.52

The Switch Foreground and Background Colors button

Switch Foreground and
Background Colors   X

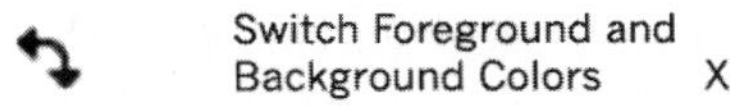

The Eraser and Magic Eraser tools paint the background in color instead of transparent when background layers or layers have transparency locked. When you increase the canvas size of an image, the additional area is filled with the background color. To change the background color, click the Background Color box and choose a color in the Color Picker, or with the Color Picker open, click on a color in the image. You can also click the Switch Foreground and Background Colors button.

Figure 2.53 shows the Set Foreground Color and Set Background Color boxes.

FIGURE 2.53

The Set Foreground Color and Set Background Color boxes

   Set Foreground Color

Set Background Color

The Mode buttons

When Quick Mask Mode is active, you can use the Brush tool to paint selections onto images. In the default settings in this mode, the selected area appears clear and the unselected area appears in a transparent red (you can reverse this by double-clicking the Quick Mask Mode button and setting new options). When you're finished painting the selection, click the Quick Mask Mode button (see Figure 2.54) to leave Quick Mask Mode, and the selection will be active. The keyboard shortcut to toggle Quick Mask Mode on and off is Q.

FIGURE 2.54

The Quick Mask Mode button

     Quick Mask Mode   Q

The Screen Mode menu (see Figure 2.55) includes the following options:

- **Standard Screen Mode.** The Photoshop workspace takes up most of the screen area.
- **Full Screen Mode with Menu Bar.** The Photoshop workspace takes up all the screen area.
- **Full Screen Mode.** The image is shown on a black background and fills the screen. Other work area components are hidden.

The keyboard shortcut F cycles through the screen modes.

FIGURE 2.55

The Screen Mode menu

Summary

This chapter described the Photoshop workspace, preferences, presets, and tools. Following are key concepts:

- The Photoshop workspace consists of the Menu Bar, Tools panel, Options Bar, panels, Image Window, and, new to CS4, the Application Frame.
- The Application Frame acts as a container for the entire Photoshop workspace and functions in a similar way as an Image Window.
- Photoshop Preferences can be set to improve performance and change the appearance and some functions of the workspace.
- You can design custom workspaces, keyboard shortcuts, and menus that are optimized for certain workflows and save and load the custom workspaces.
- There are libraries of presets that come with Photoshop, including custom brushes, swatches, styles, and shapes that can be accessed and used from various menus and panels. The Preset Manager can be used to organize sets of presets. You can also make your own custom presets.
- Use tools to work directly on images and perform tasks such as making selections, moving image pixels, creating shapes, and zooming in and out of an image.

Chapter 3

Finding and Processing Images with Bridge

Since its introduction with Adobe's CS2 suite of applications, Bridge has continued to evolve into an essential part of many a creative arsenal. In addition to providing a centralized resource for file organization and sharing, Bridge includes a powerful technology called Adobe XMP (Extensible Markup Platform), which allows for metadata tagging, keywords, grouping, and rating.

The latest incarnation of Bridge brings with it a number of new features and enhancements, including a notable boost in performance. Creative Suite veterans who may have been turned off by Bridge's less-than-speedy performance in the past may want to have another look.

Bridge is a stand-alone application and can be launched by double-clicking on its icon in the file system of your PC or Mac; or you can access it from within Photoshop (or other Creative Suite applications) by using one of these methods:

- From Photoshop, click the Go to Bridge button located on the toolbar.
- Choose File ➪ Browse or press Ctrl+Alt+O (⌘+Opt+O on a Mac) on your keyboard.
- If you already have a file open and are finished working on it, choose File ➪ Close and Go To Bridge.

IN THIS CHAPTER

Finding and opening images

Adding descriptive and searchable data to images

Organizing image collections

Creating presentations

Processing batches of images and repetitive tasks

Finding and Opening Images

One of the best things about Bridge is that you can reconfigure it in countless ways to make it fit the workflow of whatever task you happen to have at hand, be it searching for photographs, reviewing and labeling images, or viewing embedded image metadata. You can reorganize the workspace to suit your needs by dragging the vertical or horizontal bar between panels to make them bigger or smaller; or just close panels that aren't useful for the task you're currently working on (you can always get them back by selecting them from the Window menu). You can also use Bridge to browse the files and folders on local hard drives, attached optical media, and networked or shared drives.

The default workspace configuration of Bridge — known as Essentials — is shown in Figure 3.1.

FIGURE 3.1

Adobe Bridge, shown here in Essentials view

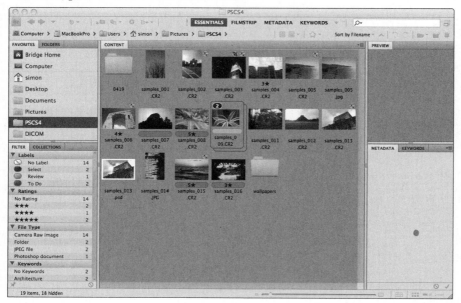

Bridge ships with eight standard workspace configurations, the first six of which can be quickly accessed by pressing the Ctrl/⌘ key in conjunction with the F1–F6 keys on your keyboard:

- **Essentials.** This view shows folder listings, favorite folders and images, image thumbnails, a larger preview of the selected image, and metadata and keywords that have been or can be applied to your images.

- **Filmstrip.** This view focuses on viewing images and their thumbnails. It displays image thumbnails in a filmstrip configuration (hence the name) either vertically along the side or horizontally along the bottom, leaving most of the workspace dominated by a large image preview.

- **Metadata.** Use this workspace for examining the metadata associated with files. The focus here is on seeing smaller thumbnails alongside such information as when the file was created, its last modification date, labels and ratings you may have applied, and other information.

- **Output.** New for Bridge CS4, the Output workspace allows you to share your photographs either as an exported PDF or as an interactive Web gallery.

- **Keywords.** This view is optimized for managing the keywords associated with your image. You can apply keywords to multiple images by Shift-clicking or Ctrl-clicking and selecting images, and then choosing the keywords to apply from the panel on the left.

- **Preview.** As the name suggests, this view is all about getting a closer look at your photos with a nice big image preview in the center of the workspace.

- **Light Table.** This view shows only thumbnails and is useful for quickly skimming through or applying keywords or ratings to a large group of photos at a time, and for selecting images for batch processing.

- **Folders.** The Folders view gives you a quick way to scan the contents of the folders on your hard drive or other volumes that are connected to your computer.

Once you've selected images or folders in Bridge, you can drag them to the Favorites panel for quick access. Use the Folders panel to move quickly within the folder structure of your computer and its connected volumes.

Depending on what you're viewing in the main Content area, the Filter panel dynamically populates with criteria on which you can narrow down your current selection of images. For instance, Figure 3.2 shows a folder containing JPEG, TIFF, and RAW files. The Filter panel shows a summary of the total number of each type of file that is present in this folder. Clicking on, say, JPEG file restricts your view to only the JPEG files in that folder. If you click additional categories in the Filter panel, those files are added to your view. To clear the filtered view, click the Clear Filter button (the circle with a line through it) located on the bottom right of the Filter panel.

You can also search your computer for images by using the search pane on the top right of the Bridge window or by choosing Edit ⇨ Find from Bridge's menu or by pressing Ctrl+F/⌘+F on the keyboard.

FIGURE 3.2

The Filter panel allows you to restrict the view in Bridge to show only files meeting certain criteria.

Importing images from a digital camera

Bridge includes a built-in program called Photo Downloader, which allows you to download images directly from a digital camera or memory card.

Opening Photo Downloader by clicking on its icon on Bridge's toolbar results in the dialog box shown in Figure 3.3. Connected cameras and memory cards are listed in the pop-up menu in the Source area at the top of the dialog box. If you don't see the device containing the images you want to download, try choosing Refresh List from the menu.

FIGURE 3.3

Photo Downloader does just that — it downloads images from cameras and memory cards connected to your computer.

The steps listed below outline the process of getting images from a camera into Bridge:

1. **Choose Get Photos from Camera from the File menu, or click the camera icon on the toolbar.** Photo Downloader launches and detects devices that are connected to your computer.

2. **Choose a location on your computer or connected hard drives to save your photos.** You can automatically create subfolders in that location, and give those folders names corresponding to the dates when the pictures were shot.

3. **Select a naming convention for the photos.** This is an optional step; you can always choose to rename the images later by using Bridge's Batch Rename.

4. **Choose other options for saving your photos, such as whether to convert them to DNG, and choose a location for backup images, such as a removable drive or a folder on your Desktop, which you can later burn to a CD or DVD.**

CROSS-REF   Learn more about DNG (Adobe's Digital Negative format) in Chapter 4.

By default, Photo Downloader opens in Standard mode, and offers limited options for downloading. For greater flexibility, you may want to work in the Advanced mode, which is accessible by clicking the Advanced dialog button at the lower left corner of the dialog box. The biggest advantages of Advanced mode are that it displays preview thumbnails of each image on the selected device and it allows you to select specific images for download, rather than automatically downloading all the available images.

You can also apply metadata such as copyright and other photographer info to your photos as they are downloaded, either by entering it in the provided fields or by choosing an existing metadata template. The Advanced dialog box is shown in Figure 3.4.

Once the download is complete, Bridge opens a window allowing you to view, label, and organize your photographs.

NOTE   If necessary, you can rotate pictures that were shot in portrait mode (with your camera turned vertically) by using the rotate icons on the toolbar.

FIGURE 3.4

Photo Downloader's Advanced dialog box gives you greater flexibility when downloading photos from a connected device.

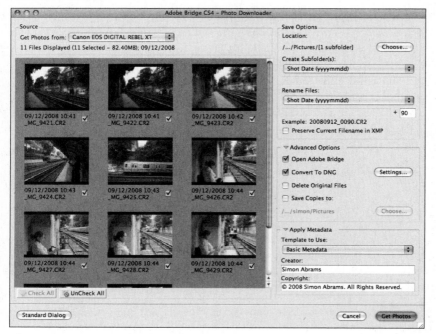

Grouping images as stacks

Because digital storage media (compact flash cards, hard drives, blank DVDs) are so inexpensive nowadays, my philosophy when taking pictures is to shoot more than I know I'll need. Sometimes I'll just leave my camera on "burst" or continuous shooting mode and fire away, especially when I'm trying to get a shot of a moving subject or of a scene I know I can't reshoot. As a result, I often end up with a series of very similar images that differ only slightly in terms of composition or camera angle, which can clutter my Bridge thumbnail area.

Enter Image Stacks. This feature, which was borrowed from Adobe Photoshop Lightroom, allows you to group a series of related images together, pick the best of the stack, then collapse the stack, hiding the remaining images out of view. If you need to see the rest of the images again, all you have to do is open up that stack. Image Stacks are shown in Figure 3.5.

FIGURE 3.5

Stacking images in Bridge lets you group similar images together, keeping your thumbnail view area free of excess clutter.

To move an image to the top of the stack, do one of the following:

- Click on the image, and from the Stacks menu, choose Promote to Top of Stack.
- Right-click (Ctrl-click if you're a Mac user with a single-button mouse) on the image and choose Stack ➪ Promote to Top of Stack.

To remove an image from a stack, click on the image and choose Ungroup From Stack from the Stacks menu.

Collapse and expand stacks by clicking the icon in the top-left corner of the thumbnail, which indicates how many images are grouped together in the stack.

You can also apply labels, keywords, and other commands to stacks, just as you can to individual images. Keep in mind that if you click on the top image in the stack, commands are applied only to that image. Alt-clicking or Option-clicking on the stack selects all the images in the stack, enabling you to apply commands to all the grouped images.

Another function of Stacks would be to work with image sequences — a series of still images that make up an animation or movie when displayed sequentially. Grouping a series of files comprising an image sequence into a stack allows you to import that stack directly into After Effects by using the File ⇨ Place in After Effects command (available if After Effects is installed on your system). You can also set the frame rate of a stack before importing it into After Effects by selecting an option from the Stacks ⇨ Frame Rate menu.

CROSS-REF Frame rates and working with image sequences in Photoshop are examined more thoroughly in Chapter 26.

Adding labels and ratings

Labels and ratings are two additional organizational tools available to you in Bridge (see Figure 3.6). When sorting through a group of images, you can assign ratings by clicking on the Label menu and choosing a value from 1 to 5 (or use Ctrl or ⌘ followed by a number from 1 to 5); or you can mark a not-so-perfect shot as a reject (don't feel bad, it happens). You can also use the following color-coded labels to further organize your photos: No Label, Select, Second, Approved, Review, and To Do.

FIGURE 3.6

These images have been assigned labels and ratings between one and five stars in Bridge. You can filter the Bridge view to show only images that have labels and ratings, or only images that haven't been rated and that need to be reviewed.

After you've added ratings and labels to your images, the labels appear as criteria you can select in the Filter menu. For instance, you can show only images that have been marked as four- and five-star selects, and export those as a PDF presentation for your client (who will be suitably impressed by your professionalism, of course).

Processing images

After you've finished organizing, labeling, rating, and otherwise weaning down the photos you're going to use for a project, you're ready to start processing the images — that is, applying any color and tonal correction, cropping, sharpening, and reducing noise — or compositing multiple images together. Bridge doesn't have built-in editing tools, but through Bridge you can access the powerful image-processing commands available in Photoshop and the other CS4 applications. You can also open images in Adobe Camera Raw and perform edits and adjustments there. For more on Camera Raw, see Chapter 4.

Adding Descriptive and Searchable Data to Images

One of the most powerful features of Bridge is its ability to wrangle file metadata to sort, group, filter, and organize large collections of images.

Metadata is information about an image such as author name, resolution, dimensions, image date, copyright, and descriptive keywords. In the case of digital photographs, most of this information is usually embedded at the time the image is captured, except for keywords, which you add during your processing workflow. Bridge allows you to edit and use this information in many ways. You can also save yourself some repetitive typing by creating metadata templates containing information that remains consistent for a group of images (such as your name and your copyright information) and applying that template to your photos in Bridge.

To edit metadata in Bridge, use either the Metadata panel or the File Info window.

Metadata panel

Figure 3.7 shows the Metadata panel, which is broken down into several subsections that may differ slightly, depending on the type of image you're working with or the capabilities of the camera you used. You can collapse and expand the different subsections by clicking on the corresponding disclosure triangles.

FIGURE 3.7

The Metadata panel in Bridge allows you to focus on the metadata embedded in your images.

- **File Properties.** This section contains basic information about the file, such as its filename, creation date, document type, file size, and image dimensions.

- **IPTC Core.** If you haven't submitted photographs to a news agency of some sort, this category might be somewhat unfamiliar to you. IPTC stands for the International Press Telecommunications Council, which is an international body of news agencies that is responsible for maintaining standards for exchanging news data.

- **Camera Data (EXIF).** EXIF data contains information about the camera that was used to shoot the photograph, and is embedded at the time the photo is taken. Camera make, model, and serial number, focal length, film speed, and whether the flash fired are examples of the kind of data available in the EXIF section of the metadata panel. EXIF data can't be modified.

- **Audio.** This section, which displays the information contained in the ID3 tags of mp3 or other music files, is populated if you view audio files in Bridge. If the Preview panel is visible, a preview of the selected audio file begins to play in Bridge (this behavior can be changed in the Bridge Preferences window).

- **Video.** Again, this section, which displays a video file's metadata, only appears if you view a video file in Bridge.

■ **GPS.** Some cameras, like Nikon's D3, automatically embed GPS location data in the metadata of each photograph that is taken. If your photos contain this information, it appears here, allowing you to search for images based on their geographical locations without having to enter that information manually (sadly, this feature won't help you with trying to navigate rush-hour traffic on the New Jersey Turnpike).

■ **DICOM.** DICOM stands for Digital Imaging and Communications in Medicine. The metadata saved in DICOM files contains information about the patient, the physician, and other medical information about the image.

CROSS-REF You'll find more information about DICOM and other technical image formats in Chapter 28.

File Info window

Adding even more information, such as suggested uses for the photograph and the photographer's Web site, goes beyond the abilities of the Metadata panel and into the realm of the File Info window (see Figure 3.8). To access the File Info window, choose File ➪ File Info. The resulting window gives you an overview of basic metadata associated with a file in its Details tab, which is displayed by default. Use the arrows or click on any of the 13 tabs at the top of the window to switch between more specific metadata categories that apply to certain types of files like audio, video, or SWF files destined for mobile devices.

FIGURE 3.8

The File Info window allows you to dig in and edit the metadata that's associated with your photographs.

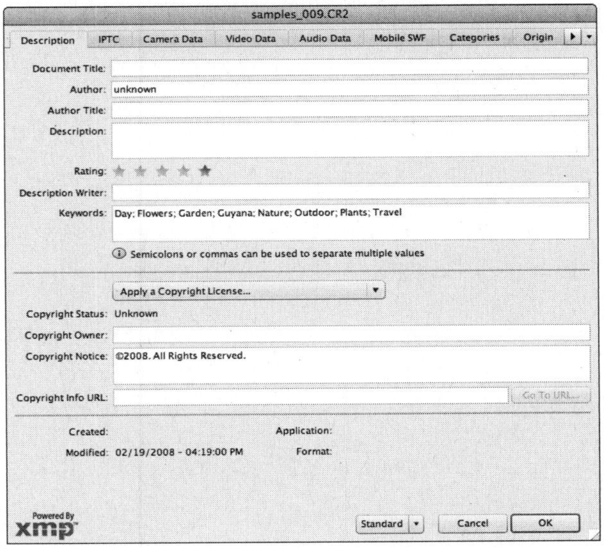

NOTE Much of the information that's embedded via the File Info window is only visible to other users if they happen to open the File Info window in Photoshop or Bridge. Therefore, if you are concerned about protecting your pictures from unauthorized use, you may want to consider adding a watermark, depending on where your pictures will be distributed.

Using Metadata templates

Now that you know all about metadata and how useful it is, you can get fancy by using templates to create boilerplate info that gets applied to images over and over, such as your name and copyright information.

To create a template, choose Create Metadata Template from the Tools menu or from the Metadata Panel menu. From the resulting Edit Metadata Template dialog box, shown in Figure 3.9, select the information that you want to store in your template. If you have an image that already has metadata that you want to use as a starting point, select that image first, and the stored information will be pre-populated in the Edit Metadata Template window.

FIGURE 3.9

Enter frequently used sets of metadata in the Edit Metadata Template window.

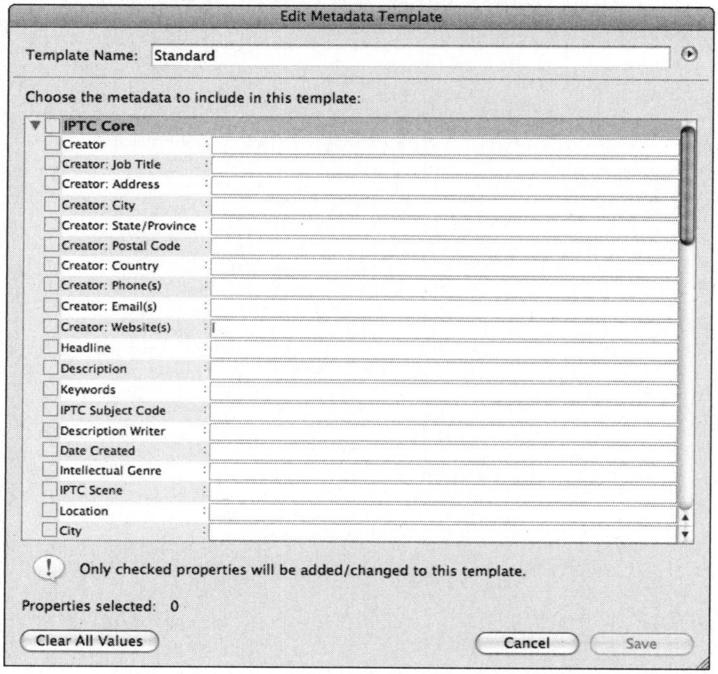

Apply your new metadata template to an image or a group of images by selecting them in Bridge and choosing Tools ⇨ Append Metadata or Replace Metadata. Append adds the metadata in your template to the existing metadata in the image; Replace overwrites any existing metadata.

Edit the data in the templates by choosing Tools ⇨ Edit Metadata Template. To see where your templates are stored on your hard drive, open the File Info window and, under the Settings menu, choose Show Templates. This is useful if you use multiple computers and want to maintain the consistent metadata templates among them.

Using keywords

Adding descriptive keywords to your images is another invaluable part of organizing your photographs, and as your digital image collection continues to grow, you will come to rely on a good keywording system for hunting down specific images. There are some sample keywords included with Bridge that you can feel free to delete if they don't apply to your images. Remember that you can add an almost unlimited number of descriptive keywords to your images. The key thing to remember is to be consistent and to use words that are most useful to you when you go back looking for your photos six months or a year down the road.

In the Keywords panel (see Figure 3.10), you'll see a list of keywords and sub-keywords (keywords that have been grouped under broader categories). Keywords that have been applied to the selected image have a check box next to them. You can add or remove keywords by selecting or deselecting the check boxes next to them.

FIGURE 3.10

The Keywords panel

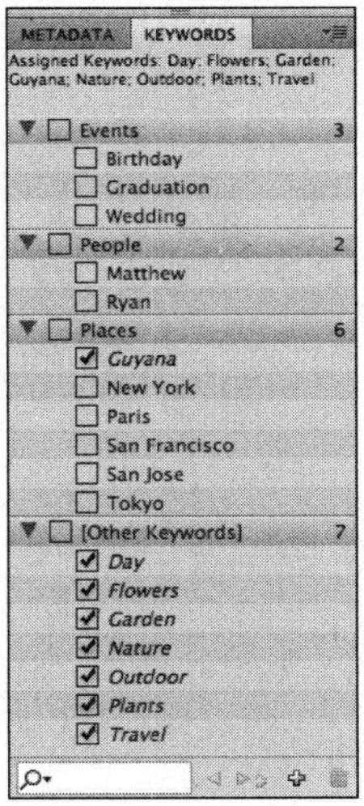

About XMP

Bridge uses a technology created by Adobe called Extensible Metadata Platform, or XMP, to read, store, and organize both standard and proprietary metadata. In most cases the metadata is embedded in the image file, where many different types of programs can access it. In cases where the information can't be embedded in the file, it's stored in what are known as *sidecar files*. These are XML-based files that can travel with the images if they are moved to different hard drives or computers, and can be read by all the applications in the Adobe Creative Suite.

Create new keywords by clicking the plus button at the bottom of the Keywords panel. You can create new sub-keywords by clicking the plus button with the little arrow next to it. Remember that because keywords are saved in Bridge's cache, they are available globally, no matter what folder or volume you're currently viewing.

To delete a keyword that you no longer need, select it and click on the little trashcan icon at the bottom right of the Keywords panel.

Organizing Image Collections

Similar to photo albums, collections are a useful way to group images together. You can make arbitrary collections of images, or you can make collections based on search results (Smart Collections).

Collections

To manage collections of images, click on the Collections panel (if it isn't visible, select it from the Window menu) and do one of the following:

- **To create a new collection:** Click the plus button at the bottom of the Collections panel and give your collection a name.

- **To add photos to a collection:** Drag images from the Content area to your collection's name in the Collections panel.

- **To remove a photo from a collection:** Select the photo and click the Remove From Collection button that appears at the top of the Content area.

- **To delete a collection:** Highlight the name of the collection and click the trashcan icon on the lower right of the panel. Note that when you delete a collection you're not actually deleting the photos it contains from your hard drive, you're just deleting that specific grouping of photos.

Smart Collections

Smart Collections are like regular collections, except they're . . . well, smart. You can build a collection based on criteria that you specify, like ISO (film speed), focal length, or keywords, and have Bridge search for images (in a specific folder, or even your entire computer) that meet those criteria. The "smart" part is that Smart Collections update dynamically, meaning that as you add or remove images that meet those criteria, they are automatically added to or removed from the collection. Follow these steps to create a Smart Collection:

1. **Click the Smart Collection button on the lower right of the Collections panel.**

2. **From the resulting Smart Collection dialog box, choose the criteria on which to base the collection.** You can add or remove criteria by clicking the plus or minus sign, as shown in Figure 3.11.

3. **In the Results section of the Smart Collection dialog box, choose whether to group images based on all or any of the specified criteria.**

FIGURE 3.11

Creating a Smart Collection

4. **You can expand your search by having Bridge search for images within subfolders of the current folder by checking the Include All Subfolders check box.**

5. **Choose whether to search folders that haven't been indexed by Bridge.** Folders get added to Bridge's cache simply by viewing their contents in Bridge. If you have Bridge search folders that haven't been indexed, it could take longer to complete the search.

You can modify the criteria that a Smart Collection is based on by clicking the Edit Smart Collection button on the lower left of the Collections panel.

Creating Presentations

Bridge is great for viewing and organizing your image collection. It's also great for providing you with a number of snazzy ways to show off your images to other people. Use Bridge to present a slide show of your photos, get them into a PDF file, or create a professional-looking Web gallery.

Creating a photo slide show couldn't be easier. From the View menu, choose Slideshow or press Ctrl+L/⌘+L on your keyboard. You can set up options such as the length of the interval between images and which transition to use in the View ➪ Slideshow Options menu.

Using the Output workspace

Newly revamped for Bridge in CS4 is the Adobe Media Gallery feature, which is now known as the Output workspace. Use the options in the Output workspace (shown in Figure 3.12) to export a PDF presentation of your photographs or create a professional-quality, Flash-based Web gallery (or an HTML version, if you prefer), which you can then upload to an ftp server.

PDF Presentation

The PDF option in Output offers you the option of creating either a regular multi-page PDF or a PDF Presentation, which will automatically launch into a full-screen slide show when opened. Use the following steps to create a PDF with Bridge's Output workspace:

1. **View a folder full of images in Bridge and click Output on the toolbar.** The Content area changes to Output Preview. This is where you can see how your final PDF will look by selecting at least one image and clicking Refresh Preview in the Output panel on the right after making adjustments to your settings.

2. **Use the Output panel to specify output options for your PDF.** You can select a template from the options provided with Bridge or customize your own settings.

3. **Under the Document section, choose your page size from the presets or enter custom dimensions.** Select whether to embed high- or low-quality images in your PDF, depending on whether your PDF is destined only for the screen or for a high-quality print. As a rule, if the final PDF is destined for on-screen display only, and not for printed output, you can opt for the lower-quality settings. This will produce a file that you won't have any trouble e-mailing to a client or colleague for review.

4. **Under Layout, specify how your images will be placed on the page.** For instance, you can have a single photo per page or you can set the number of rows and columns to place multiple images on the page.

5. **Using the Overlays section, specify which information to include with your photo and the font to display it in.**

6. **Set the Playback settings for your PDF. Deselecting all the checked options saves the PDF as a regular multi-page file.**

Web Gallery

In addition to PDF presentations, you can use the options in the Output workspace to create very nicely designed Flash-based galleries for your photographs (because, you know, I hear this Internet thing is going to be big someday). To begin creating your site, follow these steps:

1. **Making sure you're in the Output workspace, click the Web Gallery button at the top right of the Output panel (see Figure 3.12).** The Output panel populates with a number of options for customizing your gallery, and the main viewing area switches to a tabbed view with the option to switch between the Output Preview tab (what your final site will look like) and the Preview tab (an enlarged view of your selected images).

FIGURE 3.12

Bridge's Output workspace is used to create PDF presentations or to create a Web-based gallery of your images.

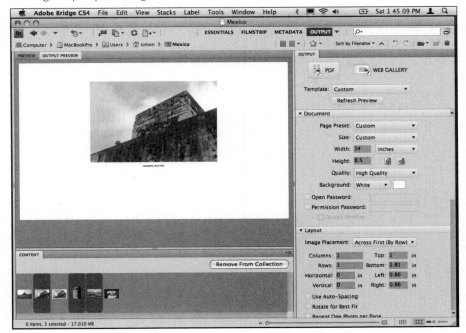

2. **Select a template for your gallery from the Template drop-down list.** Choosing from the available templates produces different options in the Style drop-down list. As you select various options, you can see a preview of your changes by clicking either of the preview buttons in the Output panel.

   ▪ **Refresh Preview:** Shows a preview right in Bridge (your main window will automatically switch to Output Preview if necessary).

   ▪ **Preview in Browser:** This button generates the files necessary to preview your gallery and saves them to a temporary location on your hard drive. It then launches your default Web browser and loads the preview of your site.

> **NOTE** Included in the list of available templates is an option to generate an HTML-based Web gallery, rather than a Flash-based site.

3. **Continue setting up your Web gallery by using the options found in the Style Information, Image Options, and Create Gallery sections of the Output panel.** Below is a brief overview of the options in the Output panel:

   ▪ **Site Info:** Use the fields in this section to change the title, description, and caption of your site. Set a contact e-mail address and phone number as well as options for the Slideshow feature of the Web gallery.

   ▪ **Color Palette:** Use the swatches in this section to choose colors for the different elements of your Web gallery (the header text, menu text, background, border, and so on). The built-in gallery templates have their own pre-defined color schemes, but you can tweak these colors and come up with combinations of your own.

   ▪ **Appearance:** The specific options in this section change depending on which template you selected for your gallery, but the general purpose of these options is to tweak the position and size of the gallery's thumbnails and main preview image.

   ▪ **Create Gallery:** Specify options for saving your gallery. To save the gallery files to a location on your hard drive, click the Save to Disk radio button. Navigate to the location where you want to save the files and click Save. From here, you can view the site locally on your hard drive by opening it in your browser of choice. You can also use ftp software to upload the files to your ftp server.

   To upload the files directly to your ftp server from Bridge, click the Upload radio button and enter your server information and credentials. The files are transferred to your server and you can see the result by entering the Web address of the site you uploaded them to in your Web browser.

Using the supplied gallery templates and tweaking the output options as described above can generate a really slick and professional-looking Web gallery for your photography. Figure 3.13 shows an example of a finished Web gallery created with the Lightroom Flash Gallery template.

FIGURE 3.13

FIGURE 3.13

This Web gallery shows an example of the Lightroom Flash Gallery template in action.

Processing Batches of Images and Repetitive Tasks

Making adjustments to a handful of images at a time is all well and good, but what happens when you want to apply a series of edits to a whole memory card full of images from Cousin Bertha's wedding in Hoboken last week? Having to make the trek to New Jersey was bad enough; spending your weekend having to make a bunch of repetitive edits only makes you resent poor Cousin Bertha even more. Instead, you can use the power of Bridge's batch-processing capabilities in conjunction with Photoshop's Actions to whip through large image collections in no time.

Batch renaming multiple images

Although it's not really an image-processing task per se, renaming a large number of images is one of the more tedious things that you'll find yourself having to do while organizing your photos, so I think it's worth covering here. Bridge's built-in, batch-renaming command is pretty simple to use and makes quick work of those often-cryptic "DSC0232.JPG" filenames that are generated by many digital cameras. To change the filenames of a group of images, follow the steps outlined below:

1. **Select the images to be renamed.** You can select specific images to be renamed by holding down Shift or Ctrl/⌘/) while clicking on them. If no images are selected, then all the images in the current Bridge window will be renamed. Choose Batch Rename from the Tools menu (or press Ctrl+Shift+R/⌘+Shift+R on your keyboard) to view the Batch Rename dialog box (see Figure 3.14).

FIGURE 3.14

The Batch Rename dialog box

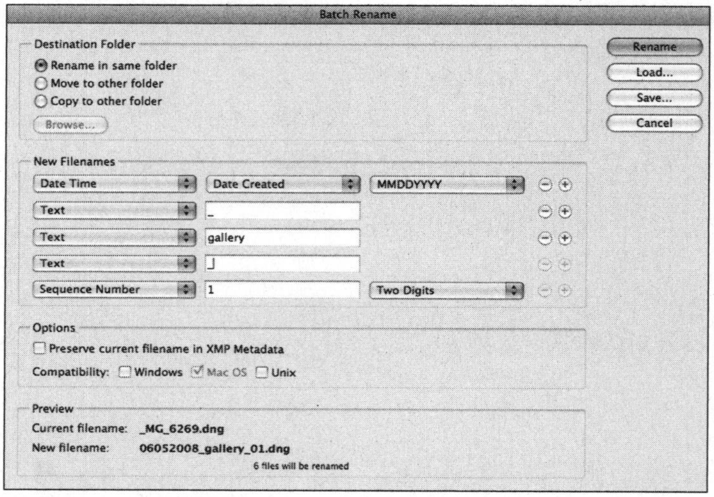

2. **Choose a destination.** You can either rename the images in their current location or choose a destination folder to either copy or move the renamed files to. Copying the files to a new destination leaves the originals where they were, while selecting the Move option renames the files and moves them to your destination folder.

3. **Customize the new filenames.** You can customize your filenames by using the drop-down lists in the New Filenames section of the dialog box. For instance, choose a prefix for your filenames by choosing Text from the first menu and entering some descriptive text. Click the plus button on the right to add more components to your filename.

4. **Set the image sequence.** Create either a numeric or alphabetic sequence of images (choose Sequence Number or Sequence Letter) from the menus. Enter a starting number or letter, and it is automatically incremented for each file that is to be renamed. You can see a preview of what the final filenames will look like at the bottom of the Batch Rename dialog box, as well as the total number of files that will be renamed.

5. **Set the Rename options.** From the Options section of the Batch Rename dialog box, choose to retain the original image filename in the file's XMP metadata, as well as the compatibility of the filename with different file systems.

Process multiple images

There are a number of useful image-processing actions available within Photoshop and the other Creative Suite components, and you can access them directly from Bridge via the Tools menu (the available options will vary depending on which Creative Suite applications you have installed).

Batch

The Batch command gives you direct access to all the actions available in Photoshop. This includes the default actions that ship with Photoshop as well as any custom actions that you may have recorded yourself or downloaded from the Internet.

Selecting this option launches Photoshop (or brings it to the foreground if it's already open), with the Batch window open and the image source set to Bridge. From here, select an action to apply to your images, specify your file-saving options, and click OK. Sit back and let the magic happen.

CROSS-REF   For more information on using actions, including how to record and save your own actions, see Chapter 8.

Image Processor

The Image Processor is an incredibly useful and versatile script that ships with Photoshop. Use the Image Processor command to quickly convert images to a different file format (or multiple formats simultaneously), resize them, and optionally, apply a Photoshop action to them. The Image Processor script's dialog box is shown in Figure 3.15.

FIGURE 3.15

Use the Photoshop's Image Processor script to resize a batch of images and change their file types.

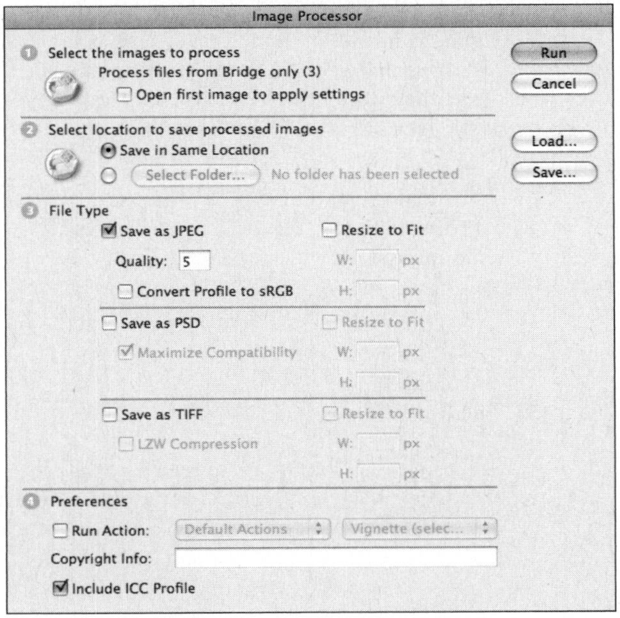

Merge to HDR

HDR is an increasingly popular advanced photographic technique, and you can use the Merge to HDR command to create your own HDR images in Photoshop.

First, a little background: HDR, or High Dynamic Range, images attempt to re-create the vast range of tonal information found in real-world scenes. They contain much more information than can be displayed on conventional monitors, or even printed on paper, and as a result, they can appear somewhat hyper-real. Typically, photographing a high-contrast scene is difficult, because you can expose either the shadows or the highlights correctly, but not both. HDR images solve this problem by combining three or more images shot at different exposures that cover the dynamic range of the scene.

Another application of HDR images is in photorealistic CG (computer generated) rendering. Because HDR images contain such a large amount of luminance information, they can be used to define light sources that emulate real-world conditions for 3-D scenes. Sadly, this topic falls outside the scope of this book.

For best results, the images should be shot with a camera mounted on a tripod, so that the alignment is exactly the same in each shot. You can use your camera's auto-bracket feature, or for more control, vary the exposure of each shot by changing your camera's shutter speed. Be sure to make the difference between each exposure at least one or two f-stops.

To create an HDR image from multiple exposures:

1. **Select the source images you want to combine in Bridge.**

2. **Choose Tools ⇨ Photoshop ⇨ Merge to HDR.**

3. **From the resulting window (shown in Figure 3.16), check or uncheck the images that you want to include in your final merged image.** You can also use the available controls to zoom in or out of the preview image.

4. **Set the bit depth of the merged image.** To retain all the dynamic range information available for the scene, merge the image, using the 32-bit option from the Bit Depth pop-up menu. Keep in mind, though, that what you will see on your screen is just a portion of all the tonal information that's available in the image — your display simply isn't capable of displaying the full dynamic range of a 32-bit image. To condense that information into a range that can accurately be displayed on-screen, choose either 8- or 16-bit from the Bit Depth pop-up menu.

5. **Preview the merged HDR image, using the slider underneath the histogram.** Moving the slider to the left darkens the HDR preview and shows the information that's contained in the bright areas of the image. Moving the slider to the right brightens the image and reveals the shadow detail. Remember that previewing the image in this way doesn't change the actual luminance data that's contained in the image; it simply shows you a subset of that information that your monitor is capable of displaying.

6. **Click OK to create the merged image.** Selecting the 32-bit option in Step 4 opens the image in Photoshop and retains the ability to preview the full dynamic range of the image by using the 32-bit preview slider at the bottom of the document window or by choosing View ⇨ 32-bit Preview Options.

FIGURE 3.16

HDR images are created by combining multiple images shot at different exposure values. Select the images to include in the composite in the Merge to HDR window.

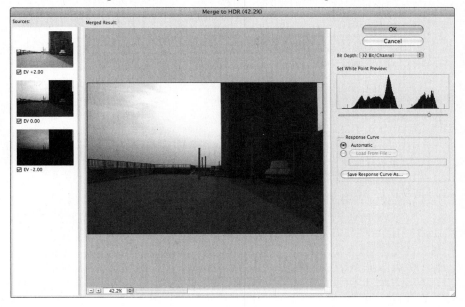

If you choose the 8- or 16-bit option from the Bit Depth menu, the HDR Conversion dialog box (shown in Figure 3.17) will open, allowing you to specify the final tonal range for your image. Again, because the dynamic range of a 32-bit HDR image is so great, you have to compress that information down to a range that 8- or 16-bit images are capable of displaying. Generally, you should try to retain as much information as possible in both the highlight and shadow areas of the image, using the methods available to you in the HDR Conversion dialog box. Choose from the following conversion methods:

- **Exposure and Gamma:** Use the sliders to adjust the brightness and contrast of the merged image.

- **Highlight Compression:** This option automatically condenses the highlight areas of the HDR image so that they fall within a range that can be displayed by an 8- or 16-bit image.

- **Equalize Histogram:** This is another automatic conversion option, which, again, compresses the dynamic range of the image so that it can be displayed by an 8- or 16-bit image file.

- **Local Adaptation:** This conversion method offers you the most control and the most creative leeway over the appearance of the final image, allowing you to adjust the brightness of local regions of the image. Use the Radius slider to set the size of the regions that will be brightened, and use the Threshold slider to specify how tonally different two pixels have to be in ordered to be considered part of different brightness regions. You can also optionally click the triangle to open the Toning Curve and Histogram, and you can adjust the curve to control the tonality of the image. The results you can produce by using this conversion method can be pretty surreal and dramatic, so feel free to experiment.

FIGURE 3.17

The HDR Conversion dialog box

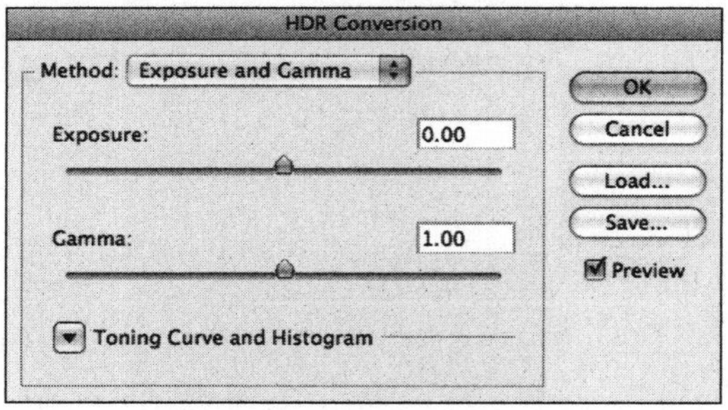

Keep in mind that 32-bit files are somewhat restricted in terms of the filters, adjustments, and other tools that you can use with them. Also 32-bit files must be saved in a file format that is capable of handling the information, such as the native Photoshop format (PSD), TIFF, or Photoshop's Large Document Format (PSB).

CROSS-REF Learn more about file formats in Chapter 7.

Photomerge

The Photomerge feature (see Figure 3.18) is used for combining several continuous, overlapping images into a panorama. As with shooting photographs for HDR images, you will get better results by using a tripod. If you do end up shooting hand-held, try to pivot from one spot while you take your pictures. Also, you should overlap each image with the next by somewhere around 20 percent or more, and keep your exposure settings consistent across all your images. If your camera automatically changes the exposure for each shot, you might need to change it to a manual setting.

1. **Select a series of images in Bridge and choose Photomerge from the Tools ➪ Photoshop menu.**

2. **Choose one of the following options for merging the images:**

   ■ **Auto:** Sit back and let Photoshop do its thing. It analyzes your photos and decides which mapping technique is best for creating the panorama.

   ■ **Perspective:** This mode selects one image (usually the center image) and sets it as the vantage point for the panorama. The other images are then transformed as necessary to match that perspective.

- **Cylindrical**: This mode is best for wide scenes. The source images are laid out on an "unwrapped" cylinder, and overlapping elements of each image are aligned.

- **Spherical**: This mode slices up a sphere and lays out the photographs. It is best for 360-degree panoramas.

- **Collage**: Choose this mode to transform the source images to match overlapping elements.

  Selecting the Blend images together check box tells Photoshop to detect the seams between each image and blend and color-match the images.

- **Reposition**: This mode aligns elements in each image, but doesn't stretch, skew, or otherwise alter the images.

FIGURE 3.18

Use the Photomerge window to select images to combine into a panorama.

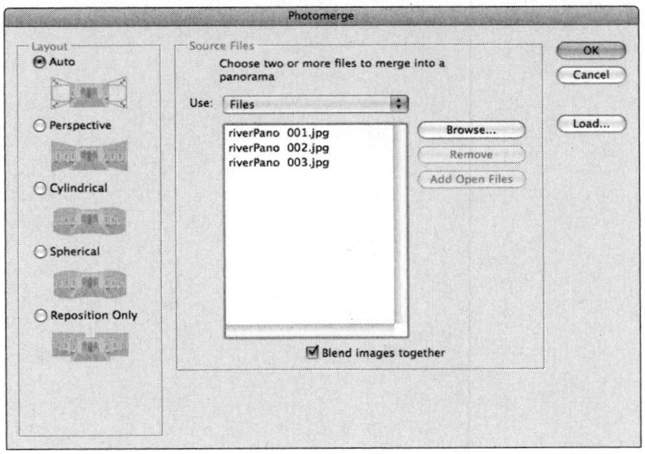

Summary

In this chapter you learned about Adobe Bridge — the powerful file management tool at the hub of Adobe's Creative Suite. You learned how to organize your images by leveraging the power of metadata and keywords and the Extensible Markup Platform. You also learned how Bridge's labeling, rating, and collections could help you to manage your library of images.

You learned how to create presentations of your images, either as PDFs or as Web galleries. Creating dramatic compositions by merging multiple exposures into HDR (High Dynamic Range) images was also covered. You also learned about using the Photomerge command to combine images into panoramas. Finally, you learned about using Bridge to automate repetitive tasks over multiple images.

Chapter 4

Camera Raw Work Area

In addition to the ubiquitous JPEG format, today's professional digital SLR (single-lens reflex) cameras, as well as many higher-end consumer cameras, are capable of saving a file format known as RAW. In this format, everything that was originally "seen" by the camera at the moment that you took the picture is still available to you when you transfer photos onto your hard drive, giving you more control in your editing process after your shoot.

IN THIS CHAPTER

The RAW format

The Camera Raw dialog box

Using Camera Raw

These high-resolution files require processing before they can be converted to JPEG, TIFF, or other commonly used file formats — that's where software like Adobe's Camera Raw comes into play. As of Photoshop CS, the Camera Raw plug-in has been bundled with Adobe's Creative Suite (you can also access it from Bridge and After Effects,) and it has evolved from its humble beginnings as a $99 add-on for Photoshop 7 into what could almost be a full-fledged, stand-alone application.

Once you've finished processing your RAW images, using the Camera Raw plug-in, they must be saved as a JPEG or TIFF file before you can bring them into Photoshop for more in-depth editing. Adobe Camera Raw can be used to perform top-level image adjustments (color correction, sharpening, and exposure corrections) or trickier image-processing tasks, particularly with the new features introduced in Adobe Camera Raw 5.0. For more in-depth manipulations, such as compositing multiple images together or applying filters and distortions to an image, you'll need to work directly in Photoshop.

TIP In addition to processing RAW files, Adobe Camera Raw can open and adjust JPEG and TIFF files.

The RAW Format

As mentioned before, RAW files are unprocessed — they contain all the image data that was originally recorded by the camera's sensor in its uncompressed, unaltered form. To get a little technical, the information is actually recorded as a grayscale image, along with a pixel-by-pixel map that corresponds to the color information in the photograph. As a result of all this information, RAW files are generally quite large in terms of size and will quickly fill up your camera's memory card, as well as your computer's hard drive.

Some of you might ask, "Well, what's the point of going through all this, if I can just set my camera to JPEG mode and be ready to go?" After all, JPEG does have its advantages:

- It requires no extra processing.

- It is an almost universally readable format.

- It can do a fantastic job of compressing photos to file sizes that are a fraction of their RAW equivalents, all the while retaining gorgeous, sharp, color detail.

You wouldn't be alone in questioning the use of RAW. In fact, this debate continues to rage in photo-related discussion forums across the Internet. To help you decide between RAW and JPEG, here is a scenario to consider. Let's say you left your camera on the default JPEG setting that it was on when you pulled it out of the box. The moment you squeeze the shutter, your camera (helpful and well-intentioned gadget that it is) applies a series of adjustments to the data it captures, based on some pretty clever methods for evaluating what it sees. It applies white balancing to make sure the colors look natural, based on the lighting conditions of your scene. It also applies contrast settings, brightness, and sharpening, and finally, it squeezes all that data down into a manageable file size.

All of this, of course, happens in mere microseconds. But if, for whatever reason, the white-balancing happens to have been set incorrectly for your scene (Tungsten mode in sunny daylight conditions? Yikes!), then you would be forced to use a good bit of post-production Photoshop work to salvage that nasty blue-tinted photo.

On the other hand, set your camera to RAW mode, and while many of those same adjustments are made at that magical moment when you squeeze the shutter, the difference is that all the original, unprocessed data remains available to you when you transfer the photos from your camera onto your hard drive. That means if you're unimpressed with the adjustments your camera automatically applied (ungrateful, aren't we?), or you need to tweak your image for any other reason, you can fire up Camera Raw and, with minimal effort, fix incorrectly white-balanced images to your heart's content (and your eye's relief).

Consider also that JPEG images contain 8 bits of color per channel, which can mean that there is a limited amount of detail in the shadows and/or highlights of your photos. If you apply lots of adjustments to this already limited data, it is possible to eventually degrade the quality of the image ("bruise" the pixels). RAW images, on the other hand, contain 12 or sometimes up to 14 bits of color per channel, resulting in a huge amount of discreet tonal levels in an image. As demonstrated in Figure 4.1, details that would have otherwise been lost in those underexposed shadows or overexposed highlights can often be coaxed back out, rescuing what at first glance might have been a rejected image.

FIGURE 4.1

Details have been lost in the shadows and highlights in the JPEG image on the left. Because the image was shot in RAW format, you can recover these details by using the Shadow and Highlight adjustment sliders in Camera Raw, as seen in the image on the right.

NOTE One of the biggest draws to shooting in RAW is that this format acts very much like an actual photographic negative, meaning that it acts as "digital film" that can be processed in any number of ways to generate unlimited prints.

When working with your photos in Camera Raw, rest assured that you're never directly modifying your original RAW file. Rather, any adjustments you make to white-balance, brightness, contrast, shadows, highlights, and sharpness are saved alongside the originals in the Camera Raw database, or as an alternative, in what's called a sidecar XMP file. You can then export the final images in a more widely compatible file format such as TIFF or JPEG, and continue to process them in Photoshop if necessary.

This is what's known as a *nondestructive* workflow — no pixels are bruised or otherwise harmed in this process. If you happen to get a little overzealous with the adjustments and your edits take a turn that you're not quite happy with (it happens to all of us at some point), or if you simply want to try a different look for one of your pictures (for instance, a black-and-white version), you can always return to the original photograph as it was shot.

The DNG format

Complicating the RAW issue is the fact that it is a *proprietary format*, meaning that it varies not only between camera manufacturers but also between individual camera models (imagine what it would be like if Canon cameras could only use Canon film, for instance). Camera manufacturers sometimes develop their own proprietary processing software for their formats, or they must provide software developers with the definitions that allow software like Adobe Camera Raw and Apple's Aperture to interpret them correctly.

The fear among many photographers who have adopted the RAW format into their workflow is that eventually, as formats change and become obsolete, that newer equipment will be unable to read their older images.

Developed by Adobe, the Digital Negative (DNG) format is a nonproprietary alternative that is intended to help address this issue. It is well documented and software developers don't need camera-specific information to allow their software to process RAW information saved in the DNG format. This makes it particularly well suited to archival purposes, as it is likely that future software packages will have no problems interpreting the data.

You can use Adobe Camera Raw to convert your photos to DNG after importing them to your hard drive and making adjustments. Or, you can convert an entire batch of RAW files from any camera's proprietary format into the DNG format by using Adobe DNG Converter, a free utility that is available from Adobe's Web site.

The Camera Raw dialog box

You can access the Camera Raw dialog box (as seen in Figure 4.2) by doing one of the following:

- Select one or more RAW images via Photoshop's Open dialog box and click Open.
- Double-click a RAW image thumbnail in Bridge.
- Select one or more RAW, TIFF, or JPEG files in Bridge and right-click (Ctrl+click on a Mac), then select Open in Camera Raw from the context menu.

FIGURE 4.2

The Camera Raw dialog box can be daunting at first glance, but it is well worth becoming familiar with.

Incorporating Bridge into your RAW image-processing workflow is probably the more efficient way to work, as you can more comfortably deal with a large number of images by taking advantage of Bridge's many view modes. Also, you have ready access to the images' metadata (see Figure 4.3), which can help you sort and group images based on very specific characteristics, such as image date, focal length, pixel dimensions, file formats, aspect ratios, or even the film speed (ISO) of each image. You can also add rate images and assign descriptive keywords to them.

FIGURE 4.3

You can view and edit your images' metadata (information about your photographs) in Bridge.

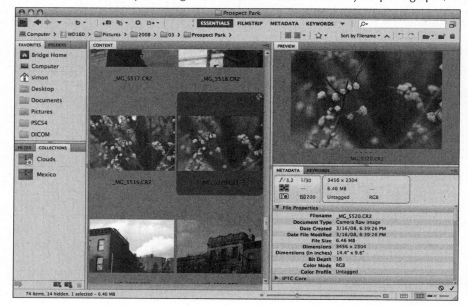

CROSS-REF Find out more about Bridge in Chapter 3.

The Camera Raw dialog box is usually separated into two areas: the main image viewing area and the image adjustment area. As you might expect, the image viewing area displays the image. It also includes controls for zooming the viewer, rotating the image, white-balancing, and removing blemishes or sensor dust.

To the right of the main image viewing area are the histogram and the image adjustment tabs and sliders, which are great ways for you to get elbow-deep in all that data that the RAW image file offers. Also in this area, nestled away under the disclosure triangle at the top of the Image Adjustment tabs, is the Camera Raw settings menu (see Figure 4.4). Here, you can reset the Camera Raw dialog box to its defaults; manage presets; and load, save, or export settings.

If you open multiple images in Camera Raw, the plug-in switches to Filmstrip view, opening a third area on the left side of the window, which displays thumbnails of your currently open group of images. You can use this mode to compare, rate, and make the same set of adjustments to multiple images.

FIGURE 4.4

The Camera Raw settings menu

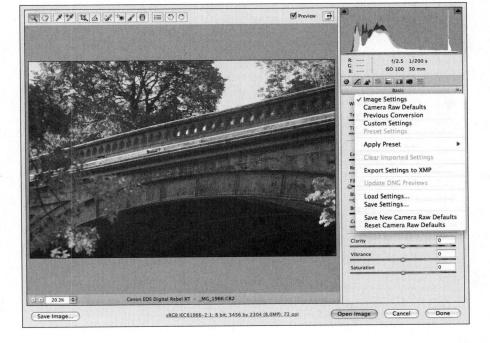

Using Adobe Camera Raw

Now that you're a believer and are ready to dive in with the RAW format, I'll get a little more specific about the various controls and tools you can use to manipulate your images with Adobe Camera Raw. Additionally, you'll learn how Camera Raw tracks your adjustments, metadata, and image thumbnails, allowing you to use Bridge to quickly browse and organize your images. Finally, you'll learn about the options you have for saving your images in other formats.

Importing RAW, JPEG, and TIFF images

You can import RAW images in several ways. Double-click a RAW file (or files) via the Open dialog box in Photoshop (or in Bridge). You can also open JPEG or TIFF images in Camera Raw by right-clicking on them in Bridge and selecting Open in Camera Raw, or by pressing Ctrl+R/⌘+R on your keyboard.

Initially when your images are opened in Camera Raw, a JPEG preview of the images appears while the image data loads and processes according to the definitions that correspond to each camera's RAW format. Unless you've made and saved adjustments to your RAW files, the JPEG preview that

Part I   **Welcome to Adobe Photoshop CS4**

you see when you first open a photo is one that was generated and embedded by your camera. The Camera Raw plug-in updates this JPEG preview as you make adjustments to the image.

Once you've adjusted the images to your liking, you may want to save those adjustments as a preset that is applied any time you import images.

TIP   To bypass the Camera Raw dialog box and open your RAW file directly in Photoshop, hold down the Shift key while double-clicking the image thumbnail. The image opens with the most recent Camera Raw settings (if you haven't used Camera Raw before, the plug-in's default settings are used instead).

Processing multiple photos

Often, when shooting multiple images with consistent lighting conditions, such as in a studio or at one location, it's useful to color-correct one image and then apply the same adjustments to all or several images from the shoot, saving yourself hours of repetitive clicking and dragging. To do this, open several files by Shift+clicking them in the File Open dialog box or in Bridge. Camera Raw opens in Filmstrip mode (as shown in Figure 4.5), displaying thumbnails of the current group of images. You can either adjust each image one at a time or select all the currently open images (by Shift+selecting their thumbnails) and apply the same set of adjustments simultaneously.

FIGURE 4.5

The Filmstrip view indicates which images are unselected, selected, or active.

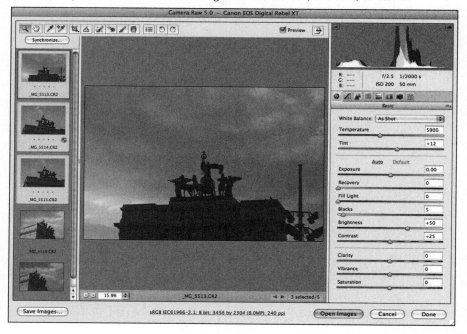

Click the Synchronize button to apply adjustments that you made to a single image to all the images that are currently opened in Camera Raw. Handily, you can choose to apply all the adjustments or you can use the check boxes in the resulting dialog box to pick and choose which adjustments to apply.

Image improvement settings

The workflow when processing RAW files usually goes from making very broad edits to the image (cropping, straightening, and adjusting white balance) to making very granular ones (for instance, making subtle tweaks to a specific range of hues). Take a closer look at the tools available in Camera Raw in the following sections.

The Camera Raw toolbar

The toolbar at the top of the Camera Raw window (see Figure 4.6) offers a number of useful tools to begin editing your photos. Here's what you'll find:

FIGURE 4.6

The Camera Raw toolbar

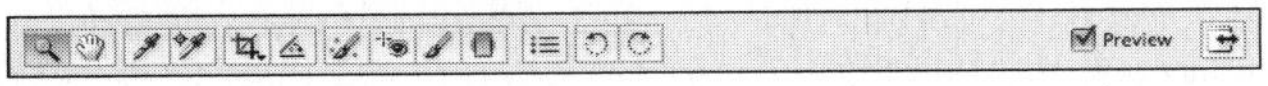

- **Zoom tool.** The Zoom tool is useful for getting an up-close look at the details of your image. To zoom out, press the Alt or Option key on your keyboard, while clicking with the Zoom tool.

- **Hand tool.** Once you're zoomed in to an image, you can use the Hand tool to pan around to look at parts of the image that have gone outside of the viewable area.

- **White Balance tool.** Use the White Balance tool to quickly adjust the color cast of an image. Click on a neutral part of the image (something that should be white or gray), and the overall colors in the image adjust to compensate. You can find additional options for adjusting the white balance of your image in the White Balance area of the Basic image adjustment tab.

- **Color Sampler.** Like the Eyedropper tool in the main Photoshop application, you can use the Color Sampler tool in Camera Raw to view color information for a specific part of your image in terms of its red, green, and blue (RGB) values. The Color Sampler tool allows you to temporarily store up to nine different samples.

- **Crop.** Use the Crop tool to trim away unwanted information in your image. Click and drag to define the region of your photo that you want to keep. The parts of the image that will be discarded are then covered with a dark overlay. Continue to adjust the crop region by using the handles at the corners until you're happy with your work. Click and hold the Crop tool's icon on the toolbar to reveal a number of presets that allow you to crop the image in different length-to-width ratios. For even greater control, select the

Custom option and use the drop-down list to enter specific dimensions in inches, pixels, or centimeters; or enter a custom aspect ratio. The crop isn't actually applied until you click Save or Open, which brings your photo directly into Photoshop.

■ **Straighten.** The Straighten tool does exactly what its name says — it helps you to straighten out those photos that might have been shot slightly off-kilter. With the Straighten tool selected, click and drag along the horizon in your image (or something that you know should be horizontal, such as a table or a roadway). When you release the mouse button, the Crop tool is activated, showing you a preview of what your image will look like when you apply the edits.

■ **Spot Removal.** The Spot Removal tool allows you to remove blemishes such as sensor dust or other unwanted elements from your image. Click Spot Removal, then adjust the radius of the tool. The Type drop-down list offers two options. The first option is Healing mode, which works by blending and overlaying pixels from a "clean" area of your image with the area that you're retouching. The second option, Clone mode, deposits pixels from your source area to your target area. You can retouch multiple spots at once, and you can go back and tweak the retouched areas after the fact as well.

■ **Red-Eye Removal.** The Red-Eye Removal tool helps get rid of red-eye — that horrible glowing red effect that sometimes afflicts your subjects when they're shot in low-light situations with a flash, and their pupils haven't had a chance to contract. To fix it, use the Red-Eye Removal tool to draw a highlight around your subject's iris, and the red is filled in with black. Use the Pupil Size and Darkness sliders to tweak the adjustment. Repeat for each eye that needs fixing.

■ **Adjustment Brush.** The Adjustment Brush is a new feature of Camera Raw 5.0, which ships along with Photoshop CS4. This tool allows you to make local image adjustments by painting them on top of your photo. Select the tool, begin painting on your photograph to define a mask, and then use the accompanying adjustment sliders to tweak your image. This new tool, along with the Graduated Filter (discussed next), is robust enough that it merits its own section, which follows this one.

■ **Graduated Filter.** The Graduated Filter tool is another new addition to the Camera Raw toolbar, and like the Adjustment Brush, you can use this tool to apply adjustments to a restricted portion of your photograph. In this case, instead of painting a mask by using brush strokes, you create a gradient to define the region of the photo that you want to adjust.

■ **Preferences.** Clicking the Preference icon opens a dialog box with a plethora of options that dictate how the Camera Raw plug-in behaves:

  ■ **General:** Choose whether to save image settings in the Camera Raw database or in sidecar XMP files.

▦ **Default Image Settings:** Use these settings to control how Camera Raw processes your images when they are first opened. For instance, you can set automatic processing for images taken by a specific camera (based on its serial number, which is embedded in the photos' metadata), or based on the ISO (film speed) setting of a particular camera. This is useful if your camera produces noisy images at a certain ISO setting.

▦ **Camera Raw Cache:** Set the location and maximum file size for the cache file that Camera Raw uses to track your image adjustments.

▦ **DNG File Handling:** If you choose to convert your RAW images to DNG format, you can save your image adjustments in the files themselves, rather than in the Camera Raw database. In this case, you can choose to ignore sidecar XMP files. You can also set how the embedded JPEG previews in the DNG files are updated and compressed. Keep in mind that higher-quality, embedded JPEG previews mean larger DNG file sizes.

▦ **JPEG and TIFF Handling:** Specify how JPEG and TIFF images opened in Camera Raw are handled.

■ **Rotate Clockwise/Counterclockwise.** Use these buttons to rotate images from landscape to portrait or vice-versa, as necessary.

■ **Toggle Full-Screen Mode.** Click this button once to switch the Camera Raw window into full-screen mode, allowing you to take advantage of the real estate of your entire display. Click it again to switch back into the (default) windowed mode.

Local adjustments in Camera Raw

Camera Raw 5.0 features numerous under-the-hood performance enhancements, but the most significant update in terms of features is the introduction of the ability to make local adjustments — that is, to restrict your adjustments to specific portions of your image, rather than making them globally. As described in the previous section, two tools are provided to make local adjustments — the Adjustment Brush and the Graduated Filter. Read on for a description of how these two tools work.

The Adjustment Brush

The Adjustment Brush brings many of the global adjustments available in Camera Raw, including exposure, brightness, contrast, saturation, and others, to a restricted portion of your image. You specify the local region you want to adjust by painting a mask over your photograph and changing the tool's sliders. The specified adjustments appear only in the area defined by the mask.

To use the Adjustment Brush, first select its icon on the Camera Raw toolbar. You'll see the Adjustment Brush tool's sliders appear below the histogram at the right of the Camera Raw dialog box (see Figure 4.7). You can choose to adjust the sliders either before or after painting on your image.

FIGURE 4.7

The Adjustment Brush allows you to make local adjustments to a photograph in Camera Raw.

When you hover your cursor over the image, you'll see that your cursor has changed — the dashed line around your cursor represents the amount of feathering that's applied to your brush. The solid black line represents the size of your brush, and the cross-hair indicates where the effect will be applied. You can change the brush size and feathering with the corresponding sliders at the right side of the dialog box.

Begin painting over the region that you want to restrict your adjustments to, to place a pin icon on your photograph representing that set of adjustments (see Figure 4.8). You can add to regions of the image that's affected by these adjustments by clicking the Add radio button above the adjustment sliders and painting additional strokes on your photo.

To create a new mask, which can have its own set of adjustments, click the New radio button and begin painting. To change the settings for an adjustment, simply click on its pin and update the sliders. Selectively remove adjustments from portions of a photograph by painting with the Erase radio button selected. You can also temporarily switch to Erase mode while painting in New or Add mode by holding down the Alt/Option key on your keyboard as you paint. Finally, to delete an adjustment mask altogether, select its pin and press the Delete key on your keyboard.

FIGURE 4.8

Making local adjustments with the Adjustment Brush in Camera Raw. Pins are placed on the canvas, indicating different adjustment masks.

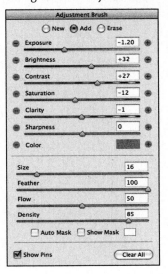

Use the Adjustment sliders to change the exposure, brightness, contrast, saturation, clarity, and sharpness of the photo. You can also add a color tint to your photo by changing the color swatch at the right of the Color slider.

To view an overlay of the current mask, either hover over its pin with your cursor or select the Show Mask check box. Change the color of the mask overlay by clicking on the color swatch next to the Show Mask check box and selecting a color from the resulting Color Picker.

The Graduated Filter

The Graduated Filter also restricts adjustments to a local region of a photograph opened in Camera Raw, but in this case, it uses a gradient rather than a free-form brush stroke to mask the image. One application for this tool would be to adjust an image with a properly exposed foreground and over-exposed background.

To use the Graduated Filter tool, select it from the Toolbox, and click and drag to define the start and end points of your gradient mask (demonstrated in Figure 4.9). The start point is represented by a green dot, and the end point is represented by a red dot. To reposition the gradient, or to change the size of the region it affects, click and drag either dot in the appropriate direction.

FIGURE 4.9

The Graduated Filter defines a local region of your image that will be affected by adjustments.

Again, use the sliders to make adjustments to the contrast, exposure, brightness, saturation, and other attributes of the photograph. Apply a colored graduated filter by choosing a color other than white from the swatch at the right of the Color slider. As described earlier, you can adjust the sliders either before or after you've defined your gradient.

Create additional graduated filters to adjust different regions of your photo by making sure the New radio button is clicked when you click and drag with your cursor. To remove a graduated filter, select it and press Delete on your keyboard. Alternately, you can remove all the filters you've created with the Graduated Filter, too, by clicking the Clear All button in the lower-right corner of the dialog box.

The histogram

The histogram (see Figure 4.10) is a quick way to see all the color and luminance (brightness) data in your image represented graphically. You can tell whether your image is over- or underexposed at a glance — Camera Raw overlays visual cues on your photo to show you exactly which areas are under- or overexposed. Camera Raw's histogram includes some of the image's metadata, such as f/stop, shutter speed, ISO, and focal length. It also includes tools to display highlight and shadow clipping.

CROSS-REF See Chapter 11 for more details regarding the histogram.

FIGURE 4.10

The histogram offers a quick graphical overview of the intensity of the color and brightness of your image.

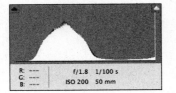

The Image Adjustment tabs

The Image Adjustment Tabs are where you'll do most of the tweaking of your RAW images. This is where you can really take advantage of all that RAW data that your fancy camera was nice enough to save for you.

TIP To return any of the sliders under the Image Adjustment tabs to their default settings, double-click the slider. To automatically adjust any of the sliders based on the embedded RAW image data, hold down Shift and double-click the slider.

Basic

In the Basic adjustments tab (see Figure 4.11), you'll find controls to adjust the color of your image. The contents of the tab are split into three general areas: white balance, exposure, and, for want of a better descriptive term, the quality of the color of your image.

FIGURE 4.11

Use the Image Adjustment sliders to tweak your image to perfection.

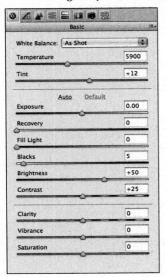

NOTE   White balance is the process of adjusting the colors of an image based on something that is known to be neutral gray or white. Often, a photographer will calibrate his camera for the lighting conditions of a specific shoot by taking a picture of a white or neutral gray piece of paper. Most cameras, though, have built-in settings that compensate for a variety of lighting conditions — sunlight, clouds, fluorescent lights, tungsten lights, and so on — and this data is embedded in the metadata of your photograph.

- **White Balance.** When you open a RAW file in Camera Raw, the white balance information is retrieved and the image is displayed "As Shot" (which is helpfully displayed on the White Balance menu). To change the white balance settings, use the White Balance menu to select a preset for different lighting conditions, or create a custom setting by using the White Balance tool on the Camera Raw toolbar.

- **Temperature.** The Temperature setting allows you to adjust the "warmth" or "coolness" of your image — that is, how red or blue it is — by using a measurement called Kelvins. To compensate for an image that is too cool, or too blue, drag the Temperature slider to the right to increase the color temperature and add some yellows to your image. Similarly, to cool down an image that has too much yellow in it, drag the slider to the left and reduce the color temperature of your image.

- **Tint.** The Tint slider is another tool you can use to remove unwanted color casts from your image. Drag the slider to the left or right to compensate for magenta or green tints in your photo.

Below the White Balance area of the Basic tab are the Exposure controls. This is where you can tweak the overall tone of the image by adjusting the following settings:

- **Exposure.** Exposure refers to the overall brightness of your photograph. To brighten your image, drag the Exposure slider to the right; to darken the image, drag the slider to the left.

- **Recovery.** The Recovery slider is a great tool to use for bringing some detail back to the blown-out highlights of an overexposed image without affecting the midtones or shadow areas of the image.

- **Fill Light.** The Fill Light control is useful for brightening up the shadow areas of your image without affecting the midtones or highlights of your image.

- **Blacks.** This control allows you to increase or decrease the richness of the black areas of your image.

- **Brightness.** The Brightness slider is similar to the Exposure slider in that it affects the overall brightness of your image. However, the difference is that the Brightness slider affects the *gamma* of your image — that is, it flattens out the shadows and expands the highlights of the photo (as demonstrated in Figure 4.12). A good workflow to follow is to make adjustments by using Exposure, Recovery, Fill Light, and Blacks first; and then use the Brightness slider to tweak the image if necessary.

- **Contrast.** This slider increases or decreases the difference between the shadows and highlights (that is, the contrast) of your photo. Contrast is a partner to the Brightness slider — it's often a good idea to use these two sliders in conjunction with each other.

FIGURE 4.12

The Brightness slider increases the overall brightness of your image and can cause the dark areas to appear gray or "flat."

At the bottom of the Basic Adjustment tab are controls for the quality of the color of your photo:

- **Clarity.** This slider enhances the *local contrast* of the pixels in an image. In other words, it adjusts the contrast of each pixel in an image based on an average of its neighboring pixels. It can help reduce haze in a photograph or get rid of the dull look that results from shooting a photo through glass.

- **Vibrance.** This control adjusts the intensity of the colors in your photograph with consideration for the surrounding colors, and without producing unnatural skin tones. It has less of an effect on the more saturated colors of your image.

- **Saturation.** This slider adjusts the intensity of the colors in your image on a global level. You can really punch up an otherwise drab image by moving the Saturation slider to the right; moving the Saturation slider all the way to the left removes all the color information from your image, making it completely monochromatic. (This isn't a good way to make a black-and-white image, though.) When increasing the saturation of an image, watch out for skin tones becoming too red and unnatural looking.

Tone Curve

After making overall tweaks to your image by using the settings in the Basic tab, you can start to fine-tune the tonal values of your image with the settings found in the Tone Curve tab. Within this tab are two ways of working with your image's tonal values: Parametric and Point. In either case, the horizontal axis of the graph represents the tonal values as they exist in your image now — that is, the input values. The vertical axis of the graph represents the output values, or the changes that you will make. Moving a point on the tone curve higher up on the graph results in a brighter value; moving a point down on the graph results in a darker value.

- **Parametric.** To adjust the tonal values, use the Highlights, Lights, Darks, and Shadows sliders to tweak these different tonal ranges of your image. You can then move the region dividers along the horizontal axis of the graph to restrict the range of tones that are affected by the tone adjustments (see Figure 4.13).

FIGURE 4.13

The Tone Curve tab, showing an image's curve in Parametric mode. Using the region dividers, you can restrict the effect of an adjustment to the shadows, midtones, and highlights of a photograph.

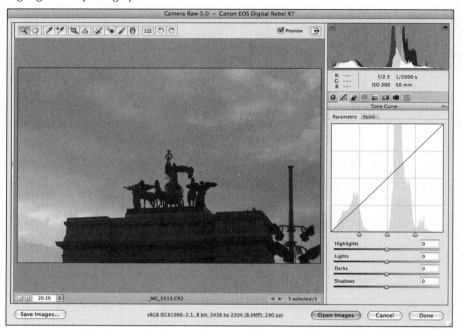

- **Point.** To adjust tonal values by using the Point tab, click on the curve and drag either up or down to brighten or darken the corresponding part of your image (highlights are on the right side of the graph, while shadows are toward the left, and midtones are affected by the middle part of the curve).

You can also use one of the presets in the Curve menu to apply commonly used adjustments to your image.

Detail

Within this section are controls for adjusting sharpness and noise in your image. Use the Sharpening tools to enhance the definition of the edges in your image. The Noise Reduction tools help get rid of the graininess or color artifacts that can appear in a photograph taken at a high ISO (light-sensitivity, or film speed) setting (see Figure 4.14).

FIGURE 4.14

Noise, or unwanted artifacts and graininess, can show up in a photograph taken in low-light conditions, as seen in the image on the left. The image on the right benefits from noise reduction, applied with the Camera Raw plug-in.

TIP It's best to view your image at actual size (100-percent zoom) before making sharpening or noise adjustments, so you can see an accurate preview of the changes you are making. To quickly set the zoom of your image to 100 percent, double-click the Zoom icon on the left side of the toolbar.

The four controls available in the Sharpening section are:

- **Amount.** Use the Amount slider to increase edge definition in your image. A higher amount of sharpening increases the intensity of the edges. Generally, you should try to be judicious with sharpening to avoid the appearance of "halos" around your edges.

- **Radius.** Radius refers to the size of the details in your image that are being sharpened. Use a smaller radius for images with lots of fine details. Using too large a radius can produce unnatural-looking results.

- **Detail.** High detail values are useful for enhancing textures in an image, while lower values can help to correct blurring along the edges.

- **Masking.** Masking affects how much information in the image receives sharpening. A value of zero means that all the edges in the image will receive the same amount of sharpening. A value of 100 means that only the areas closest to the strongest edges will receive the effect of the sharpening adjustment.

Noise in a photograph can either be *luminance* (brightness) noise or *chroma* (color) noise.

- **Luminance.** Luminance noise is found in the grayscale information of the photograph and is what makes the image look grainy. Use the Luminance slider to reduce the appearance of grain in your photo.

- **Color.** Use the Color slider to get rid of the multi-colored dots or artifacts that can show up in your photos if you took them in low-light conditions using a high ISO setting on your camera.

TIP Hold down the Alt/Option key while dragging the sliders to see a preview of the areas that will be affected by the sharpening adjustments. Note that you must be zoomed in to 100 percent to see the preview.

HSL/Grayscale

You can adjust the colors of your photograph at a very fine level by using the HSL/Grayscale sliders. HSL refers to Hue/Saturation/Luminance, and there is a corresponding tab within this area for each of those color traits.

In the Hue section, you can shift the individual colors within your image to different values without affecting other areas in your photograph by using eight different color sliders. For instance, you can make the red areas in your photograph more magenta by moving the Reds slider to the left; or you can make it more orange by moving the slider to the right. Compare the original sunset image in Figure 4.15 on the left with the image on the right — you probably can't tell from the grayscale reproduction, but the red and yellow areas of the image have been shifted to magenta and orange to create an almost dreamy look.

FIGURE 4.15

This sunset takes on a very surreal, almost dreamy quality with a few simple adjustments to the Reds and Yellows sliders under the Hue and Saturation tabs.

Similarly, to adjust the intensity of individual colors in your image, use the sliders under the Saturation tab, and to adjust the brightness of individual colors, use the sliders under the Luminance tab.

You can convert your photograph to a grayscale image by clicking — you guessed it — the Convert to Grayscale check box at the top of the HSL/Grayscale tab. Your Hue, Saturation, and Luminance tabs are replaced by a single Grayscale Mix tab (shown in Figure 4.16). This allows you to adjust the combination of the different color areas of the image in the final grayscale version.

FIGURE 4.16

When you click the Convert to Grayscale check box, the Grayscale Mix tab becomes available.

Split Toning

You can use the controls found under the Split Toning section to adjust the tone of a grayscale image. For example, to create a sepia-toned image like the one shown in Figure 4.17, follow these steps:

1. **Click the Convert to Grayscale check box under the HSL/Grayscale tab.**

2. **Under the Split Toning tab, move the Hue slider in the Highlights section to a yellow value somewhere around 60.** (Nothing happens!)

3. **Now, increase the saturation of the effect by moving the Saturation slider to the right.** (Aha — now something's happening. . . .)

4. **Repeat for the Hue and Saturation sliders under the Shadows section of the Split Toning tab until you're satisfied with the result.**

Feel free to mix it up and change the hue of the highlights of your photo to one color and the shadows to an entirely different color, resulting in an effect similar to a photographic technique called *cross processing*. Further, you can change the combination of the shadow and highlight adjustments by using the Balance slider.

FIGURE 4.17

This sepia-toned image was created using the Split Toning controls on a grayscale image.

Lens Correction

The Lens Correction controls help to compensate for *chromatic aberration* — a defect that sometimes occurs when a lens fails to correctly focus light of different frequencies in the same spot. If you were wondering about the sometimes-astronomical price differential between lenses for your camera, well, wonder no more — this type of defect is most obvious in inexpensive lenses (although all lenses are imperfect to some degree).

Chromatic aberration happens in the outer areas of your photograph, away from the center, and is typically seen as a purple or cyan color fringe around the edges of objects in your image. It's actually a result of the different color channels of your image being slightly different in size. You can also see a different type of chromatic aberration in the specular highlights of your image, particularly in bright reflections, such as reflections in the highlights of water or chrome.

- **Fix Red/Cyan Fringe.** One type of chromatic aberration that you might see in your photos is a red halo on the side of the image that's away from the center of the image, and a cyan or greenish fringe on the side of the image that's closer to the center. Use the Fix Red/Cyan Fringe slider to change the size of the red color channel in relation to green, thus reducing the size of the fringe.

- **Fix Blue/Yellow Fringe.** Similar to the Fix Red/Cyan Fringe slider, this slider can be used to fix blue and yellow fringing that appears in the corners of your photograph.

- **Defringe.** To fix color fringing around the highlights and around areas where there are drastic changes in color values, select All Edges in the Defringe menu. Click the Highlight Edges option to correct fringing only in the edges near highlights, or if using All Edges results in gray lines around the highlights.

Another type of lens defect that you might see is called *vignetting*. This shows up as dark corners around the outer parts of your photograph, as seen in Figure 4.18. You can use the Lens vignetting controls to reduce the appearance of this defect. Vignetting isn't always seen as a negative, though — you can also use the Lens vignetting slider to add this effect to your images and give them the look of photographs shot with old, inexpensive cameras.

- **Amount.** Use this slider to control the amount of correction that's applied to your photo or to add vignetting to your photograph.

- **Midpoint.** Once you've adjusted the Amount slider, the Midpoint slider becomes active, and you can slide it to the right to adjust the distance of the vignetting effect from the middle of the photo.

FIGURE 4.18

Lens vignetting — the dark areas in the corner of the photo on the left — are caused by a lens defect. Vignetting is especially obvious in images that contain large areas covered by similar colors, like in this shot of a very blue sky. The Lens vignetting slider was used to make the vignetting in this image less noticeable.

Camera Calibration

As mentioned before, different digital cameras have different sets of built-in instructions for interpreting and processing a scene when they save their sensor data to your memory card. This information is embedded in the metadata for each image along with the exact make and model of the camera itself. Also, Camera Raw comes bundled with its own set of instructions or profiles that correspond to a growing list of digital camera models.

When you open a photograph in Camera Raw, it detects these instructions and displays the image accordingly. However, like its owner, your camera might have its own quirks that cause it to behave differently from the model that was used to build the Camera Raw plug-in, in which case you may want to use the sliders under the Camera Calibration tab. For instance, your camera may apply a red color cast to the shadow areas of each photo you shoot; or maybe the greens are always a little oversaturated. Correct these with the Calibration sliders, and choose Save New Camera Raw Defaults from the Camera Raw Settings menu. You can always revert to the default profile for your camera by choosing Reset Camera Raw Defaults from the menu.

Presets

By this point, you're practically an old pro at editing your images in Camera Raw. In fact, you may have even started to develop the cranky demeanor of a grizzled veteran (hey — easy with the attitude!), and are becoming set in your ways. You might have even come up with a recipe for your own "secret sauce": a closely guarded blend of tweaks that makes your photo masterpieces look just right every time.

This is the point where it would be really handy to be able to apply those tweaks to an image, or even a whole batch of images, in one fell swoop with the click of a button. The Presets tab allows you to do just that, so select it and dive in.

Saved presets can contain every single tweak you've made to every single slider that I've talked about, or they can be subsets of settings in various combinations. Further, you can have Camera Raw apply them automatically in very specific situations. For example, you can decide that you'll reuse the Sharpening and Tone Curve settings you just came up with, and apply them automatically to every image shot at 400 ISO that you import from your Canon EOS350D camera — but apply a completely different set of adjustments to the photos from your Nikon. Cool, huh?

The Presets tab in its default state is boring because you haven't saved any presets there yet. Select the Camera Raw settings menu (tucked away under the disclosure triangle on the top-right of the Image Adjustments area — see Figure 4.4) to reveal the following options:

- **Image Settings.** This option uses the settings from the currently selected image in Camera Raw.

- **Camera Raw Defaults.** This option uses the default information that Camera Raw has about each camera model and processes the RAW image based on that information.

- **Previous Conversion.** This option applies the most recently used settings to the currently selected photograph.

- **Custom Settings.** This somewhat ambiguous menu item uses whatever settings you had concocted while fiddling around with the Image Adjustment sliders in your current Camera Raw session. In other words, these settings aren't automatically saved as a preset, so if you like what you've come up with, you should save them by choosing the Save Preset menu item.

- **Preset Settings.** This menu item is grayed out until you apply a saved preset, at which point it takes on the name of the preset you applied.

■ **Apply Preset.** This submenu grows dynamically to contain all the presets you've saved, as does the main area under the Presets tab. This means you can handily access your presets from within any of the Image Adjustment tabs without having to first click on the Presets tab.

Saving from Camera Raw

As you work in Camera Raw, the software tracks the adjustments you make. If you find that you've completely botched your photo and want a clean slate, hold down the Alt/Option key, and you'll notice that the Cancel button at the bottom of the Camera Raw window changes to a Reset button, which will take you back to the image as it was when it was first opened.

This is possible because Camera Raw is incapable of overwriting or otherwise altering the original RAW data as it was recorded by your camera's sensor. Instead, Camera Raw keeps track of your changes and saves them in one of two places: the Camera Raw Cache or sidecar XMP files.

■ **The Camera Raw cache.** Your image adjustments are tracked by default to this file that gets saved on your hard drive. You can specify its location in the Camera Raw Preferences dialog box by clicking the Preferences button on the toolbar, or by pressing Ctrl+K/⌘+K on your keyboard and choosing the Select Location button.

■ **Sidecar XMP files.** The disadvantage of the Camera Raw cache is that if you need to move your images to a different computer or if you burn them to a CD or DVD, the adjustments stay on your hard drive, and your image reverts to its original self. The way around this is to save your adjustments to a sidecar XMP file. This is a small text file that gets saved alongside each photograph (it will have the same base name as your image with an XMP file extension, as seen in Figure 4.19). Remember to keep these files with your images if you move them to a different location, such as a different hard drive.

Once you're happy with all the hard work you've been doing so far, and you're ready to free your masterpiece from the Camera Raw plug-in window, use one of the following four options available at the bottom of the Camera Raw dialog box:

■ **Save Image.** This option applies the adjustments you've just made and gives you myriad options for the output format of your file. You can save your image as a JPEG, DNG, TIFF, or PSD file. Press Alt+click/Option+click to save the image without opening a dialog box — it applies the most recently used settings or Camera Raw's defaults to the image.

■ **Open Image.** This option applies the adjustments and opens the image in Photoshop for further adjustment or processing if necessary. Press Alt+ or Option+click to open a copy of the image without altering the image's metadata.

■ **Done.** This option applies the adjustments and exits Camera Raw without opening the image. Adjustments are saved alongside the original RAW files in a sidecar XMP file.

■ **Cancel.** This option exits the Camera Raw window without applying any changes. Press Alt+ or Option+click to reset all the adjustment sliders to their defaults.

FIGURE 4.19

RAW files and their accompanying XMP files, which are a good way of ensuring that your adjustments travel with your images. To view XMP files in Bridge, choose Show Hidden Files from the View menu.

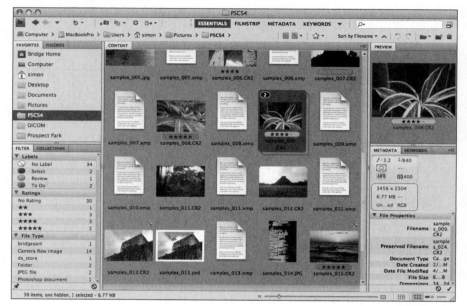

Clicking on the blue Workflow Options link at the bottom of the Camera Raw dialog box opens the Workflow Options dialog box (shown in Figure 4.20), which allows you to specify the following settings:

- **Space.** Use this option to choose between Adobe RGB, Colormatch, ProPhoto, or sRGB color profiles depending on your RGB workspace (and the final output format of your image).

- **Depth.** This refers to the bit depth of the image. Choose 8-bit or 16-bit images.

- **Size.** This link allows you to adjust the pixel dimensions of the image that will be opened into Photoshop. Again, this depends on the eventual destination of your image.

- **Resolution.** This is the pixel-per-inch resolution of the printed version of your image. You can also adjust this after you import the image into Photoshop.

FIGURE 4.20

Access the Workflow Options dialog box by clicking the link on the bottom of the Camera Raw window.

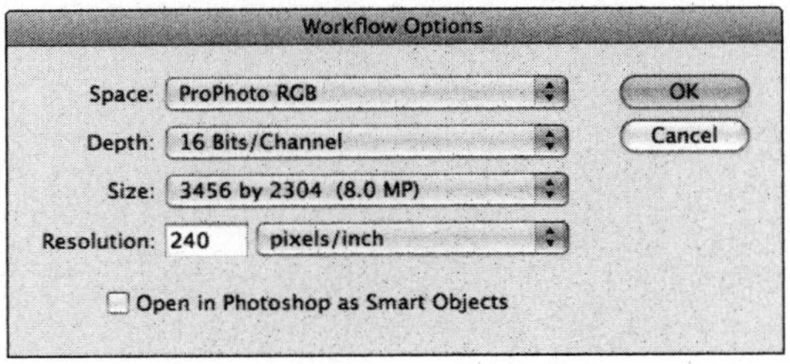

Workflow Options	
Space: ProPhoto RGB	OK
Depth: 16 Bits/Channel	Cancel
Size: 3456 by 2304 (8.0 MP)	
Resolution: 240 pixels/inch	
☐ Open in Photoshop as Smart Objects	

You can also specify whether to open the image in Photoshop as a Smart Object, ready for applying Smart Filters.

CROSS-REF To learn more about color profiles, check out Chapter 23.

Summary

In this chapter you learned about the Camera Raw dialog box and the RAW image format. I examined the pros and cons of the RAW format and discussed the workflow that is often used when processing RAW images. I also talked about the DNG format and the benefits of a nonproprietary raw image format. I covered the tools that take advantage of the vast amount of data that the RAW format includes to adjust areas such as contrast, exposure, white balancing, sharpening and noise, highlights, and shadows.

This chapter also discussed how you can apply the same edits across a batch of images, as well as how to save a set of adjustments as a preset to apply to other images later or automatically apply as default adjustments to images from a certain camera brand.

You also learned how to save your final adjusted images in various widely compatible file formats.

Part II

Working with Images

Chapter 5

Creating New Images, Resizing, and Adjusting Resolution

To create from scratch or not to create from scratch? You can start your Photoshop project by making a new blank canvas that is just the right size and resolution, or you can start with an existing image and resize it, if necessary. But you should put some thought into it before you start.

In general, it is probably more convenient and safe to start with a new document that has exactly the size, resolution, and other parameters you need. But be aware that if you bring in images that don't contain enough information to describe their detail at the new document's size, you may end up with poor quality. The same is true if you start with an existing image that doesn't have enough information and you enlarge it significantly.

If you are creating a new document from scratch and not bringing other images into it, you would start by creating the new document with exactly the parameters you need. For example, this might apply if you were creating a logo or a painting from scratch.

NOTE To test the quality of images destined for print, print a proof on a good printer; don't rely on the onscreen display to check quality. If possible, do this early in the process before you've put a lot of work into it. If you are preparing images for the Web, of course check the onscreen display of the image to determine its quality.

Getting Started with New Images

Some issues to consider before you start are these summarized facts from Chapter 1:

■ **Bitmap, or raster, images are resolution-dependent.** A bitmap, or raster, image gets its detail from the number of pixels it contains, which is referred to as resolution and measured in pixels per inch (ppi). Photos are bitmap images, and paintings or illustrations that donít have well-defined shapes are usually bitmap images. Higher resolution usually translates into greater detail; lower resolution usually translates into less detail.

■ **Ideally, pixels should be captured initially not added later.** An adequate number of pixels needed to describe a bitmap image's detail should be captured initially, not added later (because where the heck would the new pixels come from?).

■ **Vector images are resolution-independent.** A vector image gets its detail from shapes and lines that are mathematically calculated and retains its smoothness no matter how much it is resized and regardless of how many pixels it contains. Solid-color logos and type are some examples of images that would ideally be created in vector format (but often are created in bitmap format).

■ **Combination bitmap-and-vector images are resolution dependent.** Although the vector image parts don't require a certain resolution, the bitmap image parts do.

■ **Image resolution for bitmap and combination bitmap-and-vector images should usually be 300 ppi for print, 72 ppi for the Web.** Old-timers who aren't nit-picky about terminology may call this dots per inch (dpi). Adequate resolution is generally 300 ppi at the final size in inches for print and 72 ppi at the final size in pixels for onscreen display.

■ **Image resolution for vector images doesn't matter.** Worry-free resizing! The uninformed may send your 5-ppi vector image back to you and tell you they need a 300-ppi image. That's okay; you can change it to 300 ppi with no consequences, just to please them. (Upsizing that much would be disastrous for bitmap images, though!)

CROSS-REF See Appendix A for a chart that includes required resolutions for different kinds of images.

■ **Bit depth.** This describes how many different colors an image can contain. A higher bit depth hopefully translates into higher color accuracy.

■ **Ideally, bit depth is specified and created when the image is initially captured.** Changing to a higher bit depth from an original lower bit depth does not automatically increase color accuracy. But it is sometimes necessary to change a higher original bit depth to a lower bit depth in order to use some Photoshop features that won't work on a higher-bit-depth image.

■ **Color mode should be appropriate for the image's destination.** The color mode of an image specifies which basic set of colors is used to make up an image. For example, in order to maintain quality, a full-color photograph that will be printed on a printing press should be in CMYK mode, and a full-color photograph that will be displayed on the Web in JPEG format should be in RGB color mode.

CROSS-REF Bitmap and vector formats, bit depth, and color mode are discussed in detail in Chapter 1.

Let's plug some of these facts into specific situations.

If you start with a new blank Photoshop document that is 8.5 x 11 inches and 300 ppi and you bring in an image that is 8.5 x 11 inches and 72 ppi, it will appear less than one third of its size in inches after you get it into the new document because it won't have enough resolution to be at the full size (in inches) of the new document. If you enlarge the image a lot after you bring it in, you will be adding imaginary pixels (resampling up) and may end up printing an image without enough detail.

If you bring in a 16-bits-per-channel (bpc) image into a new document that is 8 bpc, you will lose some of the color accuracy (but there are times you may want to do this to access some of Photoshop's features that aren't supported in 16 bpc).

If you start with an existing image that is only 5.5 x 8.5 inches and 72 ppi and you resize it up to 8.5 x 11 inches and 300 ppi, you will be adding imaginary pixels and may end up printing an image without enough detail.

To summarize: In order to maintain quality, it's best to use images that contain the same amount of or more information than you need for your final document's size, resolution, and bit depth, whether you bring them into a new document or start with an existing image and resize it to the final size. Resizing down is generally okay; resizing up is risky. The greater you enlarge an image (make changes that increase its total file size — in megabytes, for example), the more quality you lose.

Units & Rulers Preferences

If you want to create a new image, knowing about the Units & Rulers Preferences (see Figure 5.1) can come in handy. Choose Edit ➪ Preferences ➪ Units and Rulers Preferences (Photoshop ➪ Preferences ➪ Units and Rulers Preferences on a Mac).

FIGURE 5.1

The Units & Rulers Preferences dialog box

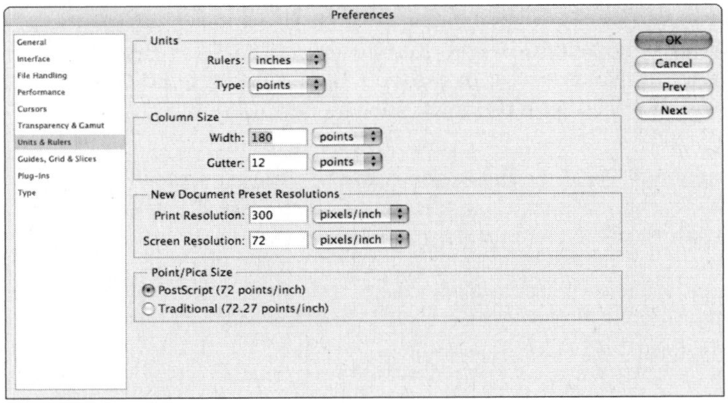

Units for rulers and type can be set in the drop-down lists. You can also set the rulers' units by right-clicking a ruler in the image window and choosing a unit. Show rulers in the image window by pressing Ctrl+R/⌘+R. In print workflows you may want to set rulers to inches or picas; in a Web workflow, you should set rulers to pixels.

You can set the width of columns, along with a gutter size, in the Column Size preference section, of the Units & Rulers Preference dialog box. Columns and gutters can be applied when you use the File ➪ New, Image ➪ Image Size, or Image ➪ canvas Size commands. In these commands, Columns is available as one of the Width and Height units of measurement in drop-down lists and you can enter a number of columns in the Width and Height boxes. But the width of the columns and gutters comes from the Column Size preference section.

Using columns can be helpful when you are preparing images for print in a publication that uses columns. In addition, or alternatively, you may want to set the ruler units to be the same as the column-size units you specified in the Column Size preference (such as inches or picas) and drag guides from the rulers into the document window to show where columns begin and end.

Choosing File ➪ New allows you to choose preset document sizes for a new document that include a resolution for the new document. Some of these presets use the resolutions you enter in the New Document Preset Resolutions preference. The paper and photo presets use the Print Resolution amount, and the Web and Film & Video presets use the Screen Resolution amount.

TIP Note that when choosing File ➪ New you can also enter custom sizes and resolutions for a new document. Choose File ➪ New ➪ Presets ➪ Custom, enter your custom size information, and click the Save Preset button to save a custom preset with a unique name.

Creating a new image

Now that you've figured out your resolution, bit-depth, and color mode, and set up your Units & Rulers preferences as you want them, you can focus on creating your new image:

1. **Choose File ➪ New to open the New dialog box, shown in Figure 5.2.**

2. **Choose a Preset or enter the Width, Height, Resolution, Color Mode, Bit Depth (8-bit is active for the U.S. Paper preset in Figure 5.2), and Background Contents (the document is initially filled with the color selected here).** Figure 5.3 shows the Preset menu in the New dialog box.

3. **In the Advanced section of the New dialog box, you can choose a Color Profile and Pixel Aspect Ratio.** Choose Square Pixels for Pixel Aspect Ratio unless you are working in a video format, in which case choose the appropriate video Pixel Aspect Ratio.

CROSS-REF See Chapters 1 and 24 for more information about color profiles and color management, and Chapter 27 for more information about working with video formats.

FIGURE 5.2

The New dialog box

New	
Name: Untitled-1	OK
Preset: U.S. Paper	Cancel
Size: Letter	Save Preset...
Width: 8.5 inches	Delete Preset...
Height: 11 inches	
Resolution: 300 pixels/inch	Device Central...
Color Mode: RGB Color / 8 bit	
Background Contents: White	Image Size: 24.1M
▲ Advanced	
Color Profile: Working RGB: Adobe RGB (1998)	
Pixel Aspect Ratio: Square Pixels	

FIGURE 5.3

The Preset menu in the New dialog box

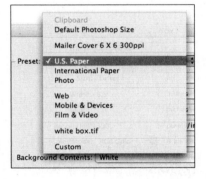

You may do projects over and over that have the same custom width, height, resolution, and so on. In those cases, you can create your own presets for the projects so they will be available in the New dialog box's Preset menu. That way, you can choose the preset when you are creating a new document and avoid re-typing all those document characteristics.

To create a new document preset:

1. **Choose File ⇨ New.**
2. **Enter the desired settings: Width, Height, Resolution, and so on.**
3. **Click the Save Preset button.** Figure 5.4 shows the New Document Preset dialog box.
4. **Enter a Preset Name and check the settings that you want to include in the Preset.**
5. **Click OK.**
6. **You can now select the preset name in the New dialog box's Preset menu.**

FIGURE 5.4

The New Document Preset dialog box

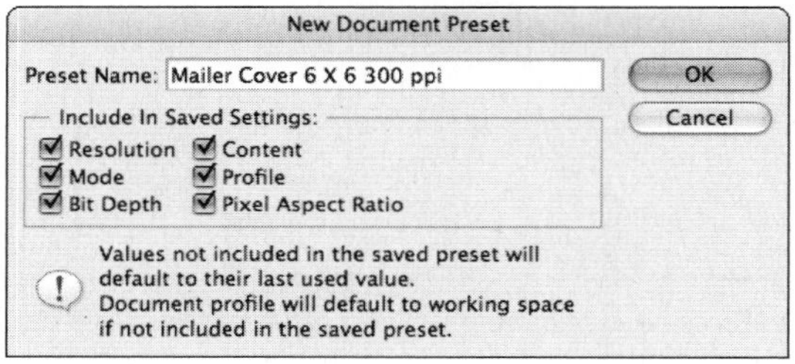

To create a new file that is the correct size and resolution for display on a mobile device, such as a cell phone:

1. **Select File ⇨ New.**
2. **Click the Device Central button.** Figure 5.5 shows the Adobe Device Central dialog box.
3. **Drag the device or devices you want to use (such as Nokia) from the Online Library section of the Adobe Device Central dialog box to the Local Library section.** If you don't see any devices in the Online Library, you may have to click a Connect button in the Online Library section to connect to the online library of devices, and of course, you must have an active internet connection.
4. **Expand the device set (such as Nokia) in the Local Library section by clicking the arrow next to the set then choose the desired device (content type) from the expanded set.**
5. **If there is just one device in the New Document section of the Adobe Device Central dialog box, click the Create button.** If there is more than one device, select the desired Device then click the Create button.
6. **Add images and/or other content to the Photoshop document.**
7. **Choose File ⇨ Save for Web and Devices.**

FIGURE 5.5

The Adobe Device Central dialog box

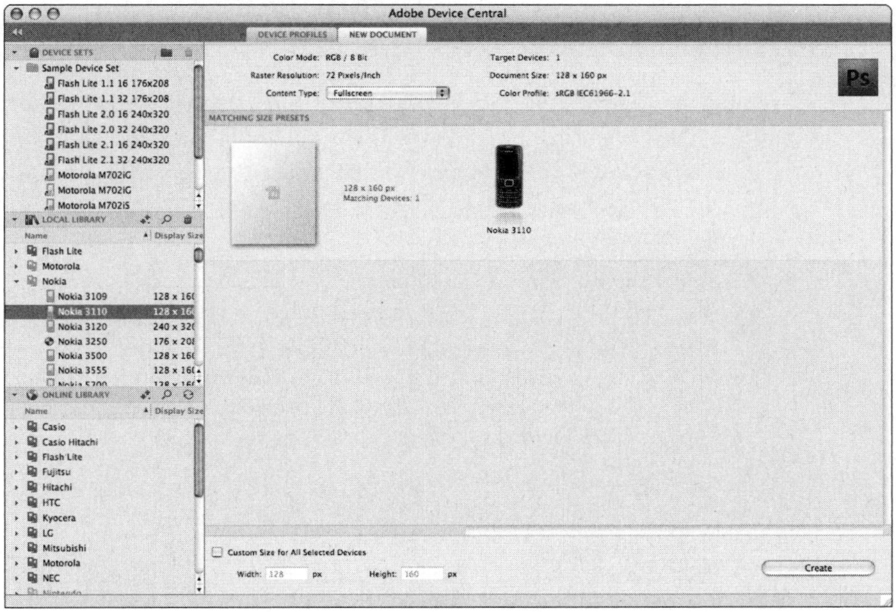

8. Select the desired Save for Web settings.

9. Click the Device Central button to preview the document in Adobe Device Central on the simulated device in the Emulator section.

10. Choose the desired the preview options on the right side of the Device Central dialog box.

11. Close the Device Central dialog box when finished.

12. Choose Save in the Save for Web dialog box.

Opening Images

You can open files by choosing File ➪ Open, by choosing File ➪ Open Recent and selecting a recently opened image's filename, or by clicking the Adobe Bridge button ("Br") in the Application Bar and using Bridge to open files.

TIP You can set how many files the Recent File list contains in File Handling Preferences.

Bridge allows you to browse thumbnails of files by navigating in the Favorites or Folders pane, or can search for filenames in the search box in the top right of the Bridge dialog box. You can see thumbnails and high-resolution previews and double-click thumbnails to open files.

CROSS-REF For more information about Adobe Bridge, see Chapter 3.

To open files with the File ⇨ Open command:

1. **Choose File ⇨ Open.** Figure 5.6 shows the Open dialog box as it appears on a Mac.

2. **Specify whether to show All Readable Documents, or if a file doesn't show up, specify All Documents.**

3. **Select the file you want to open.**

4. **If you want to open the file in a format other than its current format, select the format from the Format menu.** For example, if you want to open a Camera RAW file in Photoshop rather than in the Camera Raw dialog box, choose a different format, such as TIFF. Or, if you know Photoshop is not detecting the correct file format, which could happen if the file is mislabeled, try choosing the format you know is correct.

5. **Click the Open button.**

FIGURE 5.6

The Open dialog box

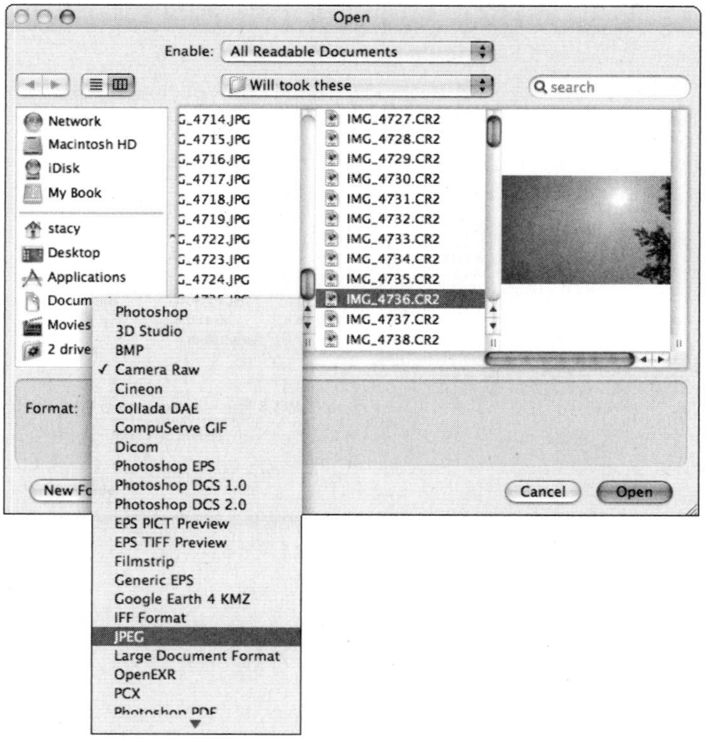

If you get a color profile warning, choose how to handle the color profile. See Chapters 1 and 23 for more information about color management. When a file format doesn't show up in the Open dialog box or after choosing File ⇨ Import, you may be able to open the file if you install a format's plug-in.

TIP Save Adobe Illustrator files as PSD files to help ensure they open correctly in Photoshop.

To open nonPhotoshop PDF files:

1. **Choose File ⇨ Open.**
2. **Select a PDF file and click Open, which displays the Import PDF dialog box shown in Figure 5.7.**

FIGURE 5.7

The Import PDF dialog box

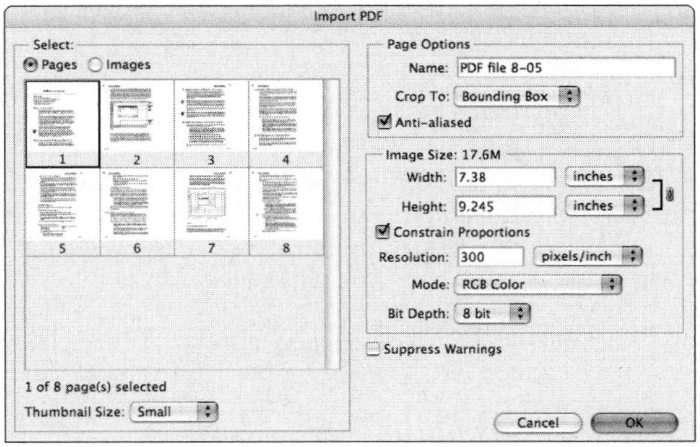

3. **Select the Pages button and select the page you want to open.** This will rasterize the file (text will not be editable). Select other options such as Resolution and Color Mode. The Crop options function as follows:

   ■ Bounding Box crops to the smallest size that includes all the text and graphics on the page (but not a background created by the source application)

   ■ Media Box crops to the original size of the page

   ■ Crop Box crops to the crop margins of the PDF file

   ■ Bleed Box crops so that prepress bleed areas are included

   ■ Trim Box crops the PDF as it would be trimmed after printing

   ■ Art Box crops to the size specified in the PDF file for placing the PDF into another application.

If you want to extract images from the PDF file instead of pages, select the Images button instead of the Pages button.

4. **Click OK.**

NOTE You can also import PDFs using the Place or Paste command, or by dragging and dropping the PDF into a Photoshop document, which places the page or image on a layer as a Smart Object.

To open an EPS file:

1. **Choose File ⇨ Open.**

2. **Select the EPS file and click the Open button.**

3. **Enter desired specifications such as dimensions and Resolution.**

4. **Select Anti-aliased if you want to make edges appear smoother.**

5. **Click OK.** The EPS is rasterized; vector data and editable type are not preserved.

NOTE You can also bring EPS files into Photoshop using the Place command, the Paste command, and the drag-and-drop feature.

To open digital camera images:

When you put either your camera's memory card into an appropriate card slot or you connect your camera to your computer with a cable, an additional drive that represents the memory card or image folder should show up on your computer. You can drag the image folder to your hard drive. You can then use Bridge or choose File ⇨ Open from within Photoshop to open the files on your hard drive (not directly from the memory card drive) into Photoshop.

After you connect your camera or memory card to your computer, you can alternatively use Adobe Bridge's Photo Downloader by following these steps:

- **In Photoshop:** Choose File ⇨ Browse (opens Bridge).

- **In Bridge:** Choose File ⇨ Get Photos from Camera.

Bridge's Photo Downloader automatically finds the camera's images and allows you to choose a location on your computer to copy the images to and create a new subfolder to put them in. Using Photo Downloader, you can also rename the images with text and a serial number as they are being copied to your computer, preserve the old filename inside the image's file information, and automatically display the images in Adobe Bridge.

Photoshop can open the following Quicktime video file formats: MPEG-1 and -4, MOV, AVI, FLV (if Flash 8 is installed), and MPEG-2 (if an MPEG-2 encoder is installed).

Photoshop can open the following image sequence formats: BMP, DICOM, JPEG, OpenEXR, PNG, PSD, Targa, TIFF, Cineon and JPEG 2000 if the plug-ins are installed.

Typical steps to get video from a digital camcorder onto your computer include:

1. **Make sure any recording media (MiniDV tape, MiniDVD disk) is in the camcorder.**

2. **Open Windows Movie Maker or iMovie.**

3. **Turn on the camcorder and make sure it is set to the video mode rather than the camera mode (which would mean it can also take still photos and save to a memory card).**

4. **Connect the camcorder to your computer with an appropriate cable.**

5. **Import the video using Windows Movie Maker or iMovie, then save to a format that Photoshop supports.** For supported video formats, import directly into Photoshop by choosing File ➪ Open, or File ➪ Import ➪ Video Frames to Layers.

CROSS-REF For information about working with video, see Chapter 26.

Placing and Pasting Images

You can use the Place command (see Figure 5.8) to add an image to your Photoshop document as a Smart Object. Smart Objects can be scaled, positioned, skewed, rotated, or warped without lowering the quality of the image. The exception is that if you enlarge the Smart Object significantly above its original size, you do risk lowering the quality, unless it contains only vector art.

FIGURE 5.8

The Place command dialog box

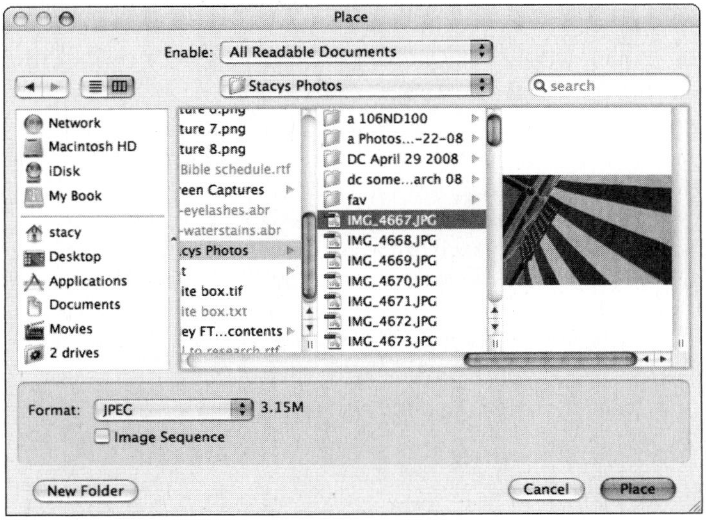

However, you can safely scale the Smart Object down and then back up to its original size any number of times without degrading the image, which you cannot do with non–Smart-Object bitmap images.

You can select an image in another document or application, copy it, then paste the image into a Photoshop document.

You can drag and drop an image with the Move tool from one Photoshop document into another or copy and paste an image from one Photoshop document into another. Either process puts the image on a separate layer in the destination Photoshop document.

It is a good idea to be aware of the Paste/Place preference before you start. Choose General Preferences ➪ Resize Image During Paste/Place to resize your image during a Place command. If this option is on when you are placing an image with larger pixel dimensions into an image with smaller pixel dimensions, the larger image's size is reduced so that you can see the entire image when you place it.

A transform box is active around the placed image so you can resize it right away, if necessary. If this option is off, you can only see part of a larger image that has been placed into the smaller one, and the transform box handles are outside the image window area (zooming out allows you to see the handles).

Following are steps to place and paste various file formats into Photoshop documents.

CROSS-REF   For more information about Smart Objects, see Chapter 8.

To place a PDF or Illustrator file in a Photoshop document:

1. **Choose File ➪ Place.**

2. **Select the PDF or Illustrator document you want to place and click the Place button.** This opens the Place PDF dialog box, shown in Figure 5.9.

3. **If the file has multiple pages, select the Page button and select the page you want to open.** Select the Image button if you want to place the page as an image, and check Preserve Clipping Path if you want to be able to access any paths in the placed image. Crop options function as follows: Bounding Box crops to the smallest size that includes all the text and graphics on the page (but not a background created by the source application), Media Box crops to the original size of the page, Crop Box crops to the crop margins of the PDF file, Bleed Box crops so that prepress bleed areas are included, Trim Box crops the PDF as it would be trimmed after printing, and Art Box crops to the size specified in the PDF file for placing the PDF into another application.

   If you want to extract images from the PDF file instead of pages, select the Image button instead of the Page button.

FIGURE 5.9

The Place PDF dialog box

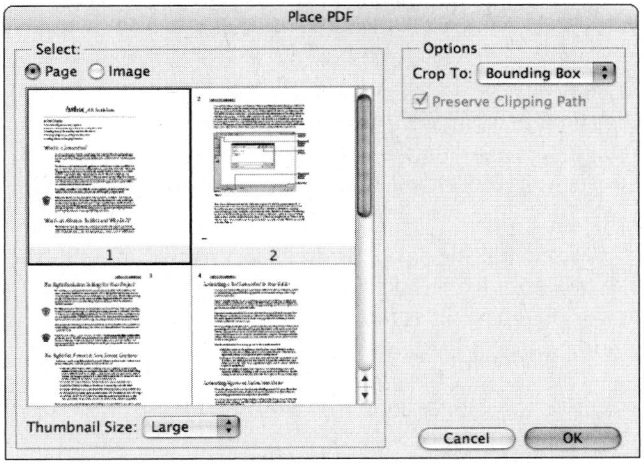

4. **Click OK to add the file as a Smart Object.** To access any paths within the placed PDF, double-click the Smart Object in the Layers palette and that will open a linked file that contains the path. You can make changes to the linked file, save it, and return to the original document. The Smart Object layer will be updated with the changes you made to its linked file.

5. **If you choose to at this point, you can transform the object while its bounding box is still active.** Drag outside of the bounding box to rotate the image, hold down the Shift key while dragging a corner handle to resize the image (release the mouse button first, then the key), and drag in the box to move the object. Or you can choose Edit ⇨ Transform and select one of the options to transform the object.

    You can also press Enter or Return and do any of the above at a later time. Just select the layer the object is on and choose Edit ⇨ Free Transform (or one of the other transform options).

    Note that if you enlarge the placed Smart Object significantly greater than its original size, you do risk lowering its quality, unless the object only contains vector information (in which case it is resolution-independent).

6. **Press Enter or Return after performing any desired transform functions.**

To place file formats other than PDF or Illustrator into a Photoshop document:

1. **Choose File ⇨ Place.**

2. **Select the document you want to place and click the Place button.**

3. **This places the object as a Smart Object in the Photoshop document, as shown in Figure 5.10.**

   If you choose to at this point, you can transform the object while its bounding box is still active. Drag outside of the bounding box to rotate the image, hold down the Shift key while dragging a corner handle to resize the image (release the mouse button first, then the key), and drag in the box to move the object. Or you can choose Edit ➪ Transform and select one of the options to transform the object.

   You can also press Enter or Return and do any of the above at a later time. Just select the layer the object is on and choose Edit ➪ Free Transform (or one of the other transform options).

   Note that if you enlarge the placed Smart Object significantly greater than its original size, you do risk lowering its quality, unless the object only contains vector information (in which case it is resolution-independent).

4. **When you are finished, press Enter or Return.**

To paste an Adobe Illustrator file into Photoshop:

1. **Set preferences in the Adobe Illustrator file:**

   If you want the artwork to be rasterized when pasting it into a Photoshop document, turn off the PDF and the AICB (No Transparency Support) options in the File Handling & Clipboard preferences.

FIGURE 5.10

A placed Smart Object with its bounding box still active and the rotate function active

If you want to have the choice of pasting the art as a Smart Object, rasterized image, path, or shape layer, turn on the PDF and the AICB (No Transparency Support) options in the File Handling & Clipboard preferences. Figure 5.11 shows the resulting Paste dialog box.

FIGURE 5.11

The Paste dialog box with Smart Object, Pixels, Path, and Shape Layer options

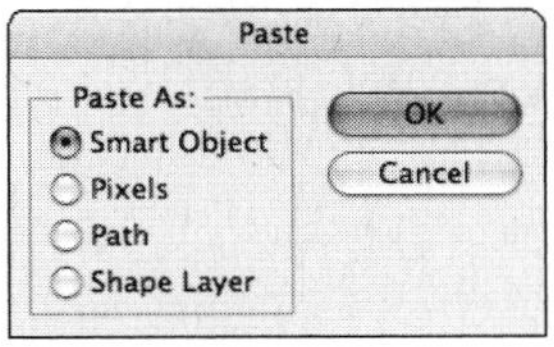

2. **Select the art in Illustrator that you want to paste into Photoshop and choose Edit ⇨ Copy.**

3. **In the Photoshop document, choose Edit ⇨ Paste.**

4. **Select one of the following in the Paste dialog box:**

   - Smart Object places art as a resolution-independent vector Smart Object.

   - Pixels pastes the Illustrator art as rasterized pixels.

   - Path pastes the Illustrator art as Photoshop paths that can be edited with the Paths tools.

   - Shape Layer pastes the art as a new shape layer (a layer filled with an easily editable color and that has a vector mask).

Image Resizing

Resizing images is one of the most commonly misunderstood functions of Photoshop, yet it is one of the most important ones. If you resize incorrectly, you can damage the quality of your image, even if the size appears to be correct. This section will describe ways to resize different types of images without reducing image quality.

You can resize entire images, rather than just parts of images, by choosing Image ⇨ Image Size. Figure 5.12 shows the Image Size dialog box.

FIGURE 5.12

The Image Size dialog box

Image Size

Pixel Dimensions: 5.80M

Width: 1688   pixels

Height: 1200   pixels

OK

Cancel

Auto...

Document Size:

Width: 5.627   inches

Height: 4   inches

Resolution: 300   pixels/inch

☑ Scale Styles
☑ Constrain Proportions
☐ Resample Image:

Bicubic Smoother (best for enlargement)

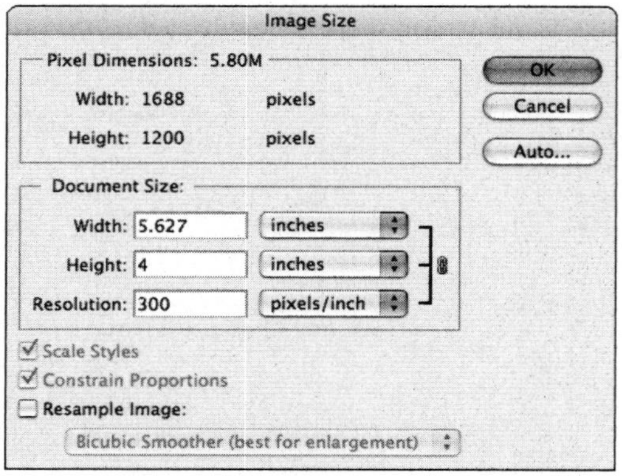

This brings us to the greatest resizing commandment of all: Uncheck the Resample Image box in the Image Size dialog box when you increase size or resolution numbers. Here's why: An adequate number of pixels needed to describe an image's detail should be captured initially; for example, at the time a digital photo is taken or a photographic print is scanned.

If the resolution is increased or the size of the image is enlarged after importing it into Photoshop, there may not be enough pixels in the image to adequately describe the image's detail at a larger resolution or size. Even though you can increase the resolution or size in Photoshop, no new pixel information that describes detail is added. Photoshop may simply guess at what kind of pixels to add, which is called resampling up or interpolation. This may result in an image that looks blurry or pixilated.

To avoid resampling up, uncheck the Resample Image box in the Image Size dialog box when you increase size or resolution numbers. Check the Resample Image box when you are decreasing an image's size; this just throws away unneeded pixels by resampling down.

To double-check that there is no resampling up happening, enter the desired numbers in the Image Size dialog box and before you click OK, check the total file size to the right of Pixel Dimensions at the top of the dialog box and make sure it does not display a new larger size along with a smaller previous size. A new larger size would indicate resampling up.

If you absolutely have to enlarge an image and resample up, the interpolation methods that you choose in the Image Size dialog box are important to preserving quality as much as possible. In order to make smooth transitions between the pixels that remain after resizing, Photoshop has to decide what colors to make the newly added in-between pixels or how to adjust the color of the pixels on the edges of areas where pixels have been thrown away. The way Photoshop resamples image pixels, in an effort to maintain image quality, is called the *interpolation method*.

The default interpolation method can be set in the General Preferences menu (but where you really want to pay attention to interpolation methods is for one-time use in the Image Size dialog box). For general purposes, you may want to leave the preference set to Bicubic and change the method in the Image Size dialog box only when necessary. In general, I recommend using Bicubic Smoother if you are enlarging an image, Bicubic Sharper if you are reducing an image, or Nearest Neighbor if you are resizing a solid-color, linear image. The most important thing is to use the interpolation method that makes your resized image look the best.

When the quality of a resized image is very important, another approach is to use the Image Size dialog box to try different interpolation methods on the same image. You can always undo the Image Size command and try a different method or save copies of images with different interpolation methods and compare images destined for print by printing them and images destined for for screen by viewing them onscreen.

Following are descriptions of the interpolation methods:

- **Nearest Neighbor.** This method is appropriate to try for images that have hard edges. It attempts to preserve hard edges and produce a smaller file. It is fast but can produce jagged effects, especially if the image is resized or distorted significantly.
- **Bilinear.** This medium-quality method averages the color values of surrounding pixels in an attempt to make smooth transitions. It is faster but less precise than the Bicubic method.
- **Bicubic.** This method is good to try for images that have smooth gradients. It is slower but more precise than bilinear and creates smoother tonal transitions than Nearest Neighbor or Bilinear.
- **Bicubic Smoother.** This high-quality method is good for enlarging images and is based on the Bicubic method but adds some contrast while also attempting to produce smoother results.
- **Bicubic Sharper.** This high-quality method is good for reducing the size of images. It is based on Bicubic interpolation but also adds some sharpening.

TIP   When quality is of ultimate importance and you need to enlarge an image significantly, you can try enlarging it 5 percent to 10 percent at a time (you can choose percentages instead of units in the Image Size dialog box), multiple times until you get it to the final size. This sometimes results in a higher-quality enlargement. If you do a lot of enlargements, you may want to purchase software made specifically for enlarging images. Be sure to check reviews and try any trial versions of upsampling software before you make a purchase.

Resizing parts of images

To resize selected parts of an image on one layer or all the pixels on one layer (when no selection is active), choose Edit ⇨ Transform. Figure 5.13 shows the transform commands.

FIGURE 5.13

Use the transform commands to resize parts of images.

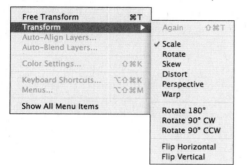

To transform the contents of multiple layers at the same time, first link the layers by selecting the layers on the Layers palette, then click the link symbol at the bottom of the Layers palette. To unlink the layers, click the link symbol again.

Significantly enlarging parts of an image can degrade image quality. Check prints from a good proofing device rather than the monitor to check quality of images destined for print.

CROSS-REF See Chapter 16 for specific examples of using the transform commands when making image collages.

Use the Ruler tool to help crop an image, measure distances in an image, or straighten an image. To measure, drag the Ruler tool across what you want to measure and see the Info palette for the measurement information. You can also click the Record Measurements button in the Measurement Log palette to record the data, which you can then export with the Measurement Log palette menu. You can also set the Measurement Scale in the Measurement Log palette menu.

To straighten an image using the Ruler tool, drag with the Ruler tool along the edge of something you know should be straight, then choose Image ➪ Image Rotation ➪ Arbitrary. Photoshop automatically calculates the angle of rotation and straightens the image.

You can also show rulers in the image window edges, then drag guides into the image from the rulers with the Move tool to help you know where to resize or crop an image. To delete guides, drag them off the image area with the Move tool.

To move the zero point of the rulers, drag the crosshairs where the rulers meet to the desired point in the image window. Double-click the box where the rulers meet to reset the zero point position.

To make moved objects and selections snap to guides, choose View ➪ Snap.

NOTE For specific examples of resizing images for the Web, see Chapter 24.

Resizing the canvas

By choosing Image ➪ Canvas Size (see Figure 5.14) you can change the canvas size independently of the image pixels that are on the canvas. If you enlarge the canvas, Photoshop leaves the objects in the image the same size and adds area to the canvas, or background area.

FIGURE 5.14

The Canvas Size dialog box

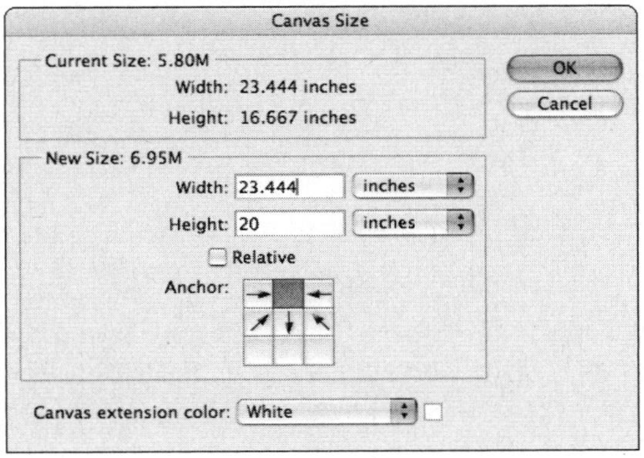

If you shrink the canvas size, the object pixels also stay the same size, but it can result in cropping away part of the objects in the image.

Enter the desired new size of the canvas in inches, pixels, percentages, and so on, or check Relative and enter a positive amount to add to the canvas size or a negative amount to subtract from the canvas size. Click an Anchor box to choose which sides the Canvas command adds to or subtracts from the canvas size.

Select the Canvas extension color to set the fill color that Photoshop uses when enlarging the canvas.

Cropping the canvas

You can use the Crop tool to crop an image, along with its canvas, to its intended size. Drag with the Crop tool, then move any of its handles to adjust the crop. Press Enter when you're finished. If you don't want to complete the crop, press ESC. Figure 5.15 shows the crop bounding box.

You can use the crop box to straighten images. Drag outside the crop box to rotate it so that its edges are parallel to any objects that need to be straightened. When you press Enter or Return, Photoshop crops out the surrounding area and straightens the object.

An active crop bounding box

If you drag the Crop tool to make a crop box, you can choose Hide in the Options Bar to hide the cropped area instead of deleting it. To get the cropped area back, choose Image ➪ Reveal All.

You can also drag the Crop tool around nonrectangular, straight-edged objects, choose Perspective in the Options Bar, and drag the bounding box handles so that the sides of the crop box are parallel to the sides of the nonrectangular, straight-edged object. When you press Enter or Return, Photoshop crops the surrounding area and makes the object rectangular.

You can enter the exact dimensions and resolution of your crop box selection in the Crop tool's Options Bar, but this can cause undesirable resampling if you are enlarging the crop box's selection and don't have enough resolution. If the Crop tool's Options Bar dimensions and resolution boxes are blank, you don't have to worry about those boxes causing resolution resizing problems.

Summary

This chapter described the importance of image resolution and how to resize images and maintain image quality. Following are key concepts:

A bitmap, or raster, image gets its detail from the number of pixels it contains, which is referred to as resolution and measured in pixels per inch (ppi). Higher resolution usually translates into greater detail; lower resolution usually translates into less detail. Vector images are resolution-independent, while combination bitmap-and-vector images are resolution-dependent. Image resolution for bitmap and combination bitmap-and-vector images should usually be 300 ppi for print, 72 ppi for the Web. Ideally, pixels should be captured initially, not added later.

You can choose Image ➪ Image Size to resize entire images. Unchecking the Resample Image box in the Image Size dialog box when you increase size or resolution numbers ensures that you don't degrade image quality when resizing with the Image Size command. You can choose Image ➪ Canvas Size to resize the canvas, or background, and Edit ➪ Transform to resize parts of images.

Chapter 6

Undoing Mistakes

We all make mistakes, but one of the great things about living in the Digital Age is that most of our flubs can be either detected for us by our smarty-pants computers, or we can zap them with the wonderful and ubiquitous Undo command.

Photoshop takes this already-invaluable concept —going back in time, before the error was made — and puts it on steroids, giving us a plethora of ways to fix our slip-ups or to change our minds. In fact, if Alexander Pope had had Photoshop, he would have said "To err is human, to undo is awesome."

In this chapter, you'll learn about the many ways Photoshop can help you go back in time and change the past.

The Undo Command

Similarly to the way it functions in most software packages, in Photoshop the Undo command removes the very last action that was performed. To use the Undo command, choose Edit ⇨ Undo, or press Ctrl+Z (⌘+Z on a Mac) on your keyboard (those keyboard shortcuts should already be etched into your muscle memory).

The Undo command is a little bit confusing, because the command itself is undoable. That means if you undo an action, and then choose Undo again, you'll undo what you just undid, making that undo into a *redo*. Make sense? Thought so. This is one area where Photoshop differs from most other software packages. Usually, choosing Undo repeatedly steps backward through the last several actions that were performed; whereas in Photoshop choosing Undo multiple times goes back and forth between undoing and redoing the last action. It might be a little disconcerting to new users of Photoshop, but fear not — there is a way to have your multiple undos in Photoshop, and it's called the History panel.

Briefly, the History panel records each action performed in Photoshop since you opened your document — up to a limit (more on that later). You can click on any of these stored states to return the document to the way it appeared when that action was performed. You can step back through the states recorded in the History panel by pressing Ctrl+Alt+Z/⌘+Option+Z and step forward by pressing Ctrl+Shift+Z/⌘+Shift+Z. You can even undo your backward and forward perambulations through the History panel.

Be aware that some commands, like closing a document, resizing a window, or opening or saving a document, can't be undone. These commands don't show up in the History panel. If an action can't be undone, the Undo turns into Can't Undo in the Edit menu.

The Revert Command

The Revert command reopens the last saved version of the file, abandoning changes that have been made since the file was last saved. Don't like the way something is turning out? Or maybe that last filter you applied made what was once a beautiful piece of art into an unfortunate mess. Simply choose File ➪ Revert or use the handy F12 keyboard shortcut to restore your document to the way it looked when you last saved it. It's kind of like Photoshop's panic button.

One of the nice things about the Revert command is that it too is undoable, just in case you change your mind. As if you weren't already given enough second chances.

> **TIP** Mac users: if you press F12 expecting Photoshop's Revert command but instead OS X's Dashboard is invoked, you can change Photoshop's default key command for Revert by choosing Edit ➪ Keyboard Shortcuts and assigning a new command for Revert. I recommend as an alternative that you re-assign OS X's default keyboard command for Dashboard by changing it in the Keyboard pane of System Preferences. See your Mac's documentation for specifics.

History Panel

Think of the History panel (shown in Figure 6.1) as Photoshop's built-in time machine. Actions that you perform in Photoshop are stored in the History panel, with new actions being placed at the bottom. Clicking on an action takes you back to the way your document appeared before you executed that command. By back stepping to an early state in your History panel, and then undoing that, you can see a nice before-and-after comparison of your document.

For an animated view of the progression of your document, you can click and drag the History state marker (the little arrow on the left of the History panel).

FIGURE 6.1

Photoshop's built-in time machine, the History panel, allows you to time-travel to different stages in a document's creation.

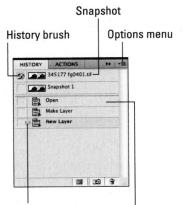

Also shown in the History panel are snapshots, which, as you may have guessed, are saved states of what your document looked like at a certain point in time. By default, a snapshot is automatically generated at the moment you open or create a new document. Using snapshots, you can temporarily save History states that you liked, and you can even create new documents from those states.

Be aware that History states and snapshots are only saved for the duration of the session; once you close your document or quit Photoshop, those states are lost.

In its default configuration, Photoshop tracks the first 20 commands you perform, and then when you perform the 21st command, the software "forgets" the oldest state at the top of the stack, shifting each subsequent state up to make room for the most recent command. This continues as you perform additional commands, freeing up valuable space in your computer's memory.

You'll soon find that 20 stored actions is just not enough, so to increase that limit open Photoshop's Preferences and choose Performance from the list on the left. Enter a higher number in the History States field by either typing it in, or using the slider that's revealed when you click the arrow on the right. The slider goes up to 1,000 states, but try not to get greedy. Things can start to get kind of sluggish if you set the maximum saved states too high — depending, of course, on your computer's capabilities. One hundred History states should be plenty for most users.

History states

As shown in Figure 6.1, the actions that you perform are referred to by the name of the tool or command that was used at that point in your document's history. By default, if you click on an earlier state of your document and then make a change to the document, the subsequent History states are removed. As mentioned earlier, you can step backward and forward through the operations saved in the History panel one at a time by pressing Shift+Ctrl+Z/Shift+⌘+Z and Ctrl+Alt+Z/⌘+Option+Z.

To remove a state select it and click the little trashcan icon at the bottom of the History panel, or drag the state you want to delete to the trashcan icon. By default, deleting a state deletes the states that follow it, but you can change this by selecting Allow Non-Linear History in the History Options dialog box. With this option enabled, deleting an operation from the History panel doesn't remove subsequent states.

Keep in mind that without Allow Non-Linear History enabled, if you select a History state and then make a change to the document, the subsequent states will be removed. You can undo this — but only once.

If you're particularly attached to the way a History state looks, you can create a new document from that state. The document is automatically given the name of the state that it was created from (shown in Figure 6.2). This is the same as clicking on the New Document from Snapshot icon at the bottom of the History panel.

To remove the stored commands from the History panel, choose Clear History from the fly-out menu. The appearance of the document isn't changed, but the History panel is cleared out, leaving only the most recent operation.

FIGURE 6.2

Here, a new document has been created from the Hue/Saturation History state, and the document has been given that name, as shown in the title bar.

NOTE As you might imagine, all of this History information that's being tracked by Photoshop has to be saved somewhere. That somewhere is your computer's memory, and there's only so much of it that Photoshop can access. If Photoshop complains that it needs more memory, you might try choosing Edit ⇨ Purge ⇨ Histories, which removes the History states from all open documents from Photoshop's cache. Note that the Purge Histories command isn't undoable.

Snapshots

As you work you can save snapshots of your document at any point in its evolution and fall back on them if you reach a point you're not happy with. You can also create new documents based on those snapshots. To create a new snapshot, click on the little camera icon at the bottom of the History panel or choose New Snapshot from the fly-out menu. To name a snapshot, after you've created it, double-click on its name in the History panel, or Alt+click/Option+click on the camera icon.

Normally, unless you've changed this in the History panel options, Photoshop automatically creates a new snapshot when you open or create a new document. You can disable this, but it can be handy to have that first snapshot to fall back on as a safety net. An instance where you may want to disable it, however, is if you're getting ready to batch-process a large number of images, and want to skip the momentary pause while Photoshop creates that first snapshot.

CROSS-REF To learn more about Batch Processing images, check out Chapter 3.

Depending on the amount of RAM your system has, you can keep on saving snapshots as often as you like. In fact, you can have Photoshop generate a new snapshot of your document every time you save it (which, if you're anything like me, is very often), by turning this option on in the History Options dialog box, which is found under the History panel's fly-out menu (see Figure 6.3).

It's worth repeating that snapshots are there only as long as you have the document open; once you close the document or quit Photoshop, those snapshots are gone. If you're particularly partial to a snapshot and want to save it permanently, create a new document from it and save that document.

FIGURE 6.3

Configure the behavior of the History panel in the History Options dialog box.

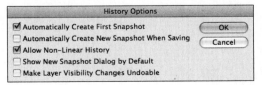

Alt+click/Option+click on the camera icon to give the snapshot a name (other than the default, which is the same as the name of the state you're creating it from), or to specify how the snapshot is created — either from the entire document or from the currently selected layer.

History Brush

To continue the time-machine analogy, the History Brush is kind of like bringing elements of the past into the future — that is, you choose a point in your document's history and paint in pixels from there to the current state of your document.

To designate the state or snapshot you want to paint from, click the History source icon to the left of the state's name in the History panel (see Figure 6.4). As you paint, the document is reverted to the source state you selected. Because it's a brush, the History Brush operates like all the other brush-based tools in Photoshop, meaning you can set a blending mode, opacity, flow, and airbrush options, all of which influence the subtlety of the effect. Try it when retouching wrinkles or blemishes to bring back some of the natural skin texture that may have been lost.

The History Brush has a caveat: If you try to set a state that is different pixel dimensions from the state that you're painting to as your source, the tool won't work. Instead, your cursor turns into a circle with the line through it (the universal symbol for "nope, sorry, try again").

FIGURE 6.4

Set the source for the History Brush by clicking the little icon to the left of any History state.

 **You can also use the Eraser tool with Erase to History checked to erase back to a previous state of the document. See Chapter 2 for a more in-depth look at the Eraser tool.**

Features with Built-In Undos

Certain features of Photoshop are designed to enable a non-destructive workflow. These features allow you the maximum flexibility in your design by enabling you to change a design that isn't working, or to satisfy the whims of even the most fickle clients. Yesterday they liked blue, but today they demand periwinkle? Not a problem.

Dialog boxes

Most dialog boxes for the tools in Photoshop allow you to undo at least the most recent action. For example, say you're using the Levels command, and you don't like the last tweak you made. You can press Ctrl+Z/⌘+Z and go back a step.

If you've made a good many tweaks within a dialog box and find that you just want to start over from scratch, holding down the Alt/Option key on your keyboard switches the Cancel button to Reset (see Figure 6.5), which restores the default settings of the dialog box.

FIGURE 6.5

Holding down Alt or Option while in most Photoshop dialog boxes changes the Cancel button to a Reset button, allowing you to remove all of your adjustments to the dialog box's settings.

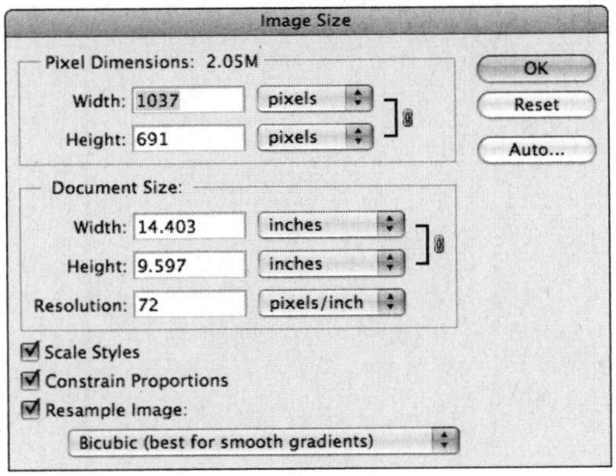

Masks

Layer masks (see Figure 6.6) are incredibly useful and a central pillar in the concept of the non-destructive workflow. Rather than deleting pixels or parts of a layer to composite it with other layers in a document, you use a mask to cover up those pixels. If you need to bring those pixels back, you simply edit the mask using any of Photoshop's brushes, filters, or selections tools; or you can remove the mask entirely to restore the layer to full view. You'll learn much, much more about masks in Chapter 8.

FIGURE 6.6

Areas that appear white in the layer mask thumbnail are revealed in this image. Areas that appear black in the thumbnail are hidden and appear transparent.

Adjustment layers

Another important tool in your non-destructive workflow is the adjustment layer. Applying any of Photoshop's image adjustment tools from the Image ➪ Adjustments menu (Brightness/Contrast or Levels, for example) affects only the currently selected layer. Adjustment layers contain color correction data and apply those color corrections to any layers that appear below them. Create a new adjustment layer by using one of the following methods:

- Choose Layer ➪ New Adjustment Layer and then choose an adjustment to apply. The New Adjustment Layer dialog box pops up, allowing you to name your adjustment layer and, optionally, choose a blending mode for it.

- Click and hold on the create new fill or adjustment layer icon on the bottom of the Layers panel (it's the little black-and-white circle), and choose an adjustment. Clicking this icon bypasses the New Adjustment Layer dialog box and applies the adjustment you just selected.

- Open the Adjustments panel (new in Photoshop CS4), and select an adjustment or one of the adjustment presets that are included with Photoshop.

A new adjustment layer appears in the Layers panel, accompanied by a thumbnail that represents the type of adjustment you just created. You can now edit your adjustment by using the sliders in the Adjustments panel (see Figure 6.7).

FIGURE 6.7

Use the sliders in the Adjustments Panel to manipulate the current adjustment layer.

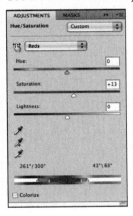

The beauty of adjustment layers is that they remain editable as long as your document is saved as any of the four file formats that recognize Photoshop's layer information (native PSD, TIFF, PSB, and PDF). You can keep editing the adjustment settings over and over again without actually affecting the pixels of the layers below your adjustment layers.

Another advantage of adjustment layers is that because they're layers, they have all the advantages of regular layers — you can change their order by dragging them up or down in the Layers panel, and so control which layers the adjustment applies to; you can change their blending modes and opacity; and you can paint or otherwise modify their built-in layer masks to determine which pixels on the layers below are affected by the adjustment.

Additionally, adjustment layers are portable — you can drag them between documents to quickly apply the same image adjustments to another image. Oh, and the icing on the cake? Because adjustment layers contain only mathematical data (as opposed to actual pixels), they won't adversely impact the file size of your document. To move an adjustment layer from one document to another, follow the steps outlined below:

1. **Make sure the source and target documents are open.** If you're not using Photoshop CS4's new Application Frame, you should align the documents next to each other so you can see them both simultaneously.

2. **Select the adjustment layer you want to move in the Layers panel.**

3. **With the Move tool selected, click anywhere on your document's canvas, and drag the layer to the destination document.** If your documents are side-by-side, simply drag from one document to the other. If you are using tabbed documents, drag from the canvas up to the tab of the document you're targeting, and pause for a second or two. The tabbed document will come to the forefront, and you can then drop the dragged layer into it.

Layer comps

Just as History states track individual actions or commands that you perform in Photoshop, layer comps (see Figure 6.8) track the state of various aspects of your Layers panel. Layer comps are often used to create different mockups or versions of a design — all within one Photoshop document — to show a client.

The Layer Comps panel tracks different attributes of the layers in your document.

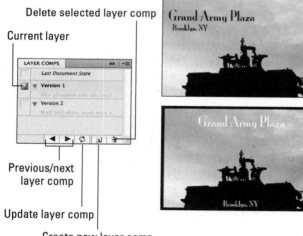

Delete selected layer comp

Current layer

Previous/next layer comp

Update layer comp

Create new layer comp

As mentioned, only certain aspects of your layers' states are tracked by layer comps, and it's important to be aware of these restrictions. Visibility, opacity, position, and layer styles and their settings are all capable of being stored and recalled. Painting on a layer, using the gradient tool, or otherwise manipulating pixels of the layer are not able to be stored across layer comps.

Open the Layer Comps panel if it's not visible by choosing it from the Window menu or by clicking its docked icon. Create a new snapshot of the current state of your document by clicking on the new layer comp icon at the bottom of the Layer Comps panel. The resulting New Layer Comp dialog box, shown in Figure 6.9, allows you to name your layer comp and enter a few notes about that version of your layout. You can also specify which attributes of your layers to track:

- **Visibility.** Selecting this option tracks the visibility of layers and layer masks.

- **Position.** This option tracks the position of your layers in relation to each other. That is, you can position a layer in the top left of your document in Comp 1, and then move it to the lower right of your document in Comp 2. Note that moving the individual pixels of a layer, say by selecting and moving them with the marquee tool, will be reflected in that layer in all of your layer comps.

- **Appearance (Layer Style).** This option stores information about the appearance of your layers including opacity, layer styles and their settings, blend modes, and knockouts.

FIGURE 6.9

The New Layer Comp dialog box allows you to specify which layer attributes are remembered.

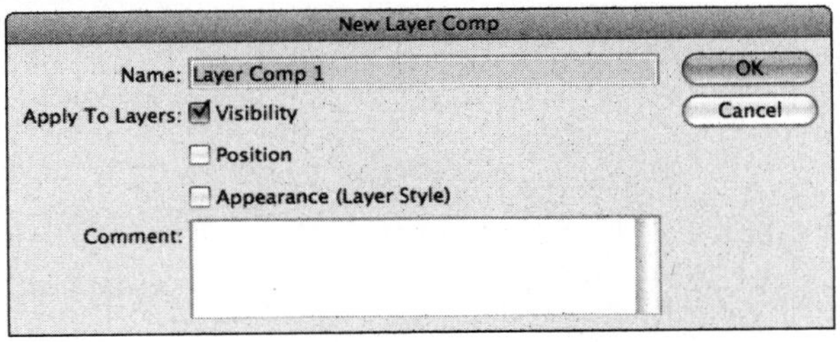

The Layer Comps panel updates with the currently selected comp indicated by the little icon on the left of the panel. If you make changes to your document that are able to be tracked by layer comps, the icon jumps back to the layer comp on the very top of the panel called Last Document State.

Managing layer comps

You can step between the different available layer comps by clicking on them or by clicking on the left- and right-facing arrows at the bottom of the Layer Comps panel. You can delete or remove layer comps by selecting them and clicking on the trashcan icon. After making changes to a selected layer comp, make sure you update the stored information by clicking the update layer comp icon (the one with the two arrows chasing each other) at the bottom of the panel.

Once you've come up with a few different design directions for your layout and you've saved them as layer comps, you can export those comps to individual files or to a multi-page PDF file. To do so, choose File ➪ Scripts… and then choose the appropriate command from the submenu.

Those fragile layer comps

If you make a change to your document that can't be tracked by the Layer Comps panel, such as deleting a layer or merging layers, a warning icon (like the ones shown in Figure 6.10) appears next to the affected layer comp (or comps).

Layer comps are kind of fragile that way — but you can either undo the offending move, or click on the warning triangle for a description of what you did to make the Layer Comps panel unhappy. You can also choose to clear the warning triangle and continue with your edits; just remember to go back and update your layer comps to reflect your new document state.

You can also clear the warning triangles by right-clicking on them and choosing to either clear that warning or clear the warnings for all layer comps.

FIGURE 6.10

Merging layers can break layer comps. To clear the warnings triangles, either undo the change that caused them, or right-click/Ctrl-click on the triangles and clear the warnings for either the selected layer comp or all layer comps.

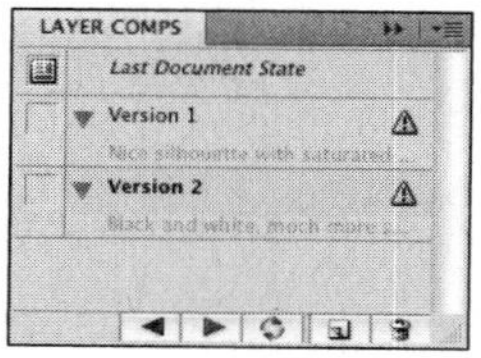

Smart Objects

Another tool in your non-destructive toolkit is the Smart Object. With Smart Objects, you take the contents of a layer or layers; or even an external document in pretty much any format that Photoshop understands, and wrap it in what is essentially a protective casing.

Once it's in there, you can transform it, warp it, or apply filters to it, all without affecting the actual contents of the Smart Object. At any time you can go back and edit the contents of the Smart Object — either in Photoshop, or in an external program, like Adobe Illustrator — and when you're done, the changes you made are updated in your original document.

To create a Smart Object, select a layer or Shift-select several layers and from the Layers menu, choose Smart Objects ➪ Convert to Smart Object. You can also create a Smart Object right from the Layers panel by right-clicking on the layer names and selecting Convert to Smart Object from the contextual menu, as shown in Figure 6.11.

Once you've got a Smart Object you can safely transform it — that is, scale, rotate, or warp it — all without affecting the actual pixels of the Smart Object (you can't use the Distort or Perspective command on a Smart Object, though). To edit the actual contents of the Smart Object, double-click its thumbnail in the Layers panel.

After a very helpful dialog box from Photoshop (see Figure 6.12), the contents of the Smart Object open up in a new PSB (large document format) file. You can edit this file using just about any of Photoshop's tools — add layers, use filters, even create new Smart Objects within this Smart Object. — and when you save it (you can even change the file format if you want), any changes you made are updated in your original document.

FIGURE 6.11

Create a Smart Object from an existing layer or layers by right-clicking in the Layers panel and choosing Create Smart Object.

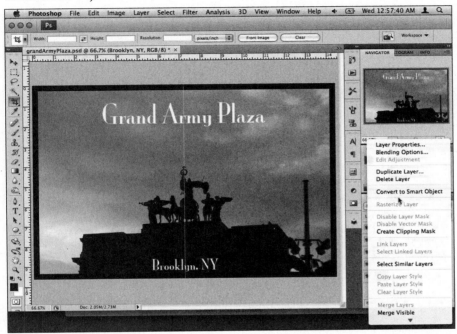

FIGURE 6.12

After editing, you can change the file format of your Smart Object, but make sure you save it in the same location so it can be properly updated in the file that references it.

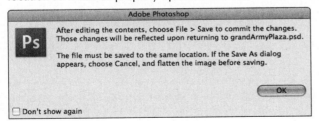

You also have the option of replacing the contents of the Smart Object with another file. To do so, right-click on your Smart Object's layer name and select Replace Contents. In the resulting dialog box, navigate to a different file and click Open. Your Smart Object is immediately replaced with the contents of the file you just selected.

Finally you can export the contents of a Smart Object to a new document by once again right-clicking (Ctrl+click on a Mac) on the Smart Object's layer name and selecting Export Contents from the contextual menu. Choose a location and a filename and click Save, and there you have it.

CROSS-REF There's more to Smart Objects (Image Stacks, anyone?) and they're covered in more detail in Chapter 8. Also, you can learn about applying non-destructive filters to Smart Objects in Chapter 20.

Crop/Reveal All

One other example of a tool in Photoshop that has a bit of a built-in undo feature is the Crop tool. You would typically use the Crop tool to get rid of parts of an image that you don't want; for example, to recompose a photograph by cropping distracting elements. Because we don't like throwing away good pixels, the Crop tool has a built-in feature that lets us get those pixels back.

For a demonstration of what I'm talking about, select the Crop tool in from the Toolbox or press the C key on your keyboard. Click and drag to define a crop region. Before accepting the crop take a look up in the toolbar. You'll notice that there are two radio buttons: Delete and Hide (see Figure 6.13). Cropping the image with Delete selected does exactly what it says — it throws away the pixels that fall outside of your crop region. Hide mode, on the other hand, covers up those pixels by leaving them outside of the new, cropped canvas area. To get them back, choose Image ⇨ Reveal All, and the canvas expands to reveal the hidden parts of your image.

FIGURE 6.13

The cropping options determine what Photoshop does with the parts of your image that fall outside of your cropping region — delete them or hide them.

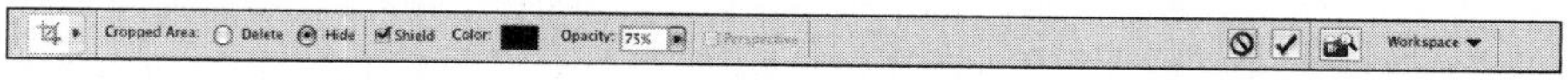

CAUTION After cropping your image, Reveal All is only available in the Image menu if your image doesn't have a background layer. To convert your image background to a regular layer, double-click on the background layer in the Layers panel and give it a name, or just click OK.

Summary

In this chapter you learned that you can indeed turn back time, at least as far as Photoshop is concerned. You learned about using the Undo and Revert commands, and how to use the History panel and History states to step back to previous stages in your document's evolution. You learned how to paint back in parts of a History state using the History Brush, effectively bringing bits of the past into the present. You saw how you could use snapshots to save History states or create new documents from them.

You also learned about non-destructive image editing and the tools that are commonly used in a non-destructive workflow, including adjustment layers, layer masks, layer comps, and Smart Objects.

Chapter 7

Saving Files

The first rule of working with any computer software is to save your work often. (The second rule is to back up your data regularly, but I'm sure you already knew that.) We've all lost data due to a software or hardware crash — or at least seen someone go through it — and it's not pretty. In this chapter you'll learn about the ins and outs of saving files in Photoshop.

You'll learn about the advantages and disadvantages of formats Photoshop is capable of saving to, including the native Photoshop file format (PSD, or Photoshop Document) and the advantages it offers. You'll also learn about the advantages and disadvantages of the various file formats, what scenarios to use them in, and how they can provide maximum compatibility when exchanging data with other software packages and devices.

Saving Files to Disk

Saving files is critical part of working with computers, no matter what software you're using. Most software packages offer at least two commands that you can use to save your files — Save and Save As — and inexperienced users are often unsure of which of these two commands to choose. Before we jump in, though, let's take a look at the configurable options in the File Handling section of Photoshop's preferences.

File handling preferences

Photoshop offers several settings that you can use to specify the way files are saved. These settings, which vary slightly depending on your operating system, include options for saving file previews, file extensions, and ensuring file compatibility across operating systems. To access them, open

Photoshop's Preferences dialog box by pressing Ctrl+K/⌘+K, then select File Handling from the list of choices on the left.

The File Handling section of the Preferences dialog box is divided into three main areas — File Saving Options, File Compatibility and Version Cue. The following options are available:

- **Image Previews.** The default Image Preview setting of Always Save embeds a tiny preview of your image into each document you save. This preview is displayed by your operating system and allows you to see what the image looks like before you open it. On the Mac you have several additional options for saving thumbnails:

  - **Icon.** Choose this option to use the image preview as a Finder icon in your Desktop.

  - **Macintosh Thumbnail.** This option generates a preview that's used in the Mac OS Open dialog box.

  - **Windows Thumbnail.** This option generates a preview that is used by Windows systems.

  - **Full Size.** This option includes a low-resolution (72ppi) version of your document for use with other applications, like page layout programs, that may not be able to open full-resolution versions of Photoshop files.

Saving icons and thumbnails along with your file means that extra data is added to the file, and as you might expect, will definitely have an effect on file size. If file size is a consideration, set the Image Preview option to Always Ask. This option displays the options discussed above in the Save dialog box (produced by selecting File ⇨ Save), allowing you to decide how which image previews to include on a case-by-case basis.

- **Append File Extension.** The file extension is the three-letter abbreviation that appears at the end of a file's name. It lets you and your computer know what kind of file it is and which software it should be associated with. On Windows systems, file extensions are included by default, but on the Mac it is optional. I highly recommend leaving this option set to Always, to ensure the maximum compatibility.

- **Use Lower Case.** This option allows you to specify the case of the file extension — for example myFile.GIF or myFile.gif. Some operating systems are case-sensitive, and would recognize the two examples given here as two completely different files, so for consistency's sake, I recommend leaving this option set to Use Lower Case.

- **Camera Raw Preferences.** This button opens up the Preferences dialog box for the Adobe Camera Raw plug-in, which is covered in depth in Chapter 4.

- **Prefer Adobe Camera Raw for Supported Raw Files.** Choose this option if you want to use Adobe Camera Raw (as opposed to other Raw processing software) to process RAW files downloaded from your camera.

- **Ignore EXIF profile tag.** Virtually all digital photos have EXIF (Exchangeable Image File) data embedded in them that describes all sorts of information, including the date and time the image was shot, the pixel dimensions of the image, and the image's color profile. Enabling this option tells Photoshop to ignore color profiles that are embedded in your images. I would leave this one checked — you can assign a color profile to an image or convert it to a different color profile any time.

- **Ask Before Saving Layered TIFF Files.** Leaving this option checked pops up a dialog box warning you that saving TIFF files with layers results in larger files.

- **Maximize PSD and PSB Compatibility.** This option is designed to make sure that older software can open files created with the most current version of Photoshop. It saves a flattened composite version of your file along with its layers, so that programs that don't understand newer Photoshop features can at least open the flattened version of the file. If there's a chance that you'll be sharing your files with other designers who might not have access to newer software, then you can leave this option set to Ask or Always.

- **Enable Version Cue.** Version Cue uses a technology called WebDAV to help organize and track shared assets in a collaborative environment. Designers check files out when they want to work on them, add notes describing their changes, and check them back into the system when they're done. The system tracks the changes, and saves backups, making it easy to revert to earlier versions when necessary. Enable this option to allow Photoshop to make use of Version Cue's features.

- **Recent File List Contains (10) Files.** Enter a number here (up to 30) to specify how many recently opened files Photoshop remembers.

The Save commands

If you're saving a document that you created from scratch, or if you're working on an existing file and you're certain that you want to overwrite it with your current revisions, use the Save command, located in the File menu, or use the keyboard shortcut Ctrl+S (⌘+S on a Mac).

The first time you save a file by using the Save command, you're presented with the Save As dialog box, shown in Figure 7.1.

FIGURE 7.1

The available options in the Save As dialog box change depending on the file format you select.

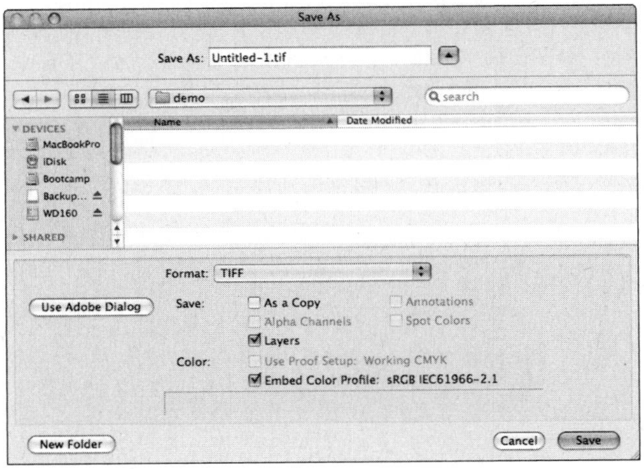

Enter a filename, navigate to a location on your hard drive to save the file to, and select a file format. As you continue to work, saving the file will immediately update the file on your hard disk with your most recent revisions, without opening the Save As dialog box.

The other version of the Save command is Save As, which can be accessed by the keyboard shortcut Ctrl+Shift+S/⌘+Shift+S, or by choosing Save As from the File menu. This command lets you save the file you're working on under a different filename or file format and keep working on that file. The original file you started with is not changed.

If, when using the Save As command, you don't change the filename, or you specify the same filename as an existing file (which there is often a perfectly legitimate reason for doing), Photoshop will alert you to this, and give you the opportunity to change your mind before overwriting the existing file, as illustrated in Figure 7.2.

Let's take a closer look at the options you can specify when saving files.

The options available to you at the bottom of the Save As dialog box depend on the file format you've chosen for your image. Options that don't apply to the current file format will be grayed out. If your image contains features that aren't compatible with your chosen file format, you'll see little warning triangles next to those options in the dialog box, indicating that those attributes are discarded in that format. The options for saving are as follows:

- **As a Copy.** This option is the equivalent of duplicating your current file, saving it, and closing the document all in one fell swoop. Your in-progress document stays open and you can continue working.

- **Alpha Channels.** Alpha channels contain information about an image's transparency. If your document contains layer masks (covered in Chapter 8), that information is preserved in file formats that understand alpha channels. These formats include the native Photoshop format (PSD), Photoshop's Large Document format (PSB), TIFF, PDF, and DCS 2.0.

- **Layers.** Again, if your image contains layers, there are only a small number of file formats that can retain this information: PSD, PSB, TIFF, and PDF.

- **Use Proof Setup.** This option is specific to Photoshop's color profiling features. Using the View menu, you can use Photoshop to preview the way colors will appear on different output devices — also known as "soft-proofing." Selecting this option converts your image to the currently active proofing space when you save it. The only file format that allows you to select this option is Photoshop PDF. Read Chapter 23 for more information on soft-proofing.

- **ICC Profile (Win)/Embed Color Profile (Mac).** Selecting this option embeds the document's current color profile (displayed alongside this option in the Save As dialog box) in the file, if the format you chose can handle that information.

- **Spot Colors.** If you created a multichannel document that contains spot colors and you want to preserve that information, select this option. The following file formats preserve this information: native PSD, PSB, TIFF, PDF, and DCS 2.0.

FIGURE 7.2

Photoshop warns you if you attempt to overwrite an existing file when using the Save As command.

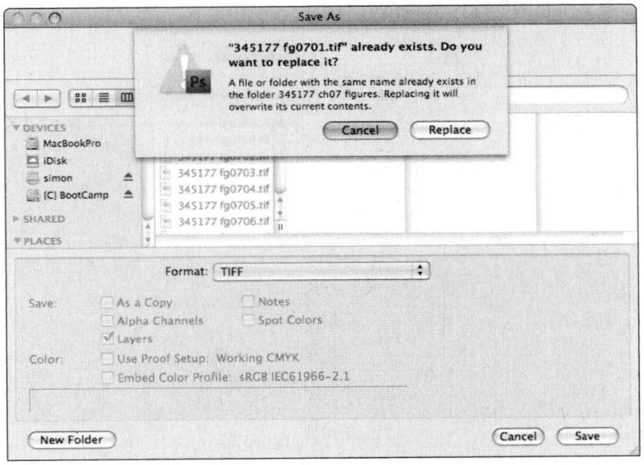

Save for Web & Devices Command

If you're saving a file that's destined for the Internet, you can use the Save for Web & Devices command (newly tweaked for Photoshop CS4 — see Figure 7.3) to output your file in one of the Web-friendly formats.

The JPEG, GIF, and PNG formats are available via the Save or Save As commands, but using Save for Web & Devices offers more intuitive access to various useful options for saving files for the Web.

- **Compare your original and optimized images side-by-side.** View your original file and simultaneously compare it to as many as three alternate versions, using different combinations of compression schemes and file format options.

- **Preview file sizes and download times.** The Save for Web & Devices dialog box displays the effect of the different file formats and their compression options on the final file size of your image. You can also view the estimated download times at different Internet connection speeds — from low-bandwidth, dial-up connections to corporate T1 connections.

- **Set the color profile used by your image.** Use this option to output the file with the document's color profile, or convert it to the standard sRGB Web color space. Learn more about color profiles in Chapter 23.

- **Resize the Web version of your image.** Want to create a smaller version of your image specifically for use on the Web? Instead of duplicating the file, then resizing it by using the Image Size command, and saving that file by using one of the Web formats, simply enter the new image dimensions in the Image Size area, select an interpolation method from the Quality pop-up menu, and click Save. Give your image a name and specify a location for the file and you're all set.

- **Send your image to Device Central.** Click the Device Central button to launch Device Central (which ships with certain versions of the Creative Suite) and preview your image on any of hundreds of different mobile devices.

The features of the Save for Web & Devices dialog box are covered in greater depth in Chapter 24.

FIGURE 7.3

The Save for Web & Devices dialog box offers lots of useful options for outputting Web-friendly images.

File Formats in Depth

Photoshop is capable of saving and opening about a billion file formats, and with the introduction of 3-D capabilities back in Photoshop CS3 (Extended edition), that number has grown substantially. Add to that the ability to extend Photoshop's capabilities by installing third-party file format plug-ins, and . . . well, you see where this is going. Some of the available formats are obscure or even defunct, but it's nice to know that Photoshop can most likely handle just about any image format you attempt to open with it.

Each file format has a purpose, and in most cases, offers some form of compression so that the file takes up less hard disk space. Let's take a look at some of the file formats available for you to choose from.

PSD: The native format

As mentioned earlier, PSD is Photoshop's default file format. It's specifically optimized for Photoshop's features and capabilities. Document attributes, such as layers, layer styles, alpha channels, spot color channels, and Smart Objects are all preserved in the PSD file format. Additionally, the close integration between Adobe's Creative Suite applications means that programs such as After Effects, Illustrator, Premiere, and Go Live can open — and in some cases, export — PSD files and preserve most of their attributes. You can also open PSD files in earlier versions of Photoshop, but features that aren't supported in those earlier versions can be lost.

To be on the safe side, if you know you'll be sharing your Photoshop documents between applications or with older versions of Photoshop, you can embed a flattened composite inside your document that can be read by these other programs while at least maintaining the visual appearance of your file.

To do so, enable the Maximize PSD and PSB File Compatibility option in the Preferences panel. Press Ctrl+K/⌘+K to open the Preferences window, then press Ctrl+3/⌘+3 to jump to the File Handling section. Under Maximize PSD and PSB File Compatibility (see Figure 7.4), select Ask to be prompted each time you save a file, or Always to automatically maximize compatibility every time you save a PSD or PSB file.

Lossy vs. Lossless

File compression schemes attempt to save disk space by compressing data. The methods they use to accomplish this can be categorized as either *lossy* or *lossless*.

Lossy data compression creates smaller file sizes by analyzing files and selectively discarding redundant data. This method often results in significant disk space savings, but lossy compression formats suffer from *generation loss* — that is, uncompressing and re-compressing the file repeatedly results in a loss of quality. JPEG is one example of a lossy compression format.

Lossless compression, on the other hand, attempts to save space by rearranging the file information more efficiently without discarding any of it. Files saved in this way do not suffer from generation loss — the data that gets uncompressed when the file is opened is the same as the data that was compressed in the first place. Some examples of lossless compression algorithms include RLE (Run Length Encoding) and LZW (Lempel-Ziv-Welch). These are some of the compression methods used by the GIF, PNG, and TIFF file formats.

FIGURE 7.4

Choose whether to embed a composite image in your PSD files for compatibility with other software or with earlier versions of Photoshop.

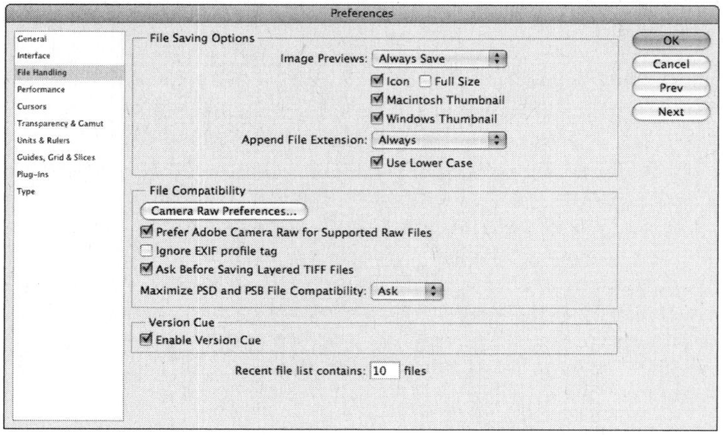

You should know that embedding this composite image in your document could have an impact on your file size, so if conserving disk space is an issue, consider disabling this feature. In many cases, it is in fact advisable to disable the Maximize Compatibility option (select Never), and instead adopt a workflow where you keep a master PSD file for yourself and save a flattened version in a specialized format that suits its intended use — for instance, as an EPS file for use with InDesign, or a JPG file for a file that's destined for the Web.

The mainstream formats

The following formats — JPEG and TIFF — are probably the most widely used of the file formats Photoshop is capable of saving, and are extremely flexible in terms of the range of software with which they are compatible and the types (and quality) of compression they offer.

JPEG

This file format was developed by and is named after the Joint Photographic Experts Group. It's most commonly used for displaying photographic images because it does a fantastic job of retaining image quality while reducing file size. In fact, most digital cameras and cell phones save their images to this format by default.

JPEG is a *lossy* format. That is, it selectively discards data to reduce the amount of disk space an image occupies. When saving a JPEG, you are presented with the JPEG Options dialog box (see Figure 7.5), where you can specify a compression amount. The more compression you apply, the more information is discarded. A very low Quality setting results in a small file, but the image quality ends up being unacceptable for most purposes.

Large Document Format (PSB)

The PSB or Large Document Format is a specialized version of the PSD format that was developed to accommodate files greater than 2 gigabytes in size. Some of you might wonder when you would ever need such a gargantuan file — and if that's you, then you probably don't work in digital video editing, high-end print design, or photo retouching.

PSB is also the default file format that Photoshop uses to store the contents of Smart Objects, which are discussed in Chapters 6 and 8.

FIGURE 7.5

The JPEG Options dialog box allows you to specify how much compression to apply to an image. Setting the Quality at Maximum (12 on the slider) applies almost no compression.

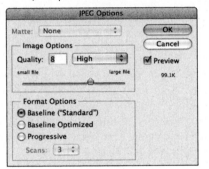

On the other hand, with the compression Quality set to Maximum — that is, hardly any compression applied at all — the difference in the visual appearance between the resulting JPEG and the original is almost undetectable, and you still benefit from a file that is significantly smaller than the original.

The radio buttons at the bottom of the JPEG Options dialog box are related to saving images that are destined for the Web. Baseline ("Standard"), which is selected by default, is the most widely used option and is compatible with most Web browsers. Baseline Optimized creates a slightly smaller file size, and Progressive compresses the image in multiple passes, so that on slower Internet connections, the image is displayed in portions as the data is downloaded.

CROSS-REF More information on preparing JPEG images for the Internet is covered in Chapter 24.

Keep in mind that JPEG compression has a cumulative effect. That is, if you save an image as a JPEG, then re-open that image and save it again as a JPEG, you will be applying additional compression to the image and thus discarding more information. The effects of this can be subtle at first, but repeatedly re-compressing a JPEG eventually results in a noticeably degraded image. On the other hand, if you're working with a JPEG image in Photoshop and you save it repeatedly during your editing session, this doesn't have a negative effect on the file, because what's being saved to disk is based on what you're seeing on your screen. An optimal workflow would be to work with a PSD or other lossless image format and save to JPEG only once when you're done with all your edits.

JPEG files are compatible with RGB, CMYK, and Grayscale color modes, and they can also retain vector paths (see Chapter 11). Alpha channels, however, aren't saved with JPEG images, and any transparent areas in your image are converted to the matte color you specify (white by default). JPEG compression is best suited to photographic images or images with areas of continuous tone. Line drawings, vector art, or images with high contrast are better suited to GIF or lossless image formats such as PNG, because the JPEG compression can result in artifacts, especially in areas of the image where there is a sharp difference between neighboring pixels.

> **NOTE** Image processing filters can exacerbate the artifacts produced by JPEG compression, so it's always a good idea to apply them to the original file before saving it as a JPEG.

TIFF

TIFF (short for Tagged Image File Format), was developed back in the 1980s by a company called Aldus in an attempt to standardize the image output of desktop scanners. Control of the TIFF specification was eventually acquired by Adobe. Today, TIFF is one of the most widely used image formats on both Mac and Windows platforms because of the broad flexibility that it provides.

In Photoshop, the TIFF format has a few extra capabilities that make it even more unrestricted. Other than the native PSD, "raw," and DCS 2.0, it is the only file format that supports images with more than four channels — in fact, TIFF can support images with 24 channels, which is the maximum for any image. You can read more about channels in Chapter 10. TIFF files are also compatible with Photoshop layers and layer styles, and can save files of just about any color space. They can also support images of up to 32 bits per channel.

> **TIP** You can save 32-bit-per-channel HDR (High Dynamic Range) images as TIFF in Photoshop. HDR images are covered in Chapter 3.

Saving an image as a TIFF file brings up the TIFF Options dialog box, shown in Figure 7.6, which allows you to specify the following options:

FIGURE 7.6

The TIFF Options dialog box allows you to specify a lossy or lossless compression scheme.

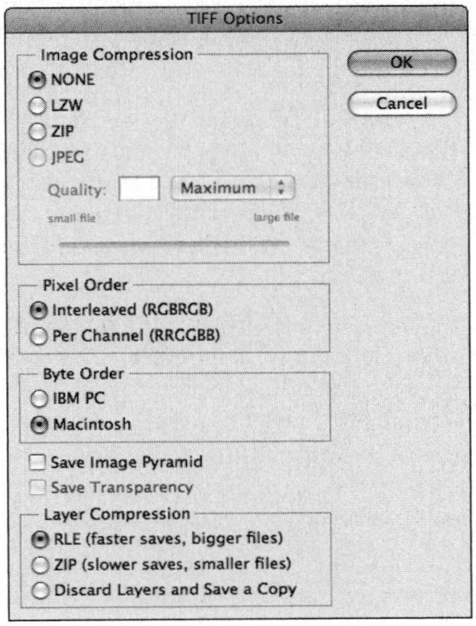

■ **Image Compression.** Choose one of three compression formats that either use lossy or lossless compression:

  ▦ **LZW:** The LZW compression technique (tip o' the hat to Messrs. Lempel, Ziv, and Welch) makes files smaller by substituting frequently used chunks of data in an image with shorter equivalent chunks. Most image-editing programs can interpret TIFF images saved by using LZW compression.

  ▦ **ZIP:** The ZIP compression algorithm was developed as a free alternative to the LZW scheme, which up until 2004 was protected by patents. ZIP compression can be more efficient than LZW and result in smaller images, but currently Photoshop remains one of the few programs that can decompress TIFF images that employ ZIP compression.

  ▦ **JPEG:** It might seem counterintuitive to use JPEG, a lossy compression scheme within a TIFF image; after all, one of the main reasons to use TIFF in the first place is to output images of the highest quality possible. But selecting JPEG with a high compression quality can result in files that are significantly smaller than the uncompressed versions and that show hardly any discernible data loss. There are purists out there, however, for whom any data loss is unacceptable; to you I say stick with LZW or ZIP.

199

> **NOTE** Some programs do not support the compression algorithms used by TIFF —
> Photoshop alerts you if you choose one of those options. For the greatest degree of
> compatibility, save your TIFF without any compression at all.

- **Pixel Order.** This option specifies the order in which to write the channel data: Interleaved or Per Channel. Previous versions of Photoshop wrote interleaved data by default, but Per Channel order is said to be read more quickly and to produce smaller files. Either choice can be read by older versions of the software.

- **Byte Order.** Mac or PC? It's a question that can incite all sorts of passion in folks, but in this case it's a simple matter of deciding which platform your file is most likely to end up on. Depending on your selection, the TIFF will be written in a way that is more efficient for that system. Either byte order is readable on both platforms, though, so ultimately it doesn't make much difference.

- **Save Image Pyramid.** Image pyramids are used for creating resolution-independent (or *multi-resolution*) files in which information for different resolution levels is stored inside a single file. It's like having a full-resolution, print-quality image as well as several smaller versions all embedded in the same document (kind of like those Russian dolls). For certain imaging tasks, the lower-resolution versions are used, but when necessary, the full-resolution version is available. Having that extra data in there can result in a 30 percent boost in file size, but in applications or image servers that support image pyramids, the gain in efficiency is worth it.

  Photoshop itself doesn't support image pyramids — it simply opens the file at the highest possible resolution. Unless you know that your image is destined for a file that supports it, don't use this option.

- **Save Transparency.** If your image contains transparent areas, select this option to preserve them. Otherwise, the image is flattened and the transparent areas become white.

- **Layer Compression.** So, you already specified a compression format for your TIFF file — now you can choose how to compress the layers within your file. As described in the dialog box, RLE is faster but saves bigger files, and ZIP has the opposite result. The Discard Layers and Save a Copy option flattens the file and discards the layer information.

> **NOTE** If you're saving a 32-bit-per-channel image, the TIFF Options dialog box also
> includes a section that allows you to specify whether to convert your image to 8- or
> 16-bit.

Specialized formats

As mentioned earlier, different file formats offer specific advantages, such as image compression, or compatibility with different applications. Following are some of the more common file formats that you can either open or save to in Photoshop. Some of the formats not covered here are either obscure, defunct, or discussed in more detail in other chapters of this book.

Photoshop EPS

EPS or Encapsulated PostScript files are compatible with virtually all page layout and image-processing programs on the market. If your document will be incorporated into a QuarkXPress or Illustrator file that will ultimately be printed on a PostScript printer, you can convert it to an EPS file in Photoshop up front. The resulting file prints faster and avoids printing problems.

EPS files also support clipping paths (covered in more detail in Chapter 11). You can use a clipping path to define the boundary of your image (you do so with the Pen tool in Photoshop). When the image is brought into a program like QuarkXPress or Illustrator, everything that falls outside of that border is treated as transparent. TIFF files also support clipping paths, but some page layout programs only recognize clipping paths embedded in EPS files.

The disadvantage of the EPS format is that the way it stores data is incredibly inefficient, and it produces files that take up far more disk space than other formats. Nevertheless, it is inarguably the most trouble-free way to prepare artwork for high-end printing.

CAUTION Windows users printing final work to a non–PostScript printer should steer clear of the EPS format, as it *causes* printing problems rather than eliminates them in this scenario. Use TIFF or JPEG instead.

To convert your artwork to an EPS, select Photoshop EPS from the Format menu in the Save As dialog box. Select from the following options in the resulting EPS Options dialog box (shown in Figure 7.7):

- **Preview.** EPS documents contain the PostScript information that gets sent to the printer, and the bitmapped preview, which is what you see on your computer screen. For a 256-color preview, select either TIFF 8-bit (if you're on a PC) or Macintosh 8-bit (if you're on a Mac) from the Preview pop-up menu. Mac users can also save a compressed 24-bit JPEG preview. The 1-bit preview options save black-and-white images and will result in smaller files. You can also opt to skip the preview image altogether.

- **Encoding.** Choose the Binary, ASCII, or JPEG option. Binary encoding (also known as *Huffman* encoding) produces a smaller file because of the way it writes the data. It uses an algorithm similar to that used by the LZW compression scheme described earlier for lossless data encoding. If you're producing a file for use with InDesign, QuarkXPress, or one of the other big layout programs, you can use this option.

  Some programs and PostScript printers don't recognize Binary encoding, in which case you must use the less-efficient ASCII format. ASCII stands for American Standard Code for Information Interchange — otherwise known as plain text. Use this method if you're printing from a Windows system, or if you're having printing problems, as ASCII encoding is more universally compatible.

  JPEG encoding is only compatible with Level 2 or later PostScript printers, but as you know, JPEG compression produces smaller files.

- **Include Halftone Screen.** Select this option if you specified a custom halftone screen for your image by clicking the Screens button in the Page Setup dialog box. Be careful using this option, though, as you can ruin your image by using it incorrectly. Read Chapter 25 to learn more about designing for print before using this option.

- **Include Transfer Function.** Clicking the Transfer button in the Page Setup dialog box allows you to specify brightness and contrast of a printed image, and you can save this information with your EPS by selecting this option. As with the Include Halftone Screen option, use this option with caution.

- **PostScript Color Management.** This option embeds a color profile to help the printer generate more accurate colors during the printing cycle. This option is only compatible with Level 2 and Level 3 PostScript printers, so if you're not outputting to one of these devices, don't select this option. Color profiles are covered in Chapter 23.

- **Include Vector Data.** If your image contains vector data such as editable text layers or vector shapes, select this option to preserve this information in the EPS file, making it available to be edited in a page layout or drawing program. If you leave this option de-selected, Photoshop rasterizes the vector information — that is, it converts it to flattened bitmap data. Reopening the EPS file in Photoshop also rasterizes the vector data.

- **Image Interpolation.** Selecting this option allows other applications like InDesign to interpolate the imported EPS file when resampling it to a different size. Scaling the EPS in InDesign generates new pixel information and results in a higher-quality file. If you leave this option deselected, scaling the imported EPS in InDesign has the same effect as increasing the size of an image by using nearest neighbor interpolation in the Image Size dialog box in Photoshop — that is, the size of the existing pixels is increased and no new pixels are generated. Learn more about interpolation in Chapter 5.

FIGURE 7.7

Select printing attributes and the type of image preview in the EPS Options dialog box.

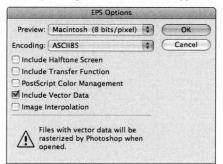

QuarkXPress DCS

DCS stands for Desktop Color Separations and was created by Quark as a variation of the EPS format. The DCS format supports saving CMYK images as color separations and is used for images that are destined for a PostScript printer. To convert an image to CMYK mode, choose Image ➪ Mode ➪ CMYK Color. DCS also supports grayscale images with spot color channels.

If your image only has the minimum four channels required to make up a CMYK image, then use DCS 1.0. However, if your image includes a Pantone color channel, you must use DCS 2.0.

Depending on whether you chose DCS 1.0 or 2.0, you'll see a different version of the DCS Options dialog box. The DCS 1.0 format (whose dialog box is shown in Figure 7.8) outputs four files, one each for the cyan, magenta, yellow, and black color channels in the image. These are the files that actually get printed. Additionally, you can create a fifth file — a color or grayscale composite file. This is the file that you would import into QuarkXPress.

FIGURE 7.8
_____

The DCS 1.0 Format dialog box

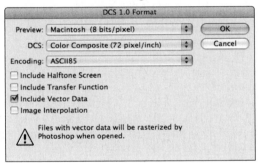

With DCS 2.0 (see Figure 7.9), you can choose to save the five files that version 1.0 saves, or you can combine them into a single file that includes all the data and that saves disk space. The single-file option is less widely compatible, however.

In either case, including the composite image (which is separate from the thumbnail image preview) definitely impacts your final file size. It is useful, however, because it enables you to print a preview of the document to a consumer-grade printer.

FIGURE 7.9

The DCS 2.0 Format dialog box

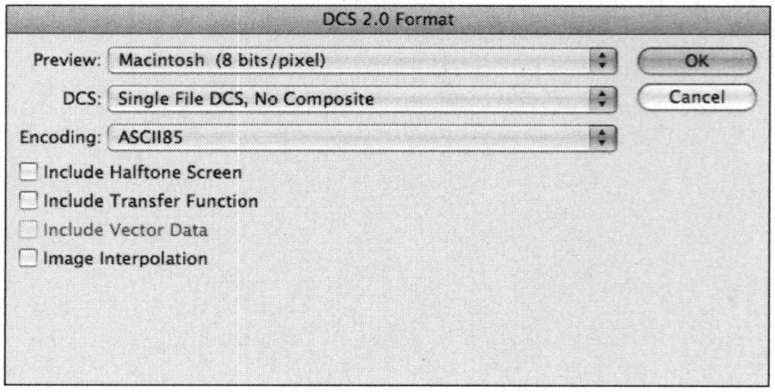

DCS 2.0 Format
Preview: Macintosh (8 bits/pixel)
DCS: Single File DCS, No Composite
Encoding: ASCII85
☐ Include Halftone Screen
☐ Include Transfer Function
☐ Include Vector Data
☐ Image Interpolation

OK
Cancel

Windows BMP

The native file format for Microsoft Paint (which is included with Windows), BMP is the standard image format on Windows and DOS-compatible computers. It supports RGB, Indexed, and gray-scale color modes. The BMP format can also support transparencies, either as a black-and-white file saved separately from the main image or as an alpha channel in a 32-bit BMP. Because the BMP format is so widely compatible, it is often used as the preferred format for the graphical elements that make up the user interface elements of software packages, and even operating systems, such as earlier versions of Windows.

To save a file as a Windows BMP, select it from the format pop-up menu in the BMP Options dialog box (shown in Figure 7.10). Specify either Windows or OS/2 format (you'll probably want to just go ahead and choose Windows), and a bit depth for the image. Usually your options for choosing a bit depth depend on the color mode you selected for the image while you were editing or creating it.

FIGURE 7.10

The BMP Options dialog box

BMP Options
File Format
⦿ Windows
○ OS/2
Depth
○ 1 Bit
○ 4 Bit
○ 8 Bit
○ 16 Bit
⦿ 24 Bit
○ 32 Bit
☐ Compress (RLE)
☐ Flip row order

OK
Cancel
Advanced Modes

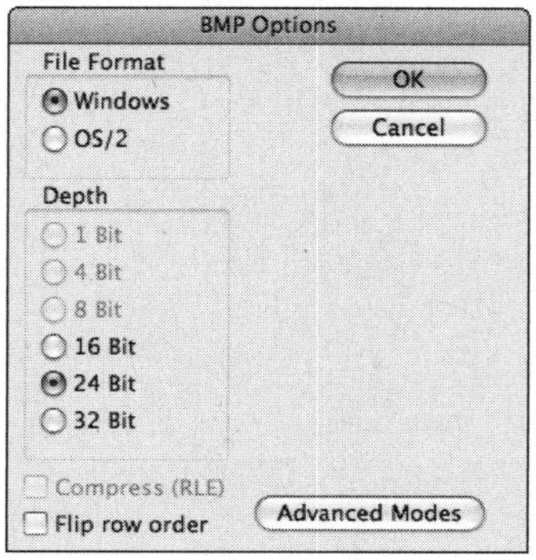

A full-color photographic image with millions of colors can be saved as 8-, 16-, or 32-bit. If your image has an alpha channel, you'll want to select 32-bit to preserve that transparency data. A grayscale image can only be saved as 4-bit, and an image that uses the Bitmap color space (that is, one with only black or white color information) can only be saved as 1-bit.

For 4- or 8-bit images, you have the option of compressing the image by using lossless RLE (Run Length Encoding) compression.

The remaining options in the BMP Options dialog box relate mostly to game developers or people working with DirectX multimedia programming.

NOTE The term "bitmap" can be somewhat confusing, as it can refer to either bitmapped, or raster, graphics, which are made up of a rectangular grid of pixels; the BMP file format; or the two-color Bitmap color space.

Cineon

Cineon is a format developed by Kodak and used for transferring computer-generated images to film. The Cineon Digital Film System was used in film production for compositing and manipulating images. Although the systems themselves were discontinued in 1997, the file format is still commonly used in the film industry.

Premiere Filmstrip

Adobe Premiere Pro is a Windows-based, video-editing program, and the Filmstrip format was developed as a means of swapping files with Photoshop. Being able to edit video files in Filmstrip format in Photoshop gives you the ability to *rotoscope*, or draw on individual frames of video.

The Filmstrip format saves a movie as a long, vertically stacked series of still frames. Each frame is separated from the next by a strip of gray. Time code (which helps identify what point in the video the current frame appears at) and the current frame number are also indicated on each frame. Once you have your video saved as a Filmstrip file, you can paint, draw, or otherwise mess around with each frame of video, save it, and re-import it in Premiere for continued video production.

Be aware that if you change the dimensions of the file in any way, you won't be able to save it back to the Filmstrip format. Similarly, using Photoshop, you can only save files to the Filmstrip format if they were originally exported as Filmstrip files from Premiere.

CompuServe GIF

CompuServe, one of the first mainstream online services, introduced the Graphics Interchange Format, or GIF, in 1987. It is one of the most commonly used formats on the Web because of its ability to compress graphical data to very small file sizes by using lossless LZW compression, and because of its support of animation. The GIF format also offers built-in support for transparencies.

One of the limitations of the format is its 256-color palette (also referred to as Indexed color mode), which makes it unsuitable for accurate display of full-color photographic images. The GIF format is best used for simple logos, line drawings, or images with minimal colors.

The GIF format will be covered in greater depth in Chapter 24.

Paintbrush PCX

The PCX format is the native file format of PC Paintbrush — the oldest paint program for DOS-based systems. PC Paintbrush later evolved into MS Paintbrush as a result of an agreement to distribute the paint program with every copy of Windows sold, which brought the PCX format into widespread use. The once-popular format has since been replaced by GIF, JPEG, and PNG because of their greater flexibility and more efficient data-compression abilities.

Adobe's Paperless PDF

PDF, or Portable Document Format, is an extension of the PostScript language. Its purpose is to accurately display documents that have been designed for print production on computer screens without having to worry about fonts, color separations, or other print issues.

PDF is an open standard, and Adobe distributes its free Acrobat Reader software on Mac, Windows, and Unix platforms, which means anyone with a computer can see your PDF as it was originally designed. Mac users also benefit from the extensive built-in support that OS X has for viewing and creating PDF files. For instance, the Print dialog box in most applications has an option to save a PDF with a single click, and just about any application designed for the Mac can use embedded PDF files.

PDF files are usually either multi-page, multi-image documents, or they contain only a single image. Using the Save As dialog box in Photoshop, you can only save single-image PDF files. To save multi-page PDF documents, you must use the PDF feature available in Adobe Bridge's Output workspace. Read more about this feature in Chapter 3.

As is the case with EPS files, PDF files are always rasterized (that is, converted to bitmap data) when opened in Photoshop. If the PDF you're opening has multiple pages, you simply pick the page you want to open in Photoshop and then specify the dimensions, resolution, and color space for the resulting file. The white-page background in the PDF is treated as a transparency in the rasterized Photoshop file, as demonstrated in Figure 7.11.

Photoshop PDF files offer broad support for a range of attributes including layers, spot colors, transparency, duotones, and more. This makes them a handy option for distributing layouts for approval while retaining the maximum amount of editability in the file.

Selecting Photoshop PDF from the Format pop-up menu in the Save As dialog box produces the Save Adobe PDF dialog box, shown in Figure 7.12. Use the options on the left to specify settings for General, Compression, Output, Security, and Summary.

You can also use the presets at the top of the dialog box to select the most appropriate scenario for the PDF you're saving — from high-quality print output to a heavily compressed file that's suitable for being e-mailed or viewed on a computer screen.

NOTE Only PostScript level 2 or higher printers can use JPEG encoding. If you specify JPEG compression for your file, you must print to a Level 2 or higher PostScript printer to avoid postscript language errors.

FIGURE 7.11

The PDF on the left is opened in Photoshop, resulting in the rasterized image on the right. Note the transparent areas where the white page showed through in the original PDF file.

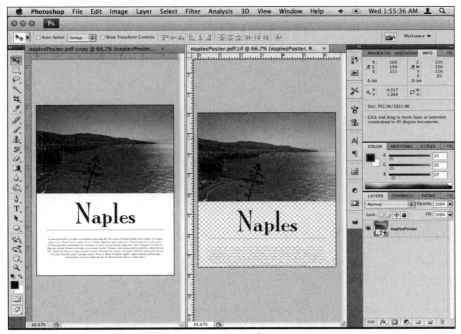

Apple's PICT

PICT (Macintosh Picture) is a Mac-only format that dates back to the pre-Mac OS X days. It was the native graphics format of QuickDraw, the core graphics system of early Mac computers, and offered a high degree of interoperability among Mac applications. The complexity of QuickDraw, and of the PICT format itself (which offers support for both vector and raster images, as well as alpha channel), prevented it from being supported on other platforms.

Apple has since adopted the PDF and PNG formats as their native graphics formats, so the only reason to use PICT is if you're saving something that you intend to use on an ancient Mac that is perhaps still hanging around for sentimental reasons.

If you are a Windows user and a PICT file comes across your desk for some reason, you can open it with Photoshop as long as you have QuickTime installed on your machine, as PICT uses QuickTime for compression.

FIGURE 7.12

The Save Adobe PDF dialog box

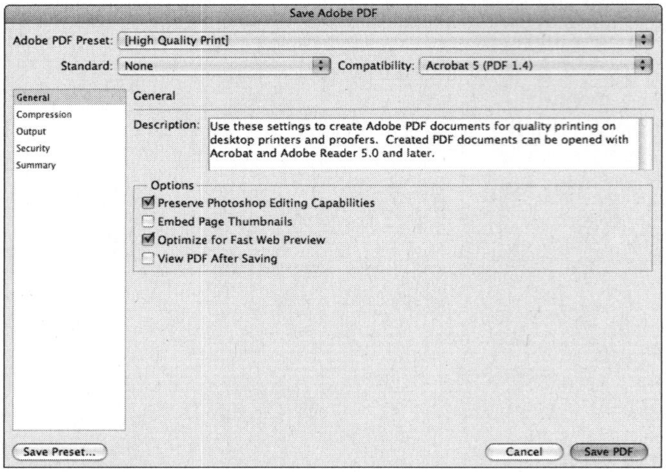

PICT Resource

The resource fork is a construct of the Mac file system. Files are split into two areas: data forks, where for example, a word-processing document might save all its text information; and resource forks, where graphics, icons, and file format information are stored. This, by the way, is one of the reasons files on a Mac don't necessarily need a file extension to open or display correctly (but it's still a good habit to get into, my Mac-using brethren).

In any case, PICT Resource files are mainly found in Mac OS 9 startup screens, and unless you're designing one, you probably won't be saving to this format.

Pixar

This is the format created by Pixar, the wildly successful computer animation studio responsible for many of the most memorable computer-generated feature films produced in recent years. Pixar uses highly customized proprietary 3-D workstations, and the Pixar format allows you to open images generated on these machines or output files for integration into a Pixar 3-D project.

PNG

PNG (pronounced *ping*) stands for Portable Network Graphic. This lossless format allows you to compress full-color photographic images in all their 16-million-color glory for use on the Web. In addition, PNG offers support for transparency through the use of alpha channels. It is becoming increasingly popular, and most of the modern Web browsers now offer support for the format.

TrueVision's TGA

Targa or TGA files were designed for use with Truevision video systems, which allow users to capture live video and overlay it with animation and computer graphics. The format originally became popular because it was one of the earliest to support 24-bit images.

WBMP

Wireless BMP, or WBMP, is the format used for those two-color images used on mobile devices like cell phones and personal digital assistants. When I say two-color, I really mean two colors — WBMP is a 1-bit format, which means it is only capable of displaying either white or black pixels.

NOTE You can also save WBMP files by using the Save for Web & Devices dialog box.

Photoshop Raw

This last file format is rarely used but deserves to be discussed, if only because of its great flexibility. When all other file format options have been exhausted, this one might be able to help you out if you need to open a stubborn file that isn't otherwise recognized, or if you need to save a file in a format for use on a device that doesn't understand the mainstream formats.

Not to be confused with RAW files saved by high-end digital cameras (see Chapter 4), Photoshop Raw is an uncompressed binary file format used for transferring files to systems that aren't capable of opening files saved in the more commonly-used formats. Photoshop can also import RAW files generated by such devices or applications.

Raw files are stripped-down, uncompressed streams of data that contain only image information and no header data, which means they have no information about color space, color palette, or pixel ordering.

Opening Raw documents

The Raw file can be a last-resort option for opening a mystery file whose origins you are unsure of, and that refuses to open, no matter how desperately you plead, coax, and cajole. Maybe you tried opening it as a TIFF, JPEG, or some other mainstream format, and Photoshop balked at it. This is the time to give the Raw format a shot. Choose File ⇨ Open As/File ⇨ Open, and make sure All Readable Documents is selected in the Enable pop-up menu.

In the resulting Photoshop Raw Options dialog box (see Figure 7.13), enter as much information as you can.

- **Width and Height.** If you know the pixel dimensions of the image, enter them here. You can click the Swap button to switch the width and height values. The maximum value you can enter is 30,000.

- **Count.** If you know the color mode of the image or how many channels it has, enter that number here. For a grayscale image, enter **1**; for RGB, enter **3**; for CMYK, enter **4**.

- **Interleaved.** This option specifies the order in which color information is stored for each pixel of data. By default, RGB images store data in the Interleaved format.

- **Bit Depth.** In most cases, images contain 8 bits per channel, so try that first.

- **Byte Order.** Choose the platform you think the image might have originated on. Most current Apple computers contain Intel chips, so this option is becoming increasingly meaningless.

- **Header.** This specifies how many bytes of information appear before the actual image data in the Raw file. The default value is zero.

- **Guess.** If you know the width and height values but not the size of the header, or vice versa, you can click the Guess button to get Photoshop to take a crack at figuring it out. It's worth a shot.

FIGURE 7.13

The Photoshop Raw Options dialog box. Enter as much information as you know and let Photoshop do its thing.

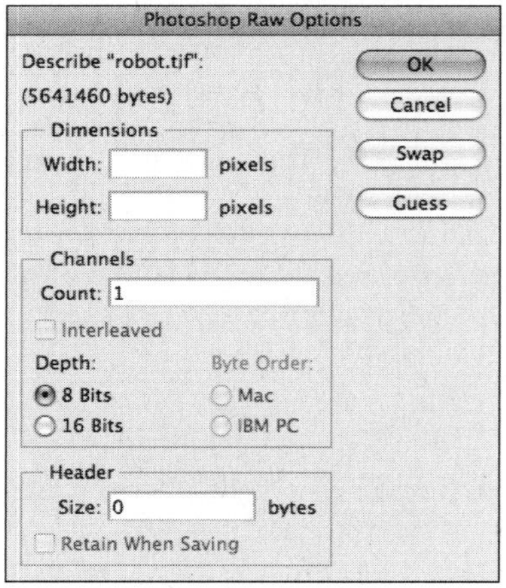

Saving Raw documents

If you need to export a file to a device or application that is incapable of reading any of the mainstream formats, you can save it as a stripped-down Raw file.

While they don't offer support for layers, Photoshop Raw files can be of any pixel dimension and can support RGB, CMYK, or grayscale color with alpha channels. They can also support lab color or multichannel images without alpha channels.

Choose File ➪ Save As, and then select Photoshop Raw from the Format pop-up menu to produce the Photoshop Raw Options dialog box, shown in Figure 7.14.

FIGURE 7.14

Use the options shown in this dialog box when saving in the Photoshop Raw file format.

Photoshop Raw Options

File Type: PRAW   OK

File Creator: 8BIM   Cancel

Header: 0

Save Channels In:
⦿ Interleaved Order
◯ Non-interleaved Order

The Photoshop Raw file format does not fully encode the image mode and size, among other things. The image may not be fully restored when you re-open the file.

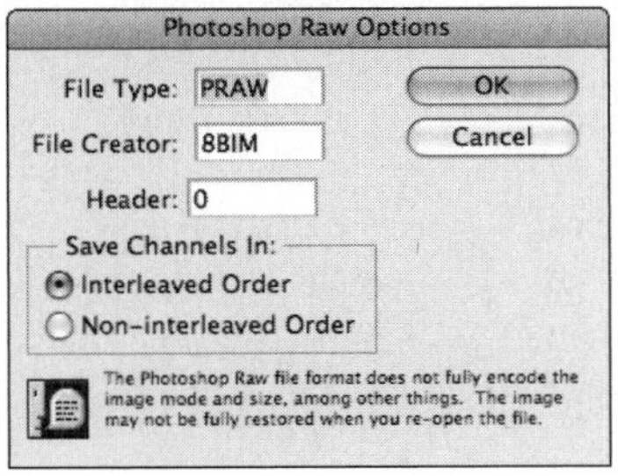

(If you're using a Mac, enter the file type and creator id. These values don't apply to the Windows platform. The file type is a four-letter code such as PICT or TIFF, and the creator id of 8BIM, which is Photoshop's code, is usually filled in by default.)

Next, you can specify a header size, but it's probably best to leave it at the default value of zero. Finally, specify the order of the color information — interleaved or not (interleaved is the default).

Save from Camera Raw

So far, we've covered saving files while editing directly in Photoshop. Saving files while editing RAW (or even JPEG or TIFF) files by using the Camera Raw plug-in is slightly different. Camera Raw is a robust enough tool that I've dedicated a whole chapter to it (wait, you mean you haven't read Chapter 4 yet?), but it's worth briefly going over the Camera Raw Save options here.

First, you should know that you cannot save a RAW file — only the camera can generate one. Because of this, whatever edits you make while working in Camera Raw are never actually saved back to the original RAW files. Instead, they're saved as metadata in the Camera Raw cache, or in a format called XMP files, alongside the original RAW files. When you've finished editing these files in Camera Raw and want to distribute them, along with the edits you just made, in another more widely compatible file format, you can use the Save Image command in Camera Raw to do so.

> **TIP** If you're broken-hearted to learn that you can't save back to the original RAW format, don't fret — you can always save your edits in the DNG, or Digital Negative, format, which is as close to RAW as you can get. For more coverage of the DNG format, refer to Chapter 4.

Clicking the Save Image button in Camera Raw presents you with a Save Options dialog box (see Figure 7.15) that looks nothing like Photoshop's Save As dialog box. You can still perform many of the same operations, though, such as navigate your hard drive and select a destination for your new file, enter a filename, and select a file format.

One of the major differences in this dialog box is that there are more options for specifying file-names for your saved images, because Camera Raw allows you to edit a batch or series of images simultaneously, so you can save them with sequential filenames. You can, for example, use the available drop-down lists to enter a descriptive filename and automatically insert the date the image was taken, followed by a sequential serial number, and finally the three-digit file extension. The example filename updates dynamically to show the results of your selections.

Also note that you're restricted to only four file formats in the Camera Raw Save Options dialog box: DNG (Digital Negative), JPEG, TIFF, and native Photoshop files. These are the formats that are most commonly used for photography, but remember that once you've saved an image in one of these formats, you can always open it back up in Photoshop and convert it to a different format by using the Save As command.

FIGURE 7.15

Camera Raw's Save Options dialog box is quite different from Photoshop's Save As dialog box.

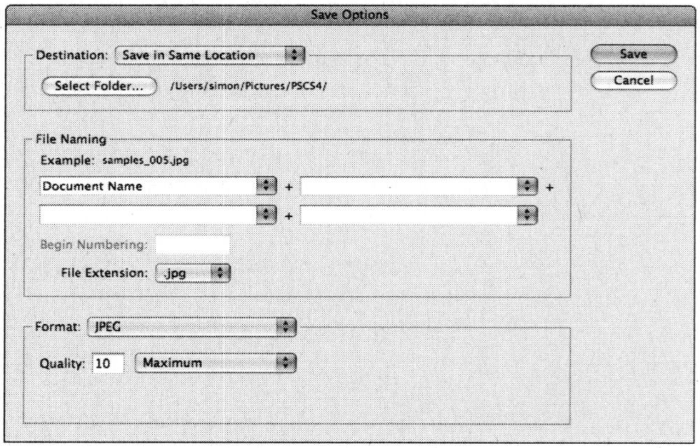

Summary

In this chapter, you learned about the ins and outs of the Save command and the different options available for saving files to disk. You also got an overview of the many file formats that Photoshop can open or save to. Finally, you got a quick review of the options for saving files from the Camera Raw plug-in.

Part III

Layers, Selections, Channels, and Curves

Chapter 8

Layers, Layer Masks, Blending Modes, and Smart Objects

Since version 2.0, Photoshop has had layers, making things much more interesting!

The flexibility you can have by using layers makes it possible for you to separate and work independently on different parts of an image (even though it still appears to be one whole image), which is very convenient. And layers are one of the main features that allow you to perform nondestructive editing to images.

Nondestructive editing means making changes to your images that you can easily undo at any time if you change your mind. And who doesn't want to be able to change his mind at one time or another?

Working with Layers

As I've mentioned, you can put objects in your Photoshop document on separate layers and, therefore, work on the objects separately. This is a huge advantage because it can help you avoid unintentionally altering other objects while you are working on the one object. If your objects start out as separate images, you can easily bring them into the document on separate layers and avoid making unnecessary selections, which you would have to do if the objects started out all jumbled together on the same layer.

Note that when layers contain transparent areas, you can see the objects on underlying layers through the transparent areas. This makes it appear as though there is only one image on one layer if you are looking at the image window, but if you look in the Layers palette, you can see small versions of the objects on the separate layers, which are the *layer thumbnails*. Figure 8.1 shows two layer thumbnails on the Layers palette.

FIGURE 8.1

Two layer thumbnails on the Layers palette, which show that there are two objects on separate layers in the Photoshop document

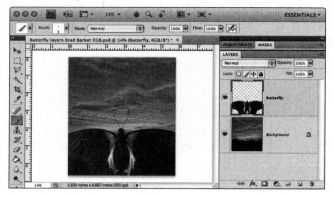

Layers also make it possible for you to use nondestructive features like adjustment layers, which can be used to lighten, darken, saturate, and desaturate and image, and more. To change an adjustment, you just double-click the adjustment layer and change its settings. Simple.

Layer masks are another huge advantage you can have when working with layers. You can use layer masks to totally or partially hide parts of an object on a layer, and you can easily show any part of the object again at any time. Layer masks make your life a lot better, and they also clean your house and wash your car (that is, they save you a whole lot of time, during which you can do other fun things).

A *Blending mode* can be applied to a layer to affect how the pixels on the layer interact, or blend, with pixels on underlying layers. For example, if you apply the Multiply Blending mode to a layer, it gives the effect of the image pixels on that layer being printed on transparency paper — the pixels look darker when combined, or multiplied, with pixels on layers underneath — but also allows you to see some of the pixels on underlying layers. Blending modes can bring out your inner artist or cater to your outer photo-retouch expert. Reducing the opacity of a layer can also be used to make a layer partially transparent, but with a different effect.

Layer styles can be used to add one or more effects to layer content, such as a drop shadow, bevel, or glow. *Smart Filters* are filters, such as the Colored Pencil artistic filter, that can be added as nondestructive effects to layers.

A *Smart Object* is another useful feature that is composed of layers. When multiple layers are converted to a Smart Object, you can resize the objects more flexibly — you can scale down the objects and later return them to their original size without losing resolution (or detail) in the objects. When scaled down, Photoshop remembers the original resolution and detail of the images that are part of the Smart Object — hence, "smart." And, when they contain certain kinds of content, Smart Objects can sometimes even do magic tricks with the help of *Stack Modes*.

Stack Modes applied to some Smart Objects can be used to miraculously delete unwanted objects or subjects in a photo in seconds, without so much as a passing thought about the Clone tool.

216

Stack Modes can also virtually eliminate undesirable image noise in certain types of Smart Objects, and it can compare images and highlight their differences, even if the differences are too subtle for the eye to detect.

The very best thing about all these features is that none of them permanently alters an image. If you save the Photoshop file as a layered PSD file, you can change any of these features even after you save, close, and open the image again. This can come in very handy in the (very unlikely) event that a client doesn't like some changes you've made to an image.

Figure 8.2 shows a file that is made up of layers, and its layers as they appear on the Layers palette.

FIGURE 8.2

A file that has parts of its image on separate layers, and its layers as they appear on the Layers palette

Getting images and image parts onto separate layers

You can put images onto separate layers by dragging them from one document into another, by selecting multiple thumbnails in Adobe Bridge and loading those images as separate layers in a new file, by copying and pasting pixels from one image into another or from one layer to another, or by using the Place command to place a file into a Photoshop document.

Following are steps to put an image onto a separate layer by dragging it from one document into another:

1. **Make sure that both the image you want and the destination image are open and you can see both images in their image windows.** (In the Application Bar, select Arrange Documents then Tile All in Grid, which shows all open image windows.)

2. **Drag the image you want from its window into the destination image's window with the Move tool.** If the image you want has multiple layers, make sure you activate the layer that has the desired content. You can also drag layer groups. When you release the mouse button, the image is automatically placed on its own separate layer in the destination document. Figure 8.3 shows an image being dragged from one document to another.

FIGURE 8.3

An image is dragged from one document into another with the Move tool, which automatically puts the dragged image on its own layer.

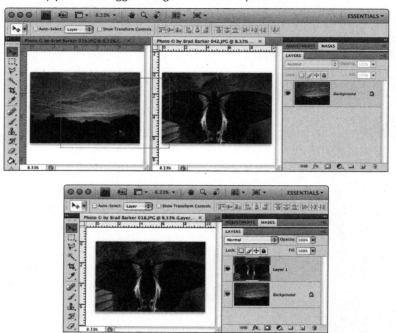

Following are steps to get multiple images onto separate layers in a new Photoshop document by using a command in Adobe Bridge:

1. **In Adobe Bridge, select the thumbnails of multiple image files you want to be on separate layers in one Photoshop document.**

2. **From the Adobe Bridge menu, choose Tools ➪ Photoshop ➪ Load Files into Photoshop Layers.** Figure 8.4 shows this menu, and Figure 8.5 shows the resulting Photoshop file and its Layers palette.

One advantage to this method is that Photoshop automatically names each layer with its former file name. If the file names were meaningful, this could make the layer file names in the new file a valuable reference.

NEW FEATURE You can use Adobe Bridge to load multiple images onto their own layers in a new Photoshop document by selecting the image thumbnails and choosing Tools ➪ Photoshop ➪ Load Files into Photoshop Layers.

FIGURE 8.4

Adobe Bridge's Load Files into Photoshop Layers menu

FIGURE 8.5

A document that was created by using Bridge's Load Files into Photoshop Layers menu option

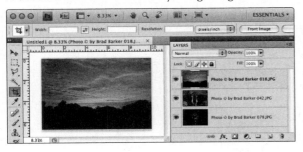

Following are steps to get an image onto a separate layer in a Photoshop document by copying and pasting:

1. **In a different Photoshop file or another application's file, or on a layer in the same Photoshop file, select part or all of an image and choose Edit ⇨ Copy, or press Ctrl+C (⌘+C on a Mac).**

2. **In the destination Photoshop document, choose Edit ⇨ Paste, or press Ctrl+V/⌘+V.** Paste automatically puts the copied pixels on their own new layer and puts the new layer just above the currently active layer. Figure 8.6 shows an image being copied and pasted into a Photoshop document.

FIGURE 8.6

An image being copied and pasted into a Photoshop document

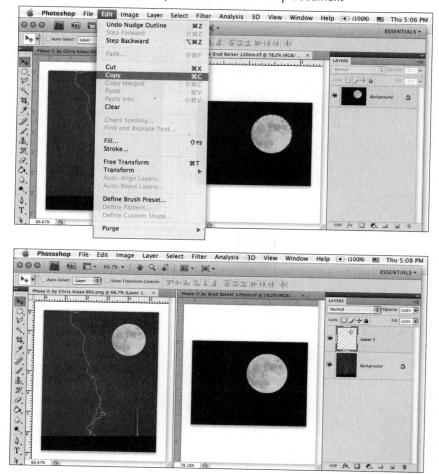

Following are steps to get an image onto a separate layer in a Photoshop document by using the Place command:

1. Choose File ⇨ Place.

2. Select the document you want to place and click the Place button.

3. This places the object as a Smart Object in the Photoshop document, as shown in Figure 8.7.

FIGURE 8.7

An image that has been placed in a Photoshop document with the Place command

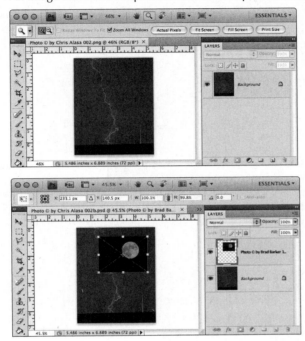

If you choose to at this point, you can transform the object while its bounding box is still active. Drag outside of the bounding box to rotate the image, hold the Shift key while dragging a corner handle to resize the image (release the mouse button first, then the key), and drag in the box to move the object, or you can choose one of the Edit ➪ Transform options to transform the object.

You can also press Enter or Return and do any of the above at a later time. Just select the layer the object is on and choose Edit ➪ Free Transform (or one of the other Transform options).

Note that if you enlarge the placed Smart Object significantly greater than its original size, you do risk lowering its quality, unless the object only contains vector information (in which case it is resolution-independent).

4. **When you're finished, press Enter or Return.**

CROSS-REF For more information about the Paste and Place commands, see Chapter 5.

Resizing images on layers

You will probably need to resize objects once you get them onto their separate layers. The handy thing about this is that if your object is on a layer by itself, you don't have to make a selection before you resize it. If you activate a layer and use a Transform command, it applies to all the pixels on the layer (but ignores transparent areas).

The images on upper layers may hide images on lower layers. To temporarily hide the layers you aren't working on, click the eye symbol next to the layer thumbnails in the Layers palette. (Click the eye symbol again to show the eye symbol and the layer contents.)

Following are ways you can transform objects that are on their own layers (first, click the layer in the Layers palette to activate the layer).

- **Edit ➪ Free Transform.** This puts a Transform bounding box around the object. To shrink or enlarge the object, hold down the Shift key while dragging a corner handle (not a side handle) of the bounding box. Release the mouse button first, then the Shift key. The Shift+click+corner handles combination maintains the object's proportions while you resize it. Figure 8.8 shows the Free Transform bounding box around an object that is to be resized.

FIGURE 8.8

An object that is ready to be resized with the Free Transform bounding box

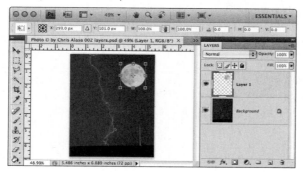

If the bounding box handles are outside the image window because the object is larger than the size of the image, you can zoom out with the Navigator palette to bring the handles into view or resize the object by entering lower width and height percentages in the Options Bar until you can see corner handles. If you use the Options Bar method, click the link symbol in between the width and height to maintain the object's proportions while you resize it.

To rotate the object, position the cursor just outside the bounding box until you see curvy arrows, then drag with the mouse. If you want to change the axis around which the object rotates, move the center bullet point (the axis) to a different position inside or outside the bounding box.

If you want to move the object while the bounding box is still active, drag inside the bounding box, but not on its center point bullet, with the mouse. The center point bullet is just the axis around which the image rotates.

If you don't want to accept the changes you made with the bounding box, press ESC. If you do want to allow the changes you made with the bounding box, press Enter or Return.

■ **Edit ➪ Transform ➪ Skew.** You can drag the side handles of a Skew Transform bounding box to slant an image. If you don't want to accept the changes you made with the bounding box, press ESC. If you do want to allow the changes you made with the bounding box, press Enter or Return. Figure 8.9 shows an object being skewed.

FIGURE 8.9

The Skew Transform bounding box around an object that is being skewed

■ **Edit ➪ Transform ➪ Distort.** You can drag a corner handle of a Distort Transform bounding box to stretch an image. If you don't want to accept the changes you made with the bounding box, press ESC. If you do want to allow the changes you made with the bounding box, press Enter or Return. Figure 8.10 shows an object being distorted.

FIGURE 8.10

A Distort Transform bounding box around an object that is being distorted

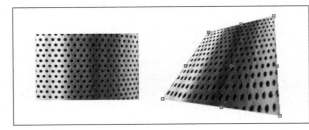

■ **Edit ➪ Transform ➪ Perspective.** You can drag a corner handle of a Perspective Transform bounding box to apply perspective to an image. If you don't want to accept the changes you made with the bounding box, press ESC. If you do want to allow the

changes you made with the bounding box, press Enter or Return. Figure 8.11 shows an object with a changed perspective.

- **Edit ⇨ Transform ⇨ Warp.** You can use the Warp Transform bounding box to push, pull, and stretch the shape of images, shapes, or paths by dragging on the Warp Transform grid lines, handles (black dots), or control points (hollow squares). If you want to rotate or resize the warp shape, you can temporarily switch to a Free Transform bounding box by clicking the Switch-between-free-transform-and-warp-modes button in the Options Bar.

FIGURE 8.11

A Perspective Transform bounding box around an object that is having its perspective transformed

To warp multiple layers at one time, do the following: Before choosing the Warp command, Shift-click or Ctrl-click/⌘-click on the layers in the Layers palette to activate them, and then choose Convert to Smart Object from the Layers palette menu. Figure 8.12 shows several layers that have been grouped into a Smart Object being warped with a custom-warp bounding box.

FIGURE 8.12

Several layers that have been grouped into a Smart Object being warped with a custom-warp bounding box

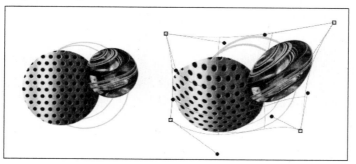

After you activate the Warp Transform bounding box, you can alternatively apply a warp shape from the Warp drop-down list in the Options Bar ("Custom" is active, by default). Warp shapes include Arc, Wave, Fisheye, and more. The bend, horizontal and vertical distortions and the orientation can be changed by using the Options in the Options Bar. Dragging the control point on the Warp Transform bounding box also changes the bend (control point is only available if there is no horizontal or vertical distortion).

If you want to rotate or resize the warp shape, you can temporarily switch to a Free Transform bounding box by clicking the Switch-between-free-transform-and-warp-modes button on the right-hand side of the Options Bar.

Figure 8.13 shows an object being warped with a warp shape, chosen from the Warp menu in the Options Bar.

FIGURE 8.13

The Options Bar and an active Wave warp-shape bounding box and object

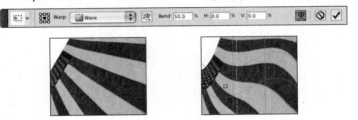

If you don't want to accept the changes you made with the bounding box, press ESC. If you do want to allow the changes you made with the bounding box, press Enter or Return.

 When you warp a bitmap image (rather than a vector image), the image gets slightly less sharp each time you warp it. So, do as many warp adjustments in one warp session as possible instead of doing several warp adjustments in several sessions.

■ **Edit ⇨ Transform ⇨ Rotate or Edit ⇨ Transform ⇨ Flip.** You can do common rotations or flip layer contents horizontally or vertically with this menu.

The Layers palette

The main area in Photoshop where you can work with layers is the Layers palette, shown in Figure 8.14.

FIGURE 8.14

The Layers palette

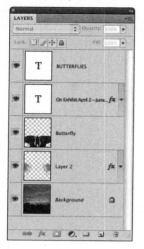

CROSS-REF   The Filter ➪ Liquify command can be used to warp images and to apply more fluid warps than the Warp command (think Salvador Dali). See Chapter 21 for more information about Liquify. You can also explore the Vanishing Point filter, discussed in Chapter 21, for information about warping images so that they conform to a particular perspective that has been defined for an object (for example, placing a logo graphic so that it spans two sides of a box and making it conform to the box's perspective). See the color insert in this book for a comparison of various methods you can use to warp objects.

In the Layers palette, you can see small versions of the layers and their content called *layer thumbnails*. You can click on a layer thumbnail to activate the layer. Shift+click and Ctrl+click/⌘+click multiple layer thumbnails to activate multiple layers, which you might want to do if you want to move them together or put them into a layer group.

You can drag layers up and down on the Layers palette to reorder layers. Figure 8.15 shows the Layers palette with an active layer, named "Layer 2," and Figure 8.16 shows how layers can be reordered by using the Layers palette.

Immediately to the left of the layer thumbnails are eye symbols. The eye symbol means the layer is visible. To temporarily hide a layer, click on the eye symbol next to the layer. To show the layer, click on the eye symbol box again.

At the top left of the Layers palette is the Blending Mode menu (the default Blending mode is Normal, which doesn't do anything special to the image). A Blending mode can be applied to a layer to affect how the pixels on the layer interact, or blend, with pixels on underlying layers.

On the top right of the Layers palette are the Opacity menu, where you can set the opacity for the active layer, and the Fill Opacity menu, which you can use if you want to set the opacity for everything on the active layer except its layer effects, such as drop shadow and glow. (Reducing the opacity in the Opacity menu affects the layer effects as well as other layer content.)

FIGURE 8.15

The Layers palette with an active layer (named "Layer 2")

FIGURE 8.16

Drag layer thumbnails to reorder layers in the Layers palette

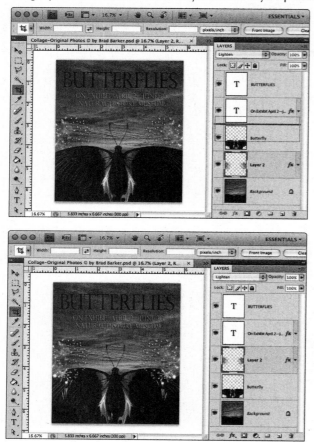

Under the Blending Mode menu is the Lock menu (see Figure 8.17). You can use this menu to protect aspects of the layer so they can't be changed. Click on a layer, then click a lock button to lock the following (listed in the order in which they appear in the menu): transparency, pixels, position of the objects on the active layer, or lock all items on the active layer. The buttons act as toggles, so to unlock the items, click the button again.

At the bottom of the Layers palette is the Background layer, which is automatically locked. To unlock the Background layer so that you can make changes or apply effects to it, you must change it to a regular layer. Double-click the Background layer in the Layers palette, then click OK to change it to a regular, unlocked layer.

FIGURE 8.17

Use the Lock menu buttons in the Layers palette to lock various items on layers so that they can't be changed.

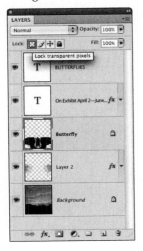

Once you start editing a layer that was formerly a Background layer, you may end up with some transparent areas (which appear as gray and white squares if there are no layers underneath with colored pixels showing through the transparent areas). In this case and in some other situations, you may want to add a layer at the bottom of the Layers palette that contains only white so that you can see white in any transparent areas instead of gray and white squares.

To add a white layer, click the Create a new layer button to the left of the Layers palette's trash can, and click OK. Then choose Edit ➪ Fill, Use: White, and click OK. Drag the white layer to the bottom or other desired position in the Layers palette.

To the right of the layer thumbnails are the layer names. Double-click a layer name and type a new name to rename a layer. Giving layers meaningful names is a good practice, especially when you have many layers or if it's hard to see the content of the layers in the layer thumbnails.

At the bottom of the Layers palette are buttons for the following (from left to right), shown in Figure 8.18.

FIGURE 8.18

The buttons at the bottom of the Layers palette

- **Link layers button (link symbol).** Shift+click or Ctrl+click/⌘+click multiple layer thumbnails to select multiple layers you want to link. When layers are linked, they resize together and move together. To unlink a layer, activate it and click the link button again. Linked layers show a link symbol to the right of the layer name in the Layers palette.

- **Layer style button (*fx* symbol).** Click on a layer to activate it, then click the layer style button and select a layer effect you want to add to the layer, such as drop shadow. This activates the Layer Style dialog box, in which you can add multiple layer effects that become part of the layer style for the active layer.

- **Layer mask button (rectangle with white circle).** Click on a layer to activate it, then click the layer mask button to add a layer mask. You can add black to the mask to hide corresponding parts of the layer and make them transparent, add gray to partially hide corresponding parts of the layer and make them partially transparent, or add white to make visible corresponding parts of the layer. You can also add a layer mask and manipulate it conveniently with the Masks palette, new to CS4.

- **Adjustment layer button (half-black, half-white circle).** Click on a layer to activate it, then click the adjustment layer button and select an adjustment, such as Curves. You can also add an adjustment layer and manipulate it conveniently with the Adjustments palette, new to CS4.

- **Create a new group button (folder symbol).** Click the create a new group button, then you can drag layer thumbnails into the layer group. You can name a layer group by double-clicking its name and typing a new one.

- **New layer button (square with corner turned up).** Click this button if you want to add a new blank layer.

- **Delete layer button (trashcan symbol).** Click this button or drag a layer on top of the button to delete a layer, or press Delete to delete an active layer or layers.

NEW FEATURE Press Delete to delete an active layer or layers. (About time, huh?)

Layers palette menu

At the top right of the Layers palette is the Layers palette menu button (lines with an arrow). The following Layers palette menu commands are commonly used:

- **Duplicate Layer.** Duplicates the active layer. You can choose a destination for the duplicate layer, including the same image, another open image, or a new image. You can also press Ctrl+J/⌘+J to duplicate an active layer.

TIP Duplicate an active layer and make it into a new document by choosing the Duplicate command in the Layers palette menu or the Layer menu. Choose File ⇨ Scripts ⇨ Export Layers to Files to open multiple layers as new Photoshop files.

- **New Group from Layers.** Creates a new layer group and puts any active layers inside it.

- **Convert to Smart Object.** Converts multiple active layers to a Smart Object. Double-clicking a Smart Object layer allows you to open the Smart Object as a separate file and edit the contents of the Smart Object (save and close when finished, and the Smart Object is updated in the original file).

- **Merge Down and Merge Visible.** Use these commands to combine multiple layers into one layer. You can also merge the active layer with the layer below it by pressing Ctrl+E/⌘+E.

> **TIP** Place a copy of a merged version of all visible layers onto a new layer by pressing **Shift+Ctrl+Alt+E/Shift+⌘+Option+E. This is referred to as** *stamping* **layers.**

- **Flatten Image.** Use this command to combine all the layers into one layer. This is recommended for final versions of files to make the final file size smaller, and is required in order to make them appear as intended in some other applications.

- **Close and Close Tab Group.** This command gives you the option to close the Layers palette or its palette group. You can also close an individual palette by dragging the palette tab out of its group then clicking the palette's close button.

> **TIP** Save the file with its layers in PSD format before you flatten a file so you can edit the layers later, if necessary.

Layer menu

There is also a Menu Bar Layer menu that contains many of the same commands as the Layers palette menu. Some Layers menu commands that aren't in the Layers palette menu are as follows:

- **Smart Filter.** Use this command to add nondestructive filters to layers. First click on the layer and choose Filter ➪ Convert for Smart Filters. Figure 8.19 shows the Smart Filter dialog box and a layer that has a Smart Filter. (For more information about filters, see Chapter 20.)

FIGURE 8.19

The Smart Filter dialog box and a layer that has a Smart Filter

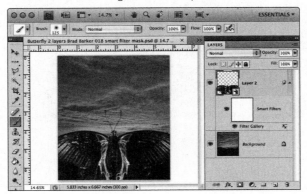

■ **Type.** This command gives you options for changing type layers, such as changing type layers into paths or shapes, setting the anti-alias method (how the edges of the type look), and updating fonts.

■ **Rasterize.** This command causes any vector information on the active layer, such as type or shapes, to be changed to bitmap, or pixel-based, information. You might want to do this when you want to add some effect or filter that doesn't work as expected on a vector object. However, you may want to first try the effect after converting the layer to a smart object (Layers palette menu ⇨ Convert to Smart Object). Often you can apply an effect or filter to a Smart Object successfully and retain the option to edit the resolution-independent vector object.

■ **New Layer-Based Slice.** This command causes slices to be made, based on where the edges of pixels are on each active layer. Slices are used in preparing images for display on the Web (see Chapter 24 for more information).

■ **Matting.** When you copy and paste a selection, it sometimes includes unwanted colors of fringe pixels around its edges. If so, you can choose Defringe to expand the selection's inner pixel colors onto the unwanted edge pixel colors. You can choose how many pixels are involved in the Defringe command. The Remove Black Matte or Remove White Matte is useful if the fringe pixels are black or white. Figure 8.20 shows the before and after shots of an image that has had its white border removed with Matting.

NOTE You can also try the Blend If sliders in the Blending Options section of the dialog box to remove fringe pixels.

FIGURE 8.20

The before and after shots of an image that has had what was left of its white background removed with the Layer ⇨ Matting command.

Layer Masks

You can use layer masks to hide or show parts of a layer. Layer masks are very flexible because they make it possible to show some or all of the hidden parts of your object again at any time you choose.

To add a layer mask to a layer, click on a layer to activate it, then do one of the following:

- Click the Add layer mask button at the bottom of the Layers palette
- Click one of the Add Mask buttons in CS4's fancy new Masks palette

  After either of the above options, you can then add black to the mask to hide corresponding parts of the layer (make them transparent), add gray to partially hide corresponding parts of the layer (make them partially transparent), or add white to make the corresponding parts of the layer visible again.

- Make a selection of the area you want to remain visible on the layer, then click the Add layer mask button at the bottom of the Layers palette. This automatically puts black on the layer mask that hides everything on the layer that was not selected.

> **NOTE** You must change a background layer to a regular layer to add a layer mask to it (double-click the Background layer in the Layers palette, then click OK).

The top image in Figure 8.21 shows a layer mask that is filled with white, allowing all the layer's contents to show. The bottom image in Figure 8.21 shows the same layer mask filled with black in areas that correspond to the greenery behind the butterfly. The greenery is not visible because the corresponding parts of the layer mask are black.

Figure 8.22 shows an image collage in which multiple layers have layer masks to hide parts of the image components and make them seem to flow together smoothly.

By default, a layer is linked to its layer mask. You can see a link symbol between the layer thumbnail and the mask. This means that if you move the contents of the layer, the contents of the mask moves along with it, and vice versa. If you want to move the layer contents separately, click the link symbol to unlink the layer and mask.

If you are using a mask to make a window for part of a photo to show through, you might want to unlink the layer and mask so you can move the photo independently, which makes a different part of the photo show through the mask "window."

Figure 8.23 shows a mask being used as a window for part of a photo and an unlinked layer and mask.

FIGURE 8.21

A layer mask filled with white shows all the contents of a layer, and a layer mask with some hides the corresponding parts of a layer.

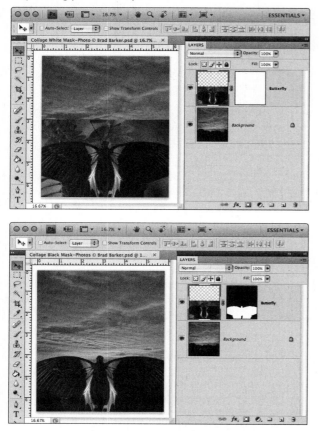

FIGURE 8.22

Masks on multiple layers can be used to hide parts of image components. This technique can be used to make an image collage whose parts seem to flow together smoothly.

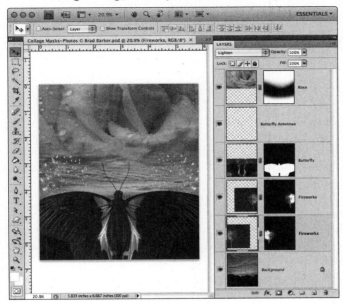

FIGURE 8.23

A mask being used as a window for part of a photo and an unlinked layer and mask. When the mask is unlinked from the layer, the layer contents can be moved separately.

To use a layer mask to hide or show parts of a layer, use any of the following techniques and tips:

- **To hide parts of an object on a layer, first click on the layer mask to activate it.** When a layer mask is active, it has a black border around the corners of the mask's thumbnail on the Layers palette.

- **After the layer mask is active, paint with black or shades of gray in the image window, or you can make a selection in the image window and choose Edit ➪ Fill to fill the selection.**

CROSS-REF See Chapter 10 for ways to make selections.

- **To reveal hidden parts of an object, add white to the mask.** It doesn't matter how you get black, white, or shades of gray on the mask — you can use any tools or methods at your disposal. When a layer mask is active and you paint or make a selection in the image window, you will really be working on the layer mask, not the pixels on the layer. You can see black, white, or shades of gray on the layer mask thumbnail when you paint on a mask.

- **To set up a brush to paint with black, choose the Brush tool and make the foreground color black.** To paint with gray, choose a reduced opacity in the Options Bar for the brush. (Shortcut: Press a number key, for example, 2, for 20 percent opacity.) To paint with white, make the foreground color white.

- **Press the D key to make the foreground color black and the background color white.** Press the X key to switch the colors.

- **Press one of the bracket keys to change the size of a brush.**

- **Press the Shift key plus a bracket key to change the hardness/softness of the brush edges.** Watch the brush edges change in the Options Bar's Brush menu. (Shift+click a bracket key four times to make the brush edge its maximum hardness or softness.)

TIP If you want to fill a selection to add paint to a layer mask, it's helpful to know these keyboard shortcuts: Alt+Delete fills with the foreground color, and Ctrl+Delete/⌘+Delete fills with the background color.

The Masks palette

The Masks palette, shown in Figure 8.24, offers lots of new ways to manage masks.

Following are ways you can use the Masks palette:

- **To add a pixel mask to a layer, click on the layer thumbnail to activate the layer, then click the add a pixel mask button in the Masks palette (the square with white circle).**

- **To add a vector mask to a layer, click on the layer thumbnail to activate the layer, then click the add a vector mask button in the Masks palette (the pen with plus sign).** Instead of painting black, white, or shades of gray on a mask, you can put a path on a vector mask to hide or show corresponding parts of the layer. You can make a path by using the Pen tool or a Shape tool with the Path option selected in the Options Bar. A vector mask is useful when you need to make a hard-edged, smooth mask, which you might need to hide the background of a hard-edged object. See Chapter 12 for more information about vector masks and paths.

■ **To change the opacity of a mask, click on a mask thumbnail to activate it, then drag the Density slider.**

■ **To feather the edges of the mask, click on a mask thumbnail to activate it, then drag the Feather slider.**

■ **To refine the edges of a mask, click on a mask thumbnail to activate it, then click the Mask Edge button to refine the edges of the mask with Refine Edge command options (see Chapter 10 for Refine Edge options).** Note that the Mask Edge button is not available if there is an active selection. Choose Select ➪ Deselect if you want to make sure there is no active selection.

■ **To base the mask contents on a range of colors in the image, click on a mask thumbnail to activate it, then click the Color Range button to access options that allow you to select a range of colors (see Chapter 10 for Color Range options).**

■ **To invert the colors on the mask, click on a mask thumbnail to activate it, then click the Invert button.** Note that the Invert button is not available if there is an active selection. Choose Select ➪ Deselect if you want to make sure there is no active selection.

■ **To load a selection of the mask contents (selects everything on the mask except black), click on a mask thumbnail to activate it, then click the load selection from mask button (the dotted circle symbol).** You can always invert the selection, if necessary, by choosing Select ➪ Inverse.

■ **To permanently apply the mask effect and delete the mask, click on a mask thumbnail to activate it, then click the apply mask button (the diamond with arrow symbol).**

■ **To toggle on and off the visibility of the mask effect, click on a mask thumbnail to activate it, then click the disable/enable mask button (the eyeball symbol).**

■ **To delete the mask and remove the mask effect, click on a mask thumbnail to activate it, then click the delete mask button (the trashcan symbol).**

FIGURE 8.24

The Masks palette

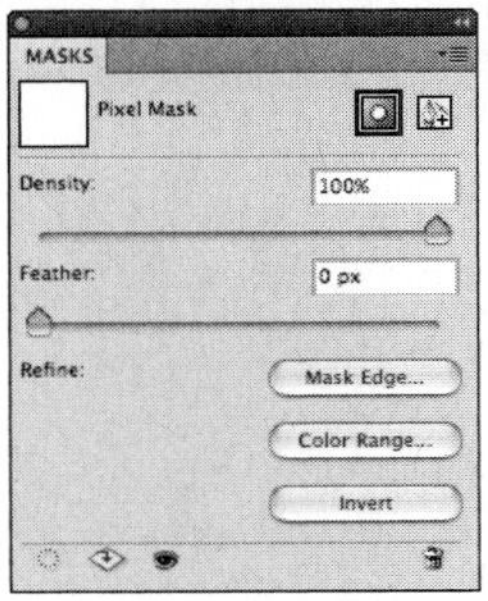

Adjustment Layers

Adjustment layers are layers that don't contain pixels but that can be used to alter how pixels on underlying layers appear. They can increase saturation, lighten and darken, make changes to colors, and more. The great thing is that you can double-click an adjustment layer's thumbnail in the Layers palette to change the adjustment at any time, or you can hide or delete an adjustment layer at any time. Figure 8.25 shows a Curves adjustment layer, which is being used to increase the contrast of the image.

> **NOTE**   **All adjustment layers are available in RGB mode and most are available in CMYK and Lab modes. Many adjustment layers are not available in Grayscale mode, and none are available in Indexed Color and Multichannel modes.**

By default, adjustment layers have masks, and adjustment layers are linked to their layer masks. You can see a link symbol between an adjustment layer thumbnail and its mask thumbnail. This means that if you move the contents of the layer, the contents of the mask move along with it, and vice versa. If you have added black or gray to the mask to hide part of the adjustment and want to move the mask contents separately from the adjustment, click the link symbol in between the adjustment layer thumbnail and its mask thumbnail to unlink them.

FIGURE 8.25

A Curves adjustment layer is used to increase the contrast of the image.

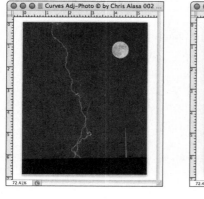 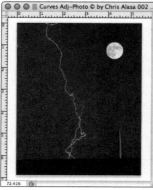 

To create an adjustment layer, follow these steps:

1. **Choose a type of adjustment layer from the Create a New Fill or Adjustment Layer menu at the bottom of the Layers palette (the half-black, half-white circle symbol).**

2. **Press and hold the button to access the menu.** Photoshop CS4 also includes a new way to create and manage adjustment layers: the Adjustments palette.

Note that the Create a New Fill or Adjustment Layer menu in the Layers palette has a few options that the Adjustments palette doesn't have: *fill layers*. A fill layer is a layer that contains only a solid color, gradient, or pattern. You can create a fill layer by selecting that option in the Create a New Fill or Adjustment Layer menu in the Layers palette.

You can easily change the color in a Solid Color fill layer by double-clicking the Color Fill layer thumbnail in the Layers palette to get the Color Picker, where you can select a new color, or, while the Color Picker is open, click on a color in the image window or Swatches palette to select a new color. Solid Color fill layers make filling a layer with a solid color relatively easy and flexible.

An alternate method is to make a new layer, select the layer, choose Edit ➪ Fill, choose the fill options (which can take several steps), and click OK. You can also press Alt+Delete to fill a layer or selection with the foreground color or Ctrl+Delete/⌘+Delete to fill with the background color. Figure 8.26 shows a Solid Color fill layer.

FIGURE 8.26

A Solid Color fill layer, which is filled with a solid color that can be edited easily

You can create a Pattern layer by selecting that option in the Create a New Fill or Adjustment Layer menu in the Layers palette. You can easily change the pattern in a Pattern fill layer by double-clicking the Pattern Fill layer thumbnail and choosing a different pattern. Figure 8.27 shows a Pattern layer.

NOTE **You can make custom patterns by making a rectangular selection of pixels in an image, and then choosing Edit ➪ Define Pattern.**

FIGURE 8.27

A Pattern fill layer, which is filled with a pattern that can be changed easily

You can create a Gradient layer by selecting that option in the Create a New Fill or Adjustment Layer menu in the Layers palette. You can easily change a gradient in a Gradient fill layer by double-clicking the Gradient Fill layer thumbnail and choosing a different gradient option in the Gradient Fill dialog box. Click in the Gradient preview in the Gradient Fill dialog box to get the Gradient Editor, which gives you more gradient options. Figure 8.28 shows a Gradient fill layer.

FIGURE 8.28

A Gradient fill layer, which is filled with a gradient that can be changed easily

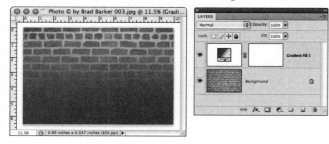

Making a Seamless Pattern

Make a seamless pattern by following these steps:

1. **Open an image you would like to make into a seamless pattern and crop it as desired.**

2. **Make a note of $^1/_2$ its horizontal and $^1/_2$ its vertical pixel measurements.**

3. **Choose Filter ⇨ Other ⇨ Offset.**

4. **In the Offset dialog box, make sure Wrap Around and Preview are checked and enter the horizontal and vertical pixel numbers you recorded.** This quarters the image and flips it so that the inside edges of each quarter are on the outside edges of the image. This also causes the edges of a pattern made from this image to flow together seamlessly.

5. **Preview the result in the image window.** Note that you will have to retouch the image so that the inner edges of the quartered image appear seamless. If you want to adjust where these inner edges meet to try to make your retouching easier, type different numbers in the horizontal and vertical boxes.

6. **Click OK.**

7. **Retouch the areas where the inner edges meet so that you can't see any seams.** The Clone tool is often helpful in this situation. See Chapter 18 for more information about retouching with the Clone tool and Chapter 15 for other retouching techniques.

8. **Choose Select ➪ Select All.**

9. **Choose Edit ➪ Define Pattern.**

You can use a pattern by making a Pattern fill layer, painting with the Pattern Stamp tool, or creating a Pattern Overlay layer style.

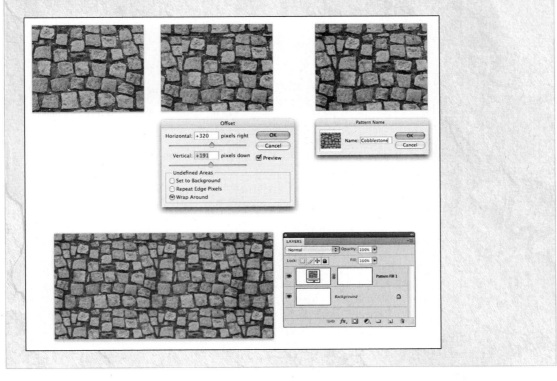

The Adjustments palette

The Adjustments palette offers a new way to create and manage adjustment layers. Figure 8.29 shows the main Add an adjustment view of the Adjustments palette.

FIGURE 8.29

The main Add an adjustment view of the Adjustments palette

Following are ways you can use the Adjustments palette:

- **To add an adjustment layer to an image, click on a layer thumbnail to activate a layer (the Adjustment layer is created right above the active layer).** Click the symbol for the desired adjustment in the Adjustments palette (hover the mouse over symbols to see the names of adjustments). The Adjustments palette shows the adjustment's options; modify the options as desired. Alternatively, you can start by selecting an Adjustment Preset in the Adjustments menu. You can modify the adjustment's options as desired.

- **To save an adjustment as a preset, activate the adjustment by clicking on the adjustment layer, if necessary, then choose Save (adjustment type) Preset in the Adjustments palette menu.**

- **To cause all future adjustment layers that you create to affect only the layer directly below it, rather than all the layers below it (the default), click the New adjustments clip to the layer button in the lower-right corner of the main Add an adjustment view in the Adjustments palette (the multiple-circles symbol).** To turn off this option, click it again. To show the Add-an-adjustment main view of the Adjustments palette, click on the Return to Adjustment List arrow at the bottom of the Adjustments palette or click on a non-adjustment layer in the Layers palette.

■ **To cause one adjustment layer to affect only the layer directly below it rather than all the layers below it (the default), click the adjustment layer in the Layers palette to activate it, then click the Click to clip to layer button in the lower left of the Adjustments palette (the double-circle symbol).** Or you can Alt+click between the adjustment layer and the layer below it in the Layers palette (click when you see the double-circle symbol under the cursor).

■ **To modify the options in (and the effect of) an existing adjustment layer, click the adjustment layer in the Layers palette and modify its options in the Adjustments palette.** For Fill and Pattern layers, double-click the Fill or Pattern layer for a dialog box that you can use to change the fill or pattern.

■ **To toggle visibility of an adjustment layer, click the eyeball visibility symbol next to the layer in the Layers palette, or click on the adjustment layer, then click on the eyeball visibility symbol in the Adjustments palette.**

■ **To view the way the image appeared right before you modified an adjustment layer's options, immediately after you make a change to the adjustment options, click and hold the Press to view previous state button at the bottom of the Adjustments palette (the eyeball with curvy arrow) or press and hold the backslash (\) key.** When you're finished viewing the previous state, release the button or key.

■ **To reset an adjustment layer to its immediately previous options, if you have just made changes to an adjustment layer's options in the Adjustments palette, click the Reset to previous state button at the bottom of the Adjustments palette (the half-circle curvy arrow).**

■ **To reset an adjustment layer to its default options, click the adjustment layer in the Layers palette to activate it, then click the Reset to adjustment defaults button at the bottom of the Adjustments palette (the full-circle curvy arrow).**

■ **To delete an adjustment layer, drag the adjustment layer to the trashcan symbol at the bottom of the Layers palette, or when the adjustment layer is active, click on the trashcan symbol in the Adjustments palette.**

The following adjustments can be made with Adjustment layers:

■ **Brightness/Contrast.** Use Brightness/Contrast (see Figure 8.30) to make simple adjustments to the tonal range of an image by making it appear brighter, darker, higher contrast, or lower contrast. A Curves adjustment offers more control. See Chapter 9 for more information about Curves.

■ **Levels.** Lighten, darken, increase contrast, and decrease contrast with Levels (see Figure 8.31). You can also use Levels to manipulate individual color channels or to set areas to gray, which can remove undesirable color casts.

The Auto Color command, which attempts to automatically correct the color and contrast in an image, can be applied by clicking the Auto button. To set Auto Color options, choose Auto Color Correction Options from the Levels palette menu. See Chapter 9 for more information about Levels and Auto Color.

FIGURE 8.30

The Brightness/Contrast adjustment palette

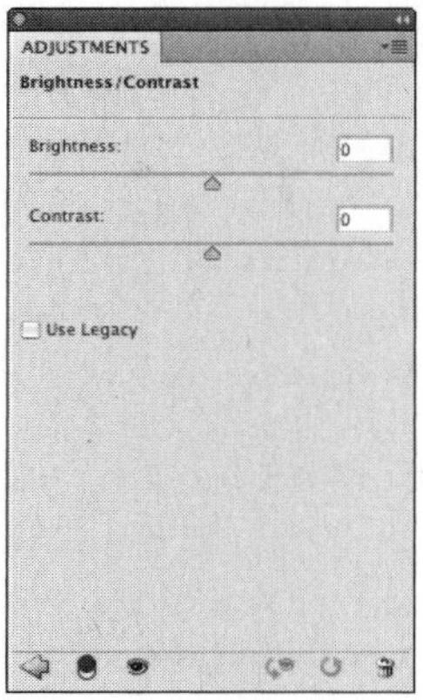

FIGURE 8.31

The Levels adjustment palette

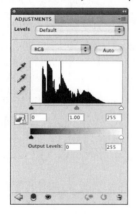

- **Curves.** Lighten, darken, increase contrast, and decrease contrast with Curves (see Figure 8.32). You can also use Curves to manipulate individual color channels or to set areas that should be gray to gray, which can remove undesirable color casts. Curves offers more control than Levels because you can put up to 14 points on a curve, whereas Levels has only three points of adjustment.

FIGURE 8.32

The Curves adjustment palette

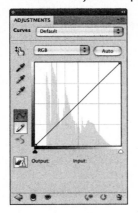

The Auto Color command, which attempts to automatically correct the color and contrast in an image, can be applied by clicking the Auto button. To set Auto Color options, choose Auto Color Correction Options from the Curves palette menu.

CROSS-REF See Chapter 9 for more information about Curves and Auto Color.

■ **Exposure.** Use Exposure (see Figure 8.33) to increase overall brightness, with a greater effect in the brighter values. Decreasing Exposure darkens an image. Exposure adjustments apply a similar effect as changing f-stops on a camera. Offset darkens mostly shadows and midtones. Gamma adjusts mostly the midtones.

FIGURE 8.33

The Exposure adjustment palette

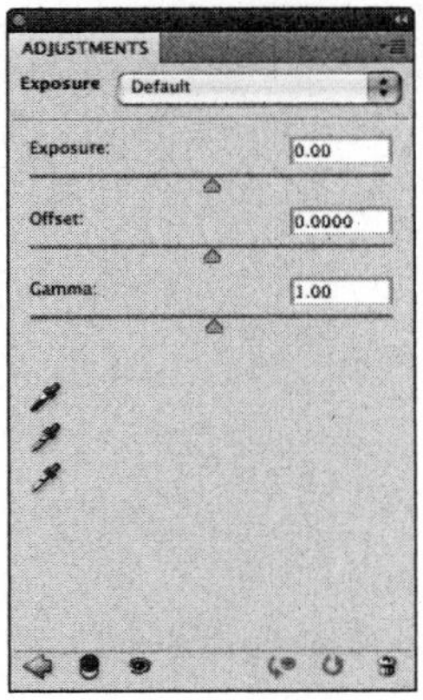

245

The Exposure eyedroppers can be used to set the black point to black, the white point to white, and the midtone point to middle gray in an image, but these eyedroppers affect only luminance, not all color channels as they do in Curves and Levels.

> **NOTE** Exposure is available in RGB mode, but not in CMYK or Lab modes.

- **Vibrance.** Use Vibrance (see Figure 8.34) to adjust the saturation of an image, with a greater effect on lower-saturated colors than on higher-saturated colors. Vibrance also attempts to prevent over-saturation of skin tones.

FIGURE 8.34

The Vibrance adjustment palette

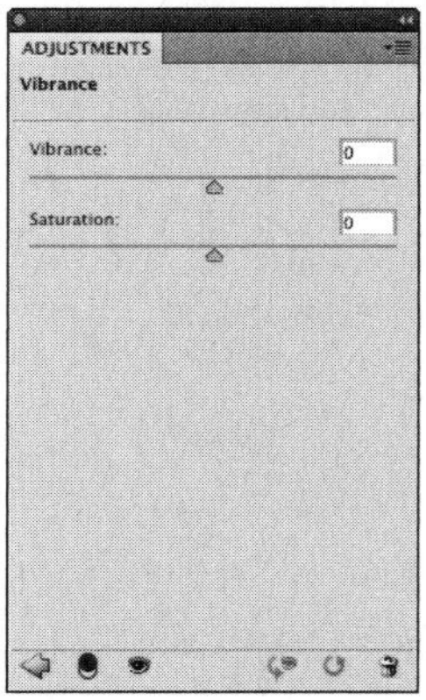

- **Hue/Saturation.** Use Hue/Saturation (see Figure 8.35) to adjust the hue, saturation, and lightness of an image or of individual colors. For more about Hue/Saturation, see Chapter 15.

> **NOTE** Vibrance is available in RGB mode, but not in CMYK or Lab modes.

- **Color Balance.** Use Color Balance (see Figure 8.36) to change the overall mixture of colors in an image, for example, so that they are more bluish, pinkish, or yellowish.

FIGURE 8.35

The Hue/Saturation adjustment palette

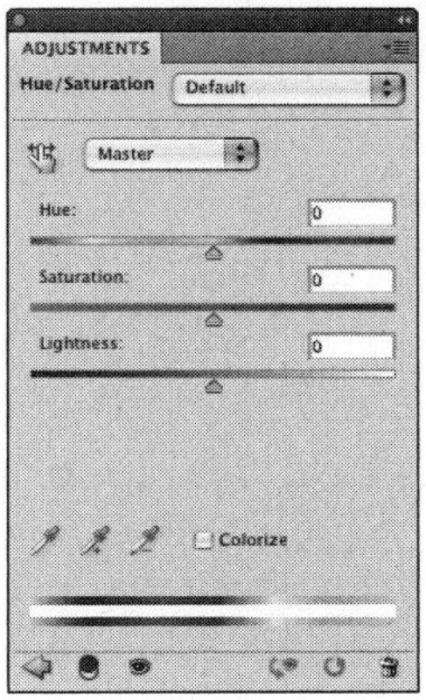

FIGURE 8.36

The Color Balance adjustment palette

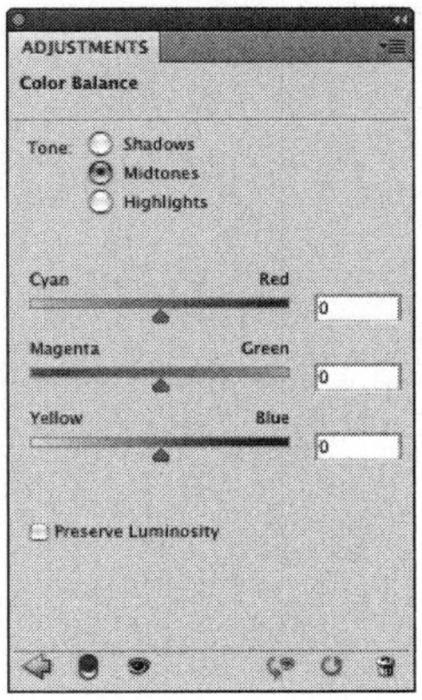

■ **The Black & White.** Use Black & White (see Figure 8.37) to convert a color image to a grayscale image and maintain control over how and which individual colors are converted to grayscale. You can also add a color tint to the grayscale image.

NOTE Black & White is available in RGB mode, but not in CMYK or Lab modes.

FIGURE 8.37

The Black & White adjustment palette

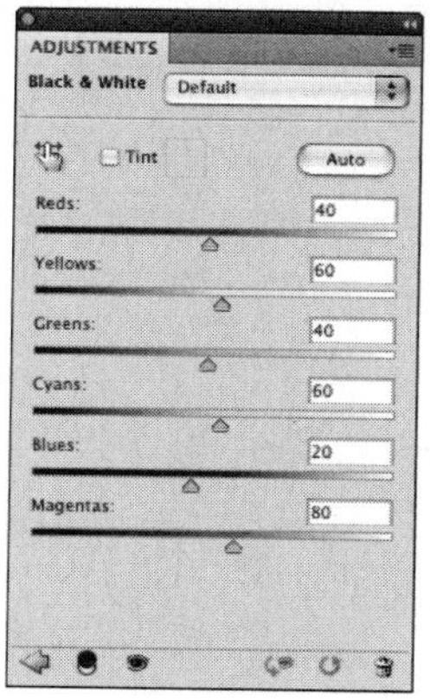

- **Photo Filter.** Use Photo Filter (see Figure 8.38) to simulate various colors and effects of camera lens filters on an image. You can use this to make an image appear warmer or cooler, for example. Choose a filter or a custom color to act as a filter. Adjusting Density increases or decreases the effect.

  Preserve Luminosity preserves the light and dark values in an image that has a photo filter applied to it. If Preserve Luminosity is unchecked, the image may get darker overall when the photo filter is applied.

FIGURE 8.38

The Photo Filter adjustment palette

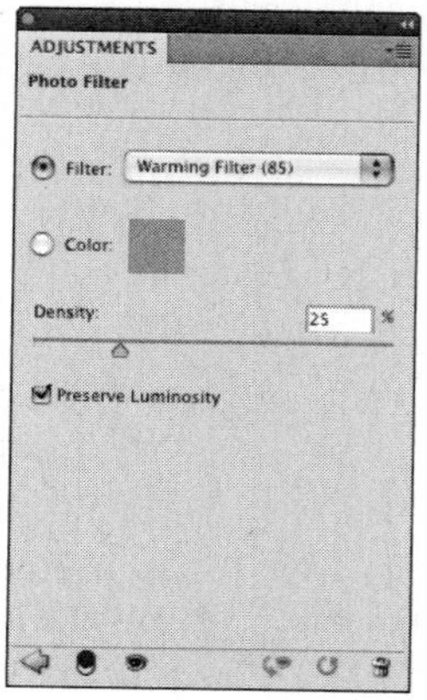

■ **Channel Mixer.** The Channel Mixer adjustment (see Figure 8.39) makes it possible for you to choose how much information from each color channel to include in an image that you are changing to grayscale. Without Channel Mixer, Photoshop uses a default formula to decide how much grayscale information comes from each color channel. Check Monochrome in Channel Mixer to make the image appear to be grayscale and preview the grayscale result in the image window while you make adjustments. (If you want to make a true grayscale-mode image, you will still need to convert to grayscale in the Image ⇨ Mode menu, after you choose Channel Mixer options.)

You can choose from the Output Channel menu the color channel that you want to use at 100 percent (or start with), then adjust the other channels — and the Output Channel — as desired to get the best result, which you can preview in the image window. Adjust the Constant option to lighten or darken overall. For more about Channel Mixer, see Chapter 19.

NOTE Channel Mixer is available in RGB and CMYK modes, but not in Lab mode.

FIGURE 8.39

The Channel Mixer adjustment palette

■ **Invert.** The Invert adjustment (see Figure 8.40) inverts the colors in a color image to their opposites on the color wheel (red to green, blue to yellow, and so on). This adjustment inverts values rather than colors in a non-color image. The Invert adjustment does not have any options for you to choose.

■ **Posterize.** Use the Posterize adjustment (see Figure 8.41) to assign the number of brightness values contained in an image. You can make an image look like it is made up of large solid-color areas rather than gradual tones. This is usually used to create a special effect.

FIGURE 8.40

The Invert adjustment palette

FIGURE 8.41

The Posterize adjustment palette

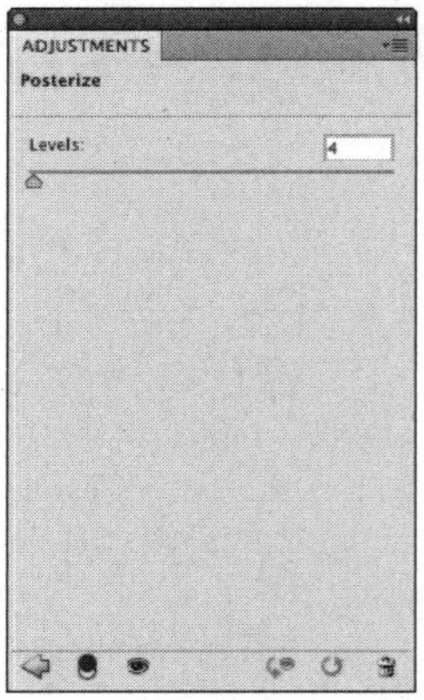

- **Threshold.** The Threshold adjustment (see Figure 8.42) converts an image so that it appears to contain only black and white (no color or shades of gray and gives you some control over which pixels become black or white. This adjustment can be applied to create a black and white effect or can be temporarily previewed without applying it to help you find the lightest and darkest areas in an image.

  The Threshold adjustment displays a histogram, a bar graph of the values in an image where 0 on the far left equals solid black, 128 in the middle equals 50 percent gray, and

255 on the far right equals white. The taller the bar at any level means there is more of that value in the image. For example, if there is a very tall bar at level 128, it means there is a lot of 50 percent gray in the image. When you set the Threshold level, you tell Photoshop to make every value in the image that is greater than or equal to the Threshold level white and every value in the image that is less than the Threshold level black.

To find and set the darkest area in an image, drag the slider to the left, almost to where the histogram bars begin. The darkest areas in the image show as black in the image window. You can use the Color Sampler tool to click on the darkest area in the image window to add a color sampler, which displays the color numbers for that part of the image in the info palette until the color sampler is deleted.

FIGURE 8.42

The Threshold adjustment palette

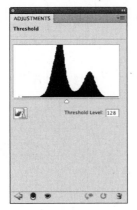

To find and set the lightest area in an image, drag the slider to the right, almost to where the histogram bars end. The lightest areas in the image show as white in the image window. You can use the Color Sampler tool to click on the lightest area in the image window to add a color sampler, which displays the color numbers for that part of the image in the info palette until the color sampler is deleted.

To delete a color sampler, activate the Color Sampler tool and right-click/Ctrl-click on the color sampler in the image window, then select Delete from the context menu.

- **Gradient Map.** The Gradient Map adjustment (see Figure 8.43) assigns, or maps, each color in a gradient that you choose to areas in the active image that are similar in value (lightness or darkness) to each color in the gradient.

The Gradient Map adjustment palette

For example, if the active image is a photo and you choose a gradient that goes from dark purple to light orange, the photo's darker areas would be changed to shades of purple and the lighter areas would be changed to shades of orange.

The photo would look like a purple-and-orange duotone. To choose a gradient, click in the gradient preview box to get the Gradient Editor. Dither attempts to make smoother transitions between the colors; Reverse reverses the colors in the image (in the example mentioned, purple would be assigned to the lighter areas and orange would be assigned to the darker areas — the opposite of the initial assignment).

An alternate method to get this same effect would be to create a duotone. Creating a duotone would also give you more control over the specific values to which the colors are assigned. Duotone, an image that is made up of two continuous-tone colors, is sometimes used as a generic term that includes monotones, tritones, and quadtones, images that are made up of one, three, or four colors. This is because in Photoshop, you access the dialog box that creates all those kinds of images by choosing Image ➪ Mode ➪ Duotone.

Note that duotones are limited to a maximum of four colors, whereas gradient maps are not limited to a certain number of colors. For more information about duotones, see Chapter 19.

- **Selective Color.** The Selective Color adjustment (see Figure 8.44) allows you to target specific colors in the image (such as reds, yellows, or magentas) and adjust the amount of process colors (Cyan, Magenta, Yellow, and Black) that the targeted color contains.

  For example, if it appears that a person's face is sunburned in a photo, you might try targeting the reds and reducing the magenta a little. Note that you can always constrain the adjustment to certain areas of an image by painting on the adjustment's layer mask.

NOTE Selective Color is available in RGB and CMYK modes, but not in Lab mode.

FIGURE 8.44

The Selective Color adjustment palette

Layer styles

You can add *layer styles*, which can contain one or more effects, to layers. Layer-style effects include drop shadows, bevels, glows, and more. Figure 8.45 shows a layer in the Layers palette that has a layer style with multiple effects.

 **You cannot add a layer style to a Background layer. First, double-click the layer name "Background" then click OK to change the layer to a regular layer.**

FIGURE 8.45

A layer in the Layers palette that has a layer style with multiple effects

You can toggle the visibility of layer styles and their effects just as you can layers by clicking the visibility eyeball symbol next to the layer style or effect. If you want to delete a layer style, drag it to the trashcan at the bottom of the Layers palette.

To add a layer style to a layer, click the layer to activate it, then do one of the following:

- Click the layer style button (*fx* symbol) at the bottom of the Layers palette and choose an effect, such as drop shadow.
- Click a layer style in the Styles palette.

When you add a layer style to a layer by clicking the layer style button, the Layer Style dialog box opens (see Figure 8.46). Use the dialog box to set options for the effects or add more effects.

FIGURE 8.46

The Layer Style dialog box

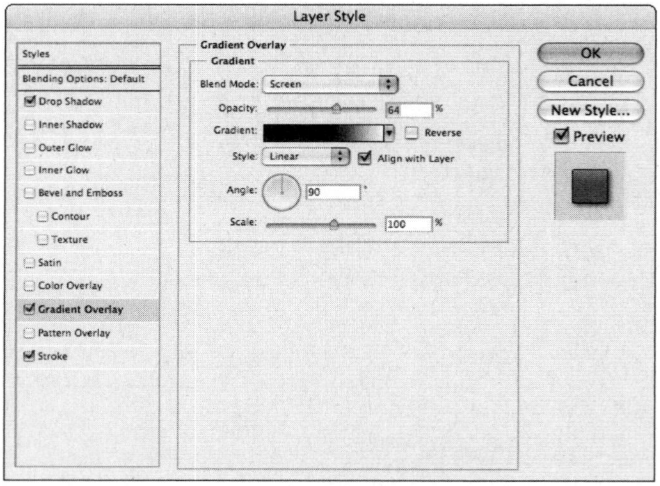

To add an effect with the Layer Style dialog box, click on the name of the effect, such as Drop Shadow. Clicking on the name of the effect, rather than just checking the box next to the name, displays the options for that effect in the Layer Style dialog box.

You can then adjust the options as desired and click OK when you are finished. If you want to edit the layer style later, just double-click the layer style in the Layers palette to bring up the Layer Style dialog box again.

To save a layer style, click the New Style button in the Layer Style dialog box, give the layer style a name, and click OK. The layer style is then included in the Styles palette and the Preset Manager.

CROSS-REF Use the Preset Manager to manage libraries of custom layer styles, brushes, color swatches, and more. For information about the Preset Manager, see Chapter 2.

Here are the effects that you can include in a layer style:

- **Drop Shadow.** Adds a shadow behind the pixels on the layer.
- **Inner Shadow.** Adds a shadow inside the edges of the layer's pixels, which gives the layer a recessed appearance.
- **Outer Glow and Inner Glow.** Adds glows that extend from the outside or inside edges of the layer's pixels.
- **Bevel and Emboss.** Adds various combinations of highlights and shadows to a layer's pixels, which gives the layer content a slightly 3-D appearance.
- **Satin.** Adds shading in the pixels on a layer to create a satiny finish.
- **Color, Gradient, and Pattern Overlay.** Fills a layer with a color, gradient, or pattern. You can use color in a layer style to assign a color to a layer's content (including type) as an alternative to adding color to content by using other palettes. This can be helpful if you need to apply the same color to content over and over again, because you can add the layer style with just a couple of clicks if you use the Styles palette, whereas it may take more steps to choose and assign a color each time by using other palettes.
- **Stroke.** Outlines the pixels, shapes, or type on the active layer using a color, gradient, or pattern.

You can set Blending Options in the Layer Style dialog box to specify how the layer style and layer blend with other layers in the document.

Blending Modes

A layer's *Blending mode* determines how the layer blends with layers underneath. Blending modes can also be used with tools that use brushes, the Fill command, and gradients. In many cases, you can choose whether to use Blending modes with tools and commands or to assign a Blending mode to a layer.

It is often more flexible if you use Blending modes on layers rather than with tools or commands because you can easily change a layer's Blending mode or opacity at any time. Figure 8.47 shows a layer with the Normal Blending mode compared to a layer with the Multiply Blending mode.

FIGURE 8.47

A layer with the Normal Blending mode compared to a layer with the Multiply Blending mode.

To assign a Blending mode to a layer, click a layer to activate it, then choose a mode from the blending mode menu at the top of the Layers palette (it will have the Normal Blending mode selected by default).

CROSS-REF See Chapters 14 and 15 for some examples of Blending mode effects.

It really requires experimenting with Blending modes on layers to get a good understanding of their effects. Here is a list of Blending modes:

- **Normal.** Pixels have their normal appearance; no Blending mode effect is applied.

- **Dissolve.** Gives the layer content a spattered, pixilated appearance.

- **Behind (available with tools but not layers).** Edits or paints on the transparent part of a layer only (the Behind blending mode won't work if Lock Transparency is turned on in the Layers palette).

- **Clear (available with tools but not layers).** Paints each pixel and makes it transparent (the Clear blending mode won't work if Lock Transparency is turned on in the Layers palette).

- **Darken.** Displays the darker of two colors: the color on the layer or the color on the layers underneath.

- **Multiply.** Makes layers look darker while preserving much of the layer's contrast. Makes the layer look transparent. Where underlying layers are white, there is no change.

- **Color Burn.** Makes the colors darker while preserving some of the layer's contrast. Makes the layer look somewhat transparent. Where underlying layers are white, there is no change.

- **Linear Burn.** Makes the colors darker overall and lowers contrast. Makes the layer look somewhat transparent. Where underlying layers are white, there is no change.

- **Lighten.** Displays the lighter of two colors: the color on the layer or the color on the layers underneath.

- **Screen.** Makes the layer lighter and preserves much of the contrast. Makes the layer look transparent. Where underlying layers are white, there is no change.

- **Color Dodge.** Lightens the layer and preserves some of the contrast. Makes the layer look somewhat transparent.

- **Linear Dodge.** Lightens the layer and lowers contrast. Makes the layer look somewhat transparent.

- **Overlay.** Multiplies or screens the colors, depending on the colors on underlying layers. Preserves much of the contrast. Makes the layer look transparent.

- **Soft Light, Hard Light, Vivid Light, Linear Light, Pin Light, Hard Mix.** These Blending modes increase contrast in varying degrees and make layers look somewhat transparent.

- **Difference.** Changes the colors in a layer and preserves much of the contrast.

- **Exclusion.** Partially changes the colors in a layer without preserving a lot of the contrast.

- **Hue.** Displays the hue of the layer but combined with the brightness and saturation of the underlying layers.

- **Saturation.** Displays the saturation of the layer but combined with the lightness and colors of the underlying layers.

- **Color.** Displays the color of the layer but combined with the lightness of the underlying layers.

- **Luminosity.** Displays the lightness of the layer but combined with the colors of the underlying layers.

- **Lighter.** Lightens a layer by displaying the lightest color in channels.

- **Darker.** Darkens a layer by displaying the darkest color in channels.

Smart Objects

Smart Objects are layers that store one or more Photoshop layers' content or an Illustrator file's content in such a way that the Smart Object remembers the contents' original characteristics, even if you transform a Smart Object layer. This makes it possible for you to make nondestructive edits to the Smart Object layer. For example, you can scale a Smart Object down and back up to its original size with no loss in resolution or detail. When you scale a regular layer down, you lose some of its resolution, which is okay if you leave it at the smaller size, but it can result in a loss of quality if you scale it back up.

To edit a Smart Object's contents, such as the text on a type layer, double-click the Smart Object. This opens a separate file in which you can see the Smart Object contents and where you can edit them. Then save and close the file. When you do that, the Smart Object layer in Photoshop is updated. This separate Smart Object file is really contained in the same Photoshop file, behind the scenes. It is not a separate file you can see in your computer's operating system.

To create a Smart Object, do one of the following:

- Open a file with the File ⇨ Open As Smart Object command.
- Place a file with the File ⇨ Place command.
- Copy and paste a file from Illustrator.
- Convert one or more active Photoshop layers to a Smart Object by using the Layers palette menu.

Figure 8.48 shows a Smart Object and its unique layer thumbnail symbol on the Layers palette.

> **TIP** You can warp several layers at the same time if you first convert the layers to one Smart Object.

FIGURE 8.48

A Smart Object and its unique layer thumbnail symbol on the Layers palette

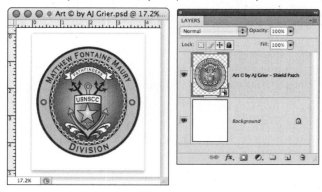

Image Stacks

An Image Stack is a Smart Object that contains two or more layers and has a Stack mode applied to it. Stack modes affect how the layers' pixels are blended together, but they blend the layers in a different way than Blending modes do.

To apply a Stack mode to the layers in a Smart Object, click on the Smart Object to activate it, then choose Layer ⇨ Smart Object ⇨ Stack Mode (choose a Stack mode).

You can use the Mean Stack mode to remove image noise in several nearly identical photos, such as photos of the same building at night, taken consecutively. Mean displays the average of the pixels in the Stack mode layers, so the difference in the pixels that make up the noise is diminished because of the averaging.

If you don't take the photos with a tripod, choose Edit ⇨ Auto-Align Layers with the Reposition Only option to align the photos on layers before you apply the Stack mode.

Use the Standard Deviation Stack mode to reveal areas in which two images that look identical are actually different. In Figure 8.49, the photo on the left is slightly different from the photo on the right in the area of the bark of the tree, although the differences are hard to see. The Standard Deviation Stack mode separates and reveals the differences in the bark, which in this case appear to form the words "Secret Code."

FIGURE 8.49

Standard Deviation Stack mode reveals that there is really a difference in these two images that appear identical.

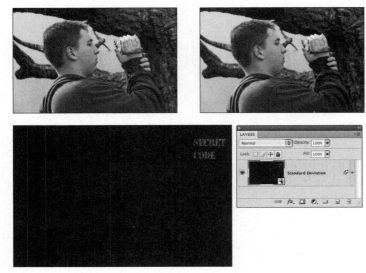

Use the Median Stack mode to blend together several photos that have an identical background and different unwanted objects or people, so that the unwanted objects "magically" disappear — as long as there are at least two photos with a clear background area in a corresponding position to each unwanted object (see Figure 8.50).

FIGURE 8.50

Unwanted objects have been removed by using the Median Stack mode.

Making nearly indiscernable changes to an image for the purpose of incorporating a secret message might be kind of fun project, but a practical application of the Standard Deviation Stack mode could be to help a photo retoucher remember where he or she retouched an image. This also can give the client a visual reference of the work that has been done. Sometimes it's not readily apparent how much work has been done to a retouched image and which parts of the image have been changed. If you put the "before" image on one layer, the "after" image on another layer, and convert the two layers into one Smart Object, you can then apply the Standard Deviation Stack mode to get a visual representation of all the areas of the image that have been changed.

Median displays the median pixel value of the Stack mode layers.

Summary

This chapter described different kinds of layers, how to use them, and how to apply various layer effects. Following are key concepts:

You can put objects in your Photoshop document on separate layers and work on the objects separately. This makes your document much more flexible and easy to change.

Layer masks are used to totally or partially hide objects on a layer, and with layer masks, you can easily show any part of the object again at any time. This is an advantage over erasing parts of an image because it is easy to undo.

Adjustment layers are layers that don't contain pixels but can be used to alter how pixels on underlying layers appear. They can increase saturation, lighten or darken, increase or decrease contrast, make changes to colors, and more. Flexibility is a big part of adjustment layers in that you can edit or delete them at any time. Layer styles can be used to add one or more effects to layer content, such as a drop shadow, bevel, or glow.

A blending mode can be applied to a layer to affect how the pixels on the layer interact, or blend, with pixels on underlying layers. Blending modes can be used to lighten, darken, affect contrast or color, and more. Commonly used blending modes include Multiply, Screen, Lighten, Darken, Color, and Luminosity.

Smart Objects are layers that store one or more layers' content or store an Illustrator file's content in such a way that it remembers the content's original characteristics, even if you transform or apply a filter to the Smart Object. You can edit Smart Objects' original content. Stack Modes applied to Smart Objects can be used to automatically delete unwanted objects in photos that have the same background, virtually eliminate image noise in a set of nearly identical photos, or compare images and highlight their differences, even if the differences are too subtle for the eye to detect.

Chapter 9

Histograms, Levels, and Curves

Most images are made up of lighter, darker, and in-between color values, which can be called tones, brightness levels, or intensities. The collection of all an image's tones is called its tonal range. A nighttime photo may have mostly dark tones in its tonal range (a low-key image), while an illustration of bright white clouds may have mostly light tones (a high-key image).

A histogram is a bar graph that shows the amount of each brightness or color intensity level in an image and illustrates the image's overall tonal range. This graph can be seen in numerous places in Photoshop, including the Histogram palette and the Levels and Curves dialog boxes. Viewing histograms, as a supplement to viewing the image itself, can be helpful in determining how to adjust an image for its intended purpose.

The Levels and Curves commands can be used to manipulate the tones in an image to make it lighter or darker, or to increase or decrease its tonal range. Grayscale images can be adjusted and color images' individual color or composite color channels can be adjusted with Levels and Curves.

The light and dark qualities of an image can be changed, as well as the color quality. By making individual color channels lighter, darker, or higher or lower in contrast, the colors in an image can be altered with Levels and Curves.

About Histograms

A histogram often looks like the solid shape of a mountain range with a jagged top, but it is actually made up of a series of adjacent vertical bars that measure the amounts of each brightness level in an image. The brightness range extends from black on the far left of the graph to white on the far right. The taller the bar in the graph, the more of its tone is present in the image.

For example, an image of mostly white clouds generates many tall bars on the right side of the graph, representing the light colors, possibly some short bars on the left side of the graph, representing a few darker tones, and it might not have any bars on the far left side if there are no very dark blacks in the image. Add some black birds in the sky, however, and there would be a bar on the far left side of the image's updated histogram.

Figure 9.1 shows a light (high-key) image, a dark (low-key) image, and each image's histogram.

Figure 9.2 shows the histogram of the lighter image when black birds are added. The relatively few additional bars on the right represent the in-between values of pixels that blend the outer edges of the birds with the sky, which would be viewable by zooming in.

FIGURE 9.1

The histogram for the lighter image does not have bars from the middle to the far left side because there are no midtones or dark tones in the image. The histogram for the darker image has shorter bars on the right side because it doesn't have many light tones.

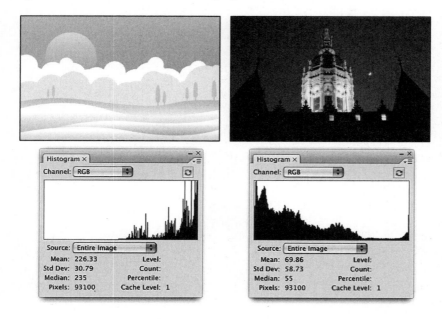

TIP Histograms: Left side represents Low light.

264

Here you see the same lighter image from Figure 9.1 with black birds added. The bar on the far left represents the solid black in the birds.

Acceptable histograms

A histogram with bars all the way across means the image contains all the available brightness levels possible, which often makes an image appear full of detail and depth. Making changes that cause bars to appear along the entire width of the histogram is a good objective if detail and depth are intended for the image, which is usually the case for photos of people and scenery.

When detail and depth are the goals, avoid changes that create significant gaps that lack bars in the histogram. When detail and depth aren't the goals for a particular image, it doesn't necessarily matter if there are gaps in the histogram.

Assume the lighter image in Figure 9.1 needs to be light overall for its purpose and looks just fine the way it is. Notice that its histogram has a huge gap — no bars from the middle all the way to the left side, which indicates there are no midtones or darker values present. Even so, its histogram looks great.

Another example of an acceptable histogram with gaps would be one that represents an image that is made up of solid shapes of only three or four colors. Its histogram would have numerous gaps because it has only a few brightness levels as opposed to a broad range of brightness levels. So, there is no one kind of histogram that is right for all images. The final tonal range represented in the histogram should be determined by the goal for the image's final appearance.

The Histogram palette

Figure 9.2 shows the Expanded View Histogram palette, as opposed to the default Compact View (not shown), which contains only a condensed bar graph and no menus. These views may be selected in the Histogram palette menu (see Figure 9.3).

FIGURE 9.3

The Histogram palette is shown with Expanded View selected in its palette menu.

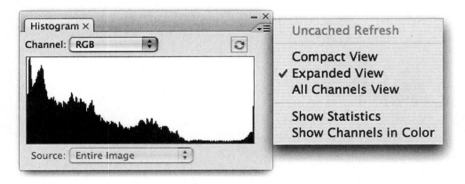

You can choose to make the histogram represent the entire image or just certain parts of the image. Figure 9.2 shows that the Entire Image option is selected in the Source menu of the Histogram palette, which means the histogram is looking at the entire image. If your image has more than one layer, you can choose which layer's information the histogram displays by activating the layer and choosing Selected Layer in the Source menu. If your image has adjustment layers, you can choose to view a histogram that represents an adjustment layer plus all the layers underneath it by activating the adjustment layer and choosing Adjustment Composite in the Source menu.

The composite color view (RGB, in this case) is shown in Figure 9.2 in the Channel menu at the top of the palette. The composite view displays a black histogram that represents the color intensities in the entire image. In this same Channels menu, you may also select an individual color channel to display a histogram that represents only the individual channel's tones; you may select Luminosity to display a histogram that represents only the light and dark qualities of the entire image (as if it were grayscale); or you may select Colors to display a color version of a histogram that shows all the color intensities in the image.

NOTE   **If a selection is active, the histogram represents only the selected area.**

Histogram Statistics

Because Histogram Statistics measure the pixels in an image in numerous ways, they can be useful in getting an idea of how much your image has changed as a result of color conversions or adjustments. Even when image changes are difficult to discern with the eye, the numbers in the Histogram palette, as well as the histogram bar graph, will reflect any changes. An interesting test that can increase your understanding of how and when images change in Photoshop is to convert an image between color modes numerous times (something that is tempting to do in certain circumstances but that sometimes degrades image quality).

Then see how much of a change in the image you can see with your eyes in the image window compared to how much the before-and-after numbers differ in the Histogram Statistics. Use the History palette to view earlier and later states of the image. The image may have changed more than you think, and the changes may affect the final quality, especially of printed images, more than you can discern when simply viewing the image onscreen.

The following are common terms for Histogram Statistics:

- **Mean.** The average brightness value.
- **Std Dev (standard deviation).** The amount of variation in brightness values.
- **Median.** The middle value in the range of brightness values.
- **Pixels.** The total number of pixels used to generate the histogram, calculated as follows: Pixels = image width in pixels x image height in pixels.
- **Level.** The brightness level of the area underneath the pointer when it is hovered over a bar in the histogram graph. Levels are expressed as 0 (black) to 255 (white).
- **Count.** The total number of pixels, including those in all channels, that correspond to the brightness level underneath the pointer when it is hovered over a bar in the histogram graph.
- **Percentile.** The cumulative number of pixels at or below the level underneath the pointer, expressed as a percentage of all the pixels in the image, from 0 percent to 100 percent. Count and Pixels are their respective values shown when the pointer is hovered over a bar in the histogram: Percentile = (Count + all Counts for all bars to the left of that bar) divided by (Pixels × number of channels).
- **Cache Level.** A cache level higher than 1 means the histogram is made from a representative sampling of pixels rather than actual pixels. This allows the histogram to update faster, but some accuracy is sacrificed. The presence of the uncached data indicator means that the histogram is not displaying the most accurate information. Clicking the uncached refresh button redraws the histogram accurately.

The All Channels View, shown in Figure 9.4, displays the Red, Green, and Blue channels in their respective colors on a color monitor.

FIGURE 9.4

The Histogram palette is shown with the All Channels View, Show Statistics, and Show Channels in Color options selected in the Histogram palette menu.

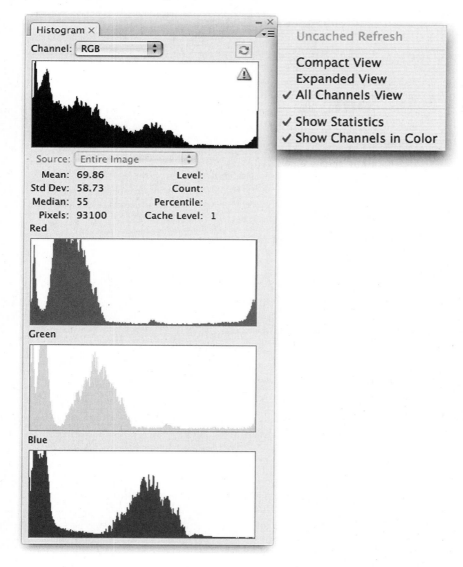

The color channels' histograms look different than the composite RGB channel's histogram because varying brightness levels in each color channel are required to make up the full color of the image represented in the histogram, which is the dark image seen in Figure 9.1.

Since there is a relatively large area of semi-dark blue sky in the color version of that photo, there are taller midtone and shadow bars in the Blue channel than there are in the Red and Green channels.

CAUTION The histogram in the Histogram palette often updates and changes accurately as you make changes to your image, but if there is an exclamation mark in the histogram graph area, it means that the tonal range display hasn't caught up with the most recent changes to the image. Click the exclamation mark or the circular uncached refresh button near the top right of the palette for an accurate tonal range display.

The Levels Command

Levels can be used to make an image look lighter, darker, or more detailed. They can also be used to adjust color. A composite channel's brightness and tonal range can be adjusted to affect lightness and the appearance of detail, and an image's individual color channels can be adjusted to create a color shift in the image. This is one way an undesirable color cast may be removed.

The Levels dialog box

Access the Levels dialog box in either of the following ways:

- Choose Image ⇨ Adjustments ⇨ Levels.
- Click the Create a New Fill or Adjustment Layer button at the bottom of the Layers Palette and choose Levels.

The Levels dialog box, shown in Figure 9.5, displays a histogram with values measured from 0 (black) to 255 (white) and a starting gamma (midtone) value of 1.00.

Numeric Input Levels are below the sliders, and numeric Output Levels are shown at the bottom of the dialog box. The Channel menu, which shows the composite RGB color channel, can be changed to cause a Levels adjustment to target individual color channels, such as Red, Green, or Blue. The Channel menu options will vary according to the color mode of the image.

Make Levels adjustments to an image by:

- Dragging any of the sliders
- Entering numeric input and output (before and after) values
- Clicking in the image with Levels eyedroppers
- Clicking the Auto button

In the Levels dialog box (see Figure 9.5), triangular shadow, gamma, and midtone sliders are directly under the histogram bar graph. Numeric Input Levels are underneath the sliders, and numeric Output Levels are shown at the bottom of the dialog box. The Channel menu, which shows the composite RGB color channel, can be changed to cause a Levels adjustment to target individual color channels, such as Red, Green, or Blue. The Channel menu options will vary according to the color mode of the image.

FIGURE 9.5

Triangular shadow, gamma, and midtone sliders are directly under the histogram bar graph.

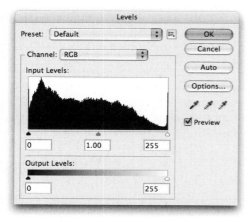

Using Levels

Shadow and highlight adjustments using Levels are made by changing an existing brightness level (Input Level) to a desired brightness level (Output Level), such as changing an Input Level of 12 (almost black) to 0 (totally black) when you want to make the darks in an image darker. When a level is changed, the other levels in an image are redistributed proportionately, including the value that the starting gamma (midtone) value of 1.00 represents.

The gamma value works a little differently than the shadow and highlight levels. Its numeric values are not represented by 0–255 in the Levels dialog box even though there are midtones in the image that can be measured in values between 0 and 255. In Levels, the gamma starts out at 1.00 and can be changed to a value greater than or less than 1.00. When a midtone brightness level has been redistributed because of an adjustment to the shadows or highlights, the change in the image's midtones is usually apparent by viewing the image in the image window.

However, the starting gamma value of 1.00 does not change to a different number until it is manually changed. If a redistributed or original midtone brightness level in the image is undesirable, you can change it by increasing or decreasing its value. While the Levels dialog box is still active, values in the 0–255 scale may be checked by hovering the pointer over the image in the image window and viewing RGB values in the Info palette.

CAUTION The histogram in the Levels dialog box doesn't reflect image changes at the time they are made, and the histogram in the Histogram palette will not fully update until you click OK in the Levels dialog box. You may also need to click the uncached refresh button in the Histogram palette to see an updated histogram.

Levels sliders

Dragging the shadow slider (the black triangle on the left) to the right darkens mostly the shadow areas of an image, as shown in Figure 9.6.

The histogram in the Levels dialog box also shows that the image's darkest shadows begin at about level 94, which is not very dark, since 0 equals black and 255 equals white. There are no bars in the histogram from about level 94 to 0, so it shows that there are no very dark shadows at all.

Dragging the shadow slider to Input Level 94, where the bars that represent the darkest shadows in the image begin, causes Photoshop to change Input Level 94 (not very dark) to Output Level 0 (black). The remaining values in the image are redistributed across the tonal range so that the shadows are darkened and the overall tonal range is increased. This makes the adjusted image on the right appear to have more detail and depth.

Dragging the shadow slider to Input Level 94, where the bars that represent the darkest shadows in the image begin, causes Photoshop to change Input Level 94 (not very dark) to Output Level 0 (black). The remaining values in the image are redistributed across the tonal range so that the shadows are darkened and the overall tonal range is increased. This makes the adjusted image on the right appear to have more detail and depth.

Dragging the highlight slider (the white triangle on the right) to the left lightens mostly the highlighted areas of an image, as shown in Figure 9.7. The right side of the Levels histogram shows very short bars in the highlight areas, which confirms that there are very few bright highlights. Dragging the highlight slider to the left lightens the highlights and in this case sets the original image level of 142 (not very bright) to 255 (white) and redistributes the image's other levels across the tonal range, which increases the image's overall tonal range. The resulting image is shown on the right.

Dragging the highlight slider to the left lightens the highlights and in this case sets the original image level of 142 (not very bright) to 255 (white) and redistributes the image's other levels across the tonal range, which increases the image's overall tonal range. The resulting image is shown on the right.

FIGURE 9.6

In this image the shadows need to be darkened, apparent by looking at the original image on the left. A Levels adjustment layer is used to darken the image.

Dragging the highlight slider to the left lightens the highlights, dragging the shadow slider to the right darkens the shadows, and dragging the midtone slider to the left lightens the midtones, as shown in Figure 9.8.

The original image of the boat on the left needs an increase in contrast, or lightening of highlights and darkening of shadows, which is achieved by dragging the highlight and shadow sliders inward toward the center of the histogram. That adjustment causes the redistributed midtones to be even darker (too dark), so the midtone slider is moved to the left to lighten mostly the midtone areas. Input Level 10 (not quite black) is changed to Output Level 0 (black), Input Level 161 (not very light) is changed to Output Level 255 (white), and the midtones are lightened from the value of 1.00 to the lighter value of 1.29. The adjusted image on the right shows more contrast, which translates to the appearance of more detail.

FIGURE 9.7

In the original image on the left, the lightest pixels in this illustration of a world map need to be lightened so that they show against the dark background. A Levels adjustment layer is used to lighten the image.

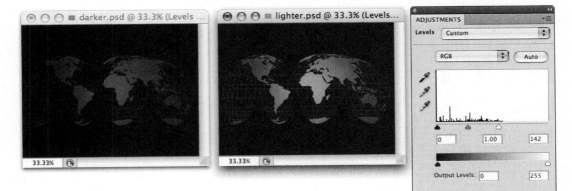

FIGURE 9.8

Contrast is increased with a Levels adjustment layer.

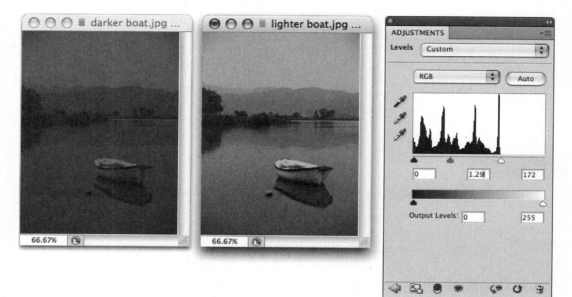

That adjustment causes the redistributed midtones to be even darker (too dark), so the midtone slider is moved to the left to lighten mostly the midtone areas.

Input Level 10 (not quite black) is changed to Output Level 0 (black), Input Level 161 (not very light) is changed to Output Level 255 (white), and the midtones are lightened from the value of 1.0 to the lighter value of 1.29. The adjusted image on the right shows more contrast, which translates to the appearance of more detail.

NOTE Output Levels don't necessarily need to be constrained to 0 (black) and 255 (white). While those values may be acceptable for images destined for on-screen viewing, images that will end up on a printing press need highlights that are a little darker than white and shadows that are a little lighter than black to preserve highlight and shadow detail, such as a shadow Output Level between 12 and 30 and a highlight Output Level between 230 and 242. The Output Levels can be used to set those values accordingly, although there are other ways to specify highlights and shadows, including the Curves command.

Levels numeric input and output values

Input and Output Levels can be entered as numeric values rather than assigned by dragging sliders. However, sometimes this means having to translate values from the destination color mode's numeric scale to the 0–255 scale, the standard measurement for RGB images and the scale used in the Levels dialog box.

One way to approximate equivalent values among color modes is to follow these steps:

1. **Open the Color Picker by clicking the Foreground Color button in the Toolbox.** Figure 9.9 shows the values available in the Color Picker (although the title of the dialog box would be Color Picker instead of the one shown if activated with the Foreground Color button).

2. **Enter the desired values in the Color Picker's color mode section that represents the image's destination color mode.** For example, values sometimes used for a CMYK mode image destined for a printing press are Highlight (C: 4, M: 2, Y: 2, K: 0) and Shadow (C: 80, M: 70, Y: 70, K: 70).

3. **Note the values that appear in the RGB section of the Color Picker after you have entered the desired destination color numbers.**

4. **Average the R, G, and B values to get the value you need to enter in the appropriate Output Levels field in the Levels dialog box.**

This won't yield exact destination values, but they should be in the ballpark. You can fine-tune values by checking values in the image with Color Samplers or the Eyedropper tool (be sure to set Sample Size to 3 x 3 in the Eyedropper Tool Options Bar) and the Info palette, then using Levels sliders or Curves to change values in the image. Fine-tuning is likely to involve manipulating colors in individual color channels in Levels or Curves.

When directly entering numeric midtone values, Levels allows you to simply change the gamma to a value greater than 1.00 to lighten midtones or less than 1.00 to darken midtones.

 **Click once in a numeric value field, then use the up and down arrow keys to raise and lower the values.**

FIGURE 9.9

Clicking a Levels eyedropper tool brings up a dialog box that includes standard Color Picker options, where values can be assigned to the Levels eyedropper tool. Clicking on the image in the image window with a Levels eyedropper tool sets that level in the image to the tool's assigned value, and other levels are redistributed proportionately.

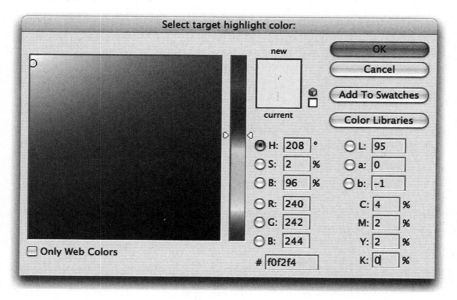

Levels eyedroppers

You can use any of the Levels eyedroppers — Set White Point tool, Set Gray Point tool, and Set Black Point tool — to change color values in the image to neutral tones (a white, gray, or black that lacks any color). You may need to use one, two, or all three eyedroppers to remove a color cast. The remaining color values in the image are redistributed proportionately. The Levels eyedroppers can remove an undesirable color cast, such as a greenish tint in a photo taken in fluorescent light, but it is sometimes tricky to determine which colors in an image are supposed to be a neutral color.

Follow these steps to use Levels eyedroppers to remove a color cast:

1. **Click on the Eyedropper tool in the Toolbox.** Set the Sample Size to 3 x 3 in the Eyedropper Tool Options Bar.

2. **Select the Levels command.** Choose Image ⇨ Adjust ⇨ Levels, or press the Create a New Fill or Adjustment Layer button at the bottom of the Layers Palette and choose Levels.

3. **Click the Set White Point Eyedropper in the Levels dialog box.**

4. **Enter desired white point values.** Values sometimes used for images destined for print are C: 4, M: 2, Y: 2, K: 0 or H: 0, S: 0, B: (between 80 and 96). Highlight values that can be used for on-screen images can range from solid white, R: 255, B: 255, B: 255, to values similar to the values for print when you need to maintain more detail in the highlights.

5. **Click OK.**

6. **Click the Set Black Point Eyedropper in the Levels dialog box.**

7. **Enter desired black point values.** Values sometimes used for images destined for print are C: 80, M: 70, Y: 70, K: 70 or H: 0, S: 0, B: (between 4 and 20). Black point values that can be used for on-screen images can range from solid black, R: 0, B: 0, G:0 to values similar to the values for print when you need to maintain more detail in the shadows.

8. **Click the Set Gray Point Eyedropper in the Levels dialog box.**

9. **Enter the desired gray point value.** If your image is an average key image — one that is not intended to be overall very light or very dark but somewhere in between — and you think part of the image should be a middle-neutral-gray color, enter RGB values of R: 128, G: 128, B: 128.

10. **Examine the image to guess which areas should be neutral, then click on a targeted area with the appropriate Levels eyedropper tool.** It may take several tries to remove a color cast, and you may need to use one, two, or all three Levels eyedroppers. If you don't like a change and the Levels dialog box is still active, you can choose Edit ⇨ Undo to undo the most recent change. If you chose Levels from the Image ⇨ Adjustments menu, you can Alt-Click the Cancel button on a PC, or Option-Click the Cancel button on a Mac, to reset the Levels dialog box values to what they were before you made any changes. If you created a Levels adjustment layer, you can click the Reset button next to the trash can at the bottom right of the Levels adjustment layer dialog box.

11. If necessary, fine-tune the color by adjusting individual color channels, which can be targeted by selecting them in the Levels Channel menu.

12. Click OK.

CROSS-REF See Chapter 15 for more about color-correcting with Levels and Curves.

The Auto and Options buttons in Levels and Curves

You can access the same Auto Color Correction Options settings by clicking the Options button in the Levels or the Curves dialog box. Use these settings to increase contrast, attempt to correct color, or cause the most extreme shadows and highlights in an image to be changed to or left as solid white or solid black (in other words, to be clipped).

These extreme values, expressed as the top percentage of the brightest highlights and darkest shadows, are assumed to be irrelevant content that doesn't contain detail. Some examples are specular highlights, such as shiny bright-white reflections or black dust specks. The goal of clipping these extreme values is to cause Photoshop to ignore them and apply the settings only to meaningful pixels, which would hopefully maximize enhancement in the parts of an image that do contain meaningful detail.

Figure 9.10 shows the Auto Color Correction Options dialog box.

Apply the Auto Color Correction Options settings that are current at a given time in either of the following ways:

■ Click the Auto button in the Levels or the Curves dialog box.

■ Click the Options button in the Levels or the Curves dialog box, make any desired changes to the options, click OK to return to the Curves or Levels dialog box, then click the OK button again.

FIGURE 9.10

The Auto Color Correction Options dialog box

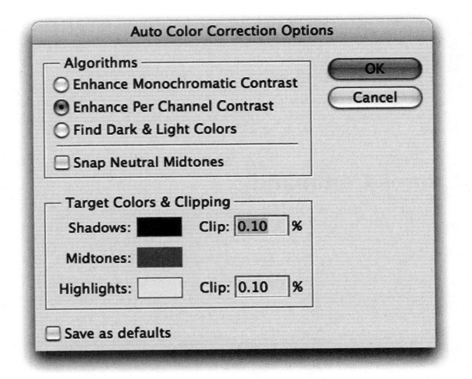

The Auto Tone, Auto Contrast, and Auto Color commands that are accessed in the Image menu also use some of the Auto Color Correction Options settings. However, instead of using the settings that are shown when the Options button is clicked, each of these Auto commands uses its own personalized version of the settings:

- **Auto Tone uses Enhance Per Channel Contrast.** The Enhance Per Channel Contrast algorithm increases contrast in each channel but may shift colors and introduce an undesirable color cast.

- **Auto Contrast uses Enhance Monochromatic Contrast.** The Enhance Monochromatic Contrast algorithm increases contrast in each channel but does not shift colors in the image.

■ **Auto Color uses Find Dark & Light Colors and Snap Neutral Midtones.** The Find Dark & Light Colors algorithm and Snap Neutral Midtones option increase contrast in each channel and change values that are close to neutral gray to a definite neutral gray.

Using the Auto commands is somewhat of a guessing game. You may want to try each one and choose the one that gives the best result for the image.

CAUTION If you change the Target Colors' Shadows, Midtones, and Highlights values in the Auto Color Correction Options dialog box, put a check mark in the Save as defaults check box, and click OK, the Auto commands in the Image menu will no longer use any of the Algorithms settings in the Auto Color Correction Options. The Auto commands will only use the values specified in the Target Colors & Clipping section, except the Auto Color command will additionally apply the Snap Neutral Midtones setting.

The Curves Command

The Curves command is one of the most powerful features in Photoshop. It can be used to make an image look lighter, darker, or more detailed. Color balance can be precisely adjusted and undesirable color casts can be removed. Composite color channels and individual color channels can be targeted, as well as any segment of an image's tonal range.

A key strength of curves is that many points along the tonal range of an image can be adjusted (up to 14), whereas Levels is limited to three points of adjustment. Finding the part of the curve that corresponds to the part of an image you want to target is very convenient when using curves.

With the Curves dialog box open, you can move your pointer over the image in the image window and hold down the mouse button on the part of the image you want to target. You can also hold down the mouse button while you drag your pointer over an area of the image. Either of these actions cause a point to temporarily display in the corresponding areas along the curve while you drag. If you want to place a point on the curve by clicking directly in the part of the image you want to target, simply press Ctrl/⌘ while you click in the image.

Both Curves and Levels can display 0–255 numeric values (black to white). This scale is also used to describe color levels in RGB color mode, a commonly used color mode for images displayed on-screen.

Curves also displays ink percentage values. Tracking ink values is essential in the adjustment of images that are destined to be printed in ink on paper, many of which will use CMYK color mode or grayscale mode.

The Curves dialog box

The Curves dialog box can be accessed by selecting either of the following:

- Choose Image ➪ Adjustments ➪ Curves.
- Press the Create a New Fill or Adjustment Layer button at the bottom of the Layers Palette and choose Curves.

The Curves dialog box displays a linear graph of the tonal levels available to an image. The initial straight diagonal baseline represents the image as it is before any Curves changes, when original Input Levels (color values) equal corresponding Output Levels. This line is called a curve, usually even when it looks straight, because it is part of the Curves command and it can be curved to cause color and brightness changes in the image.

Clicking and holding down the mouse button while dragging the curve with the pointer changes the straight line to a curved line. It also adds a point on the curve and changes color and/or brightness levels in the part of the image that corresponds to the altered part of the curve.

Each point that is added to the curve corresponds to an original Input color value and a new Output color value that displays in the Input/Output field boxes when the point is selected. Even when a point is not selected, you can simply hold the pointer over a part of the curve or curve grid without clicking the mouse button to display the Input/Output values for that area. The end points of the curve, which exist by default, may also be moved to adjust the lightest highlight and the darkest shadow areas in an image.

The initial straight diagonal baseline curve in the grid shown in Figure 9.11 represents the image with no changes. The histogram shown in the background of the grid is a bar graph that illustrates the actual tonal range in the active image.

The image it represents has none of the brightest highlights possible, which is evident because there are no vertical gray bars on the far right side of the histogram. The white point on the curve could be moved to the left a short distance to lighten the highlights and increase the tonal range.

The curve spans the entire tonal range that is possible for an image, in this case it is shown in the numeric range 0 (black) to 255 (white) because it is an RGB color mode image. In this figure, the point on the line that represents the darkest value possible for the image is at the bottom-left corner of the graph. The black point on the curve is filled with black because it is selected.

FIGURE 9.11

The Curves dialog box displays a linear graph that represents the entire tonal range possible in an image. Curves can be used to precisely change the tones and colors in images.

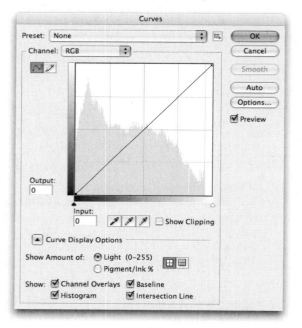

When a point on a curve is selected, its Input and Output levels show, and both levels for this black point show the value 0. The point at the top-right corner of the graph represents the white point, and its Input and Output levels are 255.

If the white point were selected, the value 255 would show in the Input and Output boxes. The middle part of a curve represents the midtones of an image, the part of the curve between the shadows and midtones represents the three-quarter tones, and the part of the curve between the midtones and highlights represents the quarter tones. A histogram is shown in the background and represents the actual tonal range of the active image.

CROSS-REF See "Auto and Options buttons in Levels and Curves" in the Levels section of this chapter. These buttons perform the same function even though they appear in both the Curves and Levels dialog boxes. For example, if you change the Auto Color Corrections Options by accessing them in Levels, you can see your changes to the options if you view them by clicking the Options button in the Curves dialog box.

The following list defines parts of the Curves dialog box:

- **Preset menu.** Pre-made curves can be selected in an attempt to improve an image or to serve as a starting point. After applying a preset curve, you can continue to adjust the curve manually.

- **Save/load preset button (to the left of OK button).** Save or load your custom curves.

- **Channel menu.** The curve affects only the composite or individual color channel selected in this menu.

- **Curve points button (at left, under Channel menu).** Must be active when you want to add points to a curve.

- **Curve pencil button (at right, under Channel menu).** Must be active when you want to draw a freeform curve.

- **Smooth button (next to the pencil button).** When the Curves pencil button is selected, the Smooth button is available. Click it to smooth the curve.

- **Tonal Input/Output bars (black-to-white bars on left and below Curve grid).** The tones on the Output bar line up with and represent the tones on the horizontal output axis; the tones on the Input bar line up with and represent the tones on the input axis.

- **Input/Output fields.** These numeric fields display values of points on the curve or Curve grid when a point on the curve is selected or the pointer is held over the curve or grid.

- **Curve.** The line that represents the entire tonal range possible in an image, which can be manipulated to change the tonal range in an image and any of its channels. The initial curve is a straight diagonal baseline that represents the image with no changes.

- **Curve grid.** The gray grid behind the curve that represents the Input/Output axes.

- **Curve histogram.** The gray histogram behind the curve that represents the actual tonal range contained in the active image.

- **Curve eyedroppers.** The Set Black Point, Set Gray Point, and Set White Point eyedroppers can be assigned a color value, and when a point in the image is clicked with one of the eyedroppers, the point changes to the assigned color and causes the other colors in the image to be redistributed proportionately.

- **Show Clipping check box.** Check box to show areas in the image that are being clipped, or changed to solid black or white.

- **Preview button.** Check box to see a preview version of the image in the image window that includes the Curves changes. Uncheck to see the image without the Curves changes.

- **Auto and Options buttons.** Click the Options button to set Auto Color Correction Options, then click OK to apply them, or click the Auto button to apply the current Auto Color Correction Options. The Auto Color Correction Options can attempt to improve an image in several ways, including increasing contrast in composite or individual channels, setting nearly neutral values to neutral to remove a color cast, and setting clipping percentages.

The following list defines Curve Display options (accessible directly in an Image ⇨ Adjustments ⇨ Curves dialog box or in the palette menu of a Curves adjustment layer dialog box):

- **Show Amount of Light.** Displays Input/Output values in 0–255, black to white.

- **Show Amount of Pigment/Ink percent.** Displays Input/Output values in 0 percent–100 percent, no ink to 100 percent solid ink, or highlights to shadows. This reverses orientation of highlights and shadows on the grid.

- **Grid buttons (to right of Pigment/Ink %).** Click the Simple Grid button on the left to display the Curve grid in 25 percent increments and click the Detailed Grid button on the right to display the Curve grid in 10 percent increments.

- **Show Channel Overlays.** Check box to show colored individual color channel curve lines, along with the normal black-colored composite channel curve line.

- **Show Baseline.** Check box to show the original curve baseline.

- **Show Histogram.** Check box to show the active image's histogram behind the curve in the Curve grid. Note that the Curves histogram appears condensed compared to the Histogram palette's histogram. The Curves histogram does not update as you alter the curve. To see an updated histogram, click OK and view the histogram in the Histogram palette — you may need to click the uncached Refresh button to update the histogram. Also, after you click OK and exit the Curves dialog box, if you reopen Curves it displays an updated histogram.

- **Show Intersection Line.** Check box to show horizontal and vertical gray lines that extend outward from a point on the curve when you drag the point. These lines can help you align the point to the grid.

CAUTION Tonal Input/Output bars and corresponding Input/Output axes change orientation in different color modes. For example, the curve would need to be moved up to lighten midtones in RGB images and down to lighten midtones in CMYK and grayscale images.

You can make Curves adjustments by using any of the following options:

- Dragging the curve line, which adds a point to the curve and adjusts corresponding levels in the tonal range of the image

- Dragging the curve end points, which adjusts shadow and highlight levels

- Clicking in the image with the Curves eyedroppers

- Adding and selecting a point by clicking on the curve or selecting an existing point on the curve and entering numeric values for the point in the Output and/or Input boxes

- Selecting a Preset Curve from the Preset menu

- Dragging the shadow and highlight sliders at the bottom of the Curves graph

- Clicking the Auto button

TIP Try drawing all sorts of doodles on the curve with the Curve pencil for artsy color effects. Be sure to click the Preview button to preview the changes. Ctrl+click/ ⌘+click the Cancel button to reset the curve to its original state (or if a Curves adjustment layer dialog box is active, click the Reset button next to the dialog box's trash can to reset the curve).

Using Curves

The curves shown in Figures 9.12 through 9.15 have been altered by clicking and holding down the mouse button while dragging the curve or its end points. Dragging the curve adds a point to the curve. Any part of the curve that is in a different position than the original diagonal baseline changes a corresponding part of the image.

Notice the relationship between the direction the curve point is moved away from its original position and the values on the Tonal Input/Output bars.

For example, if the point is moved on the grid in the direction of the shadow parts of a bar, the image darkens in its corresponding area. If you move a point vertically, notice the vertical Tonal bar, and if you move a point horizontally, notice the horizontal Tonal bar. The individual Red, Green, and Blue color channels work a little differently, which is explained in the following Note.

The captions for Figures 9.12 through 9.15 explain the effect the curves would have on an image.

TIP Undo Curves adjustments by dragging points out of the Curves grid to remove them from the curve, or Ctrl+click/⌘+click the Cancel button to reset the curve to its original state.

FIGURE 9.12

The curve on the left lightens the composite (full color) channel in this RGB image, more in the midtones than in other areas. The curve on the right darkens the composite (full color) channel in this RGB image, more in the midtones than in other areas.

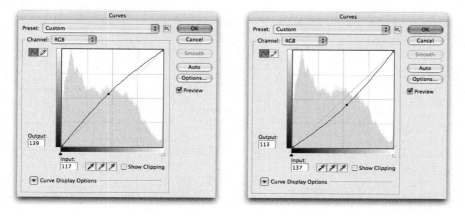

FIGURE 9.13

The curve on the left lightens the composite (full color) channel in this CMYK image, more in the midtones than in other areas. The curve on the right darkens the composite (full color) channel in this CMYK image, more in the midtones than in other areas.

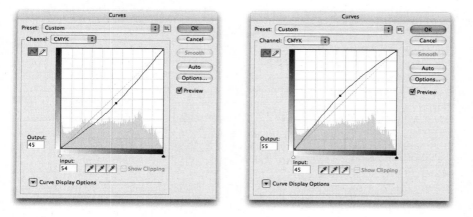

FIGURE 9.14

The curve on the left, which targets only the Blue channel, adds blue to this RGB image. It adds more in the midtones than in other areas. So, the full color image would look bluer. The curve on the right darkens only the Magenta channel in this CMYK image, more in the midtones than in other areas. So, the full color image would look more pink.

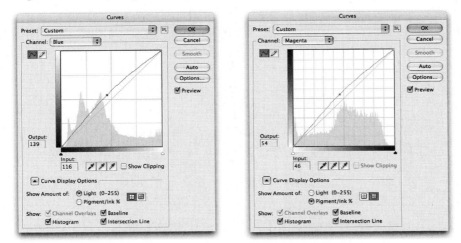

Adjusting the Curve in a Color Channel

In RGB color mode, moving the curve in an individual color channel works like a seesaw between two colors. Moving the curve up adds more of the color shown in the Channel menu. Moving the curve down subtracts the color shown in the Channel menu and therefore appears to add more of another color. The color pairs in each channel are Red-Cyan, Green-Magenta, and Blue-Yellow. It may be easier to remember by thinking about pairing up the first three letters in each of two color modes this way:

RGB

CMY

Up for red, down for cyan; up for green, down for magenta; up for blue, down for yellow.

If you forget which way you need to move an individual Red, Green, or Blue channel to affect any of those six colors, you can just make a temporary drastic move in both directions, then the direction you need to move the curve will become apparent by the color changes you see in the image.

FIGURE 9.15

The curve on the left represents a grayscale mode image, as seen in the Channel menu. Its curve darkens the highlights and lightens the shadows. The curve on the right is targeting the composite channel in an RGB image and uses the Preset: Increase Contrast (RGB). This curve increases contrast in the image, except in the highlight and shadow areas.

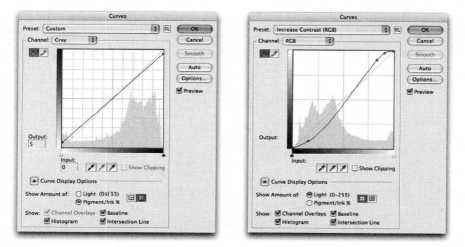

NOTE The steeper the curve, the greater the contrast. Wherever the curve is at a steeper angle than its original diagonal line, contrast is increased in the corresponding parts of the image. Wherever the curve is less steep than its original diagonal line, contrast is decreased in the corresponding parts of the image.

Figures 9.16 through 9.18 show how you can use Curves to improve the same images that were adjusted with Levels earlier in the chapter.

In Figure 9.16, the RGB mode image on the left needs the shadows darkened and the overall tonal range increased. Notice that the histogram shows there are no shadows at all in the image — no vertical bars on the left side. The black point of the curve is moved to the right, where the darkest parts of the image begin in the histogram. This forces the current darkest point in the image (see the gray value in the corresponding area of the Tonal Input bar) to change to black. The point near the top was added to keep the highlights as they were (the upper curve lines up with the original baseline). The middle point was added to steepen the curve and add contrast. All the shadow areas of the curve are moved to the right of the original baseline, which resets midtone areas to darker values. An improved image with an increased tonal range is shown on the right.

This forces the current darkest point in the image (see the gray value in the corresponding area of the Tonal Input bar) to change to black. The point near the top was added to keep the highlights as they were (the upper curve lines up with the original baseline). The middle point was added to steepen the curve and add contrast. All the shadow areas of the curve are moved to the right of the original baseline, which resets midtone areas to darker values. An improved image with an increased tonal range is shown on the right.

In the original image on the left of Figure 9.17, the lightest pixels in the illustration of a world map need to be lightened so they show against the dark background. The right side of the Curves histogram shows very short bars in the highlight areas, which confirms that there are very few bright highlights. Dragging the curve up in the highlight area lightens the highlights, and dragging the curve up in the shadows lightens some shadow areas. The resulting image is shown on the right.

TIP It is usually best to keep the curve smooth and avoid adding unnecessary points. Making too many moves in the curve can cause a loss of tonal levels.

The original image of the boat on the left of Figure 9.18 needs an increase in contrast. Highlight area points on the curve are moved up so that highlights become much lighter, midtones become somewhat lighter, and dark shadows are kept the same by keeping the lower shadow part of the curve close to its original baseline.

FIGURE 9.16

The RGB mode image on the left needs the shadows darkened and the overall tonal range increased.

FIGURE 9.17

In the original image on the left, the lightest pixels in the illustration of a world map need to be lightened so they show against the dark background.

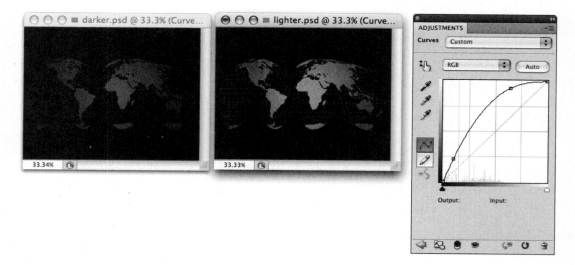

FIGURE 9.18

The original image of the boat on the left needs an increase in contrast.

Summary

This chapter described the purposes for and how to use histograms, the Levels command, and the Curves command.

Histograms are bar graphs that describe the tonal range in an image. They can be helpful in deciding what image adjustments are needed. Histograms show vertical bars of varying heights that represent the amounts of each brightness level in an image, measured from 0 (black) to 255 (white).

The Levels command and the Curves command can be used to make an image look lighter, darker, or more detailed. They can also be used for full-color composite or individual channel adjustments. Levels displays a histogram and offers 3 points of adjustment: shadow, gamma (midtones), and highlight. Curves also displays a histogram, but can have up to 14 points of adjustment. Levels uses the 0 (black) to 255 (white) scale. Curves uses either the 0 (black) to 255 (white) scale or the 0 percent to 100 percent ink level scale. Curves offers convenient ways to determine which parts of the curve correspond to specific parts of the image.

Chapter 10

Selections and Channels

IN THIS CHAPTER

Core selection tools and options

Refining selections

Understanding channels

Selections are the single most important concept to understand when working with Photoshop. The ability to quickly and accurately isolate specific parts of your image is vital to creating compelling digital art and an efficient workflow. To accomplish this, you must know how and when to use the various selection tools and refinement options that Photoshop CS4 provides.

Using the right selection tool at the right time can make Photoshop a more enjoyable and efficient process. Using the wrong tool can be an exercise in frustration at best, and can even have a negative impact on the quality of your project in some cases.

This chapter demonstrates how to use some of the most important selection tools and techniques, and also provides advice on when to use those tools. You will learn — among other things — how to use the Marquee tools, the Lasso tools, the Select menu, the Refine Edge command, and the Channels panel. Each of these items can help you to become a more proficient Photoshop user and should help make the image-editing process more enjoyable as well (at least, that's my hope!).

As you read through the chapter, it is recommended you have your laptop or computer at hand with some images open, so that you can experiment with each tool as it is discussed. It is less important that you follow the exact examples given than it is to understand the context and options that control a given selection tool. The more you experiment with each tool, the quicker they will become familiar to you.

Core Selection Tools and Options

Photoshop CS4's core selection tools are found within the main toolbar, with the exception of the Color Range function, which is found in the Select menu. Like other tools mentioned earlier in the book, each of the selection tools has additional parameters and controls that can be found on the Options Bar as you click each one.

Most of the selection tools discussed in this chapter are much easier to use with the help of a digital tablet and stylus; however, they are not required for the selection tools to function in general.

All selections — regardless of shape or the tool used to make them — will appear on the canvas as a progression of white-and-black line segments (sometimes called "marching ants") that continually move around your selected image area. You will see these marching ants in most of the chapter figures that are provided.

The Marquee tools

There are four Marquee tools available within Photoshop, shown in Figure 10.1. Located near the top of the toolbar, and easily recognized by their dotted-line icons, they are the Rectangular Marquee, Elliptical Marquee, Single Row Marquee, and Single Column Marquee.

FIGURE 10.1

The Marquee tools are a simple way to create geometric selections within your document.

These four selection tools are characterized by their ability to isolate geometric-shaped areas of the image with a minimum of steps. Among all the selection tools, they are the simplest to use and should be familiar in concept to anyone who has used the mouse for simple tasks like highlighting a range of text in a word-processing program or Web page. All you need to do is click, drag, and release.

The Rectangular Marquee tool is used to create rectangular or square selections over your image. It is most often useful when the photograph you are editing has man-made objects like road signs, bricks, or windows that need to be isolated from the rest of the image.

The Elliptical Marquee tool is used to create elliptical, circular, or semi-circular selections over your image. It is useful in a variety of situations where you need to select circular objects in photos, such as those seen in Figure 10.2, or when you would like to create circular color fills over an image area.

The Single Row and Single Column Marquee tools are typically used less often than their rectangular and elliptical siblings, but are useful for selecting a 1-pixel strip that spans the width (row) or height (column) of your image. These tools can be confusing when you look at their results because they do not appear to contain anything, but rather seem to form a single line of marching ants.

Don't let this fool you; the pixels that are selected are directly below the row or column of *ants*. To test this, make your selection and then click the Delete key one time, then press Ctrl+D (⌘+D on a Mac). This is the keyboard shortcut for deselecting the previously selected region, thereby removing the marching ants from your canvas. Once the selection is gone, you will see that the underlying pixels have been deleted, as shown in Figure 10.3.

FIGURE 10.2

The Elliptical Marquee tool is useful for selecting circular objects as well as for creating artistic touches. Circular selections can be cut in half to form semicircular selections as seen here.

To use any of the Marquee tools, follow these steps:

1. **Select the appropriate marquee from the toolbar.**

2. **Move the cursor over the point on your image where you want to start the selection.**

3. **For the Rectangular and Elliptical marquees, click and drag until the entire area you wish to select is inside the marching ants. Hold down the Shift key as you drag if you need to form a perfectly square or circular selection.** (For the Single Row and Single Column Marquees, click once on the area you wish to select.)

4. **Release the mouse button when the entire region you are targeting has been surrounded.** If making a perfect square or circle, be sure to release the mouse button before you release the Shift key, otherwise your selection will lose its symmetry (see Table 10.1).

296

FIGURE 10.3

The Single Row and Single Column Marquee tools may not appear to have selected anything, but the pixels directly below the marching ants are selected and can be manipulated or deleted just like any other selection.

Important keyboard shortcuts

There are several important modifier keys that you can hold down in different combinations to alter the behavior of your selections as you create them. These are listed in Table 10.1, and are worth practicing and committing to memory if possible. They will prove to be useful time-savers in many situations. Some of these shortcuts are described later in the chapter.

TABLE 10.1

Selection Keyboard Shortcuts

Mac Shortcut	PC Shortcut	Used With	Behavior Applied to Selection
⌘+A	Crtl+A	No area selected	Selects 100 percent of the active layer's pixels.
⌘+D	Crtl+D	All selection tools	Deselects the image region (marching ants will disappear).
Space+drag	Same	Rectangular and Elliptical Marquee tools	Allows the selection at current size to be moved to another part of the document. When you release the spacebar, the selection can still be shaped.
Shift+click+drag	Same	All selection tools	When creating an initial selection with the Rectangular or Elliptical Marquee tool, creates a perfect square or circle. For all selection tools, if an existing selection exists, the subsequent selection region is added when holding down Shift.
Option+click+drag	Alt+click+drag	All selection tools	If an existing selection exists, any overlap created is subtracted from the original selection area.
Shift+Option+click+drag	Shift+Alt+click+drag	All except Quick Selection tool	If an existing selection exists, the overlapping area becomes the new selection region.
⌘+drag	Ctrl+drag	All existing selections	Cuts, pastes, and moves the selected area.
⌘+Option+drag	Ctrl+Alt+drag	All existing selections	Moves a copy of the selected area.
⌘+Option+Shift+drag	Ctrl+Alt+Shift+drag	All existing selections	Allows multiple copies of a selection to be placed on the canvas, each one following from the previous duplicate, as you repeatedly click and drag.

Feathering selections

One of the most useful selection properties is the ability to define a feathering boundary around the periphery of your selection, using the Options Bar. By setting a feather value of 1 or more pixels, you can help ensure that any effects you are applying to the selected area, or any areas being copied and pasted, blend in more smoothly with the surrounding pixels, as seen in Figure 10.4.

FIGURE 10.4

Set a feather value to your selection in order to ensure that it blends more smoothly with the surrounding image elements, or when pasted into another document.

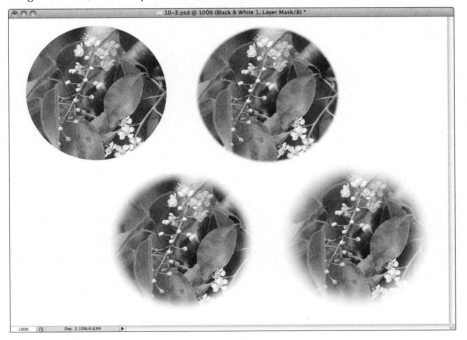

Anti-aliasing

When feathering is not an optimal solution, another helpful option is the ability to apply anti-aliased edges, as seen in Figure 10.5. Like feathering, this option allows you to smooth the boundary transition between selected and unselected image elements, but unlike feathering, it is limited to the outermost edge of your selection.

NOTE Most of the selection tools discussed in this chapter have feathering and anti-aliasing options, with the exception of Single Row and Column Marquee tools (feather only), the Quick Selection tool (neither), and the Magic Wand tool (anti-aliasing only).

FIGURE 10.5

Anti-aliasing provides a means of smoothing the edge boundaries of your selection.

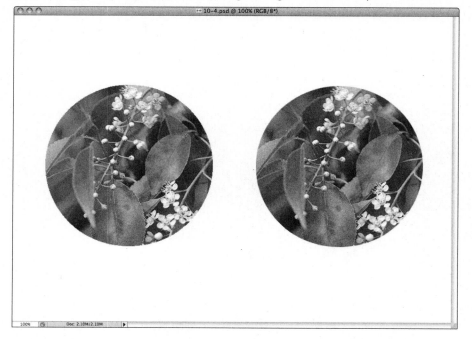

The Lasso tools

While somewhat more complex in their behavior than the Marquee tools, the Lasso tools are among the most powerful selection tools Photoshop offers. Using a digital tablet and stylus, the Lasso tools can help create precise shapes and outlines. All that's required is a bit of focus and patience. Most of the items we photograph in the real world are not perfect rectangles or ellipses, but rather, oddly proportioned and undulating shapes that require maximum flexibility in a selection tool.

The Lasso tools are all grouped together under a single button, and are located directly below the Marquee tools. They also have a variety of parameters and options for tweaking the selections they create, as seen in Figures 10.6 and 10.7.

TIP Trying to get a selection perfect on the first pass with the Lasso tool can often lead to frustration. Instead, get the selection close, then zoom in and use the Shift (add to selection) and Alt/Option shortcuts (subtract from selection) to get the selection perfected. Aside from ultimately being more precise, this method is usually quicker than attempting a perfect selection in one pass, particularly when working with complex shapes or shapes that span a large area of canvas.

FIGURE 10.6

The Lasso tools are among the Photoshop user's best friends.

FIGURE 10.7

The Lasso tool is an excellent means of selecting asymmetric regions of your photos.

Polygonal Lasso tool

The Polygonal Lasso is designed to outline the edge regions of a scene, creating a many-sided selection without having to attempt to draw the selection freehand with the Lasso tool. To create a selection, like the one seen in Figure 10.8, with the Polygonal Lasso, follow these steps:

1. **Zoom in to at least 50 percent so you can see the boundaries and angle-points of the shape you will be outlining more clearly.**

2. **Select the Polygonal Lasso and move the cursor to the first edge you wish to outline.**

3. **Click once to set down your first selection "anchor."** Now move the stylus and you will see a new selection line is created that you can angle into position along the edges you wish to select.

4. **Once you find the spot where you want to place your next anchor, click again.**

   The closer together you place the selection anchors, the more you can — in effect — create rounded selection areas. This is helpful when working around the corners of rooflines, machinery, or other man-made objects in your photos, for example.

5. **Continue this process until you've worked your way around the entire polygon.**

6. **To close the polygon and create your selection, move the cursor from your last anchor to the first one you placed.** The cursor should show a small circle to indicate you can "close the loop." Click again to create the selection.

FIGURE 10.8

The Polygonal Lasso can help you to outline many-sided geometric shapes with just a few clicks. Here two selections were added together by holding down the Shift key as the second set of selection anchors were placed.

Magnetic Lasso tool

The Magnetic Lasso operates like the standard Lasso, except that it automatically places selection anchors as you move the cursor along the edge you are targeting for selection. These anchors automatically "snap" to the points of highest contrast, and do not require you to click or hold down the mouse or stylus button. You can, however, click the mouse or stylus button to manually add a point if Photoshop does not place one where you need it.

The Magnetic Lasso is a good tool for selecting areas that have very well-defined, uninterrupted contrast relative to the surrounding image, such as in Figure 10.9. The more pronounced the contrasting edge, the better the Magnetic Lasso works. If you have an image where the area you wish to select is bordered by colors or tones with very low contrast values, you are better off not using the Magnetic Lasso; use the standard Lasso tool instead if possible.

The Magnetic Lasso has four important control parameters. Located on the Options Bar, the settings you choose (described in the following list and seen in Figure 10.9) should vary from image to image, depending on the relative contrast of the items being selected.

- **Width.** This option determines how far on either side of the Lasso cursor Photoshop will search for edge contrast. The narrower the value, the more precise your "tracking" of the edges will be. However, this option usually requires a fairly high contrast edge to be effective, as well as a steady hand. If you're likely to waver off the line a little bit, use a higher value or zoom in more to stay on track as you make selections.

303

FIGURE 10.9

The Magnetic Lasso can be useful when making selections of high-contrast image regions. Note that with high-contrast images you can use a relatively higher width and much higher contrast setting to select the edge quickly and avoid misplaced anchors.

- **Contrast.** This option defines whether the Magnetic Lasso searches for high-contrast or lower-contrast edges within the Width boundaries. The more contrast the edge regions of your image have, the higher the value should be. For example, images with nearly black-and-white contrasting regions should benefit from values between 90 and 100. For images with many midtones and not a lot of contrast, a value below 50 is a good idea. If the contrast is too low, the Magnetic Lasso tool may not be your best choice; try the standard or Polygonal Lasso in those cases.

- **Frequency.** This option defines how frequently the selection anchors are placed along the contrast edges of your image. Generally, the lower the contrast, the higher you will want this value to be and the more you will want to zoom in and try to follow the edge path as precisely as possible with your mouse or stylus. Higher-contrast edges can use lower values.

- **Tablet Pressure.** Found next to the Frequency option, this button allows you to use a stylus and tablet to change the Width value in real time by pressing harder or more lightly on the tablet as you move across the selection edge. Tablet Pressure does not have any effect when using a mouse.

Quick Selection, Magic Wand, and Color Range

The Quick Selection, Magic Wand, and Color Range tools work by detecting areas of similar color and tone to create regional color selections. While they may appear at first to look and behave similarly, the Quick Selection and Magic Wand tools are actually quite different in their approach, so you will want to become familiar with each by experimenting.

Quick Selection tool

Introduced in Photoshop CS3, the Quick Selection tool works by allowing you to slowly brush over the image, analyzing the color and contrast values as you move the cursor. As you do so, the selection begins snapping to the closest contrast edges and continues to expand as long as you hold down the mouse button or stylus on the tablet. Shown in Figure 10.10, the Quick Selection tool is a great way to quickly select a shape region without hand-drawing the shape with the Lasso tools.

FIGURE 10.10

The Quick Selection tool provides an effective means of "painting" over a region to find the nearest edges, forming an expanding selection region as you move the brush.

Once you have clicked the mouse button or picked up your stylus, the initial selection is made and the Quick Selection tool automatically switches to "add to selection" mode. As you click more or brush over more of the neighboring areas, they are added to the selection. Note that you do not have to maintain a contiguous region of selections with this tool. You can have many regions within an image selected at the same time. To subtract part of an existing selection region, hold down the Alt/Option key as you drag.

The Quick Selection tool has three parameters for controlling the degree to which things are selected. The first is the size and hardness of the brush you are using. Brushes with a higher hardness setting tend to select larger regions of the image than do softer brushes, and larger brushes also tend to select more of the surrounding image than smaller brushes. There are also a couple of items from the Options Bar that you'll want to pay attention to:

- **Sample All Layers.** This option allows the Quick Selection tool to sample the colors and contrast regions from all layers in the image, not just the active layer.

- **Auto-Enhance.** This setting attempts to create more uniform or smooth selection edges as you "paint" out the selection boundaries. While worth trying; it's not always effective. Like the standard Lasso tool, it is often the case with the Quick Selection tool that you will have to make a first pass at creating your selection area, and then go back and refine it by adding or subtracting regions of the image.

Magic Wand tool

The Magic Wand has been around since the early days of Photoshop and was for many years a reliable way of selecting regions of an image based on its colors, though it can also be used to select specific tonal regions. Shown in Figure 10.11, the Magic Wand has several options for narrowing its selection criteria, and can be quite useful with images that have well-defined regions of saturated hues.

For example, think pure blue sky rather than a multi-colored sunset. Both have saturated colors, but the pure blue sky is more uniform and doesn't contain any "transition" colors (for example, a shift from orange-red to pink or purple). The Magic Wand can work in either situation, but it creates the most precise selection on a first pass, when used on an image region with more uniform color.

FIGURE 10.11

Use the Magic Wand tool to select regions of saturated, uniform colors or tone.

The most important options for the Magic Wand are the Tolerance and Contiguous settings:

- **Tolerance.** This setting determines to what degree colors other than the one you clicked on are included in the selection. The higher the value, the more neighboring colors are selected. The default value of 32 is actually fairly liberal and tends to select more colors than just the one you clicked. Generally you will want to start out with a lower value.

  Figures 10.11 and 10.12 illustrate the difference between a moderate Tolerance value of 15 (Figure 10.11), and a very conservative value of 4 (Figure 10.12). The image was clicked in the same spot, but notice how much less of it is selected within Figure 10.12 versus Figure 10.11.

- **Contiguous.** This setting defines whether the selection contains a continuous area of color or be spread across the image in different, unconnected areas.

FIGURE 10.12

Lower Tolerance settings limit the Magic Wand's selections to similar regions of color. The Contiguous setting limits the selection to regions of connected color or tonality.

Color Range

Accessed from the Photoshop Select menu or the Masks panel, the Color Range function allows you to choose specific hues and tones to define your selection or layer mask. Shown in Figure 10.13, the Color Range dialog box is more complex than the other selection tools but well worth learning.

The Color Range dialog box has several controls (shown in Figure 10.14) that you will want to familiarize yourself with.

The following list details what each of these controls does when making your selections:

- **Select menu.** This allows you to use as the basis of your selection either one of six colors (red, green, blue, cyan, magenta, or yellow); one of three tonal levels (highlights, midtones, shadows); sampled colors from the Eyedropper (item I); or out of gamut colors. Generally, the Sampled Colors option allows for the most accurate selections.

- **Localized Color Clusters.** This feature is new for Color Range in CS4 and is designed, when used in conjunction with the Eyedropper and the Range slider (item D), to control where in the image your range of colors is used to create the selection or mask.

- **Fuzziness.** This slider works on a similar principle to the Magic Wand's Tolerance slider, defining how similar a range of colors or tones has to be in order to be included in the selection or mask. The higher the number, the more neighboring colors and partially gray areas are included in the selection.

  For example, if you use the Sampled Colors option and choose a bright yellow leaf on an autumn tree with many shades of yellow and orange, a high fuzziness value would include not only the bright yellows but the dull yellows and lighter orange colors as well. A low value would include only the brightest yellow areas.

- **Range.** This slider defines how much or little of the image is used at a given fuzziness value. Essentially this can be used to restrict the selection to one small portion of the image, by pushing the percentage under 40 and using the Eyedropper to click on a color in a specific area of the image.

  For example, if you have a picture of blue cars in a parking lot but only want the blue car on the left to be selected, push the Range slider down to around 35 percent and then click the car in question with the Eyedropper. The other blue cars are not selected until you click one of them, and then only that car is selected. Use the Add to/Subtract from Sample buttons to select more or less of the same car.

- **Selection/Image.** These buttons determine whether the image preview in the Color Range dialog box shows a color image or grayscale mask.

- **Selection Preview.** This setting determines how your image canvas displays the changes taking place in the dialog box as you work. There are five options: None leaves the image view unaltered; Grayscale temporarily displays the grayscale mask that is used on the layer in question; Black Matte displays the selected colors against a black background; White Matte displays the selected colors against a white background; and Quick Mask displays the image in Quick Mask mode.

FIGURE 10.13

Photoshop's Color Range function is a powerful way to isolate specific regions of tone and color within your image, and can also be used to quickly create layer masks for your adjustment layers.

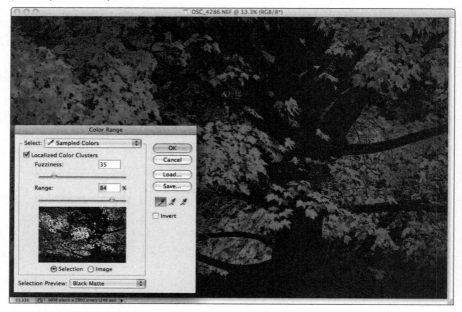

FIGURE 10.14

The Color Range dialog box has several options for refining your selection or mask, and displaying the mask. Spend a few minutes experimenting with these to find a combination you are most comfortable with.

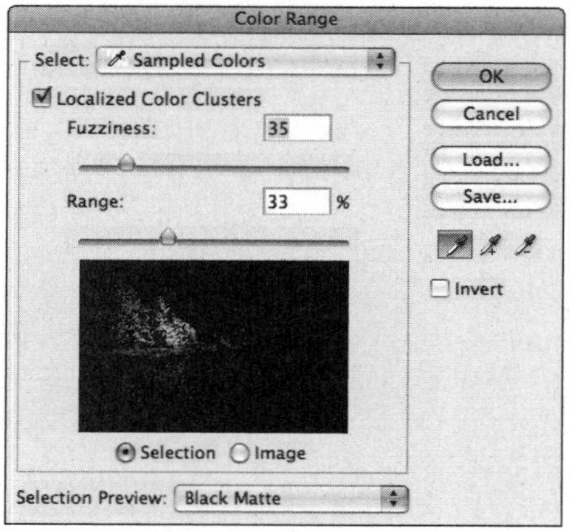

- **Invert.** Selecting this check box inverts the selection or mask to its opposite values.

- **Eyedropper.** This button, (left-most icon), is used to define which colors are included in the current selection or mask. The Eyedropper creates the initial selection or mask. Each time you click with it, a new selection is made, overwriting the prior selection.

- **Add to/Subtract from Sample.** These options (center and right-most buttons) add to or subtract from the existing selection or mask, and use the same shortcuts as other selection tools: Shift to add, Alt/Option to subtract.

Finally, you can save a given Color Range selection or mask (using the Save and Load buttons in the dialog box window) so that you can load it back into another image later, much the same way you can save a Curves or Levels session for re-use.

As mentioned earlier, the Color Range tool is also a great way to precisely target your adjustment layers so they affect only the parts of your picture that need it:

1. **Open the Adjustments panel and select the adjustment you need.** Note that the white (empty) mask icon in the adjustment layer is already selected by default.

2. **Open Color Range from the Masks panel or Select menu and use the Eyedropper and Local Color Cluster options to select the areas of the image you would like to adjust, based on its color or tonality.** Click OK when you're finished.

3. **Check the Layers panel afterward and you will see that the layer mask next to your adjustment displays the basic outline of this color range selection.**

4. **Make your adjustment and you're done!** All the changes are applied only to the unmasked portion of the layer.

> **NOTE** There is one other key tool for creating selections, and that is the Pen tool. However, because it is the most complex to use (you first need to understand paths and how to create them), the Pen tools have their own chapter (the next chapter in fact).

Refining Selections

Once you've got the general outline of your selection or mask down pat, there are several functionalities that Photoshop CS4 offers to help you perfect your selections at the single pixel level. Since all selections are actually grayscale masks underneath, you need to employ the kinds of tools that can control the boundaries of a mask to make your selections more precise.

Refine Edge

The Refine Edge dialog box (seen in Figure 10.15) was introduced in Photoshop CS3 and remains one of the most powerful tools for tweaking your selections and masks in Photoshop CS4. The Refine Edge dialog box can be accessed from multiple locations in the Photoshop user interface, some of them new to CS4.

FIGURE 10.15

The Refine Edge dialog box can be accessed by clicking the Refine Edge button on the Options Bar, when any of the selection tools are active, and a selection is present on the canvas. It can also be accessed from the Masks panel and the Select menu.

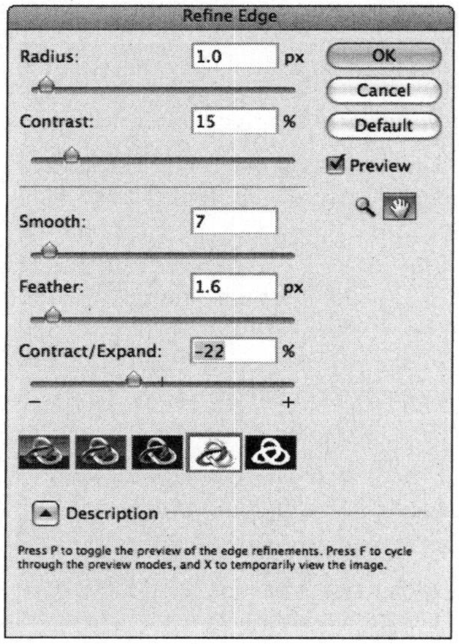

The power of Refine Edge comes from its relative simplicity, its ability to display the selection mask in several different ways, and its ability to control mask edges with pixel precision. Take some time to learn the following Refine Edge controls; you will find many uses for this helpful tool once you get comfortable with it. Don't worry if you can't remember all the details at first. Each time you roll your mouse cursor over one of the sliders you can get a detailed description at the bottom of the Refine Edge dialog box.

Figures 10.16 through 10.20 provide examples of how the Refine Edge controls can work together to improve a mask or selection.

FIGURE 10.16

The original selection seen against a black matte, no changes made yet

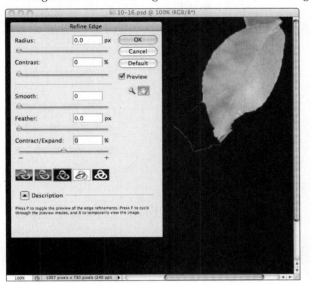

- **Radius.** This control acts as a more precise version of the feathering option described earlier in this chapter. The larger the radius value, the wider the feathering region that is applied to your selection or mask; however, unlike the standard Feather slider, the Radius slider will not muddle your colors, instead just making them more transparent as you increase the value.

- **Contrast.** This control sharpens the soft edges created by larger radius adjustments. Don't push this slider too far as it can result in crunchy or jagged edges, which defeats the purpose of using any type of feathering in the first place.

- **Smooth.** This control attempts to remove any bumps and lumps found along your selection or mask edges. Use it sparingly as it can quickly remove detail in your selection that you would not want to lose otherwise. Pulling the Radius slider back a bit may help in this case.

FIGURE 10.17

The selection after a moderate radius adjustment

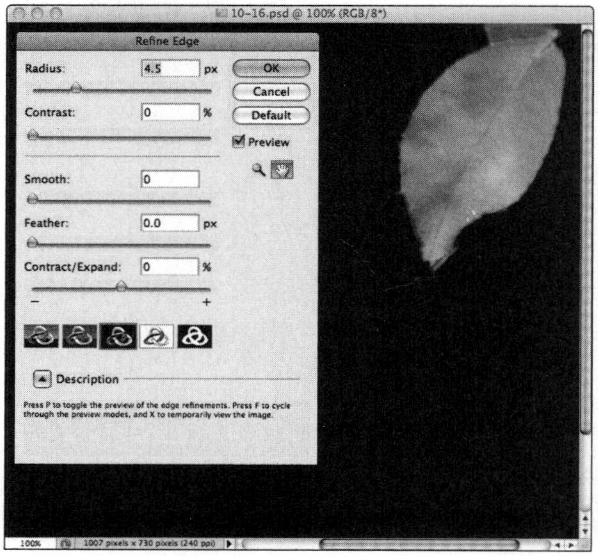

FIGURE 10.18

The selection after a large contrast adjustment (note the extraneous bits are gone)

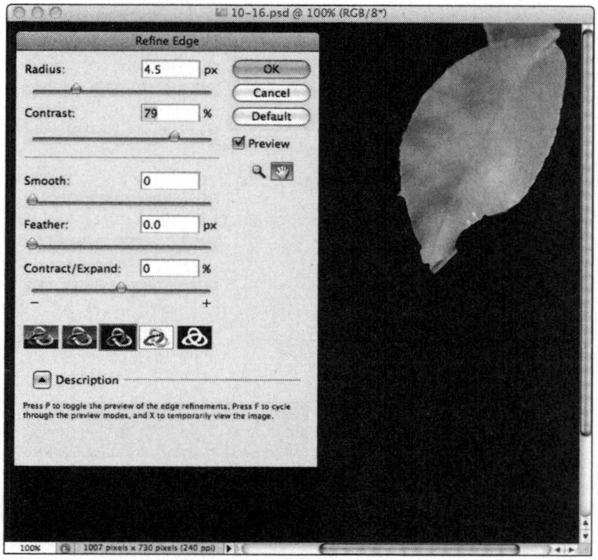

FIGURE 10.19

The selection after moderate smoothing

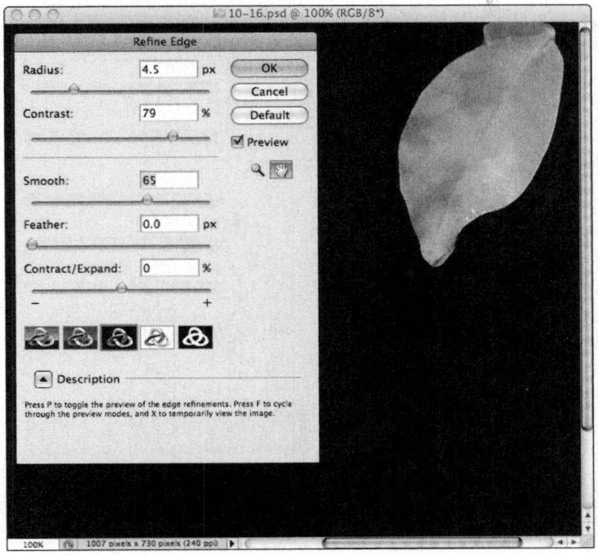

- **Feather.** This control works on the same principle as the selection feathering option discussed earlier in the chapter. Generally, you won't need to use both the Radius and Feather sliders in most cases. One or the other should suffice in producing a good selection, in conjunction with the other options on this list.

- **Contract/Expand.** This control takes the selection with its existing look (using the parameters noted above) and reduces or enlarges it to include slightly less or slightly more material in all directions. Note that using a high contract value can also cause jagged edges, so if you are pushing that slider past about −50 and are not getting the results you want, you may need to consider redefining your initial selection.

- **Preview modes.** These are, from left to right: standard selection preview (marching ants), Quick Mask mode, Black Matte, White Matte, and Grayscale Mask. Of these, for all but dark subject matter, the Black Matte is often a very easy means of seeing how your selection or mask is being affected by the changes you're making with the sliders. Try each one and see which fits your work style best.

315

FIGURE 10.20

The selection after moderate contraction

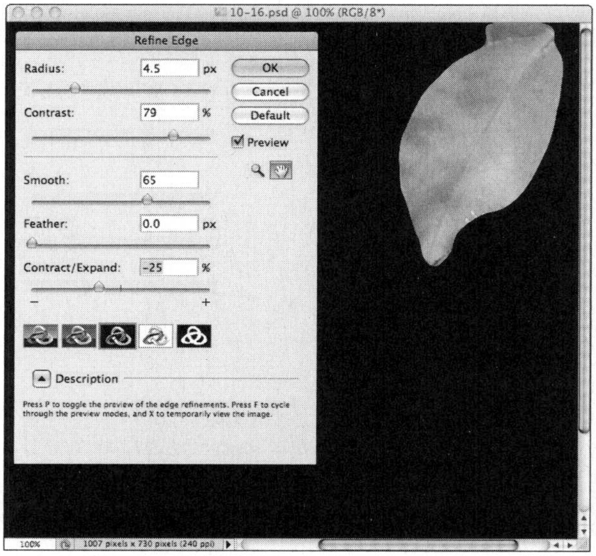

Select menu options

The Select menu also has a number of functions designed to help you quickly create and refine selections. While these are generally not as advanced or precise as the parameters found in Refine Edge, they can still be quite useful in some situations. The following list describes some of the core functions within the Select menu, which is shown in Figure 10.21.

- **(Select) All.** Keyboard shortcut Ctrl+A/⌘+A allows you to instantly select 100 percent of the pixels in your image.

- **Deselect (All).** Keyboard shortcut Ctrl+D/⌘+D does the opposite of Select All, ensuring 0 percent of pixels are selected. This is a quick way of undoing any selection.

- **Reselect.** Allows you to reselect the last region that was selected, should you accidentally lose the selection somehow.

- **Inverse.** Keyboard shortcut Ctrl+Shift+I/⌘+Shift+I allows you to take the existing selection and reverse the effect so that everything that was previously unselected becomes selected (and vice versa). This is a useful trick if the part of your image you don't want to use is much easier to select because you can quickly select all the unwanted area and then inverse with one shortcut to select the items you do want.

- **All Layers.** Keyboard shortcut Ctrl+Alt+A/⌘+Option+A selects all layers in the active document that are not locked or background layers.

FIGURE 10.21

The Select menu can be a useful tool in creating and modifying your selections.

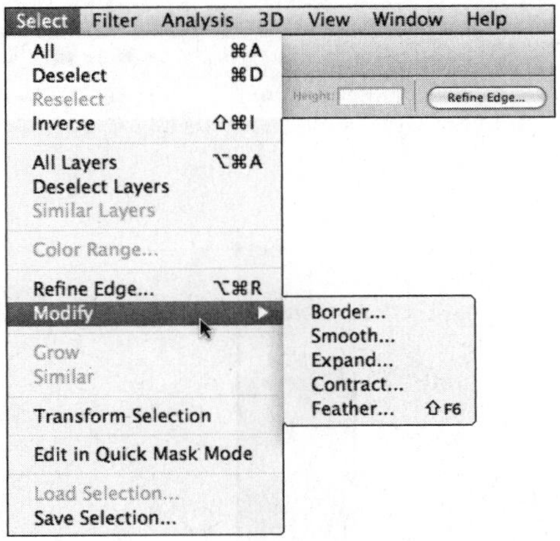

- **Deselect Layers.** Deselects all currently selected layers or layer regions.

- **Similar Layers.** Based on the active layer type seen in the Layers panel, this command will select all similar layer types found in the document. For example, if the active layer is an adjustment layer, and you have more than one of these in your document, choosing Select ➪ Similar Layers will ensure all adjustment layers are selected.

- **Modify ➪ Border.** Creates a soft-edged border selection that surrounds the former selection edge with a new selection, based on a pixel value between 1 and 200. For example, if you choose a value of 40, the new border selection covers an area (of the same shape as the original selection) that is 20 pixels inside and 20 pixels outside of the original edge, as shown in Figure 10.22.

- **Modify ➪ Smooth.** Smoothes hard corners within a selection by using the pixel value provided (between 1 and 100) to determine if the pixels that neighbor your selection edge should be included or excluded. The higher the value, the smaller your selection gets and the more rounded any corners or outcroppings will be.

- **Modify ➪ Expand.** Uses the exact shape of the existing selection and expands it in all directions by the number of pixels you specify (between 1 and 100).

- **Modify ➪ Contract.** Uses the exact shape of the existing selection and reduces it in all directions by the number of pixels you specify (between 1 and 100). Both Expand and Contract are useful when you have the right shape but just need to make the selection a bit larger or smaller.

- **Modify ➪ Feather.** Works the same as the feathering option found with any of the selection tools by creating a soft edge, between .2 and 250 pixels wide.

- **Grow.** Works in conjunction with the Tolerance value set by the Magic Wand to increase the selection area to include all adjacent colors of similar value. This is not considered a precise way to improve your selections, as the results can be fairly random.

- **Similar.** Works like the Grow command, except that the newly selected pixels are not limited to adjacent areas. All noncontiguous pixels within the Tolerance range are selected. Again, this command is not a precise means of modifying selections.

FIGURE 10.22

Choosing Select ➪ Modify ➪ Border allows you to redefine your selection so that you can manipulate its border regions to correct any problems or add styling.

- **Transform Selection.** Allows you to transform the scale (height and width) of the active selection in the same way you can transform the entire image by using the Edit ➪ Transform tools.

- **Edit in Quick Mask Mode.** Allows you to tweak your selection, using the brush tool to "paint" its exact shape, and to display non-selected pixels with a temporary red overlay called a *rubylith*. You can also access this mode by typing the letter **Q** whenever a selection is present in the active document.

The Quick Mask mode should not be confused with standard layer masks. Quick Mask is a temporary way of looking at your selection so that you can refine it with the brush tools rather than numbers and sliders, if that is a more comfortable way for you to work.

Painting with black deselects the area underneath your brush, while painting with white selects it. You can also determine whether the rubylith shows selected or unselected areas, and even change its color by double-clicking the button at the bottom of the Photoshop toolbar, as seen in Figure 10.23.

■ **Load/Save Selection.** Allows you to save and reload selections as alpha channels, which are discussed in the next section.

FIGURE 10.23

Quick Mask Mode options. Note that you can enter Quick Mask mode at any time by typing the letter **Q** as long as a selection is active in your document.

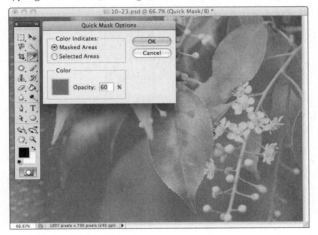

As with all selection tools, the best way to become familiar with the Select menu's functionality is to experiment with the different options and modifications. You will quickly discover which ones have value to you, based on they type of image editing you do and on your personal work style.

Understanding Channels

Many people use "alpha channels" and "channels" synonymously when referring to Photoshop; however, it's important to realize that there are actually three types of channels: color channels; alpha channels; and spot color channels. All of them have one thing in common, and that is that they are all really just grayscale images hiding beneath your canvas. There are few topics that seem to strike fear into the hearts of new Photoshop users as much as channels do, but rest assured they are actually not complicated.

Once you get past the initial hesitation, you will see that channels are an important (if somewhat obscured) part of the digital workflow and not hard to leverage at all. At worst, they take a few extra steps to create, but the benefits can be well worthwhile.

Alpha channels

An alpha channel is nothing more than a selection that is displayed as a grayscale (sometimes pure black and white) image when you activate it from the Channels panel. "Marching ant" selections, layer masks, and alpha channels are effectively all the same beast, they are just viewed and manipulated in different ways and at times are used for different purposes.

For alpha channels, the pure black areas represent the parts of the image that are not selected, while the pure white areas represent the region that is completely selected. Gray indicates areas that are partially selected (such as feathered areas or those that were modified with the Refine Edge's Radius slider).

Want to modify your alpha channel directly in the document window? Click the brush tool, size it so you can work within the selection areas comfortably, and then paint onto the mask with any shade of gray (including pure black or white) to expand or contract regions of your selection. You can also tweak your alpha channels with a Quick Mask-like overlay: Just highlight both the image's composite color channel and the alpha channel at the same time by shift-clicking.

Whether you use alpha channels or basic selections will depend on how complex the selections are and on your personal work style. There is no right or wrong choice; however, many professionals agree that when working with complex selections (ones that take 30 seconds or more to create), there is definitely a more efficient choice, and alpha channels are the clear winner.

The reason alpha channels are so useful is that unlike normal selections, alpha channels can be saved with your document, just like an image layer. They are permanent until you delete them. Every Photoshop document can store a total of 56 channels (all types included); RGB images can have a total of 53 alpha channels (plus 3 color channels — red, green, and blue). CMYK images can have 52 alpha channels (plus 4 color channels — cyan, magenta, yellow, and black).

Odds are you will never need to save that many channels in one image, but the larger point is, there's no need to limit yourself in this regard. If you have a complex set of selections in a large image, save them all as alpha channels in case you ever need to re-select parts of an image later to make additional retouches or modifications to the composition.

Creating alpha channels

The great thing about alpha channels is that they are simple to create:

1. **Use one of the selection tools to create a selection region on your image.**
2. **Open the Channels panel.**

3. **Click the Save Selection as Channel button (at the bottom of the panel, second button from left, as seen in Figure 10.24).** That's it! You have created your first alpha channel.

4. **Click on the alpha channel item to make it the active view in the document window.** Notice how the shape of the white areas in the channel exactly mimics the scale and location of your original selection.

FIGURE 10.24

The Channels panel makes it simple to create an alpha channel from your selection.

It's also possible to create a selection directly from an alpha channel:

1. **Open the Channels panel.**

2. **Click the New Channel button.**

3. **Using the brush tool and white foreground, draw a shape on the black area displayed in the document.**

4. **Click the Load Channel as Selection button, as shown in Figure 10.25.**

5. **Click the composite image channel and deselect the alpha channel's eyeball icon.** You should see a result similar to Figure 10.25, where you now have a selection in the shape of the brush strokes you made in step 3.

Keep in mind that there is no destructive effect when converting a selection to an alpha channel or vice versa; all selection detail (because it is stored as grayscale values) is maintained throughout the process unless you alter it by using one of the previously described tools or Select menu commands. Before I go any further, it's a good idea to take a close look at the Channels panel; this is where most of the channel operations take place.

FIGURE 10.25

FIGURE 10.25

Alpha channels can be converted into selections when necessary.

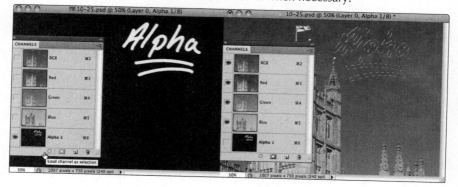

The Channels panel

The Channels panel is where all the alpha channels, color channels, and spot color channels are stored. You can also find layer masks in the Channels panel after they are created in the Layers panel. Both panels work in much the same way; if you wish to view a particular channel's content within the image window, just click the channel. To go back to the default view of the image, click the top-most channel. This is called the *composite channel* (color images only). You can also select a channel by using the keyboard shortcuts listed down the right side of the panel.

Beyond viewing a channel in the document, it's important to know the purpose and functionality of the other buttons and menus found on the Channels panel. Shown in Figure 10.26, the Channels panel has several functions that make it very easy and efficient to use.

FIGURE 10.26

The Channels panel

■ **Composite Color/Grayscale Channel.** By default, this channel represents the "combined effect" of all the other color channels in your image, and cannot be deleted. Click this channel to see the composite color image in your document window.

■ **Inactive Color Channels.** These color channels are not currently being viewed in the document.

■ **Active Color Channel.** Indicated by your system's highlight color, this is the channel(s) currently being viewed in the document window. When viewing an active color channel and an alpha channel at the same time, the alpha channel is displayed in Quick Mask mode.

■ **Load Channel as Selection.** Creates a standard selection from the contents of the active channel.

■ **Save Selection as Channel.** As described earlier, this creates an alpha channel from the active selection on the document. When clicked, these alpha channels are displayed as black-and-white or grayscale masks.

■ **Create New Channel.** Creates an empty alpha channel and provides options for naming and Quick Mask display parameters, as seen in Figure 10.27.

FIGURE 10.27

New Channel Options

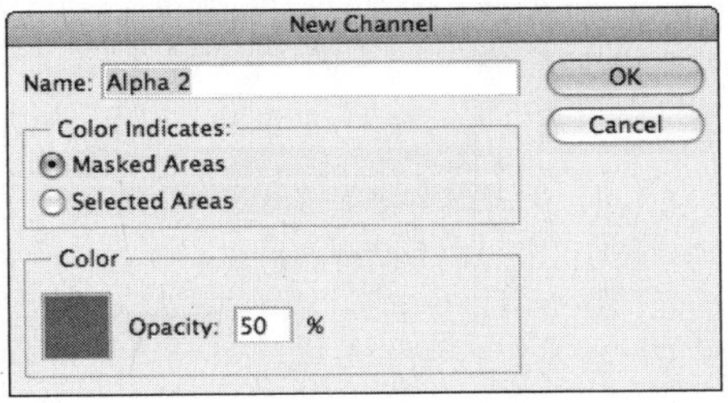

■ **Delete Current Channels.** Clears the active channels (including non-composite color channels) from the document. If you do this by mistake, don't fret; channel deletions can be undone.

■ **New Channel.** Creates an empty alpha channel.

■ **Duplicate Channel.** Creates a second copy of the currently active channel.

■ **Delete Channel.** Clears the current active channel from the document.

■ **New Spot Channel.** Creates a new spot color channel. Useful in publishing projects where you must reproduce an exact spot color in a CMYK environment. Spot channels print on a separate plate, rather than as a part of the CMYK ink process.

■ **Merge Spot Channel.** Provides users with an option for "proofing" spot color channels via inkjet printer, by merging a spot color channel into the RGB or CMYK image. Make sure your spot color channel is not solid white or you will see no change when merging into your image.

The behavior of black and white within spot color channels is the opposite from the default behaviors found in alpha channels and layer masks. If your spot color channel is solid white, it will have no effect on the document when merged or printed. Solid black areas carry the maximum effect. Gray values between solid black and white will continue to define partially selected regions but on the opposite scale. The darker the gray, the more effect the spot color will have in that region of the image.

■ **Channel Options.** Provides options for setting the properties of the active channel, based on what type of channel it is.

■ **Split Channels.** Splits the composite color channel of flattened images into separate files so that they can be saved individually. For example, an RGB image would be split into three separate Photoshop files, one for each channel in the composite.

■ **Merge Channels.** Allows you to re-blend the split apart channel images. This is often done to create interesting color and contrast effects by re-assigning channels in the new image. For example, the green channel data from the original split image can be used as red channel data in the new image.

■ **Panel Options.** Provides the ability to choose how large the Channels panel thumbnails are. You can also access this option by right-clicking on an empty area within the Channels panel.

Work smarter

The primary benefit of using alpha channels is that they are designed to make you more efficient. Photoshop pros often use alpha channels when they need to store (and potentially retrieve) a very complex selection. There are two possible workflows in this regard. One is to make the complex selection by using the tools described earlier, and then save the selection as an alpha channel. The second way is to use the image's color channels (or more specifically, their grayscale data) to create the complex selection and subsequent alpha channel. This technique, which will be described shortly, is particularly useful for selecting highly detailed objects silhouetted against the sky or other backgrounds. Trees are a very common example, as is human hair.

The only negative side effect of saving many channels within your image is that it will increase the file size to a moderate degree. However, it's common to have only a few selections per image that might require storage for later use, so unless the original file is enormous, having a few alpha channels added to the mix is not likely to cause dramatic increases in file size. Err on the side of saving more alpha channels rather than fewer. Figure 10.28 shows a complex selection and the alpha channel that was created from the selection.

FIGURE 10.28

Complex selections that you don't want to risk losing or waste time re-creating are the best candidates for being stored via alpha channel.

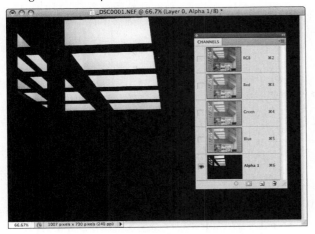

Color channels and selections

Color channels represent the grayscale data that the color image is built from. Believe it or not, digital cameras actually record your scenes as grayscale data; only later in the process are they converted to the "color composite" that you see when you open a color photograph. For example, the composite channel found in RGB images uses three color channels: red, green, and blue. CMYK images have four color channels: cyan, magenta, yellow, and black.

You can use color channels, sometimes on their own and sometimes in combination with another channel, to create a new mask that isolates complex silhouettes or other areas of an image that would otherwise take a long time to select using the tools discussed earlier in the chapter. The process for creating a selection using color channels is described in the following steps. Keep in mind that, generally, it's easier to create channel-based selections using RGB color versus CMYK color, though either can be used.

1. **Open the Channels panel and click through each of the red, green, and blue color channels.** As you do so, look carefully at the object you wish to isolate.

2. **Choose the channel that has the greatest grayscale contrast between your object and the background.** In Figure 10.29, the blue channel was used because it provided high contrast between the blue sky and the green foliage (and the building as well).

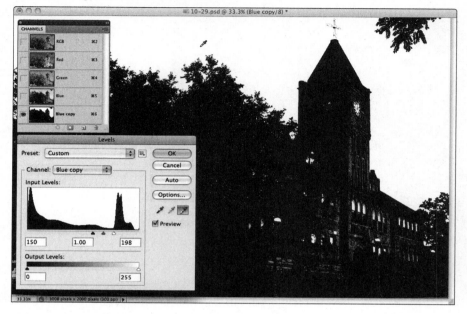

FIGURE 10.29

Using the Levels command to modify your copied color channel can help to precisely isolate one region of color from another.

3. **Drag your chosen channel to the New Channel button.** This creates a new color channel that you can work on to create the selection without changing the original.

4. **Open the Levels command.** Use the black and white pickers to isolate the darkest and lightest portions of your image from each other. For example, here the black picker was used on the lighter areas on the trees to make the foliage black. The white picker was used on the darker areas of the sky until it turned white.

5. **When you have a sharply contrasting subject and background, click OK.** You can now rename this channel as an alpha channel by double-clicking the name and changing it.

6. **With your copied channel still active, click the Load Channel as Selection button.** You should see marching ants now overlaid on your channel preview.

7. **Click the composite channel's eyeball icon to preview the selection with a Quick Mask style overlay.** This enables you to find stray areas that you will want to remove from the selection with the Lasso tool, or to paint on by using the brush tool with black as the foreground color.

8. **When finished, deselect the copied color channel's eyeball.** The final selection is shown over the composite view of the image.

Sharing channels between images

Channels can easily be shared among multiple open images. Just click and drag a channel from the Channels panel to the other image's window, and release. The channel is added to that document's collection.

You can also load alpha channels as selections (as long as the document you wish to borrow the channel from is open) by choosing Select ⇨ Load Selection, and then choose the alpha channel from the list provided, which is shown in Figure 10.30.

FIGURE 10.30

Alpha channels from one document can be loaded into another document using the Select menu.

```
┌──────────────────── Load Selection ────────────────────┐
│ ┌─ Source ─────────────────────────┐   ┌─────OK─────┐   │
│ │ Document: [ 10–29.psd        ⬍]  │   ┌───Cancel───┐   │
│ │                                   │                   │
│ │  Channel: [ Sky              ⬍]  │                   │
│ │           ☐ Invert                │                   │
│ └───────────────────────────────────┘                   │
│ ┌─ Operation ──────────────────────┐                    │
│ │ ⦿ New Selection                   │                    │
│ │ ○ Add to Selection                │                    │
│ │ ○ Subtract from Selection         │                    │
│ │ ○ Intersect with Selection        │                    │
│ └───────────────────────────────────┘                   │
└─────────────────────────────────────────────────────────┘
```

Summary

This chapter covered the core tools and skills required to make accurate selections on a wide range of image regions, including regions based on geometric shapes, amorphous shapes, color ranges, and channel data. Selections are a crucial part of any Photoshop workflow because they are usually required to modify specific parts of an image, without affecting the other parts that surround it.

After reading through this chapter and experimenting with your own images as you learned new techniques, you should be comfortable with the following concepts and techniques:

- Creating basic marquee selections
- Creating different types of Lasso selections
- Understand how to feather, add to, and subtract from a selection
- Selecting regions of color by using the Color Range command
- Modifying selection shapes with the Select menu's modify options
- Modifying selection edges by using the Refine Edge command
- Working with Quick Mask mode
- Working with channels

Part IV

Paths, Shapes, and Text

Chapter 11

Working with Paths

For many Photoshop users, paths are one of the most useful but least understood parts of the photo editing and graphic arts process. They are somewhat more complex than other selection and shape creation tools, but also extremely powerful and flexible.

While you are not likely to find much campaigning for the use of paths in quick-fix style tutorials, the one skill set that often separates the more serious Photoshop user from the dabbler is the ability to efficiently utilize paths.

Across different applications, paths can be used to make precise selections, aid in the creation of complex illustrations, and define the motion of animated objects. All that's required is a little curiosity and determination.

This chapter is broken into five primary topics, each building on the prior one to give you a solid grounding in the use of Photoshop's vector-based tools. I'll talk more about what is meant by "vector" in the coming pages, but for now open your mind, check your hesitation at the door, and prepare to experiment with paths as you read through the examples.

The best way to learn paths is by doing, so open up a new blank document and give the examples a shot. You've got nothing to lose and much to gain!

IN THIS CHAPTER

Introduction to Bézier paths

Defining paths and vector tools

Creating vector paths

Paths as selections

Introduction to Bézier Paths

Sometimes referred to as Bézier curves (after the French automobile designer Pierre Bézier, who invented the concept), paths have unique characteristics that set them apart from other computer-based graphics tools:

331

■ **Paths are common to many types of computer graphics programs and often work in much the same way.** They are used extensively in digital illustration, page layout, 3D modeling and all types of animation, and of course, in Photoshop CS4. Consequently, much of what you learn in this chapter is applicable to other programs like Adobe Illustrator or Adobe After Effects. Similarly, if you've already learned about paths from programs like Illustrator, those skills are also useful in Photoshop.

■ **Paths are mathematically defined.** This is very different from digital photos, which are fixed patterns of pixels (or bitmaps) that bear no mathematical relationship. It also means paths are not directly a part of your image, but rather sit above the image canvas.

The shape of a path is based on a mathematical concept called *vectors*. Put simply, a vector is a geometric object — usually represented by a line — that has both a direction and a defined length (see Figure 11.1).

FIGURE 11.1

A vector is a geometric object that has both a direction and defined length.

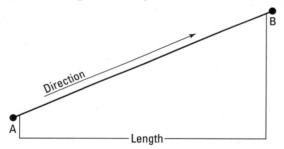

■ **Paths are resolution-independent.** This means they can be scaled up or down (repeatedly), and even be transformed, rotated, and otherwise modified without losing their visual crispness and quality in most cases.

■ **Paths are flexible.** They can be modified many times without losing their visual quality, and can even be saved as discrete objects within a Photoshop document. You can use them many times, across multiple images and applications.

■ **Creating complex paths takes practice.** Ultimately though, every minute you spend perfecting your path skills can make your images and artwork that much more compelling when ultimately displayed or printed.

The next section defines the component parts of a Photoshop path, and introduces the primary tools needed to create, control, and manage paths inside your documents.

Defining Paths and Vector Tools

This section covers the most important parts of vector paths and their basic relationships to one another. The vector tools provided in Photoshop CS4 are also discussed. Later, you learn how to create different types of paths, style those paths, or employ them as selections.

Dissecting a Photoshop path

To best understand paths, it is important to know the different types of paths, the parts that make up these paths, and the functions each part plays. Afterward, we will cover techniques for creating and manipulating the different path types.

Types of paths

Since advanced geometry is beyond the scope of this book, we won't get into the technical reasons for how and why Paths work. However, it's important for some examples and features that you understand basic geometric concepts like perimeter and area.

If your geometry is a little rusty, it couldn't hurt to do a bit of online research and look these terms up. Once you see a diagram or two, things should come back to you quickly. The first thing to understand is that there are several types of paths, as seen in Figures 11.2 and 11.3:

A straight path (left) and a curved path (right)

- **Linear vs. curved.** As seen in Figure 11.2, paths can be straight lines, wavy lines, or even simple geometric shapes like a triangle. A path then, is simply a group of linear or non-linear line segments, connected to form a particular shape or to define a specific contour found in your image or illustration.

- **Open vs. closed.** Paths can also be categorized as "open" or "closed" (Figure 11.3). An open path is one that has endpoints that do not connect. A closed path means that the final path segment you created was placed on the same coordinates as the first anchor point you created, thus "closing the loop." Closed paths are also called path components, path shapes, and sometimes shape layers, if they are applied as a mask.

CROSS-REF   Shape layers are discussed in detail in Chapter 12.

Keep in mind that straight path segments can be given curvature, and wavy path segments can have the anchor points that define their curvature removed, to form a straight segment. Nothing is set in stone until such time as the path is rasterized. Once rasterized, the path and its contents become bitmapped and thus a part of your document layer(s) and canvas.

- **Working paths.** This is the name given to a path or collection of path components that has not yet been saved. A document cannot have more than one working path at a time. Once your working path is finished, you can save the path using the Paths panel, which is discussed later in the chapter.

- **Clipping paths.** These are specialized paths used to define the visible area of an image that is used in a page layout or illustration program. They are designed to ensure that only part of the image is visible in the final layout, without deleting the parts of the image you wish to hide.

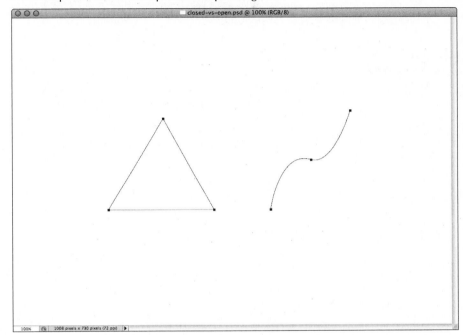

FIGURE 11.3

A closed path (left) and an open-ended path (right)

Parts of a path

The most basic linear paths can be broken into two main parts when first created, shown in Figure 11.4. The first part is the line segment itself (a); the secondary components are the two small squares attached to the far edges of the line segment (b and c), called *anchor points*. These do exactly what their name suggests: They anchor or affix that part of the line segment to the image canvas.

Anchor points can also be used along any point in a path, not just the ends. It is around these anchor points that you mold the shape of your paths.

You may notice some anchor points appear as hollow outlines of squares (b), while others appear as solid black squares (c). These two "icons" denote the difference between a selected and unselected anchor point. Selected anchor points are displayed as solid black squares and can be dragged to a new position on the canvas or manipulated to form a new curve.

Anchor points come in two varieties: smooth points (the default type whenever you create a new anchor point), and corner points. Depending on which type you are using, dragging the anchor point results in either a curved path segment or an angled path segment with the anchor point as the origin of the curvature or angle. See Figure 11.5 for examples.

FIGURE 11.4

Paths are made up of line segments (a) and anchor points (b and c). Unselected anchor points appear as hollow squares, while selected anchor points appear as solid black squares. Anchor points can be either smooth points or corner points.

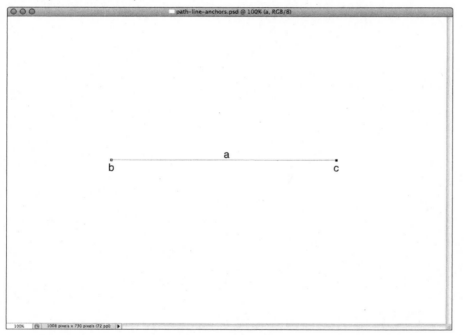

FIGURE 11.5

Notice the difference between a smooth anchor point (top) and a corner anchor point (bottom).

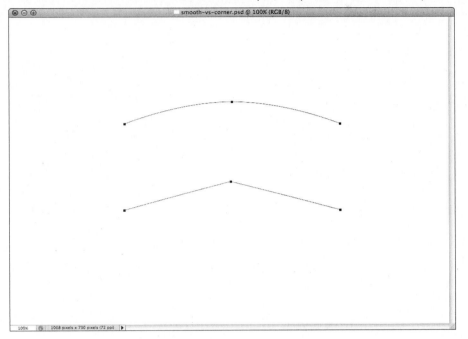

Finally, the most important parts of a path are the direction lines and direction points that are attached to all anchor points. Shown in Figure 11.6, direction lines and direction points accompany each newly created anchor point, and become visible either when the anchor point is dragged immediately after it is created or when you click on them with the Direct Selection tool.

Direction points can also be modified to behave as smooth points or corner points. Smooth direction points always work together to modify the shape of the line segment on *both sides* of the anchor point, while a corner point modifies only its side of the anchor point, leaving the other side unchanged. The use of direction lines, direction points, and more is discussed in detail later in this chapter.

FIGURE 11.6

Direction lines (d) and direction points (e) enable users to create curved and angled line segments. Direction points, like anchor points (f), can be of the smooth or corner variety.

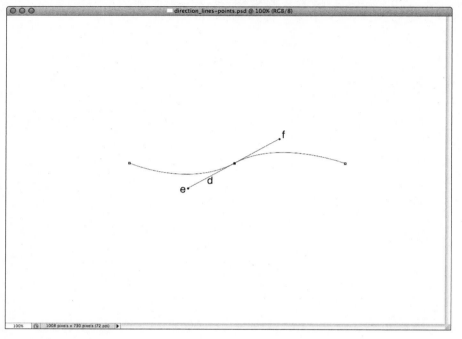

Understanding vector tools and options

Paths can be created, modified, and controlled with the use of a few tools and panels. They are the Pen tools, the Selection tools, the Options Bar, the Paths panel, and the new Masks panel. Each of these are discussed on the following pages and demonstrated where practical in the next section.

The Pen tools

The Pen tools, shown in Figure 11.7, are the most important parts of creating and manipulating vector paths.

You use them to create and modify paths from scratch, as well as to modify existing paths.

- **Pen tool.** This tool places anchor points — with a single click — onto the canvas, to define the initial coordinates of a path segment. This tool can be used to temporarily invoke the Add Anchor Point and Delete Anchor Point tools as well. The keyboard short-cut for the Pen tool is the letter P; hold down the Shift key and press P repeatedly to cycle back and forth between the Pen and Freeform Pen tools.

- **Freeform Pen tool.** This tool is used to hand-draw the approximate shape of an open or closed Path, which can then be more precisely refined using the other Pen tools discussed in this section. The Freeform Pen tool has no default shortcut, but one can be assigned.

  The Freeform Pen tool is the most intuitive and the quickest of the Path tools to use, but also somewhat more imprecise than the others initially. The use of a supported graphics tablet and stylus is recommended when using the Freeform Pen tool.

FIGURE 11.7

The Pen tools are used to create and modify vector paths.

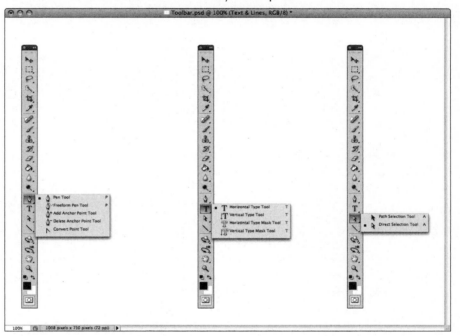

- **Add Anchor Point tool.** This tool does exactly what its name suggests, by adding anchor points anywhere along the length of an existing path segment. When you need to create a new curvature or shape from an existing segment, you will find this tool invaluable. The Add Anchor Point tool does not have a default keyboard shortcut, but one can be assigned.

- **Delete Anchor Point tool.** This tool also does what its name suggests, by removing anchor points from anywhere along the length of an existing path. You can drastically alter the shape of your path if the anchor point in question is being used to define a curved portion of the path, or to define the corner of a specific shape. The Delete Anchor Point tool does not have a default keyboard shortcut, but one can be assigned.

- **Convert Point tool.** With a single click, this tool converts smooth anchor points or direction points to corner anchor points or direction points. It can also dramatically impact your path component's shape. The Convert Point tool does not have a default keyboard shortcut, but one can be assigned.

- **Horizontal and Vertical Type tools.** Although not technically path tools, all text layers in Photoshop are vector-based. This means you can create a string of horizontal or vertical characters and convert them to a vector path using the text layer's Convert to Work Path option. The keyboard shortcut for the Type tools is the letter T.

- **Path Selection tool.** This tool is used to select, scale, or drag one or multiple path components. It is grouped with the Direct Selection tool; both use the keyboard shortcut A.

- **Direction Selection tool.** This tool is used to select and drag anchor points and direction points to form vector paths. It can be accessed from other vector tools by holding down the Ctrl key (or the ⌘ key on a Mac)

Pen and path selection tool options

When creating vector objects, both the Pen tool and Path Selection tool utilize some important path modification features, found on the Options Bar when either tool is selected. Items B, C, D, and E are available to the Pen tool, Freeform Pen tool, and the Path Selection tool.

- **Auto Add/Delete.** Used exclusively with the Pen tool, this option allows the Add Anchor Point and Delete Anchor Point tools to be automatically invoked when the Pen tool is selected if you mouse over an area of empty path segment or an existing anchor point, respectively.

- **Add to path area (+).** Shown in Figure 11.8, when this property is chosen before drawing two or more closed path components, the full perimeter and area of each is added to the active path if they are not overlapping. If they are overlapping, the active path is defined by the combined perimeter and area.

FIGURE 11.8

Path component A added to B forms a new path perimeter and area.

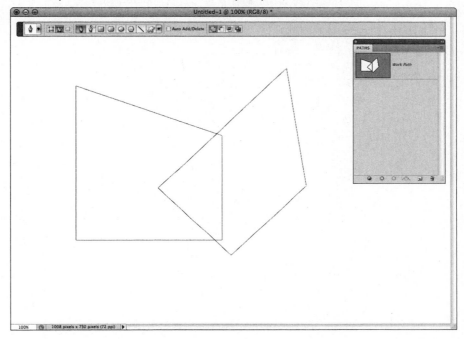

■ **Subtract from path area** (-). Shown in Figure 11.9, this property is usually applied to path components, the shape and area for which need to be removed from a pre-existing path component.

Path component A subtracted from B forms a new path perimeter and area.

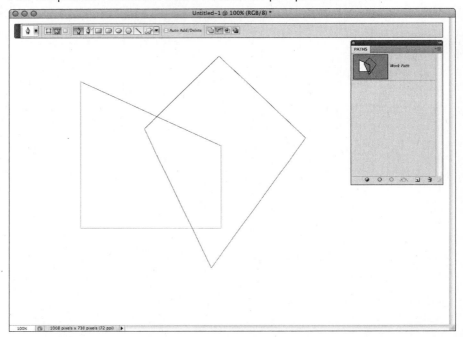

■ **Intersect path areas.** Shown in Figure 11.10, this property is usually applied to path components that are intended to redefine the shape of a path by eliminating from the new path area all other areas that do not overlap one another. Path components using this property sometimes override the others, depending on how they overlap with one another and what their properties are.

FIGURE 11.10

Intersecting regions of multiple path components can be used create a new path perimeter and area.

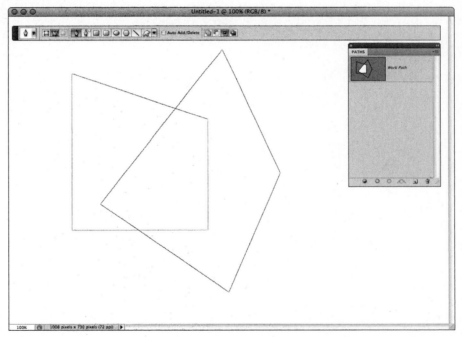

■ **Exclude overlapping path areas.** Shown in Figure 11.11, this property is usually applied to path components that are intended to redefine the shape of a path by eliminating from the new path area all areas that *do* overlap. In essence this is the opposite of creating a new path via Intersect path areas.

FIGURE 11.11

Intersecting regions of multiple path components are ignored to create a new path area.

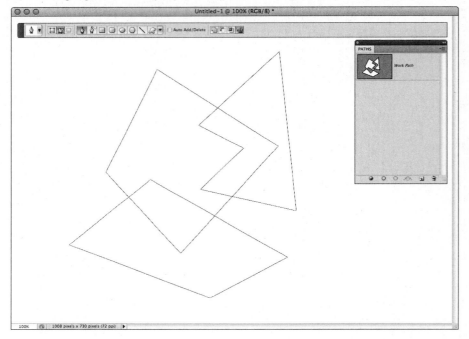

The Freeform Pen tool and Path Selection tool have additional options for modifying paths, shown in Figure 11.12, including alignment and distribution functions that work in the same way the Move tool's alignment and distribution options work for bitmap, shape, and text layers.

The Pen and Path Selection tools, combined with the Options Bar, offer an efficient means of creating crisp, complex shapes to use as selections, vector masks, and graphical elements in your photos or photo illustrations.

The Path Selection tool options include the same options for joining path components as the Pen tool, plus several path component alignment tools. The Freeform Pen tool also uses a Magnetic option to make it easier to trace over image elements when creating your path.

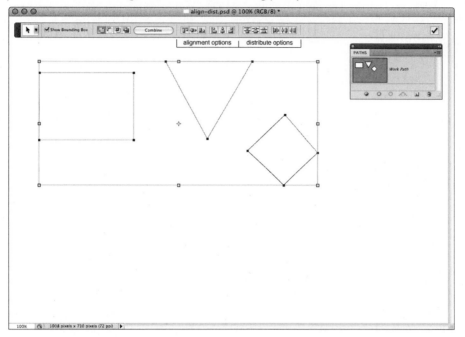

The Paths panel

Shown in Figure 11.13, the Paths panel is where all paths are stored, stylized, and applied to your document in different ways. Although it's not required to have the Paths panel open at all times while creating or modifying Paths, it's a very good idea if you have the available screen space.

FIGURE 11.13

The Paths panel is where paths are stored, stylized, and applied to your document.

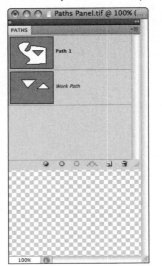

The buttons on the face of the Paths panel serve the following purposes:

- **Fill path with foreground color.** Fills either open or closed paths with the foreground color. You need at least two line segments that were created using a non-linear vector in order to apply and see the fill color.

- **Stroke path with brush.** Allows you to apply a bitmapped brush stroke below your path using the current Brush tool size and shape. Keep in mind that paths will not appear as visible shapes or contours on printed documents until they are stroked or given a fill.

- **Load path as selection.** Converts the shape of your path into a live image selection. This is an extremely useful feature when you need to create very precise but odd-shaped selections that would be difficult to draw by hand with the Lasso.

- **Make working path from selection.** Works on the opposite principle as the previous function, taking an existing live selection and turning it into a working path.

- **Create new path.** Creates and saves a new empty path that you can then define with any of the Photoshop path creation tools discussed in this chapter.

- **Delete current path.** Removes the currently selected path from the Paths panel. This operation can be undone if a path is deleted by mistake.

The Paths panel also has many useful and important options found in its popup menu, illustrated in Figure 11.14 and described below:

FIGURE 11.14

The Paths panel menu provides quick access to many useful path-related functions.

- **New Path.** Saves current work path with the option to name the path.

- **Duplicate Path.** Makes a copy of the current path. Paths can also be duplicated by dragging the current path to the create new path button at the bottom of the panel.

- **Delete Path.** Removes current path from the panel, but can be undone if necessary.

- **Make Work Path.** Performs the same task as make working path from selection.

- **Make Selection.** Converts currently active path to a live selection.

- **Fill Path.** Fills the current path with foreground color.

- **Stroke Path.** Uses Brush tool settings to place a bitmap brush stroke under the path.

- **Clipping Path.** – Creates a Clipping Path from the current active (saved) path.

- **Panel Options.** Allows you to determine the size of the thumbnail used to represent your paths inside the panel. Choosing the largest thumbnail can help you make sense of things when you're combining path components.

The path icons displayed in the Paths panel also contain an abbreviated context menu, which allows you to right-click (Ctrl+click) to access the duplicate, delete, fill, stroke, and selection commands. Whether you access these items from a button on the panel or from one of the two menus makes no difference except in terms of which one is most comfortable for you.

The Masks panel

The new Masks panel in Photoshop CS4 makes it easy to create a vector mask from the active path or working path in order to prevent a specific region of the document from being displayed. The Masks panel, shown in Figure 11.15, can also quickly modify your vector mask's density and feathering values, to help the content of the layer it is attached to, to blend in more seamlessly with the rest of the image.

FIGURE 11.15

Click the Masks panel's to add vector mask button to quickly create a vector mask over the current layer. If you have a saved path or a working path active, it will be used as the basis of the new mask.

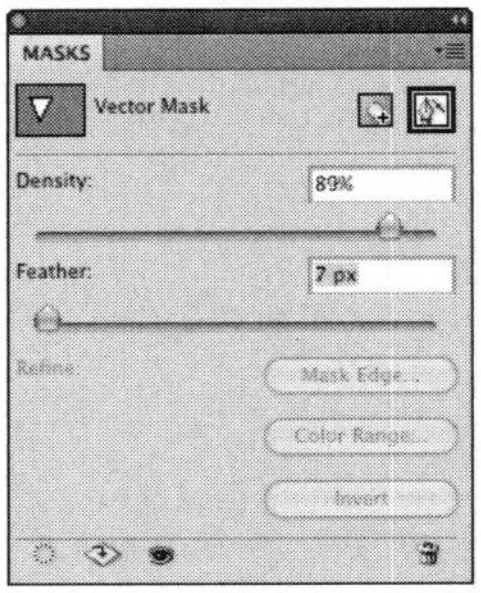

Creating Vector Paths

It may seem complicated at first, but creating paths is fairly simple once you understand the tools and options defined in the last section, and practice using them. Understand that no amount of reading will ever replace the act of opening a new Photoshop image and spending some quality time experimenting with the different vector tools, panels, and menus. Experimentation is the best way to retain the concepts you discussed in this chapter.

Making simple open and closed paths

As noted earlier, an open path is a line segment that has beginning and end points (anchor points), and which do not close the path component off from other parts of the document. For the examples that follow, keep in mind that you could, if you wanted to, create the anchor points anywhere on the document. Locations are suggested here to keep things as simple as possible the first time.

For these Pen tool exercises a digital stylus is not required. The first example is the most simplistic. Follow these steps to create a straight (open) path segment:

1. **Open a new Photoshop document and press the P key or click the Pen tool on the Toolbar.**
2. **Click anywhere on the left half of the document canvas with the Pen tool.**

3. **Move the Pen tool to the right half of the document (hold down the Shift key if you want to form a perfectly straight line segment) and click a second time with the Pen tool.** The finished path is seen in Figure 11.16.

A simple linear path segment (open path)

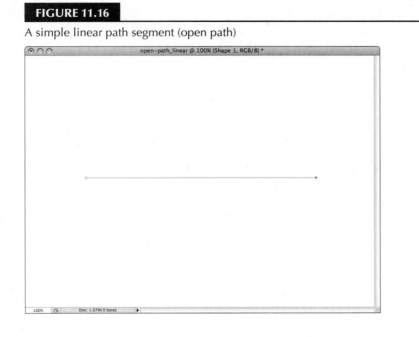

To create the basic S-curve shown in Figure 11.17 (also an open path), follow these steps:

1. **Open a new document and press the P key or click the Pen tool on the Toolbar.**

2. **Click once near the bottom left of the canvas with the Pen tool to create an anchor point.**

3. **Make a second anchor point with the Pen tool near the top right portion of the document.**

4. **If it's not already active, click the Auto Add/Delete check box on the Options Bar.**

5. **Move the Pen tool to approximately the middle of your new diagonal path segment and place the cursor directly over the path line.** Notice the plus sign (+) that appears next to your cursor; this means you can add a new anchor point at this location. Click once.

6. **With the Pen tool still active, hold down the Ctrl/⌘ key.** The Pen tool cursor should change to a white arrow — this is the Direct Selection tool.

7. **Move the Direct Selection tool to the higher of the two direction points that extend from the anchor point you created in step 5.** Click and drag this point to the left until the direction line it is attached to is vertical. You have created your first S-curve!

FIGURE 11.17

A basic S-curve can be created with just one extra click and a simple mouse-drag.

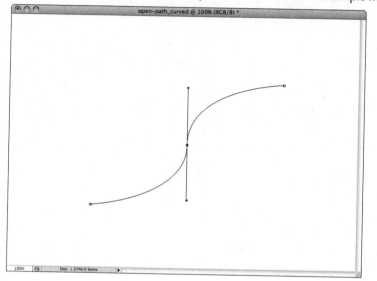

Next I'll use an example that creates a closed path by joining a straight path segment and two curved segments. The goal is to approximate the shape of a bowl, as shown in Figure 11.18.

1. **Open a new Photoshop document and press the P key or click the the Pen tool on the Toolbar.**

2. **Click once to place your first anchor point on the left half of the document, preferably about midway up from the bottom or a little higher.**

3. **Hold down the Shift key and move the Pen tool to the right half of the document and click again to place a second anchor point, creating a straight line.**

4. **Move the Pen tool about halfway to the bottom of the document and place it so that the next anchor point is in line with the middle of your original line segment.** Click and hold down the mouse button.

5. **Hold down the Shift key as well and drag the mouse straight left until your direction point is beneath your first anchor point.** Release the mouse button, then the Shift key.

6. **To complete the bowl, use the Pen tool to click inside the first anchor point.** This closes the path and should approximate a mirror image of the last curve you created.

7. **Save the Path as Bowl, then save the document as Bowl_Example.psd and close the document.** It will be used again later in the chapter.

FIGURE 11.18

Straight and curved path segments can be combined to quickly create crisp shapes of everyday objects.

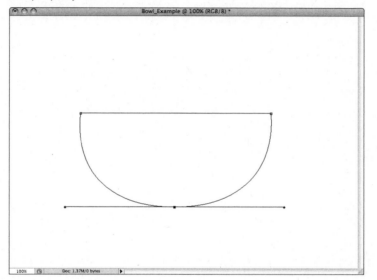

To convert the path to a selection, click the load path as selection button on the Paths panel. The entire process takes only a few minutes once you are used to creating paths, and is described in more detail in the next section. Before moving on to the next set of examples, it's a good idea to experiment on your own using the Pen tools, direction lines, and direction points to create your own simple open and closed paths.

Creating complex paths

While it's possible to use the vector-based Shape Layer tools (covered in the next chapter) to create shape paths in Photoshop, it's also possible to do so with the Pen tool and Freeform Pen tool. Making shapes improves your Pen tool skills and also enables you to make more varied types of shapes then with just the shape tools alone.

The first example shows how to create a simple triangle (closed path) with the Pen tool; the result is shown in Figure 11.19.

1. Close all (and save if you'd like to revisit them later) previous examples, then open a new Photoshop document and press the P key or click the Pen tool on the Toolbar.

2. Click once on the left side of the canvas to set your first anchor point.

3. Hold down the Shift key and click on the right side of the canvas to create the base.

4. Move your Pen tool about halfway up the document, center it over the middle of your existing path segment, and click a third time.

5. Move the Pen tool over the first anchor point and click inside of it to close the path and create the triangle. Simple!

FIGURE 11.19

A simple triangle created with the Pen tool

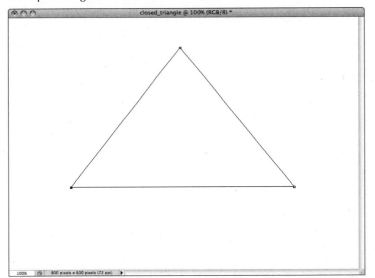

The following example shows how to create a slightly more complex shape, using guides to help you place your anchor points more accurately.

1. Open a new document and choose View ➪ Rulers.

2. Drag out one horizontal and one vertical ruler guide to the vertical and horizontal centers of your document, respectively. You should end up with four equal quadrants.

3. **Drag out two more horizontal guides, splitting the distance between the horizontal center-guide of your document and the top and bottom of your document.** Repeat the process with two more vertical guides, splitting the distance between the vertical center-guide and the left and right edges of your document, respectively.

   Your document should now have 16 equal-size squares dividing it, as shown in Figure 11.20. Note the intersection points, labeled here to simplify the example.

   FIGURE 11.20

   Taking a minute to set up ruler guides can help create more precise geometric shapes with the Pen tool.

   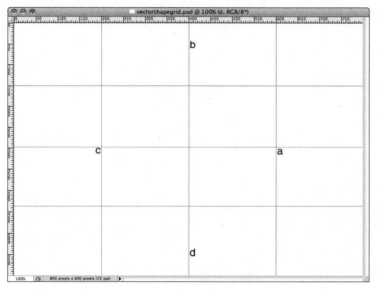

4. **Choose the Pen tool and place your first anchor point at intersection "a."** Placing anchor points or path segments on a guide has no effect on the guides themselves or the path.

5. **Place your second anchor point on the vertical line immediately to the left of the letter "b".**

6. **Place additional anchor points at the intersection of item "c," then next to item "d," and finally back to the anchor you placed at intersection "a," in that order.** The result should be a diamond, similar to the one seen in Figure 11.21.

FIGURE 11.21

The Pen tool can be used with or without guides to create any geometric 2-D shape.

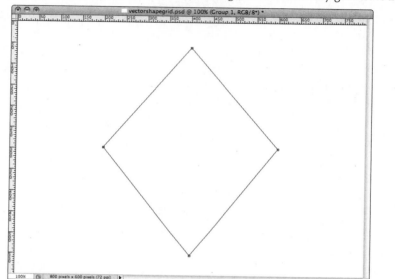

Let's take a break from the Pen tool for a moment and see how we can create vector paths using the Text tool. While it's possible to create block letters using the Pen tool (in fact, special font design programs make extensive use of advanced vector path tools), the easiest method by far is to create text paths using the Text tool and the resulting layer's context menu.

1. **Close the existing examples and save them if necessary.** Open a new document that is 1,024 pixels wide and 768 pixels tall.

2. **Choose the Type tool by pressing the T key or by choosing the Horizontal Type tool from the Toolbar.**

3. **Move the Type tool cursor near the center of the document canvas and click once.**

4. **Hold down the Shift key and type the letter G, then click the green check mark on the Options Bar.**

5. **Triple-click inside the Font Size field on the Options Bar and type 150pt and press Enter to accept the size change.**

6. **Open the Layers panel and make sure your new text layer is selected.**

7. **Right-click / Control-click on the highlighted portion of the layer (to the right of the icon and letter "G").**

8. **Choose Create Work Path from the menu.**

9. **You should now see a line that outlines the letter "G" on the canvas.** This is the new path. Note that your vector text layer is still intact. The path is a separate object that can be moved and modified as you would any other.

10. **Press the A key or choose the Path Selection tool from the Toolbar (the solid black arrow), and make sure the Show Bounding Box option is checked on the Options Bar.**

11. **Click somewhere along your new text path and the bounding box should appear. Drag the new path away from the original text layer so they don't overlap.**

12. **Hold down the Shift key, then click and drag the top-right corner of the bounding box to enlarge your text path while maintaining its normal ratios.** Save your path in the Paths panel menu. The results should look similar to Figure 11.22.

The following four examples demonstrate how to merge existing path components into a single new path, using the Pen tool, the Path Selection tool, and the Options Bar. Using the Add to path area, Subtract from path area, Intersect with path area, and Exclude overlapping path areas properties as you create new path components may not provide the result you expect at first, but they are important and useful options. Try them out on your own, as well as follow these examples. Practice makes perfect!

FIGURE 11.22

Precise text-shaped paths can be created with the Type tool and a single menu command. Text paths can then be used for creative purposes like Clipping Masks.

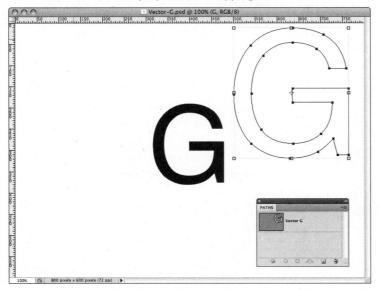

Illustrated in Figure 11.23, the first example describes how to add two closed path components using the Add to path area property with the Pen tool and Path Selection tool options.

1. **Create a new document and choose the Pen tool.** Make sure the Add to path area button is selected on the Options Bar.

2. **Using the methods you learned earlier in this section, draw two closed path component shapes, one overlapping the other.**

3. **Switch to the Path Selection tool (the black arrow) by pressing the A key or Shift+A on your keyboard if the Direct Selection tool is active (the white arrow).**

4. **Click the Combine button and notice how the path changes to form the new perimeter and path area.**

FIGURE 11.23

Two path components combined into a single path, using Add to path area

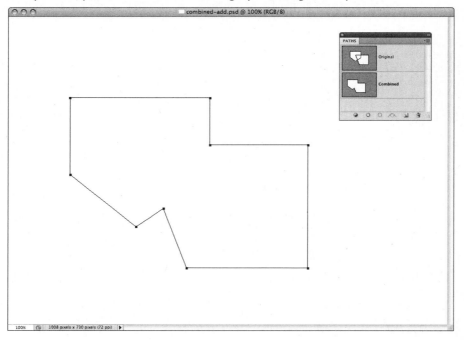

Shown in Figure 11.24, the second example describes how to subtract one closed path component from another, using the Pen tool, Subtract from path area, and the Path Selection tool options.

1. **Open a new document, making sure the Pen tool is active and that the Add to path area property is selected initially.**

2. **Draw a large closed path component on the canvas.**

3. **Click the Subtract from path area property on the Options Bar.**

4. **Draw another large closed path component, this time making sure to overlap some part of your original shape, created in step 2.** Notice part of the original shape is now omitted from the path icon shown in the Paths panel.

5. **Switch to the Path Selection tool and click the Combine button.** The subtracted areas of the second component you drew should disappear both on canvas and in the Paths panel.

FIGURE 11.24

One path component subtracted from another to create a new path, using Subtract path area from

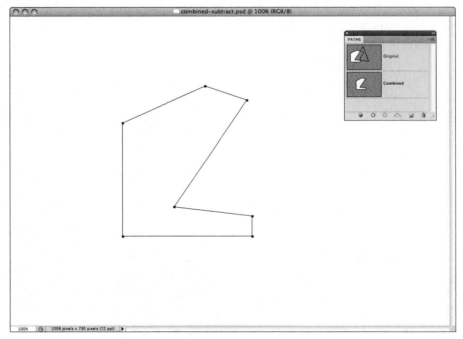

The third example, shown in Figure 11.25, describes how to intersect multiple closed path components using the Pen tool, the Intersect path areas property, and Path Selection tool options.

1. **Open a new document, making sure the Pen tool is active and that Add to path area property is selected initially.**

2. **Draw a large closed path component on the canvas.**

3. **Click the Intersect path areas property on the Options Bar.**

4. **Draw another large closed path component, this time making sure to overlap some part of your original shape, created in step 2.** Notice that only those areas where the two components overlap are now included in the active path area, and that a new perimeter has been defined as a result.

5. **Switch to the Path Selection tool and click the Combine button.** The non-overlapping areas of the second component you drew should disappear both on canvas and in the Paths panel.

FIGURE 11.25

The overlapping (or intersected) areas of two path components are combined to create a new, smaller path area and perimeter, using Intersect path areas.

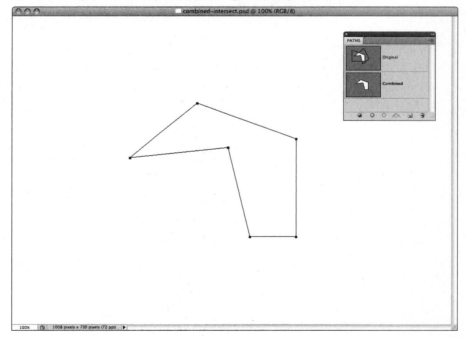

Shown in Figure 11.26, the final example describes how to omit the overlapping area of multiple, closed-path components using the Pen tool, the Exclude overlapping path areas property, and the Path Selection tool options.

1. **Open a new document, making sure the Pen tool is active and that the Add to path area property is selected initially.**

2. **Draw a large closed path component on the canvas.**

3. **Click the Exclude overlapping path areas property on the Options Bar.**

4. **Draw another large closed path component, this time making sure to overlap some part of your original shape, created in step 2.** Notice that only those areas where the two components *do not overlap* are now included in the active path area, and that a new perimeter has been defined as a result.

5. **Switch to the Path Selection tool and click the Combine button.** The overlapping areas of the second component you drew now disappear both on canvas and in the Paths panel. Note that even though the two path thumbnails in the panel appear to be the same at the end of the process, only the path labeled "original" is characterized by a single, combined shape.

FIGURE 11.26

The overlapping areas of two path components are ignored to create a new path area, using Exclude overlapping path areas.

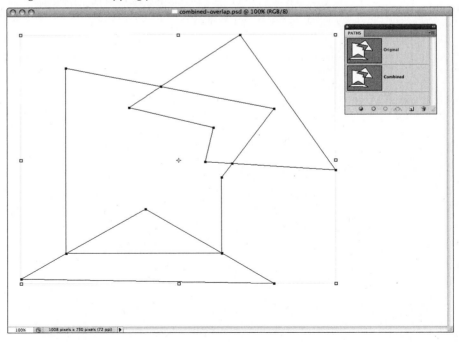

Now that you have a good idea of how simple and complex paths can be created, let's turn to the process of editing existing paths.

Editing paths

You may find that after you've saved a path and come back to it, you may need to alter the shape to suit a new creative purpose. The beauty of paths is you can alter them at any time, creating and saving new variations of the original. The primary tools used to edit paths are the Add Anchor Point, Subtract Anchor Point, Convert Point, and Direct Selection tools.

Our first example uses the same bowl shape that we created in Figure 11.18, and demonstrates how to turn that bowl into a triangle with one click of the Convert Point tool. The Convert Point tool, as noted earlier, changes smooth anchor points into corner points, and smooth direction points into corner points. This is useful for modifying a smooth path segment into something angular.

1. **Open the "Bowl_Example.psd" document you saved earlier in the chapter.**

2. **Click the path in the Paths panel to make it visible over the canvas.**

3. **Choose the Direct Selection (the white arrow) tool by pressing the A key or Shift+A if the Path Selection tool (the black arrow) is active.**

4. **Move the Direct Selection tool over the path and click one of the lines.** Three anchor points should appear.

5. **Click and hold on the Pen tool icon in the Toolbar to reveal the other tools, if you have not already defined a keyboard shortcut for the Convert Point tool.**

6. **Choose the Convert Point tool.**

7. **Click the lower anchor point that you placed to create the bowl's curvature. That same curve now turns into an angle, converting your bowl into a triangle (see Figure 11.27).**

   Had you used the Subtract Anchor Point tool instead, the line segments created by the third anchor point would've been lost completely and you would be left with a straight line. Give it a try!

8. **Leave this document open, as is, for the next exercise.**

FIGURE 11.27

The Convert Point tool removes the curvature created by smooth anchor points and their direction lines.

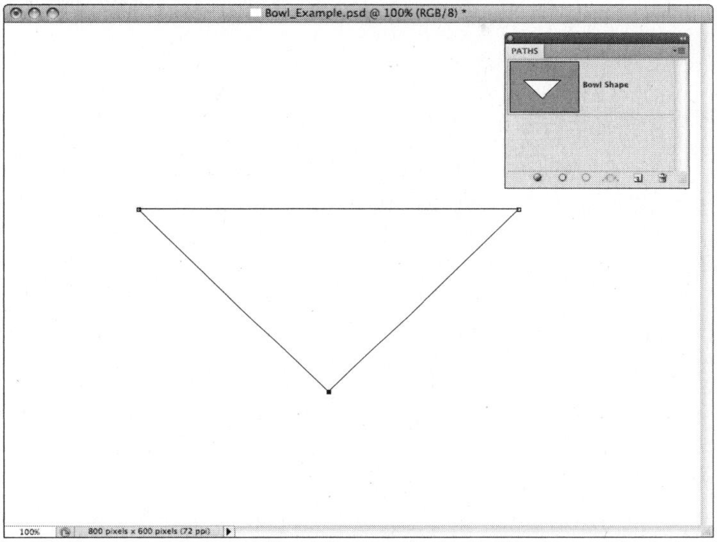

It's also common to alter the shape of a path by adding anchor points and modifying existing anchor points and direction lines with the Add Anchor Point and Direct Selection tools, respectively. The following example again uses the Bowl_Example.psd file. We will now turn it into a floating piece of paper!

1. **Press Ctrl+Z/⌘+Z to undo the converted anchor point from the previous example.** The bowl shape should reappear.

2. **Choose the Direct Selection tool and click on the empty canvas, then click on the straight line to make the three original anchor points visible.**

3. **Choose the Add Anchor Point tool or make sure it's available via the Pen tool options.**

4. **Move the cursor over the straight line on the bowl, as close to centered as you can.**

5. **Click the line to add an anchor point when you see the small plus (+) sign appear next to your cursor.**

6. **Choose the Convert Point tool and click your new anchor point.**

7. Hold down the Ctrl/⌘ key to temporarily choose the Direct Selection tool again, click the converter anchor point, and push it toward the top of the document until it creates a right angle or something approximate.

   Release the mouse button. You should now have a path that approximates the shape of an ark (front view), as seen in Figure 11.28.

FIGURE 11.28

Using new anchor points and the Direct Selection tool to modify the path's shape

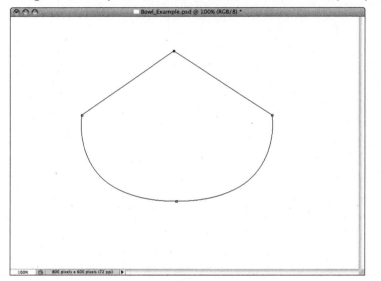

8. Choose the Pen tool or Add Anchor Point tool again, move it about halfway down the arc on the right lower corner of the path, and click.

9. Again hold down the Ctrl/⌘ key to temporarily bring up the Direct Selection tool, then click and "push" the new anchor point to the left until the line it creates starts to bend inward just a little and is parallel with the opposite line.

   Release the mouse button. You should see something like Figure 11.29.

10. Accessing the Direct Selection tool again, click on the bottom-most anchor point and "push" it toward the left-most anchor point until it is just inside the line created by the new point you made in step 9.

11. Still using the Direct Selection tool, click and drag the direction point closest to the anchor point you just moved, and rotate it clockwise until the line it controls is nearly straight but bowed slightly near the opposite left-most anchor point.

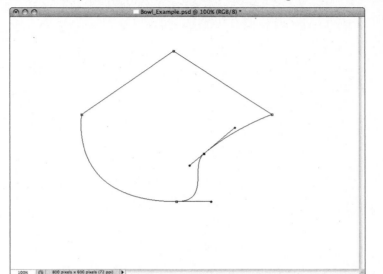

FIGURE 11.29

More anchor points and the Direct Selection tool bring the final form into view.

12. **To make the bottom right corner of the paper a little more accurate, click outside of the path with the Direct Selection tool, then click on the right edge of the paper shape near the bottom and push it inward just slightly.** The result should look something like Figure 11.30.

    You're not done with this file just yet, so save it again and leave it open for the upcoming exercises. The next section shows you how to give it a more tangible look with texture. If you haven't done so already, you can close other documents if you wish.

The final piece of the editing puzzle is to know that if you put down an anchor point on the canvas by mistake or place it in the wrong location (sometimes you may have to maneuver the direction points a bit before you realize you're in the wrong spot), the mistake is easily undone. To remove an errant anchor point and start over from the previous anchor point, do the following:

1. **Click on the anchor point you wish to delete.**
2. **Press Delete.**

That's it! The anchor point disappears and the previous anchor point becomes the active, selected point so you can try and place your next one more accurately. Similarly, if you wish to delete an entire path from the Paths panel, just highlight it and press Delete.

FIGURE 11.30

The final edits completed, the bowl has been modified with the Pen tool and Direct Selection tool into a floating sheet of paper.

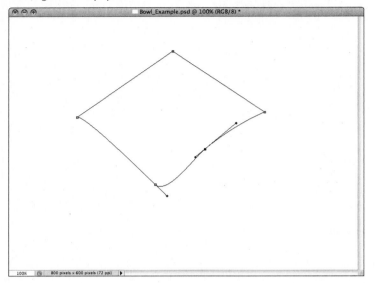

Aligning and distributing path components

The Path Selection tool has some powerful path alignment and distribution options that work in the same way as the layer alignment and distribution options.

The following example shows a simple alignment operation for three path components. For alignment to work the components have to be within the same path, because it's not possible to have more than one path active and selected at a time.

1.   **Open a new document.**

2.   **Use the Pen tool to create three simple rectangles of different sizes and shapes.**

3.   **Choose the Path Selection tool.**

4.   **Drag a marquee over all of the path components and the click the alignment option you need.** Figure 11.31 shows a variety of alignment options.

FIGURE 11.31

Various path alignment options

The vector path distribution options work in the same way as the alignment tools, except that the distance between certain parts of the path components is equalized. Note that depending on the shape of the path components and which option you have chosen, the distance between the path's edges may *not* be equal after using certain distribution options. Again, experimentation is recommended.

Path strokes and fills

As noted earlier in the chapter, regardless of what type of shape or contour you create with the Path tools, you won't see a visible path on printed documents or on final screen images until you give the path a stroke or a fill. This section show how to add some style, outline, or texture to your paths.

Path strokes

The process of giving your path a stroke is a very simple one but it's important to realize that you are not actually modifying the path, but rather the canvas below it. You are placing pixels directly onto the canvas, precisely along the bounds of the path, or in the case of Fills, which we'll talk about shortly, precisely within the bounds of the path. Use the following steps to give your path a stroke:

1. **Open a Photoshop document with vector paths you have created previously.** Choose the path you wish to outline with a stroke by clicking the path's thumbnail in the Paths

2. **Click the Paths panel menu and choose Stroke Path.** The dialog box that opens has many options for setting different types of strokes.

3. **Choose the type of option you would like to use and click OK.** Unfortunately, there is no means of previewing your path stroke, so trial and error (via the Undo command) may be necessary. Figure 11.32 shows the many different stroke types.

FIGURE 11.32

There are numerous stroke styles that can be applied to vector paths.

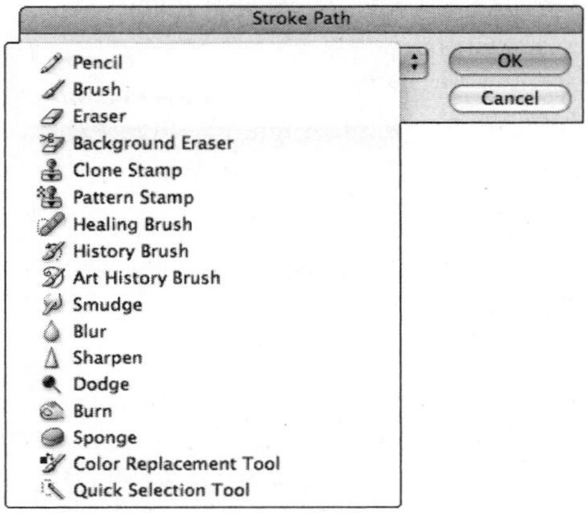

Path fills

The more powerful of the two vector "styling" options is the Fill Path command, also found in the Paths panel menu. Fill Path allows you to apply a solid color or a texture to a path's area, including the ability to specify blending mode and opacity. Again, unfortunately, you can't preview your path fills before applying them, so some trial and error may be required to achieve the desired effect.

1. **As with the prior example, select an existing path you wish to fill, by clicking on its thumbnail in the Paths panel**

2. **From the Paths panel menu choose Fill Path.**

3. **In the Contents section of the dialog box (see Figure 11.33), chose a color, pattern, history, or a shade of gray to fill the inner area of your path.**

FIGURE 11.33

Path fills actually place bitmapped pixels onto your canvas, but do so precisely within the bounds of your path, as it was located at the time of the Fill command.

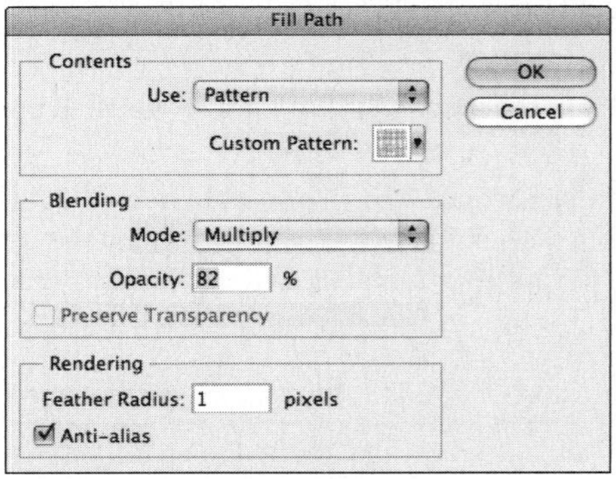

4. **Under Blending, choose a blending mode and opacity based on whatever is below your path in the document.**

5. **Check the Anti-alias option and set a feather value to smooth the fill around the edges of your path area (optional).**

6. **Click OK.** To see what your fill looks like without the path lines, just click below the active path in the Paths panel. Notice the first image layer in the stack now has a path-shaped fill of bitmapped color or texture on it.

There are many types of fills you can use, but pattern fills are among the most common, as they allow you to use any photographic or illustrative pattern available. This is a great way to make creative text effects, using a combination of the vector text example from Figure 11.22 and the Fill Path command. Multiple examples of this are shown in Figure 11.34, using the floating paper path.

Now that you are more comfortable creating, editing, and stylizing your paths, let's take a look at the biggest reason why paths are a favorite among photographic retouching and compositing pros: the ability to make precise, malleable selections that can be saved, moved between documents, and even sent to Adobe Illustrator files.

FIGURE 11.34

Examples of filled text paths

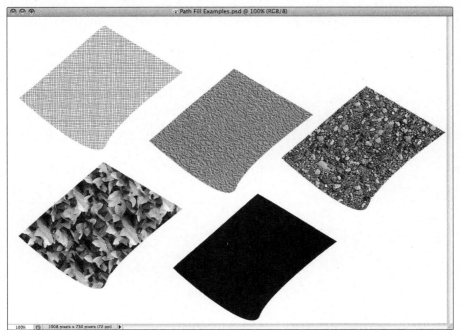

Paths as selections

Although paths can serve numerous purposes, the primary reason why they are so important to so many Photoshop pros is their power and flexibility in creating precise selections. The process of creating a path around part of an image is no different than the process of making a bowl or a piece of paper, but instead of arbitrarily placing points and making curves, you're tracing part of an image.

Creating path selections

The following example uses a combination of straight path segments and curves to create the basis for selecting the edge of a boat. To accomplish this, follow these steps:

1. **Stretch the document window slightly beyond the image boundaries, so the edges can be seen and used as guides for the left and bottom edges of the path.**

2. **Use the Pen tool to place an initial anchor point on the bottom left corner of the image.**

3. **Shift-click the Pen tool at the top edge of the boat to create a straight edge.** From this, zoom the image to 200 percent to get a better view of the boat's contour.

4. **Mentally divide the outer edge of the boat into about five or six segments, then begin by placing the first anchor point, and immediately going back half the distance to the last anchor, and placing another.**

5. **Use the Direct Selection tool to "nudge" this "middle point" upward until it conforms to the curvature of the boat hull at that location.** Repeat as many times as needed until the bottom of the boat is reached. Close off the path by Shift-clicking one final time on the original anchor point.

6. **Save the completed path.(Figure 11.35).** Click the path the Path Selection tool if you wish to make all the anchors visible for minor tweaks. Note there are many anchor points in close proximity around the chain (magnified area), to fit the contour.

7. **Choose Make Selection from the Paths panel menu.** Figure 11.36 shows the final selection around the boat.

FIGURE 11.35

The final path around the boat hull, ready to be converted to an active selection

FIGURE 11.36

The finished selection of the boat and path it was created from

From path to Alpha Channel

It's also possible to convert a path into a reusable alpha channel, giving it even more power and flexibility as a selection tool. For more information on alpha channels see Chapter 10. The following example picks up where the example from Figure 11.36 left off.

1. **With the new boat selection active, open the Channels panel.**
2. **Click the Save Selection as Channel button.** The new alpha channel is created in the shape of a boat hull.
3. **Click the alpha channel to see a black and white representation of the original path and selection, as seen in Figure 11.37.**

Alpha channels can be created indirectly from a path, by converting the path to a selection first.

Sharing paths between documents and applications

It's a common practice in photography to use the same selection shape for multiple documents; this is especially true of product and portrait photographers who may need to retouch many near-identical files. It is far more efficient to create a single precise path that can be modified slightly for each new photo than to create a brand new selection or path for each new photo being edited.

Fortunately, sharing paths between documents is as simple as saving the path and dragging it from the Paths channel of the active document onto the canvas of the target document. That's all there is to it!

Another useful path-sharing feature is the ability to export a path directly into Adobe Illustrator:

1. **Open the Photoshop document with the path you wish to export.**
2. **Click on the path in the Paths panel to make it active.**
3. **Choose File ➪ Export ➪ Paths to Illustrator.**
4. **Choose a name for the new Illustrator document, then** click Save.

5. **When you open your Illustrator document, open the Layers panel.**

6. **There should be a layer present.** Click the triangle to reveal the saved path.

Summary

In this chapter you learned about the geometric roots of the vector path (sometimes called Bézier curves) and the path's basic parts: line segments, anchor points, direction lines, and direction points. You also learned how these parts related to one another when creating vector paths.

You should also feel more familiar with the primary vector path tools and tool options, such as the ability to combine path components in different ways to create a new path area that would be difficult or time-consuming to create with only one shape. The most useful shortcuts for accessing important path tools should also be familiar to you, including: the Pen tool (P); the Path Selection and Direct Selection tools (A); and pressing the Crtl/⌘ key to access the Direct Selection tool from other tools.

You also saw examples of how to create basic and more complex paths, as well as different means for editing paths using the Convert Point tool and the Direct Selection tools in tandem. Finally, you learned about the path stroke and fill capabilities, as well as the important ability to use paths as selections, vector masks, and indirectly, alpha channels.

Chapter 12

Working with Vector Shapes

Photoshop's vector shape tools provide users with a straightforward means of creating simple shapes, symbols, and illustrative elements for their images. Vector shape elements can be stored, manipulated, and ultimately rasterized into the image itself. Their uses are wide-ranging and include tasks such as enhancing business graphics for a presentation, improving diagrams with symbols or legends, annotations for maps and directions, and of course more creative pursuits such as merging real world imagery with graphic design elements.

This chapter covers the core skills needed to create, manipulate, store, and re-use a variety of pre-built and custom vector shapes. While Photoshop's vector shapes will never be a substitute for a true digital illustration environment like Adobe Illustrator, they can be very useful in a variety of creative workflows; it would be foolish to dismiss them out of hand.

As with the Pen tools and vector path creation, the best way to integrate vector shapes into your workflow is to experiment with them firsthand as you're reading this chapter. Don't just stick to the book examples; try some new shapes and ideas of your own and see what kind of results you get.

Ultimately, vector shapes are a simple concept to grasp and master, so once you understand what they are and how they're created, you should pick up the process quickly.

IN THIS CHAPTER

Vector shapes defined

Using vector shape tools

Editing vector shape layers

Using vector shape presets

Creating new custom shapes

Creating new shape presets

Vector Shapes Defined

As it happens, while vector shapes do require vector tools for their creation, they are not really "shape objects" at all. Adobe discovered a creative way to create the appearance of solid shapes, using a color fill layer with a vector mask applied to the fill. These two elements together create what is known as a *vector shape layer*. But this is just the default setup; you can also create vector shape layers based on gradient fills and pattern fills.

I discuss how to create and use these shape layers later in the chapter, but for right now let's dissect things a bit. Figure 12.1 shows a vector path based on a Fleur de Lis shape preset, with a gradient fill layer applied to the entire document. At right, the Layers panel shows what happens when you apply the vector shape as a layer mask. The net result is that any part of the document outside of the mask is hidden, thus creating the perceived shape.

FIGURE 12.1

Though they appear to be solid-shaped objects, vector shapes are actually simple fill layers, with a vector mask that allows only a portion of that fill to show through.

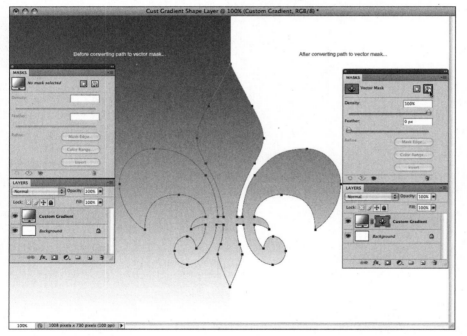

This means that whenever you alter the contours or the position of the shape layer's vector mask, you alter the shape itself as it appears over the canvas. Notice in Figure 12.2 how the shape looks different once the vector path is modified.

FIGURE 12.2

Vector shape layers can be modified by altering the shape of the mask itself, or by changing its position.

Most significantly, you are not limited to using the pre-made vector shapes that ship with Photoshop CS4. You can also use a variety of tools, including the Pen tool, to create and define your own vector shape layers. These can then be added to existing shape preset collections or form the basis of a new collection (using the Presets Manager), so that they can be re-used at any time.

Using Vector Shape Tools

While technically any tool that is capable of creating a vector path can be considered a vector shape tool, in Photoshop the term "vector shape tools" refers to a specific collection of Toolbar items. The vector shape tools have been designed to simplify the process of creating basic geometric shapes and various types of complex symbols. This means using the Pen tools for creating geometric shapes is an option, not a requirement. The vector shape tools consist of the six items shown in Figure 12.3.

- **Rectangle Tool.** Creates a vector mask that, when combined with a fill layer, results in a rectangular shape layer.

- **Rounded Rectangle Tool.** Creates a vector mask that, when combined with a fill layer, results in a rectangle with rounded corners. To control how round the corners are, use the Radius field on the Options Bar.

FIGURE 12.3

Photoshop CS4's vector shape tools simplify the process of creating graphic design elements within your images or comps.

- **Ellipse Tool.** Creates a vector mask that, when combined with a fill layer, results in an oval shaped layer.

- **Polygon Tool.** Creates a vector mask that, when combined with a fill layer, results in a polygon shape layer. To control the number of sides the polygon has, use the Sides field in the Options Bar.

- **Line Tool.** Creates a vector mask that, when combined with a fill layer, results in a single line segment shape layer.

- **Custom Shape Tool.** Creates custom-shaped vector masks that, when combined with a fill layer, result in a variety of pre-installed or pre-designed shapes or symbols. Choose the shape you need from the Custom Shape Picker menu on the Options Bar.

Each group of themed shapes is called a *preset*. You can load numerous different presets (such as animals, arrows, or ornaments) into the menu by clicking the little triangle button at the top-right portion of the Custom Shape Picker menu.

Creating vector shape layers

The vector shape tools are quite simple to use. To create a specific shape, follow these steps:

1. **Select the appropriate vector shape tool from the Toolbar.**
2. **Move the cursor over your document canvas.** It should change to a cross-hair cursor.
3. **Move the cross-hairs to the point at which you'd like to start your shape.**
4. **Click and drag (in any direction) over the area you want the shape to occupy.**
5. **Release the mouse button when the shape is the size you want.**

That's it! The result will be a new fill layer (either a color, gradient, or pattern) with a vector mask that matches the shape you made on the canvas. Together the two create a vector shape layer.

Shape layer options

Like the Pen tools, the vector shape tools take advantage of the Options Bar to help you create exactly the type of shape you need. This means in addition to the tool-specific options that are described on the following pages, you can add to, subtract from, intersect with, and ignore the overlap of existing vector shape areas. They can also be aligned and distributed by using the Path Selection tool options. The Polygon Options menu widget, shown in Figure 12.4, provides an example of options that are specific to one tool.

FIGURE 12.4

The vector shape tools' Options menu, shown here with options for the Polygon tool visible

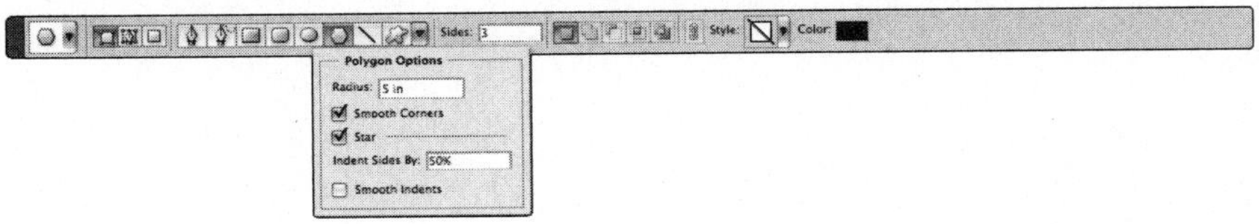

Table 12.1 shows the various Options menu items for each tool. The list that follows defines what each tool option does.

- **Unconstrained.** Allows a shape to be scaled or skewed freely in any direction, as you create it; the height and width do not maintain the same proportion.

- **Square/Circle.** Used with the Rectangle, Rounded Rectangle, and Ellipse tools, this option creates the same behavior as holding down the Shift key when you first drag out a shape mask, creating a perfect square or circle.

- **Fixed Size.** Creates a rectangle, rounded rectangle, ellipse, or custom shape that conforms to the height and width you specify.
- **Defined Size.** Creates a custom shape that fits specific dimensions.
- **Proportional.** Creates a rectangle, rounded rectangle, ellipse, or custom shape that conforms to a specific width-to-height ratio (i.e., proportion) that you specify.
- **From Center.** Creates a rectangle, rounded rectangle, ellipse, or custom shape that is drawn from the center rather than expanding from "corner to corner" as you drag.
- **Snap to Pixels.** Snaps the edges of a rectangle or rounded rectangle to the nearest grid line. For this reason, you must have your grid visible in order to use this feature.
- **Radius.** Defines the corner radius (or roundness) of rounded rectangles, or, for the Polygon tool, defines the distance from the center of the polygon to its outer points.

TABLE 12.1

Options Menu Items for Tools

	▭	▢	⬭	⬡	╲	★
Unconstrained	☒	☒	☒			☒
Square/Circle	☒	☒	☒			
Fixed Size	☒	☒	☒			☒
Defined Size						☒
Proportional	☒	☒	☒			☒
From Center	☒	☒	☒			☒
Snap to Pixels (Grid)	☒	☒				
Radius				☒		
Smooth Corners				☒		
Star Options				☒		
Arrowhead Options					☒	

- **Smooth Corners.** Renders the corners of polygons with smooth corners or indents, as shown in Figure 12.5.
- **Star Options.** Provides the option of turning a polygon into a star, with the number of sides being converted into the number of star points. Includes the ability to define the amount of indent (or how far the sides are pushed inward) and whether those indents are smooth (i.e., rounded) or angled.

- **Arrowhead Options.** Provides the option of adding starting and ending arrow points to segments created by the Line tool. Includes the ability to set the arrows' width and length as a percentage of line segment weight.

  For example, if the line segment has a weight of 2 pixels, and the arrowheads are set to 500 percent height and width, those amounts would total 10px wide and high. There is also a concavity option to specify how far the base of the arrowheads should arc inward or outward, as a percentage of length of the arrowhead, up to a value of 50 percent or –50 percent (the latter bows the arrowhead outward). Arrowhead options are shown in Figure 12.6.

FIGURE 12.5

The Polygon tool's Smooth Corners option can help to create less jagged shapes.

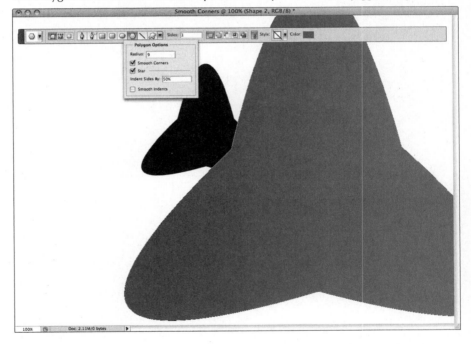

FIGURE 12.6

Arrowhead options can be combined with the Line tool to aid in the process of creating diagrams or technical illustrations.

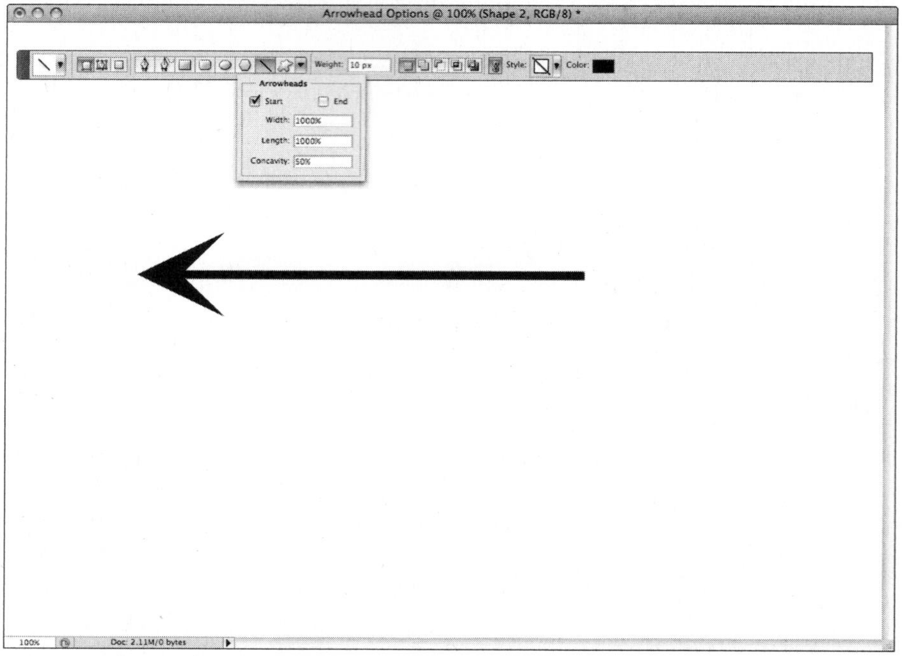

Shape layer keyboard modifiers

For the Rectangle, Rounded Rectangle, Ellipse, and Custom Shape tools, you can hold down the Shift key to constrain the proportions of your shape as you draw (the Polygon tool does so automatically). The following list contains the resultant behaviors you will see when Shift-dragging with each tool:

- **Rectangle/Rounded Rectangle.** Shift-dragging produces a perfect square/rounded square on the first attempt. Additional attempts add either square or non-square rectangles to the existing shape mask, depending on whether the unconstrained item is selected in the tool's options.

- **Ellipse.** Shift-dragging produces a perfect circle. Additional attempts add either a circular or non-circular ellipse to the existing mask, depending on whether the Constrain option is selected.

- **Line tool.** Shift-dragging constrains the line's orientation to 45, 90, or 180 degrees.

- **Custom Shape tool.** Shift-dragging constrains the exact proportions of the shape you have chosen. Unless you wish to warp the shape you've chosen, it's a good idea to use the Shift key when creating layers with the Custom Shape tool.

You can also use the Alt key (the Option key on a Mac) to subtract a shape area from the existing shape mask, as shown in Figure 12.7. If you wish to subtract a constrained shape, you should do so using the Constrain setting in the tool options, rather than using the Shift key, to maintain proportions.

FIGURE 12.7

Using the Alt/Option key in concert with the Constrain option allows you to subtract a perfect square, circle, or precisely scaled custom shape from the existing shape layer's mask.

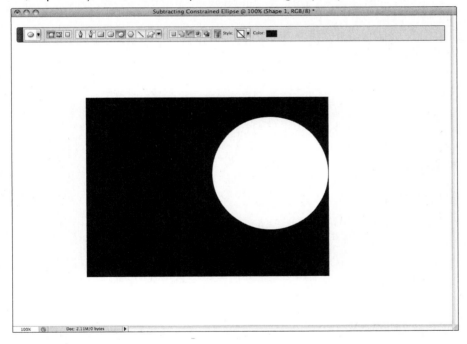

Combining shape layer areas

The same options that help you to combine individual path components or shape layers when using the Pen tool or Path Selection tool can also be used with the vector shape tools. The primary difference is, depending on whether you use Path mode or Shape mode (see Figure 12.8), the names of the combining options are slightly different.

CAUTION Both the Pen tools and vector shape tools are able to create simple paths and vector shape layers; be sure you have the right mode selected for these tools before you begin drawing!

As long as you are comfortable with options for combining path components when using the Pen tools, you will be equally comfortable using the same options for combining vector shape layers. The method for using these combining options is identical, regardless of which vector tool you are using, and regardless of whether you are creating paths or shape layers.

Table 12.2 lists the path combining options and their counterparts when using Shape Layer mode.

FIGURE 12.8

When using the Pen tool or vector shape layer tools, clicking the Shape Layers button (Options Bar, second from left) creates vector shape layers. If you click the Paths button (third from left), the same tools create a working path.

TABLE 12.2

Path Combining Options

Icon	Path Mode Name	Layer Shape Mode Name
	Not applicable	Create new shaper layer
	Add to path area	Add to shape area
	Subtract from path area	Subtract from shape area
	Intersect path areas	Intersect shape areas
	Exclude overlapping path areas	Exclude overlapping shape areas

Aligning and distributing shape layer areas

Similar to the path and shape combining functions, the path and shape alignment and distribution functions also work in exactly the same way as demonstrated in Chapter 11, and in this case there is not even a change of name. Everything works exactly the same, whether you're aligning and distributing path components or shape layer areas. Just choose the Path Selection tool as before, and these options will present themselves in the Options Bar.

Editing Vector Shape Layers

The process of editing a vector shape layer is no different than the process of editing a vector path. All the same tools and methods apply. The difference is, even though you will be working on the vector path that created the mask, you will be focused on the Layers panel rather than the Paths panel, generally speaking. There are a few tips you can take advantage of to make life easier when editing a vector mask as part of a vector shape layer. Once you have selected your shape layer:

■ **Decrease the Fill amount of your color, gradient, or pattern to 20 percent or less.** This makes it easier to see the path that you are editing, while not completely removing the effect that it creates as you edit the various anchor points and path contours. It helps in some cases to see how the fill area interacts with other parts of the document as the vector mask changes to form a modified shape.

■ **Remember to click the actual path boundaries with the Direct Selection tool, rather than clicking inside the fill area.** Clicking on the path itself automatically selects the mask in the layer being worked on, and the nearest anchor points and direction lines appear, as shown in Figure 12.9.

- When you have the shape layer's mask contoured exactly as you want it, and you have set the other layer options such as Fill and any effects blending to their final values, it's a good idea to lock the vector shape layer so that no accidental changes can be made.

- To make your shape and fill a permanent part of the bitmap image, Ctrl+click or right-click on the vector shape layer in the Layers panel and choose Rasterize Layer.

FIGURE 12.9

When editing your vector shape mask, be sure to click the path itself using the Direct Selection tool. In many cases, lowering the fill amount of your layer helps you to see the path better.

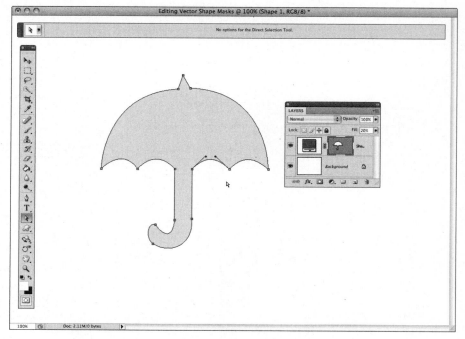

Using Vector Shape Presets

Using the Custom Shape tool, Photoshop users can quickly create a large array of pre-built vector-based shapes and symbols (called *shape presets*). These custom shapes and symbols are grouped by theme in the Custom Shape Picker dialog box, shown in Figure 12.10.

The Custom Shape tool and the preset shape you choose work the same as the other vector shape tools, creating a new vector shape layer as they are drawn onto the canvas (preset shapes are just vector masks combined with a fill layer, like those described earlier in the chapter).

The steps for producing custom shape layers are identical to those used for the other vector shape tools, except that extra steps are added so you can choose the appropriate shape:

1. **Select the Custom Shape tool from the Toolbar, making sure the Shape Layer mode is active, as shown in Figure 12.10.**

2. **Click the Custom Shape Picker button to reveal its dialog box.**

FIGURE 12.10

To access the Custom Shape tool's preset options, click the Custom Shape Picker popup menu on the Options Bar to view the different shape and symbol options available. The current or active preset and its collection of shapes are displayed as a list or group of thumbnails.

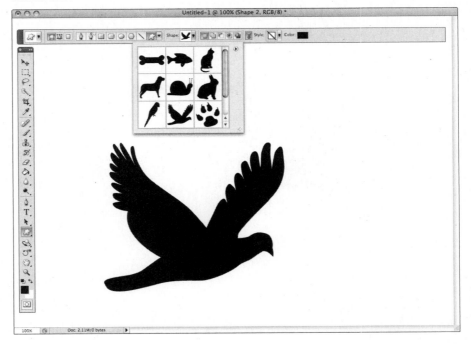

3. **If the shapes or symbols currently shown do not suit your purposes, click the Custom Shape Picker's fly-out menu (shown in Figure 12.11), and at the bottom of the menu choose All to show all shapes and symbols, or choose a different preset theme from the list.**

4. Select the shape you wish to add to your image by clicking it.

5. Choose Constrain from the Custom Shape tool's options to maintain the proper ratio.

6. Place your cross-hairs on the canvas, click and drag your custom shape to its chosen size, then release the mouse button or pick up the stylus from the tablet to release.

The Custom Shape Picker uses a fly-out menu to help you manage and view the different collections of shape presets that you create and that come with Photoshop.

Figure 12.12 shows several examples of the types of shapes that can be used, which gives you an idea of the different types of projects for which they might be applicable. Keep in mind these are just the pre-defined shape presets. As discussed in the next section, you can create your own shape presets as well.

FIGURE 12.12

Photoshop CS4 ships with a large array of pre-built shape presets that can be used with the Custom Shape tool. Common uses include general illustration and the creation of diagramming icons.

Creating New Custom Shapes

Any closed path that you create with the Pen tools, as well as any combination of shapes that you create with the vector shape tools, can be converted into a custom shape and saved with the other presets or a new preset group that you create with the Presets Manager. No special techniques or skills are required beyond the ability to work effectively with those. To create a new custom shape, follow these steps:

1. **Using the Pen tools or vector shape tools, create a new closed path in the shape that you would like to use.** It is often helpful to place an image layer containing the shape of your path into your document at a low opacity so that you can effectively trace its shape by using the vector tools. Then when you have finished closing the path or shape layer, you can discard the image you traced from.

2. Place your cursor over the new path or shape area, and Ctrl+click or right-click.

3. From the context menu that appears, choose Define Custom Shape, shown in Figure 12.13.

4. In the dialog box that opens, name your new shape and click OK.

5. Select the Custom Shape tool and then click the Custom Shape Picker.

6. **If needed, scroll to the bottom of the current Preset list.** Your new shape should appear as the last item in the group.

You can now select the new shape and apply it to your document as you would any other preset shape. To delete it, highlight your shape and choose Delete from the Custom Shape Picker's fly-out menu (refer to Figure 12.11).

FIGURE 12.13

Right-clicking or Ctrl+clicking on a new closed path or shape layer that you have created provides the option — via a context menu — to save the defining path as a custom shape.

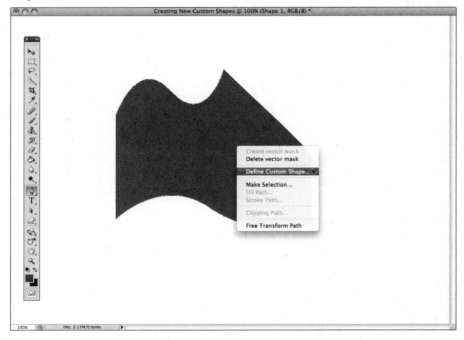

Save a Shape to a Preset Group

If you want your shape to be saved with a specific preset group, make sure you first select that group from the Custom Shape Picker's fly-out menu, and when asked, choose OK. If you choose Append, your desired preset group's shapes are added to the end of the current group's shapes in the Custom Shape Picker dialog box.

Choosing OK effectively replaces all the existing custom shape icons in the dialog box with your chosen preset's custom shape icons. The original preset and its custom shapes are not erased or deleted; it is merely a question of which shapes are displayed in the menu.

Creating New Shape Presets

The easiest way to create a brand-new preset (or group of themed custom shapes shown in the Custom Shape Picker dialog box) is to first create all your shapes so that they are available to you via the Custom Shape Picker dialog box. Then follow these steps to create the new preset by using the Photoshop CS4 Presets Manager window:

1. **Click the Custom Shape Picker's fly-out menu and choose Preset Manager.** Seen in Figure 12.14, the Preset Manager window opens with the Custom Shapes preset type selected.

FIGURE 12.14

Photoshop CS4's Preset Manager window, opened to the Custom Shapes area in preparation for creating a new custom shape preset for use in the future (Photoshop must be closed and re-launched to take advantage of newly created presets.)

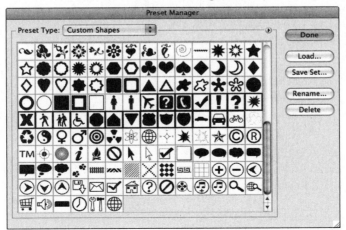

2. Scroll to the bottom of the shape list, where your new custom shapes are found.

3. Select the shape icons that represent the items you wish to include in your new pre-set, using the Shift+click/Ctrl+click (PC) or Shift+click/⌘+click (Mac) method to highlight them all simultaneously.

4. Once all your custom shape icons are selected (note you can combine the ones you made with the shapes that ship with Photoshop to create a new preset), click Save Set.

5. Name your preset according to whatever theme or purpose they serve and click Save.

6. Click Done.

7. **Save and close any open documents, and quit Photoshop.** Launch a new Photoshop session to take advantage of your new preset, which appears at the bottom of the preset list in the Custom Shape Picker's fly-out menu.

You can also use the Preset Manager to rename, redefine (by saving a new preset with the same name), or delete a custom preset by using the Rename, Save Set, and Delete buttons, respectively.

Summary

This chapter discussed and defined the concept of vector shape layers and how they can be created within your Photoshop documents. Multiple creative options for each vector shape tool were discussed, as well as important keyboard shortcuts to make your vector workflow more efficient.

Among the most important concepts you learned are that vector shape layers are created from a combination of either color, gradient, or pattern fill layer, with a vector mask applied. The shape is created when the areas outside the mask boundary are hidden from view. Also important is the fact that vector shape layers can be created with both the Pen tool and the vector shape tools, and utilize many of the same options including the ability to create either working paths or shape layers, as well as the ability to combine those path components or shapes by using the Add To, Subtract From, Intersect With, and Ignore Overlap buttons found on the Options Bar.

Alignment and distribution of vector shape layers is handled with exactly the same tools and methods as those used for aligning and distributing paths (the Path Selection tool options). Vector shape layers can also have their shapes modified by using the Direct Selection tool and Fill Slider on the Layers panel to isolate the actual path that the shape layer's mask is based upon, and editing it as you would any other path.

Finally it's important to remember that any closed path you create with Photoshop's vector tools can be made into a custom shape for inclusion in the Custom Shape Presets area. These custom shapes can be reused indefinitely.

Chapter 13

Working with Text

Type in Photoshop has come a long way. We old-timers who used Photoshop in the days of yore recall a time when the simplest type tasks involved a steady hand, a firm backbone, and a 10-mile hike barefoot in the snow (both ways); and we are very grateful for the robust type engine we have at our disposal today. Before Photoshop 5, type was created as bitmap pixels that merged directly with the background layer, and once entered, couldn't be moved or edited — it was more or less engraved in stone. Photoshop 5 finally gave us the ability to create type on its own layer, but it wasn't until version 7 that we finally had fully editable vector text. And as for creating text that deviated in any way from your basic left-to-right layout . . . well, we've come a long way, baby.

As mentioned earlier, Photoshop now supports vector-based type — type that is generated by mathematically defined outlines that you can scale, rotate, and otherwise transform without any degradation of their crisp outlines. Additionally, you can bend, stretch, and twist type with the Warp tool, all the while keeping it fully editable. Type is created on individual layers and can therefore take advantage of just about all the benefits of using layers, such as blending modes, masks, and layer styles. On top of all that, you can use the Spell Check command to ensure accuracy in over 30 different languages. Finally, the Find and Replace command makes repetitive edits a breeze.

NOTE If you create type in a document mode that doesn't support layers, the type is created as rasterized type on the background layer (Indexed, Bitmap, or Multichannel mode).

Entering Text

To create type in Photoshop, click on the Type tool in the Toolbar (shown in Figure 13.1) or press the T key on your keyboard. The Horizontal Type tool is activated by default. Click or drag anywhere in your document, and begin typing to enter text. Type is placed on a new text layer, indicated in your Layers panel by a T in the layer thumbnail.

Photoshop's Type tools and Type Options Bar

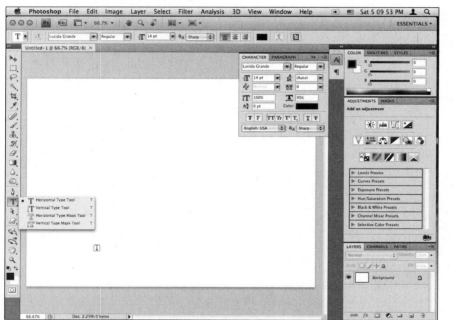

To accept the text you just entered, do one of the following:

■ Click the check mark icon in the Type Options Bar.

■ Press Enter on your numeric keypad or Ctrl+Enter (⌘+Return on a Mac) on your keyboard.

■ Click on a different layer, tool, or panel.

You'll notice that as soon as you accept the text, the name of the new type layer changes to the first 30 characters of the text you entered. You can also double-click on the name of the layer to change it to something else if you'd like.

Editing Text

To edit the text on a type layer, select the Type tool and do one of the following:

- **Hover the I-beam over the text in your document.** It changes from having a box around it to being a simple vertical bar to show that you can edit the underlying text. Click on the text to enter Edit mode.

- **Drag the cursor over text in a Photoshop document to highlight it, just as you would in a word-processing document.**

- **Double-click the T in the thumbnail of a type layer to quickly select all the text on a layer and enter Edit mode.**

You can switch between horizontal and vertical text after you've entered it by choosing Horizontal or Vertical from the Layer ⇨ Type menu (or in the context menu that appears when you right-click on the type in your document with the Type tool selected, as shown in Figure 13.2).

FIGURE 13.2

The Type tool's context menu provides convenient access to Type options. Right-click/⌘-click on text in the document or right-click/⌘-click on a type layer to access it.

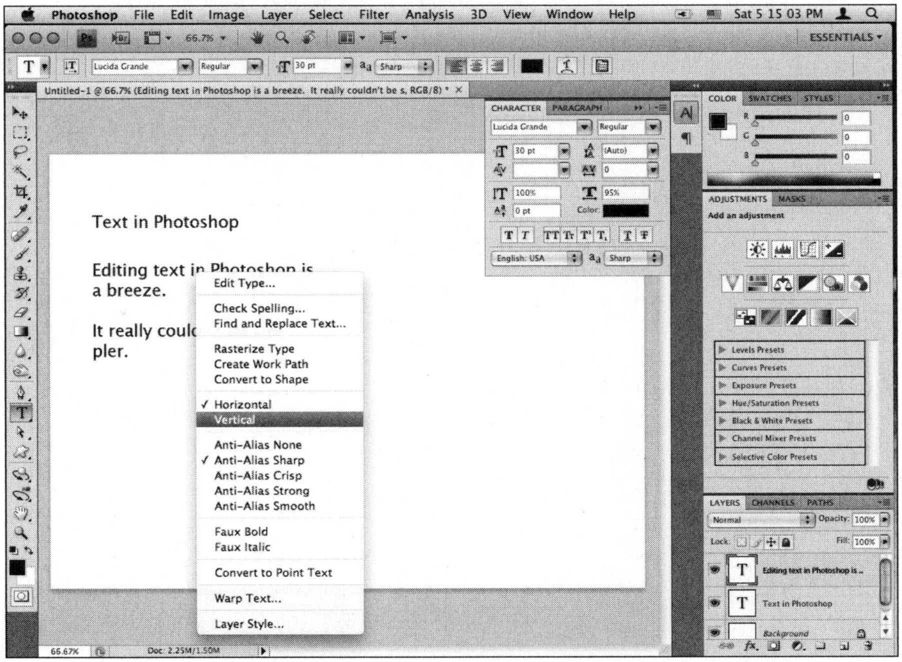

When working with vertical text, the Standard Vertical Roman Alignment option becomes available in the Character panel fly-out menu. By default, the text is automatically rotated so that each character is right-way-up. Disabling this option rotates each character 90 degrees so that it appears sideways (see Figure 13.3 for an example).

FIGURE 13.3

Enabling Standard Vertical Roman Alignment displays each character the right-way-up, while disabling it rotates each character by 90 degrees.

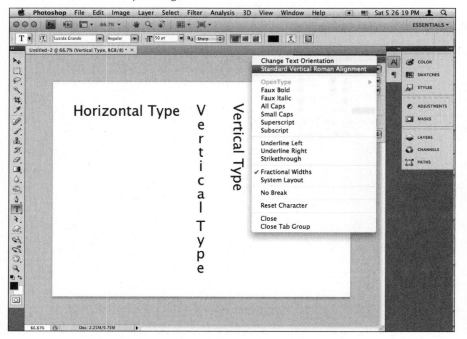

There are three ways of entering text in Photoshop — as point text, as paragraph text, or as text on or in a path. Point text is useful for adding short bits of text to a design, such as a title or caption. Paragraph text, which is text that flows within a defined rectangular frame, is more suited to adding a larger amount of text to a brochure or Web page design.

Finally, you can use a vector path or shape to create typography that flows around a free-form shape. Additionally, you can convert each character in a type layer to individual vector shapes or paths that you can manipulate. You'll learn more about using each of these different type modes later in this chapter.

About Fonts

Although the terms "font" and "typeface" are often used interchangeably, a *font* is a complete set of characters that contains letters, numbers, and symbols, and that has a common weight and style, such as Helvetica Light. A *typeface* is a collection or family of fonts that is created by the same designer, and shares an overall aesthetic appearance. The different fonts within a typeface, such as the Helvetica family, are designed to work well together and complement each other in a layout.

In addition to the characters that you can type using various combinations of the keys on your keyboard, most typefaces contain other *glyphs* — that is, a robust collection of characters (or *graphemes*, if you want to get extra-fancy) that can represent any number of things, including ornamental graphical elements, swashes, ligatures, currency symbols, fractions, and old-style figures.

Some examples of glyphs available in a typeface

¶	Pillcrow
‰	Per mille
§	Section
⟹	Arrow
₡	Cruziero
€	Euro
Œ	Ligature OE
Σ	Sigma
Ω	Omega

Generally, a typeface is comprised of a base font (usually called Roman or Regular, although this may vary depending on the typeface), and a few variants, such as a semi-bold, bold, and an italic or oblique. If the typeface you've chosen doesn't include these variants, you can apply a faux bold or italic to the base version of the typeface by using the Type palette. Generally speaking, however, most serious graphic designers avoid using faux styles, because after all, typography design is an art, and faux styles alter the design of the font — sort of like putting ketchup on filet mignon. As a rule, if a bold or italic version of a typeface is available, use it instead of the faux styles.

Type tools

There are four Type tools in Photoshop; they can be found under the Type tool fly-out menu in the Toolbar: the Horizontal Type tool, the Vertical Type tool, the Horizontal Type Mask tool, and the Vertical Type Mask tool (see Figure 13.4). The Type tools create vector-based text on type layers, while the Type Mask tools create "marching ants" selections in the shape of the characters that you type in, which you can then use as masks.

Truth be told, I've never really used the Type Mask tools, as you can achieve a similar result — that is, create a marching ants selection in the shape of your text — by creating a regular text layer and Ctrl+clicking/⌘+clicking the layer thumbnail to create a selection from the text layer. The advantage to using this method is that if you need to, you can go back and edit the type layer, for instance, changing the font or the point size of the text, and re-creating the mask as necessary. On the other hand, Type Masks are gone forever once you've created the text.

The Horizontal Text tools create text that flows from left to right and from top to bottom, while the Vertical Text tools create type that flows vertically from top to bottom, and then across the page from right to left, as it does in Japanese books.

> **TIP** You can change type options for several type layers simultaneously by Shift+clicking on them in the Layers panel, and then selecting new values in the Type Options Bar. You can also simultaneously set character options for multiple layers by using the Character panel, or you can specify paragraph options for the selected layers by using the Paragraph panel (described in greater detail later in this chapter).

FIGURE 13.4

The Type tools in the Toolbar. Press Shift+T to cycle through the four modes of the Type tool.

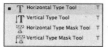

Single-Line Type

As mentioned earlier, single-line type, or point type, is useful for entering short amounts of text in your document; for example, when creating image titles or photo credits.

Create some point type by clicking anywhere in your document with the Type tool. A new type layer is created, and the blinking I-beam indicates that you're in Edit mode and ready to start typing. As you type, the text extends from the point where you initially clicked, either horizontally or vertically, depending on which Type tool you're using (see Figure 13.5).

The short, horizontal bar going across the I-beam indicates the baseline, or the imaginary horizontal line that the text rests on when using the Horizontal Type tool. When using the Vertical Type tool, it indicates the horizontal center of each character.

To resize type while in Edit mode, press Ctrl/⌘ and use the handles on the type bounding box to scale, rotate, or use other transform commands on the text. Again, because it's vector text, you can transform it to your heart's content without losing that nice crisp edge.

To accept your edits once you're finished entering text, do one of the following:

- Click the check box icon in the Type Options Bar.
- Press Ctrl+Enter/⌘+Return or press Enter.
- Click on a different tool, layer, or panel.

Or, to abandon changes, click the cancel icon in the Options Bar (it's the circle with the line through it), or press ESC.

You can convert your single-line type to paragraph type by selecting Convert to Paragraph Text either from the Layer menu or from the context menu when right-clicking on a single-line or point text layer.

FIGURE 13.5

Single-line type is best used for short amounts of text.

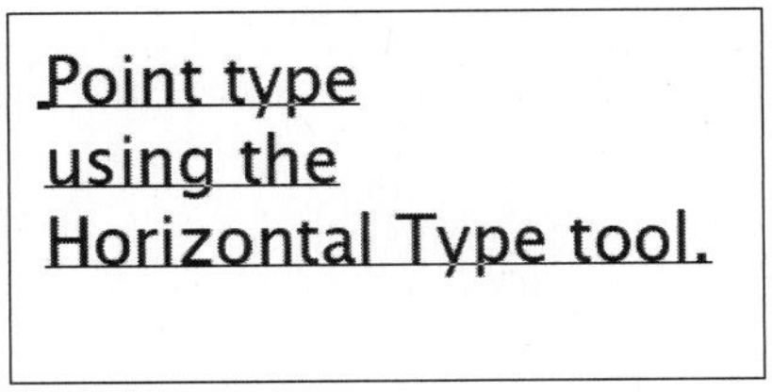

Point type
using the
Horizontal Type tool.

Paragraph Type

For laying out paragraphs of text in, say, a brochure or flyer design, use paragraph text. In this mode, you create a frame that covers the size of the area that you would like to fill with type, and the text you enter is constrained to that area or shape, as shown in Figure 13.6. You can always resize the boundaries of this frame after you've created it. To create a block of paragraph text, do either of the following:

- Click and drag with the Type tool to define a rectangle that forms the boundary of your text.
- Hold down Alt/Option and click with the Type tool, and then enter the dimensions of the text box you want to create in the Paragraph Text Size dialog box.

Begin entering type. Specify type options with the Type tool Options Bar, the Character panel, or the Paragraph panel, which is covered in more detail later in this chapter.

Pressing Enter/Return in paragraph type mode creates a new paragraph. As in the case of point type, you can also transform the bounding box of the text by using the transform handles. Drag the handles to adjust the width and height of the text box. Shift+drag to constrain the proportions of your text box.

Commit to type changes by pressing Enter, clicking the check mark in the Toolbar, or selecting another tool in the Toolbar or a different layer in the Layers panel.

Text that overflows the boundaries of the text box is indicated by a small plus sign in a square at the lower right of the boundary.

You can also convert existing point type to paragraph type as described earlier. And because you're obviously brilliant enough to be reading this book in the first place, you probably already figured out that you can convert paragraph type to single-line type in the same manner.

FIGURE 13.6

Use the handles to resize the boundaries surrounding paragraph text.

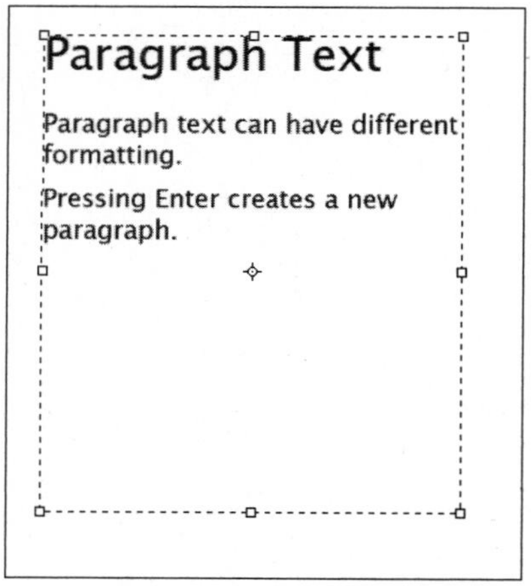

Type Tool Options Bar

The Type Tool Options Bar (see Figure 13.7) provides easy access to many of the more frequently used options found in the Character panel, including typeface, font size, anti-aliasing, and color options.

FIGURE 13.7

The Type Tool Options Bar brings these handy controls within easy reach.

The Warp tool (discussed in its own section later in this chapter) can also be accessed here. The Alignment controls (which allow you to create left-, center-, and right-aligned type) are the only controls found in the Paragraph panel that are also accessible here.

Of course, there are many more type formatting tools at your disposal, so read on to learn more about each of these controls in more detail.

Character panel

Typesetting, or manipulating the visual appearance of text characters, has been around since eleventh-century China. Wood blocks engraved with each character were manually positioned to adjust the spacing between them and to design the layout of each line of text in relation to the lines that came after it. Fortunately for us, the intervening centuries have given us the Type tool's labor-saving Character panel (see Figure 13.8). Use the Character panel to choose a typeface and font, to adjust letterspacing and leading, and to perform any number of other typesetting tasks that would have most likely taken a room full of our eleventh-century brethren weeks to complete.

If it's not visible, access the Character panel by selecting Character from the Window menu or by clicking the Character panel button in the Type Tool Options Bar.

> **TIP** To apply options from the Character panel to existing type or to specific characters on a type layer, first select the text, and then change the settings. Changing character options without selecting any text applies those settings to any new text that you create.

Choosing a font

Click the Font popup menu to display a list of the font families that are available on your system, along with a preview of what the typeface looks like (see Figure 13.9). Next to each font in the Font preview is a tiny icon that indicates the format (TrueType, OpenType, PostScript) of each font.

If you already know the name of the font you want to use, click with your cursor in the Font field and begin typing. Photoshop automatically displays the names of the installed fonts that most closely match what you're typing.

Once you've selected a font family, click the Font Style popup menu to view the available font variants within the family you've selected.

Use the Character panel and its fly-out menu to access advanced typesetting controls.

Selecting a font family from the Character panel

OpenType options

OpenType is a very flexible, standards-based font format that is designed to be compatible with both Mac and Windows computers. You can transfer these fonts seamlessly between platforms without having to worry about font substitution messin' (in strict technical terms) with the layout of your document. Photoshop now has expanded support for these fonts, which can contain well over 65,000 glyphs.

How does this affect you? Well, it means you can make use of ligatures, which are single glyphs that form when certain pairs of letters like *ff, fi,* and *ae* appear together. Fractions can also be substituted automatically when you type one number followed by a forward-slash and another number. Another feature of OpenType fonts are ordinals, or numbers followed by a superscript suffix, that indicate order, such as 1st, 2nd, or 100th. Swashes, or those fancy swooping elements of characters that sometimes flow below the baseline, are also a feature of OpenType fonts.

You can access the OpenType font options in the fly-out menu of the Character panel. Note that these options will be grayed out if you're not using an OpenType font — indicated by an "O" icon in the font popup menu. Some examples of the features available with OpenType fonts are shown in Figure 13.10.

FIGURE 13.10

Enable OpenType options to gain access to a huge number of additional glyphs.

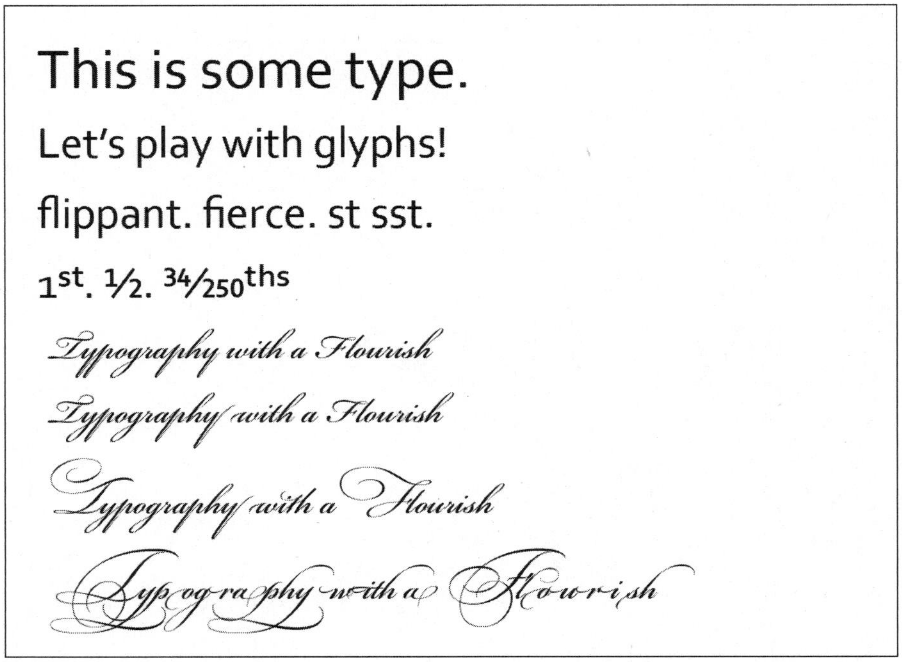

Font size

To adjust the size of your text, either click on the Size popup menu and choose one of the options, or double-click in the size field, type a new number, and press Enter/Return. You can also interactively adjust the font size by hovering over the Font Size icon until the cursor turns into a scrubber (the hand cursor with arrows on either side of it), and clicking and dragging left or right. Font size is based on the distance between the descenders (the parts of characters like "q" or "g" that hang below the baseline) and the ascenders (the tall parts of characters like "h" and "l").

Note that the actual heights of the characters can sometimes vary between fonts. Figure 13.11 shows the same sentence at the same point size in the fonts Corbel, Lucida Grande, and Aaux Pro. Notice how the text fills the 160 pixels of space differently in each case.

Text in Photoshop is measured in points (the default setting), pixels, or millimeters. To specify which unit to use, choose Preferences➪Units & Measurements and pick a new setting from the Type popup menu.

For you keyboard shortcut junkies out there, you can quickly adjust the size of selected text by pressing Ctrl+Shift+>/⌘+Shift+> or Ctrl+Shift+</⌘+Shift+< on your keyboard. This shortcut increases or decreases the type size in increments of 2 points or pixels (1 millimeter). Add the Alt/Option key to change the type size in increments of 10 pixels (5 millimeters).

FIGURE 13.11

Font size varies between different typefaces.

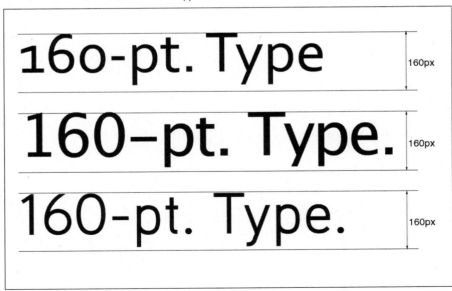

> **TIP** If the font previews in the popup menu are a little small and hard to see, you can change the size to make finding fonts a little easier on your eyes. Open Photoshop's preferences by pressing Ctrl+K/⌘+K and select Type from the options on the left. Select a suitable size from the Font Preview Size popup menu and click OK to apply your selection.

Leading

In Photoshop, *leading* (pronounced "LED-ing") refers to the amount of vertical space between the baselines of two lines of text (see Figure 13.12). The term comes from the old days of typesetting when characters were engraved on pieces of lead, and horizontal strips of the metal were used to separate lines of text.

By default, Photoshop inserts a distance of 120 percent of the current font size between lines of text. To change this default setting, open the Justification dialog box from the Character panel menu and change the Auto Leading option.

You can change the leading for all the lines of text on a type layer or on a line-by-line basis. Adjusting leading is done much in the same way as changing font size — either by selecting a value from the Leading popup menu, by double-clicking in the Leading field and typing in a new value, or by using the scrubber to adjust the value.

Of course, you can also take advantage of keyboard shortcuts to dynamically adjust leading. With text highlighted, press Alt+Down Arrow /Option+Down Arrow or Alt+Up Arrow/Option+Up Arrow to increase or decrease the leading by 2 points or pixels. Add the Ctrl/⌘ key to change the value by 10 points or pixels. Again, if you're working in millimeters, this value changes by either 1 millimeter or 5 millimeters, depending on which shortcut you use.

Kerning

Kerning refers to the amount of space between individual characters in a word. Photoshop can automatically adjust this space based on either *metrics* (the information contained in each) or optical kerning, or you can adjust it manually.

Metrics kerning

Some pairs of characters — for example *LA, Tr, Wa,* and *WA* — can be visually awkward when they are juxtaposed. Font designers take these *kern pairs* into account when designing their typefaces and include at least some information, or metrics, about how much space should appear between them. To enable metrics kerning (also called auto kerning), click on the Kerning popup menu and select Metrics.

Optical kerning

If there isn't enough information about kern pairs embedded in the font you're using, or if you're using characters from different typefaces in the same line of text, you might try using optical kerning instead. Optical kerning uses Photoshop's sophisticated algorithms (also known as software engineering magic) to analyze characters and automatically adjust the spacing between them. You can apply optical kerning to the highlighted text or to the current type layer by clicking on the Kerning pop-up menu in the Character panel, and selecting Optical.

FIGURE 13.12

Increasing the leading changes the vertical distance between the baseline of one line of text and the next.

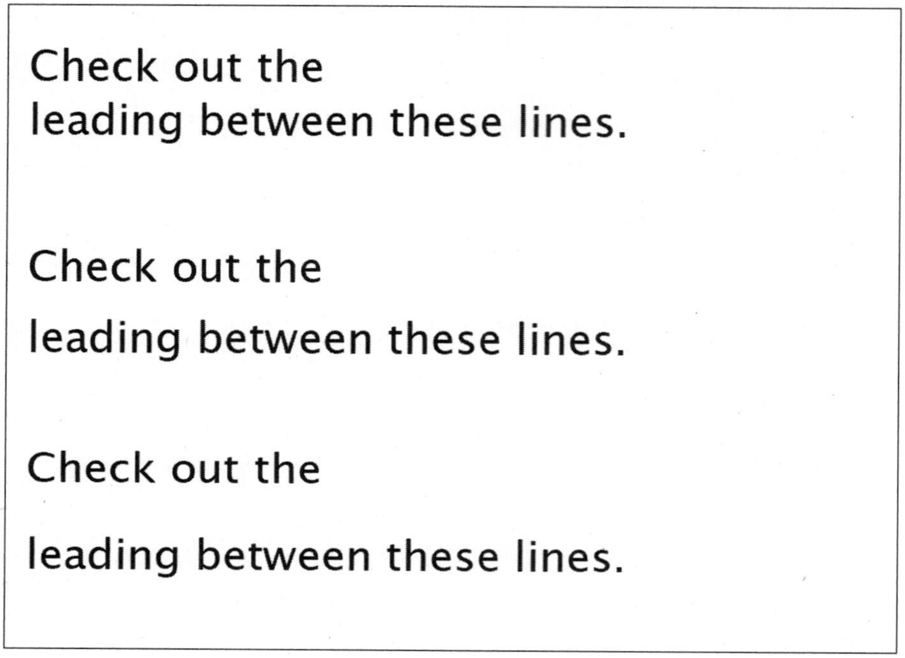

Check out the
leading between these lines.

Check out the

leading between these lines.

Check out the

leading between these lines.

Manual kerning

Of course, you can always adjust the kerning yourself if the automatic kerning options aren't doing it for you, or if you're trying to achieve a specific typographic effect. Simply position your cursor between a pair of characters and click in the kerning field, enter a number, and press Enter/Return; or choose a number other than zero from the popup menu. Negative values tighten up the amount of space between characters, while positive numbers move them farther apart.

To adjust the space between a pair of characters in increments of 20, using the keyboard, press Alt/Option in conjunction with the arrow keys on your keyboard. Press Ctrl+Alt+< or >/⌘+Option+< or > to adjust the space between characters in increments of 100.

Figure 13.13 shows some examples of the different kerning modes on pairs of characters.

FIGURE 13.13

Adjusting the spacing between different kern pairs using Photoshop's kerning modes

"Troublesome Watchdogs" is a silly phrase.

"Troublesome Watchdogs" is a silly phrase.

"Troublesome Watchdogs" is a silly phrase.

Tracking

Tracking is similar to kerning in that it refers to the spacing between characters. However, tracking usually refers to tightening or loosening the spacing of entire paragraphs of selected text. Select a type layer, or highlight some text and choose a number other than zero from the Tracking popup menu. Once again, you can also double-click the value in the Tracking field and manually enter a number, then press Enter/Return. Or, you can position your cursor in the field and use your up or down arrow key to increase or decrease the tracking for the currently selected text. Figure 13.14 shows some examples of text with different tracking values applied.

NOTE Kerning and tracking are both measured in values of 1/1000 em, one *em* being equal to the width of the lowercase *m* in the current size of the current font. Using ems to measure tracking and kerning is helpful because it allows your character spacing to remain consistent even if you later change the font or font size.

FIGURE 13.14

The first sentence has the default tracking applied. The next sentence has a tracking value of 200, while setting the tracking to –200 has tightened up the last sentence.

She sold seashells on the city streets.

She sold seashells on the city streets.

She sold seashells on the city streets.

Fractional Widths and System Layout

Another way to adjust the spacing between characters is to choose the Fractional Widths option (located in the Character panel fly-out menu). By default, the varying space between characters can include amounts smaller than whole pixels. This is designed to produce clear, readable type, and you should leave it selected most of the time. In the case of small font sizes, such as those designed for use on Web pages, it can result in awkward spacing between characters. To avoid this, turn off Fractional Widths. Note that this setting applies to all the type on a layer — you can't specify this setting for selected characters within a layer.

Another option for producing crisp, readable type at small sizes on-screen is to choose System Layout from the Character panel fly-out menu. This command performs two actions simultaneously: First, it turns off Fractional Widths to ensure consistent spacing between characters, and then it disables anti-aliasing (described later in this chapter).

Horizontal and vertical scaling

You can scale the height and width of characters by adjusting the horizontal and vertical scaling settings. A value of 100 percent is the default and means no scaling has been applied. Increasing the values makes the text grow, while decreasing the values makes the text smaller. Scaling is applied in relation to the baseline. In the case of vertical type, changing the vertical value makes each character taller or shorter, while changing the horizontal value affects the width of the column of text.

Baseline shift

You can use this setting to adjust the position of text in relation to its baseline, either raising it above the baseline by changing the value to a positive number or moving it below the baseline by changing the value to a negative number. This is useful if you're manually creating fractions or mathematical equations.

You may be saying to yourself that this sounds an awful lot like using the subscript and superscript settings (which are discussed in more detail shortly), but the difference is that by using baseline shift, you have control over the distance that the character is positioned from the baseline, as well as the character size, so use this method if you need more control. The fractions and equations in Figure 13.15 were created with various baseline shift settings.

Color

When you create type, by default it is rendered in the current foreground color. You can change the color of type by clicking on the Color swatch in the Character panel to display the Color Picker dialog box. Selecting a type layer in the Layers panel and changing the color affects all the type on a layer. You can also change the color of individual words or characters by highlighting them, then clicking on the Color swatch.

> **TIP**   **Accurately previewing the color of selected text is difficult (to say the least) because of the selection highlight. To toggle the selection highlight (as well as guides and other display aids), press Ctrl+H/⌘+H.**

FIGURE 13.15

Using the baseline shift settings to create fractions and equations

$$^1\!/125$$

$$\frac{(x+3)^2}{2x-4} - x + 6 = 0$$

$$(x+a)^n = \sum_{k=0}^{n}\binom{n}{k}x^k a^{n-k}$$

Character styles

The row of buttons at the bottom of the Character panel provides controls for applying styles to your text. All these options are also available in the Character panel fly-out menu. You can toggle them on or off by clicking the buttons or checking or un-checking the menu items.

- Faux Bold and Faux Italic allow you to create bold and italic effects when the typeface you've selected doesn't include bold or italic variants of the font (see the earlier sidebar for more information).

- Click the All Caps button to change the case of text that was entered in lower- or Mixed-case to UPPERCASE text. Clicking the Small Caps button changes text to all Uppercase Text as Well, but characters that were capitalized when entered become larger than text that was entered as lowercase.

- Superscript text appears above adjacent characters, while subscript characters appear below the baseline of adjacent characters. Use these controls to create mathematical formulas, or ordinal numbers, such as "1st" or "100th." Remember that the Subscript and Superscript buttons move and shrink the text by a predetermined amount; if you need more control, try using the method described earlier in this chapter.

- Click the Underline button to draw a line under the selected text or text layer. Note that if you're using vertical text, the Underline button doesn't change, but the Character panel menu options change to Underline Left and Underline Right. The Strikethrough option draws a line through the text.

While in Text edit mode — that is, while text is selected, or the I-beam is in text — Dynamic Shortcuts are available (see Figure 13.16).

The list of Dynamic Shortcuts appears in the Character panel menu while you're in text Edit mode, and allows you to set most of the Character style options, such as faux bold, faux underline, all caps, small caps, and so on, via the keyboard.

Check Spelling

Much like just about any word-processing or text-editing software, Photoshop can help you (or whoever is supplying you with the text for your layout) battle poor spelling with its built-in spell checker.

Select a dictionary, if necessary. If you choose a dictionary without selecting type or a type layer first, that dictionary is used throughout your document. You can also choose a dictionary on a layer-by-layer basis, or even apply different dictionaries to different bits of text within a single text layer.

To run the spell checker, choose Edit ⇨ Check Spelling. To check a single word, place your cursor in the word before running the spell checker. To check all the layers in your document, click the Check all Layers option at the bottom of the Spell Check dialog box (Photoshop only checks visible, unlocked type layers in your document).

FIGURE 13.16

Dynamic Shortcuts are only available while you're in Text edit mode.

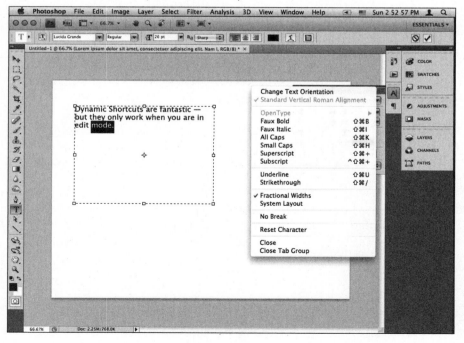

If it comes across a word that's not in the current language dictionary, you can do one of the following:

- Ignore the current word and continue searching the rest of the document. Ignore All skips over any other remaining instances of the questioned word in the rest of the document.

- Change the word to the suggested option in the Change To box. If necessary, you can enter text in the Change To box and click Change to replace the questioned word. Change All corrects all the remaining instances of the word in your document.

- If you're certain that the word exists and is indeed spelled correctly, you can click Add to store it in the current dictionary and never have it flagged as being a possible misspelling again.

Find and Replace

Another helpful editing tool is the Find and Replace function. Use this tool to quickly search through text for instances of a word or character and replace it with another. Choose Edit ➪ Find and Replace. Enter text to search for in the Find What field, and optionally, enter the text to replace it with in the Change To field. Use the check boxes to specify additional options, such as whether to ignore uppercase and lowercase letters or whether to ignore partial occurrences of the text you entered within other words.

Anti-aliasing

Anti-aliasing is a rendering technique used to smooth the edges of type on-screen. The pixels that make up the type that you see on your screen are square, and therefore can't produce a perfectly smooth curve. Anti-aliasing solves this by partially filling in the hard edges between adjacent pixels to create smooth, curved edges.

If you're designing type for a Web page or for display on a computer screen, it's often more readable if anti-aliasing is disabled, particularly at small font sizes. You may also want to disable Fractional Widths, which can cause irregular spacing between characters.

Photoshop provides five anti-aliasing options (illustrated in Figure 13.17):

- **None.** This option disables anti-aliasing and results in text with sharp, jagged edges. Avoid this option at larger type sizes (unless you're going for a specific look).
- **Sharp.** The sharpest type option.
- **Crisp.** This option produces some sharpness.
- **Strong.** Type is somewhat heavier.
- **Smooth.** Produces the smoothest edges.

The effects of the different anti-aliasing modes are most obvious at small type sizes, and again, in certain cases you're better off disabling it entirely. Play with the different options, as they tend to produce varied effects, depending on the typeface you're using.

FIGURE 13.17

Examples of Photoshop's different anti-aliasing modes

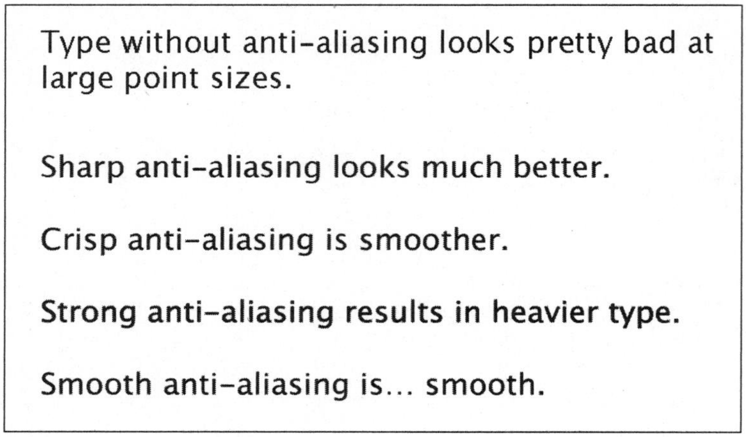

Type without anti-aliasing looks pretty bad at large point sizes.

Sharp anti-aliasing looks much better.

Crisp anti-aliasing is smoother.

Strong anti-aliasing results in heavier type.

Smooth anti-aliasing is... smooth.

Paragraph panel

So far, you've learned about formatting options that can be applied to individual characters. Now you'll learn about formatting options that can be applied to a single paragraph, or all the paragraphs on a type layer.

Select the Horizontal or Vertical Type tool by pressing the T key on your keyboard. The Paragraph panel (shown in Figure 13.18) is usually grouped with the Character panel, so you should be able to view it by clicking on the Paragraph tab of the Type options panel group. If it's not visible, choose it from the Window menu.

To format a single paragraph, click anywhere in that paragraph. To format several paragraphs, click and drag to create a selection that spans the paragraphs you want to format. To specify paragraph formatting options for an entire layer, click on that layer in the Layers panel. If you don't select any type or type layers, changing settings in the Paragraph panel affects any new type you create from that moment on.

Now that you're familiar with how to format paragraphs, let's take a closer look at the formatting options available to you.

FIGURE 13.18

The Paragraph panel is used to set type options for larger bodies of text.

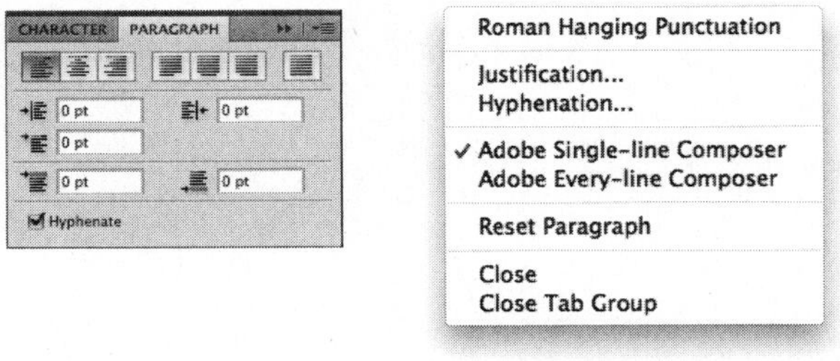

Alignment

If you're accustomed to using word-processing or other text-editing software, chances are very good that you've probably seen icons similar to the ones on the top row of the Paragraph panel. The first three icons are the alignment controls, and they are used to control how paragraph text flows in its bounding box. In the case of horizontal type, these buttons control whether text is left-, center-, or right-aligned within the text box. For instance, left-aligned text is flush against the left side of the bounding box, while the right side of the text is ragged. When using vertical type, they control the alignment relative to the top, center, or bottom of the text box.

Used with point text, the alignment buttons control how the text flows relative to the point that the text originates. Left-aligned type flows outwards from the point to the right, while right-aligned type flows out to the left.

Justification

Justified text is fully aligned against both the left and right sides of the bounding box, or in the case of vertical type, it's aligned against the top and bottom of the bounding box. The three justification options (shown in Figure 13.19) control how the last line of type in each paragraph is treated. In the case of horizontal type, justify left aligns the last line of type to the left side of the text box, justify right aligns it on the right, and justify center centers the last line between the two sides of the text box.

The fourth option, justify all (also called full or force justify in some cases), alters the spacing of the words in the last line of text to force it to fill the width of the text box. Depending on how many characters are in the last line of text, this can either result in wide, unattractive gaps, or tight, cramped text.

FIGURE 13.19

The justification buttons in the Paragraph panel, along with the Justification Options dialog box, can help you control the way paragraphs are justified within a text box.

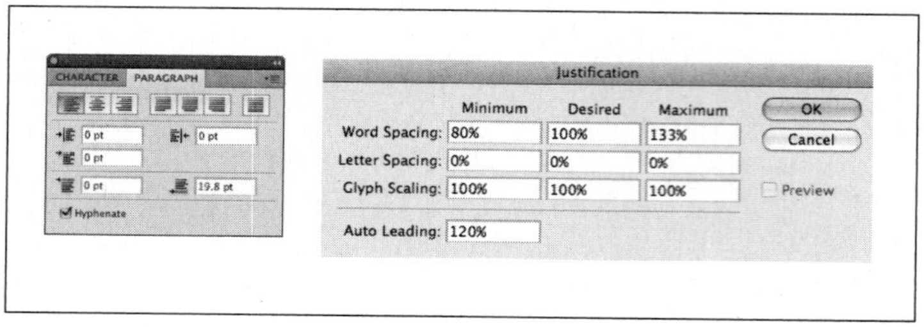

The Justification Options dialog box, found in the Paragraph panel's fly-out menu, gives you some additional control over the way type is justified. You can specify the extent to which words or letters are spaced apart when using justified text, and whether individual glyphs within a font are allowed to stretch to fill the width of the text box.

- **Word Spacing.** This controls how much extra space is inserted when you press the space bar between words. The default is 100 percent, which means that no extra space is inserted; the maximum is 1000 percent.

- **Letter Spacing.** This option controls how much space is inserted between individual characters, and adds to the kerning and tracking settings of your text. Zero percent means no extra space is inserted, and 100 percent inserts a full space between characters.

- **Glyph Scaling.** With this option, you can allow individual characters to either scale up or down from their normal size. A setting of 100 percent means no scaling is applied.

The best approach to setting up the justification options is to first specify your preferred values by typing them into the boxes under the Desired column. Then adjust the Minimum and Maximum amounts of spacing or scaling that you would be happy with, just in case Photoshop can't accommodate your preferred values in the given amount of space.

This might take some playing with, so feel free to experiment. If your text is too tight and cramped together, try increasing the Minimum values; conversely, if the text feels too "spacey" and loose, decreasing the Maximum values should help. And remember that you're not restricted to numbers larger than zero — you can type in negative values if necessary.

TIP Keep in mind that whatever you enter as the Minimum value can't be larger than the Desired value; likewise the Maximum can't be smaller than the number you entered in the Desired column.

The last option in the Justification Options dialog box, Auto Leading, specifies how much space to put between lines of text when Auto is selected in the Leading menu (found in the Character panel).

Roman Hanging Punctuation

When setting type, the casual designer may not pay much attention to how punctuation such as quotation marks, commas, or hyphens align with the sides of the text box. By default, punctuation is aligned against the edges of the text box just like any other character. The problem with this is that it pushes the other characters out of alignment, as demonstrated in Figure 13.20. To avoid this, enable Roman Hanging Punctuation, which shifts the offending punctuation marks outside of the text box so that the characters can line up correctly.

FIGURE 13.20

Text without Roman Hanging Punctuation appears on the left. Note how the punctuation falls beyond the bounding box of the text on the right, which has Roman Hanging Punctuation applied.

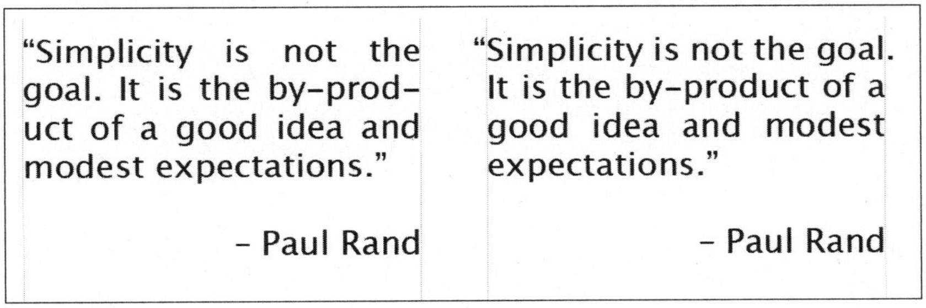

> "Simplicity is not the goal. It is the by-prod-uct of a good idea and modest expectations."
>
> – Paul Rand

> "Simplicity is not the goal. It is the by-product of a good idea and modest expectations."
>
> – Paul Rand

Indents and spacing

The next five options in the Paragraph panel (see Figure 13.21) control the amount of space between and around paragraphs and their bounding boxes. You can specify different spacing options for different paragraphs within the same type layer, or set the formatting of all paragraphs on a type layer.

- **Indent left margin/indent right margin.** Use these options to increase the distance between the left or right edge of the type and the type's bounding box.

- **Indent first line.** Use this option to indent the first line of each paragraph. Entering a positive value moves the text over to the right; a negative value moves it to the left.

- **Add space before/add space after.** These options, as you may have guessed from their names, increase the space that comes before or after a paragraph.

As is the case with most of the formatting options in the Character panel, set paragraph formatting options by entering a number and pressing Enter/Return to apply the change. You can specify these values in points, pixels, or millimeters; the default is based on the preferred unit of measurement specified in Preferences ⇨ Units & Rulers.

FIGURE 13.21

Paragraph indent options control spacing around and between paragraphs.

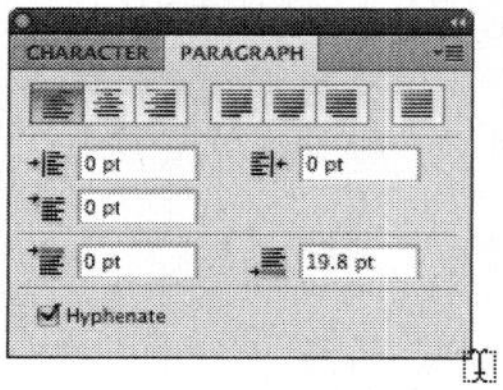

> **TIP**
>
> Remember that you can enter a different unit of measure than what's set in the document's preferences by entering a numerical value followed by the two-letter abbreviation of the unit you'd like to use. For example, if your document is set to use points, you indent the first line of type by half an inch by entering a value of .5 followed by "in" and pressing Enter. Photoshop automatically converts this to the default unit of measure, which in this example turns out to be 36 points.

Hyphenation

The hyphenation options allow you to enter settings for the way words are broken onto multiple lines. Tweak these settings to improve the look of your type layouts by specifying whether hyphenation is allowed at all, and if it is, under what circumstances.

To enable or disable automatic hyphenation, toggle the Hyphenate check box at the bottom of the Paragraph panel. Access the Hyphenation Options dialog box by choosing Hyphenation from the Paragraph panel menu (see Figure 13.22).

- **Words Longer Than.** Enter a number here to allow only hyphenation of words longer than a certain number of characters.

- **After First/Before Last.** These options allow hyphenation before or after at least the number of characters you enter here. For example, if you enter **4** for both of these values, the word "characters" would be hyphenated either as "char-acters" or as "charac-ters."

- **Hyphen Limit.** This option lets you limit the number of consecutive lines that can end in a hyphenated word, so you don't end up with multiple hyphenated lines one after the other, which isn't pretty.

- **Hyphenation Zone.** This option tells Photoshop how far from the sides of the text box it can put a hyphen.

Finally, you can allow or disallow hyphenation of capitalized words, such as proper names, by toggling the check box at the bottom of the Hyphenation Options dialog box.

FIGURE 13.22

The Hyphenation Options dialog box allows you to limit the use of hyphenation in paragraph type.

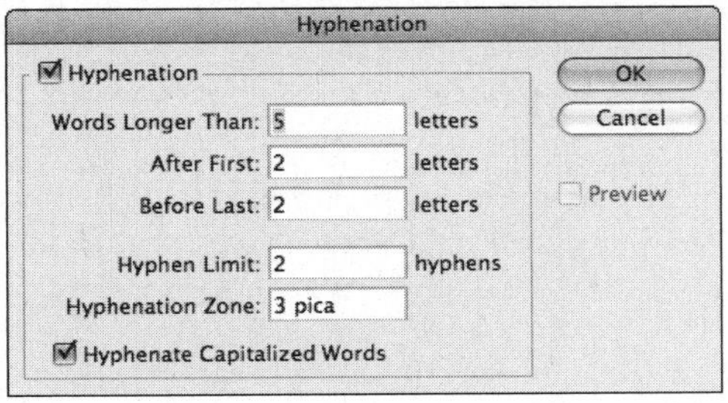

Hyphenation	
☑ Hyphenation	
Words Longer Than: 5 letters	OK
After First: 2 letters	Cancel
Before Last: 2 letters	☐ Preview
Hyphen Limit: 2 hyphens	
Hyphenation Zone: 3 pica	
☑ Hyphenate Capitalized Words	

Adobe Single-Line Composer and Every-Line Composer

Photoshop offers two ways of analyzing text to determine how to insert line breaks in paragraph type. The Single-Line and Every-Line Composers (found in the Paragraph panel fly-out menu) evaluate your kerning, alignment, hyphenation, and justification settings to detect possible line breaks for each paragraph, and decide on the best options based on the given parameters. As with most of the paragraph formatting options, you can choose different composition methods for individual paragraphs.

Single-Line Composer

As its name suggests, the Single-Line Composer analyzes each line of a paragraph to determine where to place line breaks and hyphens. Choose this option if you want more control over your line breaks. This compositing method favors more closely spaced text, rather than increasing the space between words or characters.

Every-Line Composer

The Every-Line Composer analyzes your selected paragraph or paragraphs as a whole to determine the most favorable places to insert line breaks. This option usually results in more evenly spaced text, and attempts to avoid hyphenating words.

Type on a Path

Being able to create type that flows in a straight line or within a rectangle is great, and it's exactly what you'll need for the vast majority of your design work. But we're talking about Photoshop here, so you know there's more to be had from the Type tool than standard text boxes.

One of the much-appreciated features that Photoshop CS introduced was the ability to create a vector path and flow type along that path. Fast-forward to Photoshop CS3, where this feature has become even more robust, allowing multiple, independent text layers to flow along a single vector path. On top of that, you can have text flowing in different directions along a path, you can flow text around a circle, and you can fill a vector shape with text. Let's dive in with an example.

Type on a curved, open path

Flowing type along a curved path (as illustrated in Figure 13.23) basically requires two things: a path and some text. Follow these steps to create type on a curved path:

1. **Press the P key on your keyboard to select the Pen tool (learn more about the Pen tool in Chapter 12).**

2. **Create a vector path by clicking with your mouse to lay down several points.** Clicking and dragging produces handles that allow you to create smooth curves in your path. Generally, you can achieve better results with more gradual paths — sharp turns and corners result in awkward placement of the letters. Not to worry — it is, after all, a vector path, which means you can edit it at any time by repositioning the points with the Direct Selection arrow (to activate this tool, keep pressing Shift+A on your keyboard until the hollow white arrow is selected).

3. **Press T on your keyboard to activate the Type tool.** Hover over the point on the vector path where you would like the text to begin. The I-beam cursor's horizontal baseline changes to a wavy diagonal line to show that the text will flow along a path.

4. **Click to start entering text.** The text follows the path you've drawn. Note that the text flows in the direction in which you originally created the path. In other words, if you laid down points from left to right, then that's the direction the text follows.

   If there's too much text, a small plus sign appears inside a circle at the end of the path. To fit the text, either make the path longer or choose a smaller font size.

5. **Commit the text changes by clicking the check mark on the Toolbar or by pressing Enter.**

You can change the start or end point of the text along the curve after it has been created. Select the Direct Selection tool and hover over the path. The I-beam cursor shows a small black arrow; click and drag to move the starting point of the text. Pull down to make the text flow on the bottom of the path.

If you need to reshape the path that the text follows, you can always access it from the Paths panel. Choose Window ➪ Paths, and you'll see two paths. One is the Work Path — this is the path that you first created to flow the type along. The other path should show the first several characters of the type that you entered. Highlight this path and, using the Direct Selection arrow, tweak the vector points that make up the path to change its shape, and as a result, the shape of the attached type.

> **TIP** The Work Path is special — it always represents the current vector path that you're working on. If the Work Path is not the current active selection, the next path that you create with the Pen tool or the Shape tool becomes the new Work Path, and your previous work is lost forever. If you want to hang on to that original Work Path, double-click on its name in the Paths panel and give it a name, or just press Enter/Return to accept the default name.

FIGURE 13.23

Creating text along a vector path

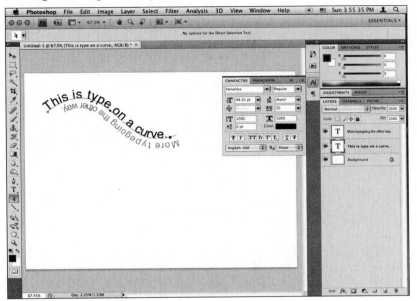

Type on a circle

Let's extend the idea of creating text along an open path to creating text that follows a closed path — in this case, a circle (see Figure 13.24). The steps are more or less the same as in the previous example, so there should be no real surprises here:

1. **Create a circular path by clicking on the Ellipse tool (not to be confused with the Elliptical Marquee tool) in the Toolbar.** The Ellipse tool is grouped with the Rectangle Shape tool; you can also activate it by repeatedly pressing Shift+U on your keyboard.

2. **From the Ellipse Tool Options Bar, select Paths mode (the second icon from the left) to draw an empty elliptical vector path.** Hold down the Shift key while dragging to constrain your path to a perfect circle.

3. **Select the Type tool by pressing T on your keyboard, and click on the circle to begin entering text.**

4. **Press Ctrl+Enter/⌘+Return to accept your text entry.**

5. **To adjust the positioning of the text on the circle, select the Direct Selection arrow and hover over the text.** The I-beam cursor shows either one or two tiny black arrows as you move it around the circle. The single-arrow mode allows you to adjust the portion of arc along the circumference the text will cover. The double-arrow mode lets you move the text around the circle to adjust where it starts from. Try pulling the I-beam either up or down to flow the text along the inside or outside of the circle.

NOTE You can use the Free Transform tool to resize text on a circle or on a path. If the vector path or circle that your text is following is active when you select the Free Transform tool, you'll only scale the vector path, and the text will remain at the same font size. If you de-select the vector path before scaling the text by clicking anywhere in the Paths panel (choose Window ⇨ Paths) other than on the path itself, you'll make the text bigger or smaller while the vector path remains the same size.

FIGURE 13.24

Flowing type around a circle is similar to flowing type along a vector path.

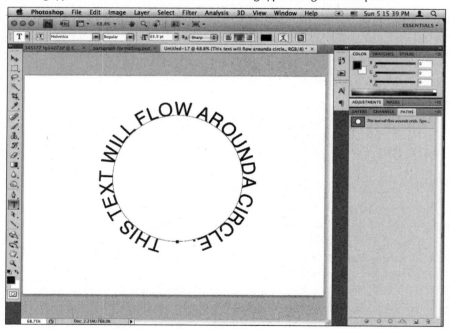

Type inside a closed shape

Taking the idea of designing with type further still, take a look at filling a closed shape with text, as illustrated in Figure 13.25. It's just like the standard rectangular text box that you know and love from working with paragraph type, but using some other shape instead:

1. **Create a shape that forms the boundary for your text.** Select the Custom Shape tool by repeatedly pressing Shift+U on your keyboard until the Shape tool icon is replaced with an amorphous blob icon. You could also draw your own shape with the Pen tool set to Path mode, or use one of the other variations of the Shape tool as a starting point, and then reshape the resulting path with the Direct Selection tool.

2. **From the Options Bar, click on the Shape popup menu and click the blobby shape from the last column of the third row of icons.** (Yes, in case you were wondering, I'm having fun with the word "blob.")

3. **Select the Type tool and hover over the shape you just created with your cursor.** You'll notice that the I-beam now looks like it has a pair of parentheses around it; this means you can click in that shape and fill it with text. So what are you waiting for? Click already.

4. **The shape you created is now an active text area — go ahead and fill it with text.** All the text-formatting tools and options can be applied, although you may have to switch from one of the automatic kerning options to manual kerning and tracking to properly deal with the curved boundaries of the text area.

> **TIP** Designers often use placeholder "lorem ipsum" text in their designs in order to have layouts approved by their client before the final copy is inserted. The reasoning is that people often become distracted from the design, and instead focus on reading the content of the text if real English is used. Where can you get some for your layouts? A quick Internet search for "lorem ipsum" should do the trick.

Warping type

Bend, twist, and reshape type by using the Warp tool, found on the Type Options Bar. The various modes of the Warp tool are all fairly self-explanatory and simple to use. With the Type tool active and a type layer selected, click on the Warp tool icon, shown in Figure 13.26. From the resulting dialog box, select an effect from the Style popup menu. Use the radio buttons to select an orientation for the effect — either horizontal or vertical (if applicable). Use the sliders to tweak the appearance of the effect by increasing or decreasing the amount of bend, or by changing the horizontal or vertical distortion. Once you're happy with the way your effect looks, click on the check mark in the Toolbar to apply it.

FIGURE 13.25

A vector shape that follows the contours of this mountain silhouette was drawn and filled with text. I used "lorem ipsum" dummy text as a placeholder.

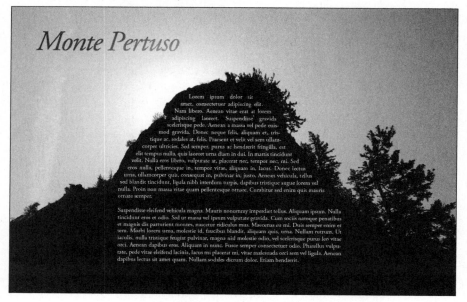

One of the great features of the Warp tool is that the text remains editable even after it has been warped, so you can go back and make changes if necessary. The Warp tool settings are also retained, so you can tweak them to your heart's content as well — that is, as long as your type layer remains a vector layer, and as long as you save your document in a format that supports layers.

 **Once a type layer has been warped, you can't apply a faux bold style to it. Conversely, you can't warp a type layer that has a faux bold style applied to it.**

To unwarp type, open the Warp Text dialog box by clicking on the Warp tool icon (or by choosing Layer ➪ Type ➪ Warp), change the Style back to None in the popup menu, and click OK.

CROSS-REF **You can also distort text layers by using the Warp mode of the Transform tool. Choose Edit ➪ Transform ➪ Warp, and choose a Style from the popup menu in the Options Bar. For more on the Transform tool, see Chapter 21.**

FIGURE 13.26

The Warp tool offers several different distortion effects. Warped text remains editable, as does the warp effect.

Type in a Smart Object

Suppose you want to create a dramatic effect where it looks like text is coming toward the viewer. You could do that by using the Perspective mode of the Transform tool (choose Edit ⇨ Transform ⇨ Perspective), but guess what — that option is grayed out if you try to select it with a vector type layer selected. What to do? Well, you could first rasterize that type layer, turning it into plain old pixels, which would let you manipulate the text as you please. But then you're stuck if you ever need to go back and edit that text, so that's not an optimal approach.

A better alternative, as demonstrated in Figure 13.27, would be to convert the type layer to a Smart Object (remember them from Chapter 6?). You can then manipulate this Smart Object by using any of the Transform tools while your vector text layer remains safely protected inside of it. If you need to edit the text, simply double-click the Smart Object thumbnail to open it as a PSB document, make your changes, and save and close it to update it in the original document.

Note that if you scale or distort the Smart Object so that it's significantly bigger than its original dimensions, you may start to notice some pixelization occurring around the edges of the text. That's because just as with a bitmap object, the Smart Object is being interpolated to generate the greater number of pixels needed to display it at a larger size. The solution? Why, make the text bigger within the Smart Object, of course. Here's how:

1. **Double-click the Smart Object's layer thumbnail to edit its contents.** Unless you've already clicked the check box to suppress it, Photoshop displays a dialog box letting you know that you should save the contents of the Smart Object in the same location to update it correctly in the originating document. Click OK to continue.

2. **Press Ctrl+T/⌘+T on your keyboard to activate the Free Transform tool.** Grab the handles at the corners of the bounding box and drag while holding down the Shift key to make the text layer bigger. Or, you can do it numerically by entering new values in the Width and Height fields in the Free Transform Options Bar. In this example (Figure 13.28), I chose 200 percent to quickly make my text twice as big.

> **TIP** Change the Width and Height values proportionally by toggling the maintain aspect ratio icon (it looks like a little chain) in the Options Bar.

3. **Quickly resize the canvas so that it's big enough by choosing Image ⇨ Reveal All.** As shown in Figure 13.28, your text is too big for your current canvas dimensions, which would cause problems if you were to update it in your original document as-is.

FIGURE 13.27

The text in this image was first embedded in a Smart Object, then given a dynamic visual treatment by using the Transform tool in Perspective mode.

FIGURE 13.28

Scaling the text by 200 percent has made it way too big for this canvas. The Reveal All command offers a quick fix.

4. **Press Ctrl+S/⌘+S followed by Ctrl+W/⌘+W to save and close the PSB document containing the contents of the Smart Object.** You'll see that the changes you made have been reflected in your original document, and you can now can go ahead and resize, distort, and tweak the perspective of your type layer until it looks just right (see Figure 13.29). In this example, I added a few layer styles (which you'll learn more about in the next section) to create the appearance of chiseled stone text.

FIGURE 13.29

Using the Perspective tool to distort type

Type with Layer Styles

Much like regular layers, type layers can have layer styles applied to them to create a huge variety of effects, such as metallic, plastic, or rubbery text. The possibilities are endless, but I'll start you off with an example that will have you well on your way to creating spectacular type effects.

1. **Choose File ➪ New Document or press Ctrl+N/⌘+N to create a new file in Photoshop.** Enter some dimensions for your file — I chose 1024 x 768 under the Web Presets for mine, because that's a standard screen resolution, and I may decide to set it as my computer's wallpaper.

2. **Create a new layer by clicking on the New Layer icon at the bottom of the Layers panel.** Press D on your keyboard to set your foreground and background colors to the defaults of black and white. Next, fill the empty layer you just created with black by pressing Alt+Delete/Option+Delete on your keyboard.

NOTE Alt+Delete/Option+Delete fills the canvas with whatever color you have selected as your foreground color. Ctrl+Delete/⌘+Delete uses your background color to fill the canvas.

3. **To make the background a little more interesting, click on the layer style button at the bottom of the Layers panel (it's the one with a tiny *fx* on it) and select Gradient Overlay from the popup menu.** Create a "spotlight" effect on your layer by selecting Radial from the Style popup menu.

   Click on the gradient to edit it so that it transitions from a dark gray to a light gray. To change the gradient colors, double-click on the leftmost color stop (it looks like a little square with a triangle on top) below the gradient. From the resulting Color Picker, choose a dark gray and click OK. Repeat for the rightmost color stop, but this time select a light gray. Click OK to close the Gradient Editor, and click OK again to save the layer style you just created. By this point you should have something that looks similar to Figure 13.30.

FIGURE 13.30

A Gradient Overlay layer style was used to create the look of a spotlight shining on a black background.

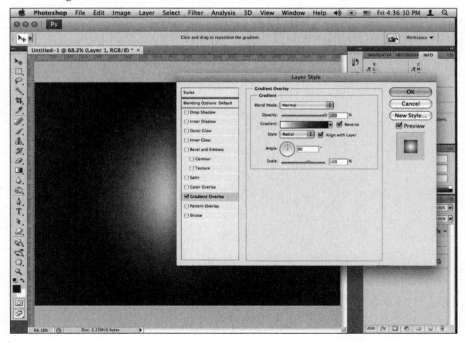

NOTE If the dark part of the gradient ends up in the middle of the page, and the light part is on the outside, open up the Gradient Overlay settings again by double-clicking on the effect's name in the Layers panel. Click in the Reverse check box to flip the gradient around so it goes the other way. Click OK to accept your changes.

4. **Now for some text. Create a new type layer and enter a word.** I chose "Shiny!" for this example. (Fitting, don't you think?) It doesn't matter what color the text is — you'll take care of that in the next step. Scale and position the text until you think it looks good, using the techniques you've learned in this chapter.

5. **Add a Gradient Overlay to the type layer you just created just as you did in the previous step.** But this time you're going to use several color stops, as shown in Figure 13.31. To add more color stops, simply click below the gradient in a spot where there isn't a color stop. Drag it left or right to adjust the gradient's color transitions.

The idea is to try and mimic the reflective surface of a chrome or silver object by adding various dark and light striations to our gradient. Don't worry about making your gradient look exactly like mine; just approximate the general look. Click OK to accept the new gradient, but don't close the Layer Style dialog box just yet.

FIGURE 13.31

The Gradient Overlay style is used to give the text a chrome or silver appearance.

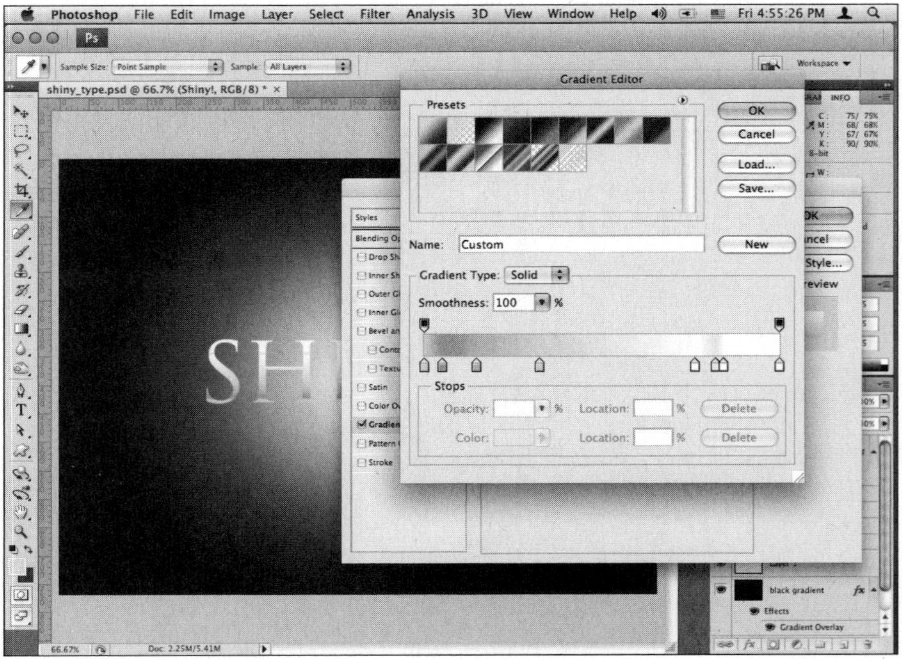

NOTE You can save gradients to reuse later — simply click the New button when you're done editing your gradient and enter a descriptive name for it. A new thumbnail representing your gradient is added to the Presets window and is available for use in other documents whenever you open Photoshop.

6. **To really sell the effect and give your type some dimension, add an outline with a gradient that simulates the effect of highlights and shadows going around the edges of your text.** Slick, huh? Select Stroke from the list of styles on the left side of the Layer Style dialog box to add an outline around the characters. Okay, so it doesn't look so hot just yet, but you're getting there. Under the Stroke settings, click in the Size field, and using the down arrow on your keyboard, change the size of the stroke to a value of 1.

Now, change the Fill Type to Gradient. Once again, edit the gradient by clicking on it, and positioning light and dark color stops so that it looks like light is hitting the edges of the text and making it shiny. Position a few dark color stops so it looks like certain parts of the edges of the text have shadows cast on them. Use Figure 13.32 as a reference. Click OK to apply the gradient, and again to apply the Stroke.

FIGURE 13.32

Once again, creative use of the Gradient Overlay style can add some highlights and shadows around the contours of the text, giving it more dimension.

7. **To give the type even more depth, I added a drop shadow to make it look like it's floating off the background (see Figure 13.33).** Click in the Drop Shadow check box and change the Distance, Blur, Spread, and Size settings until you're happy with the way the shadow looks. I also reduced the Opacity on mine to make the shadow a little bit more subtle. When you're done, click OK to save the drop shadow, then click OK to close the Layer Style dialog box.

If all went well, you should have some pretty nice-looking metallic type at this point. Feel free to experiment with other layer styles — for example, you could probably create some gold type by changing the colors of the Gradient Overlay effects to some yellows and browns. Or, create a chiseled effect by using the Bevel and Emboss effect. If you really want to go nuts, try applying a Warp to the type (but you might have to go back and tweak the Gradient Overlays if you change the size of the type too much). And remember — this is still a bona fide type layer, so it's still completely editable. Cool, huh?

FIGURE 13.33

A shadow is added to the text to separate it from its background.

CROSS-REF To delve deeper into the world of layer styles, check out Chapter 8.

Vector versus Rasterized Type

Earlier in this chapter, I mention that type remains editable in Photoshop as long as it's kept as a vector type layer — in other words, as long as it's not rasterized. There are good reasons for keeping text in vector format — for instance, so you can transform it any number of times without losing its crisp edge, and so you can change type and paragraph options, such as type styles and paragraph spacing at any time.

However, there are also occasions when you'll want to rasterize your type — in other words, convert it to pixels on a layer that you can edit. If you want to apply filters to your text, or smudge, blur, or combine it with the pixels on another layer, or partially distort type, as in Figure 13.34, you first need to rasterize the type layer.

To rasterize type, choose Layers ⇨ Type ⇨ Rasterize, or right-click (Ctrl-click if you're on a Mac with a single-button mouse) on a type layer and choose Rasterize from the context menu.

> **TIP** If you think you might want to go back and make changes to a type layer, you may want to keep a copy of your type layer before rasterizing it. Simply choose Layer ⇨ Duplicate, or drag your type layer to the New Layer icon in the Layers panel before rasterizing it.

FIGURE 13.34

A Mosaic filter has been applied to the lower portion of this type to give it a partially pixelated appearance.

Summary

In this chapter, you learned about the evolution of Photoshop's Type tool, and saw how far it has come from its humble (and often frustrating) beginnings. You learned the difference between point and paragraph type, and when it's appropriate to use them in a design. You learned to edit text, and to use Photoshop's typesetting controls to apply formatting to either individual characters or multiple paragraphs. You also learned how to use the Find and Replace tool to make easy global changes to large amounts of text; and you learned how to use Photoshop's built-in Spell Check to make sure your work is error free.

You saw several ways to use typography as design, including flowing it along a curved path or within a shape, using layer styles to create advanced text effects, and altering the shape of text by using the Warp tool.

Finally, you learned about the differences between vector and rasterized type, and the situations in which you might want to use them.

Part V

Enhancing, Correcting, and Retouching

Chapter 14

Lightening, Darkening, and Changing Contrast

I f you use Photoshop with much regularity, at some point you will need to lighten, darken, or change the contrast of an image. In fact, you will probably need to do some or all of those things to most of the images you work on.

The good news is that Photoshop provides many ways to perform these tasks; the bad news is that Photoshop provides many ways to perform these tasks. I know, just what you wanted to hear — more to learn. But variety is the spice of life, and I promise you'll be happy once you know these myriad techniques and gain the power to choose.

In addition to the many ways to create these effects, you can aply these effects to the overall image, to generally targeted areas of an image, to specifically targeted areas of an image, or to specific layers in an image. The effects can also be reduced or limited by changing their opacity or applying a blending mode. In many cases, the effects can also be changed by readjusting the settings that were initially used to create them.

When contrast is added, images seem to pop off the page and have more detail. You can decrease contrast in an image when you want to make it appear more muted or less noticeable and seem to contain less detail. Adding contrast usually involves lightening the lights and darkening the darks in some way. Reducing contrast often involves doing just the opposite — darkening the lights and lightening the darks.

IN THIS CHAPTER

Lightening

Darkening

Increasing contrast and detail

Decreasing contrast and detail

Lightening

Making images or parts of images lighter, or brighter, is a commonly needed adjustment. There are many ways to lighten an image in Photoshop. You can use a lightening process that lightens the light and/or dark qualities of an image (the luminosity or luminance) along with the colors in an image. But let's say you've got the color the way you want it — you just want to lighten part of the image and avoid risking a shift in the color while you're at it.

In that case, you can use a lightening technique that lightens only the luminosity and does not affect the colors. There are also lightening techniques that can better preserve contrast in an image, and others that may reduce contrast. You can use certain methods to make broad changes or you can use methods that allow you to target specific areas. This section will discuss all those techniques and various combinations.

Using curves to lighten

All of the following techniques require a Curves adjustment layer. To make a Curves adjustment layer, do the following:

1. **Activate the layer that you want to be just below the Curves adjustment layer you are about to make.** (An adjustment layer can affect only the layers below it.) You can activate a layer by clicking once on it in the Layers palette — clicking next to the right side of the layer name is best.

2. **Do one of the following:**

   ▥ Click the Create a new fill or adjustment layer button (the half-black, half-white circle) at the bottom of the Layers palette and choose curves.

   ▥ Click the curves button in the Adjustments palette.

3. **For some of the tasks described below, you need to activate the Curves adjustment layer and adjust it in the Adjustments palette.** For other tasks, you need to activate the Curves adjustment layer and work with it in the Layers palette.

Note that the color mode of the image determines whether you need to move the curve up or down to lighten the image. Color mode can be changed in the Image ⇨ Mode menu. You can preserve more colors in an image by adjusting it in RGB or Lab color mode.

When you convert an image to CMYK color mode, which is eventually necessary for full-color images destined for print, you lose some of the colors. Sometimes the loss of colors is noticeable, and sometimes it's not. So it's best, although not absolutely necessary, to convert to CMYK only when you are nearly finished with the image.

CROSS-REF   See Chapter 9 for more about using the curves dialog box; Chapter 1 for more about color modes; and Chapter 23 for information about color management.

CAUTION   When you are adjusting curves, be careful not to overdo it to the point that your image loses detail in areas that are important to you or that need to be preserved for reproduction on its destination device. For example, the lightest areas in images destined for print need to be a little darker than pure white and the darkest areas a little lighter than pure black to maintain print quality in a typical image.

Lightening broad areas with curves

You can lighten broad areas of an image by adjusting the curve in a Curves adjustment layer so that the majority of the curve is moved from its original straight, 45-degree-angle line in the direction of the light part of the dark-to-light bar that runs along the side of the curve.

If the resulting curve is made so that part or all of it is at a steeper angle than the original 45-degree-angle curve, the corresponding part of the image will have increased contrast. If the resulting curve is made so that part or all of it is at a less-steep angle than the original 45-degree-angle of the curve, the corresponding parts of the image will have decreased contrast.

NOTE When referring to the steepness of the curve line, the reference is to the steepness of the angle of the line, not necessarily whether the line is moved to a point that is higher than, or above, the original curve line.

Figures 14.1, 14.2, and 14.3 show before-and-after images in RGB, Lab, and CMYK color modes and the curves that lightened broad areas of the images while increasing the images' contrast. Figures 14.4, 14.5, and 14.6 show before-and-after images in RGB, Lab, and CMYK color modes and the curves that lightened broad areas of the images while reducing the images' contrast.

When you are looking at the curves in the figures, notice the direction in which the curves are moved. Curves aren't necessarily moved in the same direction to lighten or darken an image. It depends on the color mode of the image. Use the dark-to-light bar that runs along the side of the curve as a guide when you are deciding which way to move the curve. To lighten, move the curve toward the light part of the bar; to darken, move the curve toward the dark part of the bar.

FIGURE 14.1

An RGB mode image that uses a curve to lighten broad areas of the image while increasing the image's contrast. Note that part of the curve angle is steeper than it was originally and the composite color RGB channel is active in the curves dialog box.

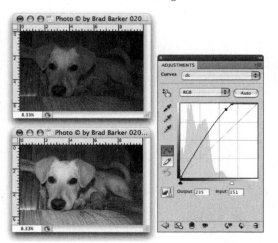

FIGURE 14.2

A Lab mode image that uses a curve to lighten broad areas of the image while increasing the image's contrast. Note that part of the curve angle is steeper than it was originally and the Lightness channel is active in the curves dialog box rather than a color channel.

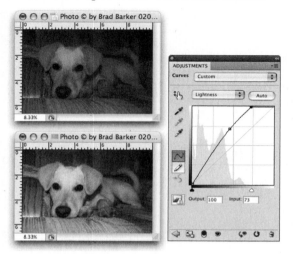

FIGURE 14.3

A CMYK mode image that uses a curve to lighten broad areas of the image while keeping some of the image's contrast. Note that part of the curve angle is steeper than it was originally and the composite color CMYK channel is active in the curves dialog box.

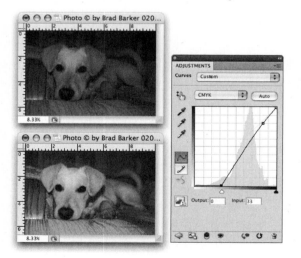

FIGURE 14.4

An RGB mode image that uses a curve to lighten broad areas of the image while reducing the image's overall contrast. Note that all of the curve angle is less steep than it was originally and the composite color RGB channel is active in the curves dialog box.

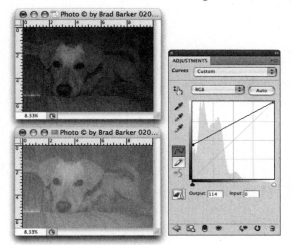

FIGURE 14.5

A Lab mode image that uses a curve to lighten broad areas of the image while reducing the image's overall contrast. Note that all of the curve angle is less steep than it was originally and the Lightness channel is active in the curves dialog box rather than a color channel.

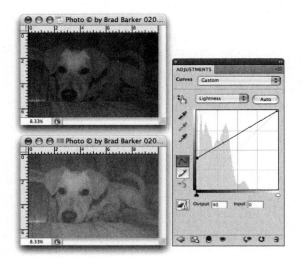

A CMYK mode image that uses a curve to lighten broad areas of the image while reducing the image's overall contrast. Note that all of the curve angle is less steep than it was originally and the composite color CMYK channel is active in the curves dialog box.

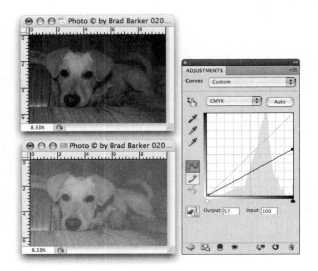

Lightening generally targeted areas with curves

You can lighten a somewhat targeted area of an image by moving part of the curve in a Curves adjustment layer in the direction of the light part of the dark-to-light bar that runs along the side of the curve but keeping another part of the curve line relatively close to its original position. This keeps part of the image the way it was originally and lightens only a portion of it.

Figures 14.7, 14.8, and 14.9 show RGB, Lab, and CMYK images and the curves that lighten generally targeted areas of an image.

FIGURE 14.7

An RGB mode image that uses a curve to lighten a generally targeted area of the image while keeping part of the image similar to the way it was originally. Note that the composite color RGB channel is active in the curves dialog box.

FIGURE 14.8

A Lab mode image that uses a curve to lighten a generally targeted area of the image while keeping part of the image similar to the way it was originally. Note that the Lightness channel is active in the curves dialog box rather than a color channel.

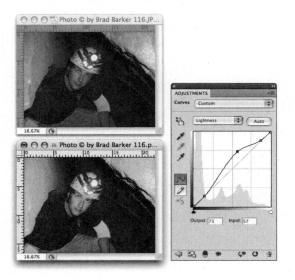

FIGURE 14.9

A CMYK mode image that uses a curve to lighten a generally targeted area of the image while keeping part of the image the same as it was originally. Note that the composite color CMYK channel is active in the curves dialog box.

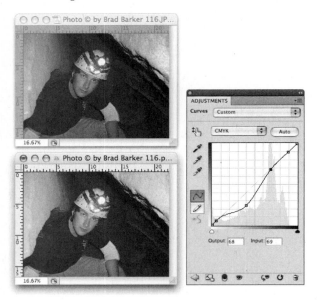

Lightening specifically targeted areas with curves

You can use the pixel mask (regular mask) or a vector mask, or a combination of the two types of masks, on a Curves adjustment layer to make the Curves adjustment apply only to a specific area in an image. The adjustment is applied to the area in the image that corresponds to the white area on the masks. For example, you could use a pixel mask to show the adjustment in a soft-edged area of the image (you could paint white and black on a pixel mask with a soft-edged brush) and use a vector mask to make the adjustment apply to a hard-edged area of the image (you could use a shape tool or the Pen tool with the Paths button active in the Options Bar to draw a hard-edged shape on the vector mask).

Figure 14.10 shows a Curves adjustment layer with a pixel mask, Figure 14.11 shows a Curves adjustment layer with a vector mask, and Figure 14.12 shows a Curves adjustment layer with both kinds of masks.

CROSS-REF See Chapter 8 for more about using layer masks, and Chapters 11 and 12 for more about using paths and shapes.

FIGURE 14.10

A Curves adjustment layer that uses a pixel mask to make the adjustment apply only to a specific area of the image

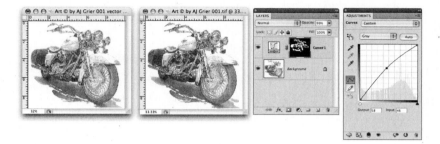

FIGURE 14.11

A Curves adjustment layer that uses a vector mask to make the adjustment apply only to a specific area of the image

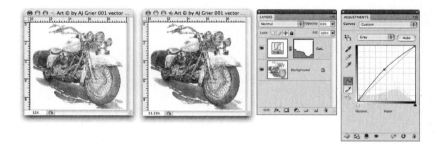

FIGURE 14.12

A Curves adjustment layer that uses pixel and vector masks to make the adjustment apply only to a specific area of the image

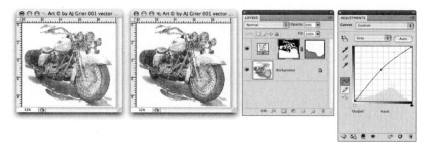

Lightening specific colors with curves

You can make a Curves adjustment in a Curves adjustment layer affect certain colors rather than the composite full color. To target a certain color, you would select the color channel you want to adjust from the drop-down list just above the curves grid. You can access the menu and grid in the Adjustments palette when a Curves adjustment layer is active.

In RGB and Lab modes, each color channel can be used to adjust two colors. In RGB mode, you use the R channel to adjust red and cyan, the G channel to adjust green and magenta, and the B channel to adjust blue and yellow. In Lab mode, you use the a channel to adjust green and magenta, and the b channel to adjust blue and yellow.

Figure 14.13 shows a curve that lightens yellow in an RGB mode image. Figure 14.14 shows a curve that lightens yellow in a Lab mode image.

FIGURE 14.13

A curve that lightens yellow in an RGB mode image. Note that the blue channel is selected. In RGB mode, you can use the blue channel to adjust yellow and blue.

The Lightness channel in Lab mode adjusts the luminosity, or light and dark values only, without affecting the color. In CMYK mode, each color channel can be used to adjust (lighten or darken), just one color: cyan, magenta, yellow, or black (K).For example, in the blue channel in RGB mode, if you drag the curve up so that you lighten (or subtract) the yellow in the image, it also darkens (or adds) blue. In the b channel in Lab mode, if you drag the curve down so that you lighten (or subtract) yellow in the image, it also darkens (or adds) blue.

In the Y channel of CMYK mode, if you drag the curve down, you lighten yellow; if you drag the curve up, you darken yellow. That can appear to add blue, but if you really want to add more blue directly while the image is in CMYK mode, you could go to the C channel and increase cyan, and the M channel and increase magenta a little bit, because in CMYK, cyan with a little magenta is blue.

FIGURE 14.14

A curve that lightens yellow in a Lab mode image. Note that the b channel is selected. In Lab mode, you can use the b channel to adjust yellow and blue.

TIP   If you forget which way to move a curve to affect a certain color when you target a specific channel, you can do a temporary drastic move of the curve in each direction, which allows you to see which colors are affected by the moves. To help you remember the colors in RGB channels, think of putting together the letters RGB and CMY: R/C, G/M, B/Y (red/cyan, green/magenta, blue/yellow). Lab mode has two of these same combinations in its two color channels: G/M (green/magenta) and B/Y (blue/yellow).

Figure 14.15 shows a curve that lightens yellow in a CMYK image.

FIGURE 14.15

A curve that lightens yellow in a CMYK mode image. Note that the yellow channel is selected. In CMYK mode, you use one individual color channel when you want to adjust one color.

Lightening with Curves eyedroppers and color numbers

If you have an image you can lighten with the Curves eyedroppers, you can get a whole lot of mileage out of a single click. You can use the Curves dialog box's Set White Point and Set Black Point eyedroppers to make a part of the image you click on with them change to the color that is assigned to them, and the other colors in the image adjust proportionally.

The Set Gray Point eyedropper changes whatever color you click on to a neutral (gray) color; you can't assign a specific color to the Set Gray Point eyedropper. This eyedropper is usually used to select a midtone area that you think should be a neutral gray but is not. This will change the area you click on to neutral and adjust the other colors in the image, which can help remove an undesirable color cast.

You can assign colors to the Set White Point and Set Black Point eyedroppers. For example, you can set them to an almost-white neutral color and an almost-black neutral color. These two eyedroppers are usually used to change the lightest and darkest points in an image that you think should be neutral (but are not) to neutral colors.

That may remove an undesirable color cast in the entire image because it corrects those two colors, and the remainder of the colors in the image adjust proportionally.

For example, if an image is too dark overall and has a pink color cast, you could click on a point in the image that you know should be the lightest white that needs to maintain some detail (like the lightest part of a white shirt) with the Set White Point eyedropper. That lightens the overall image, and if you've guessed correctly that the point you clicked on the shirt should be a bright neutral white, it may also remove the pink color cast.

You can set the White Point and Black Point eyedroppers to specific colors by double-clicking them and entering color numbers in the Color Picker dialog box. For example, a common brightest-highlight neutral color for the Set White Point eyedropper is C: 4, M: 2, Y: 2, K: 0. You can enter those numbers even if the image is in RGB mode, and they will still work. The Color Picker just converts the numbers you enter to the current color mode's numbers, and in fact, it also displays the color numbers you enter in all the other modes' equivalent numbers.

It may come in handy to note that in RGB mode, actual neutral colors have the same — and per- ceived neutral colors have approximately the same — values for R, G, and B. Neutral colors in CMYK mode have approximately the same numbers for M and Y and a little higher number for C.

Figure 14.16 shows an image that has been lightened, had its lightest point set to specific color numbers, and had its color cast removed just by clicking on it once with the Set White Point eye- dropper.

FIGURE 14.16

A before-and-after of an image that has been lightened by clicking on what needed to be changed to a very light point in the image with the Set White Point eyedropper from the curves dialog box.

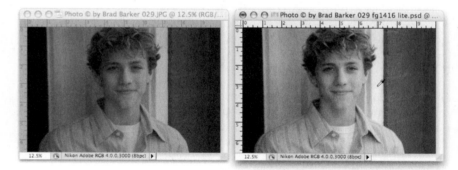

It is also possible to set the White Point and Black Point eyedroppers to colors other than neutral. You can use them to change colors in an image to custom colors, including ones that are lighter than existing image colors and that would cause the overall image to lighten. Of course, changing colors to non-neutral colors is not the Curves eyedroppers' original purpose.

But you may like to experiment occasionally for artistic purposes ... or for no particular reason. Heck, that's how I learned a lot of what I know about Photoshop.

CROSS-REF For more information about color numbers that are useful for color correction and to help ensure quality reproduction when printing, see Chapter 15.

Lightening by entering color numbers in curves

You can lighten an image by selecting a point on a curve and entering a new output number. Figure 14.17 shows a black, white, and gray image that has had its black lightened slightly.

All the pixels in the previous black part of the image were made up of R: 0, G: 0, B: 0 (pure black in RGB mode). The new black pixels are made up of R: 12, G: 12, B: 12, which are slightly lighter than pure black. In CMYK color mode, if you enter a new output value for a point on the curve when you have the composite CMYK channel selected in curves, Photoshop limits the values in any one channel to the amount of the new value, but it also may change values in all channels to values you don't expect. If you want to make individual CMYK colors conform to specific values, you first need to choose the individual color channel in curves before you type in a new output value.

FIGURE 14.17

A black, white, and gray image whose pure black pixels have been lightened slightly by selecting the darkest point on the curve and entering a new output value

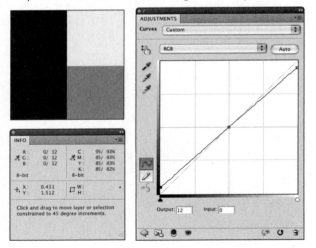

Note that if you are going to be converting from one color mode to another, the numbers in the destination color mode after the conversion may not be the numbers you expect. When Color Management is turned on, Photoshop uses color profiles to calculate color numbers that have been converted from one color mode to another.

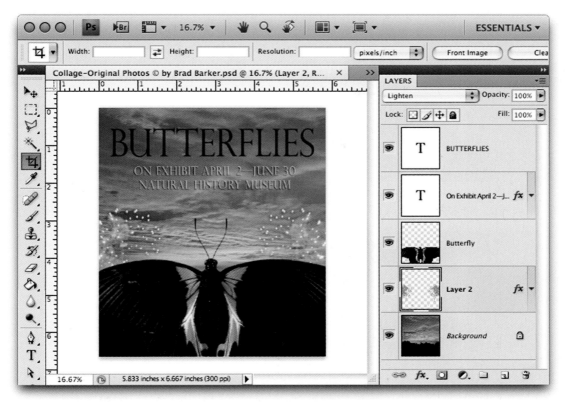

Putting different parts of an image on different layers lets you manipulate objects separately. Chapter 9 discusses layers.

There are different kinds of layers and layer accessories. Here you can see color fill and a pattern fill layers have been added to create the background, and black has been added to a layer mask on the top layer to hide the portion of the photo that falls outside the text.

Among the many ways you can manipulate colors in Photoshop is by using gradients and layer blending modes, as discussed in Chapter 15.

This graphic shows how color was changed by creating the new colors in a gradient layer set to the Hue blending mode in the Layers palette. Only the Hue from the gradient layer is used; the photo's brightness shows through from the layer underneath.

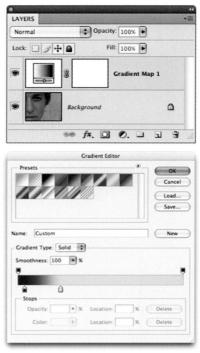

This photo has been given a special effect by using a gradient in a Gradient Map adjustment layer. This one maps the dark purple to the darkest parts of the photo and makes everything else in the photo yellow.

In this photo, the man's kimono is changed from blue to green simply by dragging the Hue slider in a Hue/Saturation adjustment layer.

Chapter 15 discusses many ways to change the color in images.

A sometimes tricky task is to change a darker color to a different lighter color. Here, a Hue/Saturation layer and a touch-up color blending mode layer are used to change the color of red flowers to yellow, and a Curves layer is used to lighten the flowers. Layer masks are used to target the flowers and leave the remainder of the image unchanged.

A Hue/Saturation adjustment layer is used to change the color of this flower.

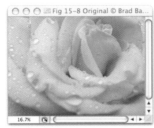

The Color Replacement Tool is used to paint this building with the color that is active in the foreground color box. This tool is smart enough to change only the color that is under the crosshairs in the center of its brush as you paint.

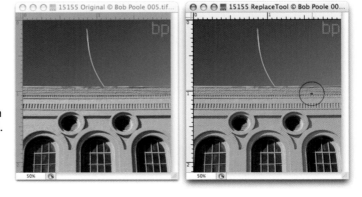

This image uses the Screen layer blending mode applied to a duplicate layer to lighten an image, as described in Chapter 14.

Multiply blending mode darkens, Luminosity blending mode uses only the brightness on the layer and not the color, and Color blending mode uses only the color on a layer and not the brightness.

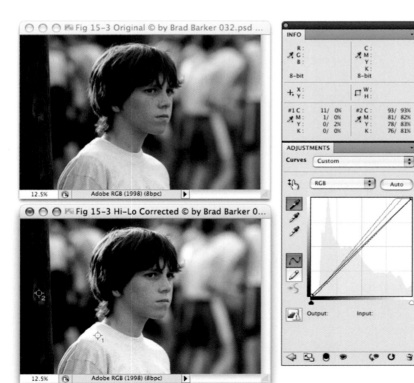

This image has been color-corrected by setting the lightest and darkest areas that should be neutral colors to neutral colors with the eyedroppers in a Curves adjustment layer. This process removed an overall undesirable color cast.

Color correction and color manipulation techniques can be found in Chapter 15.

The red hair color in this photo was enhanced by painting a more saturated red onto a layer set to Color blending mode. The red color was sampled from a red brick in the photo.

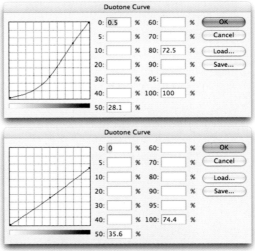

This photo was given a sepia tone look by using a Hue/Saturation adjustment layer with the Colorize option checked.

This photo was given a sepia tone look by using the Duotone method. Duotones let you use spot colors to reproduce images, for example, if you want to print a two-color brochure in black ink and brown ink. Photos can look richer if printed in black and brown rather than just one of the colors.

Chapter 15 discusses these and many other ways to manipulate color.

A Black & White adjustment layer with a layer mask was used to make part of this image appear black and white. Black & White adjustment layers let you edit the brightness of each color as it is changed to black and white. Chapter 15 discusses color changes.

The Match Color command changes the color in the second, off-color image, and matches its color to the good color in the first image. The result is the third image.

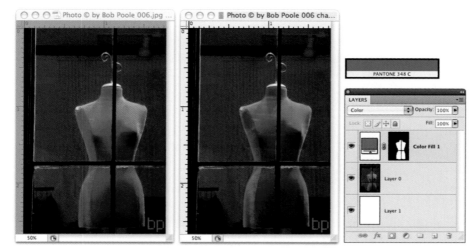

Sometime you may need to change the color of an object to a specific Pantone color. One way to do that is to use a Color Fill layer that contains the Pantone color. A layer mask can be used to target a certain area, and the Color or Hue blending mode can be applied to affect only the color and not the brightness of the image.

Curves adjustment layers were used to darken the background and lighten and increase contrast in the foreground of this image and make the focal point of the image stand out.

Chapter 14 introduces adding and reducing contrast to draw the eye to certain areas in an image.

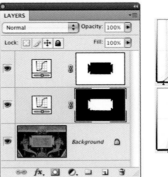 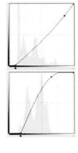

When an image lacks color variety, you can use the Lab mode and steepen the curves in the a and b channels to increase the color variety and saturation. Chapter 15 discusses color manipulation techniques.

In Lab color mode, you can easily change red to green by inverting the a curve.

Chapter 15 discusses color changes and manipulation.

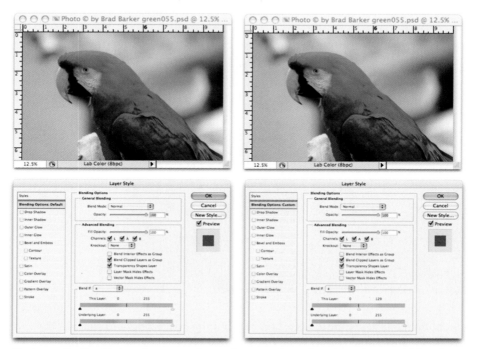

You can limit which colors on a layer show up by using the advanced blending options in the Layer Style dialog box. The options on the right limit the color that shows up within the targeted area to green (only green is between the "This Layer" sliders). This hides the red.

There are virtually limitless ways to create interesting text and distortion effects in Photoshop. See Chapter 23 for the top four effects, Chapter 13 for the center-left effect, Chapter 19 for the center-right effect, and Chapter 22 for the bottom effect.

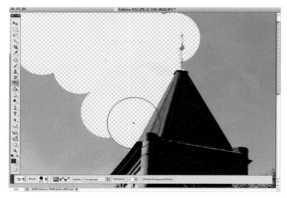

The Background Eraser tool was used to remove the sky in this photo. This tool has a Tolerance option to help the tool erase areas of similar color.

The Patch tool allows you to draw a selection around a flawed area and drag the selection on top of a good area to fix the flawed area.

A combination of techniques is often used to repair flawed images. Here, Levels, the Multiply mode, Hue/Saturation, the Clone Stamp tool, and the healing tools were used. Chapter 18 discusses repairing flawed images.

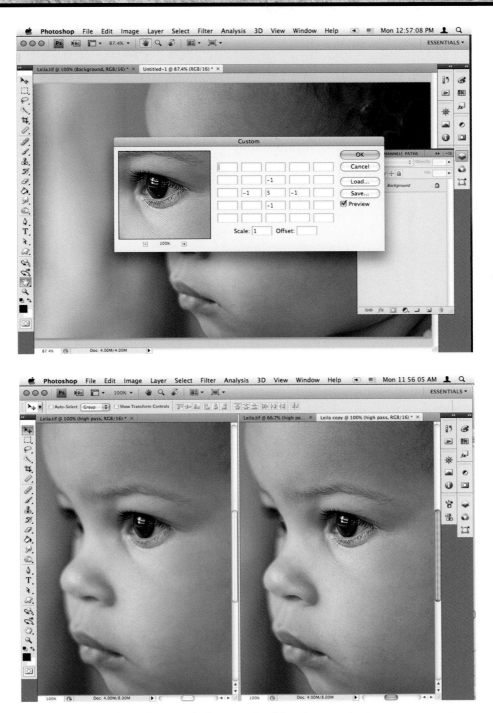

The High Pass Filter, along with the Overlay blending mode, is one approach you can use to sharpen an image. Here, you see the sharpened image on the right. Note the change in the eyes.

Ripples and zig zag filters are just a few of the types of filters Photoshop offers for distortion and other special effects. Chapter 21 discusses image distortions that use these filters and other methods.

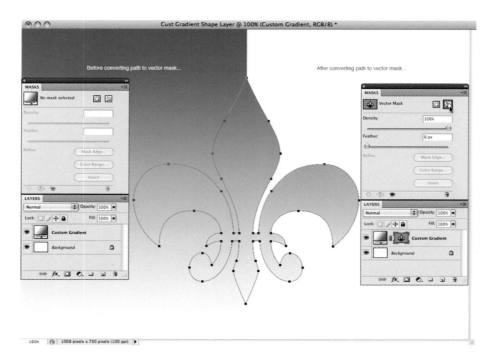

This graphic illustrates a path and a vector mask (a layer mask in which a path is used to hide part of a layer). Chapter 12 discusses shapes and vector masks. Chapter 11 discusses Paths.

Lots of fun can be had with the Liquify filter. You can use it to push, pull, expand, and contract an image as if it were made of clay. Chapter 21 discusses the Liquify filter and the other filters used below.

This cool effect uses a technique that employs the Polar Coordinates filter.

You can use the Vanishing Point filter to place straight-on images onto objects, in perspective.

The Save for Web & Devices dialog box offers options for optimizing images for use on the Web. Chapter 24 discusses preparing images for the Web and mobile devices.

Device Central allows you to preview image content on a huge number of mobile devices and gives you information about the types of media and content the device supports.

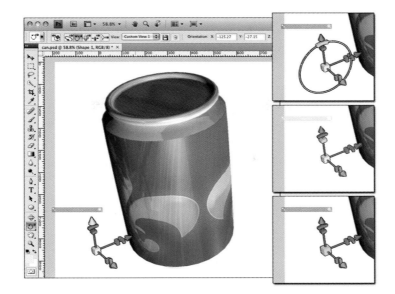

You can import 3D models directly into Photoshop for real-time compositing with our photography and designs. Chapter 27 discusses working with 3D objects.

Light guides help you see and position lights on 3D objects more accurately.

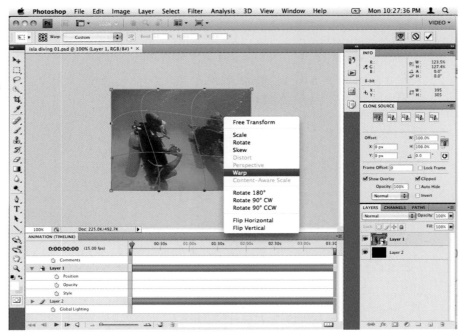

Almost anything that you can think of doing with still images — painting, compositing, masking, color-correcting, cloning — you can now do in Photoshop with imported video. Chapter 26 discusses working with video.

/Users/simon/Documents/Photoshop CS4 Bible/submissions/DICOM/digest_article/brain.dcm

DICOM is a standard for images and information generated by medical imaging devices. Photoshop can import, edit, or annotate these images. Chapter 28 discusses working with technical images.

The resulting numbers can be different depending on which color profiles are active in Color Settings. When you need more predictable color numbers, either convert the image to the destination color mode before you enter new output color numbers or turn off Color Management before you enter the new output values.

CROSS-REF   For more information about color management, see Chapter 23.

Changing a curves lighten adjustment by readjusting curves settings

Say you have used a Curves adjustment layer to lighten part of your image. You can change a Curves adjustment layer's curve by double-clicking the adjustment layer's thumbnail in the Layers palette and changing the shape of the curve in the Adjustments palette. Figure 14.18 shows the location of a Curves adjustment layer's thumbnail.

Reducing a curves lighten adjustment by reducing opacity

If you don't want to bother with fiddling with the curve and want to reduce the Curves adjustment layer's effect, you can simply reduce the opacity of the Curves adjustment layer at the top of the Layers palette. Figure 14.19 shows a Curves adjustment layer with a reduced opacity.

FIGURE 14.18

A Curves adjustment layer's thumbnail, which you can double-click if you want to change the Curves adjustment

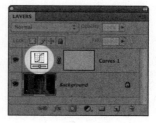

FIGURE 14.19

A Curves adjustment layer and the Layers palette Opacity box. You can lower the opacity of the Curves adjustment layer to reduce the effect of the Curves adjustment.

Confining a Curves lighten adjustment to a specific layer or set of layers

Adjustment layers can affect all the layers below it in the Layers palette but none of the layers above it. If you want a Curves adjustment layer to affect only the layer below it, double-click the adjustment layer, then click the Clip to layer button (double circle) at the bottom of the Curves adjustment layer dialog box. You can also Alt+click (Option+click) the line in between the Curves adjustment layer and the layer directly below it at the moment you see a double-circle symbol pop up as you hover the cursor over the line while holding down the Alt key. Either of these methods puts the two layers in a Clipping Group, and the layer on the bottom of the group becomes a Clipping Mask.

A Clipping Mask acts like a window that lets the content or the adjustment on the layer or layers that are above it in the Clipping Group show through the Clipping Mask layer's contents. The Clipping Group's layer or layers that are above the bottom layer of the Clipping Group — in this case, the Curves adjustment layer — will be indented and have an arrow next to its thumbnail that points to the layer below. To make the two layers become regular layers again and remove them from a Clipping Group, Alt+click or Option+click between the two layers again.

To put more layers in the Clipping Group, and therefore make the Curves adjustment layer apply to more than one layer, you can drag another layer in between the two layers in the Clipping Group. To remove one of the layers from the middle of a Clipping Group, you can drag it below the Clipping Group. You can then drag it above the Clipping Group if you need to change the order of it in the Layers palette.

Figure 14.20 shows a Clipping Group in the Layers palette with two layers, one called "make lighter" and one called "portrait." In this Clipping Group, the Curves adjustment layer affects only the layer below it.

FIGURE 14.20

In the Clipping Group shown, the Curves adjustment layer affects only the layer directly below it.

Lightening with curves without shifting color

If the color is just right in your image and you only want to lighten the image without shifting the color, you can apply the Luminosity blending mode to the Curves adjustment layer. The Luminosity blending mode tells Photoshop to use only the light and dark values on the layer (or the adjustments to the light and dark values, in this case) and not affect the color of the image.

Figure 14.21 shows a Curves adjustment layer with the Luminosity blending mode applied in the drop-down list near the top of the Layers palette.

FIGURE 14.21

A Curves adjustment layer with the Luminosity blending mode applied from the drop-down list near the top of the Layers palette. The Luminosity blending mode makes sure the layer doesn't affect the color and affects only the light and dark values in the layers below.

Increasing a curves lighten adjustment with the Screen blending mode

The Screen blending mode always lightens the layers below the layer it is applied to. If you apply the Screen blending mode to a Curves adjustment layer, it increases the lighten effect.

Figure 14.22 shows a Curves adjustment layer with the Screen blending mode applied from the drop-down list near the top of the Layers palette.

FIGURE 14.22

A Curves adjustment layer with the Screen blending mode applied from the drop-down list near the top of the Layers palette. The Screen blending mode makes the layers below even lighter.

Lightening with an original, unadjusted curve and the Screen blending mode

You can also lighten an image with an unadjusted Curves adjustment layer that is using the Screen blending mode, applied from the drop-down list near the top of the Layers palette. An unadjusted curves layer will have a curve that hasn't been changed from its original 45-degree-angle line.

This technique has the same effect as duplicating a layer and applying the Screen blending mode to it, but it doesn't increase the file size. When you duplicate a layer, it can increase the file size significantly. If the Screen effect is too light, you can reduce the opacity of the adjustment layer that is using the Screen blending mode.

Figure 14.23 shows a lightened image, a Curves adjustment layer and its unadjusted curve, and the Screen blending mode that has been applied in the Layers palette.

Increasing a lighten adjustment by duplicating Curves adjustment layers

You can use a Curves adjustment layer to lighten an image, and you can duplicate the Curves adjustment layers to increase the lighten effect. To duplicate a layer, drag it onto the New button at the bottom of the Layers palette or choose Duplicate Layer from the Layers palette menu. You can reduce the opacity of a duplicated curves layer if it makes the image too light.

FIGURE 14.23

A lightened image, a Curves adjustment layer and its unadjusted curve, and the Screen blending mode that has been applied in the Layers palette

Using duplicate layers and the Screen blending mode to lighten

You can use a duplicated layer and apply the Screen blending mode to it to lighten an image (see Figure 14.24). Each time you duplicate the layer, it increases the lighten effect. To duplicate a layer, drag it onto the New button at the bottom of the Layers palette or choose Duplicate Layer from the Layers palette menu. You can reduce the opacity of a duplicated layer if it makes the image too light. Note that each time you duplicate a layer, it increases the file size of an image.

FIGURE 14.24

This image has been lightened by duplicating a layer and applying the Screen blending mode.

You can merge the duplicated layers to reduce file size. To merge layers, Ctrl+click (⌘+click on a Mac) to select multiple layers, and choose Merge Layers from the Layers palette menu. Figure 14.24 shows an image that has been lightened by duplicating a layer and applying the Screen blending mode.

 **TIP** Press Ctrl+E (⌘+E on a Mac) to merge selected layers.

Using Levels to lighten

Using Levels to lighten images is perfectly acceptable, but you have less control with Levels than you have with curves. Levels offers two sliders that can be used to lighten an entire image or its color channels, whereas curves can lighten images with numerous control points at numerous intensity levels.

CROSS-REF   See Chapter 9 for more about using Levels and curves.

All of the following techniques require a Levels adjustment layer. To make a Levels adjustment layer, do the following:

1. **Activate the layer that you want to be just below the Levels adjustment layer you are about to make.** (An adjustment layer can affect only the layers below it.) You can activate a layer by clicking once on it in the Layers palette — clicking next to the right side of the layer name is best.

2. **Do one of the following:**
   - Click the Create a new fill or adjustment layer button (the half-black, half-white circle) at the bottom of the Layers palette and choose Levels.
   - Click the Levels button in the Adjustments palette.

3. **You can then perform the techniques described below.** For some of the tasks, you need to activate the Levels adjustment layer and adjust it in the Adjustments palette. For other tasks, you need to activate the Levels adjustment layer and work with it in the Layers palette.

Note that the color mode of the image and whether the composite or individual channels are selected in Levels determine whether you need to move the Levels sliders to the right or left to lighten the entire image or colors in individual channels. Color mode can be changed in the Image ⇨ Mode menu.

You can preserve more colors in an image by adjusting it in RGB or Lab color mode. When you convert an image to CMYK color mode, which is eventually necessary for full-color images destined for print, you lose some of the colors. Sometimes the loss of colors is noticeable, and sometimes it's not. So it's best, although not absolutely necessary, to convert to CMYK only when you are nearly finished with the image.

CROSS-REF   See Chapter 9 for more about using the Levels dialog box, Chapter 1 for more about color modes, and Chapter 23 for more about color management.

Lightening broad areas with Levels

You can lighten broad areas of an image by adjusting the Levels sliders in a Levels adjustment layer. Figures 14.25, 14.26, and 14.27 show before-and-after images in RGB, Lab, and CMYK color modes and the Levels adjustments that lightened the images.

FIGURE 14.25

An RGB mode image that uses Levels to lighten an image's composite color by dragging the midtone slider to the left. Note that RGB is selected in the Levels drop-down list.

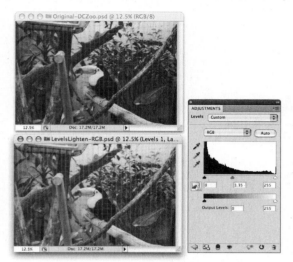

FIGURE 14.26

A Lab mode image that uses Levels to lighten the luminosity of an image by dragging the midtone slider to the left. Note that the Lightness channel is active in the Levels dialog box rather than a color channel.

FIGURE 14.27

A CMYK mode image that uses Levels to lighten the image's composite color by dragging the shadow slider to the right and the midtone slider to the left. Note that CMYK is selected in the Levels drop-down list.

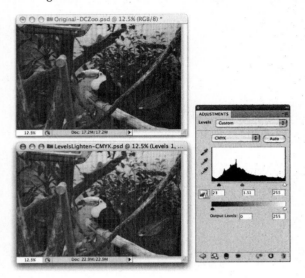

> **CAUTION** When you are adjusting Levels, be careful not to overdo it to the point that your image loses detail in areas that are important to you or that need to be preserved for reproduction on its destination device. For example, the lightest areas in images destined for print need to be a little darker than pure white and the darkest areas a little lighter than pure black to maintain print quality in a typical image.

Lightening specifically targeted areas with Levels

You can use the pixel mask (regular mask) or a vector mask, or a combination of the two types of masks, on a Levels adjustment layer to make the Levels adjustment apply only to a specific area in an image. The adjustment is applied to the area in the image that corresponds to the white area on the masks.

For example, you could use a pixel mask to show the adjustment in a soft-edged area of the image (you could paint white and black on a pixel mask with a soft-edged brush) and use a vector mask to make the adjustment apply to a hard-edged area of the image (you could use a shape tool or the Pen tool with the Paths button active in the Options Bar to draw a hard-edged shape on the vector mask).

This technique works on Levels adjustment layers just like it does on Curves adjustment layers.

Lightening specific colors with Levels

You can make a Levels adjustment in a Levels adjustment layer affect certain colors rather than the composite full color. To target a certain color, you would select the color channel you want to adjust from the drop-down list at the top of the Levels dialog box. You can access the menu and dialog box in the Adjustments palette when a Levels adjustment layer is active.

In RGB and Lab modes, each color channel can be used to adjust two colors. In RGB mode, you use the R channel to adjust red and cyan, the G channel to adjust green and magenta, and the B channel to adjust blue and yellow. In Lab mode, you use the a channel to adjust green and magenta, and the b channel to adjust blue and yellow. The Lightness channel in Lab mode adjusts the luminosity, or light and dark values only, without affecting the color. In CMYK mode, each color channel can be used to adjust (lighten or darken), just one color: cyan, magenta, yellow, or black (K).

For example, in the blue channel in RGB mode, if you drag the upper white slider to the left, you lighten (or subtract) the yellow in the image; that also darkens (or adds) blue. In the b channel in Lab mode, if you drag the upper black slider to the right, you lighten (or subtract) yellow in the image; that also darkens (or adds) blue. In the Y channel of CMYK mode, if you drag the white slider to the left, you lighten yellow; if you drag the upper black slider to the right, you darken yellow.

TIP If you forget which way to move a Levels slider to affect a certain color when you target a specific channel, you can do a temporary drastic move of the Levels sliders in each direction, which allows you to see which colors are affected by the moves. To help you remember the colors in RGB channels, think of putting together the letters RGB and CMY: R/C, G/M, B/Y (red/cyan, green/magenta, blue/yellow). Lab mode has two of these same combinations in its two color channels: G/M (green/magenta) and B/Y (blue/yellow).

Figure 14.28 shows a Levels adjustment that lightens yellow in an RGB mode image.

Figure 14.29 shows a Levels adjustment that lightens yellow in a Lab mode image.

Figure 14.30 shows a Levels adjustment that lightens yellow in a CMYK image.

FIGURE 14.28

A Levels adjustment that lightens yellow in an RGB mode image by dragging the midtone slider to the left. Note that the blue channel is selected. In RGB mode, you can use the blue channel to adjust yellow and blue.

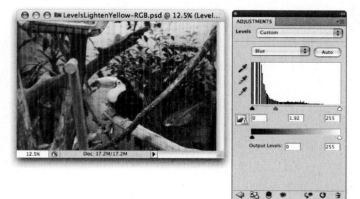

FIGURE 14.29

A Levels adjustment that lightens yellow in a Lab mode image by dragging the midtone slider to the right. Note that the b channel is selected. In Lab mode, you can use the b channel to adjust yellow and blue.

FIGURE 14.30

A Levels adjustment that lightens yellow in a CMYK mode image by dragging the midtone and highlight sliders to the left. Note that the yellow channel is selected. In CMYK mode, you use one individual color channel when you want to adjust one color.

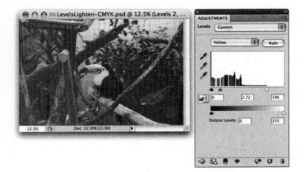

Lightening with Levels eyedroppers and color numbers

If you have an image you can lighten with the Levels eyedroppers, you can get a whole lot of mileage out of a single click. You can use the Levels dialog box's Set White Point and Set Black Point eyedroppers to make a part of the image you click on with them change to the color that is assigned to them, and the other colors in the image adjust proportionally.

You can assign specific colors to these eyedroppers by double-clicking them and entering the color numbers. The Set Gray Point eyedropper changes whatever color you click on to a neutral (or gray) color of a similar lightness; you can't assign a specific color to the Set Gray Point eyedropper.

CROSS-REF Levels eyedroppers work just like Curves eyedroppers. Details about how to use the Set White Point, Set Gray Point, and Set Black Point eyedroppers can be found in the "Lightening with Curves eyedroppers and color numbers" section in this chapter.

Lightening by entering color numbers in Levels

You can lighten an image by input color numbers in the upper boxes in Levels and output numbers in the lower boxes. Figure 14.31 shows a black, white, and gray image that has had its black lightened slightly. All the pixels in the previous black part of the image were made up of R: 0, G: 0, B: 0 (pure black in RGB mode). The new black pixels are made up of R: 12, G: 12, B: 12, which are slightly lighter than pure black.

In CMYK color mode, if you enter a new output value for a when you have the composite CMYK channel selected in Levels, Photoshop limits the values in any one channel to the amount of the new value, but it may also change values in all channels to values you don't expect. If you want to make individual CMYK colors conform to specific values, you first need to choose the individual color channel in Levels before you type in a new output value.

Note that if you are going to be converting from one color mode to another, the numbers in the destination color mode after the conversion may not be the numbers you expect. When Color Management is turned on, Photoshop uses color profiles to calculate color numbers that have been converted from one color mode to another. The resulting numbers can be different depending on which color profiles are active in Color Settings.

When you need more predictable color numbers, either convert the image to the destination color mode before you enter new output color numbers or turn off Color Management before you enter the new output values.

Changing a Levels adjustment

You can readjust a Levels adjustment layer's settings, reduce a Level adjustment layer's effect, confine a Levels adjustment to one or more layers, and lighten an image with an unadjusted Levels layer that uses the Screen blending mode. These changes can be accomplished with the same techniques that are used with Curves adjustment layers.

Using the Clone tool to lighten

One of my favorite ways to lighten an image is with the Clone tool. That may sound strange because the Clone tool is most often used to copy one part of an image onto another part of an image for the purpose of repairing it. But with the Clone tool set to Screen blending mode and a low opacity in its Options Bar, you can clone an image exactly on top of itself while lightening it at the same time. To clone an image on top of itself, start painting in the exact spot you Alt+click/Option+click on when you sample with the Clone tool and make sure Aligned is checked in the Options Bar.

FIGURE 14.31

A black, white, and gray image whose pure black pixels have been lightened slightly by entering a new output value 12 (a little lighter than pure black in RGB mode) for the input value 0 (pure black in RGB mode)

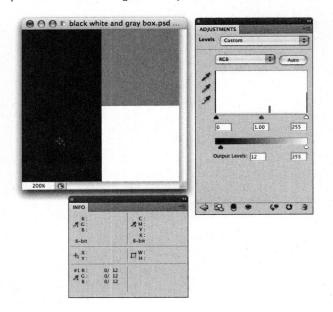

The great thing about this technique is that it's good at preserving detail while you are doing the lightening. The Clone tool is also a brush tool, so you can paint on the same spot over and over again with the Clone tool set to a soft-edged brush to slowly build up lightening. You can use a big, very soft-edged brush or a small, semi-soft-edged brush. You can be artistic with it. Just don't overdo it or the image will look weird — that's why I recommend setting the tool to a low opacity before you start. Figure 14.32 shows an image that has been lightened in the red building's windows with the Clone tool set to Screen blending mode.

Another technique you can use to lighten is to set the Clone tool to the Lighten blending mode and use it in a more traditional way — to copy from one area of the image to another. The Lighten blend mode only copies pixels if they are lighter than the destination pixels you are painting over. So, you end up copying fewer pixels, which can make the cloning look more realistic (see Figure 14.33).

One common problem you have to fix when using the Clone tool to copy from one place to another is that you can start to get repeating patterns. This technique helps avoid that because it usually doesn't copy all the pixels, just some of them. In Figure 14.33, the Clone tool was used to copy clouds from the bottom right image to the top image that has no clouds (the resulting image is shown on the lower left). Because the Clone tool was set to the Lighten blending mode, it only copied the lighter cloud pixels and not part of the sky. This technique helped avoid undesirable outlines around the copied clouds where the copied sky may have been a slightly different color than the destination sky.

FIGURE 14.32

This image's windows in the red building have been lightened with the Clone tool set to Screen blending mode. It has been used to copy an image exactly on top of itself while lightening it at the same time.

Using the Dodge tool to lighten

The Dodge tool can be used to lighten parts of images by simply painting over an image with it. The best part about this tool is that you can set it to affect mostly highlights, midtones, or shadows in the drop-down list in its Options Bar. It's also a good idea to reduce the Exposure in the Options Bar and slowly build up the effect by painting the same spot over and over until you get the effect you want. Figure 14.34 shows an image that has been lightened in some areas with the Dodge tool.

Using an Exposure adjustment to lighten

You can use an Exposure adjustment layer to increase overall brightness, with a greater effect in the brighter values. Increasing Exposure lightens an image. Exposure adjustments apply a similar effect as changing f-stops on a camera. Offset darkens mostly shadows and midtones. Gamma adjusts mostly the midtones.

FIGURE 14.33

The image on the lower left has been lightened in an area with the Clone tool set to Lighten blending mode. This tool and mode have been used to copy just the lighter cloud pixels from the image on the lower right to the image on the lower left, which previously looked like the original cloudless image at top.

FIGURE 14.34

This image has been lightened in some areas with the Dodge tool.

The Exposure eyedroppers can be used to set the black point to black, the white point to white, and midtone point to middle gray in an image, but these eyedroppers affect only luminance, not all the color channels as they do in curves and Levels. Figure 14.35 shows an image that has been lightened with an Exposure adjustment layer.

FIGURE 14.35

This image has been lightened with an Exposure adjustment layer.

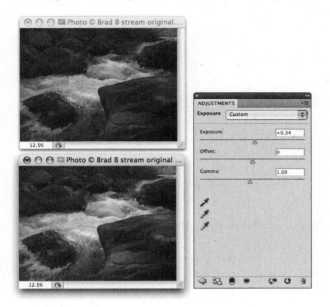

Using the Shadows/Highlights command to lighten shadows

Increasing the Shadows setting of the Shadows/Highlights command lightens the shadows while attempting to preserve some contrast. To access this command, choose Image ⇨ Adjustments ⇨ Shadows/Highlights.

It's very good at bringing out detail when the details are there but are so dark they are hard to see. This command's strength is that it can often preserve some of the contrast, but it can easily be overdone.

Usually, a conservative change looks more realistic. Figure 14.36 shows an image that has been lightened in a very dark area by increasing the Shadows setting in the Shadows/Highlights command.

Using a Brightness/Contrast adjustment to lighten

Increasing the Brightness setting in a Brightness/Contrast adjustment layer is a simple way to lighten an image but it gives you less control than other methods, such as curves. If you leave Legacy unchecked, it keeps some of the darkest colors fairly dark and preserves more contrast when lightening.

FIGURE 14.36

This image has been lightened in the shadows with the Shadows/Highlights command.

Using a Black & White adjustment with Luminosity and a mask to lighten

A Black & White adjustment is usually used to change a color image to black and white and adjust which colors in the image end up being a lighter or darker gray. If you want to lighten specific colored areas but leave them in their original color, you can use a Black & White adjustment layer and set it to Luminosity blending mode in the Layers palette.

Luminosity allows changes to lights and darks but not to color. You can paint with black on a layer mask to hide corresponding parts of the effect on the layer's image pixels. Figure 14.37 shows an image with a specific colored area that has been lightened with a Black & White adjustment layer set to Luminosity blending mode. A mask on the adjustment layer was used to hide this effect from the blues in the shirt so that just the blues in the blue jeans would be affected.

Using layers with different content and a blending mode to lighten

Fill layers, gradient layers, and layers with different objects and image pixels can be used to lighten layers underneath them. You can apply the Screen, Lighten, or Luminosity blending mode in the Layers palette or reduce the layer's opacity to try different effects.

FIGURE 14.37

This image with a specific colored area (blue) has been lightened with a Black & White adjustment layer set to Luminosity blending mode.

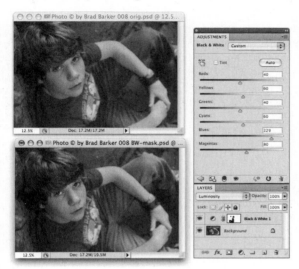

Darkening

Just as there are many ways to lighten images or parts of images in Photoshop, there are many ways to darken images, or make them less bright. This section will discuss similar techniques that were described in the Lightening section, but it will talk about how to use those techniques to darken.

Using curves to Darken

All of the following techniques require a Curves adjustment layer. To make a Curves adjustment layer, do the following:

1. **Activate the layer that you want to be just below the Curves adjustment layer you are about to make.** (An adjustment layer can affect only the layers below it.) You can activate a layer by clicking once on it in the Layers palette — clicking next to the right side of the layer name is best.

2. **Do one of the following:**

    ▪ Click the Create a new fill or adjustment layer button (the half-black, half-white circle) at the bottom of the Layers palette and choose curves.

    ▪ Click the curves button in the Adjustments palette.

3. **You can then perform the techniques described below.** For some of the tasks, you need to activate the Curves adjustment layer and adjust it in the Adjustments palette. For other tasks, you need to activate the Curves adjustment layer and work with it in the Layers palette.

Note that the color mode of the image determines whether you need to move the curve up or down to darken the image. Color mode can be changed in the Image ➪ Mode menu. You can preserve more colors in an image by adjusting it in RGB or Lab color mode. When you convert an image to CMYK color mode, which is eventually necessary for full-color images destined for print, you lose some of the colors.

Sometimes the loss of colors is noticeable, and sometimes it's not. So it's best, although not absolutely necessary, to convert to CMYK only when you are nearly finished with the image.

Darkening broad areas with curves

You can darken broad areas of an image by adjusting the curve in a Curves adjustment layer so that the majority of the curve is moved from its original straight, 45-degree-angle line in the direction of the dark part of the dark-to-light bar that runs along the side of the curve.

If the resulting curve is made so that part or all of it is at a steeper angle than the original 45-degree-angle curve, the corresponding part of the image will have increased contrast. If the resulting curve is made so that part or all of it is at a less-steep angle than the original 45-degree-angle of the curve, the corresponding parts of the image will have decreased contrast.

Figure 14.38 shows before-and-after images in RGB color mode and the curves that darkened a broad area of the images while increasing the image's contrast.

Figure 14.39 shows before-and-after images in RGB color mode and the curves that darkened the image while reducing the image's contrast.

Darkening generally targeted areas with curves

You can darken a somewhat targeted area of an image by moving part of the curve in a Curves adjustment layer in the direction of the dark part of the dark-to-light bar that runs along the side of the curve but keeping another part of the curve line relatively close to its original position. This keeps part of the image the way it was originally and darkens only a portion of it.

Figure 14.40 shows an RGB mode image that darkens a generally targeted area.

FIGURE 14.38

FIGURE 14.38

An RGB mode image that uses a curve to darken broad areas of the image while increasing the image's contrast. Note that most of the curve angle is steeper than it was originally and the composite color RGB channel is active in the curves dialog box.

FIGURE 14.39

An RGB mode image that uses a curve to darken broad areas of the image while reducing the image's overall contrast. Note that all of the curve angle is less steep than it was originally and the composite color RGB channel is active in the curves dialog box.

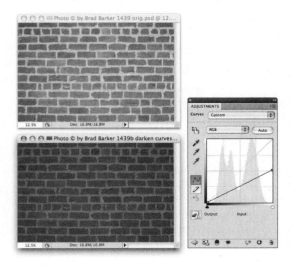

For example, you could use a pixel mask to show the adjustment in a soft-edged area of the image (you could paint white and black on a pixel mask with a soft-edged brush) and use a vector mask to make the adjustment apply to a hard-edged area of the image (you could use a shape tool or the Pen tool with the Paths button active in the Options Bar to draw a hard-edged shape on the vector mask).

Darkening specific colors with curves

You can make a Curves adjustment in a Curves adjustment layer affect certain colors rather than the composite full color. To target a certain color, you would select the color channel you want to adjust from the drop-down list just above the curves grid. You can access the menu and grid in the Adjustments palette when a Curves adjustment layer is active.

FIGURE 14.40

An RGB mode image that uses a curve to darken a generally targeted area of the image while keeping part of the image similar to the way it was originally. Note that the composite color RGB channel is active in the curves dialog box.

In RGB and Lab modes, each color channel can be used to adjust two colors. In RGB mode, you use the R channel to adjust red and cyan, the G channel to adjust green and magenta, and the B channel to adjust blue and yellow. In Lab mode, you use the a channel to adjust green and magenta and the b channel to adjust blue and yellow.

The Lightness channel in Lab mode adjusts the luminosity, or light and dark values only, without affecting the color. In CMYK mode, each color channel can be used to adjust (lighten or darken), just one color: cyan, magenta, yellow, or black (K).

For example, in the blue channel in RGB mode, if you drag the curve down so that you darken (or add) the yellow in the image, it also lightens (or subtracts) blue (see Figure 14.41). In the b channel in Lab mode, if you drag the curve up so that you darken (or add) yellow in the image, it also lightens (or subtracts) blue. In the Y channel of CMYK mode, if you drag the curve up, you darken yellow if you drag the curve down, you lighten yellow.

Darkening with Curves eyedroppers and color numbers

If you have an image you can darken with the Curves eyedroppers, you can get a lot done with a single click. You can use the curves dialog box's Set White Point and Set Black Point eyedroppers to make a part of the image you click on with them change to the color that is assigned to them, and the other colors in the image adjust proportionally.

The Set Gray Point eyedropper changes whatever color you click on to a neutral (or gray) color of a similar lightness; you can't assign a specific color to the Set Gray Point eyedropper. But you can assign colors to the Set White Point and Set Black Point eyedroppers.

These eyedroppers are usually used to change the lightest and darkest points in an image that you think should be neutral colors (but are not) to neutral colors. That can remove an undesirable color cast in the entire image, and if the color a curves eyedropper represents is darker than the point you click on in the image with that eyedropper, it darkens the image.

FIGURE 14.41

This figure shows a curve that darkens yellow in an RGB mode image. Note that the blue channel is selected. In RGB mode, you can use the blue channel to adjust yellow and blue.

For example, if an image is too light overall and has a pink color cast, you could click on a point in the image that you know should be the darkest black that needs to maintain some detail (like the darkest part of a black shirt) with the Set Black Point eyedropper. That darkens the overall image, and if you've guessed correctly that the point you clicked on the shirt should be a dark neutral black, it may also remove the pink color cast.

You can set the White Point and Black Point eyedroppers to specific colors by double-clicking them and entering color numbers in the Color Picker dialog box. For example, a common darkest-shadow neutral color for the Set Black Point eyedropper when you are working on images for print is C: 80, M: 70, Y: 70, K: 70.

These numbers can vary somewhat and can be darker, but for print images, they generally should not be as dark as 100. Limiting the darkest point in the image to a number that is less than the darkest value possible helps ensure it reproduces well during the printing process. This is because of the limitations of printing devices. In Web images, you can go darker with the black point in appropriate images since monitors don't usually have as many tonal limitations as printing devices.

Displays can vary significantly in how they display images, however. But in either case, if you want to make a neutral-color black point, C, M, and Y should have the same proportions to each other as the 80-70-70-70 numbers (M and Y equal and C a little higher). You can enter those numbers even if the image is in RGB mode, and they will still work. You can also enter three equivalent RGB numbers to get a neutral CMYK or RGB color. The Color Picker converts the numbers you enter to the current color mode's numbers, and also displays the color numbers you enter in all the other modes' equivalent numbers.

CROSS-REF See Chapter 24 for tips on how to prepare Web images so that they have the best chance at looking good on-screen.

Figure 14.42 shows an image that has been darkened, had its darkest point set to specific color numbers, and had its color cast removed just by clicking on it once with the Set Black Point eye-dropper.

FIGURE 14.42

This before-and-after image has been darkened by clicking on what needed to be changed to a very dark point in the image with the Set Black Point eyedropper from the curves dialog box.

It is also possible to set the White Point and Black Point eyedroppers to colors other than neutral. You can use them to change colors in an image to custom colors, including ones that are darker than existing image colors and that would cause the overall image to darken. Of course, changing colors to non-neutral colors is not the Curves eyedroppers' original purpose. But I believe experimentation is an important way to learn about Photoshop.

Darkening by entering color numbers in curves

You can darken an image by selecting a point on a curve and entering a new output number. Figure 14.43 shows a black, white, and gray image that has had its white darkened slightly. All the pixels in the previous white part of the image were made up of R: 255, G: 255, B: 255 (pure white in RGB mode). The new white pixels are made up of R: 242, G: 242, B: 242, which are slightly darker than pure white.

FIGURE 14.43

A black, white, and gray image whose pure white pixels have been darkened slightly by selecting the lightest point on the curve and entering a new output value. The input value was 255 and was changed to 242 by entering 242 in the Output value box.

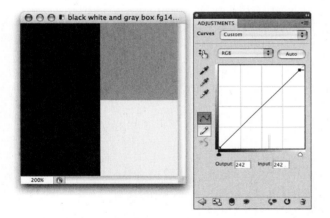

In CMYK color mode, if you enter a new output value for a point on the curve when you have the composite CMYK channel selected in curves, Photoshop limits the values in any one channel to the amount of the new value, but it also may change values in all channels to values you don't expect. If you want to make individual CMYK colors conform to specific values, you first need to choose the individual color channel in curves before you type in a new output value.

Note that if you are going to be converting from one color mode to another, the numbers in the destination color mode after the conversion may not be the numbers you expect. When Color Management is turned on, Photoshop uses color profiles to calculate color numbers that have been converted from one color mode to another.

The resulting numbers can be different depending on which color profiles are active in Color Settings. When you need more predictable color numbers, either convert the image to the destination color mode before you enter new output color numbers or turn off Color Management before you enter the new output values.

Changing a Curves darken adjustment by readjusting curves settings

Say you have used a Curves adjustment layer to darken part of your image. You can change a Curves adjustment layer's curve by double-clicking the adjustment layer's thumbnail in the Layers palette and changing the shape of the curve in the Adjustments palette.

Figure 14.44 shows the location of a Curves adjustment layer's thumbnail.

Reducing a Curves darken adjustment by reducing opacity

If you don't want to bother with fiddling with the curve and want to reduce the Curves adjustment layer's effect, you can also simply reduce the opacity of the Curves adjustment layer at the top of the Layers palette.

FIGURE 14.44

A Curves adjustment layer's thumbnail, which you can double-click if you want to change the Curves adjustment

Confining a Curves darken adjustment to a specific layer or set of layers

Adjustment layers can affect all the layers below it in the Layers palette but none of the layers above it. If you want a Curves adjustment layer to affect only the layer below it, Alt+click (Option+click) the line in between the Curves adjustment layer and the layer directly below it when you see a double-circle symbol pop up as you hover the cursor over the line while holding down the Alt key. This puts the two layers in a Clipping Group, and the layer on the bottom of the group becomes a Clipping Mask.

A Clipping Mask acts like a window that lets the content or the adjustment on the layer or layers that are above it in the Clipping Group show through the Clipping Mask layer's contents. The Clipping Group's layer or layers that are above the bottom layer of the Clipping Group — in this case, the Curves adjustment layer — will be indented in the Layers palette and have an arrow next to its thumbnail that points to the layer below. To make the two layers become regular layers again and remove them from a Clipping Group, Alt+click/Option+click) between the two layers again.

To put more layers in the Clipping Group, and therefore make the Curves adjustment layer apply to more than one layer, you can drag another layer in between the two layers in the Clipping Group. To remove one of the layers from the middle of a Clipping Group, you can drag it below the Clipping Group. You can then drag it above the Clipping Group if you need to change the order of it in the Layers palette.

In the Clipping Group with two layers, the Curves adjustment layer affects only the layer below it. In the Clipping Group with three layers, the Curves adjustment layer affects two layers below it.

Darkening with curves without shifting color

If the color is just right in your image and you only want to darken the image without shifting the color, you can apply the Luminosity blending mode to the Curves adjustment layer. The Luminosity blending mode tells Photoshop to use only the light and dark values on the layer (or the adjustments to the light and dark values, in this case) and not affect the color of the image.

Figure 14.45 shows a Curves adjustment layer with the Luminosity blending mode applied in the drop-down list near the top of the Layers palette.

FIGURE 14.45

A Curves adjustment layer with the Luminosity blending mode applied from the drop-down list near the top of the Layers palette. The Luminosity blending mode makes sure the layer doesn't affect the color and affects only the light and dark values in the layers below.

Increasing a Curves darken adjustment with the Multiply blending mode

The Multiply blending mode always darkens the layers below the layer it is applied to. If you apply the Multiply blending mode to a Curves adjustment layer, it increases the darkening effect.

If the Multiply effect is too dark, you can reduce the opacity of the adjustment layer that is using the Multiply blending mode.

Darkening with an original, unadjusted curve and the Multiply blending mode

You can also darken an image with an unadjusted Curves adjustment layer that is using the Multiply blending mode, applied from the drop-down list near the top of the Layers palette. An unadjusted curves layer will have a curve that hasn't been changed from its original 45-degree-angle line. This technique has the same effect as duplicating a layer and applying the Multiply blending mode to it, but it doesn't increase the file size.

When you duplicate a layer, it can increase the file size significantly. If the Multiply effect is too dark, you can reduce the opacity of the adjustment layer that is using the Multiply blending mode.

Figure 14.46 shows a darkened image, a Curves adjustment layer and its unadjusted curve, and the Multiply blending mode that has been applied in the Layers palette.

FIGURE 14.46

A darkened image, a Curves adjustment layer and its unadjusted curve, and the Multiply blending mode that has been applied in the Layers palette.

Increasing a Darken adjustment by duplicating Curves adjustment layers

You can use a Curves adjustment layer to darken an image, and you can duplicate the Curves adjustment layers to increase the darken effect. To duplicate a layer, drag it onto the New button at the bottom of the Layers palette or choose Duplicate Layer from the Layers palette menu. You can reduce the opacity of a duplicated curves layer if it makes the image too dark.

Using duplicate layers and the Multiply blending mode to darken

You can use a duplicated layer and apply the Multiply blending mode to it to darken an image. Each time you duplicate the layer, it increases the darken effect. To duplicate a layer, drag it onto the New button at the bottom of the Layers palette or choose Duplicate Layer from the Layers palette menu. You can reduce the opacity of a duplicated layer if it makes the image too dark. Note that each time you duplicate a layer, it increases the file size of an image.

You can merge the duplicated layers to reduce file size. To merge layers, Ctrl+click (⌘+click on a Mac) to select multiple layers, and choose Merge Layers from the Layers palette menu.

NOTE You can create the same effect as the technique described in this section without increasing the file size. See the "Darkening with an original, unadjusted curve and the Multiply blending mode" section for details.

Using Levels to darken

Using Levels to darken images works just fine, but you have less control with Levels than you have with curves. Levels offers two sliders that can be used to darken an entire image or its color channels, whereas curves can darken images with numerous control points at numerous intensity levels.

All of the following techniques require a Levels adjustment layer. To make a Levels adjustment layer, do the following:

1. **Activate the layer that you want to be just below the Levels adjustment layer you are about to make.** (An adjustment layer can affect only the layers below it.) You can activate a layer by clicking once on it in the Layers palette — clicking next to the right side of the layer name is best.

2. **Do one of the following:**

   ▪ Click the Create a new fill or adjustment layer button (the half-black, half-white circle) at the bottom of the Layers palette and choose Levels.

   ▪ Click the Levels button in the Adjustments palette.

3. **You can then perform the techniques described below.** For some of the tasks, you need to activate the Levels adjustment layer and adjust it in the Adjustments palette. For other tasks, you need to activate the Levels adjustment layer and work with it in the Layers palette.

Note that the color mode of the image and whether the composite or individual channels are selected in Levels determine whether you need to move the Levels sliders to the right or left to darken the entire image or colors in individual channels. Color mode can be changed in the Image ⇨ Mode menu. You can preserve more colors in an image by adjusting it in RGB or Lab color mode.

When you convert an image to CMYK color mode, which is eventually necessary for full-color images destined for print, you lose some of the colors. Sometimes the loss of colors is noticeable, and sometimes it's not. So it's best, although not absolutely necessary, to convert to CMYK only when you are nearly finished with the image.

Darkening broad areas with Levels

You can darken broad areas of an image by adjusting the Levels sliders in a Levels adjustment layer. Figure 14.47 shows a before-and-after image in RGB color mode and the Levels adjustments that darkened the image.

FIGURE 14.47

An RGB mode image that uses Levels to darken an image's composite color by dragging the shadows slider to the right. Note that RGB is selected in the Levels drop-down list.

Darkening specifically targeted areas with Levels

You can use the pixel mask (regular mask) or a vector mask, or a combination of the two types of masks, on a Levels adjustment layer to make the Levels adjustment apply only to a specific area in an image. The adjustment is applied to the area in the image that corresponds to the white area on the masks.

For example, you could use a pixel mask to show the adjustment in a soft-edged area of the image (you could paint white and black on a pixel mask with a soft-edged brush) and use a vector mask to make the adjustment apply to a hard-edged area of the image (you could use a shape tool or the Pen tool with the Paths button active in the Options Bar to draw a hard-edged shape on the vector mask).

This technique works on Levels adjustment layers just like it does on Curves adjustment layers.

Darkening specific colors with Levels

You can make a Levels adjustment in a Levels adjustment layer affect certain colors rather than the composite full color. To target a certain color, you would select the color channel you want to adjust from the drop-down list at the top of the Levels dialog box. You can access the menu and dialog box in the Adjustments palette when a Levels adjustment layer is active.

In RGB and Lab modes, each color channel can be used to adjust two colors. In RGB mode, you use the R channel to adjust red and cyan, the G channel to adjust green and magenta, and the B channel to adjust blue and yellow. In Lab mode, you use the a channel to adjust green and magenta and the b channel to adjust blue and yellow. The Lightness channel in Lab mode adjusts the luminosity, or light and dark values only, without affecting the color. In CMYK mode, each color channel can be used to adjust (lighten or darken), just one color: cyan, magenta, yellow, or black (K).

For example, in the blue channel in RGB mode, if you drag the upper black slider to the right, you darken (or add) the yellow in the image (see Figure 14.48); that also lightens (or subtracts) blue. In the b channel in Lab mode, if you drag the upper white slider to the left you darken (or add) yellow in the image; that also lightens (or subtracts) blue. In the Y channel of CMYK mode, if you drag the black slider to the right, you darken yellow; if you drag the upper white slider to the left, you lighten yellow.

FIGURE 14.48

A Levels adjustment that darkens yellow in an RGB mode image by dragging the shadow slider to the right. Note that the blue channel is selected. In RGB mode, you can use the blue channel to adjust yellow and blue.

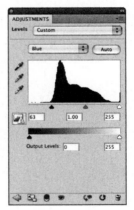

Darkening with Levels eyedroppers and color numbers

If you have an image you can darken with the Levels eyedroppers, you can accomplish a whole lot with a single click. You can use the Levels dialog box's Set White Point and Set Black Point eyedroppers to make a part of the image you click on with them change to the color that is assigned to them, and the other colors in the image adjust proportionally.

You can assign specific colors to these eyedroppers by double-clicking them and entering the color numbers. The Set Gray Point eyedropper changes whatever color you click on to a neutral (or gray) color of a similar lightness; you can't assign a specific color to the Set Gray Point eyedropper.

Darkening by entering color numbers in Levels

You can darken an image by entering input color numbers in the upper boxes in Levels and output numbers in the lower boxes. Figure 14.49 shows a black, white, and gray image that has had its white darkened slightly. All the pixels in the previous white part of the image were made up of R: 255, G: 255, B: 255 (pure white in RGB mode). The new white pixels are made up of R: 242, G: 242, B: 242, which are slightly darker than pure white.

FIGURE 14.49

A black, white, and gray image whose pure white pixels have been darkened slightly by entering a new output value 242 (a little darker than pure white in RGB mode) for the input value 255 (pure white in RGB mode)

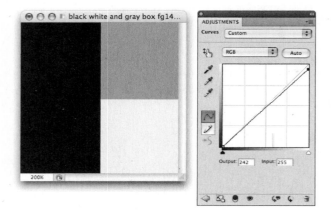

In CMYK color mode, if you enter a new output value when you have the composite CMYK channel selected in Levels, Photoshop limits the values in any one channel to the amount of the new value, but it may also change values in all channels to values you don't expect. If you want to make individual CMYK colors conform to specific values, you first need to choose the individual color channel in Levels before you type in a new output value.

Note that if you are going to be converting from one color mode to another, the numbers in the destination color mode after the conversion may not be the numbers you expect. When Color Management is turned on, Photoshop uses color profiles to calculate color numbers that have been converted from one color mode to another.

The resulting numbers can be different depending on which color profiles are active in Color Settings. When you need more predictable color numbers, either convert the image to the destination color mode before you enter new output color numbers or turn off Color Management before you enter the new output values.

Changing a Levels adjustment

You can readjust a Levels adjustment layer's settings, reduce a Levels adjustment layer's effect, confine a Levels adjustment to one or more layers, and darken an image with an unadjusted Levels layer that uses the Multiply blending mode. These changes can be accomplished with the same techniques that are used with Curves adjustment layers.

Using the Clone tool to darken

One of my favorite ways to darken an image is with the Clone tool. That may sound strange because the Clone tool is most often used to copy one part of an image onto another part of an image for the purpose of repairing it. But with the Clone tool set to Multiply blending mode and a low opacity in its Options Bar, you can clone an image exactly on top of itself while darkening it at the same time (see Figure 14.50).

FIGURE 14.50

This image has been darkened in areas with the Clone tool set to Multiply blending mode. The tool has been used to copy an image exactly on top of itself while darkening it at the same time.

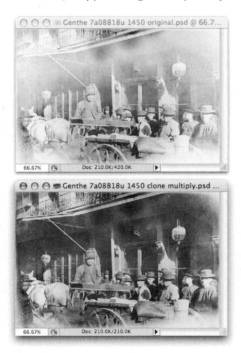

To Clone an image on top of itself, start painting in the exact spot you Alt+click/Option+click on when you sample with the Clone tool, and make sure Aligned is checked in the Options Bar. Note that this technique only works if there are at least very light pixels on the area that you want to darken. If the area contains no pixels, you might want to first try cloning from another area to that area to add some pixels.

The great thing about this technique is that it's good at preserving detail while you are doing the darkening. The Clone tool is also a brush tool, so you can paint on the same spot over and over again with the Clone tool set to a soft-edged brush to slowly build up a darkening effect. You can use a big, very soft-edged brush or a small, semi-soft-edged brush.

You can be artistic with it. Just don't overdo it or the image will look weird — that's why I recommend setting the tool to a low opacity before you start.

Another technique you can use to darken is to set the Clone tool to the Darken blending mode and use it in a more traditional way — to copy from one area of the image to another (see Figure 14.51). The top original image contains some white blemishes. The blemishes have been removed in the bottom image.

The Darken blend mode only copies pixels if they are darker than the destination pixels you are painting over. So, you end up copying fewer pixels, which can make the cloning look more realistic. One common problem you have to fix when using the Clone tool to copy from one place to another is that you can start to get repeating patterns. This technique helps avoid that because it usually doesn't copy all the pixels, just some of them.

Using the Burn tool to darken

The Burn tool can be used to darken parts of images by simply painting over an image with it (see Figure 14.52). The best part about this tool is that you can set it to affect mostly highlights, midtones, or shadows in the drop-down list in its Options Bar. It's also a good idea to reduce the Exposure in the Options Bar and slowly build up the effect by painting the same spot over and over until you get the effect you want.

Using an Exposure adjustment to darken

You can use an Exposure adjustment layer to decrease overall brightness, with a greater effect in the brighter values. Decreasing Exposure darkens an image. Exposure adjustments apply a similar effect as changing f-stops on a camera. Offset darkens mostly shadows and midtones. Gamma adjusts mostly the midtones.

Using an Exposure adjustment to darken

You can use an Exposure adjustment layer to decrease overall brightness, with a greater effect in the brighter values. Decreasing Exposure darkens an image. Exposure adjustments apply a similar effect as changing f-stops on a camera. Offset darkens mostly shadows and midtones. Gamma adjusts mostly the midtones.

The Exposure eyedroppers can be used to set the black point to black, the white point to white, and midtone point to middle gray in an image, but these eyedroppers only affect luminance, not all the color channels as they do in curves and Levels. Figure 14.53 shows an image that has been darkened with an Exposure adjustment layer.

FIGURE 14.51

This image has been darkened in some white-blemished areas with the Clone tool set to Darken blending mode. It has been used to copy just the darker pixels from close-by darker areas onto the white-blemished areas.

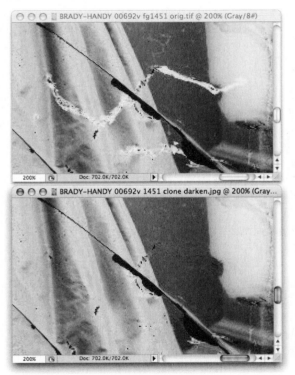

FIGURE 14.52

This image has been darkened in some areas with the Burn tool.

Using the Shadows/Highlights command to darken highlights

Increasing the Highlights setting of the Shadows/Highlights command darkens the highlights while attempting to preserve some contrast. To access this command, choose Image ➪ Adjustments ➪ Shadows/Highlights. It's very good at bringing out detail when the details are there but are so light they are hard to see. This command's strength is that it can often preserve some of the contrast, but it can easily be overdone. Usually, a conservative change looks more realistic.

Using a Brightness/Contrast adjustment to darken

Decreasing the Brightness setting in a Brightness/Contrast adjustment layer is a simple way to darken an image, but gives you less control than other methods, such as curves. If you leave Legacy unchecked, it keeps some of the lightest colors fairly light and preserves more contrast when darkening.

FIGURE 14.53

This image has been darkened with an Exposure adjustment layer.

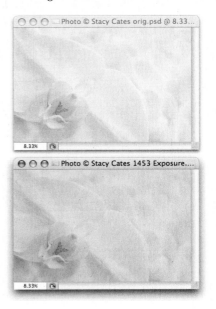

Using a Black & White adjustment with Luminosity and a mask to darken

A Black & White adjustment is usually used to change a color image to black and white and adjust which colors in the image end up being a lighter or darker gray. If you want to darken specific colored areas and leave them in their original color, you can use a Black & White adjustment layer and set it to Luminosity blending mode in the Layers palette. Luminosity allows changes to lights and darks but not to color. You can paint with black on the adjustment layer's mask to hide corresponding parts of the effect on the layer's image pixels.

Using layers with different content and a blending mode to darken

Fill layers, gradient layers, and layers with different objects and image pixels can be used to darken layers underneath them. You can apply the Multiply, Darken, or Luminosity blending modes in the Layers palette or reduce the layer's opacity to try different effects.

Increasing Contrast and Detail

Now we're getting to the good part. Increasing contrast is one of the best ways to improve images, often dramatically. Images with good contrast can seem to "pop" off the page and appear to have more detail. If you are familiar with the previous Lightening and Darkening sections in this chapter, learning about increasing contrast should be relatively painless since it basically amounts to lightening the lights and darkening the darks.

There are a few things to beware of. The main thing is to be careful not to over-lighten or over-darken any area to the point that your image loses detail in areas that are important to you or that need to be preserved for reproduction on its destination device. For example, the lightest areas in images destined for print need to be a little darker than pure white and the darkest areas a little lighter than pure black to maintain print quality in a typical image.

This is because of the limitations of the output device, such as a printing press or printer. Limiting lights and darks is not as much of an issue when you are preparing images for Web, since monitors don't usually have as many tonal limitations as printing devices. However, displays can vary significantly in how they display images.

It pays to learn how to generally or specifically target certain parts of an image when you are doing the lightening and darkening for those times when a more global adjustment doesn't do a good job. The Lightening and Darkening sections talk about many ways to do that. This section will refer to those techniques and discuss a few additional methods to target certain parts of an image when you are increasing contrast.

Using curves to increase contrast

All of the following techniques require a Curves adjustment layer. To make a Curves adjustment layer, do the following:

1. **Activate the layer that you want to be just below the Curves adjustment layer you are about to make.** (An adjustment layer can affect only the layers below it.) You can activate a layer by clicking once on it in the Layers palette — clicking next to the right side of the layer name is best.

2. **Do one of the following:**

   ▓ Click the Create a new fill or adjustment-layer button (the half-black, half-white circle) at the bottom of the Layers palette and choose curves.

   ▓ Click the curves button in the Adjustments palette.

3. **You can then perform the techniques described below.** For some of the tasks, you need to activate the Curves adjustment layer and adjust it in the Adjustments palette. For other tasks, you need to activate the Curves adjustment layer and work with it in the Layers palette.

Note that the color mode of the image determines whether you need to move the curve up or down to lighten or darken the image. Color mode can be changed in the Image ⇨ Mode menu. You can preserve more colors in an image by adjusting it in RGB or Lab color mode. When you convert an image to CMYK color mode, which is eventually necessary for full-color images destined for print, you lose some of the colors. Sometimes the loss of colors is noticeable, and sometimes it's not. So it's best, although not absolutely necessary, to convert to CMYK only when you are nearly finished with the image.

Increasing contrast in broad areas with curves

You can increase contrast in broad areas of an image by adjusting the curve in a Curves adjustment layer so that the majority of the curve is steeper than its original straight, 45-degree-angle line. When the curve has a steeper angle than it had originally, you are either lightening the lights and darkening the darks or at least increasing the difference in some of the light and dark intensities within the image. The part of the image that corresponds to the steeper-angled part of the curve will have increased contrast.

If the adjusted curve has parts that are at a less-steep angle than the original 45-degree-angle of the curve, the corresponding parts of the image will have decreased contrast.

Figure 14.54 shows a before-and-after image in Grayscale color mode and the curve that increased contrast in a broad area of the image. Note that the curve has an angle that is steeper than it was originally.

Increasing contrast in generally targeted areas with curves

You can increase contrast in a more targeted area of an image by making a smaller section of the curve angle steeper. You need to decide where in the image you want to add more contrast and find out which part of the curve corresponds to that part of the image. Pressing the I key on your keyboard activates the Eyedropper tool, and if you drag back and forth over an area in the image when the curves dialog box is open, it shows you which part of the curve corresponds to that part of the image.

You can also click the Click and drag in image to modify curves button (the hand with a double arrows symbol) in the Curves adjustment dialog box to drag in the image and affect the corresponding part of the curve directly.

NEW FEATURE When you click the Click and drag in image to modify curves button (the hand with a double arrows symbol) in the Curves adjustment dialog box, you can drag on the image and it puts a point on the corresponding part of the curve and moves the curve.

Figure 14.55 shows an RGB image and the curve that increases contrast in a generally targeted area of the image.

FIGURE 14.54

A Grayscale mode image that uses a curve to increase contrast in broad areas of the image. Note that the majority of the curve angle is steeper than it was.

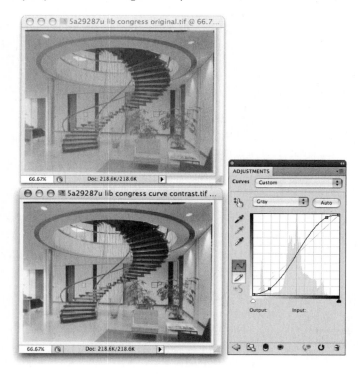

Increasing contrast in specifically targeted areas with curves

You can use the pixel mask (regular mask) or a vector mask, or a combination of the two types of masks, on a Curves adjustment layer to make the Curves adjustment apply only to a specific area in an image. The adjustment is applied to the area in the image that corresponds to the white area on the masks.

For example, you could use a pixel mask to show the adjustment in a soft-edged area of the image (you could paint white and black on a pixel mask with a soft-edged brush) and use a vector mask to make the adjustment apply to a hard-edged area of the image (you could use a shape tool or the Pen tool with the Paths button active in the Options Bar to draw a hard-edged shape on the vector mask).

Increasing contrast in specific colors with curves

You can make a Curves adjustment in a Curves adjustment layer affect certain colors rather than the composite full color. To target a certain color, you would select the color channel you want to adjust from the drop-down list just above the curves grid. You can access the menu and grid in the Adjustments palette when a Curves adjustment layer is active.

An RGB mode image that uses a curve to increase contrast in the shadow areas of the image while keeping the highlights in the image the way they were originally. Note that the composite color RGB channel is active in the curves dialog box.

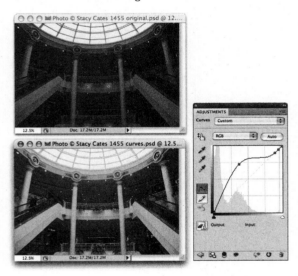

Sometimes it gives a better result to increase contrast in each color channel than to increase contrast in a composite channel. If you decide to try that, you may also try targeting the area in the image that is most important to you when you have each color channel active. You can use the Eyedropper tool in the Toolbox to find out which part of the curve corresponds to that area of the image.

Pressing the I key on your keyboard activates the Eyedropper tool, and if you drag back and forth over an area in the image when the curves dialog box is open, it shows you which part of the curve corresponds to that part of the image. You will then have an idea of which part of the curve to steepen in the active color channel.

You can also click the Click and drag in image to modify curves button in the Curves adjustment dialog box to drag in the image and affect the corresponding part of the curve directly. If you use this method, you would drag in the image to lighten the lighter area and drag again to darken the darker area.

In RGB and Lab modes, each color channel can be used to adjust two colors. In RGB mode, you use the R channel to adjust red and cyan, the G channel to adjust green and magenta, and the B channel to adjust blue and yellow. In Lab mode, you use the a channel to adjust green and magenta and the b channel to adjust blue and yellow.

In these dual color channels, you can make an S-shaped curve with the center of the curve at a steeper angle or a straight curve with a steeper angle and it will add more of each color and give the appearance of increased contrast between the two colors. It has a similar effect to saturating both of the colors.

The Lightness channel in Lab mode adjusts the luminosity, or light and dark values only, without affecting the color. If you steepen part of the Lightness channel, it is similar to steepening a Curves adjustment layer that is using the Luminosity blending mode. In CMYK mode, each color channel can be used to adjust just one color: cyan, magenta, yellow, or black (K).

Figure 14.56 shows a curve that increases the intensity of yellow and blue in an RGB mode image.

FIGURE 14.56

A curve that increases the intensity of yellow and blue in an RGB mode image. Note that the blue channel is selected. In RGB mode, you can use the blue channel to adjust yellow and blue.

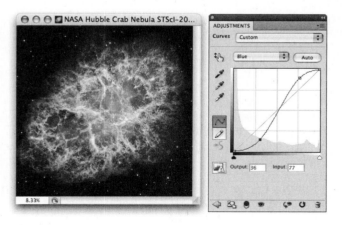

Increasing contrast with Curves eyedroppers and color numbers

You can use the Curves eyedroppers to increase contrast in an image with just a couple of clicks. You can use the curves dialog box's Set White Point and Set Black Point eyedroppers to make a part of the image you click on with them change to the color that is assigned to them, and the other colors in the image adjust proportionally.

If the image lacks contrast, often the lightest area will be too dark and the darkest area may be too light. If the Set White Point eyedropper is set to a lighter color and you click on what should be the lightest point in the image, and the Set Black Point eyedropper is set to a darker color and you click on what should be the darkest point in the image, the contrast is automatically adjusted. The other values in the image adjust proportionally. To set the eyedroppers' colors, you can double-click the eyedroppers and enter color numbers.

You can also increase contrast in an image by entering specific color numbers in the boxes in the curves dialog box. To do this, select a point on a curve and enter a new output color number in the Output number box. The numbers should be chosen so that they lighten the lighter targeted area and darken the darker targeted area.

CROSS-REF For more information about using Curves eyedroppers, see the "Lightening with Curves eyedroppers and color numbers" and "Darkening with Curves eyedroppers and color numbers" sections in this chapter.

Changing a Curves contrast adjustment by readjusting curves settings

Say you have used a Curves adjustment layer to increase contrast in part of your image. You can change a Curves adjustment layer's curve by double-clicking the adjustment layer's thumbnail in the Layers palette and changing the shape of the curve in the Adjustments palette.

Reducing a Curves contrast adjustment by reducing opacity

If you don't want to bother with fiddling with the curve and want to reduce the Curves adjustment layer's effect, you can simply reduce the opacity of the Curves adjustment layer at the top of the Layers palette.

Confining a Curves contrast adjustment to a specific layer or set of layers

Adjustment layers can affect all the layers below it in the Layers palette but none of the layers above it. If you want a Curves adjustment layer to affect only the layer below it, Alt+click/Option+click the line in between the Curves adjustment layer and the layer directly below it when you see a double-circle symbol pop up as you hover the cursor over the line while holding down the Alt key. This puts the two layers in a Clipping Group, and the layer on the bottom of the group becomes a Clipping Mask.

CROSS-REF For more information about using Clipping Masks/Clipping Groups, see the "Confining a curves darken adjustment to a specific layer or set of layers" section and Chapter 8, which discusses layers and layer masks.

In the Clipping Group with two layers, the Curves adjustment layer affects only the layer below it. In the Clipping Group with three layers, the Curves adjustment layer affects two layers below it.

Increasing Contrast with curves without shifting color

If the color is just right in your image and you only want to increase contrast in the image without shifting the color, you can apply the Luminosity blending mode to the Curves adjustment layer. The Luminosity blending mode tells Photoshop to use only the light and dark values on the layer (or the adjustments to the light and dark values, in this case) and not affect the color of the image.

Increasing contrast with an original, unadjusted curve and the Soft Light blending mode

You can also increase contrast in an image with an unadjusted Curves adjustment layer that is using the Soft Light blending mode, applied from the drop-down list near the top of the Layers palette. An unadjusted curves layer has a curve that hasn't been changed from its original 45-degree-angle line. This technique has the same effect as duplicating a layer and applying the Soft Light blending mode to it, but it doesn't increase the file size.

When you duplicate a layer, it can increase the file size significantly. If the Soft Light effect is too dark, you can reduce the opacity of the adjustment layer that is using the Soft Light blending mode. If it doesn't provide enough contrast, you can duplicate the Soft Light layer (you can merge the duplicate layers later if you need to reduce file size).

Figure 14.57 shows an image with increased contrast, a Curves adjustment layer and its unadjusted curve, and the Soft Light blending mode that has been applied in the Layers palette.

FIGURE 14.57

An image with increased contrast, a Curves adjustment layer and its unadjusted curve, and the Soft Light blending mode that has been applied in the Layers palette. Soft Light blending mode adds contrast to the image.

Using Levels to increase contrast

You can use Levels adjustment layers to increase contrast in images, but you have less control with Levels than you have with curves. To increase contrast with Levels, you can create a Levels adjustment layer and drag the upper white and black sliders toward the center. You can do this in the composite channel or individual color channels, whichever gives you the best result. Levels also has eyedroppers and color number boxes that can be used in the same way as in the curves dialog box.

Using the Clone tool to add contrast

One way you can try increasing contrast in certain parts of images is with the Clone tool. If the Clone tool is set to Soft Light blending mode, you can clone an image exactly on top of itself while increasing contrast at the same time. To Clone an image on top of itself, start painting in the exact spot you Alt+click/Option+click on when you sample with the Clone tool, and make sure Aligned is checked in the Options Bar. Note that this technique may not give the desired result on every image. It depends on the image's tones.

Using the Dodge and Burn tools to increase contrast

The Burn tool can be used to darken parts of images by simply painting over an image with it, and the Dodge tool can be used in the same way to lighten parts of an image. If you lighten lighter areas and darken darker areas that are relatively close to each other, it results in increased contrast. The best part about these tools is that you can set them to affect mostly highlights, midtones, or shadows in the drop-down list in their Options Bars.

It's also a good idea to reduce the Exposure in the Options Bar and slowly build up the effect by painting the same spot over and over until you get the effect you want. Figure 14.58 shows a before-and-after of an image that has an area with increased contrast that was applied by using the Dodge and Burn tools.

FIGURE 14.58

This image has an area with increased contrast that has been applied with the Dodge and Burn tools.

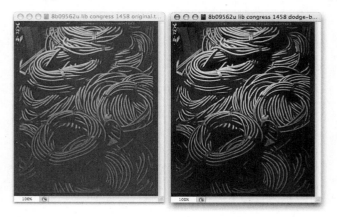

Using a Brightness/Contrast adjustment to increase contrast

Increasing the Contrast setting in a Brightness/Contrast adjustment layer is a simple way to increase contrast in an image but it gives you less control than other methods, such as curves. If you leave Legacy unchecked, it gives a smoother result. Increasing contrast with the Legacy box checked can cause the image to have a posterized look, or have a reduced tonal range so that it develops solid-color areas.

Decreasing Contrast and Detail

Sometimes you need to lower contrast in images, as odd as that may sound. Let's say you're making a collage and want a low-contrast image in the background and a high-contrast image in the foreground, or you need to create a very subtle, low-contrast pattern or photo to put behind text. The good news is that you can use most of the same techniques as those mentioned in the previous section that increase contrast — just in reverse.

Lowering contrast often means darkening the lights and lightening the darks, which is the opposite of what you do when you increase contrast. Images usually look like they contain less detail when their contrast is reduced. Images like this can help nearby high contrast and highly detailed images stand out.

The next sections talk about the differences in the techniques to lower contrast and the techniques discussed in the previous section that increase contrast. You can refer to the techniques to increase contrast for more details about how to use these methods.

Decreasing contrast with curves

You can lower contrast in images by making a curve in a Curves adjustment layer less steep than it was originally. The parts of the image that correspond to the less-steep part of the curve will have reduced contrast. Just as when you are increasing contrast, you can decrease contrast in the full-color composite channel or the individual color channels by selecting them from the drop-down list near the top of the curves dialog box. You can see the curves dialog box in the Adjustments palette when a Curves adjustment layer is active in the Layers palette.

Figure 14.59 shows a before-and-after version of an image with decreased contrast that was applied by using a less steep curve in a Curves adjustment layer.

FIGURE 14.59

This image has decreased contrast that has been applied with a less steep curve in a Curves adjustment layer.

Decreasing contrast with Levels

You can lower contrast with a Levels adjustment layer by dragging the bottom set of sliders (Output Levels) inward instead of the top set of sliders (Input Levels) that you use when you are increasing contrast. You can also enter color numbers in the Output Levels boxes instead of dragging the sliders. The numbers you enter to lower contrast would usually be values that darken a lighter part of an image and lighten a darker part of an image.

Just as when you are increasing contrast, you can decrease contrast in the full-color composite channel or the individual color channels by selecting them from the drop-down list near the top of the Levels dialog box. Figure 14.60 shows an image with decreased contrast that was applied by dragging the bottom sliders (Input Levels) inward in a Levels adjustment layer.

FIGURE 14.60

An image with decreased contrast that has been applied by dragging the bottom sliders (Input Levels) inward in a Levels adjustment layer

Using layers with different content to decrease contrast

Fill layers, gradient layers, and layers with lower-contrast objects and image pixels can be used to lower the contrast of layers underneath them. You can reduce the opacity of one of those kinds of layers in the Layers palette to let the layers underneath show through. You can also simply reduce a layer's opacity to reduce the contrast of the same layer's content. Figure 14.61 shows an image with decreased contrast that was applied by creating a white Fill layer above it and reducing the opacity of the Fill layer.

FIGURE 14.61

An image with decreased contrast that has been applied by adding a Fill layer above it and applying a reduced opacity to the Fill layer.

Using a Brightness/Contrast adjustment to decrease contrast

Decreasing the Contrast setting in a Brightness/Contrast adjustment layer is a simple way to decrease contrast in an image but it gives you less control than other methods, such as curves. There is a check box called Legacy in the Brightness?Contrast dialog box that you can select. If you leave the Legacy check box deselected, it limits the amount of contrast that the contrast adjustment can make.

For example, it won't allow you to reduce contrast so much that the image becomes completely gray, and it won't allow you to increase contrast so make that it makes the image very posterized (converted to solid blocks of color). This can be an advantage, so I recommend leaving this check box deselected.

Summary

This chapter described many ways you can lighten, darken, and change the contrast in images. Following are key concepts:

You can lighten images with Curves, Levels, the Clone tool with Screen blending mode, the Dodge tool, and with the Screen blending mode used on layers. You can darken images with Curves, Levels, the Clone tool with Multiply blending mode, the Burn tool, and with the Multiply blending mode used on layers.

Generally, increasing contrast means making lighter areas lighter and darker areas darker. An image with more contrast usually seems to have more detail and pop off the page. You can increase contrast by steepening part of a Curve, dragging the Input Levels sliders inward, using the Dodge and Burn tools, and using the Soft Light blending mode.

Decreasing contrast in an image usually makes it appear to have less detail and appear more subtle. You can decrease contrast by making part of a Curve less steep, dragging the Output Levels sliders inward, and lowering the opacity of various kinds of layers.

Chapter 15

Color Correction and Color Changes

Color is a powerful thing. You can use it to command attention, convey mood, describe your product, make a good design great, and dramatically enhance a dull image. Admittedly, deciding you will master the former in Photoshop comes with a little bit of a learning curve.

Not to worry. This chapter will show you many tools and techniques to correct images that have overall color that is just wrong, as well as ways to change individual objects' colors. I know you liked finger paints and magic markers at one time or another. Yes? Then maybe you owe it to your inner artist to discover Photoshop's color powers. No? Well, maybe you owe it to your inner expert to master its color mysteries.

Get your coffee and read on for ways to get rid of that annoying green tint from fluorescent lighting, show a one-color T-shirt in multiple colors, give a hand-tinted look to a black-and-white portrait, and make a lifeless photo come alive with vibrant color.

Preparing to Work with Color

You may be wondering how all this is going to work, considering this is mostly a black-and-white book. Many examples include objects with known colors, and the color numbers that are appropriate for those objects will be discussed. More importantly, there will be color versions of many of the examples in the color section of this book and on the book's CD.

Before you start working on the colors in an image, there are some important things to do, as discussed in the following sections.

Check the image size and resolution

It is critical to check the image size and resolution to make sure it is sufficient for the image's purpose. You wouldn't want to do a lot of color work only to find out at the end of the process that your image is too small for its purpose. Usually, 300 ppi at the final size in inches is plenty for images destined for print; 72 ppi at the final size in pixels is plenty for images destined for the Web.

When you select an image's size in the Image Size dialog box (choose Image ⇨ Image Size), the key is to deselect the Resample button in the Image Size dialog box before you increase any numbers in the box (size or resolution numbers). Then you can type in the higher numbers and the dialog box shows you the other size or resolution numbers that the image can have in order to reproduce it at a high quality.

If you need to decrease size or resolution numbers, select the Resample button. But keep in mind this throws some of the image information away — be sure you don't need the image at a larger size before you discard some of the image's detail.

CROSS-REF For more information about resolution and resizing, see Chapter 5.

Consider working on a larger master file with preserved layers

It's often a good idea to work on a larger-size image and keep it as a master file. You never know when you might need the image at a larger size. It's also a good idea to keep all the master file's layers and save the master file in Photoshop format (PSD). Use adjustment layers as opposed to commands whenever possible.

A layered version allows you to make any changes much more easily. When you finish your corrections and retouching of the master file, you can save a flattened copy (at a smaller final size, if necessary) before you sharpen. It's best to sharpen at the final size.

Think about correcting full-color images in RGB or Lab color mode

When you are working on images destined for on-screen display, such as images for the Web, the final version of the image must be in an appropriate RGB mode so that it displays properly on a computer monitor. Many desktop printers also require RGB-mode images even if the printers use CMYK inks (check your device's documentation to find out the appropriate color mode for images that will be printed on it).

Sometimes you may need to make a grayscale image and the final image will end up in Grayscale color mode, or you may want to make an image that is made up of one to four nonstandard ink colors, which will require Duotone mode.

When you are preparing a full-color image that will be printed on a standard printing press that is using standard inks, keep in mind that the required CMYK mode can't contain as many colors as RGB or Lab mode. When you convert to CMYK, the image may lose some of its colors. That is basically because CMYK mode is designed to contain only the colors that can be reproduced on printing presses, and printing presses can't reproduce as many colors as most devices that use RGB light to make up colors, such as monitors.

You can preserve more colors in an image by adjusting it in RGB color mode or Lab color mode and only converting it to CMYK when you are nearly finished with the image. You also may want to keep the master file in RGB or Lab mode. But to put this into perspective, note that sometimes the loss of colors during a CMYK conversion is noticeable, and sometimes it's not. So may choose to look at these only as guidelines to use when preserving as many colors as possible is a priority.

CAUTION Converting an image to CMYK mode over and over again may cause the image to lose more and more colors. Converting between RGB and Lab modes is much safer for preserving colors.

Lab is a standardized color mode that can contain a large number of colors and was not made to conform to any particular device's color capabilities. It is also used behind-the-scenes by Photoshop as a kind of master set of colors — an intermediate color space that helps interpret colors when Photoshop is converting from one mode to another.

Lab is good at preserving a lot of colors, but it can contain colors that can't be reproduced on some devices. So, in most cases, you will eventually need to convert to an appropriate color space for the destination device.

Set the Color Settings appropriately

You can access Color Settings by choosing Edit ⇨ Color Settings. Adobe RGB is a good RGB workspace for print, sRGB is a good RGB workspace for Web. You can choose a CMYK workspace based on what kind of paper and press an image will be printed on. Note that in the CMYK menu, "Web" means a web press (roll-fed press) as opposed to a sheetfed press.

You can use Gray Gamma 2.2 for Web images or Gray 20% Dot Gain for print, and you can leave Spot set to 20% Dot Gain. These dot gain suggestions can be used when you don't have more specific dot gain information you might get from your pressman, for example.

Photoshop's color management system, which uses these color settings, is intended to help your image maintain color consistency when it is reproduced on different devices. Sometimes color management works very well, but sometimes it doesn't. I prefer to use Photoshop's color management system in most cases; just know it is still an imperfect system.

There are times you may choose to turn off color management, such as when you want your image's colors to have very specific color numbers and you want to be sure the color management system doesn't change the color numbers to unexpected values during a color conversion. If you want to turn off color management, choose Edit ⇨ Color Settings, and choose the Off option in the Color Management Policies drop-down menu.

Create a soft-proof profile so you can proof the image on-screen as you work

It's helpful to see an image in its destination color space while you are correcting it. For example, if you are correcting in RGB or Lab mode and your image will wind up in CMYK, you can view it in CMYK while you are correcting it to see how your corrections will affect a CMYK result. This doesn't cause any colors to be lost because you haven't actually converted to CMYK yet — you're just viewing a CMYK soft-proof.

A *soft-proof* is a proof of the final image you see on-screen, and a *hard-proof* is a proof that is printed. If an RGB-mode correction adversely affects color in the CMYK soft-proof, you have the chance to improve the correction before you convert to CMYK. It's also a good idea to set the Info palette to show both the current color space's and the destination color space's color numbers so you can watch the destination mode's color numbers, if you need to, while you correct.

To soft-proof the image on-screen in the destination color space while you are correcting and retouching, follow these steps:

1. Choose View ⇨ Proof Setup.
2. **From the Proof Setup menu, choose Working (CMYK or RGB) to set the proof view to the color profile that is active in Color Settings.** Alternatively, you can choose Custom to set the proof view to a different profile, or choose Windows RGB or Mac RGB if you are preparing an image for the Web or an image that will be displayed on Mac monitors.
3. **Choose View ⇨ Proof Colors (so that Proof Colors has a check mark) to turn on the proof view and see your image in the proof view's color space.**

Calibrate your monitor

As you color-correct an image, you will want to check color numbers of certain colors in the image to see if they are reasonably proportional to typical color numbers that are seen in certain common image content (blue sky, green foliage, flesh tones, and so on). But it often involves making educated guesses on your part as to which areas should be what colors, and it's impossible to know the exact color numbers most parts of an image should be.

For these reasons, it's also important for you to be able to rely on the accuracy of the color displayed on your monitor as much as possible.

If your monitor has a pink color cast, for example, it will cause an image's color to be displayed inaccurately. The monitor's pink color cast may prompt you to erroneously reduce red or magenta in the image, which will likely introduce wrong colors.

Even though your adjustment may make the image look good on your inaccurate screen, the color probably won't look good when displayed on a different monitor or when printed. So, it's important to calibrate your monitor to a certain color standard before you start color-correcting an image.

CROSS-REF For more information about how to calibrate your monitor and use color management, see Chapter 23.

Color Correction

Sometimes images have an overall undesirable *color cast*, or color tint, such as a greenish cast caused by a photo being taken in some types of fluorescent lighting. You can use Photoshop to correct the color and remove an overall unwanted color cast or to correct colors in specific areas of images. Part of the color-correction process can involve changing the numbers that Photoshop uses to represent the colors to numbers that are closer to what they should be. In order to do this, you need to know how to measure color numbers and know some color number guidelines for common image content, like neutral-colored areas, blue sky, green foliage, and flesh tones.

Measuring color

All the colors in every Photoshop image are represented by color numbers. When you color-correct an image, you can watch the image's color numbers to help you know what kind of corrections to make. A color's numbers will change when the color mode of the image changes, even if the color looks the same to your eye.

Different color modes use different base groups of colors to make up full-color images, and those color groups use different numbering systems. You can see an image's color mode to the right of the image's name in its tab or title bar, and you can also see and/or change an image's color mode by choosing Image ➪ Mode.

CROSS-REF For more information about color modes and the numbering systems of various color modes, see Chapter 1.

The Eyedropper tool and/or Color Sampler tool can be used in conjunction with the Info palette to check the color numbers of a particular area of an image. When either of those tools is over an area in an image, that area's color numbers are displayed in the Info palette. Figure 15.1 shows the Eyedropper tool being hovered over a color in an image and the color's numbers being displayed in the Info palette.

In most cases, it's a good idea to set the Eyedropper tool to a sample size of 3 x 3 Average or 5 x 5 Average in the Options Bar. Figure 15.1 shows the Sample setting in the Options Bar. Setting the Eyedropper tool also sets the Color Sampler tool. That makes the tools measure the average color in a group of 3 x 3 pixels or 5 x 5 pixels, which helps ensure you don't accidentally get the color measurement of a tiny solid black speck you can't even see, for example.

That could happen if the Eyedropper is set to Point Sample. You also may want to make sure All Layers is selected in the Sample menu in the Eyedropper's Options Bar so that color numbers reflect all layers' information rather than just the selected layer's information.

Hovering the eyedropper tool over a color in an image displays the color's numbers in the Info palette.

To use the Eyedropper tool to measure color, simply hover it over an area of the image in the image window and look at its color numbers in the Info palette. You can set the Info palette to display the Eyedropper tool's color measurements in up to two different color modes' numbers at one time by selecting the modes in the Panel Options menu, accessed from the Info palette menu.

For example, if you are correcting in RGB or Lab color mode, you could choose to display Actual Color (the current color mode's numbers) and CMYK so that you can track the CMYK numbers while you correct in a different mode. Before-adjustments and after-adjustments numbers are separated by a slash in the Info palette.

> **TIP**   Click in the image with the Eyedropper tool to make the color you click on become the foreground color. You can then drop the color into the Swatches palette to have easy access to the color again. See Chapter 2 for more information about creating swatches, custom swatch sets, and the Preset Manager.

You can use the Color Sampler tool to click in the image and add permanent color-measuring points — they will stay in the image and display color numbers in the Info palette until you delete them. Figure 15.2 shows an image with color samplers. Up to four color samplers can exist at one time. They allow you to track, in the Info palette, how the color numbers change in the color-sampled area as you make adjustments.

You can choose which color mode's numbers a color sampler displays, regardless of the current color mode of the image. To choose which mode's numbers a sampler displays, right-click or Ctrl+click on the color sampler in the image window and choose a color mode from the menu. In this menu Actual means the current color mode and Proof Color means the soft-proof's profile that is active under View⇨Proof Setup. If you are correcting in RGB mode but will later convert to CMYK mode, you may want to display the CMYK numbers, for example.

Color samplers can be placed on colors in an image, and the Info palette continuously displays color numbers for each of the color samplers until you delete the samplers.

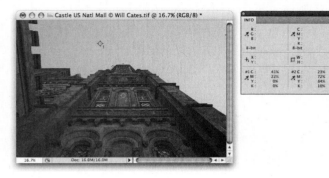

In most cases, you will want to sample different areas of an image, but it's possible to move color samplers on top of each other with the Color Sampler tool if you want to see the color numbers of the same area in an image in up to four different color mode's numbers. To delete a color sampler, make sure the Color Sampler tool is active and right-click or Ctrl+click on the sampler in the image window, then click Delete.

TIP Shift+click on the image with the Eyedropper tool to add a color sampler.

Color numbers and color correction

So how do you know what color numbers to shoot for when color-correcting? Don't worry, there are some color number suggestions in the sidebar, "Color Number Guidelines." But I emphasize that the numbers in this sidebar are just that — guidelines — not absolutes. There are many variables that affect images. Every image is different, and every device that reproduces images is different. Photos are taken in different lighting, which affects color, and you may not have any way of knowing what some colors are supposed to be.

Using Curves, Hue/Saturation, and other adjustment layers to change color numbers to the numbers they are supposed to be is an important part of color-correcting, but because you won't always know exactly what the color numbers should be, you also need to be able to rely somewhat on the color you see on your calibrated monitor.

Learning at least the basics about color management is also important. Understanding color management helps you understand how color profiles and color conversions affect images, as well as how to make decisions that affect Photoshop's method of attempting to keep an image's color consistent on different devices. It also helps you decide if there are times when you might want to turn off color management. You can find information about color management in Chapter 23, and there are other color management resources listed in Appendix B.

Your experience is also an important factor in learning how to adjust color. As you gain experience using your equipment and noticing how the views of images on your calibrated monitor compare to the way your images reproduce on other devices, you'll start to see color trends (hopefully subtle trends) and trends in the way various devices reproduce color and detail. You may want to keep collections of images printed on various devices and periodically compare them to the same images displayed on your screen.

You may also want to view images on other monitors in other rooms and compare those views to any printed materials of the same image. It's a good idea to take note how different room lighting can affect how color appears on monitors and on paper. When you are preparing images for the Web, it's helpful to view them on different monitors, operating systems, and browsers.

CROSS-REF See Chapter 9 for more information about how to use curves and levels and set their eyedroppers. See Chapter 8 for more information about using adjustment layers and layer masks.

Color Mode Tips

- **In RGB, neutral color numbers are easy to remember:** All three colors have equal values.

- **In Lab, the colors in the image are in completely separate channels (a and b) from the luminosity of the image (L), so you can adjust the colors separately from the light and dark values.** In comparison, RGB and CMYK images use a mixture of multiple colors in multiple channels to make up the light and dark qualities of an image.

- **You can adjust luminosity without affecting color in RGB and CMYK modes by applying the Luminosity blending mode to an adjustment layer.** However, that affects an image a little differently than adjusting the luminosity in the L channel of a Lab image. It's a good idea to experiment with these techniques to see the difference.

- **People sometimes find it easier to think in terms of CMYK numbers and CMYK curves when correcting skin tones, and it's okay to correct skin tones in CMYK mode.** But you could alternatively watch the CMYK-equivalent numbers in the Info palette while you are correcting in RGB mode. This is a little trickier where skin tones are concerned, but since you can preserve more colors with RGB than CMYK, it may be the best mode to use in the master file when preserving colors is a high priority.

- **In Lab, you can often easily change red objects to green or blue objects to yellow, and vice versa, by inverting the curves in the a and b channels.** You can also make colors in low-saturation images pop by steepening the curves in the a and b channels. An interesting test is to compare this technique to using Hue/Saturation to saturate colors.

- **If you want to use some color channels in CMYK mode while you are correcting or retouching in RGB or Lab without losing colors in your image by converting to CMYK, you can save a layer as a new image and change the new image to CMYK.** Then you can work on a CMYK channel in the new image, use it to help you make a selection, then save the active selection into the original open image. You can also copy what you need from a channel in the new CMYK image and paste it into the original image file. See Chapter 9 for more information.

- **To copy a layer to a new image, select the layer and choose Layer ➪ Duplicate Layer ➪ Document: New ➪ OK.**

- **To copy a flattened version of the image to a new file, you could first create a new layer that contains a flattened version of the image:** Click the top layer in the Layers palette, make sure the layers you want to include are visible, and press Shift+Ctrl+Alt (Shift+Option+⌘ on a Mac). That copies a flattened version to a new layer above the active layer.

Setting colors that should be neutral to neutral

Change any or all of the following areas that you believe should be neutral to neutral:

- The darkest point (black point)
- The middle-value point (gray point)
- The lightest point (white point)

Curves eyedroppers and curves are the methods of choice for many people when setting colors in an image to the neutral colors they should be. But there's no harm in trying the Auto Color Correction button or commands first to see if they will do a good job in a particular image. Setting the white point and black point may also improve contrast in an image.

Setting neutrals with Auto Color

You can use the Auto button in Levels or Curves or the Auto Color Correction commands as a quick way to attempt to correct color and improve contrast and tonal range. If you like the result, you can keep the changes, if you don't, you can undo and work with curves to have more control over the process. Both of these methods use either some or all of the Auto Color Correction Options settings that can be accessed by clicking the Options button in Levels or Curves.

Using the Auto button to apply the Auto Color Correction Options settings that are current at a given time can be done in either of the following ways:

- Click the Auto button in Levels or Curves.
- Click the Options button in Levels or Curves, click OK, then click the OK button in the Levels or Curves dialog box.

To use the Auto Color Correction commands, choose one or more of these commands:

- Image ➪ Adjustments ➪ Auto Levels
- Image ➪ Adjustments ➪ Auto Contrast
- Image ➪ Adjustments ➪ Auto Color

The Auto commands use some of the Auto Color Correction Options settings. However, instead of using the settings that are shown when the Options button is clicked, each of these Auto commands uses its own personalized version of the settings.

CROSS-REF See Chapter 9 for more information about setting the Auto Color Correction Options.

Setting neutrals with curves

You can use curves to help color-correct an image by moving the composite or individual channel curves and/or by using the Curves eyedroppers.

The Curves eyedroppers can be used to help you change what should be neutral colors in an image to neutral colors and set the lightest and darkest points in an image to the values they should be. Figure 15.3 shows the Curves eyedroppers. When you click on an area of an image with a Curves eyedropper, it changes the color of the point you click on, and the remaining colors in the image adjust proportionally.

If you've clicked on an area that really is supposed to be neutral, hopefully it removes an overall undesirable color cast, or color tint, in the image. The White Point eyedropper is typically used to set what should be the lightest neutral white in your image that still should contain some detail. The Black Point eyedropper is typically used to set what should be the darkest neutral black in your image that still should contain some detail.

FIGURE 15.3

The Curves eyedroppers can be used to set areas of color that should be neutral to neutral, which may remove an overall undesirable color cast.

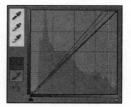

You can set the White Point and Black Point eyedroppers to be certain colors by double-clicking them and entering the desired color numbers into one of the modes in the Color Picker (RGB, CMYK, and so on). You don't set the Gray Point eyedropper to a certain color; it just changes whatever mid-range value you click on to a neutral color.

TIP You can use the Eyedropper tool (I key) plus keyboard shortcuts to set points on a curve that correspond to areas in an image. To set a point on a single curve, make that curve active in a Curves adjustment layer dialog box, and Ctrl+click/⌘+click on the part of the image you want the curve to affect. To set a point on all the individual channel's curves at once, Shift+Ctrl+click/Shift+⌘+click on the image.

When you are color-correcting and using the Curves eyedroppers to set neutral areas, the white point and black point should be set to a neutral or near-neutral color. It's not usually critical to make the colors exactly neutral. If you are using color management, color mode conversions may alter the numbers a little anyway, and often you won't be absolutely sure that a particular area in an image is supposed to be exactly neutral.

For example, if your white point in the image is in a white shirt that is lit by a sunset, that color isn't really supposed to be neutral. In that case, you may want to try increasing the yellow and maybe the magenta numbers a little in the white point to add a little yellow-orange that the sunset light adds to the white shirt.

A good way to start color-correcting an image is to follow these steps to change neutral areas to neutral:

1. **Set the White Point and Black Point eyedroppers in a Curves adjustment layer dialog box to the neutral values you want the lightest and darkest point in your image to become.** See the earlier sidebar, "Color Number Guidelines" for suggested values.

2. **Examine the image to find any areas you think should be the darkest neutral black (such as the black rim of a pair of eyeglasses), a midtone neutral gray (such as a medium-value silver piece of metal), or the lightest neutral white area (such as the lightest part of a white shirt).**

   Neutral means that a "color" is either black, white, or gray, with no color tint. The black point and white points should be areas in which you want to keep at least a little detail — not a small area that would logically be solid black or white. Very bright white reflections on metal (specular highlights) should often be solid white with no detail at all, so you wouldn't click on an area like that.

3. **Try changing the lightest and darkest areas you find to the neutral colors you think they should be by clicking on them with the White Point and Black Point eyedroppers in Curves or Levels.** You can click on a mid-range tone that you think should be neutral with the Gray Point eyedropper. If a change improves the image, keep it. If not, undo the action and try a different area, or choose not to set one or more of the three areas to neutral. Figure 15.4 shows an image that has been color-corrected by setting neutrals with the Curves eyedroppers.

After you try the Curves eyedroppers, one way to tweak colors and their numbers is by adjusting the curves of individual channels. You can also manually adjust individual curves to set neutrals instead of using the Curves eyedroppers.

Figure 15.5 shows the adjustments to the individual curves that corrected the image from Figure 15.4. These curves adjustments were made by setting the eyedroppers and clicking in the image with them, but the same curves adjustments can be made by dragging the curves manually.

FIGURE 15.4

You can often color-correct an image by setting colors that should be neutral to neutral with the Curves eyedroppers. This figure shows the before and after image and the areas that were clicked on with the Curves eyedroppers.

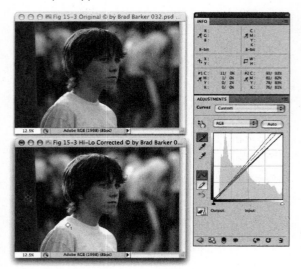

FIGURE 15.5

The individual channels' curve adjustments that corrected the image shown in Figure 15.4

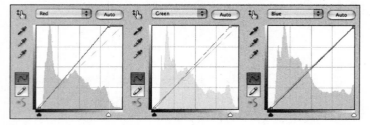

NEW FEATURE   You can select the hand-and-double-arrow symbol near the top left of a Curves adjustment layer dialog box, then simply drag in the image to simultaneously add a point to a curve and move the curve. This affects the individual curve that is active in the Curves adjustment layer dialog box.

> **TIP** To remove a point from a curve, drag the point off the curve grid. To reset the curve, including all its individual channel's curves, to the way it was before any changes were made to it, click the Reset button (the single arrow circle next to trashcan symbol) in the Curves adjustment layer dialog box.

Adjusting memory colors

Sometimes setting neutrals in an image doesn't completely remove an undesirable color cast, and sometimes there are no areas in the image that are supposed to be neutral. In these cases, you can try adjusting any known color areas in an image to the known colors' numbers.

Known colors or memory colors are colors that you remember to apply to certain things. For example, you know that on a sunny clear day, the sky is blue. So if there is blue sky in the image, you can check to see if the blue sky has color numbers that fit within the guidelines for blue and make adjustments, if necessary. Setting memory colors to the numbers they should be may remove a color cast. See the earlier sidebar, "Color Number Guidelines," for suggested color numbers for memory colors and for neutrals, including white points and black points.

> **TIP** If you are happy with the luminosity, or light and dark qualities, in an image and only want to adjust the color, apply the Color or Hue blending mode to an adjustment layer in the pull-down menu near the top of the Layers palette so that it only affects color or hue. Adjusting only the color channels of an image that is in Lab color mode also preserves the luminosity of an image.

Find the Lightest and Darkest Points

Use the Preview of the Image ⇨ Adjustments ⇨ Threshold command to find the lightest and darkest points in an image. When you choose the command, make sure Preview is checked and drag its slider all the way toward the left side until there is just a little black showing in the image window (the darkest area in the image) and toward the right until there is just a little white showing in the image window (the lightest area in the image).

With the Threshold box active, Ctrl+click/⌘+click with the Eyedropper tool in each of these areas in the image window to set a color sampler so you can remember where these areas are later. The samplers will be visible when you have the Eyedropper tool or Color Sampler tool active. Then click the Cancel button to exit the Threshold command.

Adjusting memory colors with Curves

You can adjust memory colors in an image by moving curves to make color numbers what they should be (see Figure 15.6). If you place color samplers in the image, you will be able to see the color numbers in the Info palette as you change them. As you gain more experience, you might choose not to set color samplers, and you may want to just check the color numbers periodically with the Eyedropper tool.

FIGURE 15.6

Individual channels' curves in Lab, RGB, and CMYK color modes and the directions you need to move the curves in order to add more of a certain color

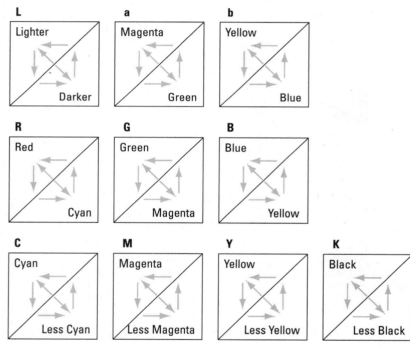

Once you are familiar with how your calibrated monitor displays color, you may also be able to rely somewhat on the color you see on your monitor. But it's always a good idea to at least double-check final color by checking color numbers.

If you don't have this chart handy, you can do a temporary drastic move with a curve to see which color that move adds. When finished, you can simply drag that point off the curve to start over. Figure 15.7 shows an image with a memory color that has been adjusted with a curve and the before-and-after color numbers involved.

Using Hue/Saturation to adjust memory colors

You can also use a Hue/Saturation adjustment layer to alter colors and their numbers.

Figure 15.8 shows an image that has had its overall hue color changed, using a Hue/Saturation adjustment layer, and the color numbers involved.

The before-and-after of an image, with a memory color that has been adjusted with curves, and the before-and-after color numbers involved

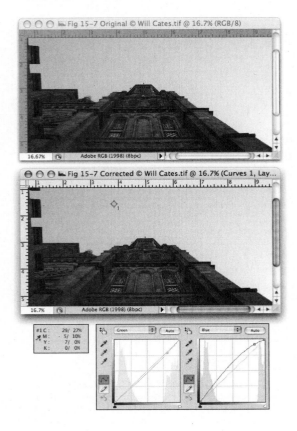

FIGURE 15.8

The overall hue of an image can be changed with a Hue/Saturation adjustment layer.

Color Changes

In addition to correcting an image's color, you may want to simply change the colors of parts of an image or even the entire image. There are many ways to accomplish this in Photoshop. It's a good idea to know about a lot of different ways to change color because some methods work much better than others, depending on the content of the image.

The more you know about various ways to change color, and the more you practice the techniques, the better you will become at choosing the best method for a particular color-change task. This can save you lots of time, so it's well worth the effort . . . and it's kind of fun, too!

CROSS-REF You can target a certain area of an image with an adjustment layer by painting or filling a selection with white, gray, or black on its layer mask. White causes the adjustment to show, gray causes it to partially show, and black hides the adjustment. See Chapter 8 for more about masks. See Chapter 10 for more about making selections.

There may be times when you want to change color for subjective rather than corrective reasons. You can change the color of specific parts of an image, make the overall colors in one image match the overall colors in another image, remove full color and make the entire image consist of different tones of the same color, or change the image so that it's made up of multiple custom colors, such as in a sepia-tone, monotone, duotone, tritone, or quadtone effect. These effects will be discussed in this section, and you can see examples of them in the color section of this book.

You may also want to use color in a more artistic way to make some values in an image one color, and other values in an image a different color; for example, make the highlights one color and the shadows a second color. Gradients can be applied to make color gradually fade from one color to another, and photo filters can be applied to introduce a color cast, such as applying a warm color cast to emulate sunset lighting.

As discussed in the previous section, you can change colors in an image by manipulating curves. This section discusses some specific curves techniques and many additional techniques that you can use to manipulate color.

Change colors by sampling and painting

You can change colors in specific areas in an image by sampling a color (Alt+click/Option+click a color in the image window with the Brush tool) or choosing a color in Swatches or the Color Picker and painting on a new layer that is set to the Color or Hue blending mode. Color blending mode preserves much of the tonal range in the image and tints the colored and neutral areas; Hue preserves even more of the tonal range and tints colored areas, but won't change the color of neutral areas.

You can also set the brush itself to the Color or Hue blending mode in its Options Bar and paint directly on the target layer. But when you paint directly on the target layer, you won't have the flexibility to adjust opacity or easily change color later like you do if you put the color on a separate layer. Figure 15.9 shows an image with color that has been changed by sampling color in another area and painting onto a separate layer that is set to Color blending mode.

Changing a darker color to a lighter color

If you want to change the color of a dark object to a much lighter color or vice versa, it's a little trickier because you may also need to change the luminosity of the object so that the color change looks realistic.

You can lighten or darken the object by using one of the following:

- Curves (you may need a layer mask)
- Screen or Multiply blending mode on a duplicate layer (you may need a layer mask)
- Selective Color adjustment-layer changes to target a darker color and lighten it by reducing the appropriate CMYK color(s)

To change the color of the object, you might want to try one or more of the following:

- Target and change the color by using a Hue/Saturation adjustment layer
- Put the new color on a Hue-blending-mode layer
- Put the new color on a Color-blending-mode layer

Each of these methods that changes the luminosity and color works in different ways, and the image content determines which way works best.

FIGURE 15.9

Areas of color can be changed by painting with a sample of the desired color onto a layer set to Color blending mode. This technique preserves most of the original luminosity. You can then adjust the opacity of the color layer, if necessary.

Changing colors with adjustment layers

You can adjust any of the layers' opacities until you get the desired result. Figure 15.10 shows a darker color that has been changed to a lighter color and the layers that were used to accomplish the change. This layered file is on the book's CD if you would like to examine it in more detail.

CROSS-REF You can make an adjustment layer affect only the layer below it by Alt+clicking/ Option+clicking in the Layers palette between the adjustment layer and the layer below it to put the layers into a clipping group. For more about clipping groups and clipping masks, see Chapter 8.

TIP Keep in mind that you can use masks on adjustment layers to target certain areas, apply the Color or Hue blending mode to a Curves adjustment layer so that it will affect only color and not luminosity, and target only one layer by putting the layer and the adjustment layer above it into a clipping group (Alt+click between the two layers). You also can adjust the opacity of adjustment layers to reduce their effect.

FIGURE 15.10

A darker color that has been changed to a lighter color and the layers that have been used to make the change

Change colors with a Hue/Saturation adjustment layer

You can use a Hue/Saturation adjustment layer to change the hue or saturation of the overall image or target any of the following colors: reds, yellows, greens, cyans, blues, and magentas. For example, if a photo subject's face has some sunburned areas that you want to deemphasize, you can use Hue/Saturation to target the reds and reduce their saturation a little. That may eliminate the need to make a selection or mask to target the red areas.

 TIP If you want to affect only the color in an image and preserve the existing luminosity, apply the Color or Hue blending mode to an adjustment layer from the pull-down menu near the top of the Layers palette so that the adjustment only affects color or hue. You can also adjust the opacity of adjustment layers to reduce their effect.

You can also use Hue/Saturation to colorize, or give a sepia-tone effect to, an image. Colorizing an image makes it look as though it is being reproduced with black plus one other color — like a tinted black-and-white photo. Hue/Saturation won't actually cause the color to be made up of only two colors, it will just give that appearance.

To create a sepia-tone image that is made up of only two colors, like brown and black, you need to create a duotone. Figure 15.11 shows a targeted color being changed by a Hue/Saturation adjustment layer, and Figure 15.12 shows an image that has been colorized with Hue/Saturation.

NOTE You can also saturate and desaturate areas in an image by using the Sponge tool set to Saturate or Desaturate in the Options Bar. The Sponge tool lets you use brushes to paint saturation in certain areas.

FIGURE 15.11

Changing a targeted color with Hue/Saturation, and the Hue/Saturation settings that were used

FIGURE 15.12

Creating a sepia-tone effect (like a black-and-white photo tinted with one color) with Hue/Saturation, and the Hue/Saturation settings that were used. This gives the appearance that the image is made up of only black and one other color (to create an image that looks tinted and is actually made up of two colors, you need to change it to Duotone mode).

Change colors with a Photo Filter adjustment layer

You can use a Photo Filter adjustment layer to add effects that look similar to using color filters with a camera. For example, if you want a photo to look warmer, like it was taken during a sunset, you can use one of the warming Photo Filters.

Change colors with a Selective Color adjustment layer

With a Selective Color adjustment layer, you can change the amount of cyan, magenta, yellow, and black within certain colors in an image: reds, yellows, greens, cyans, blues, magentas, whites, neutrals, and blacks. Selective Color can be used to target these colors even if the image is not in CMYK mode. Figure 15.13 shows a color that has been changed with Selective Color.

FIGURE 15.13

Changing a targeted color with a Selective Color adjustment layer, and the Selective Color settings that were used

Change colors with a Black and White adjustment layer

You can use a Black and White adjustment layer to make an image look black and white or grayscale. (For a true grayscale image that prints with just one color, you must change the image to Grayscale mode.) Black and White allows you to specify with sliders how light or dark the resulting grayscale values are for various original-colored areas. This gives you much more control over the distribution of luminosity than you have when you simply change an image to Grayscale mode or when you use a Channel Mixer adjustment layer to make the image look grayscale.

If you want part of the image to remain in color, paint black on the layer mask on the Black and White adjustment layer to hide part of the black and white. Note that if part of the image is to be in color, the image must remain in one of the color modes, not Grayscale mode.

You can also create a sepia-tone effect with a Black and White adjustment layer by checking the Tint box and clicking in the color box next to Tint and choosing a color for the tint. If you use a Black and White adjustment layer to tint an image, the image must remain in a color mode such as RGB or CMYK. To make a sepia-tone that will print with just two colors on a press, you must convert the image to Duotone mode and assign two ink colors in the Duotone Options dialog box.

Figure 15.14 shows an image that has been changed to appear as a grayscale image with a Black and White adjustment layer. Part of the image has been left in color by using a layer mask on the adjustment layer.

FIGURE 15.14

This image has been changed to appear as a grayscale image with a Black and White adjustment layer, but part of the image has been left in color by using a layer mask on the adjustment layer.

Change colors with the Replace Color command

The Replace Color command (Image ➪ Adjustments ➪ Replace Color) allows you to select a color that you want to change by sampling it in the image window with the Eyedropper tools that you access in the Replace Color dialog box. There is an Eyedropper tool (to click on the initial sample), an Add to Sample eyedropper tool, and a Subtract from Sample eyedropper tool in the dialog box. You can sample a color and adjust the sampled area by clicking in the image window or in the

Replace Color's black-and-white preview of the selected color (white represents the selected area) with the appropriate Eyedropper tool.

Once you have selected a majority of the targeted area, it's sometimes easier to add to or subtract from the sample by clicking in the preview area. The Fuzziness slider can be used to expand or contract the selected area while at the same time softening up the edges of the selected area.

An advantage of the Replace Color command is that after you have selected the targeted color, you can watch the color change and continue to adjust it while the dialog box is still active. You can change the color by dragging the Hue and Saturation sliders or by clicking in the Result color box and choosing a specific color in the Color Picker. With the Color Picker open, you can alternatively choose a color by clicking in the image window or in the Swatches palette. You can also resample the selected area or readjust the Fuzziness slider while the dialog box is open, even after you have selected a new result color.

The Lightness slider can be used to lighten or darken the targeted area, if necessary. If you want to change the luminosity while preserving more contrast, however, you may want to use curves or another method to lighten or darken the targeted area. Figure 15.15 shows a color that has been changed with the Replace Color command.

TIP Since there is no Replace Color adjustment layer available, the color change you make with the command is not easily changeable. Therefore, it's a good idea to use the command on a duplicate layer. That way, you at least can apply blending modes, reduce opacity, or mask parts of the layer, if necessary.

Change colors with the Color Replacement tool

You can paint on an area in an image to change its color to a new color (the foreground color). The Color Replacement tool may be hidden behind the Brush or Pencil tool. It gives the advantage of using a brush to paint with, which means you can use a very large or a very small brush or a hard-edged or soft-edged brush. It's also smarter than a regular brush — it can find and affect areas of similar color while you paint, sort of like the Magic Wand tool. You can even try making the brush larger than the object you are working on, and the tool may be able to find and change all the color you want to target with one click. Figure 15.16 shows a color that has been changed with the Color Replacement tool.

The options in the Options Bar for the Color Replacement tool can have a dramatic effect on how the tool selects and changes color:

- **Mode.** If you want to change the color of an area you paint on, choose Color or Hue. Color mode causes the tool to change existing color to the foreground color and tints any neutral areas with the new color, while attempting to preserve some of the original luminosity of the targeted area. Hue causes the tool to change existing color to the foreground color but it won't change neutral areas; so Hue preserves more of the original luminosity.

- **Sampling buttons.**
  - **Continuous:** Continuously samples, or selects, the color to be changed as you paint — it selects and changes whatever color is directly below the cross-hairs in the Color

Replacement tool cursor. If you don't want a color to be changed, don't let the cross-hairs move over it.

- **Once:** Samples only the color that the Color Replacement tool cross-hairs initially fall on, when you first click the mouse button down to drag-and-paint with the brush.

- **Background Swatch:** Causes the Color Replacement tool to change only the color that is the same as the background swatch color.

- **Limits.**

  - **Contiguous:** Causes the Color Replacement tool to find and affect only similar colors that are adjacent to each other.

  - **Find Edges:** Causes the Color Replacement tool to find the edges where a similar color ends and affects only the areas within the edges.

  - **Discontiguous:** Causes the Color Replacement tool to find and affect similar colors throughout the image, not just similar colors that are adjacent to each other.

- **Tolerance.** A higher tolerance causes the Color Replacement tool to find and affect a wider range of similar colors; a lower tolerance affects a smaller range of similar colors.

- **Anti-Alias.** Checking this option causes the edges of the new color to blend a tiny bit with adjacent colors to avoid a jagged-edge appearance where the new color meets adjacent colors.

FIGURE 15.15

Using the Replace Color command to change a color in an image. It gives you more flexibility if you use the command on a duplicate layer because you can apply blending modes, change opacity, or hide parts of the layer with masks.

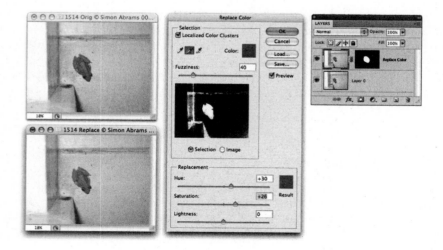

FIGURE 15.16

A color has been changed to the foreground color by painting on it with the Color Replacement tool.

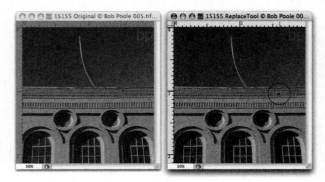

> **TIP** If you need more flexibility, you can use the Color Replacement tool on a duplicate layer. Then you can apply blending modes, reduce opacity, or mask parts of the layer, if necessary.

Change colors with filled selections or Fill layers

You can fill a selection with a color on a new layer to change the color of the visible layers below it by setting the layer to Color or Hue blending mode (you can also experiment with other blending modes). To fill a selection, choose Edit ➪ Fill or press Alt+Delete /Option+Delete to fill with the foreground color, or press Ctrl+Delete/⌘+Delete to fill with the background color. Putting color on a separate layer gives you the flexibility of reducing the layer's opacity or masking parts of the layer.

Another way to change color by putting it on a separate layer is to use a Solid Color Fill layer. The advantage of a Fill layer is that you can change the color quickly without selecting and filling. When you double-click the layer thumbnail of a Fill layer, it opens the Color Picker. Then you can change the color with the Color Picker or by clicking a swatch or another color in the image while the Color Picker is open. You can mask parts of a Fill layer, change the layer's opacity, or apply a blending mode, if necessary.

To make a Solid Color Fill layer, click the Create a new fill or adjustment layer button (the half-black, half-white circle symbol) at the bottom of the Layers palette and choose Solid Color. Figure 15.17 shows a color change made with a Fill layer.

FIGURE 15.17

This figure shows a color change made with a Fill layer that is set to Color blending mode and has a layer mask.

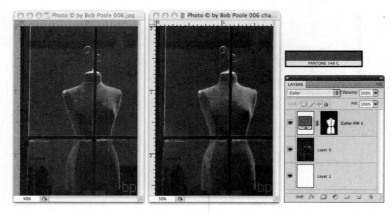

Change colors with a Color Overlay style

Changing color with a Color Overlay style gives you the advantage of being able to save a particular color as part of a style and apply it to the active layer by simply clicking on the layer style in the Styles palette. If you use the same color and drop shadow on the text layers in multiple brochures, for example, you can apply the color and shadow to the text by clicking on the style. That eliminates the steps of having to make sure you select exactly the right color and then applying the drop shadow.

You can change the color itself, the opacity, and the blending mode of the color in the Layer Style dialog box, but you can't mask a layer style directly. For that reason, applying color with a Color Overlay style can be a convenient method if the object is already separate from its background (the layer is transparent except for the object or text that is to be colored). The color applies to all the pixels on the layer and not to any transparent areas on the layer.

To apply color with a Color Overlay style, activate the layer that contains the object whose color you want to change, then click the Add a layer style button (the *fx* symbol) at the bottom of the Layers palette and choose Color Overlay. Click the Set color of overlay check box in the Color Overlay options and select the new color. You can also set the blending mode and opacity of the color in the Color Overlay options (these affect how the color interacts with the pixels on the layer, not how the entire layer interacts with the layers below it).

If you want to save the layer style that contains the Color Overlay, click the New Style button in the Layer Style dialog box, give the style a name, and click OK. Figure 15.18 shows color that has been added with a Color Overlay layer style.

CROSS-REF For more about layer styles, see Chapter 8.

FIGURE 15.18

Color has been added with a Color Overlay layer style.

Change colors with gradients

You can add a colored gradient to a new layer to change the color of layers below it. The layer's blending mode or opacity can be changed, and a layer mask can be used to hide parts of the layer, if necessary.

Using the Gradient Editor

To create a gradient on an active new layer:

1. **Select the Gradient tool (it may be hidden behind the Paint Bucket tool).**

2. **Click in the Click to edit the gradient check box near the left side of the Options Bar to bring up the Gradient Editor dialog box (see Figure 15.19).**

3. **The horizontal bar of color in the Gradient Type section shows the colors in the currently selected gradient.** The crayon-shaped opacity stops on top of the bar determine the opacity of each section of the gradient. The color stops on the bottom of the bar determine the colors in the gradient. To change opacity or color, click on the appropriate stop and make the changes. To add opacity or color stops, click in a blank area just above or below the bar.

   To remove opacity or color stops, drag them out of the Gradient Editor dialog box. If you want transparency on one side of your gradient, start by clicking the foreground to transparent gradient preset thumbnail, or click on an opacity stop and change it to 0 percent opacity.

4. **To save the gradient you created, type a name into the Name box and click the New button.** The gradient thumbnail then displays in the Presets section of the Gradient Editor. There is not a Gradients palette, but you can select saved gradient presets in the Gradient Editor.

5. **Click OK.**

6. **In the Options Bar, select the button that represents the shape you want the gradient to be (linear, radial, angle, reflected, diamond).**

FIGURE 15.19

The Gradient Editor dialog box

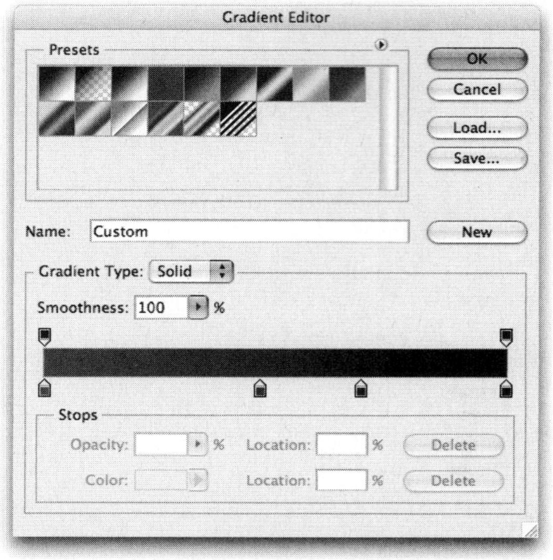

7. **Drag in the image window to apply the gradient.** Dragging a shorter or longer line, dragging in different parts of the image, or dragging in different directions will make the gradient look different. You can drag, undo, and drag again if you want to try different gradient applications.

8. **If you need to, you can apply a blending mode, such as Color, to the gradient layer, reduce its opacity, or add a layer mask.**

Figure 15.20 shows an image whose color has been changed with a gradient layer.

CROSS-REF   **For more information about saved gradients and how to use Presets, see Chapter 2.**

Change colors with Gradient Map

You can change colors in an image with a Gradient Map adjustment layer, which can be used to give an image a special-effect look. Gradient Map replaces the tones in an image with the colors in a gradient you choose — each color is applied to the parts of the image that have values similar to the values of the color. In other words, colors in the gradient are *mapped* to values in the image. For example, a gradient that contains dark purple and light yellow would cause the darker areas in an image to become purple and the lighter areas in the image to become yellow.

Gradient Map creates smooth transitions between the colors. You can reverse which tones the colors are applied to by checking Reverse in the Gradient Map dialog box in the Adjustments palette. Figure 15.21 shows an image with a Gradient Map adjustment layer applied.

FIGURE 15.20

An image whose color has been changed with a gradient layer

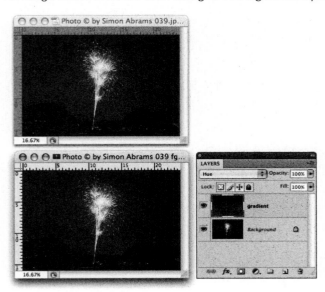

FIGURE 15.21

This image has been changed so that darker areas are made up of purple and lighter areas are made up of yellow by using a Gradient Map adjustment layer.

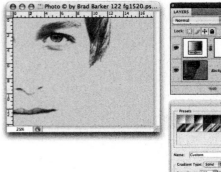

Change colors with the Posterize command

Like a Gradient Map adjustment layer, the Posterize command (Image ➪ Adjustments ➪ Posterize) can be used to give an image a special-effect look. Posterize reduces the number of colors in an image according to where you drag the Posterize slider, and the colors it uses are similar to and correspond to the colors in the image. Posterize then causes the image to be made up of solid-colored areas of the reduced number of colors.

Unlike Gradient Map, the transitions between the colors in Posterize are not smooth, and since Posterize is not available as an adjustment layer, you can't easily change its settings. Using Posterize on a duplicate layer gives you a little more flexibility.

For example, if you wanted Posterize to affect only color and you wanted the transitions to be smoother, you could set the Posterized duplicate layer to Color blending mode and use one of the Blur filters to blur it. This can give an image a glowing, otherworldly look. You can also use a layer mask to mask part of the effect on a duplicate layer.

Figure 15.22 shows a Posterized image and one on a duplicate layer that has the Color blending mode and a blur applied.

Change colors with Duotone mode

You can cause an image to be made up of just one color or an overall mixture of two, three, or four colors by using Duotone mode and specifying monotone, duotone, tritone, or quadtone. You can use special colors to make up the image, if you like, such as Pantone spot colors that can be used when printing on a printing press. If you aren't familiar with using spot colors, consult your printer about associated printing costs. Figure 15.23 shows an original image and a duotone version of the same image.

To create a duotone:

1. **Choose Image ➪ Mode ➪ Grayscale.**

2. **Choose Image ➪ Mode ➪ Duotone.**

3. **In the Duotone dialog box in the Type menu, choose monotone, duotone, tritone, or quadtone.**

4. **For each ink in the Duotone Options dialog box, click on the square color box and specify a color in the Select Ink Color dialog box.** You can choose any colors to create the appearance of a duotone and then convert the image to the appropriate color mode. But if you want to create a true duotone that will print with the specific duotone colors on press, you must choose colors that are used for printing and leave the image in Duotone mode.

   To choose a Pantone color, click the Color Libraries button in the Select Ink Color dialog box. In the Color Libraries box, select a Pantone color, then, if you want to select a color with the Color Picker, click the Picker button. When finished selecting a color, click OK.

   For fully saturated-looking colors when the duotone is printed, assign inks from the darkest (first ink) to lightest (last ink). You can alternatively choose one of the many duotone presets from the Preset menu instead of specifying your own choice of inks.

FIGURE 15.22

An image whose color has been changed with the Posterize command, and another version of the Posterized image on a duplicate layer with a blur and the Color blending mode

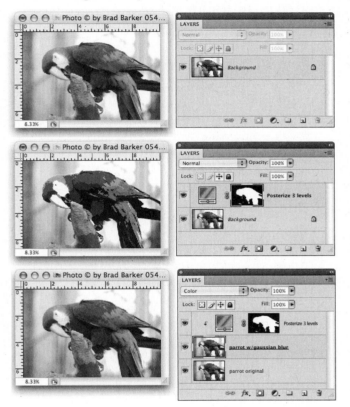

5. **For each ink in the Duotone Options dialog box, click on the square box with the diagonal line.** This brings up the Duotone Curve, where you can tell Photoshop how much, in percentages, of the color you want to use at each tone level.

   For example, if you want to use the color only in the shadows, you might put 0 percent in the 50 box and 100 percent in the 100 box. If you want the color used evenly throughout the image, which will be like giving the entire image a tint of the color, leave the numbers at the defaults: 0 percent in the 0 box and 100 percent in the 100 box.

There are special considerations when saving and printing duotones to make sure they reproduce with good quality. For more information about printing and saving duotones, see Photoshop Help.

FIGURE 15.23

An original image and a duotone version of the image, as well as the duotone settings
for the two Pantone ink colors used

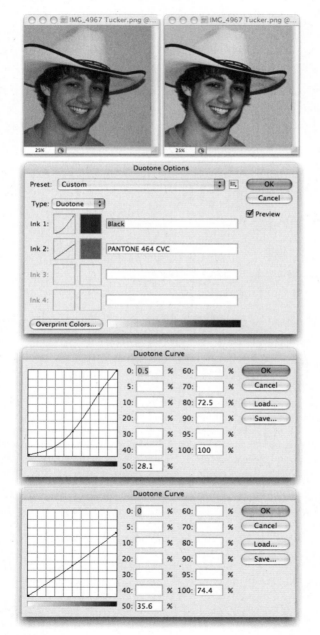

Change colors with Lab-mode curves

In Lab mode, the channels that contain color are completely separate from the colors that contain luminosity. Therefore, color changes can look more pure and can be made without affecting luminosity. Likewise, luminosity in Lab mode can be changed without affecting color.

One of the things Lab mode is particularly good at in certain situations is helping you to quickly change an object that is magenta or red to green and an object that is blue to yellow, and vice versa, especially if the object can be easily masked or if most of the other colors in the image are near-neutral.

To make these color changes, you invert the curve in the a or b channel, meaning you drag the top-right point down and the bottom-left point up. The a channel contains magenta and green and the b channel contains blue and yellow. Figure 15.24 shows an example of changing red to green by inverting the a channel's curve.

Lab mode is also good at being able to make use of the Blend-if sliders in layer Blending Options to restrict adjustments to certain colors or values in an image. This may help you avoid masking or may make masking easier. You can access Blending Options by double-clicking the blank area to the right of a Curves adjustment layer's name. Near the bottom of the Blending Options dialog box, you'll see "Blend if:" then a Channel pull-down menu, and below that "This Layer:" and sliders, and "Underlying Layer:" and sliders.

Blend (apply) the colors that are specified by this adjustment layer and are in the channel selected in the pull-down menu with the colors in the underlying layer, in the way that is specified by this layer's blending mode, only if the colors in This Layer that are between the sliders overlap the colors that are between the sliders of the Underlying Layer.

Whew.

Anyway, an example would be that if you adjust a curve in channel a to change red to green but that adjustment undesirably changes some non-red areas to green, you can use Blend-if to tell Photoshop to restrict the change to the red areas. Figure 15.25 shows an example of how the Blend-if sliders can be used to restrict changes to certain areas.

Lab mode can be used to bring more colors into an image that doesn't have a lot of color variety. You can do this by steepening the a and b channels' curves. If the change is too drastic, you can reduce the opacity of the Curves adjustment layer. Figure 15.26 shows an example of increasing color variety by steepening the a and b curves.

FIGURE 15.24

Changing red to green by inverting the a channel's curve in an Lab-mode image

FIGURE 15.25

The Blend-if sliders can restrict changes to certain colors and values in an image.

FIGURE 15.26

Increasing color variety in an image by steepening the a and b curves in an Lab-mode image

Change colors with the Match Color command

You can use the Match Color command to make the colors in one image similar to the colors in another image. This can be helpful if you have two photos of the same subject, but you need to fix the undesirable color cast in one of the photos. Another use of Match Color could be to make multiple photos in a design be made up of the same colors so the colors will coordinate.

To match the color in two images:

1. **Make sure that both the image you want to change and the image that contains the colors you want to match are open, and make sure the image you want to change is the active image.**

2. **Choose Image ⇨ Adjustments ⇨ Match Color.**

3. **In the Match Color dialog box's Source pull-down menu, select the name of the image that contains the colors you want to apply to the active image.**

4. **Adjust the Match Color settings as desired.** Luminance affects the brightness of the image, but you can maintain more contrast in the image by changing the brightness with a Curves adjustment layer. Color Intensity affects the saturation of the colors, and Fade can be used to bring back some of the original color. If you check Neutralize, Photoshop tries to guess which parts of the image should be neutral and it makes them neutral — sometimes this improves the image, and sometimes it doesn't.

You can also match colors in only a selected area in either the Source image or the Target image, or both, by selecting the area(s) and checking the appropriate Use Selection boxes in the Image Statistics area of the Match Color dialog box (see Figure 15.27).

FIGURE 15.27

The Match Color dialog box

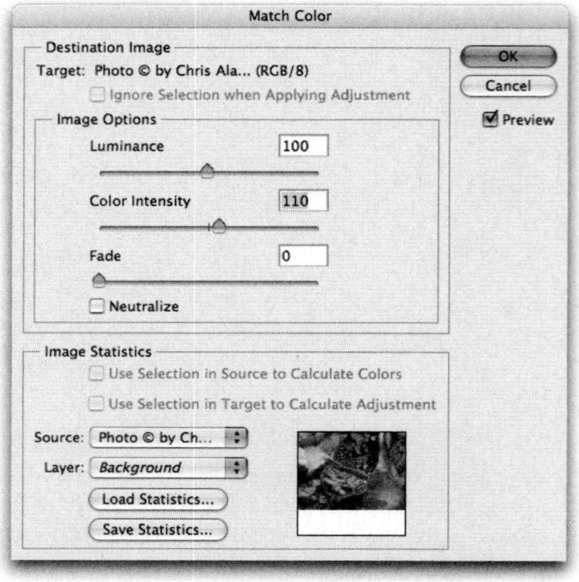

If you want to save an image's set of colors and how they are distributed in the image so you can apply the colors over and over again to other images, click the Save Statistics button. Save Statistics saves the colors of the active image in the location of your choice. If you want to apply the colors to another image, open the image and click the Load Statistics button in the Match Color dialog box, then find and select the color statistics you want to apply. In this situation, you won't select a Source image.

The colors will come from the loaded statistics. Figure 15.28 shows three images: one butterfly photo that has good color, another photo of the same butterfly that has a bad color cast, and a version of the second butterfly that shows how the cast was removed by matching the color of the first butterfly.

FIGURE 15.28

Three images: one butterfly photo that has good color, a photo of the same butterfly that has bad color, and a version of the second butterfly whose color was improved by matching the color of the first butterfly

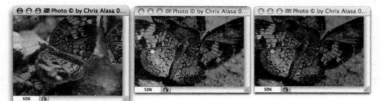

Color Number Guidelines

This section lists color numbers for memory colors, or typical color numbers for common image content. Keep in mind these are guidelines rather than absolutes.

Fleshtones

- RGB: R is greater than G is greater than B
- CMYK: Y is a little greater than or equal to M, and C is much less than Y or M (except in shadow areas)

Blues

- RGB: B is greater than G is greater than R
- CMYK: C is greater than M and there is much less or no Y

Greens

- RGB: G is higher than R and B
- CMYK: Y is greater than or equal to C and there is much less or no M

Yellows

- RGB: R is greater than G and there is much less or no B
- CMYK: Y is much higher than other colors; much less or no C; the more M, the more orange

Reds

- RGB: R is much greater than G and B
- CMYK: Y and M are high and roughly equal; much less or no C

Neutrals

- RGB: R, G, and B are equal
- CMYK: M is equal to Y; C is a little higher

Summary

This chapter described ways you can correct the color of images, change colors in images, and add colors to images. Following are key concepts:

- Some images have an undesirable color cast (an undesirable color tint) that needs to be corrected.

- Before you start color-correcting an image, it's a good idea to do the following:

  - Check the image size and resolution.

  - Consider working on a larger master file with preserved layers.

  - Think about correcting full-color images in RGB or Lab color mode.

  - Set Photoshop's Color Settings appropriately.

  - Create a soft-proof profile so you can proof the image on-screen as you work.

  - Calibrate your monitor.

- A good approach to color correction involves changing color numbers that represent the colors in an image to known color-number values (memory colors), such as those for neutral-colored areas, green foliage, blue sky, and flesh tones. When you change known colors to the values they should be, the other colors in the image often adjust proportionately to the correct colors.

- You can measure colors in an image by sampling them with the Eyedropper tool and/or the Color Sampler tool and observing the color numbers in the Info palette. Before-adjustments and after-adjustments numbers are separated by a slash in the Info palette.

- A common way to change color numbers is by using the White Point, Gray Point, and Black Point eyedroppers in a Curves adjustment layer dialog box to set neutral colors to what they should be and by adjusting the curves in a Curves adjustment layer to adjust any other known colors to the color numbers they should be. To refine colors, you can also use a Hue/Saturation adjustment layer. If you want to attempt an initial quick fix, you can try the Auto Color command.

- When you want to change colors in an image or add colors to an image — for reasons other than simply to correct color — Photoshop offers many ways to do this, including Curves, Hue/Saturation, Photo Filter, Selective Color, and Black and White adjustment layers. You can also paint colors with the brush tool, replace colors with the Replace Color command or the Color Replacement tool, add colors with Fill adjustment layers or with gradients, change color with a Color Overlay contained in a layer style, create special-effect colors with a Gradient Map adjustment layer or the Posterize command, or create images tinted with and made up of specific colors by using Duotone mode.

- The Color and Hue blending modes can be applied to layers or adjustment layers to make Photoshop use only the color or hue characteristics of a layer and not use any luminosity characteristics of the layer. This is useful when the luminosity appears as desired and you only want to change color.

Chapter 16

Transparency, Opacity, Silhouettes, and Image Collages

I f you've worked hard and trudged through the nuts and bolts of Photoshop, it's definitely time to start having some fun. You can make beautiful artistic imagery, as well as practical day-to-day images, by combining images into collages using various Photoshop techniques to change opacity and transparency, and creating crisp, clean silhouettes of people or objects. This is where you can really start putting together all the foundational Photoshop techniques you've learned and make stunning image combinations.

The techniques in this chapter make use of layers, layer masks, and selection methods, so if you aren't familiar with those aspects of Photoshop, you may want to review Chapters 9 and 10.

To begin with, I'd like to talk about some of the techniques you can use to make image objects look like they flow together: transparency, opacity, and silhouetting.

IN THIS CHAPTER

Transparency and opacity

Silhouetting

Combining images into a collage

Drawing the eye to certain areas

Transparency and Opacity

Transparency and opacity in image combinations can make image parts seem to gradually change from one object to another or just look like they are adjacent to one another. You can also make it appear as though smooth or hard-edged shapes are cut out of an image combination — like you might need to do at the bottom of a Web site banner graphic that contains multiple photos, for example. Another common use for transparency is simply knocking out the background behind people or objects, or silhouetting.

You can make smooth, hard-edged transitions or very gradual transitions between transparent and opaque areas. The transitions can be painted on in a random or flowing artistic way or they can be made in a very precise way that runs along the edge of an object.

You can use numerous methods and tools in Photoshop to make parts of images transparent or partially transparent. There are a few common good practices to use when you are doing this, though, and they give you a lot of flexibility when working with transparency and opacity.

First, it's a very good idea, and in many cases necessary, to put the objects in an image on their own separate layers. When an object is on its own layer, you can activate the layer in the Layers palette, and you will be working on the object that is on that layer. If all of your objects were on one layer, you would have to select an object and work within the selection, which would in most cases turn out to be a whole lot of trouble.

TIP   Dragging images from one document into another with the Move tool and selecting-and-copying in one image and pasting into another automatically puts the moved or pasted object on a separate layer.

NOTE   Objects on underlying layers show through a transparent or partially transparent object on an upper layer.

Second, use layer masks to hide parts of an object — make parts of it transparent or semi-transparent — rather than selecting and deleting or erasing parts of the object with the Eraser tool. Layer masks are very flexible because they make it possible to show some or all the hidden parts of your object again at any time you choose.

Making an image transparent

There are various ways to make an image transparent.

You can click on the layer in the Layers palette that contains the object to activate the layer. Then you can add a layer mask and add black or shades of gray to the layer mask to hide or partially hide parts of the object on the layer.

To add black or shades of gray, you can activate the layer mask thumbnail and paint in the image window with a hard-edged or soft-edged brush, or a custom-shaped brush. You can also make a hard-edged or soft-edged selection in the image window, and when the layer mask is active fill it with black or gray. To show parts of an object again, add white to the layer mask. Figure 16.1 shows a layer mask that is used to create transparency on one layer.

NOTE   You must change a background layer to a regular layer to add transparency or a layer mask to it (double-click the layer name "Background," then click OK).

Try adding a layer mask to a layer group in the Layers palette. The mask can be used to hide corresponding areas in all the layers contained in a group, rather than just one layer. Figure 16.3 shows a layer mask that is used to create transparency in a group of layers.

FIGURE 16.1

Transparency created on a layer with a layer mask, used to hide corresponding parts of an object on a layer. The layer mask is active, as indicated by the black border around it. A soft-edged brush was used to paint on the mask and make corresponding parts of the layer transparent.

FIGURE 16.2

Transparency created to make a custom border by painting on a layer mask with a custom-shaped brush and hiding the center portion of the pixels on the layer

You can also create transparency by reducing the opacity of the entire layer (see the menu at the top right of the Layers palette), as shown in Figure 16.4.

A blending mode can make the layer partially transparent (and adds other special effects); select a blending mode from the menu at the top left of the Layers palette. The default blending mode is Normal. Some commonly used blending modes are Multiply, Luminosity, and Screen. For more about blending modes, see Chapter 9. Figure 16.5 shows transparency created by assigning a blending mode to a layer.

Another method for making an image transparent is to make a selection and press Delete or the backspace key, or paint with the Eraser tool. Other methods are more flexible than these methods, however. For example, you can make a new layer and create a gradient with the Gradient tool and Gradient Editor that contains transparency. Figure 16.6 shows a gradient with transparency.

FIGURE 16.3

Transparency created in a group of layers with a layer mask. This layer mask hides the same area in all the layers in the group. Black was added to the mask by making a rectangular selection with the Rectangular Marquee tool and filling it with black.

FIGURE 16.4

Transparency created on a layer by reducing its opacity in the Layers palette.

FIGURE 16.5

Transparency created by applying the Multiply blending mode to the layer in the Layers palette.

You can also make a shape layer that has filled shapes and transparent areas. See Chapter 13 for information about shape layers. Figure 16.7 shows a shape layer that has transparency.

Try bringing an image that contains transparency into the Photoshop document from another Photoshop document or another application, such as Adobe Illustrator. The white background area and overlapping shapes that are set to Exclude Overlapping Shape Areas in Illustrator come into Photoshop as transparency unless you flatten the object or rasterize it.

FIGURE 16.6

A gradient with transparency on a layer. The layer underneath shows through the transparent area.

FIGURE 16.7

A shape layer that has transparency

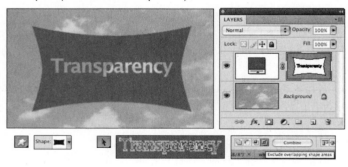

For example, you can save the object from Illustrator as an Illustrator file or export it as a PSD file and paste or place it in Photoshop, and it maintains transparent areas.

Figure 16.8 shows an Illustrator file that has been placed in Photoshop and contains transparency.

Placing an Illustrator file that contains transparency into a Photoshop document.

Creating and painting on layer masks

To make a layer mask, activate a layer and click the layer mask button at the bottom of the Layers palette.

You must change a background layer to a regular layer to add transparency or a layer mask to it (double-click the layer name "Background," then click OK).

To hide parts of an object on a layer, click on the layer mask to activate it and paint with black or shades of gray in the image window. To reveal hidden parts of an object, do the same, except paint with white.

To set up a brush to paint with black, choose the Brush tool and make the foreground color black. To paint with gray, choose a reduced opacity in the Options Bar for the brush. (Shortcut: Press a number key, for example, 2, for 20 percent opacity.) To paint with white, make white the foreground color.

- Press the D key to make the foreground color black and the background color white. Press the X key to switch the colors.
- Press one of the bracket keys to change the size of a brush.
- Press the Shift key plus a bracket key to change the hardness/softness of the brush edges. Watch the brush edges change in the Options Bar's Brush menu. (Shift+clicking a bracket key four times makes the brush edge its maximum hardness or softness.)

CROSS-REF See Chapter 9 for more information about layers and layer masks.

Silhouetting

Let's say you want to precisely silhouette a photo of a person or object. That makes things a little trickier. A good way to approach this is to do the following:

1. **Make a selection of the object's background area.**
2. **Use the selection to fill a layer mask with black to hide the background area.**

Therefore, it helps to be very familiar with many selection techniques because somehow, some way, you have to isolate the object from its background. Knowledge about selection methods, of course, helps you avoid spending more time than necessary to make the selection and helps you make the selection as precise as it needs to be. Figure 16.9 shows a silhouetted object.

CROSS-REF See Chapter 10 for information about selections and channels.

FIGURE 16.9

A silhouetted object

When you are trying to decide on the quickest and best way to make a selection, it's good to examine the full-color version of an image and its individual channels in the Channels palette to see if there is good contrast between the object and its background in one of these locations. You can even temporarily change color modes to examine different color modes' channels.

If you find good contrast somewhere, you can use that contrast, along with a selection tool such as the Magic Wand, to help you make a selection. The Magic Wand selects colors that are similar to the color you click on with it, so if the background color is different enough from the object's colors, the Magic Wand might be able to select the background. Figure 16.10 shows the Channels palette.

Tips for making selections

Selections are not bound to a specific layer or place in Photoshop. They apply to the layer, layer mask, or channel that is currently active. So, a selection can be made when an individual channel is active, then the same active selection can be applied to a full-color composite channel when you activate the composite channel and the appropriate layer.

You can save selections and load them, or at a later time add new selections to them or subtract new selections from them, by choosing Select ➪ Save Selection or Load Selection.

If you find that in the full-color composite version of an image there is good contrast in one part of the image and in an individual channel there is good contrast in another part of the image, you can make separate selections and save them. You can load one of the selections then load-and-add the other selection to make a composite selection.

Saved selections are stored in channels that appear below the composite and individual color channels in the Channels palette.

If an object is selected but you actually want everything except the object to be selected (like its background), you can invert the selection by choosing Select ➪ Inverse, or by pressing Shift+Ctrl+I/ ⌘+I (on a Mac). You can invert the colors on a channel by choosing Image ➪ Adjustments ➪ Invert, or by pressing Ctrl+I/⌘+I.

FIGURE 16.10

The Channels palette, which you may want to examine to look for high-contrast areas you can use to help you make a selection

Another method of making a selection of an object's background is to make a duplicate of a channel that has high contrast between the object and its background (choose Duplicate Channel on the Channels palette menu), and work on the duplicate channel to increase its contrast until it contains only black and white (with the Curves command and painting on it with black and white, for example). You can then load the channel as a selection by clicking the Load Channel as a Selection button at the bottom of the Channels palette.

Areas that are white (or transparent) in the channel will be the selected area after the channel is loaded as a selection. Photoshop sees a duplicate channel as the same thing as a saved selection because saved selections are also stored as duplicate channels.

Duplicate channels that you make with the Channels palette rather than by choosing Select ➪ Save Selection can also be loaded as a selection by choosing Select ➪ Load Selection. Figure 16.11 shows the Channels palette with a manipulated duplicate channel.

If your object is wispy and detailed — for example, fireworks and their smoke, curly hair, or delicate grasses — you may benefit from using the Extract filter, which erases the background area and makes it transparent.

If there is no good contrast in your full-color image or its channels, you have some more choices. If the object's edges don't have to be very hard or precise, you can use Quick Mask mode to paint a selection onto the image with brush tools. Although this might be tedious and less precise when making hard-edged selections, Quick Mask is a great, quick way to make soft-edged selections.

FIGURE 16.11

The Channels palette with a manipulated duplicate channel that can be loaded as a selection by clicking the Load Channel as a Selection button at the bottom of the Channels palette

If the object has hard, smooth, straight, and curved edges, you can make a precise path around it with the Pen tool, then load the path as a selection by clicking the Load Path as a Selection button at the bottom of the Paths palette. Figure 16.12 shows an object that has a path around its edges.

CROSS-REF See Chapter 11 for information about making paths.

If the object has only straight edges and no curved edges, the Polygon tool may be sufficiently precise to make the selection. To select with the Polygon tool, click on each corner of the object until you get back to the start point. When you click on the start point, it closes the selection.

FIGURE 16.12

An object that has a path around its edges. The path can be loaded as a selection by clicking the Load Path as a Selection button at the bottom of the Paths palette.

Exporting transparency from Photoshop

Some applications, such as Adobe InDesign and Adobe Illustrator, support PSD files and can preserve their layers and transparency. In these cases, you can save Photoshop files with transparency and layers in the PSD format before you bring them into these applications.

For some other applications, you must first save an image (especially a color image) as a Photoshop EPS file that contains a closed clipping path that fully surrounds the object that you want to be visible. Everything else in the Photoshop image will be transparent when it gets into the other application. It's not necessary to delete the pixels in the Photoshop document that are outside the object that is surrounded by the clipping path. To make a clipping path, activate a path in the Paths palette, select Clipping Path in the Paths palette menu, and click OK. In the EPS Options Save dialog box, be sure to select the correct preview for the operating system — don't select a Macintosh preview if the image will be going to a PC. (Some software also supports clipping paths saved within TIFF-format files.)

If you save a bitmap-color-mode image — an image that can contain only black and white pixels — as a TIFF (PC-format TIFF to make compatible with PCs), some applications, such as Quark Express page layout software, let you apply a color of your choice to the black part of the image and transparency or another color to the white part of the image (may be referred to as the background color in the other application).

If you save a grayscale-color-mode image — an image that can contain black, white, and gray pixels — as a TIFF (PC-format TIFF to make compatible with PCs), some applications, such as Quark Express page layout software, let you apply a color of your choice to the image and another color to the background of the box that contains the image. The image appears somewhat transparent and lets the box's background color show through. If a color other than white is assigned to the background, it gives the image an appearance of a "faux" duotone in the other application. A "real" duotone is a two-color image made by choosing Image ⇨ Mode ⇨ Duotone in Photoshop. (See Chapter 26 for more information about duotones.)

For additional information, check the destination software's documentation for details about how it can import transparency. See Chapter 7 for more information about saving files from Photoshop.

Combining Images into a Collage

When you want to make an image collage, you usually gather a collection of images and bring them into Photoshop on separate layers. From there, you can resize the individual images on the layers with Transform commands, if necessary. Then you can add layer masks and use them to hide parts of the image you don't want.

Custom collages using layers and layer masks

Let's say you want to use three images to make a 4.5 x 3-inch collage at 300 ppi in CMYK mode for a magazine. Figure 16.13 shows the three original images that will be used in the collage.

Here are the typical steps you might follow to make a three-image collage:

1. **Create a new Photoshop document by choosing File ⇨ New.** Make a 4.5 x 3-inch, 300 ppi, RGB document (it will be changed to CMYK later). Leave this document open.

   FIGURE 16.13

   Three images that will be used in a collage.

2. **Click the Maximize button at the top of the Photoshop Application Frame to make the workspace as large as possible.** You can click the Minimize button if you need to temporarily get it out of the way.

3. **Open the three images and make sure they have at least enough size and resolution to maintain their quality at their final size in the collage.** See Chapter 5 for resizing and resolution.

4. **Click the Arrange Documents button in the Application Bar, then click the Tile All in Grid button to see all four open documents.** Figure 16.14 shows the four tiled open documents.

5. **One at a time, drag each of the three images from their image window to the new document's window with the Move tool.** This should automatically put each image on its own layer in the destination document. (You don't need to make a selection before you drag an image, but if an image has multiple layers, you will need to activate the appropriate layer or layer group, or flatten the image before you drag it into the new document.)

To automate bringing multiple images onto separate layers into one Photoshop document, you can use Adobe Bridge. Select multiple image thumbnails in Bridge and choose Tools ⇨ Photoshop ⇨ Load files into Photoshop Layers. Change the resulting Photoshop document's canvas size, and its image resolution, if necessary, while keeping in mind resolution requirements and good practices when resizing.

6. Close the three original images by clicking the close button on their window tabs so that only the new document is open.

7. Click the Arrange Documents button in the Application Bar, then click the Fit on Screen button so you can be sure you are seeing the entire document.

8. **Move each object by activating its layer in the Layers palette then dragging the object around in the image window with the Move tool.** You don't have to make a selection, because dragging in a layer moves all of the layer's contents if there is no selection active. Putting only one object on the layer saves you the hassle of selecting the object to move or resize it. Figure 16.15 shows the moved objects.

FIGURE 16.14

All four documents: the new destination document and the three open images that will be moved to the new document and used in the collage

544

FIGURE 16.15

The collage with the objects that have been moved

9. **If you need to resize an object, choose Edit ⇨ Free Transform.** This puts a Transform bounding box around the object. To shrink or enlarge the object, hold down the Shift key while you drag a corner handle (not side handle) of the bounding box. Release the mouse button first, then the Shift key. The key-mouse-corner handles combination maintains the object's proportions while you resize it.

NOTE You can copy and paste or choose File ⇨ Place an image into a Photoshop document instead of dragging it with the Move tool. The Move tool is quicker, but paste and place give you the option of bringing the object in as a Smart Object. Smart Objects can give you more flexibility when resizing objects and editing objects' original contents (see Chapter 9). If you choose to paste or place, putting a check mark next to the General Preferences ⇨ Resize Image During Paste/Place preference causes a larger placed or pasted image to resize down to the destination image's size so that the Transform bounding box handles are automatically in view and not outside the image window.

10. **To hide parts of an image, activate the object's layer and click the Add Layer Mask button at the bottom of the Layers palette.** Make sure the layer mask is active and not the layer thumbnail (it has a black border around it if it is active), and paint or select-and-fill with black or gray in the image window to hide corresponding parts of the object. To show the image parts again, put white on the mask. Figure 16.16 shows the collage and its layer masks.

And you're finished creating the collage!

Final steps for saving for printing in a magazine would include changing the image mode to CMYK, sharpening, flattening, and saving in PC TIFF format.

The image collage and its layer masks that have been used to hide parts of the objects on the layers

To design a collage for the Web, the main differences are to set the resolution to 72 ppi instead of 300 ppi, set the measurements in pixels instead of inches, leave the image in RGB mode, and save as a JPEG or GIF.

CROSS-REF   For more information about preparing images for the Web, see Chapter 24.

Transforming objects in a collage

Following are ways you can transform objects that are on their own layers in a collage (first, click the layer in the Layers palette to activate it):

Edit ⇨ Free Transform

This puts a Transform bounding box around the object. To shrink or enlarge the object, hold down the Shift key while you drag a corner handle (not side handle) of the bounding box. Release the mouse button first, then the Shift key. The key-mouse-corner handles combination maintains the object's proportions while you resize it. Figure 16.17 shows the Free Transform bounding box around an object that is to be resized.

If the bounding box handles are outside the image window because the object is larger than the size of the image, you can zoom out with the Navigator palette to bring the handles into view or resize the object by entering lower width and height percentages in the Options Bar until you can see corner handles. If you use the Options Bar method, click on the link symbol in between the width and height to maintain the object's proportions while you resize it.

To rotate the object, position the cursor just outside the bounding box until you see curvy arrows, then drag with the mouse. If you want to change the axis around which the object rotates, move the center bullet point (the axis) to a different position inside or outside the bounding box.

FIGURE 16.17

The Free Transform bounding box around an object that is to be resized

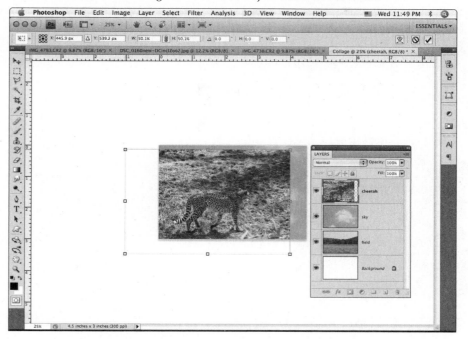

If you want to move the object while the bounding box is still active, drag inside the bounding box, but not on its center point bullet, with the mouse. The center point bullet is just the axis around which the image rotates.

If you don't want to accept the changes you made with the bounding box, press ESC. If you do want to allow the changes you made with the bounding box, press Enter or Return.

Edit ⇨ Transform ⇨ Skew

You can drag the side handles of a Skew Transform bounding box to slant an image. If you don't want to accept the changes you made with the bounding box, press ESC. If you do want to allow the changes you made with the bounding box, press Enter or Return. Figure 16.18 shows an object being skewed.

Edit ⇨ Transform ⇨ Distort

You can drag a corner handle of a Distort Transform bounding box to stretch an image. If you don't want to accept the changes you made with the bounding box, press ESC. If you do want to allow the changes you made with the bounding box, press Enter or Return. Figure 16.19 shows an object being distorted.

FIGURE 16.18

The Skew Transform bounding box around an object that is being skewed

FIGURE 16.19

A Distort Transform bounding box around an object that is being distorted

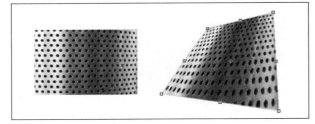

Edit ➪ Transform ➪ Perspective

You can drag a corner handle of a Perspective Transform bounding box to apply perspective to an image. If you don't want to accept the changes you made with the bounding box, press ESC. If you do want to allow the changes you made with the bounding box, press Enter or Return. Figure 16.20 shows an object with a changed perspective.

FIGURE 16.20

A Perspective Transform bounding box around an object that is having its perspective transformed

Edit ➪ Transform ➪ Warp

You can use the Warp Transform bounding to push, pull, and stretch the shape of images, shapes, or paths by dragging on the Warp Transform gridlines, handles (black dots), or control points (hollow squares). If you want to rotate or resize the warp shape, you can temporarily switch to a Free Transform bounding box by clicking the Switch between free transform and warp modes button in the Options Bar.

To warp multiple layers at one time, before choosing the Warp command, Shift+click or Ctrl+click/⌘+click on the layers in the Layers palette to activate them. Choose Convert to Smart Object from the Layers palette menu. Figure 16.21 shows several layers that have been grouped into a Smart Object being warped with a custom warp bounding box.

Several layers that have been grouped into a Smart Object being warped with a custom warp bounding box

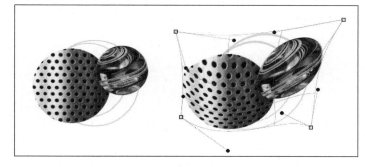

After you activate the Warp Transform box, you can alternatively apply a warp shape from in the Warp drop-down list in the Options Bar (by default, "Custom" is active). Warp shapes include Arc, Wave, Fisheye, and more. The bend, horizontal and vertical distortion, and orientation can be changed using the options in the Options Bar. Dragging the control point on the warp-shape bounding box also changes the bend (control point is only available if there is no horizontal or vertical distortion). If you want to rotate or resize the warp shape, you can temporarily switch to a Free Transform bounding box by clicking the Switch between free transform and warp modes button in the Options Bar.

Figure 16.22 shows an object being warped with a warp shape, chosen from the Warp menu in the Options Bar.

If you don't want to accept the changes you made with the bounding box, press ESC. If you do want to allow the changes you made with the bounding box, press Enter or Return.

FIGURE 16.22

The Options Bar and an active Wave warp-shape bounding box and object

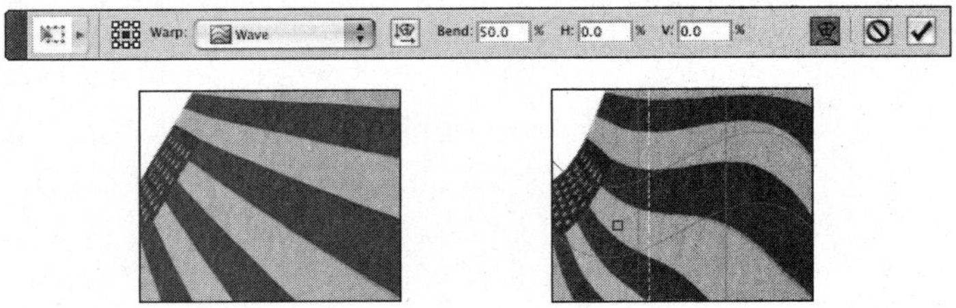

> **NOTE**
> When you warp a bitmap image (rather than a vector image), the image gets slightly less sharp each time you warp it. So, do as many warp adjustments in one warp session as possible instead of doing several warp adjustments in several sessions.

Edit ⇨ Transform ⇨ (Rotate or Flip)

You can do common rotations or flip layer contents horizontally or vertically with this menu.

> **CROSS-REF**
> The Filter ⇨ Liquify command can also be used to warp images and apply more fluid warps than the Warp command. See Chapter 21 for more information about Liquify. You can also explore the Vanishing Point filter in Chapter 21 for information about warping images so that they conform to a particular perspective that has been defined for an object (as in placing a logo graphic so that it spans two sides of a box and making it conform to the box's perspective).

Collages of panoramas using the Photomerge command

You can use the Photomerge command to automatically combine multiple photos that have overlapping content into one photo.

- In Photoshop:

  1. Choose File ⇨ Automate ⇨ Photomerge (see Figure 16.23).

  2. Add the Source Files.

  3. Choose a layout method.

  4. Click OK.

- In Adobe Bridge:

  1. Select multiple image thumbnails.

  2. Choose Tools ⇨ Photoshop ⇨ Photomerge.

  3. Choose a layout method.

  4. Click OK.

FIGURE 16.23

The Photomerge dialog box

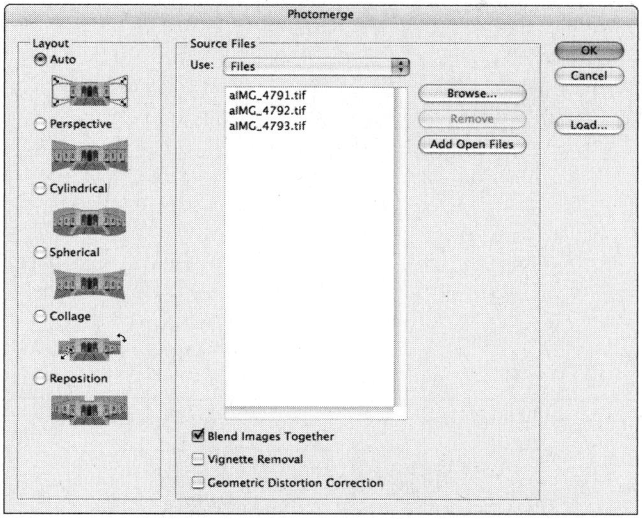

> **Photomerge**
>
> **Layout**
> - ⦿ Auto
> - ○ Perspective
> - ○ Cylindrical
> - ○ Spherical
> - ○ Collage
> - ○ Reposition
>
> **Source Files**
> Use: [Files ▾]
>
> aIMG_4791.tif
> aIMG_4792.tif
> aIMG_4793.tif
>
> [Browse...]
> [Remove]
> [Add Open Files]
>
> [OK]
> [Cancel]
> [Load...]
>
> ☑ Blend Images Together
> ☐ Vignette Removal
> ☐ Geometric Distortion Correction

In my experience, the Auto layout method usually works best, and checking Blend Images Together causes Photoshop to choose the optimum areas for the seams where images are to be stitched together and match tone and color along the seams. If the blend option doesn't produce good results, you could try it again with that option off and edit the layer masks in the resulting composition by hand to produce the desired blending.

Photomerge creates one multi-layer image from the source images and adds layer masks as needed to create blending where the images overlap.

Figures 16.24 and 16.25 show source images and various Photomerged result files of a field and hills, using different layout methods in Photomerge.

FIGURE 16.24

Source images of a field and hills

FIGURE 16.25

Photomerged results

Figures 16.26 and 16.27 show source images of different sizes and rotations and the Photomerged result files of the Hollywood sign and hills.

FIGURE 16.26

Source images of different sizes and rotations of the Hollywood sign and hills

Your Photomerged result may need some refinement. In most cases, you will need to crop out some uneven edge areas with the Crop tool.

If the image is still too dark or light in some areas so that the transitions between the combined images don't look realistic, one method to correct this is to use a soft-edged Clone tool that is set to Multiply or Screen mode with a very low opacity to clone the image directly on top of itself. The Multiply mode makes the cloned parts darker; the Screen mode makes the cloned parts lighter.

To clone the image directly on top of itself, be sure to start cloning in exactly the same position as the Clone source point (Alt+click or Option+click with the Clone tool to define a source point). Paint over areas with the Clone tool multiple times to increase the effect. You may also need to make color changes or edit the layer masks to fine-tune the Photomerged file.

CROSS-REF For more information about lightening and darkening images, see Chapter 14. For information about editing the color of images, see Chapter 15. For information about working with layer masks, see Chapter 8.

You can also do a Photomerge with different commands. If the overlapping image source files already exist on separate layers in the same Photoshop document, you can select the source-file layers in the Layers palette and choose Edit ➪ Auto-Align Layers with the Auto layout method active. You can then choose Edit ➪ Auto-Blend Layers with the Panorama option active to better blend the stitched seams of the images.

FIGURE 16.27

The resulting Photomerged (Auto layout) file and its layers and masks

Here are some tips for taking panorama source photos to use with the Photomerge command:

- Images should overlap by about 25 percent to 40 percent to increase the chances of a successful Photomerge.

- If possible, use one focal length.

- Try to keep the camera as level as possible while you are shooting the source images. Using a tripod is not absolutely necessary, but it helps.

- Try not to change your position as you take a series of photographs, so that the pictures are from the same viewpoint.

- Avoid using fisheye and other distortion lenses that can interfere with Photomerge.

- Maintain the same exposure. The blending feature in Photomerge helps smooth out different exposures, but extreme differences can cause a bad result.

Collages to remove unwanted image content

If you have taken multiple shots of the same scene that are nearly identical but each photo has some unwanted feature, you can combine the photos and show only the desirable features. For example, you may have a group portrait of three people that is nearly identical except that a different person has his or her eyes closed in each photo.

You can bring the images onto separate layers into a Photoshop document and choose Edit ⇨ Auto-Align Layers with the Reposition only option turned on. This aligns the images based on their content so that they are exactly on top of each other. Then you can add layer masks and use them to hide unwanted parts of the images to let the desirable features show through from the other photos that are on layers underneath.

If you have taken multiple photos of the same scene that has unwanted moving objects coming and going in each photo, you may be able to use Image Stacks to automatically remove the unwanted objects so that you are left with just the background objects. An example would be if you took multiple photos of a storefront in a mall but all the photos had at least one person walking in or out, and you want to eliminate all the people from the photo.

You can also use Image Stacks to create a photo that has very little noise but is derived from multiple noisy, nearly identical photos.

CROSS-REF   See Chapter 8 for more information about Image Stacks.

Drawing the Eye to Certain Areas

When you are putting together a collage or even in a single image, you don't have to settle for the default attention-getting areas. You can use some tricks to direct the viewer's eyes to specific parts of the image.

Use blur and sharpen

You can sharpen an area that you want viewers to notice first and blur an area that you want to be less attention-getting. Figure 16.28 shows a photo that makes use of this technique and the layers and layer masks that were applied to facilitate it.

Add contrast and reduce contrast

Adding contrast to a section of an image draws the eye to it, especially if you decrease contrast in a less important area. Curves adjustment layers with masks are great for this purpose. Figure 16.29 shows an image that makes use of this technique and the layers and layer masks that were used to apply it.

Use color to draw attention

Warm and highly saturated colors often appear to be closer and cool and low-saturation colors farther away. Figure 16.30 shows an image that makes use of this technique to draw the eye to a certain area. See the color section of this book for the color version.

FIGURE 16.28

An image that uses blur and sharpen to direct the viewer's eye to the sharper area

FIGURE 16.29

An image that uses high contrast and low contrast to direct the viewer's eye to the high-contrast area

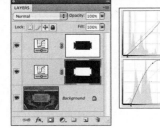

FIGURE 16.30

An image that draws the eye to areas with warm, saturated colors when combined with cool, less saturated colors

Summary

This chapter described uses of transparency and opacity in Photoshop, silhouetting, combining images into a collage, and drawing the eye to certain parts of an image. Following are key concepts:

- Transparency and opacity can be used to make image parts seem like they flow together in an image collage.

- Transparency can be used when silhouetting an object and can be exported from Photoshop by using clipping paths, the bitmap image mode, and in layered PSD format files for the external applications that support PSD format.

- Custom image collages can be created for combining images in an artistic or practical way or in special ways that help you easily remove unwanted objects or noise.

- You can use blurring and sharpening, increasing and decreasing contrast, and combinations of warm, saturated colors and cool, low-saturation colors to draw the eye to certain parts of an image.

Chapter 17

Noise, Grain, Dust, Pixelization, and Jagged Edges

In photographic terms, noise refers to the grainy dots that can sometimes appear, particularly in the dark areas of pictures taken in low-light conditions. Noise can be either good or bad, though — sometimes it can add to the mood of a photograph, creating a classic, timeless feel; or, especially in the case of digital photos taken at a high film speed (ISO) setting, it can produce distracting multi-colored blobs.

Pixelization, dust, and halftone patterns (which are sometimes introduced when scanning images) are examples of other undesirable artifacts that can show up in your images. In this chapter, you'll learn how to combat unwanted noise and pixelization by using various filters and other techniques.

Get Rid of Overall Pixelated Look

Noise, that excessive grain in an image, can result from using a high film speed (ISO) setting, from shooting in low-light conditions, or it can be introduced when scanning images on a flatbed scanner. Most point-and-shoot digital cameras produce noisy images with ISO settings above 400 — or less, in some cases. Some current high-end SLR (single-lens reflex) digital cameras, on the other hand, can shoot noise-free up to an ISO of 1600.

There are two types of noise: color noise and luminance noise. Color noise, which is also referred to as *chroma* noise, appears as colored blobs that become really obvious when you zoom into the image. Trust me, once you know what to look for, they're all you'll be able to see when you look at images shot with cheap digital cameras. As its name would suggest, color noise is visible in one or more color channels of a photograph — most often the blue one. Click on the Channels panel's tab, or choose

Windows ⇨ Channels, and click around between the different color channels of the image to examine where most of the color noise occurs. Luminance noise more closely resembles traditional film grain, and as a result, is often more tolerable than color noise.

Reducing noise

Photoshop offers five options under the Noise section of the Filters menu. The first, Add Noise, is the only one that's used to introduce noise or grain into an image, while the remaining filters are used to get rid of artifacts and blemishes.

Despeckle

The Despeckle filter is one of several that operate by applying a predefined effect to your image, without any options for configuring it. In this case, the filter detects all the areas of sharp transition between colors — the edges, that is — and ignores them. The areas between the edges are blurred to reduce the appearance of noise.

With this filter, you have no control over just how much blurring is applied, or over what is considered an edge or not, so you may have varying degrees of success with this filter. One way to mitigate the effect of the Despeckle filter would be to choose Edit ⇨ Fade (Ctrl+Shift+F/⌘+Shift+F on a Mac) immediately after applying it, and reducing the opacity, or changing the blending mode of the filter. The results of applying the Despeckle filter are illustrated in Figure 17.1.

The original image, shown on the left, has some visible noise in the shadows. The Despeckle filter was used (middle) to smooth out some of the noise. The image on the far right was subjected to the Despeckle filter five times, which has gotten rid of lots of noise, but also resulted in loss of important details.

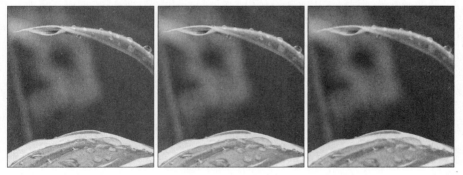

Median

The Median filter examines the each pixel in relation to its neighbors within a given radius and figures out the median brightness value of those pixels (see Figure 17.2). It then applies that value to the center pixel. Pixels that vary too much from their neighbors within a selection are ignored, so they don't skew the median value. Increasing the value of the Radius slider above a radius of 3, quickly obliterates any detail within the image, so it might be useful to combine the Median filter with the Fade command, or apply it to a duplicate of the background layer. You can then change the opacity and blending mode of the blurred layer, or mitigate its effect by using a layer mask.

FIGURE 17.2

The effects of the Median filter, applied at settings 3, 5, and 25 respectively

Reduce Noise

The most flexible of the filters available to combat image noise is the Reduce Noise filter. Choose Filter ➪ Noise ➪ Reduce Noise to launch its dialog box (see Figure 17.3). Once again, you are able to preview your adjustments to the filter's settings via the Preview window and the main document window. The Reduce Noise filter has a Basic mode for straightforward noise reduction, and an Advanced mode that offers some added options for configuring the filter's effect.

The following options are available in the Basic tab of the Reduce Noise dialog box:

- **Strength.** The Strength slider controls the amount of luminance noise reduction that the filter applies. Specifically, it increases or decreases the intensity of the overall noise reduction that the filter attempts to apply to all of the image's color channels.

- **Preserve Details.** The process of reducing noise inherently results in some blurring. To protect the fine details in your photograph such as in hair or textured areas, adjust the Preserve Details slider. A value of 0 percent doesn't preserve any of the detail in the image — every pixel receives the full-force noise-reducing effect. Increasing this number reduces the number of pixels that are impacted by the filter.

- **Reduce Color Noise.** This option focuses on color or chroma noise, reducing the appearance of colored artifacts in the image.

- **Sharpen Details.** As mentioned, the process of noise reduction tends to introduce some fuzziness into the image during the course of smoothing out artifacts and grain. The Sharpen Details slider helps you counter this smoothing by adding some contrast along the edges and other detailed areas of your image. Of course, as an alternative, you can choose to leave this slider set to 0 percent and instead sharpen your image with one of Photoshop's other sharpening filters.

■ **Remove JPEG Artifact.** One of the by-products of saving images using the JPEG file format is the blocky artifacts created when the compression algorithm crunches the image data into a smaller file size (for a refresher on JPEG and other file formats, see Chapter 2). Click in this check box to reduce the appearance of these artifacts and halos.

Switching to the Reduce Noise filter's Advanced mode adds a Channels tab, which allows you to click through each of the image's color channels and apply the filter where it is needed most. Adjust the strength of the effect and choose how much of the image detail is preserved by using the sliders for each channel.

FIGURE 17.3

The Reduce Noise filter has plenty of configurable options through its Basic and Advanced modes.

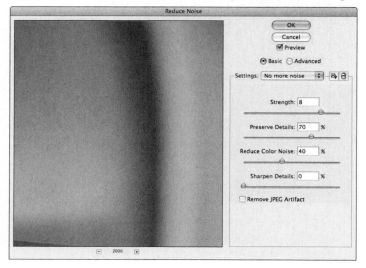

Anti-aliasing an image

If you have an image that is plagued with a pixelated appearance, such as a GIF image from the Internet or some scanned line art that you want to smooth out, you can use the Image Size command to anti-alias the entire image. As you'll remember from Chapter 5, using this command to make images larger than their original size works by applying interpolation — that is, by "guessing" at the data that's required to make the new larger image — which has a blurring effect. Normally, you'd want to avoid this blurring, but in this case, you can use it to your advantage.

Open the offending image and choose Image ➪ Image Size, and resize the image to 200 percent (you can change the popup menus next to the width and height dimensions to percent instead of pixels or inches). Make sure the Resample Image option is set to Bicubic or Bicubic Smoother, and click OK. Then, choose Image ⇨ Image Size again, but this time, reduce the size by 50 percent, and choose Bicubic Sharper as the Resample Image setting.

You should notice that any areas that were previously blocky or pixelated are now much smoother than they were initially (see Figure 17.4) — that's because the interpolation that's applied when the image size is doubled blends pixels and smoothes the transitions between them.

> **TIP** Ideally, you should scan your drawings at a resolution of at least 600dpi by using the Line Art setting (or its equivalent) in your scanner software. Clean up any stray lines or pixels in the scanned document, then downsample the image to a lower resolution as needed.

FIGURE 17.4

The original scanned art on the left has jagged lines and edges. The art was cleaned up with some anti-aliasing by using the Image Size command, followed by Gaussian blurring and Levels to increase the contrast. Finally, larger stray lines were cleaned up with the Eraser tool.

You might need to apply this procedure a few times for particularly pixelated images, keeping in mind that you are degrading the overall image quality in the process. For best results, you can use this technique in combination with blurring, applying the Levels command to increase contrast, and sharpening with Unsharp Mask or Smart Sharpen.

Fix Undesirable Edges

So far the focus has been on noise or grain in an image. Now, you'll learn how to get rid of unwanted pixels in a few other relatively common situations.

Remove unwanted edge pixels

When faced with the very specific situation of copying or moving a selection that was anti-aliased against a black or white background, and placing it on a different colored background, you can end up with unwanted pixels around the edge of your selection, as shown in Figure 17.5. You can replace those black or white fringe pixels by choosing Layer ➪ Matting ➪ Defringe. Defringe searches the edge pixels of a layer for colors that aren't the background color, and replaces them with the colors that exist further in from the edge. Use the Radius setting to specify the size of the area in which to search for pixels by entering a number in the Defringe dialog box.

FIGURE 17.5

Zoomed to about 800 percent, the text on top of this illustration shows some white fringe pixels, as it was copied off of a white background. The Defringe command with a radius of 1 pixel was applied to the second line of text, eliminating the white fringe.

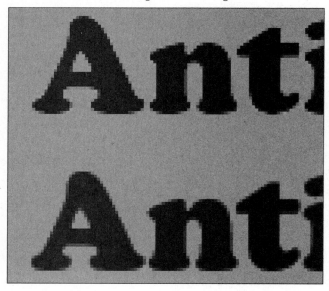

Photoshop also offers options specifically for removing black or white edge pixels via the Remove Black Matte and Remove White Matte commands under the Layer ➪ Matting menu.

Smooth jagged edge pixels

Sometimes parts of an image copied to another layer or image can have harsh, jagged edges. You can avoid this by using the Pen tool, which assures you of perfectly smooth selection edges. For quick selections made with the Magic Wand or Quick Selection tool, the Refine Edge command can work wonders. Figure 17.6 shows a portion of an image that was copied from the original. The selection used to define this area was made — hastily — with the Quick Selection tool, resulting in harsh, jagged edges.

FIGURE 17.6

The robot in this illustration was copied from the source image by using the Quick Selection tool. Note the rough, jagged edges.

This jagged-edged abomination could have been avoided if I had used the Refine Edge command. With one of the selection tools highlighted in the Toolbar and a "marching ants" selection active in your document, do one of the following:

- Click the Refine button in the Options Bar.
- Choose Select ➪ Refine Edge.
- Right-click/Ctrl+click anywhere within the document and choose Refine from the context menu.

Upon launching the tool, your main document window is updated with a preview of what your selection will look like as you make changes to the controls in the Refine Edge dialog box (see Figure 17.7). Here's an overview of the available controls within the Refine Edge dialog box:

- **Radius.** Use this slider to change the size of the region around your selection boundary that will be refined. Use a larger radius for areas with blurry edges, or for fine details like hair or grass.

- **Contrast.** Increase the contrast to create crisp selection edges with this slider.

- **Smooth.** As its name suggests, this setting smooths out irregular selection boundaries.

- **Feather.** Use this slider to create a softer transition between the selected region and its surrounding pixels.

- **Contract/Expand.** Decrease or increase the size of the selection boundary with this slider.

The five icons at the bottom of the Refine Edge dialog box control the way the selection preview is displayed.

Finally, at the bottom of the dialog box is a Description area, which you can toggle on or off, that gives a short description of each tool within the dialog box. When you click OK to accept your changes, you're returned to your document with the newly refined selection active — you can now either copy or move the selected area to a new layer or document.

FIGURE 17.7

The Refine Edge command displays a preview of your refined selection as you change the settings in the dialog box.

Dust Removal

Dust removal is a fairly common problem if you're scanning images that have damage or if the scanner itself has particles on its flatbed. One of the first tools to reach for to remove dust is the Dust & Scratches filter. This filter finds pixels that are drastically different from the surrounding pixels and eliminates them by blurring them to match their neighbors.

In addition to dust, it's designed to help with removing hair, halftone dots, and other blemishes from scanned images. Your success with this filter may vary depending on the image — in some cases, it might get everything right on the first try; in others, you might have to retouch the image manually by using the Healing Brush and other techniques discussed in Chapter 18.

Open the filter's dialog box (see Figure 17.8) by choosing Filter➪Dust & Scratches. Adjust the Radius slider (the maximum value is 100 pixels) to increase the size of the area that is examined for dissimilar pixels. The Threshold slider controls which pixels receive the effect of the filter — a lower threshold setting restricts the filter to just those pixels that are dramatically different from their neighbors.

When applying the Dust & Scratches filter, it's best to stick with fairly low values for the Radius — anything below 16 should be enough. Once you've found a Radius value that reduces the most noticeable blemishes, slowly increase the Threshold value until a sufficient amount of detail is brought back into the photograph. Figure 17.9 shows a scanned photo from the '50s that's a little worse for the wear.

I applied the Dust & Scratches filter with a Radius of 1 and a Threshold of 14, which helped get rid of some of the smaller flaws in the photograph, and the result is shown in the center image. The larger creases and wrinkles that remained had to be taken care of manually with the Healing Brush and Cloning Stamp tools. To finish off the restoration of this photo, I boosted the contrast and applied the Unsharp Mask to counter some of the blurring that the Dust & Scratches filter produced.

The Dust & Scratches filter also helps to diminish the moiré pattern that is sometimes visible in images scanned from books and magazines. For best results when working with images from these sources, you should scan them at a higher resolution than you actually need, and then down sample the image to the appropriate resolution. This will help to blur the halftone dots, while keeping detail in the photograph. You can then apply the Dust & Scratches filter until the moiré is reduced further and finish with some sharpening.

FIGURE 17.8

The Dust & Scratches dialog box. The Radius slider controls the size of the area to search for dissimilar pixels. Adjust the Threshold to widen or narrow the range of pixels that is affected by the filter.

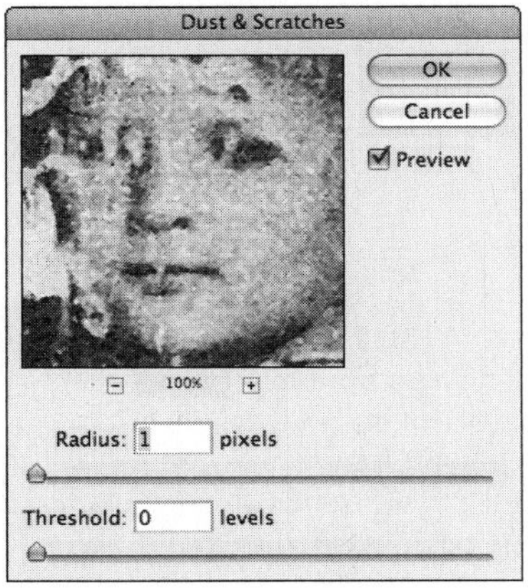

FIGURE 17.9

The original image on the left, which was scanned from an old photograph, is marred by the effects of time. The center image shows the result of using the Dust & Scratches filter to get rid of the smaller blemishes. The image on the right was sharpened and retouched manually with the Healing Brush and Cloning Stamp.

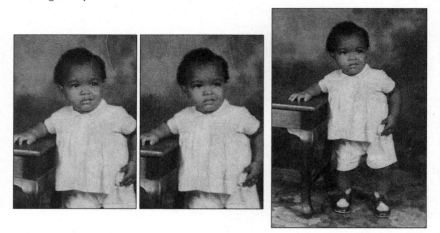

Blurring

Instinctively, blurring seems like the last thing you would want to do to enhance a photograph — after all, it's usually ingrained in us very early on that most pictures look their best when they are crystal clear and everything is in focus.

Nevertheless, blurring can be a useful way to reduce the appearance of grain or other artifacts in an image. Blurring can also be used creatively to emphasize specific areas of an image or to create a specific atmosphere by toning down distracting background elements.

Blurring works by reducing the contrast between pixels and smoothing out transitions between colored areas. Pixels are examined and manipulated in relation to their neighbors. Two of the major blurring tools — Gaussian Blur and Lens Blur — are covered in this chapter, while the remaining filters in the Blur subcategory of the Filter menu are covered in Chapter 20.

Gaussian blur

Despite (or maybe because of) its simplicity, the Gaussian Blur filter is the one that most Photoshop users reach for first to satisfy their blurring needs. Selecting it from the Filters ➪ Blur menu produces a rather simplistic dialog box with a Preview window and single slider labeled Radius, which controls the amount of blur that is applied to the image.

Enter a value from 1.0 to 250, and a blur is calculated based on a bell-shaped curve. To illustrate the effect of the Gaussian Blur filter in Figure 17.10, I used a mask to protect the flower, and applied the blur only to the leaves in the background of the image. In the last image, a blur setting of 50 pixels completely obscures the leaves.

FIGURE 17.10

The leaves behind the flower in this image were subjected to a Gaussian blur at six different settings. As the Radius value increases, the leaves become less and less recognizable.

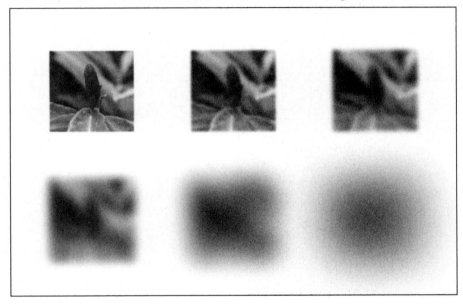

Lens blur

Lens blur is used to add some depth to your image by giving it a shallower depth-of-field. Some settings, such as landscapes and architectural subjects, benefit from being tack-sharp throughout the image, but there are cases where a photo can benefit from selected areas being out of focus. Photographers achieve this by varying the lenses they use with their cameras, but if you use a point-and-shoot, this filter can help you out.

The Lens Blur filter works by using transparency information to figure out how to blur pixels relative to their distance from the camera (that is, to create depth-of-field). With that in mind, you should set up a layer mask or an alpha channel that represents the depth-of-field you want to create before you launch the filter.

For the photo of the yellow buses shown in Figure 17.11, I created a new alpha channel in the Channels panel, and filled it with a reflected gradient that goes from white to black to white again.

In the Lens Blur dialog box, I used this alpha channel as the source of my blur, with the result that the parts of the photo that correspond to the black part of the gradient are in focus, and the rest of the image is blurred. If this sounds confusing, read on for a more in-depth explanation.

Choose Filter ➪ Blur ➪ Lens Blur and the Lens Blur dialog box opens, filling your entire screen. By default, your photograph is zoomed to fit the space available in the Preview area, but you can use the zoom controls to change that as necessary. Don't let the apparent complexity of this window put you off — only a minimal amount of fiddling with its settings is needed to produce a very convincing depth-of-field effect.

FIGURE 17.11

The Lens Blur window helps you refine the depth-of-field of your image.

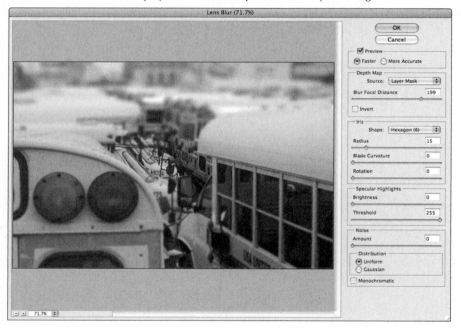

The options in the Lens Blur dialog box are described here:

- **Preview.** The Preview check box allows you to decide whether the photograph is continually updated as you make changes to the Lens Blur settings. Also, you can opt for a Faster or More Accurate preview by clicking those radio buttons. On slower computers, while making particularly complex lens blur calculations, you may want to consider disabling Preview — or at least opting for the faster preview option.

- **Depth Map.** Set a depth map source to define which parts of your photo should be treated as in focus or out of focus. The default setting of None results in your entire image being blurred equally — which doesn't really help if you're trying to emulate a shallow depth-of-field.

  Choosing Transparency as the Depth Map source sets the blurring based on the transparency values of your selected layer. (Hint: If your layer doesn't contain any transparent pixels, then everything is blurred equally, as with the previous option.)

  Selecting the Layer Mask option bases the amount of blur that's applied on the grayscale information in the layer mask of the selected layer. Black areas of the layer mask indicate in-focus elements, and white areas represent the parts of the photo that will receive the most blurring, although you can reverse this behavior by checking the Invert check box. Similarly, if you created an alpha channel, you can set that as the source of your Depth Map.

  The Blur Focal Distance slider allows you to specify the depth at which pixels are in focus. Pixels closer to this distance are in focus, while pixels farther away are out of focus. To adjust the blur focal distance interactively, simply click anywhere in the preview window. The Lens Blur filter analyzes the depth map info for the pixel you clicked on, and based on the specified depth map source, the focal distance is updated accordingly.

- **Iris.** The options in the Iris section allow you to simulate the various characteristics of actual lenses, affecting the quality of the lens blur that is produced. In real lenses, the shape of the iris (the mechanism in the lens that expands or contracts to control the amount of light that is allowed to enter the lens), the blade curvature (the "roundness" of the blades that form the iris), and the rotation of the iris all combine to produce different effects, which are most noticeable in the specular highlights of the photograph. Experiment with the corresponding sliders to achieve a greater degree of realism.

  The Radius slider, which has the most noticeable effect of the options in this section, allows you to control the maximum amount of blur that is generated, much as the focal length, or f-stop, of an actual lens would.

- **Specular Highlights.** In photography, specular highlights are the brightest areas of the photograph that are pure white. These areas can turn gray when blurred using the other blur filters — a dead giveaway that the image has been manipulated. To help maintain realism in the effect, you can use the Brightness slider to boost the intensity of the highlights. Use the Threshold slider to designate which pixels receive the brightness boost. Anything above the slider value is treated as a highlight and brightened.

- **Noise.** Blurring an image tends to smooth out all the detail and film grain in an image. To counter this and thus make the lens blur effect more convincing, you can add back in some noise. Use the Amount slider to add noise until it matches the in-focus parts of the photo. Choose a noise type — either Uniform or Gaussian — then, select Monochromatic if you want to add noise without affecting the color in your image.

Blur tool

Another way to blur specific areas of an image is to use the brush-based Blur tool, which is grouped alongside the Sharpen and Smudge tools in the Toolbox. To use the Blur tool, adjust the radius and hardness of the brush from the tool's Options Bar, and then set the intensity of the effect by using the Strength slider.

You can also specify the painting mode by using the options in the Mode popup menu. Click and drag to paint over areas in your image that need softening. The advantage of working with this tool is that you can be very specific about which areas are smoothed, and you can also precisely control the intensity of the effect, rather than applying a blanket setting for the entire image.

CROSS-REF For more about the Blur tool and its painting modes, see Chapter 19. For more information on the remaining blurring filters, check out Chapter 20.

Summary

This chapter explored the different ways to reduce the appearance of noise and pixelization in images. You learned about the different ways noise can be introduced into an image, from high ISO settings to scanner dust or halftone patterns. You learned about the Noise Reduction, Dust & Scratches, and other filters that help to reduce undesirable image artifacts. You also learned about using blur filters to smooth transitions between pixels and to lead the viewer's eye through an image.

Chapter 18

Retouching and Restoring Digital Images

IN THIS CHAPTER

Core retouching tools

Sample retouching workflows

The term retouching can refer to many processes that you might use when making improvements to a digital image. While there is no precise or standardized definition, fundamentally retouching is about making the image better. What "better" means depends on the person you ask. A fine art photographer will have a very different answer than a post-production artist at an advertising firm! But whether your goal is to make the people, places, or things in your photos more realistic or even surrealistic — with perfect skin, figures, and hair — Photoshop CS4 provides many useful tools for getting that job done.

This chapter will cover several of the most commonly used retouching tools, including the Clone Stamp, the Patch tool, the History Brush, the Dodge and Burn tools, and a few others. It's important to note that these aren't the only tools in Photoshop that can help you with retouching, merely the ones that are most frequently used in the typical retouching workflow.

Also, this chapter does not endeavor to make you the next great fashion magazine makeover artist, but rather provides examples more typical of the average photographer and digital hobbyist. We will cover things like how to remove blemishes, smooth eye lines, brighten eyes, and remove various kinds of unwanted objects from your images. Most importantly, these techniques will be shown with an eye toward a realistic-looking edit, rather than an idealized edit (the favorite of magazine publishers everywhere).

We will also cover these examples in a start-to-finish workflow so you can get an idea of how things can work for your set of images. Finally, we will discuss a few useful tips for restoring old scanned photographs by removing some cracks and creases, removing yellowish tones, and bringing back some long-lost details.

Core Retouching Tools

There are many useful retouching tools and commands within Photoshop CS4. Generally you can go a long way by learning how to use the most popular ones, then adding others to your repertoire as needed. Retouching in this context means making changes to the content of the image beyond global changes to tonality or color (such as running the Levels command or the Hue & Saturation command on the entire image).

More specifically, most of these tools change the appearance of details or textures within your image. Pixels are modified, moved, scrunched, and smoothed in various ways to create a slightly new variation of your image. The trick is to use the retouching tools in a way that does not produce out-of-place or unrealistic-looking images. Those in the fashion photography world not withstanding, the goal of a good photo retoucher is to create improvements that blend in with the original textures and character of the image, without drawing unwanted attention to themselves.

The most important thing to remember when retouching with any of the tools you're about to learn? Work on a separate image layer! By maintaining your original background layer in its unaltered condition, you always have a reference point in your file to fall back on should you need to start over or revert part of the image to its original state.

Clone Stamp

The Clone Stamp (see Figure 18.1) is a long-time favorite of Photoshop users. Its purpose is simple: to copy a region of the image that you specify as a source, and then paint that source region and the adjacent areas over your targeted pixels, thereby replacing them.

The word "paint" is used here because the Clone Stamp uses the same brush setting, blending modes, and dynamics (described in Chapter 19) as the Brush tool. Technically it's a cloning brush rather than a stamp.

This is an important distinction, as the brush settings can have a big impact on the quality of your cloned regions, especially when experimenting with brush shape and hardness. Brushes that are slightly soft and that don't have a perfectly symmetrical shape can often produce more subtle results than those with 100-percent hardness that are perfectly round, for example.

The best way to know which brush settings are right for your image is simply to experiment until you find a cloned appearance that you like.

The Clone Stamp tool is a great way to replicate textured areas or regions of repetitive and somewhat random detail. For example, if you needed to clone some grass from one area of a yard to another, the Clone Stamp would be the perfect tool because grass is a collection of randomly spaced and randomly sized details.

FIGURE 18.1

The Clone Stamp tool uses the same brush types and dynamics as the Brush tool, but it paints with the specified regions of your image, rather than solid colors. Also seen here is the Clone Source panel, which is discussed in the next section.

Another good example is something like pebbles, which are arranged randomly on the ground. As you replicate them from one place to another in your document, the placement of such details is less likely to draw the scrutiny of your viewers.

If you attempt to clone something that has an obvious, less random pattern to it, and "paint" it onto a nearby part of the document, this often creates a repetitive visual pattern within the image, such as the one seen in Figure 18.2. This is something you want to avoid when creating photorealistic retouches for your imagery.

Using the same image but different source points and destination, Figure 18.3 shows a good example of cloning randomly patterned areas into a nearby region. Note that it's much harder to see where the cloning has taken place in this example.

FIGURE 18.2

It's important when using the Clone Stamp to choose a source that has enough randomness that it fits into the surrounding target area. Here, the willow tree stands out because the pattern is easily recognized from the nearby source point.

Another purpose of the Clone Stamp is to remove unwanted objects with surrounding (and again somewhat random) texture or details. Figure 18.4 shows tree branches in the foreground that are replaced by the lake waters.

To perform a simple Clone Stamp operation, follow these steps:

1. **With your image open, click the Clone Source tool (press the S key on your keyboard or press Shift+S).**

2. **Move the Clone tool's brush cursor over the part of the image you wish to clone, and choose your brush settings.**

3. **Hold down the Alt key (or the Option key on a Mac); the cursor changes to a cross-hair. Click once to set the clone source point.**

4. **Release the Alt/Option key and move the cursor to another location on the document.**

5. **Click and drag the mouse or move the stylus along the tablet, and the source point material is replicated wherever you move the brush.**

FIGURE 18.3

FIGURE 18.3

Here more carefully chosen source points with random detail allow the cloned region to blend in better, without drawing attention to what has been done.

Clone Source panel

The Clone Source panel was introduced to Photoshop users with version CS3. This panel (shown in Figure 18.5) is designed for use with the Clone Stamp and Healing Brush (also discussed later in the chapter). Use this panel to set and store multiple source locations, preview your cloning or healing changes before you actually apply them, and manipulate the cloned data so that it fits the target location (for example, you can rotate and scale the cloned source region before using it).

The Clone Source panel's functionality includes:

- **Clone Source buttons.** Each of these five buttons can store a separate clone source. To store a clone source area, click one of the buttons and then Alt+click/Option+click the source point on the image. Note that these buttons may reflect source points from multiple open documents, not just the active document.

- **Offset.** As you move the Clone Tool's brush cursor away from the source origin, the current values for X (left is negative, right is positive) and Y (above is negative, below is positive) are displayed relative to the original coordinates. For example, if you move the cursor 36 pixels below and 20 pixels to the left of where you clicked the source point, the X and Y fields display –20 px and 36 px, respectively.

FIGURE 18.4

The Clone Stamp tool is a great way to remove unwanted objects around the edges of your image with neighboring texture detail. Here the tree branch at the bottom right was replaced with water detail from three or four source locations around the branch.

FIGURE 18.5

The Clone Source panel is a great way to manage and modify the cloned source area before it is applied to other regions of the image.

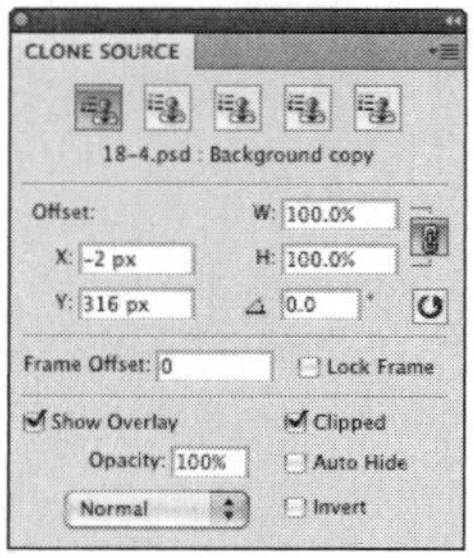

- **Frame Offset and Lock Frame (Extended edition only).** Used to define offset between video frames that are used in cloning operations.

- **Show Overlay.** Shows you the actual source pixels overlaid on your target area. Helpful in aligning cloned elements to other parts of the image. When unclipped, the preview is the same size as the original document and can be somewhat unwieldy.

- **Opacity.** Defines the opacity of the clone source Overlay.

- **Blend options.** Defines whether the Overlay is displayed using Normal, Darken, Lighten, or Difference blending modes. These are helpful when contrast issues exist between source and target locations.

- **Invert.** Inverts the tonal values of the Overlay area (like a photo negative), making it easier to see.

- **Auto Hide.** When the Clipped item is unchecked, this option hides the full document Overlay as you perform the cloning or healing operation.

- **Clipped (New in CS4).** This reduces the Overlay preview to the size of the active brush cursor. You'll want this option checked most of the time when using the source Overlay.

- **Clone Source Angle.** Used to rotate the original clone source to a new angle that matches the target region. This angle can be unique with each stored clone or healing source.

- **Reset.** Use this button (rotating arrow icon) to reset the Clone Source Angle and Clone Source Scaling options.

- **Scale width and height.** Use these fields to scale the source information up or down to a desired percentage. Click the chain link icon to ensure both width (W) and height (H) use the same value. Width and height scaling can also be unique to each stored source.

- **Clone Source panel menu.** Shows secondary access points for commonly used items.

To use the Clone Source panel, set the parameters you need and then use the Clone tool or Healing Brush as you normally would. For the purpose of illustration, Figure 18.6 provides a simple demonstration of what happens when you modify the rotation and scale in the Clone Source panel and then apply that source point to different areas of the image.

The Healing and Spot Healing Brushes

The Healing Brush and Spot Healing Brush are among the most valuable Photoshop tools for retouching photographs in a realistic way. Like the Clone Stamp tool, they use image data from a source point to perform tasks like reducing wrinkles and removing dust and scratch lines. However, instead of replicating the source texture, the Healing Brushes (and the Patch tool, which will be covered shortly) blend the source texture into the target area. This "healing effect" produces a more natural appearance than the Clone Stamp, especially when working on portraits or fine details that are not part of a random pattern or texture.

FIGURE 18.6

The Clone Source panel provides a variety of options for tweaking your clone source regions, including the ability to scale and rotate them when needed. Here three different scales and rotation are used with a single source point, and stored as three separate items.

Healing Brush

Shown in Figure 18.7, the Healing Brush operates similarly to the Clone Stamp tool. Follow the steps below to begin experimenting with this extremely useful retouching tool. Here, the smoother skin under the wrinkles was used as a source, and then we painted across a few of them with one quick stroke apiece. A freckle was also removed.

CAUTION Keep in mind that removing all wrinkles or imperfections would create an unrealistic representation of the picture you are retouching. Don't overdo it!

NOTE Be sure your brush size just covers the width of the area you are correcting, with maybe 2 to 5 pixels extra. Trying to match the brush width too precisely can cause distortions or dark streaks.

To use the Healing Brush, follow these steps:

1. Select the Healing Brush (press the J key on your keyboard or press Shift+J).
2. Move the brush cursor over the part of the image you wish to base your correction on.

FIGURE 18.7

The Healing Brush is a great tool for making image corrections (left) that require source texture from elsewhere in the image, but which need to be blended into the target region. Be sure to choose the Sampled option from the Source selector.

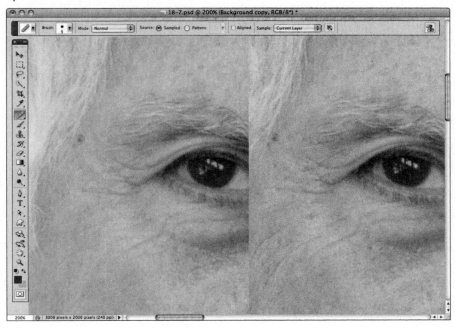

3. **Alt+click/Option+click your source area. Use the Clone Source panel to assign multiple sources from your image(s).**

4. **Move the Healing Brush to the point where you'd like to make a correction and brush over it.** For multiple corrections to areas such as part of a face, use multiple source locations close to the areas you are correcting. This can create a more even-toned result, because skin tone often changes in subtle ways from one region of a portrait to another. You want the areas being blended to be as similar in tone as possible.

Healing Brush options

Also seen in Figure 18.7 within the Options Bar, there are a few options you can use to modify the effect of the strokes applied with the Healing Brush:

■ **Brush options.** Like other brush tools, you have the option to change the brush's shape, diameter, hardness, spacing, angle, and roundness. The only option you don't have is changing the brush shape, unfortunately.

■ **Blending modes.** These can be used to modify the manner in which your source and target regions are blended together. These modes include Multiply, Screen, Darken, Lighten, Color, and Luminosity.

CROSS-REF For more information on blending modes, see Chapters 14 and 15.

There are two blending modes that have specific meaning in this context that are different than other times you may see them. Normal ensures that source and target are blended together. Replace causes the Healing Brush to act exactly like the Clone Stamp tool. This can be useful in making your cloning and healing operations more efficient, since you can use one tool to provide both types of edits, and both use the Clone Source panel.

■ **Source options.** These define what type of image source you are using. Sampled is the best option for retouching. Pattern uses a pattern preset to blend into your targeted image regions; this can be useful for creative artwork or illustration purposes.

■ **Aligned.** This defines the offset used with your brush strokes. Leaving this unchecked allows you to draw all brush strokes from the same source point. If Aligned is checked, the source point shifts depending on where your cursor is on the canvas.

■ **Sample menu.** This defines whether the source sample utilizes information from only the active layer, the active layer plus the layer below it, or all layers.

Spot Healing Brush

The Spot Healing Brush (shown in Figure 18.8) works in much the same way as the Healing Brush. The main difference is that you do not need to set a source point. Instead, the Spot Healing Brush attempts to pull information from the areas around your brushed region to make a blended correction.

The Spot Healing Brush is most useful making corrections to very small regions of pixels. Dust, freckles, acne, and other "specks" that occupy a region of the image where they don't belong or aren't wanted all qualify as good uses for the Spot Healing Brush.

Many of the options for the Spot Healing Brush are also the same as the standard Healing Brush. One slight difference is that instead of having a Source option, there is a Type option that allows you to define your corrected regions as either a Proximity Match (giving a more blended result from areas around your target region) or a Create Texture (giving a result more like a Clone Stamp, using the surrounding areas as a source).

Patch tool

Though it has few options to modify its behavior, the Patch tool works exactly like a combination of the Healing Brush and the Lasso tool. Instead of setting a source point and brushing over the areas you wish to correct, use the lasso-like cursor to encircle the area you wish to correct. Then, drag the lasso over the source area you wish to use, as seen in Figure 18.9. Once you find a good spot, release the mouse button or pick up the stylus from the tablet, and the correction appears after a second or two, depending on how large the area being blended is.

FIGURE 18.8

The Spot Healing Brush is a great tool for cleaning up sensor or lens dust and other small artifacts.

The Patch tool is very handy for correcting lots of small blemishes or artifacts that are clustered in a relatively small area. The trick to using the Patch tool is to avoid blending two regions of very high contrast (light and dark). If you do this, or try to patch by using regions from the edges of your image, a smudge is likely to result (see Figure 8.10).

The Patch tool options, also shown in Figure 18.9, are fairly limited. The main option you need to be familiar with is the ability to define your selected region (before you drag) as either the source or the destination.

The default mode is Destination and is somewhat preferable in that as you drag the selection around (prior to releasing the mouse button or stylus from the tablet), you can see how the region you are using as a source fits texture-wise, because it is previewed live in the destination area.

When you have found the region of image you wish to apply as the source, just release the mouse button or pick up the stylus from the tablet. Generally, the larger and more varied the area you are patching, the more likely you will need to undo the first couple of attempts and try again before you get things just right. It's also common to "clean up" around a patched area with the Spot Healing Brush.

FIGURE 18.9

The Patch tool allows you to draw a marquee around your selected target or source region and then drag to the source or target region to complete the correction. If you default to selecting the target region and dragging to a source area with a cleaner texture (as in this example), a preview of the source data that will be blended into the target area shows inside the marquee in real time.

Magic and Background Eraser tools

While the concept of permanently erasing pixels to see what's underneath is never preferable to using a layer mask to accomplish the same task, there are times when using the Magic and Background Eraser tools in Photoshop can be a more efficient (and destructive) way to accomplish this goal.

Magic Eraser tool

Seen in Figure 18.11, the Magic Eraser works on exactly the same principle as the Magic Wand tool, but in reverse. Instead of selecting large swaths of an image based on your chosen source point's color and tone, it erases large swaths of an image.

It even uses the same options: Tolerance, Anti-alias, Contiguous, and Sample All Layers. Put another way: If you know how to use the Magic Wand, you also know how to use the Magic Eraser tool. Unfortunately, the Magic Eraser has about the same amount of first-click-precision as the Magic Wand — not a great deal.

FIGURE 18.10

Trying to patch high-contrast areas or regions along the very edge of an image can often result in blurry smudges instead of two cleanly blended image regions.

FIGURE 18.11

The Magic Eraser works on the same principle as the Magic Wand tool, except that it erases pixels instead of selecting them.

If you are working on an important image, I suggest you not use the Magic Eraser, as it is somewhat imprecise and permanently deletes the pixels it erases (once the document is saved and closed). Use a layer mask instead for important images.

For less important images, if you have large areas of generally uniform color that you wish to remove, then the Magic Eraser can be a convenient option.

Background Eraser tool

The Background Eraser tool is a more precise option for removing large regions of color from an image because it allows you to use the control of a brush tool. Essentially, the Background Eraser (see Figure 18.12) also works on the same principle as the wand tools, by employing a Tolerance slider to tell Photoshop how different a color has to be before it is not subject to erasing.

Though more precise than the Magic Eraser, it is no less destructive in terms of how it handles image pixels.

The trick to getting the Background Eraser right is to make sure you have significant regions of uninterrupted color, make sure you are using a large enough brush to overlap areas you wish to erase without placing the cross-hair on a color you wish to maintain, and experiment with the Tolerance slider. There are other useful options for the Background Eraser, shown in Figure 18.12:

- **Continuous Sampling.** The third button from the left on the Options bar, this setting is the default (and most effective). It allows the Background Eraser to continue sampling the colors that are underneath the cross-hair as you move it. This is why it's important to make sure you don't move the cross-hair over regions that you want to maintain. If those regions are sampled accidentally, then whatever similar colors that fall within the brush diameter will be erased.

- **Sample Once.** The fourth button from the left, this uses the first point you click on as the basis of its color detection. It can be useful where you have areas of one continuous color that you wish to erase.

- **Background Swatch.** The fifth button from the left, Background Swatch uses the background color as the basis for erasing colors.

    Discontiguous (Limits menu). This option erases colors that meet the tolerance criteria, whether they are connected or not. The only requirement is that you move the brush cursor over them.

- **Contiguous (Limits menu).** This option does not erase colors that meet the tolerance criteria, unless they are connected to other regions of the same color that are under the brush cursor.

- **Find Edge (Limits menu).** This option bases the erased region on where the contrast edges between your color and neighboring colors lie. This option is useful for working around man-made structures (such as rooftops against a blue sky) because the edges are very pronounced.

FIGURE 18.12

The Background Eraser provides more control than the Magic Eraser tool; however, it is still preferable to use a layer mask for important images because, like all eraser tools, it permanently discards the pixels.

Dodge and Burn tools

The Dodge and Burn tools used to require a very conservative approach in day-to-day use because both tools were adept at removing all the detail and color accuracy in the areas where they were applied too liberally. For example, users often had to lower the Exposure slider under 10 percent, and just live with whatever moderate changes to those exposure levels were created. However, with the advent of one very useful item on the Options Bar, Dodge and Burn are now much more useful in CS4.

NOTE Both the Dodge and Burn tools should be considered when you have relatively small areas that you need to adjust the tonality for in subtle ways. If you need to make changes across 20 percent or more of your image, you are better off using an adjustment layer and masking out the part of the image you do not wish to apply the changes to.

Dodge

As in a traditional darkroom, the Dodge tool allows you to selectively brighten small areas that are underexposed or caught in shadow. Shown in Figure 18.13, the Dodge tool works like any other brush tool except that you use the Options Bar to set which of the three tonal regions you wish to apply your brightening to (shadows, midtones, or highlights) and to set which Exposure value (1 to 100 percent) you wish to use. The most important option is the Protect Tones check box (far right). This little wonder allows you to use much higher exposure settings, without wiping out all the detail and color in that region.

The Dodge tool is now particularly useful as a means of brightening teeth and the whites of people's eyes (but again, don't go overboard!), because it does not destroy the fine details by turning things pure white or creating a white haze.

FIGURE 18.13

The Dodge tool is now much more accurate and powerful when brightening small areas of your image, if you use the Protect Tones option. Here, the top-left portion of the clock was brightened with Protect Tones, while the top-right portion uses the same exposure setting in legacy mode (no tonal protection).

Burn

The Burn tool is also a traditional darkroom favorite, and it also works with similar options as the Dodge tool (including Protect Tones). The obvious difference is that it darkens small areas of the image that have been slightly overexposed, though the best way to bring back details from bright areas that have been overexposed is still the Recovery slider in Adobe Camera Raw. Figure 18.14 shows what the new Burn tool can do at higher exposure settings (using Protect Tones), as compared to without (legacy mode).

FIGURE 18.14

The Burn tool also benefits greatly from the new Protect Tones option. The right side of the window frame has been burned with the legacy mode, while the left side was burned at the same exposure with Protect Tones active to help even out the harsh highlights around the window. It's still a good idea to use more conservative exposure values with Burn as compared to the Dodge tool.

Sponge tool

The Sponge tool — which is grouped with the Dodge and Burn tools on the main toolbar — is used to increase or decrease the saturation within a specific region of your image. Like the Dodge and Burn tools, the Sponge tool is best used somewhat sparingly, on relatively smaller regions of your image. If you need to make saturation changes to 20 percent or more of your image, you are probably better off using the Vibrance Adjustment Layer and masking out the portions of the image you do not want to affect.

Seen in Figure 18.15, the Sponge tool has a few simple options: a Mode menu that defines whether you are going to saturate or de-saturate an area of color; a Flow slider, which controls the intensity of the effect you are applying to the image; and a Vibrance check box, which is new in CS4. Vibrance is the Sponge tool's analog to the Protect Tones option with Dodge and Burn. When checked, it prevents fully saturated or de-saturated colors from clipping when brushing over them.

FIGURE 18.15

The Sponge tool has improved accuracy in Photoshop CS4 with the Vibrance option, which prevents fully saturated or de-saturated colors from clipping. Here the top-left side of the image was enhanced by using the Saturate and Vibrance settings. This combination is often useful for taking the "haze" out of blue skies.

Content Aware Scaling

A brand-new tool for Photoshop CS4 is the Content Aware Scale option found in the Edit menu. Content Aware Scaling works like the standard Transform ➪ Scale option, except that you can protect certain areas of the image from being stretched or crunched, while the rest of the image scales normally. This is sometimes called *Seam Carving*.

Figures 18.16 and 18.17 demonstrate the effect. For this image, the area from the right edge of the image over to the left third has been protected by using an alpha channel. The rest has been scaled in toward the right and upward from the bottom to make a smaller image, but without distorting the important part of the scene. More details on how this is done follow.

FIGURE 18.16

The Content Aware Scale command allows you to protect part of your image by using an alpha channel and the Amount slider.

The easiest way to use Content Aware Scaling is as follows:

1. **Select your image and use the Marquee or Lasso tool to select the parts of the image for which you want the least amount of distortion when you are finished.** The closer to the inside edge of your selection something is, the less it will be protected.

2. **Create an alpha channel from your selection.**

3. **Deactivate the selection by pressing Ctrl+D/⌘+D.** This is important because if you leave the selection active, the transform commands will only act on what is inside the selection.

4. **From the Edit menu, choose Content Aware Scale.**

5. **In the Protect menu (Options Bar), choose your alpha channel.**

6. **To protect the boundary areas around your alpha channel selection, adjust the Amount slider value accordingly.** You may have to experiment a bit with this setting.

7. **If there are people in your image, click the Protect Skin Tones button (human icon).**

8. **Click Enter or the check button (Options Bar) to accept the changes.**

FIGURE 18.17

Here the finished product after scaling is complete. Note that you cannot perform Content Aware Scaling on a background layer.

Lens Correction

Photoshop CS4 offers many transform tools in the Edit menu; however, not all of these are used in a typical retouching session. Some are much better suited to creative deformation of an image than traditional retouching (the Skew and Warp commands are two prime examples). Luckily for us, Adobe was good enough to create a set of its most useful transform capabilities and wrap them up in a single filter window called Lens Correction, seen in Figure 18.18.

Shown in Figure 18.18, the Lens Correction dialog box packs a lot of functionality into one window. The following list details the various controls and what operations they perform on your image. Note that the first five items are located along the top-left portion of the window, listed from top to bottom.

- **Remove Distortion Tool.** When you click and drag this tool across the image preview, it moves the Remove Distortion slider near the top of the Settings area. This is used to correct barrel distortion.

- **Straighten Tool.** Works in the same way as the Straighten tool in Adobe Camera Raw. Click on one edge of the horizon and then drag a line to the other edge and release.

- **Move Grid Tool.** Allows you to grab and move the grid overlay, which can be useful for aligning things before a rotation or keystone correction.

- **Hand Tool.** Works the same as the Hand tool on the main Photoshop toolbar.
- **Zoom Tool.** Works the same as the standard Photoshop Zoom tool.
- **Magnification Settings.** Use the + and – buttons to zoom in or out, or use the magnification preset menu to choose the best magnification level.

FIGURE 18.18

The Lens Correction filter is a great way to minimize distortions and other flaws in an image that were caused by the physical properties of the lens. The most common are barrel distortion, keystone distortion, chromatic aberration (or color fringing), and dark regions in the corners of an image (vignettes). Lens Correction also handles image rotation problems caused by tilted cameras.

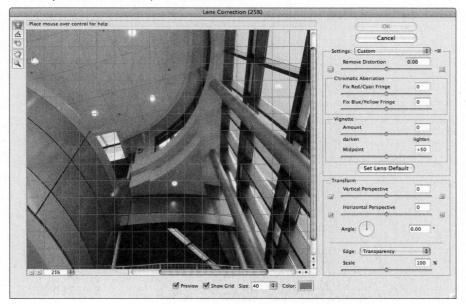

- **Preview.** Turns the preview of your current settings on and off. Use this before clicking OK, as the Lens Correction filter can take a while to render out a final image correction.
- **Show Grid.** Turns the grid overlay on and off.
- **Size.** Defines the size of the grid squares in pixels.
- **Color.** Defines the grid's color.
- **Edge/Scale.** Allows you to artificially scale the edges of the image to compensate for truncations that occur when the Transform tools are used. Typically the best setting is the default (Transparency), which shows transparency behind the truncated areas. It is very difficult to get an accurate result by using Edge Extension. Background Color can be useful if you wish to matte the image (uncropped) onto a specific color.

- **Angle.** Allows you to correct improper image rotation caused by tripod misalignment.

- **Horizontal/Vertical Perspective.** Allows for correction of keystone distortions caused by camera or tripod tilt.

- **Set Lens Default.** Allows you to set a default correction value for Vignette, Chromatic Aberration, and Remove Distortion. First, note the camera, lens, *and* focal length used on the shot, then make your settings and click the Default button when they provide the level of correction you need. Then, the next time you open an image into Lens Correction that has the same camera, lens, and focal length settings, it automatically gives you the option to apply the Lens Default via the Settings menu.

- **Vignette.** Allows you to remove dark areas from the corners or edges of your image, caused by light fall-off from the lens. This phenomenon is fairly common in close-ups and macro images. The Amount slider provides the level of intensity or brightness applied, while the Midpoint slider controls how far from the corners or edges the amount is applied. The higher the setting the more the correction sticks to the corners and edges.

- **Chromatic Aberration.** Corrects the red/cyan or blue/yellow fringes sometimes visible along high-contrast edges of an image (such as a roofline, tree limbs, or other subjects silhouetted against the sky, or even hair/hats). Zoom in to 100 percent or more to get the best indication of whether Chromatic Aberration is present in your image; if it is, note the color and push the appropriate slider until the effect begins to visibly lessen or disappear.

  Note that images that are slightly soft and have Chromatic Aberration may not be able to be repaired. This function works best with very crisp images and edges.

- **Remove Distortion.** Used to remove barrel distortion caused by wide-angle lenses.

- **Settings menu.** Used to apply either custom settings, the previous correction, or the Lens Default, if stored from a previous session.

- **Settings popup.** Allows you to save all settings as a preset and load them later. Saved settings show up in the Settings menu.

Figures 18.19 through 18.26 show corrections for barrel distortion, vignettes, keystone distortions, and rotation issues, respectively.

You can combine these types of corrections in a single image session — and often you need to — but for the purposes of illustration, they're separated here. You may not get things precisely right on the first try, so use a smart filter layer that allows you to go back and tweak your initial Lens Correction settings non-destructively.

FIGURE 18.19

Wide-angle distortions are present, caused by the curvature of the lens.

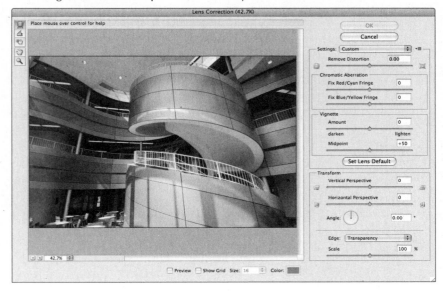

FIGURE 18.20

Here the distortion is lessened, giving a more realistic depiction of the staircase. In most cases, it's necessary to crop the transparent areas out of your image after applying distortion corrections.

FIGURE 18.21

Vignettes (or darkened corners) sometimes accompany shots taken with certain lenses or focal lengths.

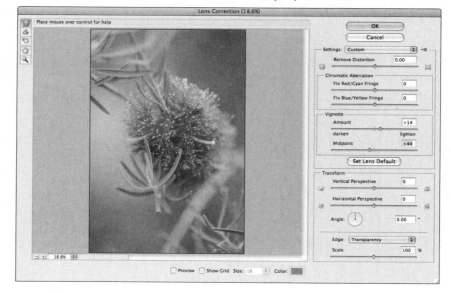

FIGURE 18.22

Here the vignette areas in the corners and along the top have been brightened up.

FIGURE 18.23

Keystone distortions (which give a trapezoid-like appearance) are a common problem for pictures that were taken with the camera tilted or shifted at odd angles relative to the subject.

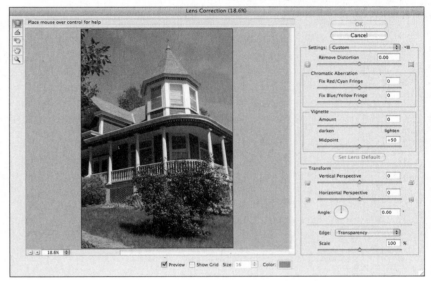

FIGURE 18.24

Here the image needed to be both rotated and given a keystone correction since the camera was tilted sharply upward when the picture was taken.

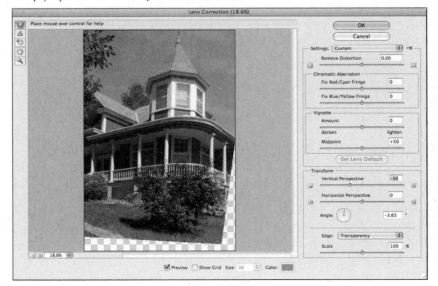

FIGURE 18.25

Pictures that require a slight degree of rotation in order to be "squared" with the subject are very common.

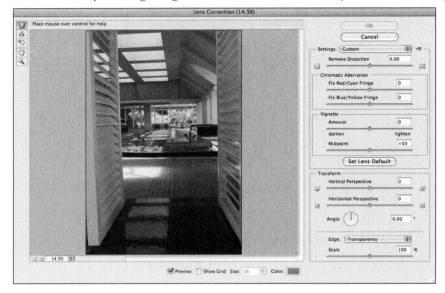

FIGURE 18.26

Here the image has been rotated to square the image, and a slight barrel distortion correction has been made as well to straighten the shutters a bit.

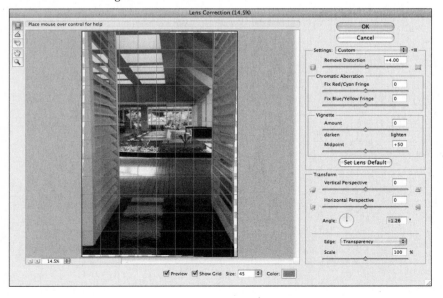

Sample Retouching Workflows

To give you some idea of how a basic retouching workflow might look from start to finish, this section details two quick examples of how a typical image might be corrected, using a variety of the tools demonstrated earlier in the chapter. The first example focuses on general retouching, the second on restoring an old image that was scanned into Photoshop. Both examples also make use of some tools you learned earlier in the book, such as the Levels command.

Image retouching

The general progression for retouching an image should follow this pattern once you have completed your initial edits in Adobe Camera Raw (ACR):

1. **Noise reduction**
2. **Global tweaks to image tonality and color**
3. **Retouching**
4. **Output Sharpening**
5. **Output (prints, Web, and so on)**

For this example, I will assume all work in ACR and all noise reduction has been completed, and all output sharpening and output processes will be handled later. In other words, you're focusing strictly on the Retouching components of the process.

Assuming you have made some useful corrections to your overall color, tonality, and contrast in ACR, and that you have a relatively noise-free image, the first thing to do is make any final corrections or stylistic changes (perhaps to influence the mood of the photo) to the image's tonality.

Figures 18.27 through 18.31 illustrate the progression of your demo image from its original opened state, through final tonal correction, retouching, and then final sharpening.

Image restoration

This example demonstrates how to use the tools discussed in this chapter (and tools from previous chapters) to improve the appearance of an old, faded photograph. The assumption here is that the image was a paper print acquired digitally with a flatbed scanner at 16 bits per channel and 300 ppi. Figures 18.32 through 18.36 illustrate a restoration process that goes from the original unaltered scan, through Levels corrections, to color corrections (to decrease the yellow cast), to defect removal, and finally on to sharpening.

FIGURE 18.27

The sample image in its original condition, after primary edits in ACR, but prior to basic retouches like tonal corrections, cloning, healing, and sharpening

FIGURE 18.28

Parts of the initially corrected image remained too dark, so the Levels command was used to set new black and white points to improve contrast, and the midtone slider brightened the brick areas significantly.

FIGURE 18.29

The next step was to move the lens dust and streaks that appeared on the reflected sky (in the mirror), and remove the skid marks from the surface of the intersection (also seen in the mirror). The dust and streaks were removed with the Healing Brush, while the skid marks were first cloned over with clean pavement, and then patched to blend together more naturally.

FIGURE 18.30

To sharpen the detail in the side of the building and the reflection in the mirror, a High Pass sharpen technique was used. To use High Pass, duplicate your finished retouching layer and choose Filter ⇨ Other ⇨ High Pass. Try a value somewhere between 1 and 4 pixels until you can see the detail in your image being outlined in light gray (right half). Click OK, then apply the Overlay blending mode to your sharpening layer, which brings back the normal view (left half). Click the layer visibility on and off to see the difference.

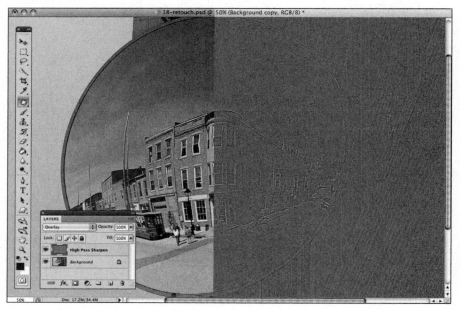

FIGURE 18.31

The final image after basic retouches have been applied

FIGURE 18.32

The original scanned image with defects

FIGURE 18.33

To bring back the detail in the clothes and make the exposure of the clothes more even in relation to the surrounding image, the clothes were selected and formed the basis of a layer mask. From there, I used Levels in the Multiply mode to bring back the detail and even out the tonality. The second Levels command was used to handle the contrast of the entire scene, including the corrected clothes.

FIGURE 18.34

Because the photo was still too yellow (particularly the clothes and skin tones) after the Levels correction, Hue and Saturation were used to completely remove saturation and lightness in the yellow channel. Note this type of change is not recommended unless the scanned photo is very old and weathered, as it can introduce banding and other artifacts when you move any of the Hue and Saturation sliders more than 30 to 40 points.

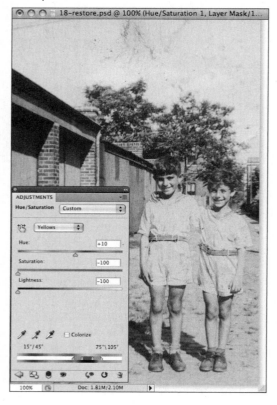

FIGURE 18.35

A duplicate of the original background was created, and from that, all the scratches and splotchy areas were removed with a combination of cloning and patching. A few pits that were on the surface of the original image (which show up as inky blue) were removed with the Spot Healing Brush.

FIGURE 18.36

I sharpened the image by duplicating the finished retouch layer, and applied the High Pass method with a value between 2 and 3 pixels.

Summary

This chapter demonstrated several methods of replacing, smoothing, and removing unwanted defects in an image, as well as methods of selectively brightening and darkening small regions of an exposure, without losing detail. Methods of accurately scaling an image without distorting or compressing important details were also shown with Content Aware Scaling, and flaws that come from lenses were diminished by using Lens Correction.

Among the most fundamental retouching tools are the Clone Stamp and the Clone Source panel, which allow you to effectively replace small bits and pieces of the image with surrounding texture. These tools can be especially useful in shots where you are trying to replace regions of the image with other, random details such as grass, sand, or tree leaves — things which have detail, but no particular order and allow for barren areas to be covered up in a realistic way. The Clone Stamp is also a useful tool for removing dust and spots caused by debris on your lens or digital camera sensor.

The Healing Brush and Spot Healing Brush are excellent tools for smoothing over facial imperfections or other areas where the texture from neighboring image regions must be used in a convincing way. Reducing wrinkles or removing spots and blemishes are the bread and butter for the healing brushes, and typically the results are fantastic if you watch what you're doing and take advantage of the Fade command to ensure that things don't get too perfectly smooth. Another tool used for blending image regions is the Patch tool, and its uses can be as varied as removing acne to removing a wall socket on an interior design photograph.

If you need to remove background regions from your image, the Magic Eraser and Background Eraser tools can be a big help in this regard, though like the Magic Wand tool (which they are loosely based on), the results are not always precise, so you may need to make multiple attempts to get the effect just right.

Photoshop CS4 has brought new life to the Dodge and Burn tools, enabling photographers and retouchers to brush on very localized tonal corrections, without damaging the texture or color nearly as much as the prior versions of these tools. Dodge can be used for brightening teeth or the whites of people's eyes (provided you don't use too aggressive a value in the Options Bar), while Burn can be used to tone down specular distractions or overly bright regions that still maintain some detail. The Sponge tool has also been improved by allowing you to selectively saturate or desaturate regions of color without clipping colors.

The Lens Distortion filter is an extremely powerful way to deal with the imperfections in your image caused by wide-angle lenses, digital sensor alignment issues, and perspective issues.

Content Aware Scaling is a brand-new technique for Photoshop CS4 (sometimes called Seam Carving) that allows you to scale or nudge in one part of an image, while protecting other parts by using an alpha channel to define the protected region. This allows for some very interesting effects, such as cramming tall buildings together on a skyline, without actually warping the buildings' shapes.

You also learned about basic retouching workflow that included localized tonal corrections using a masked Levels adjustment layer in Multiply mode to bring back faded details, global Levels and Hue and Saturation corrections, as well as removal of scratches and defects with a combination of Clone Stamp, Healing Brushes, and the Patch tool. High Pass sharpening techniques were also covered, allowing you to better define the edge regions in your images.

Part VI

Painting and Special Effects

Chapter 19

Painting

There are numerous options as far as painting software goes on both the Mac and Windows, but because of its robust features, Photoshop remains one of the premier choices. At its core, Photoshop is engineered as image-editing software, but skilled artists can create beautiful, painterly images from scratch by using only Photoshop's brush tools. These same tools are also part of the core toolset of digital photographers, retouchers, graphic artists, and many other creative professionals.

Part of what makes Photoshop's painting toolset so versatile is its capability to heavily customize almost every aspect of the brush tools. There is also the huge number of brush presets that ship with Photoshop — which, with the custom brushes that you can create or download from the Internet, make for almost limitless possibilities.

Photoshop and its brushes have features that are designed to work especially well with drawing tablets such as those created by Wacom (www.wacom.com), and can respond to the pressure, angle, and rotation of the pens used with these devices.

Many of Photoshop's tools, including the Clone Stamp, the Healing Brush, and the History Brush, are brush-based, but in this chapter you'll learn about those tools that more closely resemble traditional painting implements.

To fully dive into using the painting tools, it might not be a bad idea to switch Photoshop's panels and tools into the new workflow-based Painting Workspace by selecting Painting from the Workspace menu at the top right of the Application Frame, or from the Window ⇨ Workspace menu.

611

Brushes and Tools That Work Like Brushes

Photoshop's painting tools fall into two classes: those that apply color, and those that manipulate or edit existing colors. These tools are shown in Figure 19.1. You'll notice that many of the tools appear grouped in the Tools panel — for example, the Brush, Pencil, and Color Replacement tools all fall under the Brush tool's fly-out menu. The tiny black triangle in the lower-right corner of the tool's icon is your cue that there are more tools hiding under the icons in the Tools panel; simply click and hold down the mouse button on these icons to reveal them.

Painting tools

Photoshop's two primary painting tools — the Brush and the Pencil — are very similar to their analog counterparts. They work, as you'd probably expect, by laying down strokes with the foreground color while you drag with your mouse or stylus across the canvas.

The Brush tool lays down soft-edged strokes (using anti-aliasing — a technique that draws partially transparent pixels to create smooth edges), while the Pencil tool creates crisp, hard-edged strokes.

FIGURE 19.1

The painting and editing tools in Photoshop's Tools panel

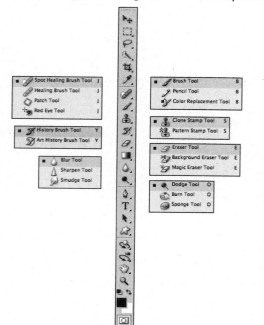

You can draw freehand by simply dragging with your mouse or stylus. You can also draw perfectly straight lines by first clicking to define a starting point, then holding down the Shift key and clicking again where you want the line to end. Or, to constrain your brush strokes to horizontal or vertical lines, hold down the Shift key before clicking with the mouse. Figure 19.2 shows a variety of brush strokes created with the Brush and Pencil tools.

FIGURE 19.2

These strokes were created with the Brush and Pencil tools. Shift+clicking constrains the Brush tool, drawing perfectly straight strokes.

Editing tools

The editing tools manipulate existing pixels, rather than laying down color on the canvas. Aside from this difference, they function in a very similar manner to the painting tools in that to use them, you adjust the tip size, and drag with the mouse button or stylus held down on the canvas. Here's an in-depth look at the editing tools.

Dodge/Burn

The Dodge and Burn tools (see Figure 19.3) are based on traditional darkroom techniques used to control the amount of exposure that selected parts of a photograph receive. The Dodge tool is used to brighten areas of an image, while painting an area with the Burn tool darkens it.

To brighten or darken certain regions of an image, select the Dodge or Burn tool from the Tools panel, or press O (or Shift+O repeatedly to cycle through the tools that share this keyboard shortcut). In the Options panel, select whether to affect the Shadows, Midtones, or Highlights of the image by using the Range pop-up menu. You can adjust the intensity of the effect by increasing or decreasing the Exposure setting, with a higher number resulting in a more intense effect and a lower setting resulting in a less obvious change. I recommend starting with a lower number and gradually building from there.

Sponge

The Sponge tool can be used to either increase or decrease the intensity of the colors in an image. Select the Sponge tool (which shares a tool grouping with the Dodge and Burn tools) and then select the mode. Paint over a part of your image to either soak up some of the color from the area (Desaturate), or add more intensity (Saturate). See Figure 19.3 for an example. The Vibrance check box protects the colors in the image from being oversaturated to the point that they fall beyond the gamut, or range that can be handled by your document's color profile (refer to Chapter 24 for more on color profiles).

FIGURE 19.3

This image shows the effect of the Dodge, Burn, and Sponge tools. Compare the three samples to the original image (shown on top): in the first instance (bottom left), the Dodge tool was used to brighten the boat; in the second case (middle), the Burn tool was used to darken the water and the background sky; and the Sponge tool was used to saturate the sky and desaturate the water in the third example (bottom right).

Sharpen/Blur

Painting with the Sharpen tool increases the contrast between neighboring pixels, thereby increasing the sharpness of the details in that region. The Blur tool has the opposite effect, reducing contrast between edges and pixels, resulting in reduced detail (see Figure 19.4). Use the Mode pop-up menu to specify the way the effect is combined with the existing image pixels. Blending modes get more coverage later in this chapter.

FIGURE 19.4

The image on the left was painted with the Sharpen tool (excessively, just to make the effect more obvious). On the right, the Blur tool was used to soften the boat and foreground, as well as the setting sun.

Smudge

The Smudge tool (see Figure 19.5) allows you to push colors and pixels around in your image.

Pixels are picked up from the point where you initially click your mouse, and pushed through the image in the direction that you move the cursor until you release the mouse button. You can change the intensity of the effect with the Strength setting. It's sort of like finger painting; in fact, the Smudge tool actually has a Finger Painting option. Enabling this option in the Options Bar smudges the current foreground color into the existing pixels.

Color Replacement

The Color Replacement tool is a great way to replace an existing color in an image by painting over it in a different color. Select a foreground color, and begin painting over the color that you'd like to replace. The three icons next to the Mode pop-up menu (shown in Figure 19.6) specify how Photoshop identifies the color that you want to replace.

- **Continuous Sampling.** Continuous Sampling does what it sounds like — that is, as you drag your cursor in your image, it continually detects the color that's under your cursor and replaces it with the foreground color.

- **Once.** Setting the sampling mode to Once samples the color that you initially click on, and only replaces that color in the areas that you paint over.

- **Background Swatch.** Background Swatch replaces the colors that you paint over with whatever color is set as your background color.

FIGURE 19.5

Use the Smudge tool to push pixels around in your image. I set my foreground color to red and enabled Finger Painting to create the swirling effect around the sun.

FIGURE 19.6

The Color Replacement tool's Options Bar controls

The options under the Limits pop-up menu control how colors are replaced:

- **Discontiguous.** This option replaces the sampled color wherever it occurs under your brush.
- **Contiguous.** This option replaces colors that are immediately adjacent to the color that's under your brush.
- **Find Edges.** This option replaces colors while keeping the edges of shapes distinct.

Although the Color Replacement tool offers four blending modes, it generally works best when set to Color.

Eraser

The Eraser tool is more versatile than its name would imply. Its most basic function is to remove pixels from the canvas, but as you'll see shortly, there are two other flavors of the Eraser tool that offer some very convenient functionality (see Figure 19.7).

FIGURE 19.7

The Eraser, Background Eraser, and Magic Eraser tools are shown here along with their respective Options Bars.

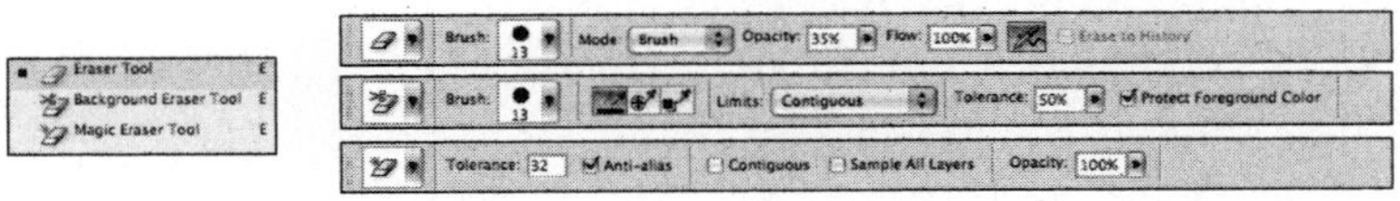

In its basic form, the Eraser tool gets rid of pixels either by making them transparent, or by replacing them with the current background color, if you're working on the background layer (or on a layer with transparency locked).

Here's what you need to know about the Eraser tool:

- **Brush and Pencil modes.** The Eraser tool has three options under its Mode menu. The first two — Brush and Pencil — behave just like the corresponding modes of the Brush tool. Brush mode erases using smooth, anti-aliased edges, while Pencil mode produces jagged strokes. These two modes also offer options for Opacity and Flow. Additionally, the Airbrush option can be used with Brush mode.
- **Block mode.** The somewhat-limited Block mode literally turns your cursor into a square with no sizing or transparency options. Frankly, I'd forgotten this mode even existed, since I don't remember seeing or using it since probably sometime around Photoshop 4. Suffice it to say, you can get by without it.
- **Erase to History.** To erase to an earlier state of your document, set a History State or snapshot in the History panel (choose Window ➪ History, if it's not visible), then click the Erase to History check box and begin painting.

TIP To temporarily enable the Erase to History option, hold down the Alt key (Option key on a Mac) while erasing.

Two additional tools are grouped with the Eraser in the Tools panel:

- **Background Eraser.** The Background Eraser is very much like the Color Replacement tool in the way it functions, except that instead of laying down color, it removes pixels. The Options Bar controls are practically identical, except there are no Color modes for this tool — which makes sense. Refer to the description of the Color Replacement tool for more information on how the Background Eraser works.

- **Magic Eraser.** Clicking with this tool detects similar pixels in your document and erases them. If you click on the background layer, it's converted to a regular layer, and pixels that match the one you clicked on become transparent. If, however, you click on a layer with locked transparency, then the matching pixels are filled in with the background color. Use the Options Bar to control the way the Magic Eraser works:

  - **Tolerance:** A high tolerance means a wide range of colors outside the one you clicked on are targeted for deletion. A low tolerance selects only colors that are very similar to the one you initially clicked.

  - **Anti-Alias:** This term should be familiar by this point — it refers to the technique that's used to produce smooth edges on-screen. Used with the Magic Eraser, it creates a smooth transition between the pixels that are erased and the ones that remain. If disabled, hard, jagged edges result.

  - **Contiguous:** Enable this option to select regions of color that are adjacent to each other. Disabling it could result in larger areas of color being deleted.

  - **Sample All Layers:** If this option is disabled, then only the current layer is analyzed when you click to delete pixels. Disabling it causes all the layers in your document to be taken into consideration when deleting.

Brush tool Options Bar

The Options Bar allows for quick and convenient access to settings for the painting and editing tools. The Brush tool's Options Bar is shown in Figure 19.8, but the available controls vary depending on which tool is selected. Here is a quick rundown of some of the settings you can change:

- **Mode.** Choose a mode to specify the manner in which new pixels that you paint are combined with the underlying pixels. The modes available vary depending on which of the painting tools you have selected, and are based on the 27 blending modes available in Photoshop (refer to Chapter 8 for more on blending modes).

- **Opacity.** This setting controls the transparency of the "paint" or color being laid down. While holding down the mouse button and painting, paint is only applied up to the transparency that you specify using this control. For example, set the Opacity to 40 percent, and any pixels you lay down with the Brush tool are only 40 percent opaque until you release the mouse button. If you paint over that stroke, the pixels build up in opacity until they eventually reach 100 percent.

■ **Flow.** This setting controls the amount of paint that is being laid down with each stroke. A low setting means that a low amount of color is applied. Painting over the area repeatedly eventually increases the coverage of color until it reaches the foreground color.

TIP You can set Opacity and Flow values by using the number keys on your keyboard. Pressing 5 sets the Opacity to 50 percent, 1 sets the Opacity to 10 percent, and so on. Press 0 to set the Opacity to 100 percent. Pressing the Shift key and pressing the numbers sets the Flow value.

■ **Airbrush.** Enable airbrushing capabilities by clicking the Airbrush icon in the Brush tool's Options Bar. This causes the brush to behave as a traditional airbrush would — holding down the mouse button is equivalent to holding down the trigger on an actual airbrush, causing the color to accumulate. To toggle Airbrush mode, press Shift+Alt+P/ Shift+Option+P.

■ **Auto Erase (Pencil tool only).** This option allows you to automatically toggle between drawing pencil strokes using the foreground color, or if you go over strokes that have already been drawn, erasing the strokes by drawing over them with the background color.

FIGURE 19.8

The Brush tool's Options Bar allows quick access to frequently used controls.

TIP Once you've come up with that magical combination of opacity, blending mode, and flow settings, use a tool preset to save it so you can reuse it. To do so, click the Brush Preset icon at the very left side of the Brush tool's Options Bar, and then click the New Tool Preset button. Give your preset a name, and click OK to save it. The difference between tool presets and brush presets (which I cover shortly) is that the opacity, flow, blending mode, and even the foreground color can all be saved with the tool preset — but these settings are specific to the selected tool. Brush presets save brush tip settings such as size, rotation, noise, and dynamics, but they can be applied to any painting or editing tool.

Presets panel

If you want to quickly adjust the size or hardness of the current brush tool without having to deal with the numerous options of the Brushes panel, click the Brush pop-up menu in the Options Bar to reveal the Presets panel (see Figure 19.9).

Use the Master Diameter slider to increase or decrease the diameter of the brush. Use the Hardness slider to increase or decrease the softness of the edge of the brush. Or, select a different brush preset from the thumbnails below. Hover momentarily over the thumbnails for a description of each brush.

FIGURE 19.9

The Presets panel offers the basics for choosing brush tips and for setting frequently used brush options.

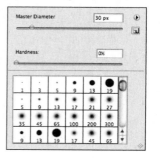

Adjust the brush size in increments of 5 by pressing the left and right bracket keys ([and]) on your keyboard. Press the Shift key and bracket keys to change the Hardness setting: Shift+[for a softer edge, and Shift+] to increase the hardness. Those of you with computers featuring OpenGL-capable graphics cards can take advantage of a new feature in Photoshop CS4: interactively change the Master Diameter of the brush by pressing and holding down Alt while right-clicking and dragging your mouse left or right (on a Mac, press Ctrl+Option while clicking and dragging).

Add the Shift/Option key to this combo to interactively increase or decrease the hardness of the brush. In both cases, a red circular overlay will appear, giving you a visual representation of the size of your brush. Personally, I don't know how I ever got by without this functionality.

TIP Right-clicking/Ctrl-clicking anywhere in the canvas with one of the brush tools active also displays the Presets panel, positioned conveniently under your cursor.

Brushes Panel

Up until this point, you've been learning about the painting tools and what they do on a relatively basic level. Now it's time to step it up and learn where their real power lies — in customizing them. The Brushes panel is the place to do that.

Open the Brushes panel (shown in Figure 19.10) if it's not already visible by choosing Windows ➪ Brushes, or by pressing the F5 key on your keyboard, and click on Brush Presets at the top left of the Brushes panel if it's not already selected.

On the right of the Brushes panel, you'll see thumbnails of all the preset brushes that come with Photoshop, and below that, a preview of what brush strokes made with each brush tip looks like. On the left side of the Brushes panel is a list of brush attributes that you can enable or disable with check boxes, as well as tweak in innumerable ways to adjust the effect of each brush tip.

FIGURE 19.10

The Brushes panel is the place to customize every aspect of the painting tools' behavior.

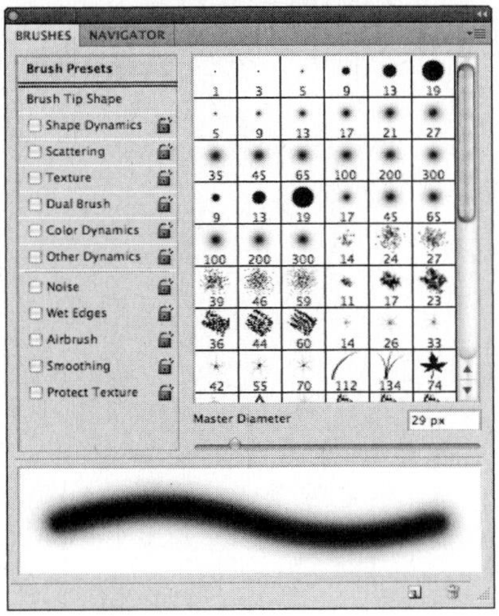

The Brushes panel's fly-out menu offers you options on customizing the appearance of the Brushes panel, as well as controls for loading additional custom brushes and saving your own brush customizations. I cover customizing brushes shortly, but first take a closer look at all those brush tip options (it's not as overwhelming as it looks).

Brush options

Using these options, you can control the characteristics of the brush tips until they're perfectly tuned to let your inner Matisse out. By combining the varying options — from the diameter, opacity, and wetness of the brush, to the way it responds to input from a stylus and tablet — you can make your brush behave like chalk on a blackboard or like a watercolor brush on canvas.

Be aware that some of these options may not be available, depending on which tool is currently selected. For example, the Color Dynamics setting is grayed out while the Dodge or Burn tool is active, and the Wet Edges and Airbrush settings are disabled for the Pencil tool.

Another good thing to know as you experiment with the brush options is that each tool has its own set of default options, so the settings you enable for one tool won't be applied if you switch to other tools.

Brush presets

As mentioned earlier, this is where you'll find all the default brush tip presets that ship with Photoshop. You can use these as starting points for your own brush customizations. Go ahead and experiment with them, as any changes you make are temporary — if you don't like what you've ended up with, you can always reset them by re-selecting the brush preset you started with.

From the Brush Presets section of the Brushes panel, you can specify the Master Diameter of the brush if you need it to be something other than its default value.

 **Quickly switch between brush presets even if the Brushes panel is hidden by pressing the . (period) or , (comma) key on your keyboard. The period key goes forward through the presets, while the comma key switches to the previous preset.**

Brush tip shape

Under this section, you can modify such attributes as the hardness, roundness, angle, and spacing of a selected brush preset to come up with your own customized version of the brush.

- **Diameter.** Use this setting to change the size of the brush tip in pixels. A larger diameter creates a bigger brush stroke, and you can either use the slider or type in a value up to 2,500 pixels.

  Note that you can change the way the cursor represents the brush tip in Photoshop's general preferences. Press Ctrl+K/⌘+K, followed by Ctrl+5/⌘+5 to select the Cursors preferences (see Figure 19.11). From there, under Painting Cursors, you can choose the Standard cursor, which is a throwback to the earliest versions of Photoshop and displays your brush as a tiny little paintbrush icon (frankly, it's pretty useless, and I wouldn't recommend it); or the Precise cursor, which displays your brush tip as a cross-hair on the screen (again, I wouldn't use this, because pressing the Caps Lock key on your keyboard has the same effect).

FIGURE 19.11

The Preferences dialog box for Cursors lets you choose the size and color of your paintbrush.

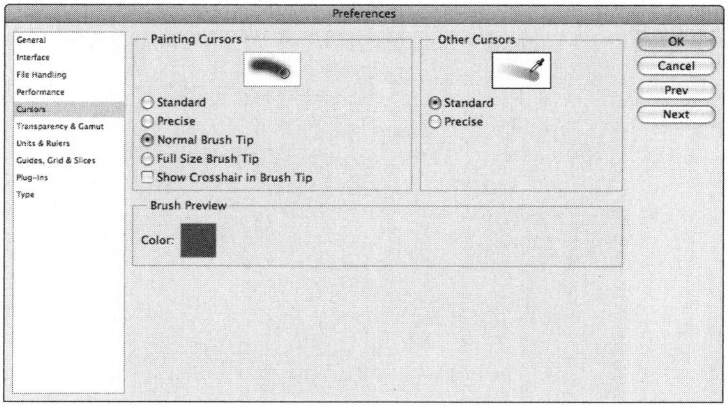

The two more useful options to choose from are Normal Brush Tip (the default) and Full Size Brush Tip. Setting the brush tip to Normal restricts the size of your cursor to the areas of your brush that have at least 50 percent opacity.

This means that with soft-edged brushes, the parts of the brush that are more than 50 percent transparent won't be represented. Setting the brush tip to Full Size causes the cursor to be as big as the area that will be affected by the brush, including the transparent areas of soft-edged brushes. Finally, checking the Show Crosshair in Brush Tip check box can also be useful, as it gives you a visual indication of where the center of your brush is.

■ **Flip X/Y.** This option, which is really only useful with non-round brushes, allows you to change the orientation of the brush tip. Flipping a brush tip on its X-axis turns it upside down, while flipping it on its Y-axis mirrors it horizontally.

■ **Angle.** This option rotates the brush tip around an invisible Z-axis. Again, this option is more useful with brushes that aren't round. Type a number into the Angle field, use the scrubber to change the value, or drag the gray arrow in the brush tip preview to change the angle of the brush interactively. Hold down the Shift key while dragging to change the value in increments of 15 degrees.

■ **Roundness.** A value of 100 percent means the brush tip is a perfect circle (if the currently selected brush preset is round). Reducing the roundness value produces an elliptical shape, which is useful if you want to create a chiseled brush effect. Adjust the roundness either numerically or by dragging either of the two round handles in the brush tip preview area.

■ **Hardness.** Except in the case of the Pencil tool, strokes with any of the brush-based tools have a smooth, anti-aliased edge, even if the hardness is set to 100 percent. That said, decreasing the hardness setting introduces transparency and feathering to the edge of the brush tip. Remember that as you decrease the softness of a brush, the actual radius of the brush increases somewhat to account for the feathered edges.

So a brush with a diameter of 200 pixels and a hardness setting of 0 percent actually occupies significantly more than 200 pixels on-screen, as demonstrated in Figure 19.12.

■ **Spacing.** When you paint a brush stroke in Photoshop, you're really laying down a series of blobs of color in whatever shape the brush tip is set to. The Spacing setting controls the distance between those blobs of color: the greater the number, the greater the distance, in relation to the diameter of the brush, as demonstrated in Figure 19.13.

You can disable the Spacing control by removing the check mark from the check box above the Spacing slider, in which case the distance between brush marks is controlled by the speed of your mouse or pen movement.

FIGURE 19.12

Both of these brushes have a diameter of 200 pixels, but the one on the left has a hardness of 100 percent, while the one on the right has a hardness of 0 percent. The light gray circle indicates the total area occupied by the brush.

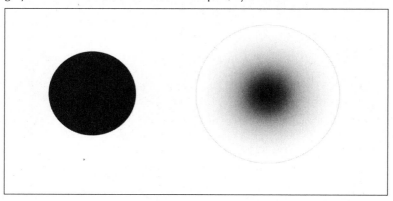

FIGURE 19.13

Going from top to bottom, these three strokes were made with a 15-pixel brush by using a Spacing setting of 25, 125, and 250 percent, respectively.

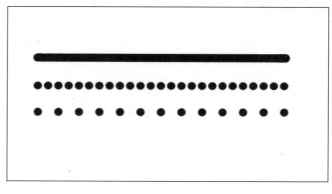

Dynamic brush tips

Adding some dynamic elements to the mix generates many of Photoshop's more interesting brush-based effects. For instance, imagine randomly varying the size, angle, or texture of the brush tip as you paint. Better still, imagine randomly varying those elements based on the angle of your stylus or the amount of pressure you apply to your tablet.

Clicking on any of the Dynamics settings on the left side of the Brushes panel displays options for changing the way your brush tip behaves. Once you've come up with a combination of settings you like, you can click the padlock next to each setting to prevent those options from changing if you select a different brush tip shape or brush preset. Remember, though, that the dynamic settings are specific to each tool — they won't carry over if you switch from, say, the Brush tool to the Blur tool.

Also keep in mind that you can either enable or disable dynamic elements without making any customizations to their options by toggling the check boxes next to each setting's name.

There are two main components you need to pay attention to when adding dynamic elements to your brushes. The first is Jitter, which is somewhat synonymous with randomness when it comes to dynamic elements. A setting of 0 percent means there is no variation in the elements as you paint with the brush; a setting of 100 percent means that the elements change with the maximum randomness.

The second component is the Control pop-up menu. Using this menu, you can choose what controls the dynamic effect:

- **Off.** This disables any variations for the current effect.
- **Fade.** Selecting this option causes the dynamic effect to fade over the course of a brush stroke.
- **Pen Pressure, Tilt, and Stylus Wheel.** The amount of variation is controlled by the amount of pressure applied, the angle the stylus is held at, or rotating the stylus wheel when a brush stroke is created with a stylus. As you might guess, these options are designed to only work when a pen tablet is attached to your computer; you'll see a warning triangle appear if you try to use these when a tablet is not connected.

Now that you're clear on the basics, take a look at each of the dynamic elements in detail.

Shape Dynamics

Click on the Shape Dynamics setting (shown in Figure 19.14) to access sliders that allow you to control variations in the size of the brush stroke. Here are the controls you'll find under the Shape Dynamics setting:

- **Size Jitter/Minimum Diameter.** This is where you control the variation of the brush tip's size over the course of painting a brush stroke. A Size Jitter setting of 0 percent means there is no change in the size of the brush while you paint, while a setting of 100 percent results in the maximum variation. Use the options under the Control pop-up menu (discussed previously) to determine how you'll control the variations in size.

   Once you've set how much variation will happen in the size of your brush tip, use the Minimum Diameter slider to specify the smallest diameter that the brush tip will be allowed to reach. Either type in a value or use the slider to enter a number that is a percentage of the brush tip's maximum diameter.

The Shape Dynamics panel

For example, if the brush has a maximum diameter of 200 pixels, and you enter a minimum diameter setting of 50 percent, that means the brush won't get any smaller than 100 pixels over the course of the brush stroke. Logically, this setting only becomes available if you have enabled Size Jitter, or selected one of the controls in the Size Jitter pop-up menu.

■ **Tilt Scale.** This setting only works with pen tablets that detect the angle that you're holding your pen at as you draw, and lets you vary the brush tip size based on that angle — just as you could if you were using an actual paintbrush. Select Pen Tilt in the Control pop-up menu (if your tablet isn't tilt sensitive you'll see a warning triangle), then you can control the size of the brush stroke based on the angle of your pen in relation to the tablet. As with the Minimum Diameter setting, this is a percentage of the diameter of the brush tip.

■ **Angle Jitter.** This setting lets you vary the angle of your brush as you paint. Of course, you won't notice any effect if you're using a 100 percent round brush tip. This setting is based on rotating the brush tip by a percentage of 360 degrees, so if you set a really small number, your brush only rotates by a few degrees; if you set it to 100 percent, your brush is allowed to rotate through a full circle. The Angle Jitter Control pop-up menu adds several options for controlling the variation of your brush tip's angle:

  ▦ **Rotation:** If your tablet detects pen rotation, you can interactively rotate the brush tip by rotating your pen.

  ▦ **Initial Direction:** This bases the rotation of the brush on the initial direction that you move your mouse or pen to make your brush stroke.

  ▦ **Direction:** Similar to the previous option, this control bases the variation of the brush tip's rotation on the direction that you're moving your mouse. The difference is subtle, but in this case the rotation is based not on the initial mouse or pen movement, but instead updates continuously based on the current direction that your mouse or pen is moving.

- **Roundness Jitter/Minimum Roundness:** Use this to control how much the roundness of your brush tip varies during a stroke. This controls the variation between the maximum roundness (0 percent) and whatever value that you set with the Minimum Roundness control. Speaking of which, the Minimum Roundness setting lets you specify the ratio of the shorter axis of the brush tip to its longer axis, which has the effect of squashing the brush tip. A smaller value means the brush tip can be squashed more over the duration of your strokes; the closer you get to 100 percent, the less your brush will squash.

Additional dynamic settings

The Shape Dynamics setting is probably where you'll end up doing the most customizations, and once you familiarize yourself with the way its options work, the remaining dynamic settings will become more intuitive to you. Here's a quick rundown of the rest of the dynamic settings:

- **Scattering.** This option lets you create scattered brush marks over the course of a stroke — sort of like using a can of spray paint. You can change the randomness of the scattering by increasing the value of the Scatter option. A higher Count creates more particles, resulting in a denser concentration of brush marks, and you can vary the Count by increasing the Count Jitter setting (see Figure 19.15).

FIGURE 19.15

In this example, the top stroke was made with Scattering disabled. The bottom stroke was made with Scattering set to 500 percent along both axes, with a count of 5. Size Jitter was also enabled.

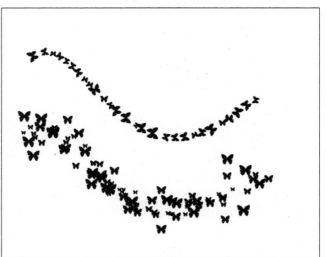

Enabling the Both Axes option sprays brush marks in all directions, radiating out from the center of your brush tip. Disabling this option restricts scattering so that it only occurs perpendicular to the direction of your stroke — so if you're painting a vertical stroke, the particles only scatter to the left and right, while they scatter above and below your stroke if you're painting horizontally.

■ **Texture.** Use this setting to apply a pattern to your brush strokes as you paint, creating, for example, the appearance of painting on canvas or watercolor paper. Photoshop already ships with a nice selection of patterns that you can choose from, but you can also define your own, which means the effects that you can create are virtually limitless.

As Figure 19.16 demonstrates, the Texture setting is most effective when used with a soft-edged brush.

FIGURE 19.16

This brush stroke was made with a brush preset loaded from the Wet Media collection that ships with Photoshop.

■ **Dual Brush.** This setting allows you to draw brush strokes by using a combination of two brush tips. Select your second brush tip from the presets shown on the right, and select how the strokes combine or blend by choosing an option from the Mode pop-up menu.

You'll recognize the eight modes available here, as they correspond to some of the blending modes seen in the Layers panel and in the Options Bar for many of the brush-based tools. Other options you can set for your second brush include Diameter, Spacing, Scattering, and Count.

- **Color Dynamics.** This setting changes the color of your brush stroke from the foreground to the background color as you paint. As with the other settings, use the Fade, Stylus Pressure, or Stylus Wheel setting to control the variation of the color in your brush strokes.

  The additional sliders under the Color Dynamics section allow you to tweak the percentage by which the hue, saturation, and brightness of the color can vary. Finally, the Purity slider increases or decreases the saturation of the color.

- **Other Dynamics.** Only two options are available in this section: Opacity and Flow Jitter. Using these two options, you can add some randomness to these two attributes of your brush strokes. And as is the case with the other dynamic elements, you can use their respective Control pop-up menus to specify how to control these two options.

Other settings

The remaining five options in the Brushes panel can only be turned on or off — they don't have any configurable options. They also function the same whether you're using a mouse or a tablet.

- **Noise.** Introduce some random noise to your brush strokes with this option. A soft-edged brush is needed to see the effects of this option.
- **Wet Edges.** Using this option adds dark edges to your brush strokes to simulate using a watercolor brush.
- **Airbrush.** This is your old friend the Airbrush icon from the Options Bar making another appearance here in the Brushes panel. Just in case you need a refresher, its function is to add a pooling effect to the brush-based tools.
- **Smoothing.** When painting with a pen tablet, the Smoothing option helps to ensure that quickly drawn strokes stay smooth. You may notice a bit of a delay at times, however, as Photoshop works on rendering your brush strokes.
- **Protect Texture.** When using textured brushes, this setting helps to keep the texture consistent by applying the same settings whenever you use a textured brush tip — even when you switch between different brush presets.

Custom brushes

By now, you're probably already hugely impressed (or maybe even overwhelmed) by the sheer number of options Photoshop offers you in terms of brush tips. Well, take a deep breath and regain your composure, because it doesn't stop there. Let's take a look at some ways of adding even more brush options to Photoshop, including creating and saving your own libraries of presets.

Predefined brush sets

Photoshop ships with several robust brush preset libraries, which you'll find listed in the Brushes panel fly-out menu (see Figure 19.17).

FIGURE 19.17

The Brushes panel fly-out menu gives you access to the many brush preset collections that ship with Photoshop.

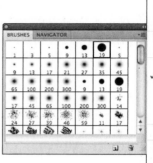

Select one of these pre-defined sets of brushes, and Photoshop asks you whether you'd like to append the brushes to the currently loaded set, or if you'd like to completely replace the current set. Not to worry if you've inadvertently replaced the default set of brushes — you can always get them back by choosing Reset Brushes from the Brushes panel menu.

CAUTION If you do choose to reset the default brushes, you're given one chance to save any custom brushes you've created; otherwise they're gone for good.

Creating and saving brush sets

As mentioned earlier, a great way of coming up with custom brushes is to use the default brush presets as a starting point for your own creations. To store your brush as a preset that is accessible whenever you are working in Photoshop, click the Create New Brush icon at the lower-right side of the Brushes panel, or select New Brush Preset from the Brushes panel menu.

Yet another way of making a custom brush would be to create one from scratch by selecting a drawing or a portion of an image and defining that as a brush. Start with a white background and experiment with creating something you think would make a good brush stroke. Using one of the Marquee tools, make a selection around your drawing. There's no need to be too perfect; Photoshop automatically distinguishes between your drawing and the white background. Choose Edit ➪ Define Brush Preset, give your brush a descriptive name, and click OK. Your brush is now stored with the Brush Presets and is available whenever you use Photoshop.

Once you've defined your own brush, you can tweak its settings just as you would any other brush. The Hardness setting is grayed out for brushes created with this method, though, so that's an attribute you'll have to build into your preset beforehand. One thing to note is that if you increase the size of the brush beyond the size it was originally created at (that is, its Sample size), you'll start to notice some blurring of the edges of the brush. You can always reset the brush to its original size by clicking the Use Sample Size button in the Brush Tip Shape window.

If you have several custom brushes that you've created, it's probably a good idea to save them as a brush set so you can use them on different computers, and so that you won't lose them if, for some reason, you end up having to re-install Photoshop on your machine. To save all the brushes that are currently loaded in the Brush Presets window, select Save Brushes from the Brushes panel menu. If you want to be selective and save specific brushes in their own set, use the Preset Manager (shown in Figure 19.18), which you can access from the Edit menu (or from the Brushes panel menu — just be sure to select Brush Presets first, or it will be grayed out).

With the Preset Manager open, select Brushes from the Preset Type pop-up menu, or press Ctrl+ 1/⌘+1 to view the Brush Presets. Click on the thumbnails of the brushes you want to save, using Shift to select multiple contiguous brushes, or Ctrl/⌘ to select multiple noncontiguous brushes. Click Save Set and navigate to a location on your hard drive to save your brushes as an ABR file.

FIGURE 19.18

The Preset Manager is the central location for custom brushes, patterns, and other presets in Photoshop.

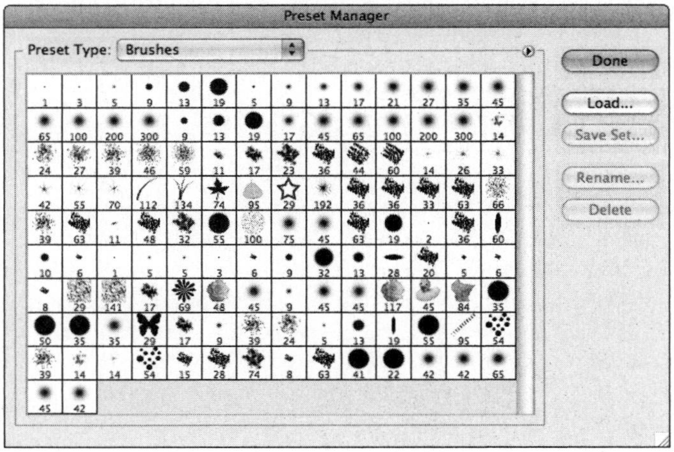

While we're here, let's talk about some of the other ways you can manage your brush collection by using either the Preset Manager or the options in the Brushes panel menu:

- **Reset.** If you find that you need a fresh start, or if you simply want to return to the default collection of presets that Photoshop ships with, select Reset Brushes from the Brushes panel menu. If you're working in the Preset Manager, you'll find the Reset command under the triangle menu in the upper right of the window. Chose Replace to clear out all the currently loaded presets and start from scratch, or choose Append to add the defaults to the end of the presets window.

- **Replace.** This option allows you to clear away all the current brush presets and load a different group of brushes in their place. This is useful if you know there are brushes you won't need during a particular session.

- **Delete.** Changed your mind about a brush preset? Get rid of it by selecting it (or Shift+ selecting multiple presets), clicking the trashcan icon in the Preset Manager, and then choosing the Delete command from the Presets menu. Note that you can't delete any of the brushes that shipped with Photoshop — you'll find the delete commands grayed out if you try. You can only permanently get rid of brushes that you've created or loaded from custom collections.

- **Rename.** Use this option to change the name of a brush in your collection. Here's a quick shortcut: Double-click any brush thumbnail in the Presets window and enter a new name in the resulting dialog box.

Downloading brush sets

You can also find collections of custom brushes distributed as freebies out there on the Internet. Let me first say that I trust you'll take all the necessary precautions before downloading *anything* from untrusted sites on the Internet.

That said, there are plenty of legitimate sites out there dedicated to the art of creating custom Photoshop brushes that offer their collections as freebies in ABR format. Once you've downloaded a collection that you like, select Load Brushes from the Brushes panel menu and navigate to the collection's location on your hard drive. Select the ABR file and click Open.

Brushes Used with Blending Modes

As you learned in Chapter 8 (which I'm sure you've read studiously by this point), layers can be combined in a number of complex ways by using Photoshop's blending modes. These same modes (with slight differences in the way they function) can be applied to some of the painting and editing tools, adding a whole other dimension to the way you work in Photoshop. While layer-based blending modes affect the interaction between colors on different layers, brush-based modes affect how colors mix on one layer.

There are 27 available blending modes — divided into six groups — that can be used with the Paintbrush and Pencil tools. Depending on which of the other painting or editing tools you have selected, the available blending modes will vary (see Figure 19.19 for an illustration of which modes are available with which tools). As was covered earlier in this chapter, Dodge, Burn, and Sponge have their own specific modes that don't show up anywhere else.

FIGURE 19.19

The 27 blending modes available to Photoshop's brush-based tools

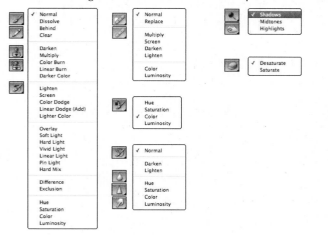

As shown in Figure 19.20, only a handful of modes are available when working with 32-bit images. Not only that, the Dodge, Burn, and Sponge tools aren't available at all in 32-bit mode, so you'll need to convert your image to 16- or 8-bit mode to use any of these tools.

Just as you can cycle between layer-based blending modes by using the Shift+plus (+) and Shift+minus (-) keys while the Move tool or one of the selection tools is active, you can cycle between brush modes by using those same keyboard shortcuts when one of the brush tools is active.

As an alternative, you can jump straight to a specific blending mode by using the combination Shift+Alt/Shift+Option and the key shown in parentheses next to each of the following blending modes. For example, pressing Shift+Alt+N/Shift+Option+N jumps you straight to Normal mode.

FIGURE 19.20

When working in 32-bit image mode, only a handful of blending modes are available to the painting and editing tools.

Photoshop's 27 blending modes are described below. Again, all these blending modes are available to the Brush tool and the Pencil tool; the number of available blending modes will vary when using other brush-based tools.

■ **Normal (N).** This is the default mode for the painting and editing tools. When the painting tools are used in Normal mode, the foreground color is applied, and its appearance is controlled by the Opacity, Flow, Airbrush, and other brush settings. In the case of the editing tools, existing colors in the image are manipulated normally, and again, the brush settings govern the tools' output.

When you're working in Indexed or Bitmapped mode, Normal mode becomes Threshold mode. Because of the very limited number of colors available in these image formats, strokes that you paint have harsh, aliased edges, similar to those normally produced by the Pencil tool.

■ **Dissolve (I).** Similar to Normal mode, Dissolve edits or paints with the foreground color, but it adds in a random blend of the foreground color and either existing colors in the current layer or transparency. It has the effect of creating a dithered, or speckled, look. Normal and Dissolve modes were used to produce the brush strokes shown in Figure 19.21.

FIGURE 19.21

The Normal (left) and Dissolve (right) blending modes were used to create the strokes around the flower shape in this illustration.

- **Behind (Q).** This mode, which really only works with layers with areas of transparency, allows you to paint only on translucent parts of the layer without affecting existing areas of color.

- **Clear (R).** The Clear mode works on layers other than the background layers, and lets you edit existing pixels by turning them transparent. This is pretty much the same functionality that is provided by the Eraser tool, so it's a matter of preference which of the two tools you use. It can be useful when used with the Fill or Stroke tool, however.

- **Darken (K).** This mode falls in the group of darkening effects. Darken (shown in Figure 19.22) examines the pixels in the image under the brush and only affects pixels that are brighter in value than the foreground color. More specifically, it evaluates pixels on a channel-by-channel basis, which means that pixels on the red channel might be affected, while pixels on other channels might be left alone, depending on their brightness or value.

- **Darker Color.** This mode works by comparing the values of all the color channels for the existing pixels with the foreground color, and displaying the darker value. Technically, this differs from the Darken mode because it evaluates the total values of the channels rather than working on a channel-by-channel basis. You may want to experiment with these two modes, though, to see which one results in the effect you're after.

FIGURE 19.22

From left to right: The flower was painted with the brush set to Darken, Darker Color, and Multiply blending modes.

- **Multiply (M).** This color mode multiplies the foreground color by the existing colors in the image to produce a third color that is darker than either of the starting colors. Multiplying any color by black always results in black, while multiplying by white results in unchanged colors.

- **Color Burn (B)/Linear Burn (A).** Color Burn converts existing colors in the image to a darker version of the foreground color by increasing contrast. Linear Burn creates a similar effect, but by reducing the brightness of the existing pixels. In either case, blending with white as the foreground color doesn't have any effect.

- **Lighten (G).** This mode is the first of the lightening group (as you may have guessed). Lighten works just like Darken does, but instead it only affects pixels that are darker than the foreground color.

- **Lighter Color.** This mode is analogous to its darkening equivalent: It adds up the channel values in the foreground color, compares them to the values for the existing image colors, and paints with the brighter value.

- **Screen (S).** The yin to the Multiply mode's yang, if you will, Screen combines the inverse of the foreground and the base, or existing pixel colors, to create a third color that is lighter than either of the original colors.

- **Color Dodge (D)/Linear Dodge (W).** These modes are cousins of the plain-vanilla version of the Dodge tool. Color Dodge manipulates colors that exist in the image into a lighter version of the foreground color by reducing contrast. Linear Dodge has a similar effect, but achieves it by increasing brightness. In either case, blending with black has no effect. Color Dodge and Linear Dodge are shown in Figure 19.23.

- **Overlay (O).** Overlay, along with the next seven blending modes, acts in different ways to darken dark pixels and brighten light pixels. Overlay either multiplies or screens the base colors while retaining shadow and highlight detail. The resulting effect is an increase in overall saturation and contrast.

FIGURE 19.23

Color Dodge (left) and Linear Dodge (right) are shown in this example.

- **Soft Light (F)/Hard Light (H).** Soft Light brightens or darkens existing colors in an image (similar to dodging or burning), depending on the foreground color. The resulting effect is soft and diffused. If the foreground color is brighter than 50 percent gray, it lightens the base colors; if it's darker, it darkens the base colors. Hard Light works like Soft Light, but instead multiplies or screens colors in the image, creating greater contrast for a much stronger, harsher effect.

- **Vivid Light (V)/Linear Light (J).** Both of these modes dodge or burn existing colors in an image: Dark colors get darker and light colors get lighter. Where Vivid Light works by increasing or decreasing contrast, Linear Light operates by using brightness.

- **Pin Light (Z).** Continuing the darkening/lightening theme of this group of blending modes, Pin Light replaces colors that are darker than the foreground color, without affecting brighter colors when the foreground color is lighter than 50 percent gray. The opposite is true when the foreground color is darker than 50 percent gray: Colors that are lighter than the foreground are changed, while darker tones remain unaffected.

- **Hard Mix (L).** This mode starts by combining the red, green, and blue color channel values of the foreground color with those of the existing pixel colors. It then sets the value of those channel colors to either 0 (black) or 255 (white), with the result being that each pixel is one of the eight primary colors: red, green, blue, cyan, magenta, yellow, white, or black. It's a fairly harsh, high-contrast effect, but it can be used to produce some nice effects with a soft, transparent brush.

- **Difference (E).** Painting with Difference mode (see Figure 19.24) calculates the difference between the brightness of the foreground color and the brightness of the existing colors. If the result of this calculation is a negative number, then its positive equivalent is used. The result of this operation is to invert the original colors. Blending with black has no effect.

- **Exclusion (X).** Exclusion creates an effect that is close to but less high-contrast than Difference.

FIGURE 19.24

Difference (left) and Exclusion (right) are shown in this illustration.

- **Hue (U).** Hue applies the currently selected foreground color to the pixels in an image, without changing their existing value (brightness) or saturation (intensity).

- **Saturation (T).** Paint with Saturation mode to apply the intensity of the foreground color to the existing pixels; the hue and brightness are unaffected.

- **Color (C).** This blending mode, which is often used to restore color to black-and-white photographs, applies a combination of the hue and saturation of the foreground color while leaving the brightness value of the original pixels intact. To add color to a black-and-white photo, first ensure that it's in RGB Color mode (choose Images ➪ Mode ➪ RGB Color). Then set your Brush tool to the Color mode, select a color, and begin painting.

- **Luminosity (Y).** This mode produces a color that has the brightness of the foreground color and, as you've probably already guessed, retains the hue and saturation of the existing colors. Examples of these last four blending modes are shown in Figure 19.25.

FIGURE 19.25

Clockwise from top left: Hue, Saturation, Luminosity, and Color modes.

Painting Techniques

You've learned a lot so far about the way the painting and editing tools function in Photoshop. It would be wrong to just dump all that information on you without giving you some context for it. Now you'll learn how to apply what you know about the brush-based tools to some sophisticated painting techniques.

Painting straight lines

Okay, admittedly, this one doesn't sound so sophisticated, but you'd be surprised how much you can do with this deceptively simple technique.

There are a couple of different ways to draw straight lines with the brush tools in Photoshop. To connect two points with a straight line, click where the line should start, then hold down the Shift key and click where the line should end. A perfectly straight line joins the two places where you clicked. Continue Shift+clicking to draw additional lines from each point to the next. All the characteristics of the brush you are using are respected — Opacity, Flow, Airbrush, and even all the dynamic settings.

The other way to draw straight lines is by holding down the Shift key before you start painting — this constrains your brush strokes to horizontal or vertical lines. Using combinations of these techniques with varying brush tips can yield surprisingly complex results, as shown in Figure 19.26.

FIGURE 19.26

To create this stylized effect, I held down the Shift key while clicking to draw straight lines following the edges of this ancient Mayan temple.

Once you've got your painted outlines drawn (on a separate layer, of course), you can manipulate them by using any number of layer styles, filters, and blending modes. In Figure 19.27, I used the Bevel and Emboss layer style and set my layer's mode to Overlay to create the effect of chiseled stone.

FIGURE 19.27

With the Overlay mode, the temple takes on a more chiseled look.

Undoing your strokes

As you experiment with releasing your inner da Vinci, you're going to find yourself making mistakes. The good news is that, unlike the Renaissance masters, you have Photoshop. A misplaced brush stroke (or several) can be undone with a few clicks and no messy cleanup. A single stroke can be undone by pressing Ctrl+Z/⌘+Z on your keyboard.

Take note that often, especially when using a pen tablet, what might seem like one stroke to you can register as several to Photoshop. In that case, you can undo several strokes by selecting an earlier state from the History panel, or by repeatedly pressing Ctrl+Alt+Z/⌘+Option+Z.

CROSS-REF **For more on the History panel and History States, check out Chapter 6.**

Creating Special Effects with Painting

In this section you'll learn a few more tricks to creating interesting effects with Photoshop's painting tools and editing tools. I start you off with a couple of step by step examples, which should give you a real feel for how to put everything that's been covered so far into practice. From here, you really are only limited by your imagination, as you can use these techniques in endless combinations to create art in a multitude of styles.

Painting with the Path tool

Another useful technique is to create a vector path and automatically trace it with a brush stroke. This technique can even simulate the effects of varying pen pressure — with or without a tablet connected to your computer — to create a very dynamic brush stroke.

CROSS-REF Paths are covered in much more detail in Chapter 11.

1. Begin by creating a vector path. You can use any of the Shape tools or the Pen tool set to Path mode (click the second icon on the Options Bar). I chose one of the preset shapes available under the Custom Shape tool, as shown in Figure 19.28.

FIGURE 19.28

For this example, I chose a vector shape preset, found in the Options Bar of the Custom Shape tool. You can create a vector path from scratch, if you like.

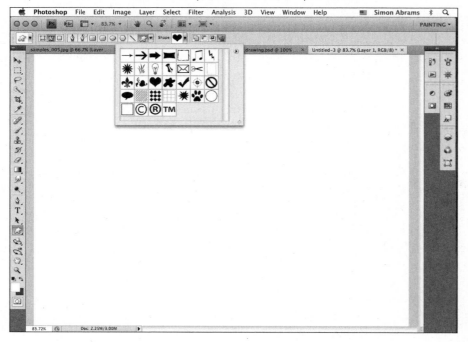

2. Switch to one of the painting tools — in this example, I used the good old Brush tool, set to 70 percent Opacity. I also chose the Rough Round Bristle brush preset, and left its default settings (see Figure 19.29). You can also select a foreground color other than black if you'd like.

TIP   **You can even create a vector path from a "marching ants" selection made with any of the selection tools. Create a selection, then select Create Work Path from Selection from the Paths panel menu.**

3. Click on the Paths panel tab and select your path's name to make sure it's active. From the Paths panel menu, choose Stroke Path, and in the resulting dialog box, select the Brush tool. Place a check in the Simulate Pen Pressure check box and click OK.

The result is shown in Figure 19.30.

FIGURE 19.29

I chose the Rough Round Bristle preset for this example, but feel free to experiment with different presets to produce varied results.

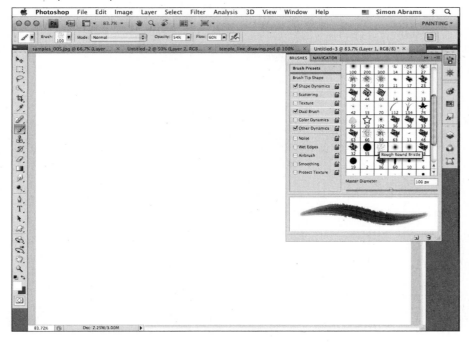

FIGURE 19.30

The final brush stroke, created from a vector path

This is only the beginning — since I created this on its own layer, I'm free to push this effect even further by adding layer styles, experimenting with blending modes, and so on, until I'm happy with the result.

Creating a chalkboard effect

Here's a convincing chalkboard effect, which you can create fairly simply by using only a few textured brushes.

1. Create a new document by pressing Ctrl+N/⌘+N. Enter the image dimensions or choose a preset (I set mine at 1024 x 768) and click OK.

2. Create the base color for your chalkboard. I like green, so that's the color I went with for this example. Click on the foreground color swatch and use the Color Picker to select an appropriate green and click OK. Fill your background layer with green by pressing Alt+Delete/Option+Delete.

3. Currently the chalkboard looks too pristine. To really sell the effect, create some faded chalk marks, so it looks like it gets some regular use. Click the Create New Layer icon on the bottom of the Layers panel to make a new layer.

With a little experimentation, I discovered that there's a certain brush preset I like in the Dry Media Brushes collection. Select Dry Media Brushes from the Brushes panel menu and click Append in the resulting dialog box to load the collection (see Figure 19.31).

FIGURE 19.31

Loading the Dry Media Brushes collection

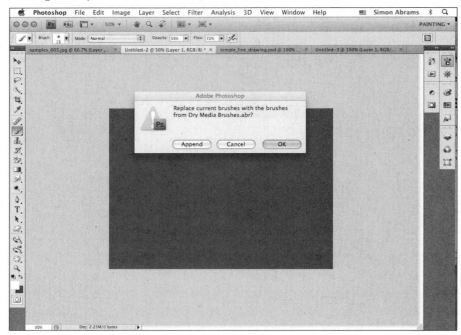

There's no rule that says you can only use the brushes to create the effects that their description says they're for. With that in mind, select the very last of the Dry Media Brushes, which is called Pastel Medium Tip.

TIP Hover over each preset to see its name. You could also select Text Mode, Small List, or Large List from the Brushes panel menu to make it really easy to see the brush names.

4. Increase the brush size by dragging the Diameter slider in the Brush Tip Presets window until it's fairly large. I made mine about 140 pixels. Set your foreground color to white, and begin painting in broad strokes (see Figure 19.32).

5. This doesn't look like much yet, so go ahead and drop the layer's opacity down to about 8–10 percent. To add more dimension, you could repeat this procedure so there are several layers of erased brush marks.

FIGURE 19.32

Making some chalk dust marks

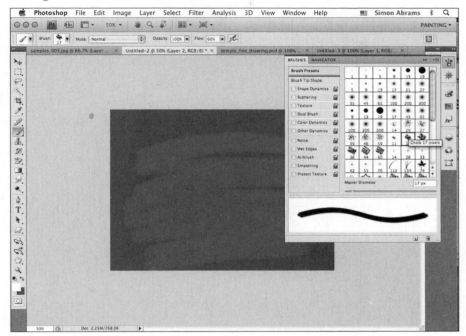

6. Next, you need to make your chalk to write on the board with. There are several pre-defined chalk presets, and they make as good a starting point as any. Click on Brush Presets at the top of the Brushes panel and find the 17-pixel Chalk preset. As I said, it's a good preset as-is, but I think it could use a little more texture.

   Select Texture under the Brush Tip Shape settings. Open the Texture swatch to reveal additional texture thumbnails. From the small triangle menu, load the Rock Pattern collection, and select Granite (200 x 200 pixels) from the newly added thumbnails.

7. Create a new layer and have fun experimenting with your piece of chalk. From here on out, I leave it to you to experiment with settings such as changing the opacity of the brush, adjusting the scale of the granite pattern, or maybe adding some noise to the brush stroke. My final result is shown in Figure 19.33.

 **TIP** Don't forget to save your brush presets once you're happy with what you come up with.

FIGURE 19.33

The final chalkboard effect. The nice thing about the color of the chalkboard being on its own layer is that you could decide that you want a blackboard after all by simply filling the background layer with black.

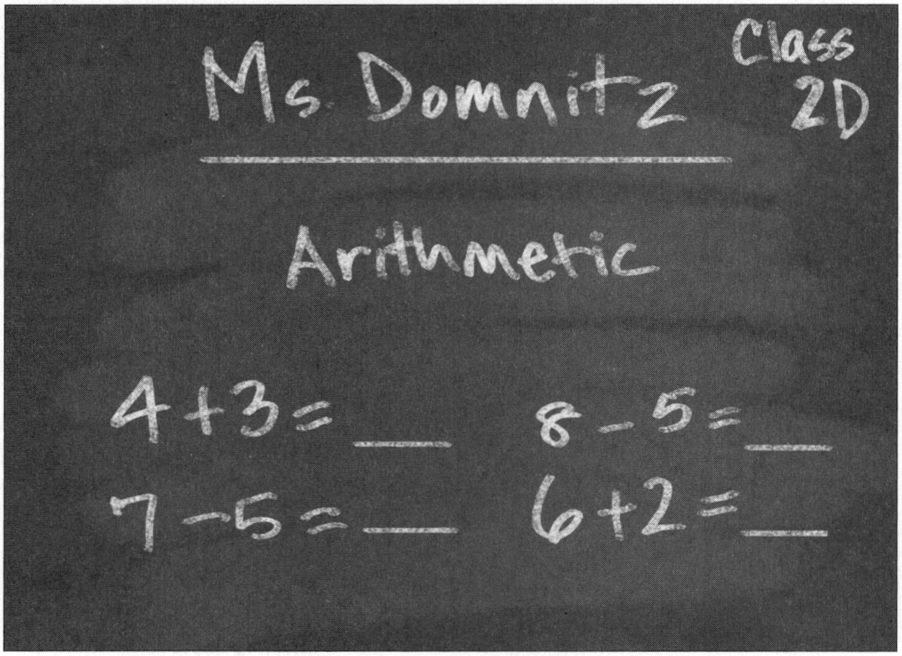

Summary

This chapter gave you an in-depth look at Photoshop's painting and editing tools. You learned how to customize the tools using the settings available in the Options Bar and in the Brushes panel. You saw how to load, create, and save brush presets. You also learned about using Photoshop's many blending modes with the brush-based tools to create advanced painting effects.

Chapter 20

Filters and Layer Styles

When speaking about Photoshop, the immediate association for many is with the special effects and visual eye candy that it is capable of creating through its robust collection of filters. In most cases, the association is positive, and for good reason, as some truly spectacular visual effects can be produced when filters are skillfully combined. On the other hand, many first-time Photoshop users make a bee-line straight for the Filters menu and seem to do their darndest to see just how many effects they can squeeze into a single design — with nausea-inducing results. If you're reading this, congratulations are in order: You've already taken a solid first step toward ensuring that you don't end up in that group of filter-abusers.

Photoshop's filters can be loosely broken down into two categories — those that perform corrective image-editing tasks, and those that are used to create special effects. Coverage of these filters will be spread out over the next several chapters, although frankly, it would be impossible to cover every single filter that's included in Photoshop within these pages without significantly increasing the size of this already substantial tome.

Fear not, though — once you get used to using the filters that do receive coverage here, you'll feel comfortable striking out on your own and experimenting with the ones that I don't cover. And if, after reading the filter-related chapters in this book, you're still feeling somewhat unsure, or you're determined to become a filter expert and simply must have more information, there are books out there that are dedicated to filters and their every nuance that you might want to check out.

About Filters

There are a huge number of filters that come preinstalled with Photoshop. If that doesn't satisfy your filter appetite, don't worry — an even larger number of filters can be downloaded from third-party developers, such as Alien Skin. Some third-party filters are free, but remember — in many cases you get what you pay for. The filters that are loaded when you fire up Photoshop come from the Plug-ins ⇨ Filters folder in Photoshop's application folder, so to install additional filters, drop them in that folder and restart Photoshop.

Using filters

To apply a filter to an image, simply choose it from the Filters menu. If a selection is active, the filter is applied only to the selected region, without affecting the rest of your image. If you want to apply a filter to your entire image, make sure there are no active selections before choosing a filter.

When choosing an effect from the Filters menu, you'll find that some filters display a dialog box where you can specify options to control the effect; others, such as Blur and Solarize, can't be configured and are applied instantly when you choose them from the menu. An easy way to tell which ones will let you configure them is to pay attention to whether they have ellipses (". . .") after their names in the menu. The ones with ellipses have options that can be configured; the ones without ellipses don't.

Be aware of the bit-depth of your images when working with filters. All filters can be applied to 8-bit images, while 16- and 32-bit images are restricted to a handful of filters.

Previewing filter effects

With a few exceptions, the filters that do have configurable options allow you to see a preview of the filter's effect on your image in the Preview window of the filter's dialog box (see Figure 20.1). Click and drag within this window to pan and scroll to different parts of your image. Or, if you move your mouse outside of the dialog box, you can click anywhere in your main image window to focus the Preview window around that part of your image.

You can also change zoom levels within the Preview window by clicking on the + and - buttons, although I'd recommend leaving the zoom at least at 100 percent, so you can see an accurate representation of the effect on your image.

What Happened to Extract and Pattern Maker?

Users of the earlier versions of Photoshop might be alarmed to notice that the Extract and Pattern Maker filters have vanished from their old spot near the top of the Filters menu. Well, the engineers at Adobe have decided not to include those two old veterans in the default installation of Photoshop. Don't worry — they're still available as optional downloads from Adobe's Web site (www.adobe.com).

FIGURE 20.1

Most filters' dialog boxes feature the ability to see a real-time preview of the filter's effects on your image.

Most of the filters' dialog boxes offer the option to preview the filter in the main image window by enabling the Preview check box. As you adjust the filter's options, the main image display updates continually, giving you a big-picture view of your changes. Note that some filters take longer than others to update; in these cases you'll notice a progress indicator blinking underneath the Zoom value in the dialog box. If you're working on a slow computer, you can disable the Preview check box to speed things along.

TIP   While working in filters' dialog boxes, you can use the standard Zoom and Hand tool shortcuts in the full image window. Press Ctrl+the plus or minus keys (⌘+the plus or minus keys on a Mac) to zoom in or out; press Ctrl+Alt+00/⌘+Option+0 to quickly zoom to 100 percent. Finally, hold down the spacebar while you click and drag to move around your main image window.

NOTE   The Preview check box doesn't have any effect on the Preview window within the dialog box — it only applies to whether or not the main image window is updated as you change the filter's options.

Repeatedly applying filters

To re-apply the most recently used filter, either in the same document or in a different document, press Ctrl+F/⌘+F or select the first menu item from the Filters menu. This reapplies the filter with the most recently used settings. Press Ctrl+Alt+F/⌘+Option+F to display the dialog box for the most recently used filter, so you can apply it again, but with different options.

Note that this option is only available for filters that have actually been applied, even if you undo the filter after applying it. However, canceling out of a filter's dialog box, then pressing Ctrl+Alt+F/⌘+Option+F applies the last filter that wasn't canceled.

Using the Filter Gallery

Making its first appearance in Photoshop CS, the Filter Gallery (see Figure 20.2) offers several benefits. The most obvious one is that it displays thumbnails of what each filter looks like, giving you a rough idea of how each filter will affect your image. The other real advantage of the Filter Gallery is that it allows you to apply multiple filters for a cumulative effect. The Filter Gallery is covered in greater detail later in this chapter.

FIGURE 20.2

Photoshop's Filter Gallery offers thumbnails of nearly 50 filter effects, and the ability to blend those filters in various combinations.

Fading and blending filters

You may find that the filter you just applied is too intense, and you wish you had a way to dial it back a bit. The Fade command allows you to do just that. Choose Edit ➪ Fade to display the Fade dialog box for the most recently used filter (see Figure 20.3). You have only two options in the Fade dialog box: Opacity and Mode. Opacity allows you to change the transparency of the filter, allowing more of the original image to show through. Under the Mode menu, you'll find most of the blending modes that you've already learned about in Chapter 8, with the exception of the Behind and Clear modes.

TIP The Fade command isn't only available when using Filters — you can also apply it after using the Stroke command to apply a brush stroke to a Path via the Path panel menu. Select a vector path, then select Stroke Path from the Path panel menu. Choose a tool to stroke the path with and click OK. Then select Fade from the Edit menu to fade the brush stroke.

There are a couple of catches to using the Fade command: First, you must use it immediately after applying a filter. Any other action — even if it's just saving your document — results in the option being grayed out in the Edit menu. Also, you can't use the Fade command on Smart Filters, which are coming up in the next section.

FIGURE 20.3

I applied a Radial Blur to this image, then selected the Fade command and changed the blending mode to produce the result you see here.

Destructive vs. Nondestructive Workflows

In a typical workflow, when working with filters, the filter is applied to a layer or selection, and each pixel is directly manipulated. Once applied, if for some reason your History States aren't available, or if you close and reopen the document, there's no going back. This is known as a destructive workflow, and though it's perfectly acceptable for quick-and-dirty tweaks, it's generally not an ideal way to work on larger projects where you would want to have as much flexibility and editability as possible.

A welcome addition to Photoshop CS3 is the ability to work with filters in a non-destructive manner, using what are known as Smart Filters. Smart Filters are similar to adjustment layers or layer styles. Once applied, their settings can be changed at any time, they can be selectively applied to portions of a layer, and they can be copied between documents. And like adjustment layers and layer styles, Smart Filters are preserved in any file format that recognizes layers (for a file format refresher, check out Chapter 7).

Applying filters, the Smart way

The first step in working with Smart Filters is to prepare your image or layer(s). To do so, choose Filters ➪ Convert for Smart Filters. Photoshop displays a dialog box that lets you know that the layer you selected will be converted to a Smart Object in order to work with Smart Filters. Click OK. Now when you select a filter from the Filters menu and apply it to your image, you'll see a Smart Filters object listed under the thumbnail for your layer in the Layers panel (see Figure 20.4).

FIGURE 20.4

Smart Filters are displayed in the Layers panel just like layer styles. Click the arrow at the far right of the layer to collapse the list of Smart Filters, and save a little real estate in your Layers panel.

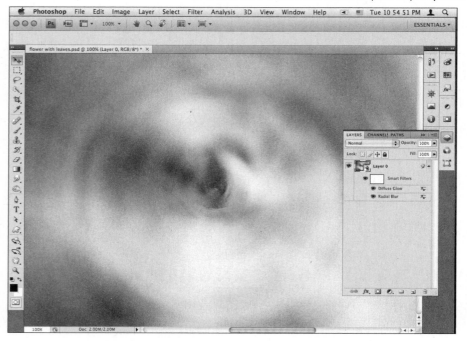

If you apply additional filters, they appear in the Layers panel under the Smart Filters object. As is the case with the Filter Gallery, you can reorder Smart Filters by dragging them up or down to change their position in the Layers panel, and changing their effect on the image.

Double-click the filter name in the Layers panel to display the filter's dialog box and make changes to its settings. If you have multiple Smart Filters in a stack, Photoshop displays a dialog box letting you know that filters appearing higher in the stack than the one you're trying to edit will not be previewed while you're making changes.

> **TIP** Smart Filters applied using the Filter Gallery appear as one item in the stack in the Layers panel — even if you layered multiple consecutive filters. Double-clicking this single item takes you back to the Filter Gallery window, where you'll find all your layered filters intact.

Blending and masking

Double-clicking the icon at the far right of the Smart Filter's name (it looks like two tiny sliders) opens the filter Blending Options window (shown in Figure 20.5). Here, you can change the opacity of the filter, and blend it with the original image by choosing one of the familiar blending modes from the options listed here.

FIGURE 20.5

The Blending Options window allows you to set the opacity and blending mode of each Smart Filter.

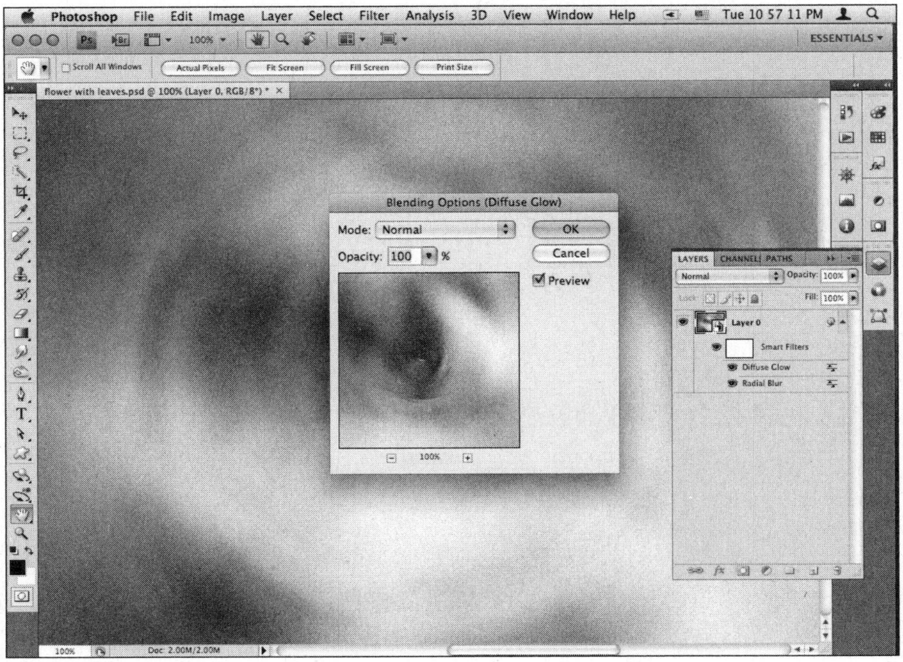

You may have noticed that the Smart Filter object in the Layers panel has a thumbnail that looks suspiciously like a layer mask. That's because it is a layer mask, and you can use it to selectively apply Smart Filters to portions of a layer. By default, Photoshop creates Smart Filters with a mask that's all white — meaning it reveals all the effect.

Add black to the filter mask with the brush, fill, gradient, or selection tools to hide the effect in certain parts of your image, as demonstrated in Figure 20.6.

FIGURE 20.6

I painted on the Smart Filter's layer mask with my foreground set to black to obscure the filter in the central part of this image.

To display only the filter mask, Alt+click/Option+click the thumbnail; Alt+click/Option+click again to restore the image. To temporarily hide the effects of the filter mask, Shift+click on the mask's thumbnail. A red X across the thumbnail icon indicates that the mask has been disabled. Shift+click again to restore the filter mask. You can also hide the Smart Filters outright by clicking on the eye icon at the left of the thumbnail in the Layers panel.

Enough talk about filters — let's move on to actually using them.

Blurring and Sharpening

A pair of complementary techniques — blurring and sharpening — are often used to repair or correct images. Blurring works by reducing contrast between pixels, thereby smoothing out trouble spots, while sharpening enhances contrast between pixels, producing crisp images. In this section, these two techniques are examined in detail.

Blur

Two of the powerhouses of the Blur family of filters — Gaussian Blur and Lens Blur — have already been covered in Chapter 17, in the context of removing noise and pixelization. To recap quickly, the Gaussian Blur filter analyzes pixels in relation to their neighbors, and reduces the contrast between them based on a bell-shaped curve. Enter a value from 1.0 to 250 to increase the intensity of the blur.

Lens Blur, a more complex filter, is used to bring specific areas of an image into or out of focus, giving you the ability to simulate shallow depth-of-field effects that are normally performed by photographers in-camera, through the use of lenses with wide apertures. The areas of the photo that are in focus can be determined either by a depth map based on a layer's transparency, its layer mask, or an alpha channel.

In the following sections, the remaining variations of the blur filters are covered in more detail.

CROSS-REF For more on the Gaussian Blur and Lens Blur filters, refer to Chapter 17.

Smart Blur

Smart Blur is designed to blur low-contrast areas in a photo while preserving edges, making it useful for reducing the appearance of noise and artifacts; the details, in the meantime, are left alone (see Figure 20.7). The Radius slider controls the size of the area containing the pixels that are examined when calculating the amount of blur to apply. The Threshold value determines how similar pixels should be to be included in the blur effect; a high threshold allows more pixels to be included. Pixels that are excluded are considered edges.

FIGURE 20.7

Smart Blur softens the low-contrast areas of an image while retaining the detail in the edges.

The Quality setting applies to edges, with a higher setting producing smoother edges, along with the expected slower processing time. The Mode menu includes two settings other than Normal: Edge Only and Overlay Edge. Edge Only displays the edges resulting from the smart blur effect as a black-and-white image. Overlay Edge combines the resulting image with the white edges generated by the filter.

> **TIP** While the Edge Only effect is not quite what one would expect from a blur filter, you could use the resulting black-and-white image to create a line-drawing effect. Select a low radius and a high threshold to produce edges with less detail, and then combine the black-and-white image with underlying layers using different blending modes. Try inverting the edge only image (press Ctrl+I/⌘+I) and change the layer's blending mode to Multiply.

Other blur filters

Here's a quick rundown of the remaining filters available under the Blur menu:

- **Average.** This filter finds the average of the colors in an image or selection, and fills it solidly with that color — and I mean solidly, as demonstrated in Figure 20.8.

  The photograph of the school buses on the left is predominantly yellow, and the result of the Average filter being applied is shown on the right. This might not seem useful — after all, who wants their photo turned into a mustard-brown mass of color? — but using the Fade command to change the blending options for this filter or creating a soft-edged selection before applying the Average command can yield interesting results, as shown in Figure 20.9.

- **Blur/Blur More.** These two filters apply a pre-defined amount of smoothing to your image. They're designed to work on areas of transition between colors. Honestly, I have to say that most people forgo both of these filters in favor of the more configurable options available.

FIGURE 20.8

Without an active selection, the Average filter turned my photo of these parked yellow school buses into a solid mass of mustard-brown, which isn't a very practical application of the filter.

FIGURE 20.9

To punch up the water in this image, I choose Select ⇨ Color Range to pick some of the tones in the foreground of the image. I then applied the Average filter, and followed that immediately with the Fade command with the mode set to Overlay and the opacity set to 65 percent.

■ **Box Blur.** Like most of the other blurring filters, this method takes neighboring pixels into consideration when blurring an image. However, in this case, it analyzes the pixels to the left, right, above, and below each pixel to create an average value — hence the name "Box" Blur. Like the Gaussian Blur, this filter has only a single slider, allowing you to adjust the radius to affect the amount of blur that is applied. Figure 20.10 provides a comparison between a Gaussian Blur and a Box Blur.

FIGURE 20.10

A Gaussian Blur was applied to the image on the left, while a Box Blur was applied to the image on the right. In both cases, a radius of 20 was used.

■ **Motion Blur.** Use this filter to apply movement to an image. Specify the angle of the motion in degrees, and enter a number from 1 to 1,000 in the Distance field to control the intensity of the effect. Figure 20.11 shows the results of the Motion filter using several different settings.

FIGURE 20.11

The Motion filter with distance settings of 25, 50, 150, and 500, respectively. The first example is the original photo.

■ **Radial Blur.** The Radial Blur emulates a photographic technique where the camera is zoomed or rotated while the photograph is being taken. Choose Blur ⇨ Radial, and select either Spin or Zoom as the Blur Method. Unfortunately, this filter's dialog box doesn't offer a live preview of the effect on your image, so you'll have to do some experimenting. Better yet, apply it as a Smart Filter, so you can go back and tweak the effects as often as necessary.

Selecting Spin has the effect of concentric blurring around a central point. Zoom results in a linear blur converging toward a central point. Figure 20.12 shows a comparison of the Zoom and Spin settings. In either case, pixels near the blur's origin are affected less than those farthest away from the center. Click and drag in the Blur Center preview box to specify the point about which the blur occurs.

FIGURE 20.12

Radial Blur was applied using the Zoom (left image) and Spin (right image) settings. In both cases, the amount was set to 40 and the quality was set to Good.

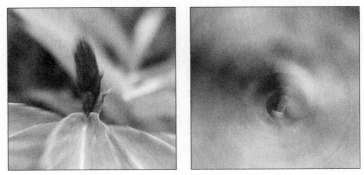

Finally, choose a Quality setting to determine how the blur is applied to the image. Draft quality is fast, but produces grainy, diffuse results. The Good and Best options produce smooth results, using different interpolation methods (bilinear and bicubic, respectively — see Chapter 5 for a refresher, if necessary).

As you would expect, the use of either of these higher-quality settings comes at the expense of longer processing time, with Best taking significantly longer than Good.

- **Shape Blur.** This filter generates a blur based on a custom shape. In principle, it's the same as the Box Blur, except the way the pixels are analyzed is dictated by the shape you choose in the filter's dialog box.

  Incidentally, you should recognize those shapes — they're the same as the ones that appear in the Custom Shape tool's Options Bar. Just as with that tool, there are a number of additional shape presets that you can load from the triangle menu, giving you many more options to choose from.

  Choose a shape and change the radius to change the amount of blur. Higher settings increase the amount of blur, but beyond a certain amount, the effect of the shape on the blur begins to get somewhat indistinct (see Figure 20.13).

- **Surface Blur.** This filter is intended for use with photographs containing shiny, reflective surfaces, such as water, glass, or chrome. It preserves edges while smoothing out underlying grain or noise.

  As Figure 20.14 illustrates, the filter is great for removing excess detail in the shiny reflections in the paint job of this car. As with many of the other filters we've discussed so far, the Radius slider affects the intensity of the blur, while the Threshold slider determines which pixels are affected by or ignored by the blur.

FIGURE 20.13

These blurs were generated with the Shape Blur filter, using different custom shapes, at a radius of 10 pixels.

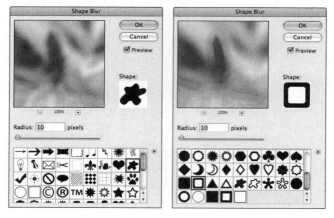

FIGURE 20.14

Using the Surface Blur tool, some of the excess detail in the reflections in the photo was eliminated. Use low threshold and radius settings for a more subtle effect.

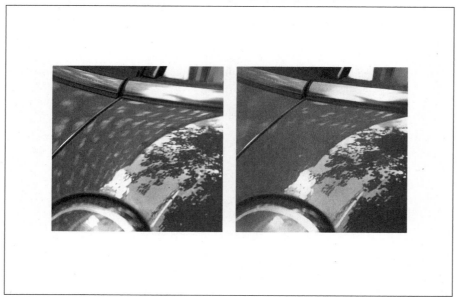

Sharpen

Up until this point, all the filters we've covered smooth detail in images by reducing contrast between neighboring pixels. Now you'll learn about the filters that perform the opposite task — enhancing contrast between pixels to sharpen images.

Why sharpen?

Quite simply, the answer is because sharpening makes photographs look better. The photographs produced by most digital cameras need some degree of sharpening, despite the fact that sharpening is one of the operations that is applied in-camera at the moment you press the shutter release button. This is because, even when working with a high-end camera with a sophisticated sensor, the amount of detail that can be recorded is always less than what really exists, and the processing that your camera applies to compensate for this results in a slightly fuzzy appearance.

Of course, half of the battle is to shoot a sharp, properly focused photograph in the first place, by setting your aperture, shutter speed, and film speed correctly (if your camera allows it), and by using a tripod, particularly in low-light situations. The Sharpen filters in Photoshop can work wonders, but only up to a limit — if you shot a picture out the window of a Jeep while off-roading at twilight, then, well . . . best of luck to you.

Working with sharpening filters

The other thing to know about sharpening is that it should be the last corrective step that you perform on your photograph. Fix the contrast and saturation, remove any blemishes, whiten teeth, remove noise, and then sharpen the image. The reason for this is that any imperfections or noise tends to be magnified by sharpening, leading to undesirable results.

TIP   If you use Smart Filters, you can always change the order in which the filters are applied, making sure that sharpening is the last step: yet another argument for adopting a non-destructive workflow.

One final consideration: The amount of sharpening that you apply is determined to a degree by the size of the image and its destination — whether it will be printed on an inkjet printer at home, whether it's going to a prepress facility, or whether it will be displayed on the Web. There's no one magic number that works for all these situations, so your best bet is to save a corrected, unsharpened master version of your photograph, then output different versions with different degrees of sharpening for different uses.

With that said, here's what you need to know about the Sharpen filters (also see Figure 20.15):

FIGURE 20.15

Here, you can compare the effects of the Sharpen, Sharpen More, and Sharpen Edges filters. The original image is on the top-left.

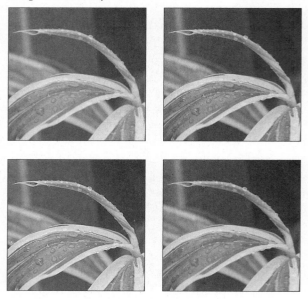

- **Sharpen/Sharpen More.** Just like the Blur and Blur More filters, these two filters apply a pre-defined amount of sharpening, with Sharpen More (predictably) applying a higher degree of sharpening. In either case, you may have to apply these filters repeatedly to achieve a noticeable effect. Again, most people opt for one of the Sharpen filters that offers more precise control of how much sharpening is being applied.

- **Sharpen Edges.** The purpose of this filter is to find the areas of greatest transition between pixels — in other words, the edges — and increase the contrast between them and their neighboring pixels, while preserving smoothness in the rest of the image. This filter also applies a pre-defined amount of sharpening.

- **Unsharp Mask.** If there were such a thing as a rock star in the world of sharpening filters, then Unsharp Mask would be it (see Figure 20.16).

  Some might argue that the recently introduced Smart Sharpen filter is better because of the additional customization it offers, but in terms of sheer name recognition, Unsharp Mask wins hands down. And speaking of names, don't let the term "unsharp" throw you off. The name comes from a traditional photography technique that exaggerates the contrast between light and dark areas of a photograph by using a piece of glass to soften (or "unsharp") the focus of a mask.

FIGURE 20.16

The effect of the Unsharp Mask filter at various settings is demonstrated in these images. In the two-toned gray thumbnails, you can see the effect that the higher Radius and Threshold settings have along the border between the two colors. The corresponding photographs have each been sharpened using the same settings.

Choose Filters ⇨ Sharpen ⇨ Unsharp Mask to display the filter's settings. Below the familiar Preview window and zoom controls you'll see the three sliders that control the filter's effects:

- **Amount:** The Amount slider controls the intensity of the contrast that is applied to edge pixels. The values you can enter range from 1 to 500 percent. At an area of transition between light and dark pixels, a lighter colored line is added to the light area, and a darker color is added to the dark area, on either side of the boundary between the two colors. This enhances the edge and results in a sharper image.

- **Radius:** The Radius slider controls the distance that the sharpening effect extends from each pixel that is being sharpened.

- **Threshold:** Threshold controls how similar pixels have to be to adjacent pixels before they are affected by the Sharpen filter. A value of 0 means that all the pixels in the image are analyzed as the Unsharp Mask filter attempts to detect edges. Raising this value excludes pixels that are similar to each other from the sharpening effect.

Many Photoshop pros recommend starting with a value of 0 for the Threshold, as increasing this number too much can result in patchy areas in your image. If you are determined to increase the Threshold settings, stick with values below 5. I also recommend using small values for the Radius — numbers smaller than 2 should be plenty for home inkjet printers. Speaking of printing, you can often get away with a degree of over-sharpening when printing on consumer-level inkjet printers, since the spreading of the inks masks any halos that you might see on-screen. Images destined for the Web can be sharpened with a radius in the area of .5 pixels.

■ **Smart Sharpen.** Introduced in Photoshop CS2, Smart Sharpen (see Figure 20.17) offers some controls not available to the venerable Unsharp Mask tool. Choose Filter ➪ Sharpen ➪ Smart Sharpen to bring forth the filter's dialog box, where you can preview the effects both in the Preview area and in your document window.

FIGURE 20.17

The original image, and the results of the Smart Sharpen filter.

Notice that there are two modes to the Smart Sharpen filter: Basic and Advanced. Under the Basic mode, you see the familiar Amount and Radius sliders that behave as they do in the Unsharp Mask filter.

The Remove menu allows you to specify the algorithm used to sharpen the image. The default option, Gaussian, is the same method used by Unsharp Mask to reduce blurring in an image. The Lens Blur option sharpens details with more precision, while avoiding the halos that sometimes result from too much sharpening. The third method attempts to compensate from motion blur caused by either the subject or the camera's movement. Enter the angle of the movement in the photo to counter the blurring.

Clicking in the More Accurate check box causes the Smart Sharpen filter to more slowly process the image for more accurate results. Be aware that in some instances this extra processing can add unwanted sharpening to noise and artifacts that exist in the image.

Clicking the Advanced radio button at the top of the Smart Sharpen dialog box produces two additional tabs labeled Shadows and Highlight. The sliders found in the Shadow and Highlight tabs are identically labeled, and allow you to adjust the sharpening effect in the dark and light areas of your image:

- **Fade Amount:** Setting this slider to an amount of 100 percent conceals the sharpening effect in either the shadows or the highlights of the image. Smaller numbers gradually fade out the visible effect of the sharpening. So if your image is looking a little too crisp after adjusting the Amount and Radius settings in the Sharpen tab, you can moderate the effect here.

- **Tonal Width:** This slider controls the range of tones in either the shadows or highlights that are modified by the Fade Amount. Smaller numbers result in a narrower range of tones being treated as shadows or highlights, and vice versa.

- **Radius:** As with the Unsharp Mask filter, the Radius sets the size of the area around each pixel that determines whether it is in shadows or highlights.

  After you've tweaked the settings in the Smart Sharpen dialog box, you can save them as a preset using the save icon next to the Settings menu. Delete saved settings by selecting them in the menu and clicking the trashcan icon.

> **TIP** Want to be more accurate about the angle of motion blurring in your photo? Use the Ruler tool, which is grouped with the Eyedropper tool to draw a line that follows the movement of the blurring in the image, and note its angle in the Ruler tool's Options Bar. Enter this value in the Angle field of the Smart Sharpen filter's dialog box.

Alternative sharpening techniques

As you've learned, Photoshop offers several perfectly good ways to sharpen your photos in the Sharpen section of the Filters menu. There are a few additional filters lurking outside of the officially designated sharpening group that can add a few additional techniques to your arsenal.

The Custom filter

Nestled in the Filters ⇨ Other menu is one of the earliest sharpening tools: the Custom filter. It's complicated and obscure enough that it doesn't merit a position with the other sharpening filters, but it's effective, and in the interest of being thorough, I cover it here.

Choose Filters ⇨ Other ⇨ Custom to reveal the rather complicated-looking dialog box shown in Figure 20.18. The Custom filter works by applying a *convolution kernel* to your image, which is determined by the values entered in the 25 fields in the dialog box. The boxes represent a grid of any 25 pixels in your image. The default values mean that the center pixel becomes five times as bright, while the pixels immediately above, below, and to either side of it lose a level of brightness. The net result is an overall sharpening of your image.

Increasing the amount of sharpening that's applied is a matter of juggling the brightness values in each box so that they always ultimately add up to at least 1. For instance, placing a value of −1 in the corner boxes around the center pixel immediately plunges the photo into darkness; that's because the net brightness of the pixels is now −3. To compensate, raise the value of the center box to 9, bringing the total back to 1 and increasing the level of sharpening dramatically.

FIGURE 20.18

The Custom filter allows you to create and save your own sharpening filter — with some effort.

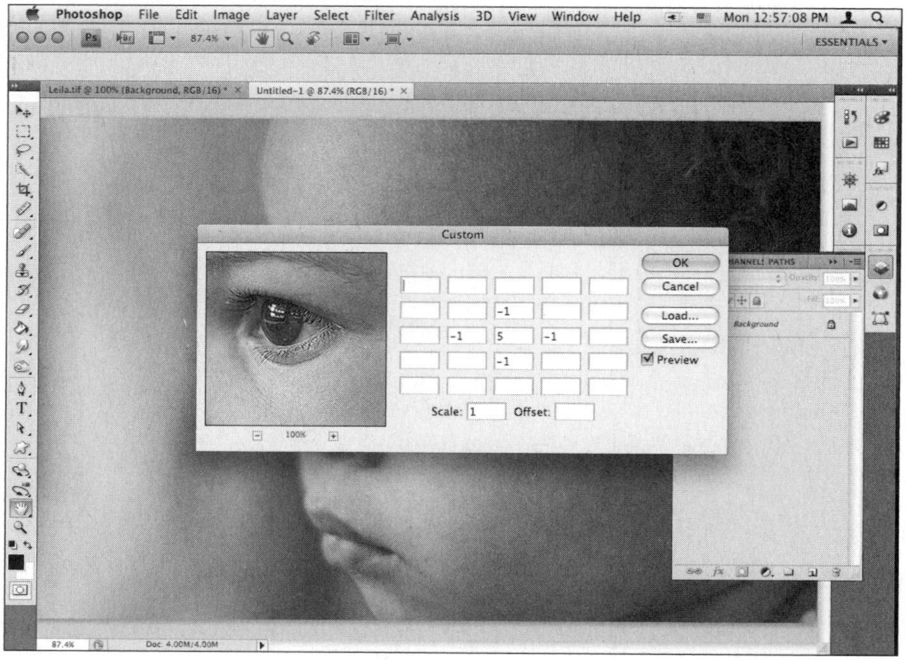

Working with those principles in mind, you can tweak the values in the boxes between –999 and 999. The value in the Scale field is what the sum of the values in the boxes will be divided by. So if values in the boxes add up to, say, 4, you can compensate by changing the Scale value to 4 for a total brightness of 1. The value in the Offset field is added to the result of the Scale calculation. Once you've found the magic setting that works for you, click Save to enter a name for your filter, and select a location for it on your hard drive.

One thing to keep in mind about the Custom filter is that it applies its effect to every single pixel in your image indiscriminately, which can exacerbate noise, pores, blemishes, and all the other stuff you'd rather conceal. As mentioned before, it's hard to justify using the Custom filter when Photoshop offers so many superior and easier-to-use options. Nonetheless, there it is.

Using the High Pass filter

One of the more unintuitive sharpening methods is to use the High Pass filter to emphasize contrast between edges. Portrait photographers often use this technique to reduce the appearance of pores and blemishes, and produce really crisp details in the catch lights of the subject's eyes.

1. Open an image that could benefit from some sharpening. I chose the portrait of my niece shown in Figure 20.19.

FIGURE 20.19

The original unsharpened image looks pretty good, but it will look outstanding once it's been sharpened.

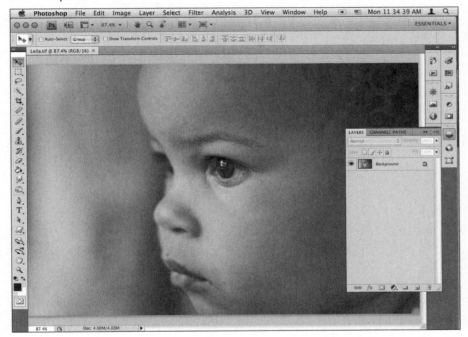

2. Duplicate the background layer by pressing Ctrl+J/⌘+J. This is the layer that's going to receive the sharpening effect via the High Pass filter.

3. Choose Filters ➪ Other ➪ High Pass. What this filter does — other than turn most of your photo a lovely shade of gray as in Figure 20.20 — is look for details along edges and other places where sharp color transitions occur.

   The Radius slider adjusts the width of the edges that the filter detects. A setting of 0.1 pixels keeps only the barest minimum of edge detail, which isn't particularly useful. Increase the radius to somewhere between 1.5 and 2 pixels.

FIGURE 20.20

The High Pass filter turns your photo a lovely shade of gray — that is, except for the edges.

4. Change the blending mode of the high pass layer you just created to Overlay. Make sure you're zoomed in to 100 percent (select Actual Pixels from the View menu, or press Ctrl+1/⌘+1) to see the result of the sharpening.

If you feel the effect is a little too intense, you can always dial down the opacity of the high-pass layer. The final result is shown next to the original image in Figure 20.21.

FIGURE 20.21

The original unsharpened image appears on the left, while the sharpened version is on the right. Detail around the eyelashes and the highlights in the eyes look much crisper.

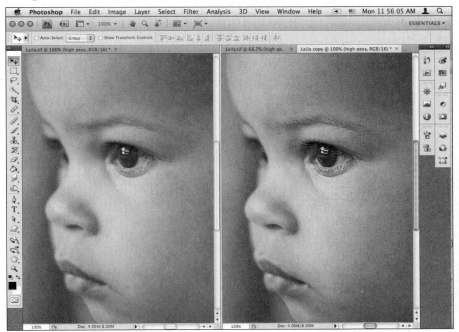

Special Effects Filters

One of the best ways to experiment with the almost 50 Special Effects filters is to use the Filter Gallery to browse through their thumbnails and click on them to see what effect they'll have on your image. Access the Filter Gallery by selecting it from the Filters menu. Choosing almost any of the filters in the Artistic, Brush Strokes, Distort, Sketch, Stylize, or Texture submenus of the Filters menu also launches the Filter Gallery. Some of the filters found in those categories, such as Lens Blur, Ripple, and Pinch, which are under the Distort menu, have their own standard dialog boxes.

The way the Filter Gallery works is simple: Launch the Filter Gallery using either of the two methods discussed above. Here's what you need to know about working in the Filter Gallery:

- **Choose a filter by clicking on one of the thumbnails in any of the six filter categories listed.** Use the settings in the panel on the left to customize the filter's effect. Switch to a different filter by simply clicking on a different thumbnail or by choosing one from the popup menu at the top of the settings area. As with other dialog boxes, you can see the effects of your changes reflected in the preview area on the left, and you can change the magnification of the preview area using the zoom controls.

669

- **Stack multiple filters to create complex effects by clicking the New Effect Layer icon in the lower right of the Filter Gallery window.** You can continue to stack filters on top of each other, but you'll soon begin to see a lag in processing time as your effects get more and more complex. Remember that selecting a different filter replaces the effect for the current effect layer — I've often unintentionally switched a filter I liked to a different filter, when what I intended was to add another filter on top of it.

- **To change the order in which the filters are applied, drag the filter layers just as you would drag regular layers in the Layers panel.** The top-most layer in the stack represents the most recently applied filter.

- **To get rid of an effect, highlight its filter layer and click the trashcan icon at the bottom of the Filter Gallery window.**

- **When using the Filter Gallery with a Smart Object, multiple stacked effects become a single Smart Filter item in the Layers panel.** Double-clicking on this item (listed as Filter Gallery in Figure 20.22) re-opens the Filter Gallery's interface, where you can adjust the settings again.

The other advantage to working with Smart Filters in the Filter Gallery is that each effect's opacity and blending mode can be changed individually (see Figure 20.23 for examples of several Smart Filters). And remember that you can add a layer mask and paint on it to apply the Special Effects filters to selected portions of your image.

FIGURE 20.22

The Filter Gallery interface. Combine filters and rearrange their stacking order to create complex effects.

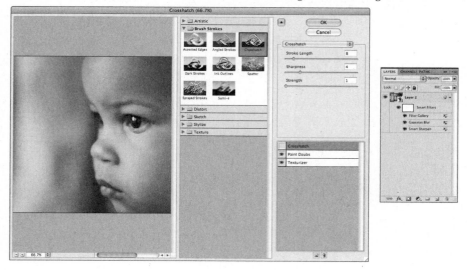

NOTE The Filter Gallery is unavailable if your image is in anything higher than 8-bit mode. Choose Image ⇨ Mode ⇨ 8-bits/Channel to change it. There's a way around this limitation, though: Turn your image into a Smart Filter first, then convert your image to 8-bit mode. That way, you can use the Filter Gallery, but the high bit depth of your image is preserved within the Smart Object. Double-click on the Smart Object's thumbnail to edit the image in all its 16-bit glory. Sneaky, huh?

FIGURE 20.23

Nine samples of the many Special Effects filters available in the Filter Gallery. From left to right: Texture, Chalk & Charcoal, Diffuse Glow, Glass, Ink Outlines, Crosshatch, Angled Strokes, Palette Knife, Plastic Wrap.

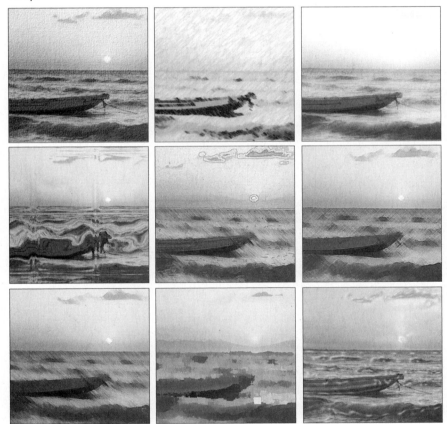

Creating Clouds and Fire

I end this introduction to Photoshop's filters with a few demonstrations of how you can combine filters with layer styles to produce some very impressive visual effects. During the course of these examples, I introduce you to some other effects filters that I may not have specifically covered in the earlier sections of this chapter.

The techniques in these examples make heavy use of such principles as layer styles, layer masks, blending modes, and levels. It might be worth it to do a quick review of some of the earlier chapters of this book that cover these topics.

Clouds

Photoshop has two built-in filters that create random cloud patterns — the Clouds and Difference Clouds filters, located under the Filters ➪ Render menu. Neither of these filters used by itself produces satisfying results if you're looking to produce realistic clouds, but they can be useful as a starting point.

The Clouds filter generates a random pattern that varies between the foreground and background color. Set your foreground and background color and choose Filter ➪ Clouds to fill the current layer or selection with the cloud pattern. The contents of the current layer will be replaced by the pattern, so create an empty layer if necessary.

The Difference Clouds filter works slightly . . . differently. For one, the target layer can't be empty, because Difference Clouds works by blending the foreground and background color values with the existing contents of the selected layer, the same way the Difference blending mode does. So either select a layer that has some non-transparent pixels on it, or create a new layer and fill it with a color.

The results of the Clouds and Difference Clouds filters are shown in Figure 20.24.

Creating clouds can be a tricky effect to pull off convincingly, but it's something that's very useful to know.

I started with the photograph of the Bay of Naples shown in Figure 20.25. It is a perfectly decent photograph, but the sky is kind of flat and could use some texture. Bring on the clouds! Follow these steps to learn how to play weatherman and create some perfectly puffy clouds for your photos.

FIGURE 20.24

Clouds and Difference Clouds blend the foreground and background colors in random values to generate a soft cloudy pattern. To get the Difference Clouds effect on the right, I applied the filter repeatedly about five times.

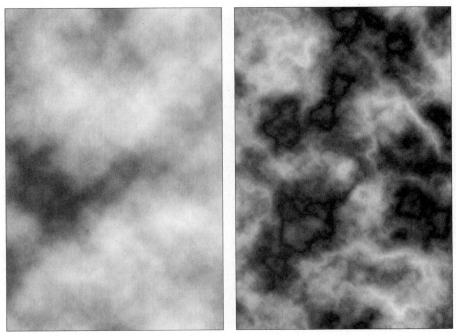

1. Click on the background color swatch and use the eyedropper to select a color somewhere in the upper part of your sky.

2. Do the same for the foreground color swatch, only this time, select a color somewhere near the lower part of your sky (see Figure 20.26).

3. Create a new layer by pressing **Ctrl+Alt+Shift+N/⌘+Option+Shift+N**. Fill this layer with black by pressing Shift+Delete on your keyboard and selecting Black from the Use menu. Be sure that Preserve Transparency is unchecked. Click OK.

4. **Double-click the layer thumbnail and select Gradient Overlay from the list of styles on the left.** Ensure that the gradient is a blend of your foreground and background colors by clicking on the gradient picker arrow on the right of the gradient swatch and selecting the Foreground to Background swatch on the top right. Click OK to apply the layer style.

TIP If you selected your colors in the reverse order — that is, if the top of your sky gradient is brighter than the bottom — simply open the Gradient Overlay settings again and click in the Reverse check box.

FIGURE 20.25

The sky in this photo of the Bay of Naples could sure use some detail.

FIGURE 20.26

To create a gradient background for my clouds, I sampled the colors in my original photo.

5. **To bring on some cloud action, press D on your keyboard to set your foreground and background colors to the default black and white.** Create a new empty layer and choose Filters ⇨ Render ⇨ Clouds. For organizational purposes, double-click the layer name and change it to Clouds.

6. **To give these clouds a little extra punch, go ahead and run the Difference Clouds filter on it (choose Filters ⇨ Render ⇨ Difference Clouds).** You should have something similar to Figure 20.27 by this point.

7. **Use the Levels command (press Ctrl+L/⌘+L) to increase the contrast of the cloud layer.** Drag the sliders at either end of the Input Levels graph toward the middle to boost the highlights and dark areas of the clouds until they are fairly high-contrast, and change the blending mode of the cloud layer to Screen. Aha — it's starting to take shape!

8. **Now we'll add some depth to the clouds, as they're currently a little flat.** With the cloud layer selected, press Ctrl+A/⌘+A to select the whole canvas, and then press Ctrl+C/⌘+C to copy everything to the clipboard.

9. **Create a new layer and name it Shadows.**

FIGURE 20.27

Clouds followed by Difference Clouds produced the soft texture shown here.

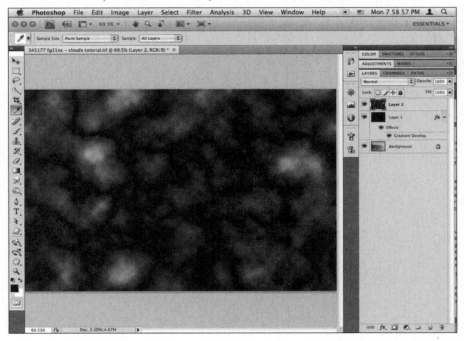

10. **Toggle Quick Mask mode by pressing the Q key on your keyboard, and press Ctrl+V/⌘+V on your keyboard to paste in the clouds that you just copied.** You should now see a red overlay with white areas where your clouds are (see Figure 20.28).

FIGURE 20.28

Quick Mask allows you to paint selections using any of the brush or selection tools, but in this case, it was used to make a quick selection that matched the clouds from the cloud layer.

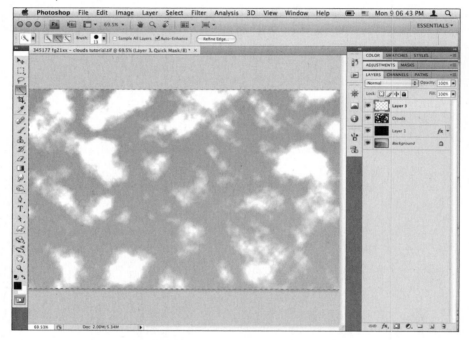

11. **Press Q again to switch out of Quick Mask mode and fill the active selections with white by pressing Ctrl+Delete/⌘+Delete on your keyboard.**

12. **To add shadows, double-click the shadow layer's thumbnail and choose Inner Shadow from the list of layer styles (see Figure 20.29).** Reduce the opacity of the shadow to around 20 percent, and make sure that the Distance and Choke are set to 0.

13. **Finally, bring the Size of the shadow down to about 5 pixels.** I added a little Noise using the slider at the bottom of the dialog box to introduce a little randomness to the shadow.

FIGURE 20.29

The Inner Shadow layer style was used to add a little bit of dimension to the clouds.

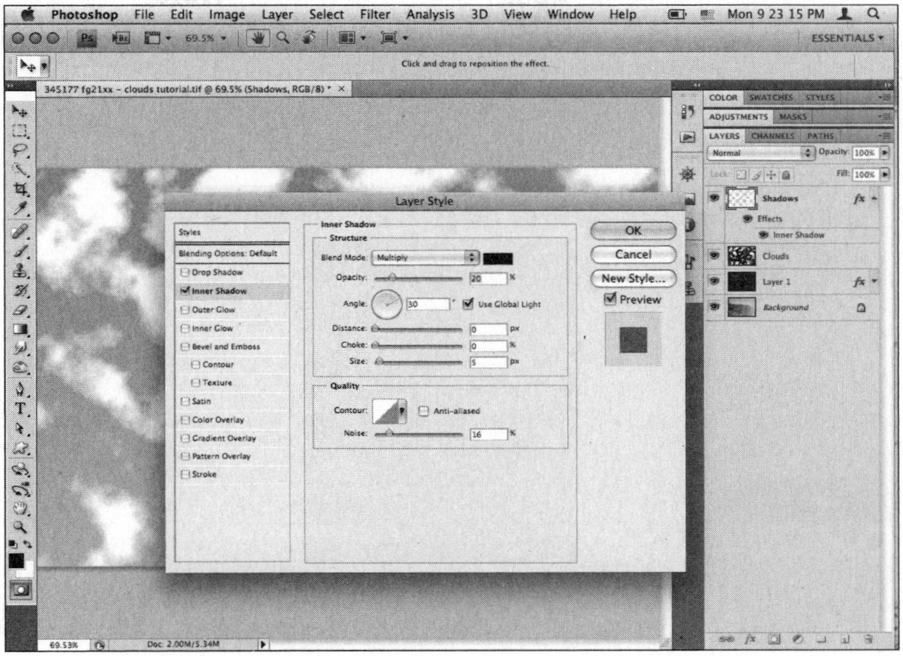

You now have some reasonable-looking clouds. You could spend a little time adding still more dimension to the clouds by using the Brush or Burn tool with a soft-edged tip, and add in some shadows, but I leave that up to you.

For now, you need to know how to blend your clouds with the original image.

14. **Start by combining your background gradient and your cloud and shadow layers into a Smart Object (choose Convert to Smart Object from the Layers panel menu).** This gives you a little flexibility with editing the cloud elements later, if necessary. I renamed mine to Clouds, just to keep things tidy.

15. **Click the Add Layer Mask icon at the bottom of the Layers panel to mask the Smart Object.** By default, the mask is filled with white, which reveals all the contents of the layer.

16. **Make sure the layer mask thumbnail is selected (you should see four brackets highlighting its thumbnail icon), and select the Gradient tool by pressing Shift+G on your keyboard until it's selected in the Toolbar.** Make sure the Gradient tool options are set to 100 percent opacity, and the Reverse and Dither options are checked.

17. Draw a gradient so that there's white at the top of the mask, gradually fading to black, revealing the clouds at the top of the image.

18. Finally, change the Clouds Smart Object layer's blending mode to Lighten.

Depending on what your background looks like, you might want to use a different tool to create or refine your mask, like a brush or one of the selection tools.

As you can see in Figure 20.30, I touched up the mask in my example with a large brush to make it match the mountains in the background.

The possibilities for tweaking this effect even further are endless — remember, you put the clouds in a Smart Object, which opens up the world of Smart Filters to you. Also, if your gradient background doesn't quite match the original photo, or if you just want to adjust the saturation of the colors, you can always double-click on the Smart Object and edit the Gradient Overlay layer style on the clouds' background layer.

I added a Water Paper Smart Filter with its opacity dropped to 50 percent to my cloud layer, which helped to soften the effect a bit. I also added a Noise filter to try and match the grain in the original photograph. The final result is shown along with the original in Figure 20.31.

FIGURE 20.30

Refining the mask with the Brush tool on the Smart Object helped to enhance the cloud illusion.

FIGURE 20.31

The original photograph is shown here alongside the retouched final image.

Playing with fire

Here's another one of those effects that often pops up, and that can be tricky to execute convincingly. Try this somewhat advanced technique to stoke some flames in your designs. The effect I'll be demonstrating here creates a wall of flames rather than something small like a candle flame, but once you get the basic idea, you should be able to come up with some fire of your own.

1. To start your conflagration, create a new document with a black background layer.

2. With your foreground and background colors set to the defaults black and white (press D on your keyboard), choose Filters ➪ Render ➪ Fibers. The Fibers filter (see Figure 20.32) creates the appearance of woven fibers by creating a blend of the foreground and background colors with the existing colors of the selected layer. The Variance slider controls the length of the fibers, while the Strength slider affects the look of each fiber. I used settings of 25 and 4 for Variance and Strength, respectively.

FIGURE 20.32

The Fibers filter is used to generate the basis of what will become a wall of flames.

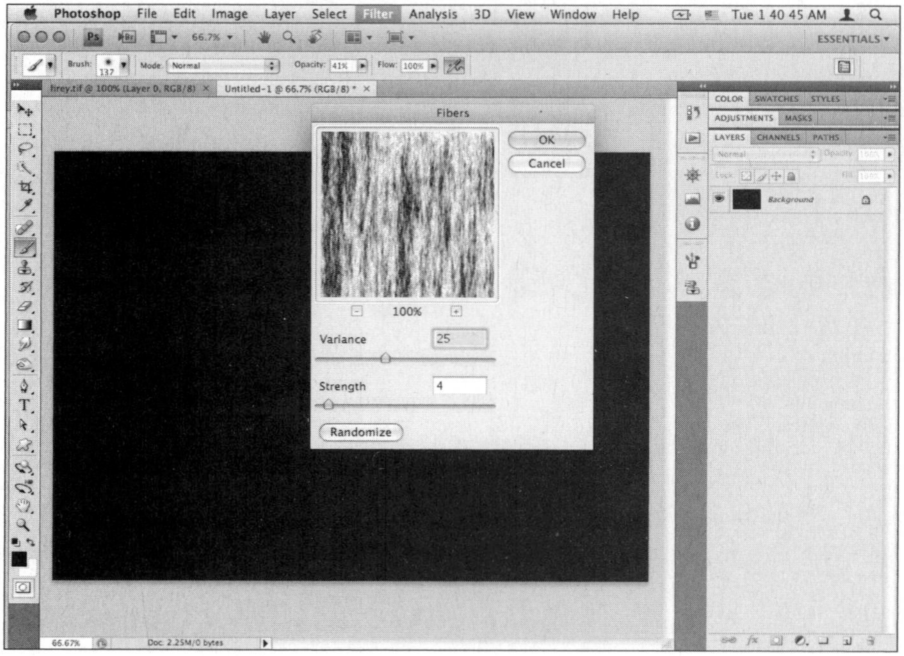

3. Click the Randomize button to generate a random fiber pattern, then click OK. You're looking for a pattern with some fairly dense areas of white (which will eventually become your flames).

4. Blur your fibers using a Gaussian Blur setting of around 6, then increase the contrast of the blurred fibers using the Levels command, as shown in Figure 20.33.

5. **Select the Gradient tool and set your foreground color to black.** Right now, the flames should be running from top to bottom of your document, so to get rid of the top half of them, you can fade them out with a gradient.

6. **In the Gradient tool Options Bar, open the gradient swatches and pick the second thumbnail to fade from the foreground color to transparent.** Draw a gradient from top to bottom, to fade out the top half of the fibers.

FIGURE 20.33

Blurring the fibers and reducing the detail produces the basis for the flames in this effect.

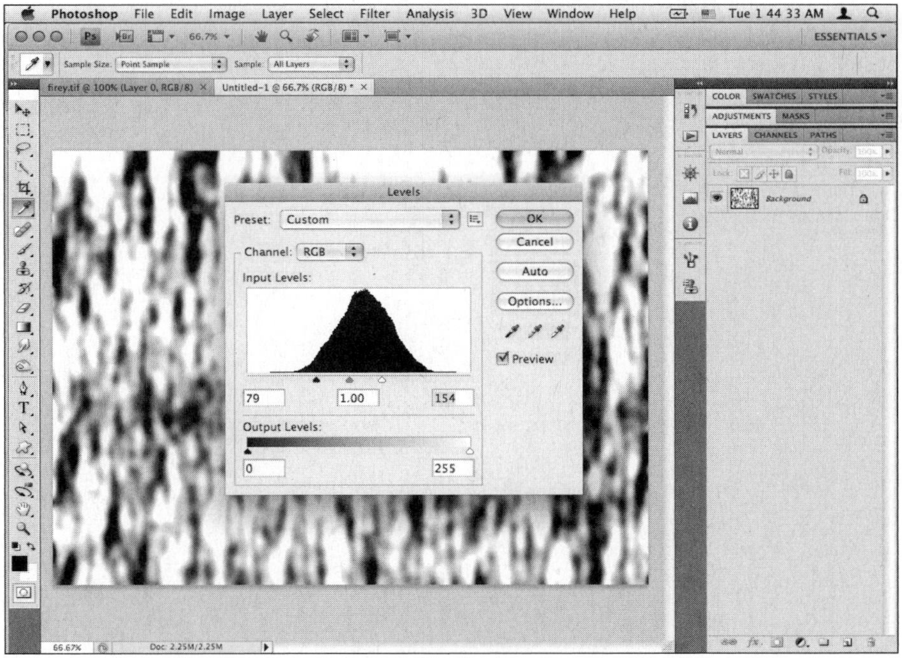

7. **Add some color to the flames by pressing Ctrl+U/⌘+U to launch the Hue/Saturation dialog box — or create a Hue/Saturation adjustment layer by clicking its icon in the Adjustments panel (see Figure 20.34).** Click the Colorize check box and set the Hue to a reddish-orange color. Bump the Saturation slider way up to 100, and click OK.

8. **Press Ctrl+Alt+Shift+E/⌘+Option+Shift+E to merge the visible layers to a new layer above the others.** Use Hue/Saturation again to change the color of this new layer to a reddish hue (no need to check the Colorize box this time).

9. **Change the blending mode of the layer you just created to Color Dodge, and press Ctrl+Shift+E/⌘+Shift+E to merge all the layers together.** Starting to look pretty fiery, huh?

FIGURE 20.34

Coloring the flames with the Hue/Saturation command has made a huge difference already.

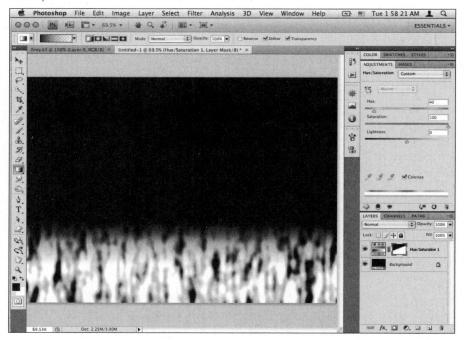

10. **To start shaping the flames, select Liquify from the Filters menu.** This filter overlays a mesh of points on top of your image (see Figure 20.35).

    You can then distort the image by moving those mesh points around. Click in the Show Mesh check box under the View Options section to view the mesh. This filter is covered in depth in Chapter 21.

11. **Click on the Forward Warp tool (which is normally selected by default), and set your Brush Size to around 70.** Begin slowly painting the tops of the flames to stretch them upward in a flame-like fashion. If you go too far, don't sweat it — one of the coolest things about the Liquify filter is its Reconstruct tool (the second icon in the filter's Toolbox), which lets you gradually restore the points of the mesh to their original positions.

FIGURE 20.35

The Liquify tool is used to pull the tops of these flames into shape.

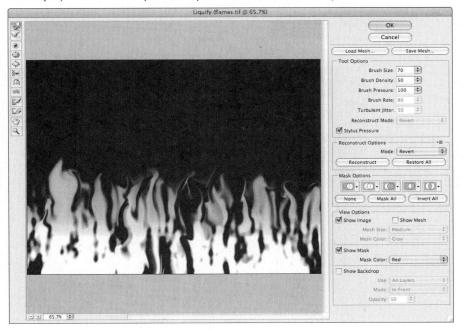

12. Once you've got some nice flames licking upward, click OK to exit the dialog box and distort your image.

13. **To add a glow to the effect, duplicate the liquified flames layer and apply a Gaussian Blur at a radius setting of about 8.** Set the blending mode of your duplicate flames to Screen, and drop the opacity setting, if necessary, until it looks right to you (see Figure 20.36).

14. **You can combine the flames with another image.** Press Ctrl+A/⌘+A to select your entire canvas, then press Ctrl+Shift+C/⌘+Shift+C to copy the merged contents of all the layers (you can also find this command under Edit ➪ Copy Merged).

15. **Open the image you want to combine the flames with (I chose a photo of a row of apartment buildings in Figure 2.37), and press Ctrl+V/⌘+V to paste in the flames.** To blend in the black background, change the flames' blending mode to Screen or Lighten.

FIGURE 20.36

The flames in their final state

As usual, there's nothing to stop you from pushing this effect even further. Once again, I applied a Ripple Smart Filter to my background to add a little heat distortion, and painted in the layer mask to restrict the distortion to the parts of the buildings that are directly behind the flames.

FIGURE 20.37

The composite image combines the flames I created with a row of buildings.

Summary

This chapter introduced you to Photoshop's plethora of Filter effects. You learned about the group of filters used to perform tasks like sharpening and blurring, and you learned about the wide variety of creative effects that can be produced by the Special Effects filters.

Additionally, you saw how you could create complex combinations of effects using the Filter Gallery, and you learned how to apply effects non-destructively through the use of Smart Filters. You finished up by learning a few advanced special effects techniques, combining the use of filters and layer styles to create clouds and fire.

Chapter 21

Distortion Effects

In the preceding chapter, you were introduced to a sampling of the filters that make up part of Photoshop's image manipulation arsenal. This chapter continues that theme, this time focusing on some of the filters that allow you to warp, twist, melt, and otherwise distort images.

Some of these filters, like Vanishing Point or Lens Correction, have obvious technical applications. Others can be used to create eye-catching special effects, but there is often a temptation to dismiss some of them as novelty filters. Take the Liquify Filter, for example — at first glance it seems like all it would be good for would be to create funhouse mirror effects as a gag. In the hands of professional retouchers, though, the Liquify Tool is a virtual surgical scalpel, trimming, nipping, and tucking to produce magazine cover-worthy photos.

By the end of this chapter you should be armed with enough information to make the most of these filters — either to create fun special effects or realistic visual sleight-of-hand.

Liquify

One of the more robust of the distortion filters is the Liquify filter, which you were introduced to briefly back in Chapter 20. There you saw how the Liquify filter could be used to distort pixels, creating flames; now we'll take a step back and examine how the filter works more closely.

Liquify is one of the few stand-alone filters in the Filters menu, appearing alongside Vanishing Point (covered in the next section of this chapter) outside of any of the filter categories. It was added to Photoshop back in version 6, and has since proved to be a highly useful part of any digital artist's toolset. It works by overlaying a mesh or grid over your image, and associating the pixels in your image with points on the grid. When you're distorting the image, you're really moving the grid points around, and the corresponding pixels in the image follow.

The Liquify tool's dialog box, which you can access by choosing Filter ⇨ Liquify, is shown in Figure 21.1. As is the case with most of the other filter dialog boxes, you can change the zoom level and move around the preview area using the provided controls. On the left side of the dialog box, you'll find an array of tools used to apply the distortion, and on the right are numerous settings used to modify the Liquify tools.

FIGURE 21.1

The Liquify filter is robust enough to be its own application.

Distortion tools

Ready to start liquifying? Here are the tools you'll find within the window's Toolbox. The keyboard shortcut for each tool is also shown in parentheses next to the tool's name. Figure 21.2 shows the crazy effects you can create with each tool.

FIGURE 21.2

The results of using the Liquify filter's various distortion tools

- **Forward Warp (W)/Reconstruct (R).** This is the main distortion tool. Holding down your mouse button and dragging with this tool causes pixels to be pushed forward, away from the center of your cursor. The effect lessens as pixels get farther away from the center of the brush. As with the other brush-based tools, clicking, then holding down the Shift key and clicking again, distorts pixels in a straight line between the two points.

  The Reconstruct tool allows you to reverse any distortions you've made by painting back in the image as it originally was. You can also select the Reconstruct tool from the Toolbox, which appears directly below the Forward Warp tool.

  To temporarily switch to the Reconstruct tool while using the Forward Warp tool, hold down the Alt/Option key on your keyboard. This key command works in reverse when you're using the Reconstruct tool.

- **Twirl (C)/Pucker (S)/Bloat (B).** The Twirl tool rotates pixels clockwise around your cursor. Alt/Option-clicking rotates pixels counterclockwise.

  The Pucker tool pulls pixels in toward the center of your cursor, and the Bloat tool pushes pixels outward. In all three cases, the effect is applied while dragging your mouse or when you click and hold down the mouse button.

- **Push Left (O).** Dragging upward with this tool pushes pixels under your cursor to the left, while dragging down pushes them to the right. Dragging horizontally pushes the pixels either above or below the cursor, depending on the direction you're dragging. The Push

Left tool can be used to enlarge or shrink an object: Drag in a clockwise circle to enlarge, and drag counterclockwise to shrink.

To temporarily invert the tool's behavior (that is, to push the pixels in the opposite direction that they normally move), hold down the Alt/Option key while dragging.

■ **Mirror (M).** The Mirror tool reflects the pixels that are perpendicular to the direction of the brush stroke as you paint. So, while painting left to right, the area above the cursor is mirrored, and top-to-bottom strokes mirror the area to the right of the cursor. Again, to invert the default behavior, paint with the Alt/Option key held down.

■ **Turbulence (T).** This tool smoothly jumbles the pixels that you're painting over. You can also distort with the Turbulence tool by clicking and holding down your mouse button.

■ **Freeze Mask (F)/Thaw Mask (D).** To refine your distortions, it's helpful to "freeze" some areas of the image that you don't want to modify. To do so, select the Freeze Mask tool from the Toolbox. As you paint with the Freeze Mask tool, a semi-transparent red overlay is applied to the areas of the image that you don't want to distort.

To enable distortions in those frozen areas, you would naturally want to "unfreeze" those areas — and there's a Thaw Mask tool that does just that. Select the Thaw Mask tool and paint over frozen areas to allow distortion.

Distortion options

Over on the right side of the Liquify tool's dialog box are settings that control how distortions are applied to your image, how the preview image is displayed, masking options, and more.

Tool options

Within this section you'll find options to modify the behavior of the Liquify tool's brush. Some of the options apply only to specific tools — for example, the Turbulent Jitter tool is grayed out unless the Turbulence tool is active.

■ **Brush Size.** As you may have guessed, this setting adjusts the diameter of your brush and can be set as high as 600 pixels.

■ **Brush Density.** This setting refers to the intensity of the distortion as you go further from the center of the brush. It's analogous to the Hardness control of Photoshop's other brush-based tools.

■ **Brush Pressure.** Use this option to control the speed of the distortions. The Brush Pressure slider covers a range from 0 to 100 — higher settings will apply distortions very rapidly, while a lower setting allows you to distort your image more slowly and with more control.

■ **Brush Rate.** This option controls the amount of distortion that's applied when you click and hold your brush in place.

■ **Turbulent Jitter.** This option is only available with the Turbulence tool selected. It controls how tightly the pixels are scrambled when you paint with the Turbulence tool. A setting of 1 scrambles pixels more smoothly, while a high setting — up in the range of 50–100 — applies a lot of movement to the distorted pixels.

Reconstruction

So you've distorted your image, and now you need to bring it back from the precipice. Or maybe you just want to make your distortions more subtle and believable. The Liquify tool gives you several ways to remove distortions that you've added to your image, or change the way that those distortions have been applied.

The first way would be to undo a distortion by pressing Ctrl+Z (⌘+Z on a Mac) to undo the most recent distortion (repeating the key command undoes the undo, turning it into a redo). The commands for stepping backward (Ctrl+Alt+Z/⌘+Option+Z) and forward (Ctrl+Shift+Z/⌘+Shift+Z) through History States also work here.

To take it a step further, you can remove distortions in specific areas of your image by using the Reconstruct tool, or you can use the buttons in the Reconstruct Options area to affect your entire image.

Choose one of the settings in the Reconstruct Mode menu to specify how the Reconstruct tool removes distortions:

- **Revert.** This mode restores the original image, completely removing any distortions.
- **Rigid.** Right angles are restored in portions of the grid that lie near the borders between frozen and unfrozen areas. This almost (but not quite) restores distorted areas back to the original image.
- **Stiff.** This mode reduces the distortions as you move farther away from the borders between frozen and unfrozen areas. At the borders, unfrozen areas take on some of the distortions of the frozen areas.
- **Smooth/Loose.** These two modes both apply distortions that occur in frozen areas to unfrozen areas. Loose applies the distortions with more continuity. If your frozen areas don't have any distortions, you won't notice any change when you use the Reconstruct tool with either of these two modes.

The Displace, Amplitwist, and Affine modes are unique to the Reconstruct tool. They allow you to sample distortion in one part of your image and propagate that same distortion throughout your image. The same distortion sample is used as long as you hold down the mouse button. Every time you click and release, a new sample is defined. Pick Displace to move pixels from the source point. Amplitwist matches displacements as well as scaling and rotation information, while Affine reconstructs thawed areas to match all distortions of the source area including displacement, scaling, rotation, and skewing.

Protecting parts of your image

You've already seen how you can use the Freeze Mask tool to paint in a mask that protects specific areas of your image. The buttons in the Mask Options area of the Liquify tool's dialog box provide additional masking tools.

The five mask options allow you to generate a mask for your image using any of the following: an existing layer selection (that is, if you had a selection active when you first launched the Liquify filter); transparent pixels in your image; or a layer mask. From left to right, each button does the following:

- **Replace Selection.** Clears any mask you've created with the Freeze Mask tool and replaces it with a mask based on the layer's selection, transparency, or layer mask.
- **Add to Selection.** Keeps the currently thawed areas of your image and thaws additional areas based on the source you select.
- **Subtract from Selection.** Keeps the currently thawed areas of your image and freezes the areas that correspond to the source you select.
- **Intersect with Selection.** Finds thawed areas in your current selection that overlap with thawed areas in the selection, transparency, or layer mask.
- **Invert Selection.** Inverts the currently thawed areas, but only within the corresponding areas of the selection, transparency, or layer mask.

Additionally, the three buttons at the bottom of the Mask Options area allow you to fill the preview image with a mask, remove any currently frozen areas (the equivalent of thawing the entire image), or swap the areas that are currently frozen with the unfrozen areas.

View options

The last set of options in the Liquify filter's dialog box control the viewing options for the preview area:

- **Show Image.** Use this to toggle the preview image on or off. This is useful if you want to clearly see what your mask looks like or if you want to see what distortions you've applied to the pixel mesh.
- **Show Mesh.** Toggle the pixel mesh — the grid on which your distortions are based — on or off using this button. The menus below offer controls for the size (use a smaller grid for finer distortion, and a larger grid for coarser changes) and color of the mesh.
- **Show Mask.** Choose a color for the mask overlay. The default is red, but you can try other colors if you find that it's too close to the colors in your image.
- **Show Backdrop.** Display either the active layer or a combination of other layers in your document in the preview area. If you choose to display other layers, you can specify whether they appear in front of, behind, or blended with the preview of the distorted image. Enter a number in the Opacity field, or click the double arrows next to it to reveal the Opacity slider, which controls the visibility of the backdrop. This is a helpful way to see how your distortions compare with the original image.

Vanishing Point

Introduced in CS2, the Vanishing Point filter is another mini-application within Photoshop. It's used to manipulate objects by distorting them accurately to maintain correct perspective. You can still use the Perspective mode of the Transform tool to manipulate layers or images in perspective, but that's pretty much as far as that tool goes.

The capabilities of the Vanishing Point filter include the ability to bend and rotate objects around corners, measure objects in perspective, and export information for use in CAD or 3D applications (in DXF or 3DS formats). In Photoshop CS4 Extended, you can also create a 3D layer from the perspective information generated by the Vanishing Point filter. To access these extra features, open the settings menu by clicking the little triangle icon in the upper-left corner of the dialog box.

The best way to learn about this somewhat complex filter is to dive in and use it. To demonstrate, I chose this photograph of the side of a building in my neighborhood. There's a huge half-painted space on it that used to be covered by an ad of some sort, but is now just an eyesore (see Figure 21.3). I'm going to make those apartment owners very happy by giving them some additional windows on that north-facing wall.

FIGURE 21.3

The apartment building before its makeover.

To edit in perspective using the Vanishing Point, follow these steps:

1. **Create a blank layer.** The Vanishing Point filter applies its distortions to the currently active layer. For this reason, it's generally good practice to work on a blank layer so you can change the blending mode, opacity, or otherwise manipulate your work after the fact if necessary. You can also work on a duplicate of the image's background layer (highlight it in the Layers panel and press Ctrl-J/⌘-J on your keyboard).

2. **Choose Filter ⇨ Vanishing Point to launch the filter's dialog box.** By default, the Create Plane tool is already selected. Click on the four corners of a rectangular object in the photograph.

   In this example, I used the area where the ad used to be as a guide. Getting this first plane right is pretty important. That said, you can always zoom in to the preview area and manipulate the corners of your grid (by pressing Ctrl/⌘ and dragging) to make sure they're lining up correctly.

   Stretch out the sides of your first plane as necessary (see Figure 21.4). You can make your perspective planes taller or wider by dragging the stretch nodes found on each side.

FIGURE 21.4

Align your first plane with something rectangular in your photograph.

---

3. **Create additional planes.** Ctrl-click/⌘-click on the stretch nodes of the plane to drag out new planes perpendicular to the first one. To change the angle between the new plane and its parent to something other than 90 degrees, use the Angle slider that appears in the options area of the dialog box, or Alt-click/Option-click on one of the handles on the sides of the plane.

For my example, I only needed one additional plane (see Figure 21.5), but feel free to continue adding more planes if you need them.

4. **Save your perspective planes.** This would be a good place to save your work. To do so, click OK to accept the perspective grids you just made, close the filter's dialog box, and then save your document in PSD, TIFF, or JPEG format.

Re-launch the Vanishing Point tool. Note that up to this point, you haven't manipulated any pixels yet. Just in case you were wondering why your image looks exactly the same as it did when you started — don't worry, you'll start distorting in the next step.

> **TIP** True, the Vanishing Point filter supports multiple undos, but if you were to begin editing and suddenly decided that you didn't like a change you had made, pressing the undo key repeatedly would also get rid of the grid you created, which would be a drag.

FIGURE 21.5

Create additional planes by pressing Ctrl/⌘ and dragging out from the sides of your original plane.

5. **Start cloning windows.** I used the Vanishing Point filter's version of the Cloning Stamp tool to clone windows from the front of the building to the windowless side. Just as with the regular Cloning Stamp tool, Alt-click/Option-click to define a source. In this case, I clicked on one of the windows that I wanted to copy and began painting in the destination area.

   By default, the Cloning Stamp paints with Heal turned on, which preserves the original texture of the plane you're painting on. In my case, the wall is a different color, so I've disabled the Heal option.

   The Aligned check box keeps the Cloning brush synced up with the source you selected, which in this example, allowed me to paint the windows and fire escapes from the front of the building onto the side, all the while maintaining correct perspective (see Figure 21.6).

6. **Click OK to exit the Vanishing Point filter and apply the distortion to your image.** Again, any changes you made will be applied to the layer that was active when you launched the filter, which is why you created a new blank layer (or duplicated the background layer) in the first step.

FIGURE 21.6

This instant architectural makeover was achieved with the Cloning Stamp tool.

The possibilities for manipulating images with this tool are vast, and to discover them all, you'll have to be prepared to experiment on your own.

Here's an additional tip, though: You can bring text or other images into your document and position them in perspective with a simple copy and paste. Copy your source image, launch the Vanishing Point filter in your destination document, and press Ctrl+V/⌘+V to paste the image into the filter's dialog box.

You can then drag it into position in one of your perspective planes. As demonstrated in Figure 21.7, I decided to pretty up that building with a giant photo of my niece, because who wouldn't love a giant photo of a 6-year-old eating ice cream on the side of their building?

FIGURE 21.7

Awww . . . much better than the original two-toned brick wall, isn't it?

Warping Objects

Photoshop offers several ways of warping images. The Text tool has its own built-in Warp function in its Options Bar, as I covered in Chapter 13. To extend that ability beyond text and warp any item, the Transform tool also offers a Warp mode that uses a mesh to manipulate pixels.

Warping with the Transform tool

As mentioned, the Transform tool allows you to warp any object, not just text. Choose Edit ➪ Transform ➪ Warp, or press Ctrl+T/⌘+T to activate the Free Transform tool and select the Warp icon, which is up toward the right side of the Options Bar. This button acts as a toggle so you can switch back and forth between Transform and Warp modes.

When in Warp mode, the first thing you'll notice is that a mesh is placed over the bounding box of the layer that you're currently working with. The pixels in your image are mapped to the points on this mesh so that when you move the mesh, the pixels follow it. It's the same principle that the Liquify tool works on. A Warp menu also appears in the Options Bar, offering the same presets that you'll find under the Text tool's Warp mode. These are the two ways you can apply a warp distortion to your image.

Creating a custom Warp

To warp an object in a freeform manner, click and drag on any of the mesh points (the places where the lines intersect) to distort the part of the image that falls under that location. The corner points also have handles that you can drag, giving you still more control over the distortion (see Figure 21.8). When you're happy with your modification, click the check mark icon in the Options Bar or press Enter/Return on your keyboard to accept the effect.

FIGURE 21.8

Using the mesh points, a custom warp was created to distort this image.

Using Warp presets

The alternative to creating a custom warp is to use the presets available in the Warp menu in the Options Bar (see Figure 21.9).

FIGURE 21.9

The Flag, Arc Lower, and Shell Upper presets were used to produce these images.

Select a preset to apply it to the current object. You can adjust the settings for each preset using the controls provided in the Options Bar, changing the orientation, Bend, and Horizontal and Vertical distortion of the warp. You can also adjust the effect interactively by clicking and dragging the control point that appears on the mesh.

You can use any of the warp presets as a starting point for your own custom distortion. Choose a preset, then select Custom from the Warp menu. Click and drag the mesh control points to modify the distortion.

NOTE The control point disappears if you change the horizontal or vertical distortion value.

Remember that you can switch back and forth between the Transform and Warp modes to apply multiple changes to your image. Be aware, though, that once you commit to the transformation, the warp settings are lost.

CAUTION Repeatedly warping — or applying any transformation, for that matter — gradually reduces the sharpness of the image, so try to make all your warping and transforming edits in one session with the tool, rather than warping and transforming in separate sessions.

Warping multiple layers

One of the features that the Warp tool lacks is the ability to warp the contents of several layers simultaneously (go ahead and try it, I'll wait . . . See? Told you). The solution to this dilemma, as is so often the case, is to use a Smart Object. Select the layers to be warped, right-click (Ctrl-click if you have a single-button mouse on a Mac) on the layers, and select Create Smart Object, then activate the Warp tool as described in the previous section.

There are a couple of things to take note of when warping with Smart Objects:

- Resizing or warping beyond the original size of the contents of the Smart Object results in blurring, since Photoshop has to interpolate the information necessary to display it at a larger size.

- You can always go back into the Smart Object and edit the individual layers within. When you save your edits (as long as you don't save the file in a different location), the Smart Object is updated to reflect them in the original document.

- Unlike single layers, Smart Objects do retain the warp settings, so if you decide that you want a do-over, simply activate the Warp tool and have at it.

Warping with Filters

To round off the coverage of warping objects in Photoshop, here's an overview of some of the available filters that fall within the warping category.

Lens Correction

Depending on the lens used to shoot a picture, any number of defects such as barrel distortion (see Figure 21.10), vignetting, or chromatic aberration can show up in a photograph. That's where the Lens Correction filter comes in. Lens Correction is another filter that feels more like an application than a plug-in, given its robust set of options. To launch it, choose Filter ⇨ Distort ⇨ Lens Distortion.

NOTE The Lens Correction filter is only available for 8- and 16-bit images.

FIGURE 21.10

The Lens Correction filter helps to remove lens distortions from photographs.

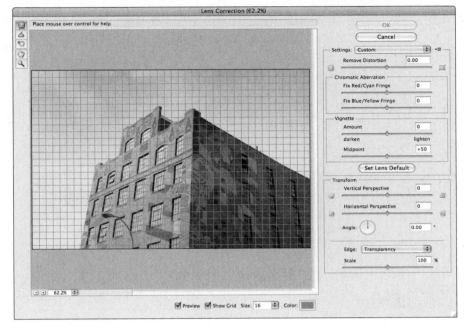

Below is a description of the controls found in the Lens Correction filter's dialog box:

- **Settings.** Select a preset for correcting lens distortion from this menu. The Lens Default option is only available if you click the Set Lens Defaults button to save information specific to a particular camera, lens, f-stop, and focal length combination (more on this in a moment).

  You can also use the settings from a previous conversion, or you can save any number of other custom presets.

- **Remove Distortion.** Use this slider to correct barrel and pincushion distortion in your photograph. An image is said to have barrel distortion if lines that should be vertical are curved outward at the middle. Pincushion distortion is the opposite effect — vertical lines appear to cave in (see Figure 21.11). Drag the slider to the left to fix pincushion distortion and to the right to fix barrel distortion.

- **Chromatic Aberration.** The sliders in this section can be used to remove a defect that can occur with inexpensive lenses, where edges in a photograph are fringed with color. This is a result of variations in the way the lens focuses on different colors of light.

FIGURE 21.11

Compare the example of pincushion distortion on the left with barrel distortion on the right.

■ **Vignette.** Some lenses produce darkened colors in the outer areas of the image, particularly in the corners (see Figure 21.12).

FIGURE 21.12

The figure on the left has no vignetting, while the figure on the right has some added.

In some cases, though, vignetting is actually desirable and fits the aesthetic of a photograph, so you can either remove or apply vignetting with the Lens Correction filter. Moving the Amount slider either adds or removes darkness in the outer areas of the photograph, while the Midpoint slider controls how far from the center of the photograph the vignetting starts.

- **Set Lens Default.** Once you've made adjustments to compensate for distortion, chromatic aberration, and vignetting, you can save these settings as a lens default. Next time you open an image that has the same camera, lens, focal distance, and f-stop information, the Lens Default option becomes available in the Settings menu. Note that the Set Lens Default option isn't available if your image doesn't have all the necessary EXIF data embedded in it.

- **Vertical and Horizontal Perspective.** Use these sliders to compensate for perspective distortions by making vertical or horizontal lines parallel to each other. As demonstrated in Figure 21.13, tilting the camera up to take a photograph of a tall building from the ground can result in the sides of the building appearing as though they are leaning in toward each other, giving the impression that the building is falling away from you. You can use the Vertical Perspective slider to correct this, bringing the building back upright.

FIGURE 21.13

In the original image, the building looks as though it's about to tip over. Using the Vertical Perspective slider helps to bring the building into correct perspective.

- **Angle.** The Angle control allows you to rotate the image to compensate for a camera that wasn't held perfectly straight when the photograph was taken. You can also use the Straighten tool to make the same adjustment — simply click and drag along the horizon or a line that should be horizontal to straighten out your image.

- **Edge and Scale.** Making changes to the pincushion, perspective, or angle settings in your image results in transparent edges, and the two remaining controls allow you to specify how those transparent edges are dealt with. You can fill the areas with a transparency, the current background color, or stretch the edge pixels (which works only if the edges of the image are a solid color).

  The other option is to scale the corrected image up to hide the transparent edges using the Scale slider. This option is the equivalent of using the Crop tool to crop out the transparent parts, then scaling the corrected image up to fill in the original image dimensions. Be aware that this method interpolates the image, which can result in some loss of sharpness.

Other distortions

To round off coverage of the wacky world of warping (say that five times fast), here's a quick look at some of the other options you'll find in the Filters menu:

- **Glass.** Use this filter to make an image look as though it was shot through a window (see Figure 21.14). Four types of glass textures are available under the Texture popup menu by default, but you can also load your own Photoshop files as textures. Use the filter's Distortion, Smoothness, and Scaling sliders to adjust the amount of distortion that is applied and the size of the texture.

FIGURE 21.14

The Blocks, Canvas, Frosted, and Tiny Lens textures were used to distort this photograph of a truckload of mangoes. In each case, the distortion was set to 5, the smoothness was set to 3, and scaling was at 100 percent.

- **Pinch.** The Pinch filter either squeezes pixels inward or pushes them outward based on a temporary mesh (similar to the Liquify filter's Pucker and Bloat tools) as shown in Figure 21.15. The filter offers a single slider with a maximum of 100 percent in either a positive or negative direction; a positive number sucks pixels in, and a negative amount has the opposite effect.

- **Spherize.** The Spherize tool creates an almost three-dimensional effect, stretching and distorting pixels by wrapping them around a sphere (see Figure 21.16). As with the Pinch filter, you can use the slider to set an amount ranging from −100 to 100 percent. The Spherize filter also offers a Mode menu, which controls whether the distortion occurs on both axes (the default setting), or along either a horizontal or vertical axis.

- **Polar Coordinates.** The Polar Coordinates filter converts a selected image from rectangular to polar coordinates, or vice versa. What does this mean to you? Well, for one, you can use it to create your own version of the popular eighteenth-century artform *cylinder anamorphosis*, which is a technique in which a circular grid is used to create a distorted image that looks normal when viewed in a cylindrical mirror.

FIGURE 21.15

The effects of the Pinch filter

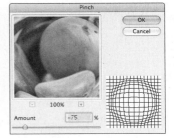

FIGURE 21.16

The effects of the Spherize filter at settings of 75 and –75 percent

Too esoteric for you? Another fun technique is to create little planets using a 360-degree panoramic image (see Figure 21.17). Here's how:

FIGURE 21.17

I used a series of four photos I shot in my local park to generate the panorama shown here. I then made the image square, flipped it 180 degrees, and ran the Polar Coordinates filter on it. Because my starting image wasn't a full 360-degree panorama, I had to do some cloning and healing to smooth out the seams.

1. **Shoot a panoramic scene.** For best results, it should really be a 360-degree panorama, but you can get away with less — at the very least, it should be at least twice as wide as it is tall, and the left and right sides of the image should match somewhat. Also, you'll make things easier on yourself if you photograph a scene where the lower part of the image is more or less a continuous texture, like water or grass, and the sky is also a continuous tone, like an overexposed white or a solid blue. Either way, use a tripod to align the images properly.

2. **Merge the images using Photomerge.** Once your images are imported from your camera, you can easily stitch them together by choosing File ➪ Automate ➪ Photomerge (for more, see Chapter 26).

3. **Make the image into a perfect square.** Choose Image ➪ Image Size and deselect the Constrain Proportions option, then make the height the same as the width of the image (it's better to scale up the height than the other way around).

4. **Rotate the image 180 degrees.** Choose Edit ➪ Transform ➪ Rotate 180° to flip the image around.

5. **Apply the Polar Coordinates filter.** Choose Filter ➪ Distort ➪ Polar Coordinates and make sure the Rectangular to Polar button is checked. There you have it. You can take it a step further by using the Healing Brush or Cloning Stamp tool to smooth out any seams.

■ **Shear.** Use the Shear filter to define a curve along which to distort an image or selection. Figure 21.18 shows the dialog box for the Shear filter. Dragging the control points at either end of the curve shown in the grid controls the distortion of the image. Clicking anywhere along the curve defines additional control points, allowing you to create complex distortion curves.

FIGURE 21.18

The Shear filter's dialog box, showing the default state on the left, followed by two manipulations of the distortion curve

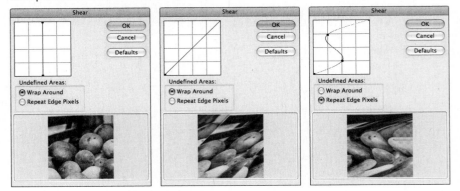

The preview area at the bottom of the dialog box updates continuously to reflect your changes. Choose one of the two radio buttons to decide what to do with the seams of the image — either repeat the edge pixels, or wrap them around from one side to the other.

- **Twirl.** This filter spins the pixels of an image or selection about a central point (see Figure 21.19). The single slider available covers a range of angles from –999 to 999 degrees, allowing you to control how many full rotations the pixels make around the center. The distortion is greatest at the center point, gradually tapering off as the distance from the center increases.

FIGURE 21.19

The Twirl filter set at 50 (the default), 300, and 600 degrees

> **TIP**   The Twirl filter (and many of the others covered in this chapter) begins its distortions from the center of your document if there isn't an active selection. If you find that your twirl effect is not originating where you expect — that is, from the center of a layer — try first selecting the pixels on your layer by Ctrl-clicking/⌘-clicking on the layer thumbnail, then running the filter.

Waves

So far in this chapter, you've seen tools that liquify and warp, and even tools to manipulate objects in perspective. Now it's time to start making some waves (pun intended).

Ocean Ripple vs. Ripple

The difference between these two filters seems subtle at first glance, but each serves a distinct purpose. The Ocean Ripple filter is designed to apply a random distortion to the image to make it seem as though it is underwater, while the Ripple filter creates an effect similar to movement of water across the surface of a pond (see Figure 21.20).

FIGURE 21.20

The Ocean Ripple and (plain old) Ripple filters applied with various settings

The Ocean Ripple filter launches you into the Filter Gallery, where the available settings include Ripple Size, which doesn't make a whole lot of discernible difference no matter what number you set it to, and Ripple Magnitude, which is where all the action is as far as this filter is concerned. For best results, set the Ripple Magnitude fairly low or the effect begins to look suspiciously like the Frosted setting of the Glass filter.

The Ripple filter's dialog box is of the more standard variety, and its two controls adjust the amount of distortion and the size of the ripples (Small, Medium, or Large). In this case, to get effects that more closely resemble water, stick with either Medium or Large ripples, since the ones generated by the Small setting more closely resemble a cross-hatching effect, and if that was what you wanted, you'd probably just use the Filter Gallery's Cross Hatch filter.

ZigZag

The ZigZag filter applies its distortions in a radial fashion from the center of the image. To apply the ZigZag filter, choose Filter ➪ Distort ➪ ZigZag. The effect, which produces a series of concentric ripples emanating from a central point (see Figure 21.21), varies depending on the setting used:

FIGURE 21.21

Various settings of the ZigZag filter were used to produce these distortions.

- **Amount.** Adjust this slider to control the intensity of the distortion. You can enter a value between −99 and 100 to produce ripples that either protrude upward or sink downward below the surface being distorted.
- **Ridges.** This slider controls the number of times the distortion is repeated, from 1 to 20.
- **Style.** Choose from the options in this menu to specify how the pixels are displaced — twisted in a true zigzag pattern around the center (Around Center), radiating outward from the center (Out from Center), or a combination of the two (Pond Ripples).

Wave

One of the more complex of the distortion tools, the Wave filter takes you from the idyllic rippling of ponds and places you at the mercy of the open sea. Choose Filter ➪ Distort ➪ Wave to reveal the dialog box shown in Figure 21.22.

FIGURE 21.22

The Wave filter's dialog box offers a great deal of control for generating wave distortions.

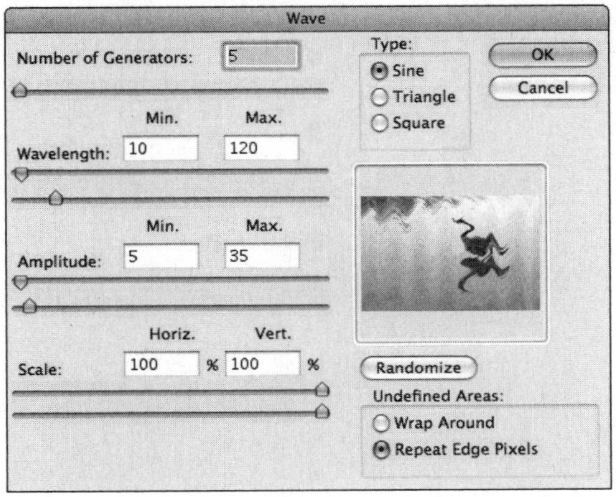

The Wave Dialog box features the following controls:

- **Number of Generators.** This option adds more sources of distortion to the image. The more sources, the more complex and extreme the distortion (see Figure 21.23).

- **Wavelength/Amplitude.** Set the distance between the tops of each wave (Wavelength) and the height of the waves (Amplitude) with these sliders. The pair of sliders allows you to enter maximum and minimum values, adding randomness to the effect (see Figure 21.24).

- **Scale.** Control the Horizontal and Vertical scaling of the waves with this pair of sliders.

- **Type.** Choose from three types of waves in this section. Sine produces standard, rolling waves, Triangle produces waves that appear in a triangular zigzag pattern, and Square produces a pattern based on rectangular shapes (see Figure 21.25).

- **Randomize.** If you don't like the effects you've come up with, or you'd simply like to leave things to chance, click this button (or the preview thumbnail) repeatedly to keep generating random combinations of settings until you see one that you like.

- **Undefined Areas.** Decide what to do with any areas of transparency created by the Wave filter's distortions. Either repeat edge pixels or wrap parts of the image around from one side to the next.

FIGURE 21.23

The effect of different numbers of generators, set at 1, 2, 5, and 25, is shown in these images. All other settings remained constant.

FIGURE 21.24

The effects of different Wavelength (distance) and Amplitude (height) values are shown in these images. The number of generators remained at 1.

FIGURE 21.25

The Sine, Triangle, and Square wave types were used to produce these distortions.

Bump Maps

In the world of 3D animation, *bump* or *displacement maps* refer to grayscale images that tell the software how to render a smooth surface so that it appears to have a three-dimensional texture. This is an efficient way to produce bumpy surfaces such as brick walls, gravel, and tree bark without having to physically create each bump and crevice on a surface.

In the world of Photoshop, we achieve similar sleight-of-hand (or sleight-of-mouse, if you prefer) using displacement maps with the Displace filter.

When working with displacement maps (also called *dmaps*), the color value of the dmap — a value from 0–255 — determines the direction of the movement of displaced pixels. If we were to start at 50 percent neutral gray (a value of 128) and increase the brightness of the color in the dmap, pixels would shift farther up or to the left. Going in the other direction — that is, darkening the values of the dmap — pixels would shift down or to the right. And what about a value of 128? Those pixels would stay exactly where they are.

Photoshop only recognizes displacements maps saved as flattened native PSD files. They can be created from single-channel grayscale files, in which case the direction of the displacement is both up and to the left, or down and to the right. Complicating things somewhat, displacement maps can also be generated as RGB files, in which case the grayscale contents of the first channel — the red one — control the horizontal movement, and the green channel controls the vertical movement of displaced pixels.

Launch the Displace filter by choosing Filter ➪ Distort ➪ Displace. The dialog box is deceptively simple, as illustrated in Figure 21.26.

FIGURE 21.26

The Displace filter's dialog box offers relatively few options for a fairly complex effect.

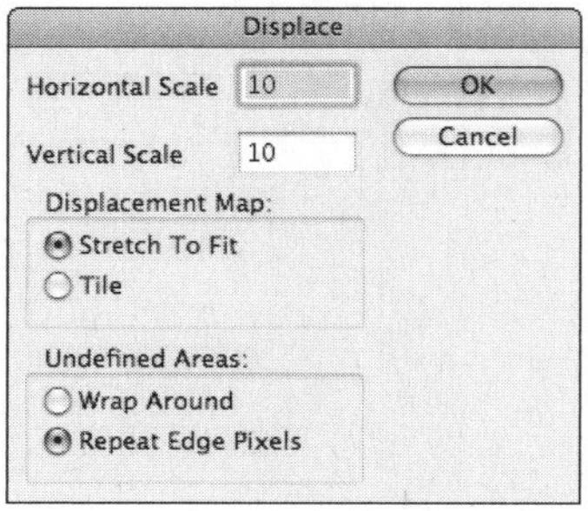

- **Horizontal and Vertical Scale.** These two values control how far pixels move when the Displace filter is applied. The values you can enter range from –999 to 999.

- **Displacement Map.** If the displacement map is smaller than the size of the image or selection being displaced, you have a few options you can choose from before proceeding. You can stretch the displacement map to fit the size of the area being distorted, or you can tile or repeat the displacement map until it completely covers the size of the area being displaced.

- **Undefined Areas.** As is the case with many of the filters that move and distort pixels, the Displace filter can create seams or transparent areas if it moves pixels away from the edges of the selection. The options in the Undefined Areas section specify how to treat those transparent areas — either wrapping pixels and repeating them from one side of the image to the next, or stretching the single row of pixels that lies at the edge of the selection to fill any transparent areas.

Clicking OK brings up a dialog box that prompts you to locate the dmap you want to use. Navigate to the location of your displacement map on your hard drive and press Open. Photoshop ships with a fairly large collection of pre-made displacement maps, which are saved in the program's Plug-ins/ Displacement Maps folder. If you take a look at the channels of these supplied displacement maps, you'll see that the red and green channels have information, but the blue channel is filled with white, because it's ignored by the Displace filter. Some of the files have a recommended scaling value, in which case you'll see it listed in parentheses after the filename.

Again, this is one of those filters that requires an example to really drive home how it works. To illustrate this, I'll show you how to make a waving flag using a simple displacement map.

1. **Create a new document.** I chose a resolution of 1024 x 768 because I'll probably want to put this on the Web at some point.

2. **Create a flag shape.** Press Shift+U on your keyboard until the Rectangle tool is active, and draw a rectangle to form the base for your flag. You can decorate your flag however you like; I decided that my flag would be the banner of the proud land of Photoshop. You can see my simple flag in Figure 21.27.

FIGURE 21.27

Here's the beginning stage of my flag, which represents the imaginary land of Photoshop.

3. **Create a Smart Object containing all your flag's elements.** To make it easy to distort all the flag elements at the same time, select all the necessary layers and choose Convert to Smart Object from the Layers panel menu.

4. **Create a distortion map.** Create a new document using the same dimensions as your flag document, but choose Grayscale under the Color Mode popup menu. Activate the Gradient tool (press Shift+G on the keyboard until it's selected), and from the gradient thumbnails in the Options Bar choose a stripe-y preset. It doesn't matter what color it is because you'll be using it in a grayscale document. Dragging from the upper-left to the lower-right side of the screen, create a gradient that fills the canvas, and that looks like the ripples in a flag (see Figure 21.28).

FIGURE 21.28

Using the Gradient tool, I filled my canvas with a gradient to create a displacement map for my flag.

Remember that values near middle gray will not receive any distortion, so adjust the contrast of your gradient with the Levels command or by dodging and burning. If you're feeling particularly inspired, you could also try using the Warp tool to add some irregularity to your displacement map. Save the file in Photoshop's native format in a location you'll remember.

5. **Displace the flag.** Switch back to your flag, and choose Filter ➪ Distort ➪ Displace. The defaults should work for this example (refer to Figure 21.26). Click OK, select the displacement map you saved in the previous step, and press Open. Your flag should start to look a little wavy around the edges, but if, like me, you used a flat color for your flag's background, you won't be able to see the distortion within the body of the flag (see Figure 21.29). Don't worry — you'll fix that in the next step.

6. **Add some shadows and highlights to the flag.** Go back to your displacement map (reopen the file, if necessary) and press Ctrl+A/⌘+All followed by Ctrl+C/⌘+C to copy the gradient. Back in the flag document, press Ctrl+V/⌘+V to paste the gradient as a new layer directly above your flag's layer. Right-click on the gradient's layer in the Layers panel, and select Create Clipping Mask to use the flag layer as a mask for the gradient layer (for a refresher on Clipping Masks, see Chapter 8). Switch the gradient layer's blending mode to Overlay. At this point your flag should look something like the example in Figure 21.30. It's looking good, but still needs a couple of finishing touches.

FIGURE 21.29

The flag is beginning to wave, thanks to the Displace filter, but it needs some shadows and highlights.

FIGURE 21.30

With freshly added shadows and highlights, the flag is looking pretty good.

7. **Give the flag a drop shadow.** To lift the flag off of its background, create a Drop Shadow layer style. I gave mine a fairly large distance of 33 and set the size to 50. Reduce the opacity of the shadow to make it less intense.

8. **Add a little texture.** For a touch more realism, the flag needs some texture. Choose Filter ➪ Texture ➪ Texturizer and adjust the settings until your texture looks good. I used a canvas texture with a scaling setting of 50 percent, and relief set to 1. Press OK to apply the filter and admire your work (see Figure 21.31). Remember, it's a Smart Filter, so you can always go back and tweak it later if necessary.

FIGURE 21.31

The Texturizer filter was used to add a subtle canvas texture to the flag.

You should now have a pretty nice-looking flag, but as usual, I leave it to you to continue pushing the effect further. For instance, if your flag has any areas of pure white, like mine does, you'll notice that the gradient overlay has no effect on those areas. You might want to go into the Smart Object and darken up the brightness of the white parts of the flag just slightly, so they're not pure white. I used a Gradient Overlay layer style to add some shadows to mine.

I also added a lighting effect by choosing Filter ➪ Render ➪ Lighting Effects and making a spotlight to add a little life to my flag. The final image is shown in Figure 21.32.

CROSS-REF Baffled by the Lighting Effects filter's dialog box? Check out Chapter 20.

FIGURE 21.32

The final flag effect. The denizens of Photoshop land should be proud!

Summary

This chapter continued the coverage of Photoshop's filters, focusing on the filters that are used to distort pixels. You saw how the Liquify tool works, and how it can be used either for humorous effects or for subtle retouching work. You learned about the Vanishing Point tool, and how to use it to modify images while retaining correct perspective. You also learned about warping objects with the Transform tool and with various filters. The Lens Correction filter was also covered, as were various ripple and wave filters. Finally, you learned how to use the Displace filter to add depth to images.

Chapter 22

Text Effects

As you'll remember, the ins and outs of creating type in Photoshop were covered back in Chapter 13. In this chapter, you'll take what you already know about type a step further by learning to combine layer styles with type layers to create some eye-catching effects. The beauty of these techniques is that in most cases, as long as you save your files in a format that supports layers, such as PSD or TIFF, these effects will remain editable so you can always go back and make changes whenever necessary.

The focus of this chapter is on creating text effects, but you can definitely take the concepts you learn here and apply them to any kind of layer content.

Wood burn effect

This example demonstrates how a few creatively placed layer styles can be used to create the look of type burned into wood — sort of like something you'd find on a ranch, or in a frontier town in the Old West. As a bonus, you'll also learn a quick way to create your own wood texture in Photoshop, which you'll use as a base to burn the text into.

1. **Create a new document.** Choose File ⇨ New and enter your document's dimensions, or use one of the provided document presets and click OK. I chose 1024 x 768 from the Web presets for this example.

2. **Create a new blank layer and fill it with a yellowish-brown color.** To create a new layer, click the New Layer icon at the bottom of the Layers panel. This layer will form the base color

of your wood texture. Choose a color that suits the type of wood you prefer — maybe a pale birch, or a more orange-ish beech — it's up to you.

I'm a firm believer in keeping the layers in my Photoshop documents well organized by naming them descriptively, and grouping them into folders as necessary. With that in mind, rename your base layer by double-clicking the layer's name, and changing it to wood base.

3. **Start creating the wood grain by adding some noise.** With your wood base layer selected, choose Filter ➪ Noise ➪ Add Noise. The Noise filter adds random pixels to your image, and is a common starting point when creating textures from scratch. Set the Amount to somewhere around five pixels, then select Gaussian as the distribution method. Finally, to ensure that the noise isn't multicolored, make sure the Monochromatic check-box is checked. Figure 22.1 shows the Noise filter in action.

NOTE   If you selected a high resolution (like 150 or 300 ppi) when you created your document, you might need to use higher values for the Noise setting than those I've suggested here. Experiment!

FIGURE 22.1

The Noise filter is used to create the beginnings of a wood grain texture

4. **Use the Motion Blur filter to make the grain texture.** Choose Filter ➪ Blur ➪ Motion Blur to display the filter's dialog box. To create grain that flows from left to right, enter an angle of 0 degrees, and set the distance to around 30 pixels. Click OK to apply the filter. Now you should have a nice background grain texture.

5. **Create some grain rings for your wood background.** Create another blank layer, and rename it to grain rings. Press B to select the Brush tool. Right-click/Ctrl+click anywhere on the canvas to show the Brush tool's contextual menu and set the Master Diameter to about 7 pixels. Set the Hardness to 100 percent and press Enter/Return, or click anywhere on the canvas to dismiss the Contextual menu. Set your foreground color to a dark-ish brown and draw some horizontal lines going across your canvas. To keep the brush strokes you're drawing perfectly straight, hold the Shift key while you draw. Try to vary the length of the lines, and the amount of space between them, as illustrated in Figure 22.2. For even more variation in the grain, you can reduce the brush diameter and add some additional lines.

FIGURE 22.2

The horizontal lines going across the will become the dark rings in the wood grain.

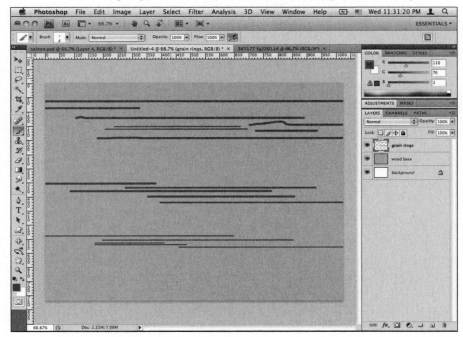

6. **Use the Liquify tool to add some distortion to the wood grain rings.** Choose Filter ➪ Liquify (or press Ctrl+Shift+X/⌘+Shift+X) to open the Liquify tool's dialog box. Select the Twirl Clockwise Tool (press C on the keyboard) and set the brush size to around 150. Begin painting over the lines to shape them into the wood grain rings (see Figure 22.3). You can also switch to the Forward Warp tool (the first icon in the Toolbar on the left) and push the lines into shape. If the distortions are getting a little out of hand, select the Reconstruct tool (just below the Forward Warp tool) and set the Reconstruct Mode to Revert to erase the distortion.

   Once you're happy with the your wood grain rings, click OK. To make the grain a bit more subtle, set the Opacity of the grain rings layer to about 12 percent.

7. **Add text and begin styling it so it looks burned into the wood.** Press T on your keyboard to activate the Text tool, and then choose a good western font from the Font menu in the Options Bar (an Internet search for "free western font" should produce ample results if you don't have anything suitable installed on your system). Click on your canvas and enter some text as shown in Figure 22.4. If necessary, change the text color clicking on the color swatch in the Options Bar and choosing a brown color from the resulting color picker.

FIGURE 22.3

Using the Liquify tool to shape the wood grain rings

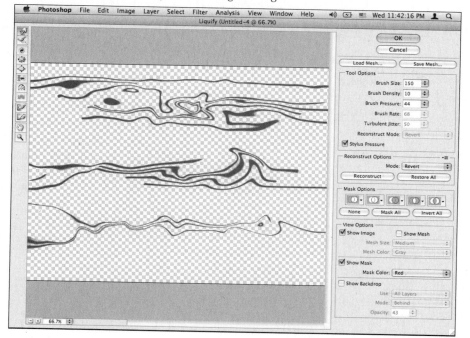

FIGURE 22.4

The text (set in Rockwell Extra Bold) overlaid on top of the wood grain texture

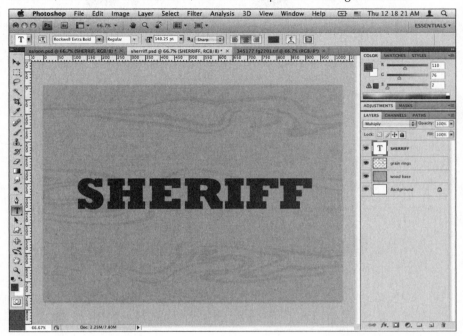

You can quickly resize and position the text with the Free Transform tool. Press Ctrl+T/ ⌘+T to launch the Free Transform tool, then Drag the corners of the bounding box while holding the Shift key to maintain the proportions of your text. Once the text size looks good, press Enter on your keyboard to accept the transformation.

Since the text is being burned into the wood, you want some of the wood grain to be visible through the text. To do this, set the text layer's blending mode to Multiply, and change the layer's Fill to about 95 percent. Setting the Fill reduces the opacity of the text without affecting the opacity of layer styles that have been applied — which is what you'll do in the next step.

8. **Continue styling the text layer with layer styles.** Double-click in the space next to the text layer's name to launch the Layer Style dialog box. Select Inner Shadow from the list on the left (the default settings should work just fine) to give the text some depth. Next, to add a scorched effect around the letters, click on the Outer Glow tool. Click on the color swatch and set the color to Black, then set the Blend Mode of the glow to Multiply. Reduce the size of the glow to about 3 pixels.

The text should be looking good by this point, but to finish, add some more shading to the inner part of the text by selecting Inner Glow from the list of layer styles on the left. Drag the Opacity slicer to about 18 percent, and set the size of the glow to about 18 pixels. Click OK to close the Layer Style dialog box.

From here on, you can add as many adornments as you like to continue building this into a Western-themed design. (Maybe a Wanted poster? How about some bullet holes?) I found a star shape I liked in the Custom Shape Picker (press Shift+U to cycle through the Shape Layer tools until you get to the blobby shape that represents the Custom Shape tool). Load additional Custom Shape Presets by clicking on the tiny triangle icon at the right of the Custom Shape Picker, and choosing from the presets listed at the bottom of the menu.

To copy the layer styles from one layer to another, click on the layer you want to copy from, then select Layer ⇨ Layer Style ⇨ Copy Layer Style. Next, highlight the layer you want to apply the style to, and choose Layer ⇨ Layer Style ⇨ Paste Style. Don't forget to set the blending mode of the star to Multiply, and reduce its Fill to match the text layer. Figure 22.5 shows the final shows my final illustration.

FIGURE 22.5

The final styled text

Bevel and Emboss

The Bevel and Emboss layer style is an incredibly versatile effect. At its most basic, you can use it to add dimension to text, making it look like the text is carved out of stone or forged from some type of metal. With a little creative manipulation of the effect's settings, you can go beyond that to create some unexpected looks, including glass or shiny plastic.

Choose Layer ⇨ Layer Style ⇨ Bevel and Emboss. You'll find two types of bevel and three emboss styles available under the Styles menu. Depending on the options you select in the Structure section of the Layer Style settings window, you can create the look of text that was chiseled from stone, or stamped into a sheet of metal, like a license plate.

This is all achieved by applying a shadow and highlight in various ways, which you can manipulate in the Shading section of the settings window. Figure 22.6 shows the different basic types of bevel and emboss effects that are found in the Styles menu.

FIGURE 22.6

The Bevel and Emboss layer style offers the five styles shown here. Note that for the Pillow Emboss and Stroke Emboss examples, the Layer Fill was set to 0, so that the background gradient shows through the type. The Stroke Emboss example requires a Stroke effect to be applied to the layer.

Offering some additional control over the way the different styles appear are the three options in the Technique menu. Smooth creates a smooth transition between the shading and the base color of the text or background. Somewhat counter-intuitively, Chisel Hard and Chisel Soft both produce sharper angles and transitions, the difference being that Chisel Hard works best on shapes with crisp edges, like text or Shape Layers, while Chisel Soft can be used with a variety of shapes. Chisel Hard and Chisel soft both preserve detail along the edges of shapes that are beveled using this technique.

It's not too difficult to take the metallic type example from Chapter 13 and use a Bevel and Emboss effect to change the look of the type from delicate silver text to heavy stainless-steel text, as illustrated in Figure 22.7.

The first step in creating this effect was changing the typeface to something with a little more authority — in this case, Aachen Bold. Making sure that Bevel and Emboss was enabled under the Styles menu, I chose Inner Bevel from the Styles menu and set the Technique to Chisel Hard. I set the Depth to 500 to give the bevel a nice steep angle, and set the Size to 5.

FIGURE 22.7

Starting with the silver text created in the previous example, a Bevel and Emboss layer style is added to create the heavy steel text.

The most important element in this example, however, is the Gloss Contour setting (see Figure 22.8). Changing the Gloss Contour allows you to sculpt the shape of the shadows created by the effect; in this case I used the Cone contour preset to create the high-contrast look that really drives the effect home.

FIGURE 22.8

The Gloss Contour settings of the Bevel and Emboss layer style

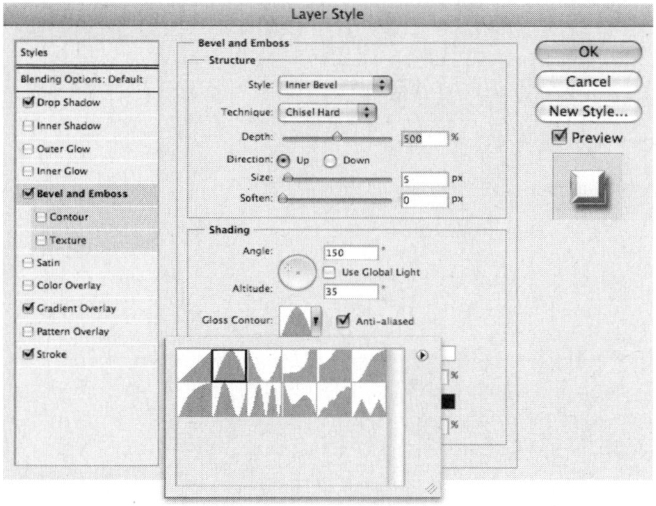

> **TIP** None of the Gloss Contour presets doing it for you? You can create your own by clicking on the contour's preview and manipulating the curve in the resulting Contour Editor window by dragging or adding points.

Figure 22.9 shows another example of the use of the Bevel and Emboss layer style. In this case, the base of the license plate was created with the Rounded Rectangle tool. The base is made up of two rectangles, the smaller of which was given some depth with an outer bevel layer style.

A subtle Gradient Overlay layer style added some texture to the two base shapes as well. A quick Internet search yielded a free license plate typeface, and that was also given an outer bevel treatment. For a finishing touch, four white circles with an Inner Shadow layer style were used to make the holes in the license plate.

FIGURE 22.9

Making a license plate is quite easy, using nothing more than a few Bevel and Emboss effects.

Flaming Type

Fire is one of the trickiest things to create convincingly in Photoshop from scratch, but following these steps should produce some reasonable flaming text. As you'll see, this example is one of the few cases where you'll need to directly manipulate the pixels of a rasterized type layer, which means sacrificing some editability.

1. **Create a new document.** Out of habit, I set mine at 1024 x 768 pixels, and 72 pixels per inch, which is a handy size for images destined for the Internet. . Fill the background layer with black by pressing Shift+Backspace/Shift+Delete on your keyboard and choosing Black from the Use pop-up menu.

2. **Add some text.** Select the Type tool from the Toolbox, or press the T key on your keyboard. Select a typeface that you think looks good from the Options Bar (I chose one that was pre-installed on my Mac, called Herculanum), and make sure the type color is set to white. Click on your canvas and enter some text — in this example I used the word "fire."

   Duplicate the type layer by pressing Ctrl+J/⌘+J), and turn off visibility of the duplicate you just made by clicking on the eyeball icon at the left of the layer's thumbnail. By this point, your document should look like the illustration in Figure 22.10.

FIGURE 22.10

A simple radial gradient was used to produce the background for the fire effect.

3. **Start making some flames.** Click on the first of your two text layers in the Layers panel. You'll use this layer to make a base for the flame effect. You'll need to manipulate the actual pixels of the text to get them to look like flames, in which case the type layer has to be rasterized. Right-click/Ctrl+click on the bottom copy of the type layer in the Layers panel, and choose Rasterize Type.

    Select the Smudge tool from the Toolbox and set the strength to 30. With a soft-edged brush, begin painting in short upward strokes, gradually pulling the pixels of the text so that it starts to look like flames (see Figure 22.11).

4. **Using a layer style, add some dimension to the flames.** Double-click on the flames layer's thumbnail to open the Layer Style window and select Gradient Overlay from the list of styles on the left. Click on the gradient swatch and create a gradient from orange to yellow.

    Click OK to return to the Gradient Overlay settings, and then click on Satin in the Styles list. The Satin layer style is designed to add shading and highlights to the layer, creating the appearance of shiny fabric. In this example, it's used to add some shadows and dimension to the flames.

FIGURE 22.11

The rasterized type layer has been manipulated with the Smudge tool to produce the beginnings of some flames.

Click in the color swatch to change the color from the default black to a dark orange. Experiment with the contour to change the way the shadows interact with the flames. Click on the tiny arrow at the right of the contour thumbnail to reveal the contour presets. The Gaussian preset (hover over each preset's thumbnail for a second or two to see it's name) was used to achieve the result shown in Figure 22.12.

5. **Begin styling the main text layer.** Now you'll add some effects to the editable type layer to finish the effect. Turn the visibility of the upper type layer back on and select Gradient Overlay from the Layer Styles icon at the bottom of the Layers panel.

   As in the previous step, create a gradient that goes from black to dark orange to yellow to color the text. To give the text a nice hot glow around the contours, add a Stroke and change the color to a bright yellow, and set the blending mode of the stroke to Screen.

   As a final touch, click on Outer Glow under the list of styles and set the color to a dark orange-red. Increase the size of the glow to about 10–15 to achieve the result shown in Figure 22.13.

FIGURE 22.12

A combination of a Gradient Overlay and the Satin layer style was used to add some dimension and color to the flames.

FIGURE 22.13

A Gradient Overlay, Stroke, and Outer Glow have been added to produce this effect.

As usual, the effect doesn't have to stop here. By all means, experiment with adding additional styles to the text to give it more depth and realism. To change the text to say something other than "fire," edit the type layer, then duplicate it and follow the previous steps to recreate the flame texture.

 **Save any of the layer styles you've created as presets by clicking the Create New Style icon at the bottom of the Styles palette. Enter a name and click OK.**

Glows

Inner and Outer Glow are two basic styles that can be used to punch up your text. As their names would suggest, they produce a glowing effect either within each character on a type layer, or expanding outside of the type. Used in conjunction with other layer styles, these two simple styles can be used to produce some very slick typographic effects. Figure 22.14 shows the basic effects of the Inner and Outer glow styles.

FIGURE 22.14

Outer and Inner Glow

Both Inner and Outer Glow allow you to control the color and blending mode of the effect using the options found within the Structure settings of the dialog box. Use the settings under the Elements section to determine the shape and size of the glow, and use the Contour settings to change the shapes of the glow effects.

Ready to create some glowing text of your own? Follow these steps to produce a great glassy text effect.

1. **Create a new document and add some text.** As usual, the dimensions are up to you, but I'm sticking with my 1024 x 768 canvas. Press T on your keyboard to activate the Type tool. Select a typeface and enter the text to which you will be applying the glassy effect (see Figure 22.15).

2. **Color the text with a Gradient Overlay layer style.** Click the Add Layer Style button at the bottom of the Layers panel and select Gradient Overlay. Set Reflected as the gradient style and edit the colors of the gradient to your liking. I chose a gradient that goes from dark to light green for this example (although you probably can't tell from this grayscale image) (see Figure 22.16).

FIGURE 22.15

Getting set up to apply the glassy text effect

FIGURE 22.16

Applying a gradient overlay to the text

3. **Begin adding dimension with an Inner Glow effect.** Click on Inner Glow from the list of styles on the left side of the dialog box, and under the Elements section, make sure Center is selected as the source of the glow. Change the color of the glow to a version of your gradient's base color. In Figure 22.17, I used a medium green. Increase the size of the glow to about 30.

FIGURE 22.17

An Inner Glow was added to begin building some dimension to the glass effect.

4. **Continue building texture using additional layer styles.** Add a nice reflective highlight with a Bevel and Emboss style (see Figure 22.18). Turn the opacity of the shadow all the way down to 0 and reduce the highlight opacity to 20. Increase the Depth and Size settings of the bevel to 700 and 80, respectively. Click the little arrow next to the Gloss Contour setting and select the Cove–Deep preset (again, hover over each preset for a few seconds to see the preset names). Finish the effect by adding a drop shadow to lift your text off the background.

Note that these values are subjective — use them as starting points, but definitely tweak them so they look good for your design.

FIGURE 22.18

A Bevel and Emboss style was used to create the crisp reflections on the text in this illustration.

As a bonus, to create the reflected wet floor look that's all the rage these days, duplicate your type layer and choose Edit ➪ Transform ➪ Flip Vertical. Use the Move tool (press V on your keyboard) to move the upside-down type layer so it's just touching the bottoms of the characters on your original layer.

Add a layer mask by clicking the Layer Mask icon at the bottom of the Layers panel, and fill the layer mask with a gradient going from white on the top to black on the bottom. Finally, reduce the opacity of this reflected layer to about 60. The result is shown in Figure 22.19.

FIGURE 22.19

The final glassy text effect is shown, complete with a reflection effect.

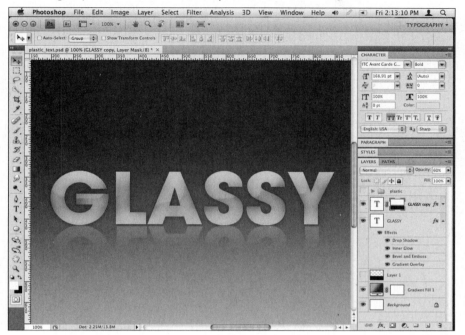

Textures

Using textures can make the difference between ho-hum text and a really eye-catching effect. You can apply textures with layer styles either by using the Pattern Overlay style or by using the Texture option of the Bevel and Emboss style to apply a texture to that effect.

To use the Pattern Overlay style, select it from the list of styles in the Blending Options window and choose a pattern preset from the triangle menu next to the swatch. As is the case with brushes, color swatches, gradients, and many other presets, Photoshop ships with several collections of pattern presets, which you can load by clicking on the tiny triangle menu in the Pattern preview window (see Figure 22.20). You can also create your own patterns by choosing Edit ➪ Define Pattern while any "marching ants" selection is active in a document.

Once you've selected a pattern, you can change its blending mode to modify the way it combines with the underlying text's color. You can also use the Scale slider directly below the pattern's thumbnail to change the size of the pattern, but keep in mind that if you increase the scale, after a certain point the pattern will begin to look blurry and pixelated. On the other hand, reducing the size too drastically can make the repeated pattern look too obvious.

FIGURE 22.20

Additional pattern libraries can be loaded via the fly-out menu in the Pattern Overlay settings window.

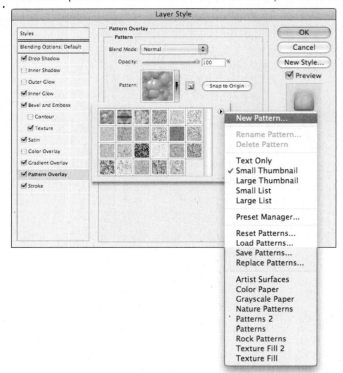

To create the effect shown in Figure 22.21, I filled a layer with white and applied a Pattern Overlay effect using Kraft Paper as my texture (found in the Color Paper library). I then created my text layer using a stencil typeface (AG Book, if you're curious), and applied an Inner Shadow and Pattern Overlay (White with Wood Fibers this time, also from the Color Paper library).

Clicking the Textures option under Bevel and Emboss uses the selected pattern as a basis for the effect, giving your text a three-dimensional textured appearance. In this case, a grayscale version of the pattern is used, so there aren't any color blending options; instead, you can adjust the depth of the texture using the Depth slider.

FIGURE 22.21

I used a Pattern Overlay effect in combination with an Inner Shadow to make it look as though this text was cut out of a paper bag, revealing a wood or particle-board surface below.

Check out Figure 22.22 for a quick example of adding a texture to the Bevel and Emboss effect. Here, I converted the text from the "Heavy Metal" example created earlier from smooth steel to a pitted, brushed metal simply by applying the Frosted Glass pattern (found in the Texture Fill pattern library) with a shallow depth to the bevel effect.

FIGURE 22.22

With a simple addition of a texture to the bevel effect, this text went from smooth to pitted, dimpled metal.

Summary

This chapter explored some of the ways to make creative, illustrative text effects with layer styles. You learned how to create a wood burn text effect with a few simple text style and a custom created background texture. You saw how the Bevel and Emboss layer style could be used to create dimensional type effects. You also learned about combining several layer styles on multiple layers to create flaming type. Further examples of text effects were created using the various glow layer styles. Finally, you learned how to load additional pattern presets for use with the Pattern Overlay layer style.

Part VII

Color Management and Workflow

Chapter 23

Color Management

C olor management is one of the most confusing aspects of designing on a computer. Color can be a fickle thing — and the devices that reproduce color can be even more fickle, with any number of variables from ambient light, to the condition of the connecting cables, to inconsistencies in the batch of inks in your printer all affecting the final appearance of the colors that are produced. The word "morass" comes to mind.

But there is a light at the end of the tunnel. A color-managed workflow can help to ensure consistency between what you see on your screen, and what gets output to your printer, or published on the Internet.

In this chapter, you'll learn to make sense of the somewhat bewildering elements of color management, from calibrating your devices, to embedding and converting color profiles in your documents, and previewing what they'll look like on different devices. So take a deep breath and dive in.

Color Accuracy and Consistency

Color is completely subjective, and looks different across devices. Different ambient lighting conditions also affect the perception of colors — daylight, tungsten, and fluorescent light all add shifts in color appearance. Type of paper (for example, newsprint versus magazine), age or type of monitor, and software interpretation of color values all affect differences in color appearance. Even variations between batches of paper or inks can affect color perception. Add to all this the fact that the human eye — flexible and adaptable thing that it is — can quickly adjust its perception of colors in an image so that you become accustomed to color shifts, and you'll realize that it can't be trusted.

So where does that leave us? Color management, that's where. The first step to a color-managed workflow is calibrating your monitor using either software or a hardware device. Follow that by adding color profiles that describe how color will appear on the various output devices you'll be using.

Next, you'll want to set up color management in your Adobe software (and other color-aware applications). You can preview the way images will be output by using the proofing options available in Photoshop and other Creative Suite applications. Finally, you'll want to ensure that you're saving your color management information along with your documents, and when printing or outputting images for the Web.

ICC color profiles

The path to consistent color starts with color profiles, which mathematically define the way a device interprets or "sees" numerical color values. Defined by the ICC (International Color Consortium), color profiles define the *gamut*, or range, of colors that devices are capable of reproducing.

Color profiles are used by Color Management Modules (CMMs) such as Apple's ColorSync or Microsoft's Windows Color System to match or convert a document's colors between its source profile (that is, the characteristics of the device it was created on) and the destination profile (the profile describing the output device the image is destined for).

Where do profiles come from? Well, as you'll learn shortly, in most cases hardware such as monitors and printers ship with their own generic profiles that are automatically installed along with their drivers (if you're on a Mac, then monitor profiles are built in to the operating system).

These profiles are usually good enough for most users, but for true color accuracy, you'll want to generate profiles that are specific to your own setup, taking into consideration such factors as ambient light and paper and ink combinations. Prepress facilities for high-end printing can also provide profiles so you can accurately preview what your final output will look like.

Embedding color profiles

Certain file types including PSD (the native Photoshop format), JPEG, TIFF, EPS, and PSB can support embedded color profiles, which ensure that images are displayed correctly when transferred between devices. When saving a color managed document, the option to embed the profile in the document becomes available in the File ⇨ Save As dialog box, as long as you select one of the compatible file formats.

The Save for Web & Devices dialog box (File ⇨ Save for Web & Devices) also offers a check box allowing you to embed the color profile in the final optimized file. Additionally, by default, images are automatically converted to the sRGB color profile when working with Save for Web & Devices, as this profile is the most commonly used for Web production (you'll read more about sRGB shortly).

In the case of images destined for the Web, only Apple's Safari (as of version 2.0) and Mozilla Firefox (as of version 3.0) actually support color-managed images. Keep in mind, though, that in Firefox, color management isn't enabled by default, so chances that the majority of users will be using it are slim.

Device-dependent versus device-independent

Now you know that profiles are used by CMMs to help convert color information so that it's displayed correctly from one device to another. The tricky part is that RGB and CMYK colors vary depending on different devices — that is, they're *device-dependent*, which makes for inaccurate translation between color spaces.

That's why the CIE (Commission Internationale d'Eclairage) stepped in and created a group of device-independent color models like CIE L*a*b and CIE XYZ, which are based on the way the human eye perceives color, and which are used as interim spaces when converting between device profiles.

Whew! Still awake? Good — because now that you've read all this theory, you'll learn how to actually put it into practice and take advantage of the color management features that the Adobe applications offer.

Calibrating Devices, Such as Monitors and Printers

As mentioned, the first step toward achieving color-management nirvana is calibrating your monitor. If you're using a Mac, you can do this using Apple's Display Calibrator Assistant (see Figure 23.1), which is located in the Displays pane of System Preferences. Windows users have access to Adobe Gamma, which is a utility that's installed along with the Creative Suite.

For more accurate calibration, vendors such as Gretag-Macbeth and ColorVision sell hardware called a *colorimeter* that you place on your monitor to measure the color values produced by your actual hardware. The profiles generated using these devices are far more accurate than the calibration software provided by your computer's operating system, because they take into consideration your device and all its display characteristics, as well as other conditions such as ambient light.

If you were really, really, *really* after the most accurate results possible, you'd paint your walls neutral gray, and wear neutral gray overalls while you work in a room with no daylight-balanced lights (or no lights at all) — but personally, I think that's going a bit far, unless you're in a high-end facility doing work that's absolutely color-critical. You should try to calibrate your monitor in a darkened room, or if that's not practical (for instance, if you work in a wide open space with giant windows and lots of fluorescent lights, like I do), at least avoid having light shining directly on your display, and change your desktop wallpaper to a neutral color before beginning.

FIGURE 23.1

Mac users can do some quick-and-dirty monitor calibration via the built-in Display Calibrator Assistant.

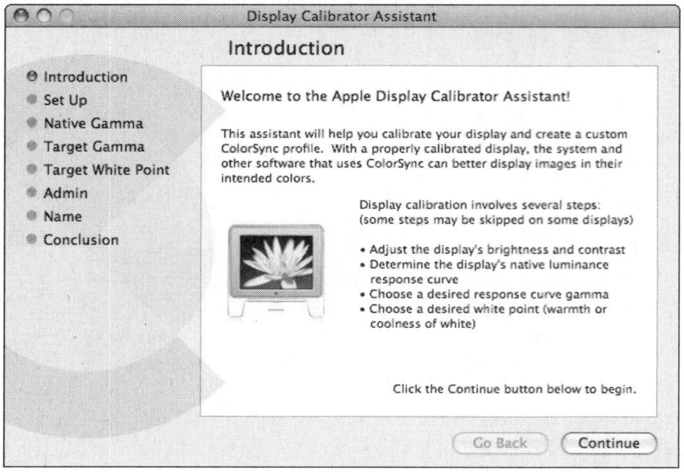

> **TIP** Keep in mind that as displays age, their performance changes, so it is often recommended that you perform calibration regularly — say, once a month.

The Debate To Use Color Management

Given all the ins and outs of color management, it's no wonder many people just throw their hands up in the air and pretend it's not there. And to be perfectly frank, if you are working within a controlled environment — that is, you work strictly with your own calibrated scanners, monitors, cameras, and printers — you can probably safely skip color management. Plus, most modern monitors and operating systems come with preinstalled monitor profiles that produce good-looking color under a fairly wide range of scenarios.

On the other hand, in scenarios where accurate color reproduction is crucial — say, for printing top-quality wedding or fine-art photography, or when producing images to be used in a high-end printing environment — color management is crucial. Yes, it's tedious, but once you understand it and incorporate it into your workflow, its there working for you, and your work will definitely benefit from it.

Calibrating printers generates profiles that describe how a particular piece of hardware will output color, and specific profiles are generated for varying ink and paper combinations. The procedure involves printing out a *target* — that is, a supplied image consisting of neutral colors — and using a device called a *spectrophotometer* to analyze the color values produced by the printer. These devices are expensive and can be somewhat cost-ineffective especially for small studios or individual designers, but there are service bureaus that will generate printer profiles for you, based on a printed sample you send them. The cost for these custom printer profiles is fairly reasonable — a quick search on the Internet yielded prices ranging from US $20 — $40.

Specifying and Using Color Settings

Once you've generated a color profile for your monitor (which you actually did, because you've been convinced to embrace color management, right?), it's time to bring Photoshop (and eventually, your other installed Creative Suite apps) into the picture. Choose Edit ➪ Color Settings, or press Ctrl+Shift+K (⌘+Shift+K on a Mac) to open the somewhat daunting Color Settings window, shown in Figure 23.2. The following sections describe the functions available in the Color Settings window.

FIGURE 23.2

Photoshop's Color Settings window is your friend, if you've decided to hop on board with color management.

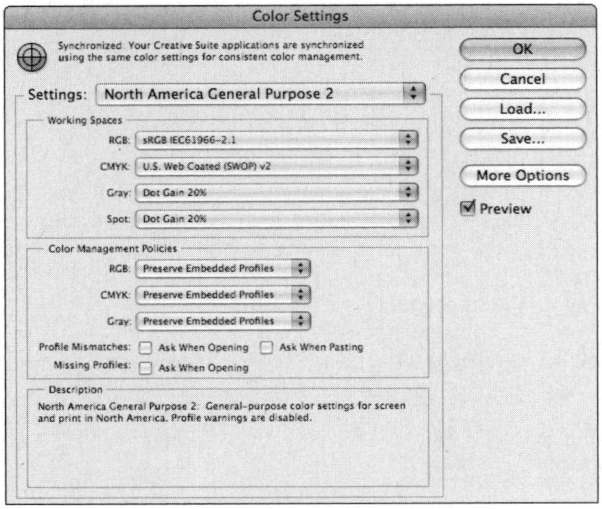

Color Settings

If you're not ready to jump into the deep end and customize every aspect of your color workflow, the Color Settings window offers several presets for the most common working scenarios under the Settings popup menu.

Using color settings presets

The most commonly used CSFs (Color Settings Files) are North America General Purpose 2, North America Prepress 2, and North America Web/Internet. Here's the skinny of it: If you're mostly producing graphics for the Web, use the North America Web/Internet preset. This sets the RGB working space to sRGB, which is the standard color space for viewing images on the Internet.

If you mostly work with print images, you probably want to use the North America Prepress 2 preset, which sets your working RGB color space to Adobe RGB, which, because of its wider gamut, is capable of displaying colors that the sRGB space can't define. Also, CMYK profiles, which are usually device-dependent settings specific to certain paper and ink combinations, are preserved.

If you vary between producing work for the Internet and print, then use the North America General Purpose 2 preset, which also uses the sRGB profile as its default RGB working space. This preset is more relaxed about color management in that it doesn't give you any warnings when you open documents that are untagged with color profile information or that don't match the current working space.

Of course, if you don't live in North America, you should choose a CSF that corresponds to your printing situation.

Loading and saving custom presets

There's nothing to stop you from tweaking the color settings to your own specifications and saving these settings for use on different machines, or across Adobe Creative Suite applications. To save your custom configuration, click the Save button at the right of the Color Settings window, and enter a name for your CSF. Save the file in the default location to ensure that your preset shows up automatically as an option in the Color Settings menu. If you save the file in a different location, you have to first load it (by clicking the Load button on the right side of the Color Settings window and navigating to its location on your hard drive) for it to be recognized by the Color Settings menu. The default locations for color settings files are:

- `/Users/<yourusername>/Library/Application Support/Adobe/Color/ Settings` (Mac)

- `Users/ [Username] / AppData/ Roaming/ Adobe/ Adobe Photoshop CS3/ Adobe Photoshop CS3 Settings` (Windows)

An additional advantage to saving the CSF files in the default locations is that you can access them in Bridge and the other Creative Suite applications, for a fully synchronized color workflow.

Working Spaces

Under this area, you can define a default working space for images that use the RGB, CMYK, Gray, or Spot color models. By default, new documents that you create, or documents that you open which aren't tagged with profile information, will use the settings specified here.

RGB profiles

Under the RGB menu, you'll find several profile options, but the most commonly used are Adobe RGB (1998) and sRGB-IEC61966-2.1. What's the difference? Well, apart from having a less human-friendly name, sRGB is designed to reproduce the gamut of colors that can be displayed by the broadest range of displays and monitors in use today.

It is often used as the default (or only) space built in to digital cameras, scanners, and other capture devices, which is quickly making it the default RGB color space. Because of its ubiquity, it's perfect for Web use — but its small gamut can result in dull colors, which makes it less than ideal for high-quality print work.

Adobe RGB, on the other hand, has a larger gamut than sRGB, and its easy conversion to CMYK makes it well-suited for print production. Figure 23.3 illustrates the gamut of the sRGB and Adobe RGB color profiles, and how they compare to each other.

FIGURE 23.3

The gamut of the sRGB and Adobe 1998 profiles are shown on the left. The figure on the right shows how these two color profiles compare to each other. As you can see, sRGB fits mostly within the Adobe RGB gamut.

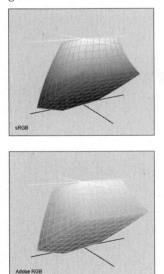

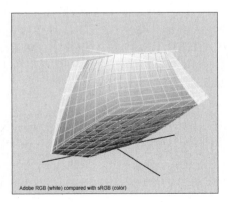

CMYK profiles

Each of the available working space profiles for the CMYK color model corresponds to an actual paper and ink combination. Converting images from RGB to CMYK via the Image ⇨ Mode command uses the working CMYK space as the basis for this conversion. The default CMYK profile, U.S. Web Coated (SWOP) v2, is the standard printing on North American offset presses.

Color Management Policies

This section of the Color Settings window governs how Photoshop color manages RGB, CMYK, and grayscale images that you open. Of course, Photoshop is happy to simultaneously display multiple documents, each using its own embedded color space information no matter what the default working space is set to. As an alternative, you could choose to have the images converted to the working space, or if no embedded profile information is present, Photoshop can assign one.

Choose from the following options to specify how Photoshop handles color management:

- **Off.** With this setting selected, Photoshop doesn't color manage documents that you open or create. Images without color information are left as-is, and embedded profiles are ignored. Be aware that when color management is off, if you move colors, or copy and paste elements between documents of different profiles, the color numbers are preserved, but not necessarily the color appearance. This can result in fairly significant — and undesirable — color shifts.

- **Preserve Embedded Profiles.** Use this option to maintain embedded profiles when you open files. This option ensures the most consistent colors, so you should probably leave it selected in most cases.

- **Convert to Working Profile.** Select this option to convert the colors in an image to the working profile when opening or importing files. When using this option, the color appearance is maintained by shifting the numerical values so that they fit within the working space's gamut.

Additionally, you can let Photoshop give you a warning when opening or pasting images that are either missing profile information, or whose profiles don't match the working space. If you choose to be alerted, you'll be given the opportunity to convert the colors to the working space via the dialog box shown in Figure 23.4. Choosing the Don't convert option can result in drastic color shifts.

Description

This is probably the most useful area of the Color Settings window. As you select or hover your cursor over the various menu options and settings, a brief description is displayed here. This is probably the best way to learn about the various color management options available to you.

With Photoshop set to warn you about profile mismatches, pasting an sRGB image into an Adobe RGB document resulted in the Paste Profile Mismatch dialog box appearing.

Advanced options

If you really want to get into the nitty-gritty of how colors are converted from one profile to the next, access the advanced color settings by clicking the More Options button on the right of the window. Figure 23.5 shows the additional settings available in the advanced mode of the Color Settings window.

Additional color settings offer control over conversion options.

Conversion Options

The options in this section have to do with the way color conversion is performed between spaces:

- **Engine.** Select a Color Conversion Module (CMM) here. At least one of the available options depends on your operating system. Adobe's ACE is available whether you use a Mac or a Windows PC. In either case, the engine is a software algorithm that converts between color profiles.

- **Intent.** Also referred to as rendering intents, these four choices affect how the conversion engine represents colors between spaces:

  - **Saturation:** This is probably the least-used rendering intent. This mode moves out-of-gamut colors in the source profile to the closest values in the destination profile, without taking neighboring pixels into consideration. The result is a shift in color and an overall increase in saturation. This rendering intent is really only useful for images made up mostly of solid colors, such as charts and graphs.

  - **Perceptual:** When using this rendering intent, all the colors in the source profile are compressed to fit within the gamut of the destination profile. This method takes neighboring pixels into consideration, adjusting colors proportionally to make room for all the colors in the destination space. This results in very accurate translations of colors from one space to another. That's why this is one of the more commonly used rendering intents.

  - **Relative Colorimetric:** This intent translates colors between spaces by converting the white point of the source to the destination's white point, and shifting all the colors that are out of gamut to match. This is the other commonly used rendering intent; however, you should be careful when using it to convert from a smaller color space (like CMYK) to a larger color space, as it could produce banding and dithering in the shadow areas of your image.

  - **Absolute Colorimetric:** This intent is used mostly for device proofing, or simulating what output will look like on a specific printer or other device. To do this, it makes the white point in the destination color space match up to the white point of the source color space. For example, to simulate newsprint on your monitor, you could soft-proof your image with Absolute Colorimetric, which would result in the whites being shifted to the yellowish white of newsprint. Avoid outputting hard copies using this intent for this reason — in the newsprint example, printing the simulated yellowish color on top of actual newsprint paper would just be a big mess.

Three options remain within the Conversion Options section:

- **Use Black Point Compensation.** When checked, this option simulates the entire dynamic range of the printer (or output device), allowing you to ensure that detail is being preserved in the shadow areas of your image. It's recommended by the good folks at Adobe that you keep this checked.

- **Use Dither.** This selection reduces banding in areas of transitions between colors when converting 8-bit images (which will probably be most of the images you're working on) between color spaces. Again, keep this one checked.

- **Compensate for Scene-referred Profiles.** This option is new to Photoshop CS4, and refers strictly to video production. It allows you to match the default color management setup in After Effects CS4, so if you're working with that software, you probably want to keep this checked as well.

Advanced Controls

The remaining two controls within the Advanced section of the Color Settings window are pretty esoteric, but good to know about nevertheless:

- **Desaturate Monitor Colors By.** Enter a number to desaturate the colors on your monitor, so that they visually match the colors available in a color profile that has a larger gamut than your display is capable of showing. When the colors in the larger gamut are toned down, more detail is visible in areas that would have otherwise been flat. This is only useful for viewing images on-screen, though, as enabling this option causes your screen to no longer match printed output. It's recommended that you leave this option on its default unchecked setting, in most cases.

- **Blend RGB Colors Using Gamma.** Select this option to blend colors in the document based on the specified gamma (1.0 is considered colorimetrically correct; 2.2 is standard on Windows machines), rather than on the default gamma of the working space. I would suggest using this option only if you know what you're doing, as using this option results in layered documents that look different in Photoshop than they do in other applications.

Assigning, converting, and embedding color profiles

When working with an image that doesn't match the current working space (or that isn't tagged with a color profile at all), you have a few choices: You can assign a color profile to the image, you can convert the image from one color profile to the next, or you can choose not to color manage the image at all.

- **Assign Profile.** The color numbers in your image remain the same, but a new profile is applied. This method of changing the image's profile makes no attempt to maintain visual consistency during the conversion process, so be aware that a dramatic visual shift can occur. To change the profile, choose Edit ➪ Assign Profile, and select one of the three available options (shown in Figure 23.6):

  - **Don't Color Manage This Document:** This option removes an image's embedded color profile entirely, and displays it according to the working color space options.

  - **Working RGB [Color Model: Working Space]:** This option applies the current profile that matches the working space.

  - **Profile:** Use this option to choose from any installed color profile.

- **Convert to Profile.** To change an image from one color profile to another, while preserving the appearance of the colors by shifting the colors' numerical values, choose Edit ➪ Convert to Profile, and select a Destination Space profile from the popup menu (see Figure 23.7).

If you took a peek at the Advanced section of the Color Settings window (click More Options to reveal this section), then the Conversion Options section of the Convert to Profile dialog box should look somewhat familiar to you. Choose a conversion engine and a rendering intent setting, and enable the remaining settings as applicable.

FIGURE 23.6

The Assign Profile options window

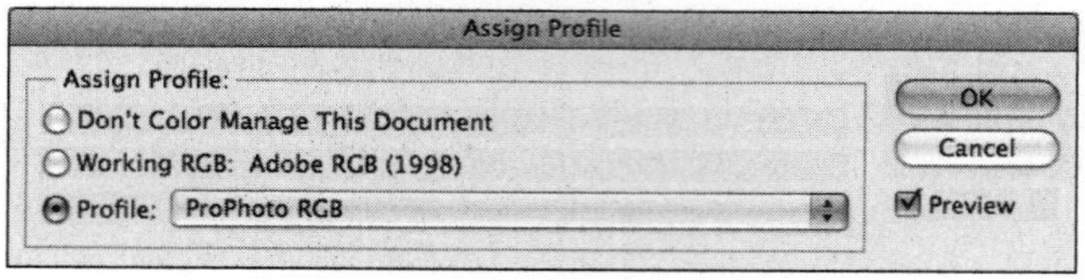

FIGURE 23.7

The Convert to Profile options window

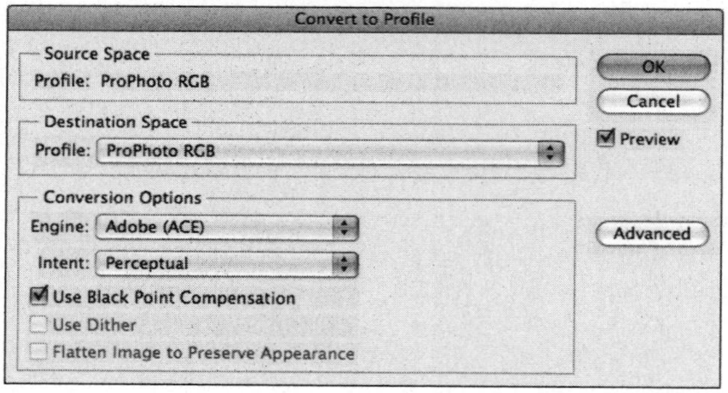

Synchronizing color using Bridge

The real benefit of color management is being able to take advantage of consistent colors across multiple applications. For example, you could import pictures from your digital camera, retouch them in Photoshop, create custom vector artwork in Illustrator, and scan printed reference materials or slides.

You've now got a mixed CMYK and RGB workflow, but you can be assured of seeing consistent colors no matter which application you're using, by synchronizing your Creative Suite color settings in Adobe Bridge. Open Bridge by clicking its icon in Photoshop's Application Bar, and press Ctrl+Shift+K/⌘+Shift+K) to launch the Suite Color Settings dialog box shown in Figure 23.8.

FIGURE 23.8

Adobe Bridge provides a centralized means of synchronizing the color settings across all your installed Creative Suite applications.

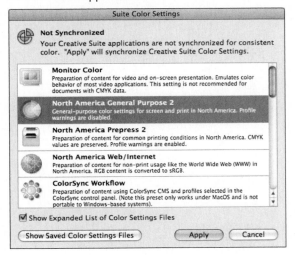

By default, only a handful of presets are displayed, but you can click the check box at the bottom of the window to show all the installed CSFs.

NOTE Perform advanced color setting tweaks in Photoshop, then save your settings as a preset, which you can apply to the other Creative Suite applications from Bridge's Color Settings menu.

Printing Using Color Management

There are three ways of approaching color management when it comes to printing and keeping the output consistent with what you're seeing on your screen. You can let your printer handle color management, in which case, Photoshop sends all the necessary information to the printer for accurate color conversion. As mentioned before, most modern inkjet printers supply accurate profiles for specific paper-ink combinations along with their drivers. This option is the most straightforward, although you have to remember to enable color management options in your printer driver. This process varies depending on the printer manufacturer, so consult your device's manual for more information.

In the second scenario, Photoshop performs color management using the supplied printer profiles to covert colors from your image's color space to the printer's gamut. This option relies on accurate

ICC profiles, such as those supplied by a service bureau. When using this option, you have to make sure that the printer driver isn't also trying to manage color, because the resulting output can be unpredictable.

The third option is to print without color management, which is most often used only when generating test targets for use with calibration devices, or to send to service bureaus to produce custom ICC profiles.

The Print dialog box appears in Figure 23.9. If they're not already visible, access the color management options by choosing Color Management from the popup menu on the right side of the dialog box.

FIGURE 23.9

Photoshop's Print dialog box lets you specify how color management should be handled.

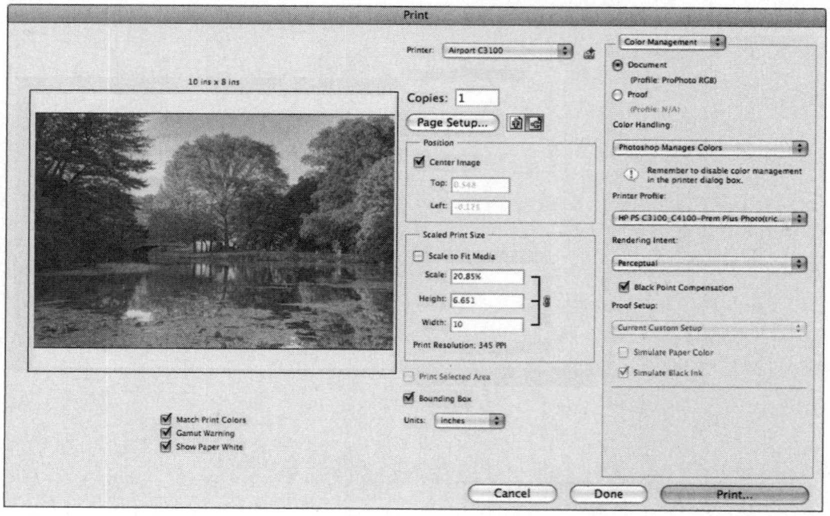

Here's a summary of the color management controls found in the Print dialog box:

- **Document/Proof.** Choose Document to print your image using its embedded color profile, or, if no profile is present, choose the default working space as specified in the Color Settings dialog box. To emulate the output from a different profile — that is, to see how the document would look if printed on a different device — choose Proof. If Color Handling (discussed next) is set to allow Photoshop to manage colors, this uses the custom proofing settings specified in View ⇨ Proof Setup.

■ **Color Handling.** From this menu, you can select one of the three color management scenarios discussed above — Photoshop manages colors, the printer manages colors, or no color management is performed at all. The subsequent options available will change depending on which color-handling scenario you have selected.

> **TIP** Photoshop provides a handy reminder to either disable or enable color management in your printer driver's dialog box, depending on which color-handling option you choose.

■ **Printer Profile.** If you've chosen to let Photoshop handle color management, this is where you choose the ICC profile that matches your paper and ink combination.

■ **Rendering Intent.** Select an intent depending on how you want Photoshop to convert colors from the document's color profile to that of the device you're printing to. Typically, when printing photographic material, use either Perceptual or Relative Colorimetric. Rendering intents are discussed in detail earlier in this chapter.

■ **Black Point Compensation.** This option helps maintain smooth color tone transitions by matching the black point of the document's profile to that of the destination device. It's usually recommended that you leave this option checked.

■ **Proof Setup.** If Proof is selected at the top of the print settings window, you can choose to emulate the custom setup specified in View ⇨ Proof Setup ⇨ Custom or choose the current CMYK working space.

■ **Simulate Paper Color.** Use this option to change the colors to emulate the paper that the final output will be produced on.

■ **Simulate Black Ink.** Select this option to emulate the darkness of the black ink of the selected device. This option is automatically checked when Simulate Paper Color is selected.

Summary

In this chapter you learned what color management is and why it's necessary for producing consistent color. You learned about calibrating your devices and about using color profiles to determine how colors will appear in different scenarios. You learned about using Adobe's color management options in Photoshop and Bridge for a consistent color workflow. Finally, you learned how to embed or change color profiles and how to predict printed output by using color management with your printer.

Chapter 24

Designing for the Web

I n this chapter you'll learn some of the ins and outs of working with images destined for the Web. Whether you're simply saving an image that you want to upload to a Web site or designing a Web page, this chapter covers the tools available to get the job done in Photoshop.

You'll review the file formats that are favored by the Web, as well as learn how to best optimize your images so they download quickly and efficiently even on the slowest Internet connections. Finally, you'll wrap up with a few examples of producing Web content in the form of a Web banner and an actual Web page.

Exploring Web Workflows

For the uninitiated, there is sometimes confusion when first dipping a toe into the pool of Web publishing (sorry for the terrible metaphor). People often confuse the tasks of producing Web graphics and producing the HTML code that makes up the foundation of a Web page. This section aims to clear up any misconceptions by outlining a typical workflow for producing a Web site and clarifying the roles that Photoshop and Dreamweaver play in that workflow.

When producing a Web site, the place to start is with pencil and paper. Decide the purpose of your site, look at similar sites, and take note of the things that you think they got right (and what you think they got wrong). Is it easy to find information? Is the navigation simple and straightforward? How many top-level pages are there on the site (put another way, how many links are on the main navigation)? How about the use of typography and imagery? Once you've got a basic idea of those sorts of things, get your site's architecture (that is, the pages that make up your Web site) nailed down and sketch them out, so you have an idea of how everything fits together.

Next is visualization. Most Web designers will produce a "flat," nonworking version of what the site will look like, coming up with a color palette and type treatment that make up the visual language of the site. Design the headers, navigation links, position any photography or graphics you'll be using, add "dummy" text, and make everything look really pretty. At this stage, if you were working with clients, you'd show this to them and get their feedback, and make necessary revisions and tweaks. Once the design is finalized, you're ready to go into production mode, where you actually generate the working parts that will make up the Web site.

So how do Photoshop and HTML editors such as Dreamweaver fit into this scenario? Well, step back for a second and take a look at how Web pages work. Most Web sites are made up of *HTML* (short for Hypertext Markup Language) code that runs behind the scenes, giving Web browsers instructions on how to render the text, images, links, and other elements that make up the Web page. HTML is saved in text files with the extension .html or .htm, and because they are just text files, you could actually create them using basic text editors like NotePad on Windows systems, or TextEdit on a Mac.

More complex sites can use *CSS* (Cascading Style Sheets) for positioning and text styling, as well as other scripting languages to generate dynamic content; or Flash for video and interactivity. But let's not get distracted — that stuff is mostly beyond the scope of this book.

In a nutshell, Photoshop is usually used to handle all the graphical aspects of the Web production process. Producing design comps, or mockups, of the Web page; resizing images; and optimizing and exporting images in Web-friendly formats — these tasks are all handled by Photoshop.

Incorporating these graphical elements in the HTML code is then achieved using an editor such as Dreamweaver. For those who are unfamiliar with it, Dreamweaver is a Web development application. On the one hand, it is what's known as a WYSIWYG ("what you see is what you get") editor, allowing you to assemble Web pages visually, which appeals to designers and those who aren't experienced with writing code. On the other hand, hardcore Web developers can use it to produce advanced scripting, so it's got the whole gamut of users covered.

Here's the thing — Photoshop, being the jack-of-all-trades that it is, is also capable of generating the HTML (and/or CSS/JavaScript, if necessary) that makes up a Web page, as you'll see later in this chapter. You could easily take a designed mockup and export the graphical elements and the supporting HTML code from Photoshop, all in one fell swoop.

There are pros and cons to this approach, though. Using Photoshop to generate HTML is fast, easy, and it works. For those who have no experience with HTML, you can create a Web page without once touching a line of code. On the other hand, if your site is more complex than a page or two, it can be cumbersome to manage and update these pages, as even simple tweaks would require re-exporting everything from Photoshop. By contrast, Dreamweaver provides tools that make it easy to make global updates to every single page in a Web site by executing a simple search-and-replace command.

I would recommend using Photoshop to do the graphics portion of the site, and stick to software such as Dreamweaver — or even simple text-editing software (after all, HTML is really just text) — for generating the HTML.

Preparing Images for the Web

If you cast your memory back to the early days of the World Wide Web when 56K dial-up connections were the norm, you probably remember gnashing your teeth, waiting for what seemed like an eternity for Web pages to load. By necessity, Web designers had to optimize their images so that their pages would be fast and lean, or impatient viewers would be certain to turn away in disgust. With the ubiquity of broadband connection speeds, it's not as much of an issue now as it was even as recently as five years ago, but it's still a good practice to keep an eye on file sizes and compress your graphics properly. After all, many people are now connecting to Web sites via mobile devices, and you want your site's visitors to have a good experience no matter where they're coming from.

What follows is an examination of many of the most important things to consider when preparing images for use on the Web.

Web image file formats

As discussed back in Chapter 7, there are a few standard image formats that Web browsers can display: GIF, JPEG, PNG, and in rare cases, WBMP. Here's a quick review:

- **GIF.** Short for Graphic Interchange Format, GIF is one of the bread-and-butter formats for displaying images on the Internet. Capable of displaying images with a maximum of 256 colors (or 8 bits per channel), this format is great at handling images with sharp distinctions between areas of solid color, such as line drawings, logos, or text.

  The colors that are used in a GIF are indexed and stored in a color lookup table (CLUT), which is why GIFs are sometimes referred to as indexed color files. Converting an image to indexed color mode results in each original color being shifted to the values in the color lookup table. If a color in the original doesn't exist in the lookup table, it's shifted to the closest value, or emulated by a combination of values from the table.

  GIF usually produces files that are quite a bit smaller than the original un-optimized source files because the format features built-in lossless LZW compression. Named after some really smart guys named Lempel, Ziv, and Welch, the LZW compression algorithm makes files smaller by rearranging their data in a more efficient manner.

  The GIF format supports transparency, allowing you to, for example, overlay an image over a patterned background in a Web page. The transparency is limited to pixels being either on or off — you can't have varying levels of transparency, so images' drop shadows or semitransparent pixels will appear jagged and harsh.

- **JPEG.** Named after its developer, the Joint Photographic Experts Group, JPEG is best at compressing photographic images or those that contain areas of continuous tone. The

JPEG format is capable of displaying up to 16.7 million colors, and is one of the most commonly used file formats because of its ability to preserve much of the original appearance of the image while significantly reducing the file size. JPEG uses what's known as *lossy* compression — that is, it selectively discards data to make files smaller. Applying a small amount of compression results in an image that hardly looks any different from the original, even though file sizes become much smaller. As you increase the compression, the file size drops even more sharply, but there is a corresponding deterioration of image quality. Typically, you wouldn't want to use JPEG for images with large areas of solid color, because the compression artifacts that the format can introduce start to become more noticeable. Also, while JPEG images do preserve vector paths, they don't support animation or alpha channels.

■ **PNG-8 and PNG-24.** PNG (Portable Network Graphic) has only relatively recently started to gain popularity, as some older browsers weren't capable of displaying them correctly. Pronounced "ping," PNG images are kind of a best-of-both-worlds scenario in that they offer some of the features of both the JPEG and GIF formats.

The 8-bit flavor of PNG is very similar to the GIF format and can be used to compress the same types of images that you would use a GIF for. It also supports a maximum of 256 colors, and binary transparency, just like GIF images.

The 24-bit version of the format is more like JPEG, saving images with millions of colors. However, files saved in this format are much larger than their JPEG counterparts, because of the lossless compression algorithm that PNG uses. On the other hand, PNG images don't suffer from the compression artifacts that JPEG can produce. Also, the 24-bit support means that you can have pixels that range from fully opaque to completely transparent, with 254 varying steps of transparency in between, for a total of 256 levels — perfect for preserving soft drop shadows. Another benefit of the lossless PNG-24 format is that saving, then opening and re-saving, a PNG won't result in continuous degradation, as is the case with JPEG images.

■ **WBMP.** WBMP stands for Wireless Bitmap format. This 1-bit format is primarily used for mobile devices that are only capable of displaying either black or white pixels. These devices are becoming more and more rare, but there is still occasionally a need for images in this format.

Web work area

When working with Web images, you may find it convenient to use the Web workspace, which the good folks at Adobe have designed to place most of the tools and panels you'll need most frequently right at your fingertips, while tucking the extraneous stuff away to avoid clutter. If working with Animations, however, you'll need to enable the Animation panel from the Window menu. In fact, if you frequently work with animated Web graphics, you may want to save your own custom version of the Web workspace that includes the Animation panel.

 When working in the Web workspace — or any workspace, for that matter — if you don't see a menu item that you're absolutely positive was there just yesterday, don't panic, you're not going crazy. Switching workspaces results in some menu items that are less relevant to the task at hand being hidden. To get at these hidden menu items, select the Show all Menu Items command that appears at the bottom of each menu.

The demise of ImageReady

Speaking of Web tools, it used to be that Photoshop didn't really include that many tools for working with Web graphics and Web sites, but instead, most of those duties were handled by a separate software package called Adobe ImageReady. ImageReady was introduced alongside Photoshop 5.5, and featured very specific tools for exporting Web images, such as the ability to create JavaScript rollovers for buttons. As the versions of Photoshop progressed, more and more of ImageReady's specialized Web tools, such as slices and the ability to work with animation, were included in Photoshop, until version CS3, when ImageReady was put out to pasture.

Unfortunately, there are one or two ImageReady features that still haven't made it into the current version of Photoshop, including the ability to create rollovers, and the ability to save a group of slices as a table (although Photoshop will still read this information from a legacy ImageReady PSD file). Also, if you try to open an animated GIF file in Photoshop, you'll only be able to view the first frame of the animation. This becomes a problem if you've created an animation and want to edit the optimized GIF file, and no longer have the source PSD file that you used to create it. The solution to these missing features would be to use Adobe Fireworks, if you have access to that software.

Units and document resolution

Many designers who come from a print-oriented background tend to bring over some of their habits when they first start designing for the Internet. This isn't necessarily a bad thing, but there are one or two things you should be aware of when getting into Web design. Measurements for the Web (or any screen) are done in pixels, so it's best to set your default document units to pixels, rather than inches. To ensure that your document is set to use pixels, either choose pixels as the default units in the new document window, or, if you're already working on a document, open Photoshop's preferences by pressing Ctrl+K (⌘+K on a Mac), select Units and Rulers, and set the Rulers popup menu to Pixels.

You'll also want to make sure you're working at a pixel resolution of 72 pixels/inch (ppi). This is the default resolution for any screen, so if you design your content at a higher resolution, and you're not careful, you'll eventually find that you're plagued by mismatches in size. The good news is that the Save for Web & Devices command automatically resamples your image down to 72 ppi when you use it to export images. If you use the Save As command, you're on your own.

Color settings

In this section you'll learn a little bit about color and color spaces when preparing images to be published for the Web.

RGB color mode

First and foremost, you will want to ensure that any images that you create for the Web are in the RGB color mode. RGB is the default color mode for screens of all kinds, so you'll want to make sure that if you bring content over from other programs such as Adobe Illustrator, your documents are set to RGB color, not CMYK, which is the default for prepress work. To convert an image to RGB color from a different color mode, choose Image ⇨ Mode ⇨ RGB Color. You can tell what color mode your document is in by looking it up — the color mode is displayed next to the document's title either in the Tab bar or in the document's Title bar if you're working with floated windows.

The sRGB color space

Those of you who have already read Chapter 23 on color management might find this a little repetitive. For the uninitiated, the default color profile for images used on the Internet is sRGB. To back up a bit, a color profile is a description of how colors are represented on input and output devices such as monitors, printers, and scanners. The sRGB color profile (whose full name is actually sRGB IEC61966-2.1) is designed to describe the range of colors that can be displayed by most monitors in use today. So, since you can't personally go around making sure everyone who sees your images on the Internet has a correctly calibrated display, the next best thing is to use the sRGB format for your images. You can set your default working color space as sRGB using the Color Settings window. For images that are already tagged with another color profile, choose Edit ⇨ Convert to Profile.

Proofing color displays

Monitors display colors differently depending on the operating system that's being used. Windows-based systems use a *gamma* of 2.2, while Macs have a default gamma of 1.8. To overly simplify things, gamma is a complex term referring to brightness and luminance, which essentially means that on Windows machines, images created on Mac systems appear darker, while on Macintosh systems, Windows-generated colors appear somewhat washed out. To preview how your images will look on different systems, you can choose proofing options from the Proof Setup menu. Choose View ⇨ Proof Setup ⇨ Macintosh or Windows RGB to simulate how your image will look on a typical Mac or Windows setup.

The Save for Web & Devices dialog box offers options for dealing with color profiles and proofing different color scenarios. Learn more later in this chapter.

CROSS-REF Refer to Chapter 23 for information about converting and assigning color profiles, and on proofing colors.

Slices

Web browsers and HTML were originally designed to display information in a tabular format — after all, in the early days, Web pages were all text, and it made sense to present it in tables. Web browsers have come a long way since then, but the underlying structure of Web pages remains the same. When exporting elements of a Web page designed in Photoshop for use in HTML, slices make it easy to divide your layout into rectangular sections containing images, text, headers, footers, and navigation elements — each of which can be saved using different optimization settings (discussed in the next section).

The image in Figure 24.1 is a design for a detail view of an imaginary gadget Web site's catalog.

FIGURE 24.1

A design for a detail page of a gadget Web site's catalog

The design features several distinct regions: a header area with the title of the page, a photograph and accompanying item title, a description of the item, and a footer area. The Slice tool is used to divide the image along these regions into a table structure, as shown in Figure 24.2.

Photoshop features the Slice tool for slicing images, and the Slice Select tool for selecting and resizing slices. As of Photoshop CS4, the Slice tool and the Slice Select tool are grouped with the Crop tool, and share C as a keyboard shortcut (see Figure 24.3).

To create a slice, select the Slice tool and draw a rectangle around the portion of the image that you want to treat as a distinct region. Use the Shift key to constrain the slice to a square shape. You can reposition the slice on the fly as you're drawing it by holding down the spacebar and moving the slice to its new position. Release the spacebar to drop the slice and continue drawing.

FIGURE 24.2

The Slice tool is used to divide the elements on the page into distinct areas that will be reassembled into a table with HTML.

FIGURE 24.3

The Slice and Slice Select tools are grouped under the Crop tool's fly-out menu.

It's a good practice to divide your image using as few slices as possible, as this creates the cleanest HTML code. Avoid having slices overlap each other, and try not to leave gaps between slices, as this forces Photoshop to draw additional auto slices to fill in the gaps. To have the slices snap to each other as you draw them, choose View ⇨ Snap To ⇨ Slices.

Types of slices

Slices fall into different types based on how they were created and the type of content within them. The four types of slices in Photoshop are user slices, layer-based slices, no-image slices, and auto slices. Figure 24.2 contains several of the different types of slices that Photoshop provides. The badges that indicate the different types of slices are shown in Figure 24.4.

FIGURE 24.4

The badges for the four types of slices that Photoshop uses to distinguish content in a page that's destined for the Internet From top to bottom: user slice, layer based slice, no image slice and auto slice.

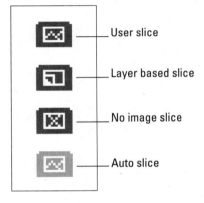

User slices

User slices, as you may have guessed, are slices that are manually drawn. A solid blue outline and a blue badge in the upper-left corner denote them.

Layer-based slices

You can create a different type of user slice that matches the boundaries of the content of a layer by choosing Layer ⇨ New Layer Based Slice. Layer based slices show a blue badge with a with a tiny icon representing a layer in the upper left corner. These slices adjust their boundaries dynamically if the content of the layer changes, which is useful if you add content to a layer or change the properties of a layer effect (for example, making a drop shadow or glow bigger).

No-image slices

To go back to the Gadgetland example in Figure 24.1, the text description of the gadget should be implemented as HTML text. It could be saved as a GIF, keeping the text legible and crisp, but for an actual Web site, there are several reasons why you'd want to put body copy in the HTML rather than in an image. For one, search engines can't read the text within images, which means your site would be less likely to show up in Web searches. Also, if your visitor wanted to copy and paste a portion of the text to use in an e-mail, or save as a reference, that would be impossible if the text were embedded in an image. To tell Photoshop not to save this region as an image, but rather as HTML-coded text, you need to convert it into a no-image slice. No image slices are denoted by a blue badge with an x through it in the upper left corner.

Auto slices

Auto slices are those that Photoshop automatically creates to divide the remaining areas of the page. These slices have gray badges and dotted blue outlines.

> **TIP** You can toggle the visibility of slices by choosing View ⇨ Show ⇨ Slices. To hide the slice numbers and badge overlays from view, but keep slices themselves visible, open Photoshop's preferences (press Ctrl+K/⌘+K), choose Guides, Grids and Slices from the list on the left, then Uncheck Show Slice Numbers.

With the Slice Select tool active, either right-click (Ctrl+click if you're a Mac user with a one-button mouse) and choose Slice Options, or simply double-click on the slice you want to change. From the Slice Type menu, choose No Image, and enter the text that should be displayed in that region of your page, as demonstrated in Figure 24.5.

FIGURE 24.5

Convert your slice to a no-image slice to add HTML-coded text to your final optimized design.

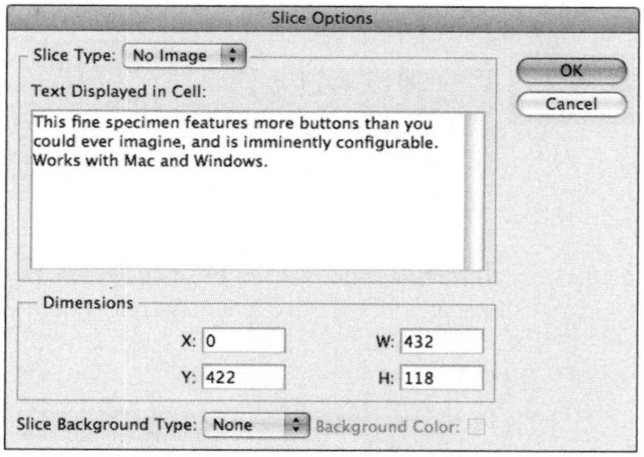

When you click OK, you won't see any obvious changes to your Photoshop file, except the slice's badge will change to indicate that it's a no-image slice. To see what the final exported page will look like, choose File ➪ Save for Web & Devices, then click the Preview button in the lower left corner of the dialog box to display the page in a Web browser.

TIP You can use HTML tags, such as `<font>`, `<b>`, and `<i>`, to style your text.

Setting slice options

The Slice Options window (see Figure 24.6) offers several other useful controls for your slices:

- **Slice Type.** You've already seen how you can use this option to switch between slices that contain images and those that contain HTML-coded content. The third option, Table, is grayed out, and only applies to legacy content created in ImageReady 2 (which has been discontinued as of Creative Suite 3).

The Slice Options window

- **Name.** By default, the name of the optimized file corresponding to each slice is automatically set to the document name followed by an underscore and the slice number. To customize the slice name, and eventual output filename, enter a new value in the Name field.

- **URL.** Use this field to assign a link to a slice, making the entire slice area clickable in the exported Web page. Clicking on the slice area causes the browser to navigate to the specified Web address.

- **Target.** If the slice has an assigned Web address, enter a value in the Target field to specify how the browser handles the link. Enter `self` to open the Web address in the same browser window as the originating page; enter `blank` to signal the browser to spawn a new window with the linked page, leaving the originating page as is. Advanced users who are comfortable using HTML frames can use -parent or -top to target specific frames within the frameset. For more information on framesets, consult an HTML reference book.

- **Message Text.** The text entered here appears in the status bar of a Web browser when the user rolls over a link. If you leave this area blank, the Web address that the link is pointing to is displayed here instead.

- **Alt Tag.** An alt tag (also known as alt text) is displayed by the browser in place of an image that hasn't completely downloaded. Alt text is also displayed in some browsers as a tool tip when the user hovers over a link, and is read by search engines and screen readers.

- **Dimensions.** Use the fields here to precisely position and set the dimensions of the selected slice or slices.

- **Slice Background Type.** Use this popup menu to set the background color for a slice. The background color shows through the transparent areas of an image slice, or the entire slice if you're using a no-image slice. Choose None if you want the default background of your Web page to show through, or choose one of the color options to specify a colored background.

Changing slice types

Of the various slice types in Photoshop, user slices are the most flexible — you can resize and reposition them at will. The other slice types are more restrictive because their size and position depend on either the content of the layer (in the case of layer-based slices), or the position of the surrounding slices (in the case of auto slices). To take matters completely into your own hands and resize and reposition at will, you need to first convert or promote these slices into user slices. To do so, select a slice and click the Promote button in the Options Bar.

> **NOTE** You've already seen an example of another type of slice conversion — the conversion between image and no-image slices.

Dividing slices

Sometimes it's useful to split a slice into several equally sized slices — either to create rows or columns of distinct content, or to divide both horizontally and vertically at the same time, creating a grid. A good example would be to create a slice for each button in the navigation of a Web page. Simply draw one big slice that encompasses the navigation buttons, then use the Divide command to subdivide it (see Figure 24.7).

To divide a slice, make sure the Slice Select tool is active and either click the Divide button in the Options Bar or right-click and choose Divide from the resulting context menu. Select either horizontal or vertical (or both) to determine how the slice is divided, enter either the size of each resulting slice in pixels or the number of slices you want to produce, and click OK.

FIGURE 24.7

In this example, what was one large slice has been divided into five smaller slices using the Divide command.

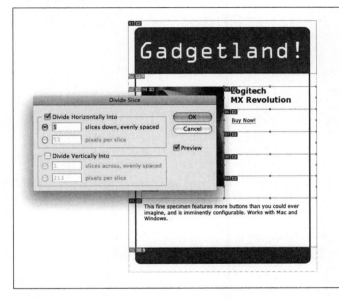

Save for Web & Devices

Save for Web & Devices performs essentially the same function as if you were to choose File ⇨ Save As, then check the Save a Copy check box — except that it also gives you precise control over how the file or files are optimized and saved. If you're already familiar with Save for Web & Devices, it's gotten a bit of a makeover and a few newly added features in Photoshop CS4, so read on for an overview.

To launch the Save for Web & Devices window (shown in Figure 24.8), select it from the File menu, or use the following finger-twisting keyboard shortcut: Ctrl+Shift+Alt+S/⌘+Shift+Option+S.

Like many other Photoshop dialog boxes, Save for Web & Devices offers a large Preview area, which allows you to see the results of your changes as you make them. In addition to panning and zooming within the Preview area using the Hand and Magnify tools, you can preview up to three differently optimized versions of the original image by using the tabs at the top of the Preview area.

FIGURE 24.8

The Save for Web & Devices dialog box offers many options for optimizing images for use on the Web.

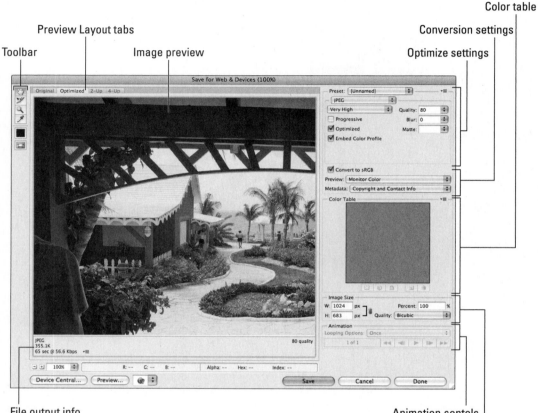

Toolbar

Preview Layout tabs

Image preview

Color table

Conversion settings

Optimize settings

File output info

Animation contols

Image size settings

The area directly below the Preview area displays information about the current image or slice, including the selected output format, the optimized file size, and the download times at various connection speeds. To change the download speed that's being emulated, click the small fly-out menu icon to the right of the download speed, and select a different setting (see Figure 24.9).

FIGURE 24.9

The Save for Web & Devices dialog box can give you estimated download times for various connection speeds.

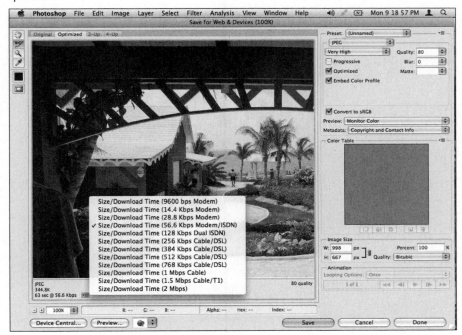

Optimize settings

The area on the upper left side of the Save for Web & Devices dialog box is where you'll spend most of your time when saving images for Web output. Using the controls here, you can choose the output format of your image (or the slices that make up your image), and specify the compression settings that are used. The options in this section will be covered in more detail later in this chapter, but for now, here's a quick overview:

■ The Preset menu at the top of the Save for Web & Devices dialog box is populated with optimization settings for saving images using the four commonly used Web formats (JPEG, GIF, PNG, and WBMP). Most of the available presets contain variations of settings for the GIF format, but you can save your own custom configurations here as well.

■ Select a file format from the menu directly below the Preset menu. The options in the Optimize settings area change depending on which file format is selected.

■ If you have a target file size that you need to optimize to, choose Optimize to File Size from the fly-out menu at the top right of the Save for Web & Devices dialog box. Enter your target file size in kilobytes and select a file format for your image. Next, choose to optimize either the current slice or the entire image, and click OK. Photoshop automatically runs through various combinations of optimization settings, reducing the number of colors in the image or increasing the compression that's applied until it gets as close as it can to your target file size. Be warned that in some cases the results aren't pretty — you may have to go back and edit your original image by simplifying the design, or reducing the pixel dimensions of the image, in order to meet file size requirements.

Conversion options

If you've read Chapter 23, you already know how important a color-managed workflow is (if you haven't, what are you waiting for?). Color management is the key to being able to produce consistent color across devices. The problem with monitors (which is where the Internet is viewed, for the most part) is that in most cases, they haven't been calibrated, and they display wildly varying colors, depending on the hardware in question. The options in this section help you maintain consistent color as you send your images to the unruly chaos that is the World Wide Web.

■ **Convert to sRGB.** sRGB is the default color profile for images being displayed on the Internet. If you are exporting color-managed files for use on the Web, or if you have untagged images (that is, images without embedded color profile information), you can use this option to translate the images' colors to the sRGB color profile. Note that converting to the sRGB space increases the final file size, but usually only by a negligible amount.

■ **Preview.** Gamma, when talking about optimizing images for the Web, has nothing to do with mild-mannered scientists being transformed into giant green behemoths with anger management problems. In this context, gamma is related to screen brightness, which differs depending on the operating system and calibration of the monitor being used. Windows systems use a gamma value of 2.2, while the default gamma of Mac OS systems is 1.8. This means that images created on a Mac tend to look darker when viewed on Windows systems, and images created on a Windows machine can sometimes look washed-out when viewed on a Mac.

The options under the Preview menu can simulate viewing your images under these different conditions. Keep in mind that these are only simulations — the actual colors of your original document and the exported image are unchanged.

▪ **Use Monitor Color:** This displays the image as it appears with no color management.

▪ **Macintosh (No Color Management):** This option gives a preview of what the image would look like on an uncalibrated Mac display using factory settings.

▪ **Windows (No Color Management):** This option previews the gamma of a standard Windows system.

▪ **Use Document Profile:** If your image is color-managed, this option displays the image using its embedded color profile.

Metadata

Metadata refers to information embedded in a file relating to a wide variety of its properties, such as the type of camera used to take the picture, whether the flash was fired or not, the focal length of the lens used, and even, in some cases, the longitude and latitude of the location where the picture was taken. Photographers can also embed their personal information, such as address, phone number, Web site, e-mail address, and copyright information. All this information is great, but if you don't want to make all that information available for whatever reason, in Photoshop CS4 you now have the ability to strip some or all of that information when exporting images for the Web. (Prior to this version of Photoshop, you could only achieve this with third-party software.)

Choose None to remove all the metadata from the image. You'll notice that a small warning triangle appears next to the Save button as a reminder that no copyright information will be included with the image. On the other extreme, choose All to include every bit of metadata that is embedded in the image. Select one of the in-between options to include a portion of the metadata — Copyright, Copyright and Contact, or All Except Camera Info, which strips out the make, model, and serial number of the camera used to take the picture.

Resizing images

The controls under the Image Size section of the dialog box (shown in Figure 24.10) allow you to change the dimensions of the optimized copy of the image while saving it, leaving the original image untouched. You should already be familiar with these controls, since they're essentially the same as the ones found in the Pixel Dimensions area of the Image Size dialog box. Enter the image dimensions in pixels or as a percentage, and then select an interpolation method to use (Bicubic or Bicubic Sharper, if you're scaling the image down).

FIGURE 24.10

Resize the optimized version of your image using the Image Size controls.

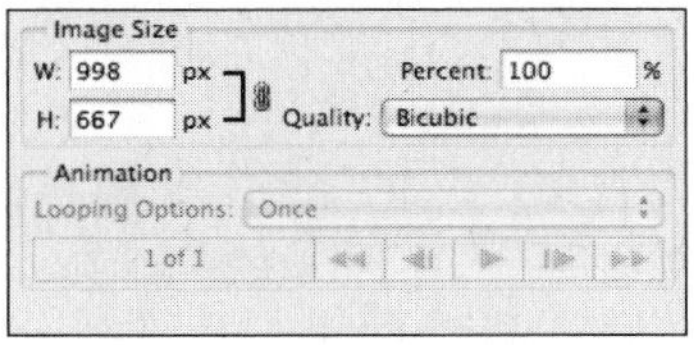

CROSS-REF For a review of the Image Size command, refer to Chapter 5.

Animation

If you're working with a document that contains animation information, the controls in the Animation area of the Save for Web & Devices dialog box will become available (see Figure 24.11).

FIGURE 24.11

Preview animated images using the controls in the Animation area of the Save for Web & Devices dialog box.

Play, pause, rewind, fast-forward, or step through each frame of the animation, and set the maximum amount of times the animation should loop through its playback. Working with video and animation is covered in more detail in Chapter 26.

CAUTION   **You may see a discrepancy between the playback performance in the Save for Web & Devices dialog box and various Web browsers. Since a browser is where most people view your work, be sure to preview your animation in at least two different Web browsers, and adjust the timing of the animation as necessary.**

Slices

When exporting slices with the Save for Web tool, you can specify compression settings on a global or a slice-by-slice basis. To select individual slices, click on the Slice Select tool or press the C key on your keyboard, then click on a slice to change its settings. As you might expect, you can Shift+ click to select multiple slices and edit their optimization settings simultaneously.

To temporarily disable the visibility of the slices so you can see what your optimized page looks like without distraction, click the Slice Visibility button or press the Q key on your keyboard.

You can also edit Slice options while in the Save for Web & Devices dialog box. Simply select the Slice Select tool and double-click the slice whose options you want to change. The Slice Options dialog box that appears is almost identical to the one you have access to while editing your image in Photoshop's main window, with the exception of the missing dimension fields.

Device Central

As mobile devices become more and more prevalent, the need to develop content for them increases as well. The huge variety of new devices that are released on the market in what seems like every other minute brings with it a flurry of new dimensions and device specifications that are pretty much impossible to keep up with. That's where Device Central comes into play.

The huge variety of new devices that are released on the market brings with it a flurry of new dimensions and device specifications thhat are pretty much impossible to keep up with.

Click the Device Central button to launch the program (shown in Figure 24.12).

FIGURE 24.12

Device Central features a huge library of profiles for emulating different mobile devices.

Select a device template from the list on the lower-left portion of the screen, and then click on the Emulator tab at the top of the window to preview what the actual phone looks like and to see what your content looks like on the device's screen. You can even preview what effect reflections will have on the appearance of the image.

Device Central CS4 offers access to an online library of device profiles. You can also create local sets of devices that you work with regularly.

The functionality of Device Central goes far beyond what's covered here, but this should give you a little taste of what is possible.

Previewing optimized images in a Web browser

Different browsers can sometimes render HTML content inconsistently. Add different operating systems into the mix, and your optimized Web pages can be fairly unpredictable. Fortunately, the Save for Web & Devices dialog box offers the ability to preview your image in any browser installed on your computer.

Click the Preview button at the bottom of the Save for Web & Devices dialog box to preview your optimized page or graphic in the default browser on your system. To get additional installed browsers to show up in the popup menu to the right, open the menu and click Edit List. Choose Add from the resulting dialog box, and then navigate to each browser's location on your hard drive.

It's a good practice to preview your work on as many browsers as possible, on both Windows and Mac-based systems, before putting it out there for public consumption, and this feature offers you the first step in that direction.

Saving files

Once you've set up all your optimization options, you're ready to save your files. Press the Save button (the Done button simply pops you back out to the main Photoshop document window, while preserving your Save for Web settings) to produce the somewhat familiar Save As dialog box depicted in Figure 24.13.

FIGURE 24.13

The Save Optimized As dialog box sports a few variations from the regular Save As window.

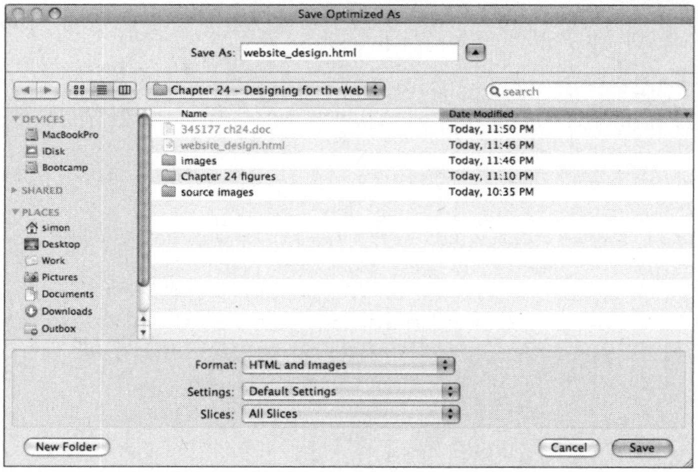

Here's what you should know about saving options from the Save Optimized As dialog box:

- **Format.** Choose whether to save just images, just HTML, or both images and HTML. If you've decided to go the do-it-yourself route, and are coding the page yourself, then select the Images only option. If you want Photoshop to do all the work, then select the images and HTML format.

TIP   If you're using the Images Only option, the image filenames are based on the values in the Slice Options window. As a result, the filename you enter in the Save As field doesn't do anything, and you may as well leave it to the default, which is based on your document's name. When using one of the HTML options, the name you enter in the Save As field determines the name of your HTML file.

■ **Settings.** Photoshop offers a plethora of options for specifying how the HTML and accompanying image files are saved. You can either stick with the defaults or use the Other option to launch the Output Settings dialog box shown in Figure 24.14 to customize the file saving options (you can also access this dialog box by selecting it from the fly-out menu at the top right of the Save for Web window). Most users are perfectly happy with the basic settings, but if you're familiar with HTML and need more control, the Output Settings dialog box offers the following sections (accessible by clicking the Previous and Next buttons at the right of the dialog box):

■ **HTML:** Use this section to customize HTML formatting options.

■ **Slices:** Select whether to use tables or `<div>` tags (used to denote sections of a Web page) with CSS when outputting the final HTML for your site. You can also set up custom naming conventions for your slices, using the popup menus in the area at the bottom of the window. Use this option to change the default name that shows up in the Slice Options window.

■ **Background:** Specify a background image for the entire Web page by clicking Choose and navigating to an image file. You can also specify a matte color for any transparencies.

■ **Saving Files:** In this area of the Output Settings dialog box, you can set up options for how files are saved. Again, set up a naming convention, this time for the actual output filenames for the images and HTML files. In the Optimized Files section of the window, you can choose to put the saved images in their own folder and specify a name for it. If you specified a background image, you can click the Copy Background Image When Saving check box to include it in the folder with the rest of the saved images.

FIGURE 24.14

The Output Settings dialog box

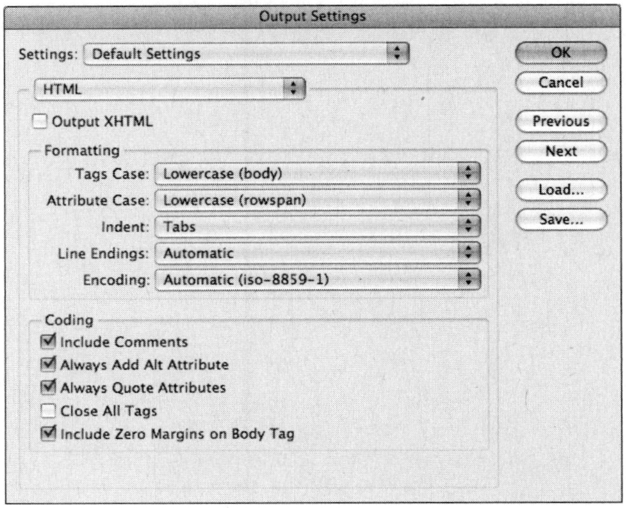

■ **Slices.** Use the options in this menu (refer to Figure 24.13) to specify which slices to save — all of them, only the user-created slices, or the slices that were selected in the document before you launched the Save for Web & Devices window.

Optimizing images for the Web

Optimizing images is an art that involves finding the balance between reducing an image's file size and keeping it looking as close to the original version as possible. There are two ways to save files in the favored Web formats: Save As and Save for Web & Devices. The Save As command is great, but it doesn't offer you the same level of control that you can find in the Save for Web & Devices window. Read on to learn how to finesse your optimized images so that they look great and download fast.

Optimizing GIF and PNG-8 images

Exporting images in the GIF format is all about throwing away colors while keeping the image looking as good as possible. Start by gradually reducing the number of colors while keeping an eye on the resulting file size. You can either enter a number manually or use the popup menu to the right of the Colors field. The compression options that appear when using the GIF (or PNG-8) format are shown in Figure 24.15.

FIGURE 24.15

The options for compressing images in the GIF format. Choosing PNG-8 offers exactly the same options.

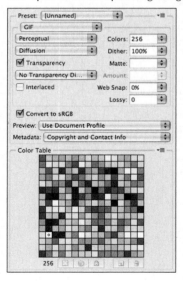

Color reduction

The Color Reduction menu offers several options for generating the color table, or the colors that will make up the final image. The following options are available:

- **Perceptual.** This option generates the color table based on colors that are favored by the human eye.

- **Selective.** This option generates colors similar to the Perceptual option, but works to preserve broad areas of flat colors, as well as "Web-safe" colors — that is, colors that fit within the standard 216-color palette common to both Windows and Mac computers. This option produces the most accurate colors, and is selected by default.

- **Adaptive.** This option produces a color table based on the dominant colors in the image; for example, if the image or slice is predominantly made up of oranges and yellows, the color table also contains these colors.

- **Restrictive (Web).** Choosing this color reduction method uses the standard 216-color, Web-safe palette. These colors are common to Windows and Mac systems, and to all browsers on these systems. Using this option can produce larger file sizes.

- **Custom.** Choosing this option creates a set grouping of colors that doesn't change regardless of the colors that are in the image. Set a number of colors between 2 and 256 using the Colors popup menu, and customize the swatches in the color table by double-clicking on them. If you want to include transparency in your color table, map transparency to one of the color swatches by clicking on the checkerboard icon below the color table.

Once you've settled on the perfect grouping of colors, you can save it using the fly-out menu at the right of the color table. For consistent colors between images, you can also load and apply saved color tables.

The remaining options (Black — White, Grayscale, Mac OS, and Window) are set palettes, and are rarely used.

Dithering options

Because GIF and PNG-8 images can have only 256 colors at most, it's often impossible to display smooth transitions between colors. The result is *banding* — solid areas of color with abrupt transitions between them. *Dithering* refers to the patterns that are applied to create the illusion of smooth transitions between colors, or to simulate colors outside of the current color palette. Figure 24.16 shows an example of a dithering pattern.

NOTE Dithering can also occur if the user's monitor is set to 8-bit color or to a palette of 256 colors. In this case, the browser applies dithering to try and display all the colors in the image. These days, however, most monitors are capable of displaying at least 24-bit color (16.7 million colors), so browser dithering is rarely an issue.

FIGURE 24.16

The two images on top show the banding effect caused by disabling dithering. The images on the bottom show an example of a dithering pattern applied to smooth the transitions between colors.

Four options are available within the Dither menu:

- **No Dither.** Choose this option to forgo applying any dithering pattern. You might need to use this option if reducing file size is critical.

- **Diffusion.** This dithering algorithm attempts to smooth transitions by not producing an obvious pattern, but instead diffusing pixels of two neighboring colors. You can increase the amount of scattering by increasing the percentage in the Dither field on the right. Note that a high dither setting increases file size.

- **Pattern.** This option dithers using a defined pattern of pixels to produce intermediate colors.

- **Noise.** The Noise algorithm dithers by producing random pixels.

The illustration in Figure 24.17 shows a comparison between the three dithering algorithms.

FIGURE 24.17

From left to right, the effect of Diffusion, Pattern, and Noise dithering

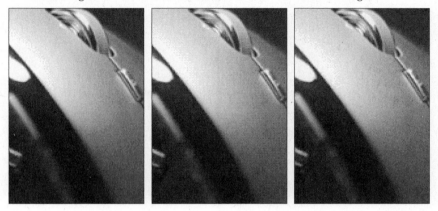

You can also control the percentage of dithering that's applied via the Dither field at the right of the GIF settings area. The default setting of 100 percent means that adjacent colors are blended as much as possible, while 0 percent is the same as disabling dithering altogether. Reduce the dithering percentage by changing the number in the Dither field or click the double arrows at the right and use the slider instead.

Transparency and matte settings

Transparent GIF and PNG-8 files are only capable of displaying either opaque or transparent pixels. In images that use partially transparent pixels (such as images with drop shadows), Photoshop deals with these semitransparent pixels based on the color that you specify for the matte. Optimally, you would select the exact same color for the matte color as the Web page's background. This is easy when your Web page has a solid-color background. Simply click in the Transparency check box to preserve the state of all transparent pixels, and choose a color for the matte from one of the options in the popup menu:

- **None.** Disable the matte color with this option. Pixels are either made completely opaque or transparent depending on their opacity in the original image.

- **Eyedropper.** This option uses the current color displayed in the color swatch at the left of the Save for Web & Devices dialog box. Set this color either by using the Eyedropper tool or by clicking in the color swatch to display the familiar Adobe Color Picker and choosing a color.

- **Black, White, Other.** These options set the matte color to black, white, or a custom color chosen in the Color Picker.

If your Web page has a gradient or patterned background, setting a matte color becomes much more of a challenge, as there will be portions of the matte that don't match the background. In these cases, try to use a PNG if possible, but if the option isn't available, you may have to experiment with selecting a somewhat neutral color and hoping for the best. Figure 24.18 shows some examples of transparency and matting.

Transparency dithering

Transparency dithering works based on the same principle as dithering, except that it relates to the areas of transparent and non-transparent pixels in the image. Enabling transparency dithering applies a pattern to the semitransparent pixels to blend them with their neighbors, and reduces the harsh edges that can result from applying a matte to an image. To enable it, select one of the three dithering algorithms from the popup menu. If using Diffusion Transparency dithering, you can specify an amount with the slider on the right.

FIGURE 24.18

This image shows matting set to a custom color (top right), none (bottom left), and transparency disabled with a colored matte (bottom right). The original image is on the top left.

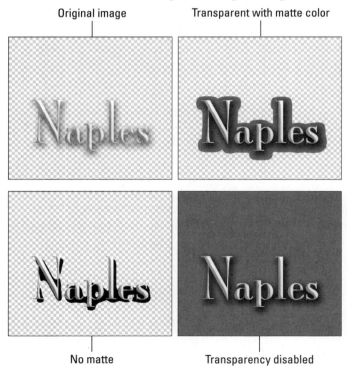

Original image
Transparent with matte color

No matte
Transparency disabled

Interlaced images

Interlacing images displays a low-resolution version of the image in the browser while the image continues downloading. It's intended to reassure your page viewers that something is happening, rather than leaving big rectangular holes in your page where the not-fully downloaded images are supposed to be. However, enabling interlacing results in a larger file size, so it's not used very often these days.

Optimizing JPEG and PNG-24 images

JPEG and PNG-24 are used to compress full-color, 24-bit images for the Web. Their ability to handle 16.7 million colors without significant loss of image quality makes them perfect for photographs and other continuous tone images. In the case of PNG, true transparency is supported, meaning pixels can be fully opaque, fully transparent, or any of 254 different states of semitransparency in between.

Figure 24.19 shows the JPEG and PNG optimization settings found in the Save for Web & Devices dialog box.

FIGURE 24.19

The options for saving JPEG (left) and PNG-24 (right) are fairly simple.

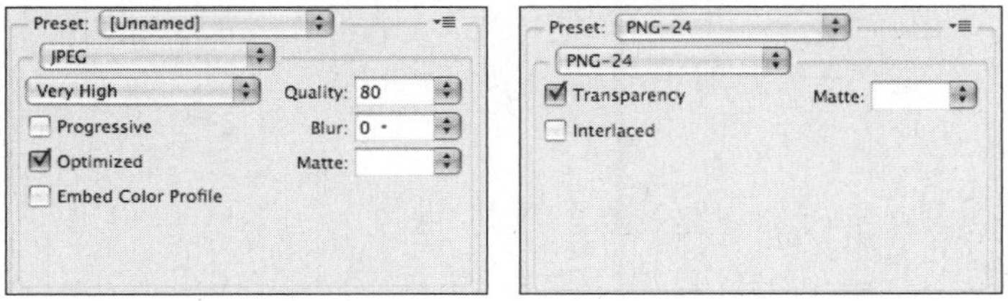

Compressing JPEG images

In the Save for Web & Devices dialog box, JPEG compression is represented on a scale of 0 to 100, with 100 representing no compression (full-quality) and 0 representing maximum compression — and an image so degraded as to be completely unusable. To set the JPEG quality, either use the Compression Quality menu or enter a number using the slider to the right. One of the reasons the JPEG format is so popular is that even at a quality setting of 100, the compressed file size is often significantly smaller than the uncompressed file size, with no visual degradation of the image quality, as demonstrated in Figure 24.20. Note that the file size of the optimized JPEG is only 37K, compared to the original image, which is 175K.

Enabling the Optimized option produces a smaller file size, so it's recommended that you keep this checked. If you're using a color-managed workflow (and you probably should be), you can embed the document's ICC color profile in the optimized JPEG by checking the Embed Color Profile check box.

FIGURE 24.20

The original image is shown on the left, and the optimized JPEG using a compression quality of 100 appears on the right.

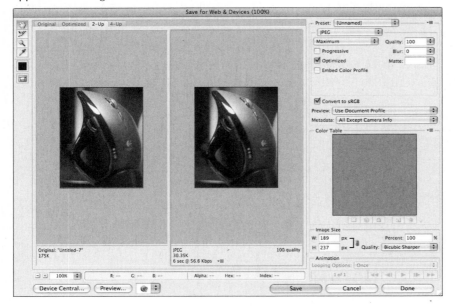

Transparency and matte settings for JPEG and PNG-24

Unlike GIF and both flavors of PNG, JPEG doesn't support transparency. When outputting images that contain transparent pixels as JPEG, the only option is to substitute a solid background color for those transparent pixels. Use the matte options to select what color should be used, as described earlier in the section on GIF and PNG-8.

PNG-24, on the other hand, supports full transparency, so the Matte menu doesn't serve any purpose here. Since most modern browsers can display PNG images, you should opt for this format when saving images that require smooth transparencies. Be sure to preview your images in multiple browsers just to be sure.

Interlaced PNG-24 and progressive JPEG images

As with GIF and PNG-8, PNG-24 offers the option to save an interlaced image, in which case the browser displays a low-resolution version of the image while the rest of the image data downloads. In the case of JPEG, enabling the Progressive check box has the same effect. Again, using these options isn't recommended because it results in larger file sizes.

Zoomify

As you've learned, images must generally be resized to a smaller size and compressed before they are uploaded to the Web. There are cases where you would want to upload images in a larger size than is normally acceptable for the Web, and Photoshop ships with a third-party plug-in called Zoomify that enables you to do just that.

Zoomify converts a high-resolution image into a format that can be zoomed and panned by embedding a scaled-down version of the image in an interactive Flash movie and chopping the original high-resolution image into tiles of varying sizes. As you navigate the image, using the provided controls for zooming and panning, the controller seamlessly swaps in the high-resolution tiles that correspond to the portion of the image you're currently viewing.

Because the tiles are small, and only portions of the image that are currently being viewed are downloaded, this can occur pretty quickly, even on a slow Internet connection. The disadvantage is that you still can't view the highest-resolution version on the screen all at once, but this method is still a good option.

To export an image using the Zoomify plug-in, choose File ➪ Export ➪ Zoomify. The resulting dialog box is shown in Figure 24.21. Here's what you need to know about the plug-in:

FIGURE 24.21

The Zoomify Export dialog box

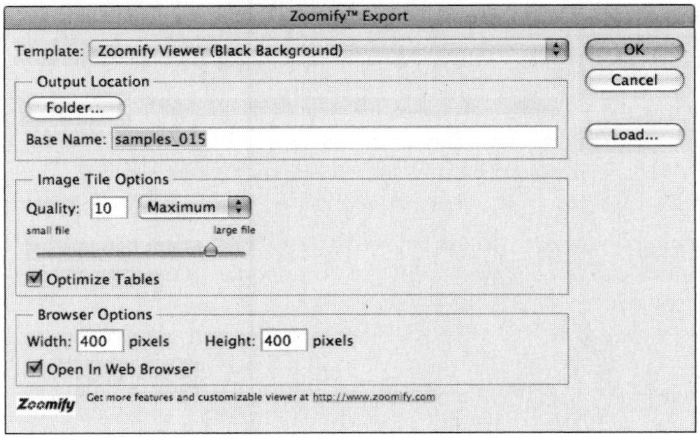

- **Template.** Select a template from the six available options to customize the appearance of the exported HTML page in which the image will be embedded.
- **Folder.** Choose an output location for the HTML, the tiled image, and other associated files by clicking the Folder button and navigating to a suitable place on your hard drive.

- **Image Tile Options.** Enter a level of JPEG compression for each image tile that's generated. This compression scale works on a level of 1 to 12, with 12 being the highest quality available.

- **Browser Options.** Use these settings to specify the dimensions of the resulting image and controller. Try to stick to widths bigger than 400 pixels to make sure there's enough room for the Zoomify navigation controls.

Click OK to export the files. If the Open In Web Browser check box is checked, the exported image is opened in a browser window for you to preview. If you're happy with the way it looks, you can upload the HTML and associated files to a Web server for viewing on the Internet.

Creating a Web Banner

Advertising is one of the biggest money-makers on the Internet. Sure, many people go out of their way to ignore those annoying banners that often surround the content on Web pages, but the fact remains, they do bring traffic to the advertisers' sites, and for that reason, they'll keep paying ad agencies to produce them. These days, most Web ads are created in Flash — after all, Flash supports interactivity and can add all sorts of bells and whistles that entertain the user while benefiting the advertiser. But every Flash Web ad that gets delivered to a publisher's site is accompanied by an animated backup GIF version just in case. That said, making an animated Web banner is a useful thing to know how to do, and you'll learn how in this section.

There are a couple things you should keep in mind when creating Web banners:

- **File-size is critical.** Web publishers (such as Yahoo!, the *New York Times*, iVillage.com, and about a billion others) normally restrict the size of the ads on their sites, because it would make a terrible experience for visitors if they had to wait longer than expected for the site to load due to bloated ads. A common file-size limit for animated GIF images is 30 kilobytes. Some common file-size killers include photography, gradients, too many frames of animation, and dramatic changes between one frame of the banner and the next.

- **The simplest way to create frame-by-frame animation is to create a storyboard in Photoshop.** Create a layer group that corresponds to the visual layout of each frame of animation, then when your layout is finalized and it's time to create the animation, you can simply enable or disable the visibility of the layer group on each frame.

In this example, the client is the fictional Gadgetland site. They want a banner that promotes their great deals on wireless peripherals. We'll be careful to maintain a consistent look with their Web site by using similar colors and fonts, and we'll include a strong call to action to encourage the user to click on the Web site and take advantage of those great deals. We'll accomplish this in three frames of animation, and within the standard file-size limit of 30K.

Creating an animated banner

The steps below outline the process of creating a Web banner:

1. **Create a new document.** The IAB (Interactive Advertising Bureau), which is a group that sets standards for the online advertising industry, has come up with some default sizes for different ad units. You'll see some of these default sizes saved as presets in Photoshop's New Document dialog box.

2. **Choose Web from the Preset menu, select Medium Rectangle from the Size menu, and click OK.**

3. **Lay out the first frame of your banner.** Figure 24.22 shows the layout for the first frame of the Gadgetland banner. In direct contradiction to my own advice, I snuck a small-ish photographic image in there, because I plan to restrict the animation to only three frames, and everything else in the ad is pretty simple by comparison.

FIGURE 24.22

The first frame of my animated banner

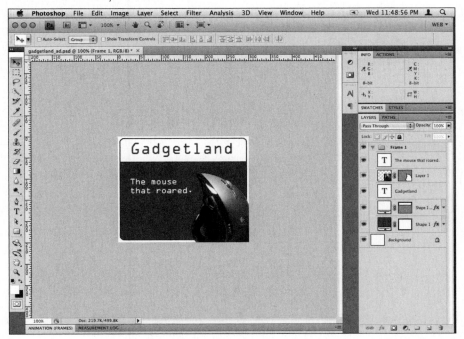

4. **Once the layout is complete, group all the layers that comprise the first frame by Shift+selecting them in the Layers panel and pressing Ctrl+G/⌘+G.** To keep things neat, double-click the layer group's name and rename it Frame 1.

5. **Duplicate the Frame 1 group, and modify it to make the second frame layout.** In Figure 24.23, you'll see that I added a line of text. Rename the layer group Frame 2.

FIGURE 24.23

Frame 2 of my animated banner features an additional line of text, keeping the changes between frames one and two to a minimum.

6. **Repeat step 5 for the third frame of animation.** In Figure 24.24, you'll see that for this frame, I've removed the first two lines of text and added a call to action, prompting the viewer to visit the Gadgetland site.

7. **To begin animating the banner, open the Animation panel by choosing it from the Window menu.** By default, the Animation panel opens in Timeline mode, which is useful for editing video (see Chapter 26 for more coverage).

FIGURE 24.24

The layout for the final frame of the animation

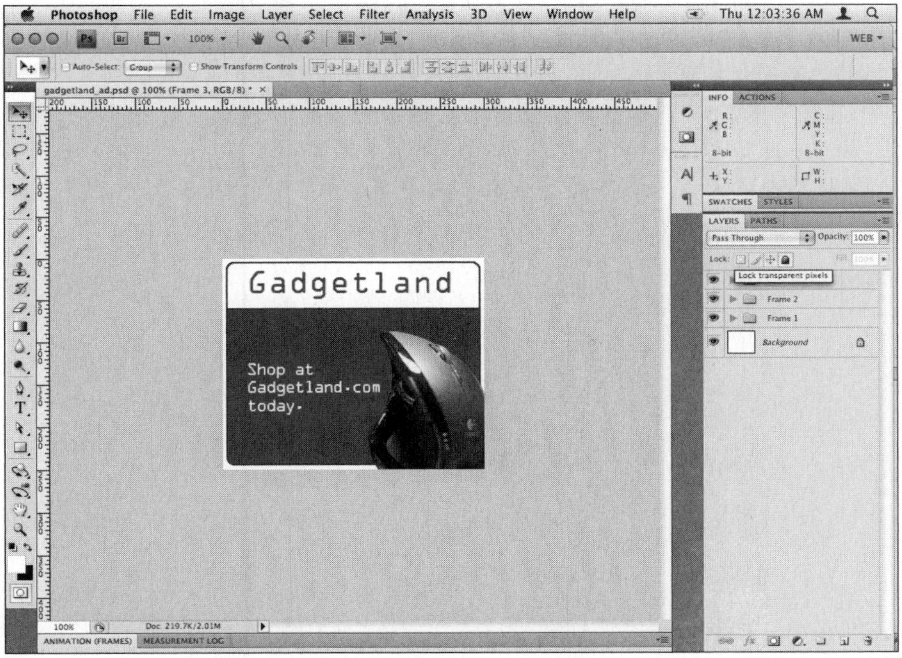

8. **For frame-based animation, click the icon at the bottom-right corner of the panel to switch it to Frame mode.** You should already have one frame of animation visible in the panel, reflecting the current state of your document.

9. Turn off the visibility of Frames 2 and 3 so that the thumbnail of the first frame in the Animation panel matches the content of the first frame that you laid out (see Figure 24.25).

10. To add a delay so your viewer can read the message text, click the Delay popup at the bottom of the first frame's thumbnail in the Animation panel. It should currently read 0 sec., indicating that the banner will not pause on the first frame before advancing to the next frame — which definitely won't be readable for your viewers. Choose 2 seconds from the presets in the Delay menu.

FIGURE 24.25

The first frame of animation is now set up correctly in the Animation panel.

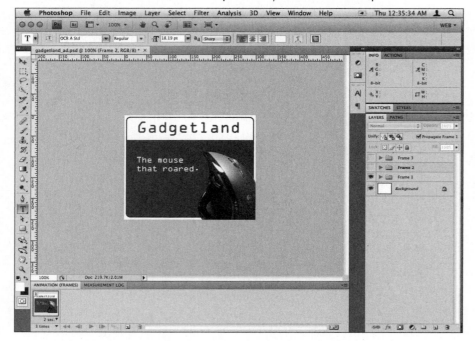

11. **Duplicate the current frame by clicking the icon that looks like the corner of a piece of paper at the bottom of the Animation panel.** In the Layers panel, make sure that the Frame 2 layer group is the only one that's visible (see Figure 24.26).

    Note that when you duplicated the first frame, the delay settings were maintained. Change the delay if necessary to maintain readability and the pace of the animation. You can preview the animation by clicking the play button at the bottom of the Animation panel.

12. **To create the final frame of animation, duplicate the second frame in the Animation panel as described in the previous step, and turn off all but the Frame 3 layer group in the Layers panel.** By default, the animation should play once and then stop, but you can specify how many times the animation should play by setting the looping options.

FIGURE 24.26

Frame 2 of the animation is enabled.

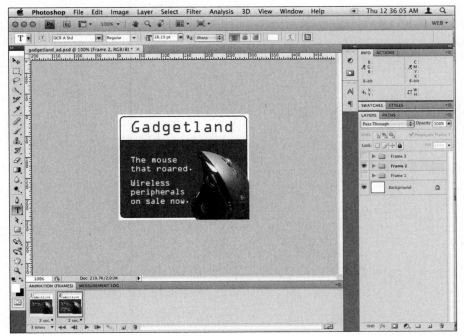

13. **Click the popup menu at the bottom left of the Animation panel, and select Once to have the animation play once, select 3 Times to loop through three times and then stop, or select Forever to have the animation loop continuously.** You can select Other to enter a set number of times that the animation should play. Most site publishers don't like to have animations flashing continuously because it's distracting to the site's visitors, so they require that an animation only play a maximum of three times. With that in mind, set your looping options to 3 Times (see Figure 24.27).

FIGURE 24.27

The final three-frame animation setup is complete in the Animation panel.

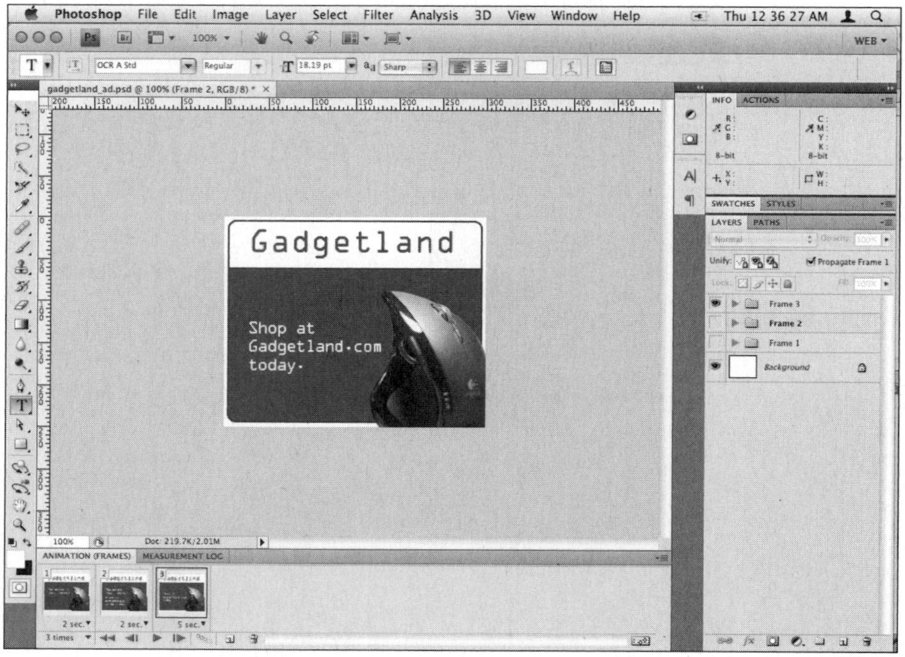

14. **Press Ctrl+Alt+Shift+S/⌘+Option+Shift+S) to open the Save for Web & Devices dialog box to set your optimization settings (see Figure 24.28).** Keep an eye on the file size at the bottom of the dialog box. In my example, the file size is at a perfectly respectable 18.67K even with my colors set to the maximum value of 256. Excellent — that means I don't have to do anything. If the file size were higher than my target 30K, I would have had to start reducing colors to bring it within the limit.

FIGURE 24.28

The banner's optimization settings in the Save for Web & Devices dialog box

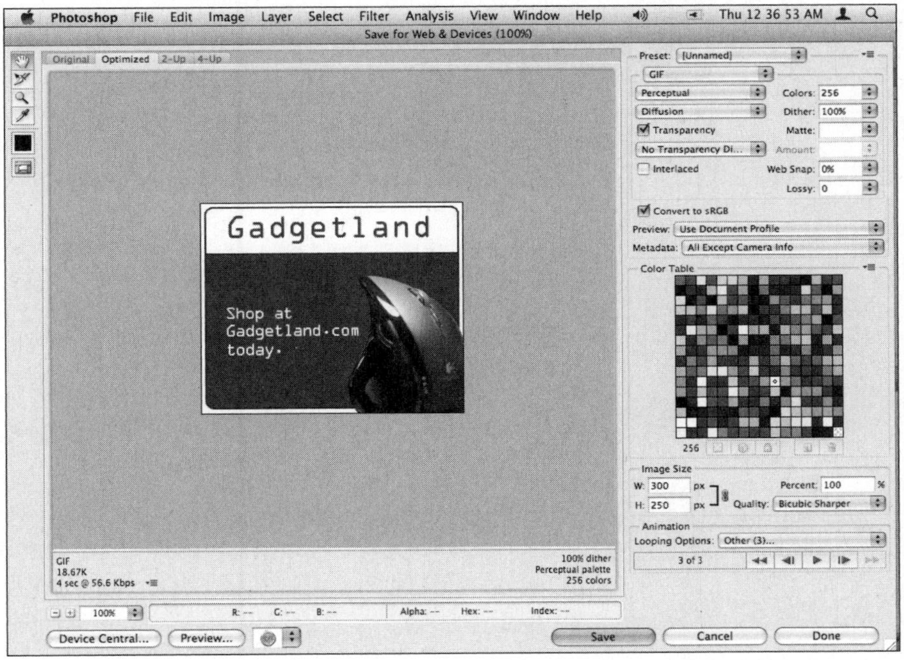

15. **To preview the animation in a Web browser, press the Preview button at the bottom of the dialog box (see Figure 24.29).** Pay attention to the animation's pacing — read the text aloud to make sure you have enough time to view the banner's messaging. Go back and adjust the delay if necessary. Once you're happy with the animation, press Save to save your optimized animation.

FIGURE 24.29

The browser preview of the animation offers a plethora of information, including a summary of the optimization settings.

If this ad were being produced for an actual client, it would now be ready for client approval and then to be shipped off to the various sites that have been selected for the campaign. This particular example is exceedingly simple, but you should now have some understanding of how to create a simple animation using Photoshop.

Using Tweens

Tweening is based on traditional animation techniques, and it involves generating a transition between two states of animation. To return to the example used in the previous section, given that I'm well within my file-size limit, I could start experimenting with using a tween to fade those lines of text in and out.

To use the Tween command, follow these steps:

1. **Click on its icon at the bottom of the Animation panel (it looks like a series of fading squares) to display the dialog box shown in Figure 24.30.** The Tween command allows you to transition between position, transparency, or layer styles, meaning you could use a tween to move an object across the screen, fade it in or out, or make a drop shadow or glow grow over time.

FIGURE 24.30

The Tween feature allows you to tween the position, opacity, and layer style of any layer.

Tween
Tween With: Next Frame ⇕   OK
Frames to Add: 5   Cancel
Layers
⦿ All Layers
○ Selected Layers
Parameters
☑ Position
☑ Opacity
☑ Effects

2. **To set the duration of the tween, specify how many frames should be added between your starting frame and the end frame of the transition.**

3. **To fade the line of text in, duplicate the second frame of animation by clicking the Duplicate Selected Frame button.** Now you have two identical frames side by side in the Animation Panel, both with that second line of text visible.

4. **Select Frame 2 in the Animation panel and set the opacity of your second line of text to 0.**

5. **Click the Tween button.** I chose to add two frames (remember, I still had the final file size of my animation in mind), and made sure to select Next Frame from the Tween With menu.

6. **Click OK to produce the updated Animation panel shown in Figure 24.31, which now has a total of six frames.**

FIGURE 24.31

The animation now has two transition frames, over the course of which the text gradually becomes more opaque.

If you select either of the two transition frames that were added by the Tween command, and then click on the layer for that line of text that was just tweened, you'll notice that its opacity setting gradually increases over the duration of the transition.

7. **The last step is to change the timing of the transition frames, as by default, each transition frame picked up the 2-second duration of the frame you started your tween from.** Shift+select both frames and click on the duration to change that to a duration of 0.1 seconds, which results in a nice fluid fade (see Figure 24.32).

FIGURE 24.32

The final frames of my animation

Returning to the Save for Web & Devices dialog box, I noticed that my animation jumped up in file size a bit to 22.89K, which is still under the limit. I can now send it out to a very happy client.

Creating a Web Page

There are many fine, free, Web-publishing tools, but if you're reading this chapter, the assumption can be made that you're at least considering taking the do-it-yourself approach to creating a Web site from scratch. Good for you! This section briefly outlines the process behind planning, designing, and exporting an optimized Web page. Use the following steps to guide you in creating your own page:

1. **Determine the purpose of your site, and sketch out its basic layout.** In this example, I'm making a personal Web page that features some of my photography and a little bit of information about myself. Ultimately, the site will be very simple, and won't feature any complex functionality like e-commerce.

   Following the principles outlined earlier in this chapter, I've come up with a sketch of what my site's structure will look like. As shown in Figure 24.33, I've also developed that sketch into what's called a *wireframe* — a simple schematic representation of my Web page that denotes its main structural parts. I also worked out the basic navigational structure of my site, deciding that it will have a total of four pages, including the homepage.

2. **Design the look and feel of your site.** This is the art direction phase of creating the site, and, for many, it's also the hardest — and most subjective — part of the process. Be prepared to spend some time picking out color schemes, experimenting with type treatments, and deciding on imagery to use. It's also a good idea to use books, magazines, and other Web sites as visual references and inspiration for your own designs (just as long as you're not copying designs wholesale).

FIGURE 24.33

Wireframes help to visualize how the elements of a Web page will fit together structurally.

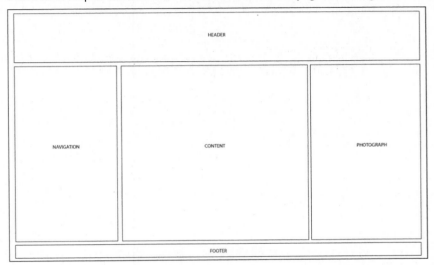

Using other sites as reference (and after lots of trial and error), I came up with some color combinations and button treatments I liked. I then created the various header, footer, and button elements resulting in the final design comp shown in Figure 24.34. All the elements that comprise this design are simple shapes created with the Shape tool, a few layer styles, and a couple of type layers.

You may have noticed that the text in my site is in Latin — that's not because I'm some kind of language scholar. Using dummy text (also called *lorem ipsum* text, or "Greeking") is a common practice that designers use while they are finalizing art direction. The intention is that the client doesn't get hung up on reading and pointing out changes to the text, but rather stays focused on approving the visuals. Once the visuals are locked down and approved, the dummy text comes out and is replaced with the real text that will be used on the final design.

TIP It's often useful to set up a grid against which to create the layout for your Web page. To show the grid in Photoshop, choose View➪ Show➪ Grid, or click the View Extras button on the Application Bar. To change the size of the grid's divisions, press Ctrl+K/⌘+K followed by Ctrl+8/⌘+8 to view and change the Units and Rulers settings.

FIGURE 24.34

My final site design comp. Only when the design is finalized do I actually begin work on getting the pieces ready to be exported for Web publishing.

3. **Use the Slice tool to start dividing the site into its distinct elements for the final version that will be output to the Web.** Using a combination of the Slice tool and the New Layer Based Slice command, I created slices for the main elements of my Web page — the header and footer, each navigation button, the text, and the photograph. Photoshop filled in the rest of my page with auto slices. Figure 24.35 shows what my sliced page looks like. Remember, to temporarily hide the auto slices, click the Hide Auto Slices button in the Slice tool's Options Bar.

4. **Edit the slice options.** For the sake of neatness, and to make it easy on yourself if you ever decide to open the final HTML document for this page and edit it manually using Dreamweaver, you should open the Slice Options window for each slice you created, and change the names of the slices to something more intuitive than "website_design_03."

    Figure 24.36 shows the Slice Options dialog box for my Web page's header slice. You'll notice that I entered the Web site's address as the link for the site's header, which is common practice. I also filled in the remaining options in the dialog box.

5. **Export the final page using Save for Web & Devices.** Choose File ➪ Save for Web & Devices and specify the optimization settings for each slice. Remember, if you need to make last-minute changes to any slice options, simply double-click the slice with the Slice Select tool active. Also, remember to take a look at how your site will appear in various Web browsers by using the Preview button.

FIGURE 24.35

My final sliced layout, ready to be optimized and exported for Web publishing

FIGURE 24.36

The filled-in Slice Options dialog box for my Web page's header slice

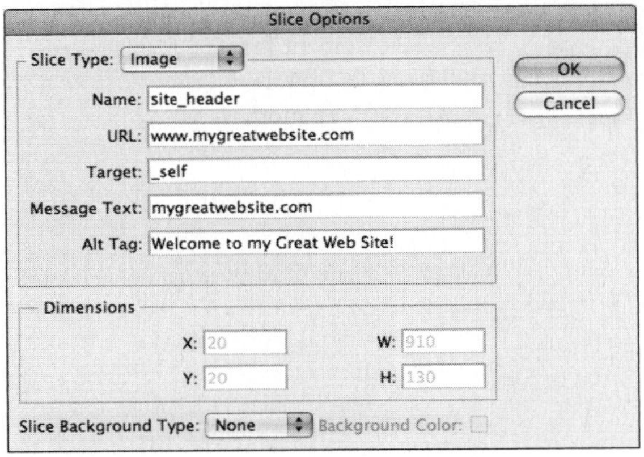

6. **When everything looks good, click Save and use the Format menu to choose to export both images and HTML.** Since the names of all the images that are saved are determined by the values in the Slice Options dialog box, the filename you enter in the Save As field refers to the HTML file. Navigate to an appropriate location on your hard drive, and click Save. By default, the images are all saved in a folder called "images" alongside your HTML file.

7. **To view the Web page in a browser, simply drag the HTML page to an open browser window.** To publish the Web page so that it's accessible on the Internet, you'll have to use an FTP (File Transfer Protocol) program to upload the final files to a Web server.

There you have it. You should have a nice, working Web page, which you can use as a basis for the remaining pages on your site. If you do add pages, it's a good idea to set up all the linkable buttons that will appear globally on the first page, before creating the subpages.

Summary

This chapter covered many aspects of Web publishing. You learned about Web publishing workflows and how Photoshop is used alongside programs such as Dreamweaver to create Web content. You also learned about the image formats used on the Web and how to optimize them using the Save for Web & Devices dialog box. You saw how slices can be used to divide a Web page layout into distinct regions and be exported as HTML tables. You learned how to export large, high-resolution images using the Zoomify plug-in. Finally, you examined the steps involved in creating a typical Web banner and a simple Web page.

Chapter 25

Digital Workflow Overview and Automating Processes

The word workflow generally refers to a sequence of steps or processes that one should follow in order to create high-quality digital photographs or artwork. There are many types of workflows, ranging from the very specific to the very general. For example, there are color workflows, intended to carefully manage the color quality of an image from its inception to final printing and screen output. There are also Web workflows, which can refer to optimizing a finished image for the Web or creating an entire Web site design within Photoshop.

The key point to remember is that workflow is about process: using the right tools (often in a specific sequence) to get the best possible result.

The first part of this chapter provides a high-level overview of a typical digital photography workflow, and includes components of other workflows such as color management, image retouching, and Web optimization. The second part of this chapter deals with functions and features that can make parts of your Photoshop workflow more efficient.

It is not uncommon for many Photoshop users to find themselves in situations where they must perform the same task repeatedly on many images. Doing so manually can quickly become so time-intensive that you fall behind schedule. Given that scenario, you'll see how Actions, Droplets, Scripts, and the Photoshop Image Processor can help you stay on track!

IN THIS CHAPTER

Digital workflow overview

Automating Photoshop processes

Digital Workflow Overview

The first part of this chapter focuses on different things you can do throughout the entire Photoshop workflow to get better results from your images, stay better organized, and hopefully be as efficient as possible. The topics covered include Adobe Camera Raw (ACR), workflow setup, file naming and saving tips, general editing sequence, leveraging layers and edit history, Web-related workflow features, general printing tips, and more.

Adobe Camera Raw

One of the most important things you can do in ACR is set the Workflow Options (Figure 25.1) to match your desired output type before opening your image in Photoshop and saving it.

FIGURE 25.1

Use the ACR Workflow Options to define your file's color space, bit depth, size, and resolution. The settings shown here reflect a file that is intended for minimal retouching and quick output to the Web.

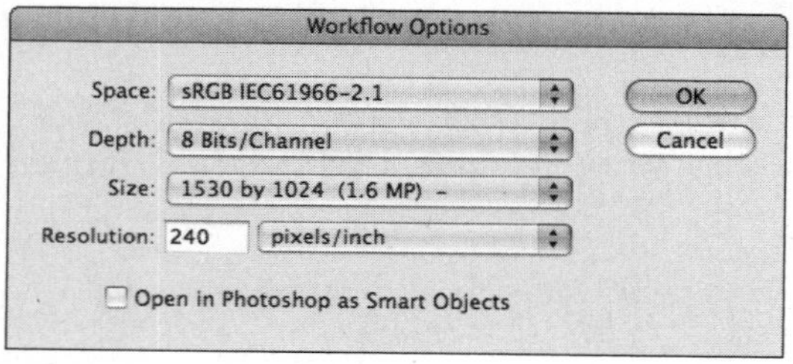

> **TIP**   To open the Workflow Options dialog box, click on the blue "dialog link" near the bottom of the ACR window. The link will list whatever the current settings are. For example: "Adobe RGB (1998); 8-bit; 3000x2008 (6 MP); 240 ppi."

If you choose to ignore your workflow options, you may end up tagging your document with a color profile that does not match your working RGB space in Photoshop, thus requiring extra conversions later. You can also hurt your cause by rendering your image out of ACR with the wrong bit-depth, depending on what your goals are.

For images that require minimal retouching that are headed to the Web, applying a color space of sRGB and a depth of 8 bits can save you extra steps later. Depending on the situation, it may also make sense to reduce the Size setting by choosing smaller pixel dimensions. For cameras with 8+ megapixels, even the smallest ACR size setting is likely to be larger than your final Web image, so you may have to resize it again later with the Photoshop Image Size command.

For pictures that require significant retouching or that may be output to multiple mediums (inkjet, Web, or CMYK), try the Adobe RGB 1998 color space and a depth of 16 bits. These two settings give you a wider color gamut than sRGB to leverage while editing, as well as more tonal data, respectively. Both can help eliminate clipping, banding, and other unwanted side effects that may occur if you really need to push your Curves or other tonal and color manipulation functions.

Use ColorMatch RGB when you are working with third parties and are unsure of which color spaces they are utilizing in their workflow, or if you are unsure of their color management policies.

ProPhoto RGB is best used when the file in question will never leave your control and you want to ensure that no colors recorded by your camera are lost in editing. HDR imaging is one example of when you can benefit from using the ProPhoto color space, as well as when creating archival quality prints. Even when using the highest-quality large format inkjet systems, some colors may be lost when printing a ProPhoto file. It is an enormous color space that expands even beyond the limits of human perception.

CROSS-REF ProPhoto RGB is not a great choice for images that are destined primarily for a CMYK press, as many colors can be lost during the profile conversion process.

Histogram highlight and shadow clipping previews

Another important benefit you can provide to your images while using ACR is to pay attention to the histogram's Clipping previews, particularly as you move any of the following sliders:

TIP You can activate the Clipping previews for image Highlights and Shadows by clicking the two small triangles (top-left and -right corners of the Histogram). When you do this, you will see that any part of your image that approaches pure white or black is given a false color overlay (such as bright red or yellow) to let you know that you are close to clipping a highlight or shadow region.

- Temperature
- Tint
- Exposure
- Recovery
- Fill Light
- Blacks
- Brightness
- Contrast

Clipping highlight or shadow regions in your image to pure white or black (respectively) is generally not a desirable thing and should be avoided if possible to maintain the widest tonal range possible. The wider range you are able to maintain, the more you also reduce the likelihood of clipping highlights or shadows later on, when editing with Photoshop's Levels or Curves function.

Also with respect to the Histogram, keep in mind the kinds of edits you will be making after ACR, and whether those edits may require more color data being present in a particular tonal region. The Camera Raw histogram provides feedback not only on highlight and shadow values in your image, but also on the relative distribution of primary and secondary color data throughout the tonal range. For example, you can determine whether most of the blues in your image fall within the highlights, mid-tones, or shadow regions. The same is true of red, green, yellow, and cyan tones. There is a lot of information about your image's color and tonal character in the ACR histogram, so it's to your advantage to make use of it whenever you can!

Saving ACR presets

There are a couple of great time-savers when using ACR, and one of these is the ability to save an entire edit session as a preset so you can later apply that same set of corrections to very similar images. Taking an extra moment to save and carefully name an ACR preset can save you hours as you work through your other selected shots in ACR. For more information on presets in the Camera Raw environment, see Chapter 4.

Synchronize

The other great time-saver in ACR is the Synchronize function. When you open multiple RAW files into a single ACR session, if the files are very similar in their tonal properties and color characteristics (and you intend the same look for each), you can Select All, click the Synchronize button, and make sure that any edits you make to the main preview image are made to all images when they are saved or output to Photoshop.

Just a minute or two of setup time with Synchronize can save you many hours of effort. Using a combination of Synchronize and presets can save you even more time!

Noise reduction and sharpening

ACR can both reduce camera noise levels and sharpen your digital photos, before you open them in Photoshop (Figure 25.2).

Whether you should use these features at the start of your workflow depends on image quality and whether you use third-party plug-ins such as Noiseware, Noise Ninja, or Photokit Sharpener as part of your workflow.

These plug-ins are often very effective at what they do. It may not be necessary to perform noise reduction or sharpening in ACR if your original images look clean and crisp when viewed at 100 percent magnification, but you can employ these more powerful plug-ins later should you need them.

Photoshop Workflow Setup

Before you begin making all your post-ACR edits in Photoshop, it's a good idea take a few minutes to set things up in ways that make important features more accessible and speed up the editing process. While there are no absolutes — every experienced Photoshop user has a unique combination of settings he or she prefers — it's important to consider these options before you begin.

Preferences — General

The most important items to consider within the General section of Photoshop's Preferences dialog box are the default Image Interpolation options and the History Log options.

For Image Interpolation, if you often find that you need to reduce the size of your images while editing, choose Bicubic Sharper as your default. If you often find that you need to increase the size of your images, choose Bicubic Smoother as your default.

The ACR Sharpening and Noise Reduction sliders can produce a crisper and clearer image to use as a foundation for subsequent Photoshop edits.

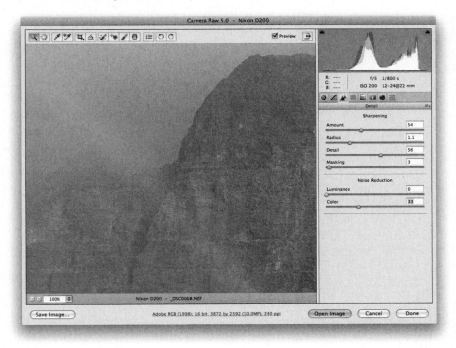

Adobe realized that it's easy to overlook which resizing algorithm is active when you open the Image Size dialog box, thereby causing some users to resize with the wrong algorithm by mistake. This preference gives you the choice ahead of time so fewer instances occur where you must undo an image size operation in order to set the correct algorithm and re-apply the image size operation.

The History Log is a preference that is often overlooked; however, it can be useful in situations in which you (or someone else working on the same image) need to revisit the changes made to a given image. Adding history tracking to your documents can provide you with information about the tools and settings used to make those changes. Many professionals choose to save their history settings to metadata (no extra files to track), and do so using the Detailed setting under Edit Log Items.

Preferences — File Handling

Depending on workflow type and intended output, the settings under File Compatibility (Figure 25.3) and Version Cue vary for most Photoshop users. One thing that doesn't vary is that all users must take steps to ensure their computers can make sense of the Photoshop files they create and share with others. For that reason it's important to select and click (to activate) the following File Saving Options:

- Image Previews — Always Save
- Icon
- Macintosh Thumbnail
- Windows Thumbnail
- Append File Extension — Always
- Use Lower Case

FIGURE 25.3

Choose OS-friendly settings for the Photoshop File Saving Options. .

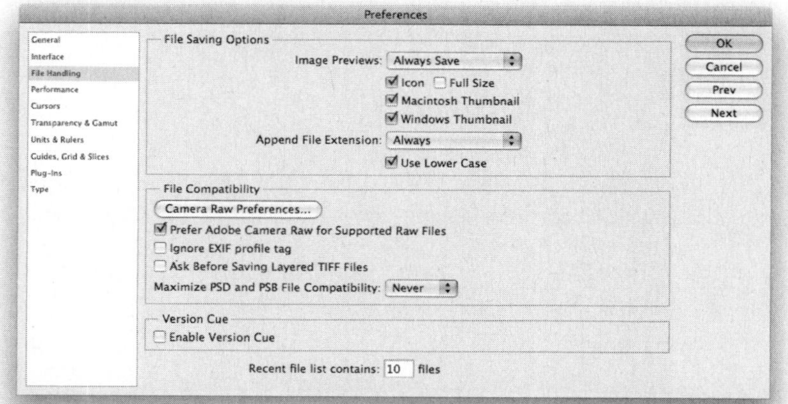

Preferences — Performance

Some significant changes have been added to Photoshop CS4 in the way images can be displayed and manipulated on your screen. The Rotate Preview functionality in particular makes brushing operations a more efficient process, as it alleviates the common reflex of turning your head in order to orient your eyes to a specific part of the image that is situated at an odd angle (such as a diagonal). This feature ensures the image preview can be oriented to your eyes, not the other way around.

Additionally, there are some long-standing practices you should try to adhere to as much as your computer hardware and budget allow for. Within the Performance section of Photoshop's Preferences dialog box (see Figure 25.4), keep the following items in mind:

FIGURE 25.4

Performance preferences in Photoshop can have a big impact on the responsiveness of your edits and on how fluidly you can view and manipulate your image on-screen.

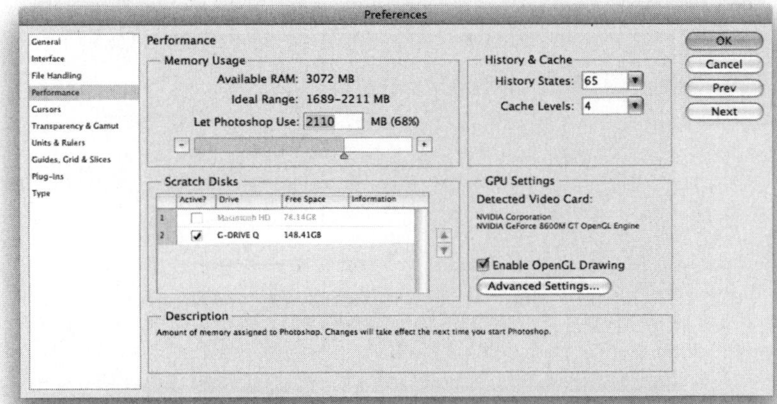

- **Memory Usage.** The single most important Photoshop performance variable after processor speed is memory. The more memory (or RAM) you have that you can dedicate directly to Photoshop, the better off you'll be. Generally it's a good idea to set Memory Usage to a value between about 55 and 70 percent. Use the Ideal Range indicator to make your machine-specific assessment.

- **History & Cache.** Increasing the number of History States means more of your assigned RAM gets used up more quickly, but many people like to operate between roughly 50 and 100 History States. Some people even go well beyond that. If you have plenty of memory, it can be a good idea to use a higher value. This is especially true if your retouching consists of large numbers of repetitive brush strokes; such workflows can quickly use up your available History States.

  Cache levels should generally remain at their default value.

- **Scratch Disks.** If your computer has an extra internal hard drive that is empty or an external FireWire or USB 2 hard drive that is empty, using it as a Photoshop scratch disk will greatly improve performance. This is probably the most often overlooked improvement for newcomers, but it is very important in speeding up many operations.

- **GPU Settings.** If available, clicking in the Enable OpenGL Drawing check box gives you access to some very useful new features in Photoshop CS4, such as the ability to rotate your image preview on-the-fly, zoom and pan over a highly magnified document, and others. If you have the option, activate this setting.

> **TIP** If you are working with a Mac and have 5 gigabytes or more of RAM installed, and you do not plan to use other RAM-hungry apps concurrently with Photoshop, you can safely move the slider to 100 percent, thereby giving Photoshop the maximum possible allocation on a Mac (3 gigabytes, or roughly 3,072MB). For PCs running a 64-bit operating system, there is no longer a maximum RAM limit for Photoshop, so you can assign even more than 3 gigabytes to Photoshop if you need to.

Color management considerations

It is often assumed that as a Photoshop user, you are safe using the default color settings Adobe has provided for you in the Color Settings dialog box. This is not always the case. There are two situations where you might consider making a few changes and saving your new collection of color settings as your new default.

If you are using ACR as part of your workflow and understand the basic workflow options, you should use those as the basis for your Photoshop color settings on the RGB side of things. For example, if you often output files using the Adobe RGB 1998 color space from ACR, it makes sense to choose Adobe RGB as your default RGB working space in the Color Settings dialog box. Leaving the CMYK settings as-is will not result in problems for most users.

The second consideration is handling missing or mismatched profiles. Since the settings you use may be different from the settings other people you work with use, it makes sense to set your Profile Mismatches and Missing Profiles settings to Ask, as shown in Figure 25.5.

This way if you open or attempt to paste image data with a missing profile or a profile that does not match your default working space, you are given options for how to manage that document or content before continuing.

Keyboard shortcuts and menus

Remembering all of Photoshop's keyboard shortcuts (Figure 25.6) can be daunting. The beauty of shortcuts is that they can save you time, but there are a lot of them! However, if you take a few moments to customize these time-savers, using and remembering your most important shortcuts becomes much easier.

For example, people who rarely use the Last Filter command (pressing Ctrl+F, ⌘+F on a Mac) might instead use that same shortcut for the Flatten Layers command, which is something used in almost every workflow. Similarly, if there are menu options you rarely use, take the time to hide them during your initial setup so your interface is personalized and more streamlined to your workflow.

FIGURE 25.5

The Color Settings dialog box with all options displayed

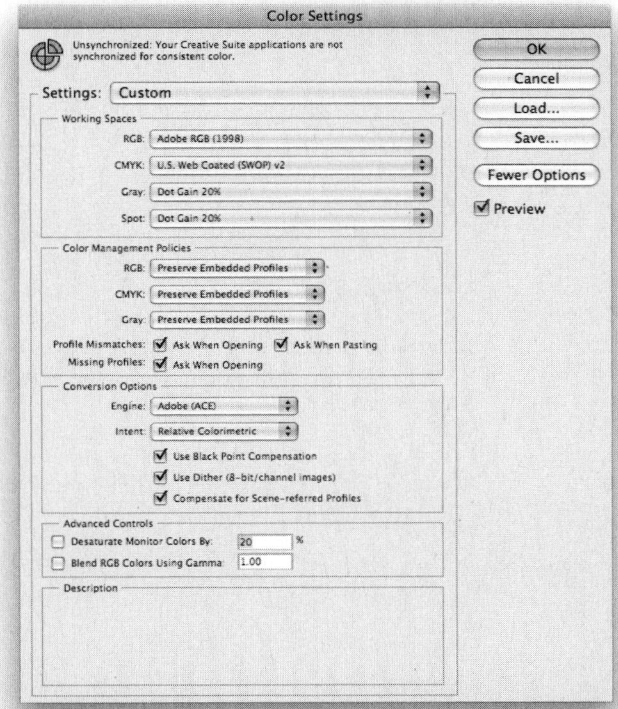

Custom workspaces

Once you've worked your way around the new Photoshop CS4 user interface and experimented with the default workspace configurations, try moving things around. Set up the panels that you need most along the right edge (or on a second monitor). This will be your main panel dock.

Next, drag and drop a few important but less frequently used panels to the left of your main panel dock and resize them as icons. This should maximize the room you have to operate and also speed your workflow, as you won't have to search the Window menu for secondary panels.

FIGURE 25.6

Use the Keyboard Shortcuts and Menus dialog box to make things more accessible to your personal work style.

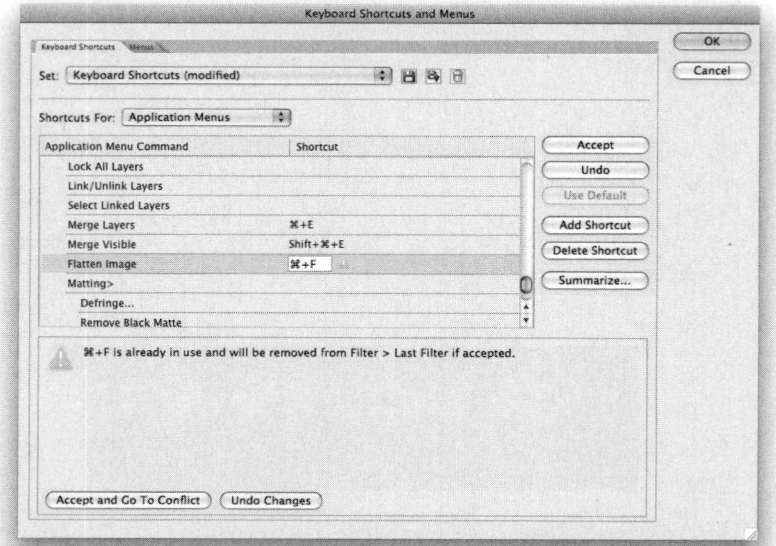

When you've got everything the way you like it, save that workspace under a new name. This allows you to select the original workspace you used and reset it, so that you again have access to that default option. Custom workspaces are one of the very best ways to streamline your Photoshop experience. Don't forget to include your custom keyboard shortcuts and menu visibility options (Figure 25.7)!

FIGURE 25.7

Saving custom keyboard shortcuts and menu visibility settings with a new workspace

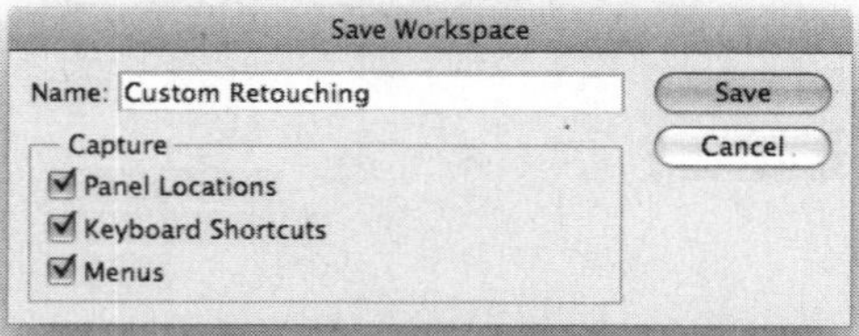

File saving and naming tips

Staying organized is also very important for any Photoshop workflow. Two commonly overlooked aspects of staying organized are making sure you've named your files appropriately and using the correct file format for your desired workflow and output types. All names and formats are not created equal, so take the time to find out which ones work best for your purposes. Otherwise you may find yourself with different files that have similar names, or worse, multiple versions of the same file because you had to "Save As" multiple times after discovering you started with the wrong format.

Important file formats

There are many file format options when working with Photoshop, but generally, for each type of workflow, there are a few favorites among seasoned pros. Table 25.1 gives examples of some common workflows and some of the more popular formats used in those scenarios.

TABLE 25.1

Common Workflow Formats

Workflow	Popular Formats
Photo Editing	Photoshop (.psd); TIFF (.tif)
Graphic Design	Photoshop (.psd); EPS (.eps)
Video	Photoshop (.psd); Targa (.tga)
HDR Imaging	Photoshop (.psd); Radiance (.hdr); OpenEXR (.exr); TIFF (.tif)

See any patterns emerging? The reason many Photoshop professionals save the majority of their work in the native Photoshop Document (PSD) format stems from its versatility and uncompressed, non-destructive qualities. With huge hard drives now commonly holding hundreds of gigabytes and even terabytes, there is little reason to be concerned about the slightly larger file size of PSD files in most circumstances. When in doubt, save to PSD.

Note that if you are frequently using Photoshop document files and also are working with people who use older versions of Photoshop, setting the Maximize PSD and PSB File Compatibility menu to Always in Photoshop preferences (File Handling) can be a good way to avoid problems.

Naming your files

Another important consideration is how to name your Photoshop files. It is often useful to not only mention the subject in the filename, but also the file's purpose or a characteristic that sets it apart from other similar images you have created and stored on your hard drive.

For example, when creating multiple versions of an image, many photographers use names that help them remember how the document is used when they encounter it later in file searches. The alphanumeric characters in the middle of the name denote the bit depth and presence or absence of layers (see Table 25.2). So, for example, "16bL" means the document is saved as a 16-bit file, with layers intact. "8bF" means the file is saved in 8-bit and is flattened, having only a background layer.

TABLE 25.2

File Name Examples

File Purpose	File Name
Master edit version	Oceantraveler_16bL_Edits.psd
Version for prepress	Oceantraveler_8bF_Press.psd
Version for AfterEffects	Oceantraveler_8bL_AEffects.psd

General workflow sequence

When editing your digital photographs, there are different workflow paths that you can take to wind up with a great result. However, certain tasks are generally carried out before others to ensure image data integrity and maximum quality. These are the cornerstones common to most picture-editing sessions, and they are often applied in the following order:

1. **ACR processing (including initial noise reduction and sharpening)**
2. **Additional Noise reduction (if needed)**
3. **Levels/Curves/Shadow-Highlight localized tonal corrections**
4. **Localized color corrections**
5. **Clone/Heal/Patch brushed corrections**
6. **Perspective corrections**
7. **Sharpening**
8. **Printing/output for video, Web, or 3-D**

The most important concept to note among this list of general steps is that noise reduction should be performed early in the process to avoid duplicating regions of noise or exacerbating noise when making tonal or color corrections. Following that same logic, global sharpening is often applied at the very end of the workflow process to avoid magnifying any noise or other problems that need fixing.

Also, in some cases, small amounts of print sharpening are applied to existing, already-sharp images. This can help inkjet prints to exhibit the same crisp appearance as the screen image. Results vary from printer to printer; experiment on printing sharpened and unsharpened images before settling on a final workflow for your images and printer type.

Ultimately, the exact order of your workflow and what you include or exclude become a matter of personal experience and preference, but the previous sequence is a good starting point for many users.

Leveraging Photoshop layers

Layers are perhaps the single most important component of the Photoshop editing process. A great deal of the creative control that you have begins with the appropriate application of layers within your documents. Some important tips for getting the most out of Photoshop layers are provided in this section.

Use adjustment layers

Instead of using the Levels or Curves function directly on your pixel-based layers, try using an adjustment layer instead. Adjustment layers give you a lot of extra flexibility because you can make your desired changes, save the document, and then open the adjustment layer later and still maintain total control over the original correction. Conversely, once you apply a tonal or color command to a pixel-based layer, and then save and close that document, you can no longer undo those changes; with adjustment layers, you can.

Another benefit of adjustment layers is that they allow you to apply layer masks to the correction so that it can be localized to a very small or unusually shaped area of the image, leaving other areas unaltered. This greatly impacts the quality of your final output, as precise, localized changes often provide a more realistic effect than global image modifications.

Consider also that Adobe has improved the efficiency of adjustment layers in Photoshop CS4 with the Adjustments panel (see Figure 25.8), making it easier to apply, preview, and adjust your settings on-the-fly.

FIGURE 25.8

The new Adjustments panel in Photoshop CS4

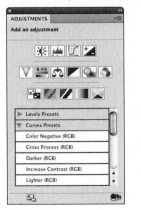

Use Smart Object layers

Smart Object layers are a great way to increase your creative flexibility. They are often used by compositing artists, whose work requires frequent trial and error. Using Smart Object layers allows these artists to experiment non-destructively, alleviating the need to create many duplicates or versions of an image, in order to experiment with different visual effects without ruining the original.

Smart Filter layers are helpful because they allow you to go reopen your chosen filter's dialog box and change the look of your layer after the initial filter use without degrading the image quality.

Adobe has increased the flexibility and power of Smart Object layers in Photoshop CS4, improving mask linking behaviors as well as integrating the popular Transform functions. This means, for example, that you can turn your image layer into a Smart Object before performing a perspective correction. Then you can go back later and modify the transformation without degrading image quality.

This is a significant capability for those who photograph at very wide angles on a regular basis, because they no longer have to lose portions of the original image data when applying perspective transforms. They can simply reopen the Transform dialog box and either modify the existing settings or remove the changes altogether. This means they can redo the transform as many times as they like, rather than each time modifying the previously transformed canvas until it loses its visual integrity.

Use iterative image layers to stay non-destructive

When you are retouching a photograph, the worst thing you can do is to apply things like cloning, brush strokes, patching, transforms, or other "destructive" edits to the original background layer. This leaves you with very little recourse should you make a mistake and save the document, or run out of History States to undo the mistake you made. For this reason, always maintaining your original background layer should always be your starting point when editing images in Photoshop.

A wiser approach when retouching or restoring an image, assuming you have set yourself up with plenty of hard drive storage for your images, is to maintain as much control over your edits as possible, using multiple image layers and the Layers panel (Figure 25.9).

To do this, consider the following suggestions as you work:

- Duplicate the initial background layer before you perform any edits.
- Name new duplicate layers after the steps you will perform.
- Create new duplicates from the layer immediately below in the layer stack.
- If you have a series of layers you wish to apply an effect to, group them in a folder first.
- Isolate all liquify and warping operations onto their own image layers if possible.
- When using filters, duplicate the target layer, then convert it to a Smart Filter first.

FIGURE 25.9

Taking full advantage of layers and the Layers panel can make your workflow more flexible and productive, resulting in higher-quality images.

Leveraging history

One of the most powerful features in Photoshop is the ability to step back in "document time" and improve the look of your image by removing unwanted changes from the history. Many Photoshop pros use the History panel like a supercharged undo function, allowing them to experiment in ways that would otherwise not be possible, without making many copies of a given file.

Using the History States is also a very powerful way of reaching back to a prior image state and painting it back onto selected parts of your image without "undoing" the intermediate steps that have been applied to the image. For those who do serious retouching or compositing work, the History panel and History Brush are essential in their workflows.

NOTE Using 50 or more History States can require a significant amount of memory (or RAM), so if you can budget for it, have enough RAM installed to allocate 3-4GB directly to Photoshop. For Photoshop users, having systems with a total of 6-8GB of RAM installed is not uncommon. Theoretically, this means the user could have roughly 4GB of RAM assigned to Photoshop and the remaining 2-4GB assigned to the system and other programs so that they can run simultaneously without slowing down to share RAM.

General editing tips

The items that follow are not particular to a specific workflow, but are easily overlooked when working in Photoshop. Keep them in mind. There are many situations where they can help you to maximize the quality of your work and minimize the time required to get those results.

Use the Fade command

Often, you may find that a specific image correction comes close to achieving your desired result, but is too much of a good thing. However, undoing and redoing the same correction many times, making incremental changes as you go, can be tedious. Instead, if you find that your initial correction is close to correct but a bit much, use the Fade command (choose Edit ➪ Fade), shown in Figure 25.10.

FIGURE 25.10

The Fade command's simple but effective dialog box and slider control

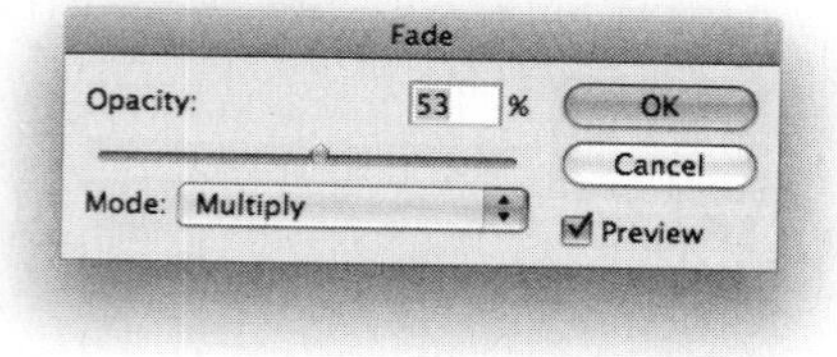

This feature allows you to take the full effect of the most recent change and scale it back from 1 to 99 percent, allowing for very fine control. Fade is designed to be used with any image adjustment or brush stroke, and can help you get the results you want more quickly than trying many iterations of the same adjustment or stroke. As you might suspect, the Fade command cannot be used with any type of function that is an "all or nothing" proposition, such as transforms, warps, paths, or selections. Note however, that if you are applying a filter to a Smart Object layer, you will not be able to fade that command.

Experiment with brush dynamics

As you apply various brush-based corrections to your image, you may discover that the effect is a little bit off the mark. In these cases, instead of switching tools and finding other workarounds, experiment with brush dynamics such as Shape, Jitter, and Angle, as well as basic parameters like hardness and opacity, to achieve your desired effect. Sometimes a simple brush modification is all that is needed to arrive at the perfect result.

Experiment with blending modes

One of the most overlooked aspects of Photoshop is the power of blending modes, not only over your brush strokes but over your layers as well. While some blending modes lend themselves only to the creative side of digital imaging and not to the realism side, you'll be amazed at the added range of effects you can achieve in a given situation.

They can be daunting at first, but the more you use blending modes, the more you'll gain an instinctive feel for when to use them. For compositing projects in particular, where you are blending parts of multiple images together to form a whole, experimenting with blending modes can be invaluable to achieving the right result. For more information on specific blending modes, see Chapter 8.

Photoshop's Web features

Photoshop and Bridge CS4 offer tools that streamline the process of moving your images to the Web. When you should use these features depends on your level of Web expertise and on how much time you have to get something online. While Photoshop will not replace a tool like Dreamweaver for creating complex Web pages and sites, its Web tools are important.

Save for Web

This is a core tool when it comes to getting your images online, looking right. Save for Web (see Figure 25.11) handles all the popular Web formats, provides a large array of options to fine-tune your image quality and compression, and provides a means of visually comparing different output settings. If you have any interest in optimizing images for the Web so that they look great but are as compact as possible, you should know how to use Save for Web. To access Save for Web, choose File ⇨ Save for Web.

FIGURE 25.11

One of the most important features in Photoshop: Save for Web. Use it to compare your original image (left) with the image you have applied compression settings to (right) before you save the final Web file.

Adobe Output Module

New to CS4 is the Adobe Output Module (AOM), which is found in Bridge CS4 under the newly added Output workspace. AOM (see Figure 25.12) replaces previous Web templates in Photoshop and Bridge, such as the AMG (Adobe Media Gallery).

This module provides the ability to select a folder or range of images and automatically create static or flash-based Web galleries. Generally, users find these galleries to have more of a professional look than prior templates, and the process of choosing your gallery options is more streamlined. Everything is available from a single panel in Bridge, rather than from a complex dialog box buried in the Photoshop File menu. You can even upload the files directly from Bridge if you have the appropriate bits of information handy.

FIGURE 25.12

The new Adobe Output Module makes it easy to create professional-looking galleries and slide shows. It even allows you to upload your gallery files directly from Bridge, which further streamlines the gallery production process.

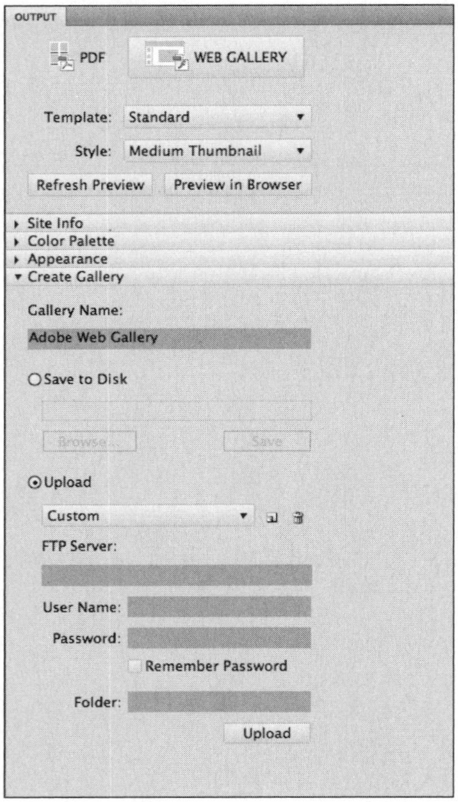

```
OUTPUT
     [ ] PDF        [ ] WEB GALLERY

  Template:  Standard              ▼
     Style:  Medium Thumbnail      ▼
  [ Refresh Preview ]  [ Preview in Browser ]

▸ Site Info
▸ Color Palette
▸ Appearance
▾ Create Gallery

 Gallery Name:
 Adobe Web Gallery

 ○ Save to Disk

   [ Browse ]              [ Save ]

 ⊙ Upload
   Custom              ▼  ⬜ ⬛
 FTP Server:

 User Name:
 Password:
           ☐ Remember Password

 Folder:
                        [ Upload ]
```

If you want to display your images in a professional-looking gallery for family, friends, or clients, taking a few minutes to learn AOM is a good investment of your time.

General printing and proofing tips

Printing is one of the more complex and time-consuming processes in any Photoshop workflow, but if you keep a few important tips in mind, you should be able to achieve success with fewer hiccups.

Page Setup

You might be surprised how many erroneous prints could be avoided by simply choosing the right printer, paper and feed type, and paper orientation from your Page Setup dialog box. When you're ready to print, this is the first thing you should check.

Handling print color issues

Many problems with color accuracy can be solved by checking a few key settings in the Photoshop Print dialog box and in your printer's driver dialog box. The following settings, found under the Color Management pop-up menu (top right, Print dialog box), assume a color inkjet workflow and are listed in the order in which you will encounter them:

- **Color Handling.** The best setting here is Photoshop Manages Colors. Photoshop does a much better job than your printer of handling the colors between computer and printer in most circumstances.

- **Printer Profile.** Make sure this is set to a printer-specific profile or a paper-specific profile you have created. Do not set this to a working space like Adobe RGB 1998, or the colors in your printed image will look very different from the version you see on your screen.

- **Rendering Intent.** Relative Colorimetric or Perceptual works for most photographs.

- **Driver Color Management.** Within your printer's driver software, turn off any available Color management options, allowing only Photoshop to manage the colors in your document.

Profiling your printer and paper type

If you are following the suggested settings for managing print color but are still getting unusual results, then it's possible your printer and paper type need to be profiled.

Profiling printers accurately and quickly is a more affordable process than in the past with the advent of products like the X-Rite ColorMunki system, which can profile your monitor, printer, and even projector for under $500. While not cheap, it is definitely a worthwhile investment if accurate color matching from screen to printer is important to you.

Soft-proofing

When you need documents printed on a four-color press (CMYK), you should do everything you can within Photoshop, to get as close a color match in the final print run as possible. A big part of this process is communication between you and the press specialist. No CMYK press is likely to match the vibrancy or color range of a high-end inkjet printer, but you can get much better results with good communication and soft-proofing.

The following questions are important general considerations; however, they may not apply in all instances. It is assumed that you have a properly calibrated monitor and that you are working with a knowledgeable press provider. If these minimum conditions are not in place, your chances of a successful print run are reduced.

- If you performed your primary image edits in RGB mode, have you made a separate CMYK version of the image and handled any separations your press provider might have suggested?

- Did the press provider suggest any special settings for your file, such as a specific CMYK profile, dot gain settings, or black ink limits? If so, have you implemented them as suggested? You may need to create a custom CMYK Working Space (Edit ⇨ Color Settings) that includes the recommended CMYK Ink Options and Separation Options.

- Under your custom proof setup (View ➪ Proof Setup ➪ Custom), are the options to Simulate Paper Color and Simulate Black Ink checked (see Figure 25.13)? Leaving these unchecked often gives you an unrealistic result for making assessments.

- When making your final CMYK Curves adjustment, was the Proof Colors command checked? Making color corrections for the press without the proofing preview to guide your decisions is a shot in the dark. Remember to use an adjustment layer for this correction until you're ready to send the file. Making multiple CMYK corrections directly to the background layer can degrade image quality.

FIGURE 25.13

Having the proper Custom Proof Condition can make all the difference when working with four-color press situations.

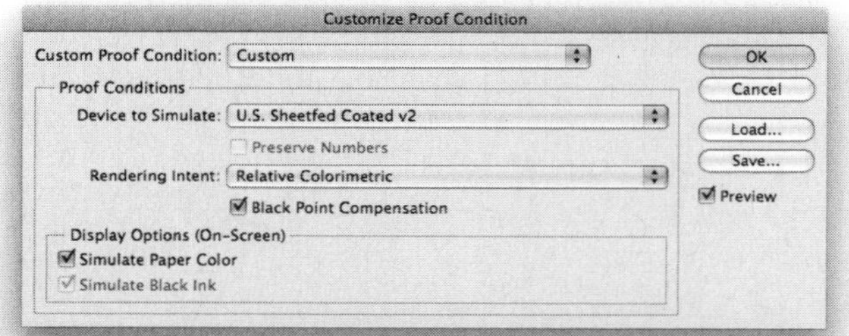

- When making your final CMYK Curves adjustment, did you have the final RGB image open to make comparisons?

Considering these factors as you prepare your CMYK files can help you to avoid common problems such as muddy or faded colors on the final print run.

Automating Photoshop Processes

When retouching or working with large numbers of images, it's not uncommon to encounter the same task many times as you apply it to different images. This can become a time-consuming and, frankly, uninteresting process. Fortunately, Adobe has provided Photoshop users with some excellent tools to help automate repetitive tasks, getting them done much more efficiently.

Using Actions

The most robust of Photoshop's automation tools is the concept of Actions and managing those through the Actions panel. They may seem a little intimidating at first, but they're quite easy to use once you become familiar with the user interface and general concept.

Actions are essentially a collection of individual editing commands. These commands are strung together (or recorded) in a particular sequence — which you define — along with special instructions to open or ignore any dialog boxes associated with those commands. When you play back an Action, Photoshop applies the entire sequence of editing commands before moving on to the next file. It may seem abstract, but once you create an Action and watch it run, you will quickly gain confidence.

Understanding the Actions panel

The Actions panel is a relatively simple concept that operates on principles similar to most video recording devices, along with a few extra items to keep your Actions organized. Figure 25.14 shows the Actions panel with each area labeled; descriptions of each item's purpose and usage follow.

FIGURE 25.14

The Actions panel and its component parts

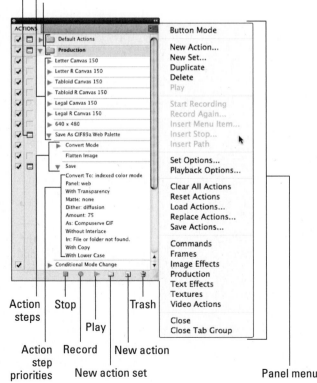

- **Action Sets.** These are collections of related Actions. Photoshop CS4 ships with eight Action Sets: Default, Commands, Frames, Image Effects, Production, Text Effects, Textures, and Video Actions.

- **Action.** Clicking the triangle next to the Action's name shows you all the steps involved. Highlighting an action and then clicking the Play button starts the Action. To move an Action to a new set, drag and drop it onto the chosen Action Set folder.

- **Action Shortcut.** When you create Actions, you have the option of assigning a keyboard shortcut so that you can access it quickly when working outside of the Actions panel. See Figure 25.15.

- **Action Step.** One component of a recorded action, such as a menu command, image adjustment, or brush stroke.

- **Action Step Properties.** All the functional options that are applied as result of the Action step.

- **Actions Panel Menu.** Controls all the functions that relate to the recording and organization of Actions, the creation and visibility of Action Sets, and even the appearance of the Actions panel, which can display Actions as buttons, if needed.

- **Trash.** Click this button to delete unwanted Actions, Sets, or individual Action steps.

- **New Action Button.** Use this to create new Actions by clicking and defining the basic properties shown in Figure 25.15. You can also duplicate an Action by dragging and dropping it onto this button.

FIGURE 25.15

When creating a new Action, take a moment to give it a descriptive name and place it inside whichever Action Set makes the most sense. If you'll use this Action on a regular basis, give it a keyboard shortcut for quicker access.

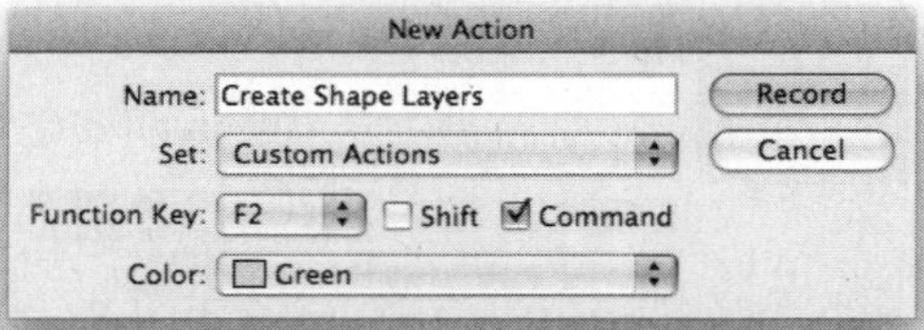

- **New Action Set Button.** Use this item to create a new Action Set Folder. To add an Action to an Action Set, drag and drop the Action onto the desired Action Set folder.

- **Play Button.** When you are ready to use an Action, highlight it and click this button.

- **Record Button.** Click this to begin recording your Action or continue recording from a stop. This records only applied menu commends, image adjustments, and changes made with Toolbar items. Recording Actions is not time-based, so whether you record your three steps in 15 seconds or 15 minutes, the resulting action will be exactly the same when you're done.

■ **Stop Button.** If you make a mistake while recording, don't worry! You can stop the recording, delete your erroneous step, and begin recording again from that point. You can also use Stop in conjunction with the Insert Stop, Insert Menu Item, and Insert Path commands to add a user message, menu action, or vector path, respectively, into your recorded Action.

■ **Modal Dialog Controls.** If your action uses commands that require a modal dialog box in order to make specific settings to the image, this box will be filled with an icon. If you see a red icon, that means one but not all of the commands in your action are modal, or that one but not all of the actions within a set contain a modal command.

■ **Action On/Off Toggle.** Turns on or off all the steps in a given Action.

Creating a New Action

Now that you are more familiar with the Actions panel, walk through the steps of creating a simple Action. Remember: Actions can be made to manipulate existing documents, or create new ones. For this example, you'll take an existing photograph and prepare it for the Web by resizing it, creating a black border, converting the color profile to the Web-safe sRGB, adding a copyright line into the border area, and finally flattening the image. Since you want to optimize each image individually in Save for Web (based on its content), I leave that as a manual step.

1. **Create a new Action Set for your custom actions if you haven't already, and make sure the first image you wish to prepare for the Web is open.**

2. **Click the New Action button and fill in the options similar to those shown in Figure 25.15.**

3. **When you have the correct steps in mind, click the Record button.**

4. **Choose Image ➪ Image Size, set the image to 600 (long dimension) x 480 pixels, and use Bicubic Sharper resampling, because the original image is larger than 600 x 480. Click OK.**

5. **Choose Image ➪ Canvas Size, and expand the image in all directions by 40 pixels, filling with black. Click OK.**

6. **Choose Edit ➪ Convert to Profile, click the RGB section, then choose sRGB from the menu. Click OK.**

7. **Click the Type tool and set the color to white from the Options Bar color well or from the Character panel's color well.** Zoom in to the document as much as needed so you can see clearly. Using the Text tool, drag out a text box in the black lower border area and enter your copyright text. When you're finished, click the green check mark in the Options Bar.

   If you need to have non-image-modifying menu commands like Zoom In or Zoom Out as part of your Action, click Stop and then choose the Insert Menu Item command. This allows you to select the menu item in question and have it record as an Action Item once you click OK in the Insert Menu Item dialog box, shown in Figure 25.16.

The Insert Menu Item dialog box, found in the Actions panel menu, allows you to add commands like Zoom In and Zoom Out to your Actions, because they are not recorded by default.

8. Choose Layer ⇨ Flatten Layer.
9. Click Stop to end the recording of the action.

That's it! You're finished recording your Action. From this point you would manually open the Save for Web dialog box and apply custom quality and compression settings for each file, then give it a unique name when saving it.

Now that you've created your Action, it's time to put it into practice.

Playing Actions

Playing an Action is as simple as highlighting the Action's name in the Actions panel, making sure the image you want to affect (if any) is open, and clicking the Play button. Beyond that, all you need to determine is whether you are targeting one image or many, or even using the Action to create new images from scratch, in which case no images need to be open at all. Each Action finishes within a few seconds, in most cases, and you can either continue with your few remaining tasks, or the Action moves on to the next image if you've targeted a folder of images. This can be accomplished using Droplets, the Batch command, or the Image Processor, all of which I discuss next.

Creating Droplets

Droplets are Actions that have been saved into a self-contained application file. Droplets allow you to perform their enclosed Action on any image or image folder by dragging and dropping them onto the Droplet. Many Photoshop users place the file icon for their Droplet on their Desktop for easy access.

You create Droplets using the Create Droplet dialog box, which is found in the Automate submenu of Photoshop CS4's main File menu. The following list provides an overview of Droplet creation options, as shown in Figure 25.17. Once you've set the options, click OK to create the Droplet.

FIGURE 25.17

Use the Create Droplet dialog box to make self-contained Action applications. Once created, you can drag and drop images directly onto a Droplet icon to speed up your workflow.

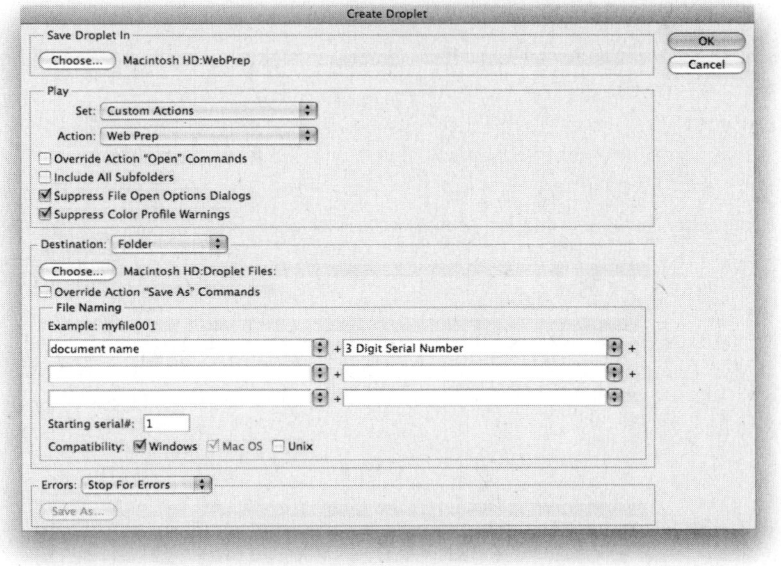

- **Save Droplet In.** Click the Choose button to place the finished Droplet into your folder of choice; the Desktop is a popular location.

- **Set.** Choose the Action Set where your targeted Action is found.

- **Action.** Choose the Action you wish to use.

- **Override Action "Open" Commands.** Check this box to disregard any Open file commands within your recorded action that specify a particular file being opened.

- **Include All Subfolders.** Check this box to ensure that any subfolders containing images, within the main folder you dragged onto the Droplet, are processed.

- **Suppress File Open Options Dialogs.** Check this box if you don't wish to see or set options for the files being processed as they are opened.

- **Suppress Color Profile Warnings.** Check this box if you don't wish to see color profile mismatch or missing profile warning dialog boxes as images are processed.

- **Destination.** Options for what to do with your processed images. There are three options:

    - **None:** This leaves your processed images open in Photoshop without further action.

■ **Save and Close:** This saves the changed images to their original location and closes them.

■ **Folder:** This allows you to choose a new location to save your modified images.

■ **Override Action "Save As" Commands.** Check this box to disregard any Save As commands found within your recorded action that specify a specific filename and location.

■ **File Naming.** Choose options for how your file is named, including numeric sequencing, dates, and other data types.

■ **Starting serial #.** Tells the Droplet which number to start with if you choose a serial number option in your filename. For example, if you type a **5** in this box and chose "3 Digit Serial Number" as a naming option, the first file is saved with an 005 in the name.

■ **Compatibility.** Makes sure filenames are compatible with the operating systems you use.

■ **Errors.** Chooses the behavior when errors are encountered during the processing of files.

■ **Stop For Errors.** Suspends the Action until you dismiss the error dialog box.

■ **Log Errors.** Logs errors to a special file without stopping the Action.

Droplets (Figure 25.18) are a very convenient way of leveraging the power of Actions without spending time inside the Actions panel.

FIGURE 25.18

Droplet icons look like blue arrows with the Photoshop brand mark (Ps) on them. Naming a Droplet is important, as the icons all look alike.

As you create more Droplets, it's a good idea to designate a Droplets folder on your Desktop and make sure that folder's view options use relatively large icons or list items. This way, when you drag and drop files or folders onto your Droplet, there is less chance of you dropping them on the wrong item.

Batch processing Actions

The Batch command, which is also found in the Automation submenu of Photoshop CS4's main File menu, performs exactly the same task as a Droplet, but without creating the Droplet application or icon. The Batch dialog box options, shown in Figure 25.19, serve the same purposes as those in the Create Droplet dialog box. Use the Batch processing function when you want to apply an Action to a large number of files but on an intermittent basis.

FIGURE 25.19

The Batch processing dialog box

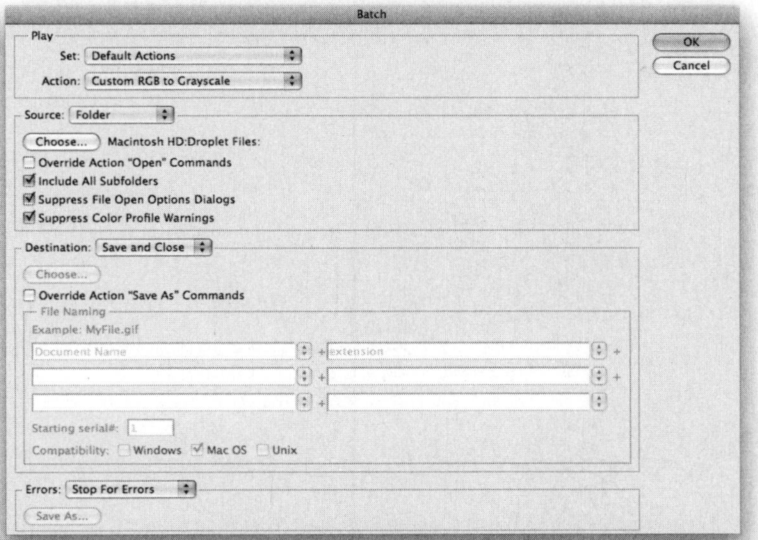

Photoshop scripts

The extensible architecture of Photoshop allows developers and advanced users to create original automation processes within Photoshop's collection of functionalities, called *scripts*. While the creation of scripts generally requires some programming knowledge (JavaScript, for example) and is therefore beyond the scope of this book, there are a few useful scripts that Adobe provides for us.

The most useful among these, in terms of making workflow more efficient, is the Image Processor. We will also discuss briefly the Export Layers to Files script and the Load Files into Stack script. All scripts can be found under File ➪ Scripts.

Image Processor

The Image Processor is a special script that combines many common image-processing tasks, as well as the possibility of using select Actions, into a single dialog box. The Image Processor, shown in Figure 25.20, is a great tool if you often need to resize and save large numbers of images and save them to a new format. You can also use this tool as part of your Camera Raw workflow. The basic steps for using the Image Processor are listed below.

FIGURE 25.20

The Image Processor is a great way to make common workflow tasks easier, such as resizing images and applying simple image commands or color profiles to larger numbers of images. You can even add your copyright information to file metadata.

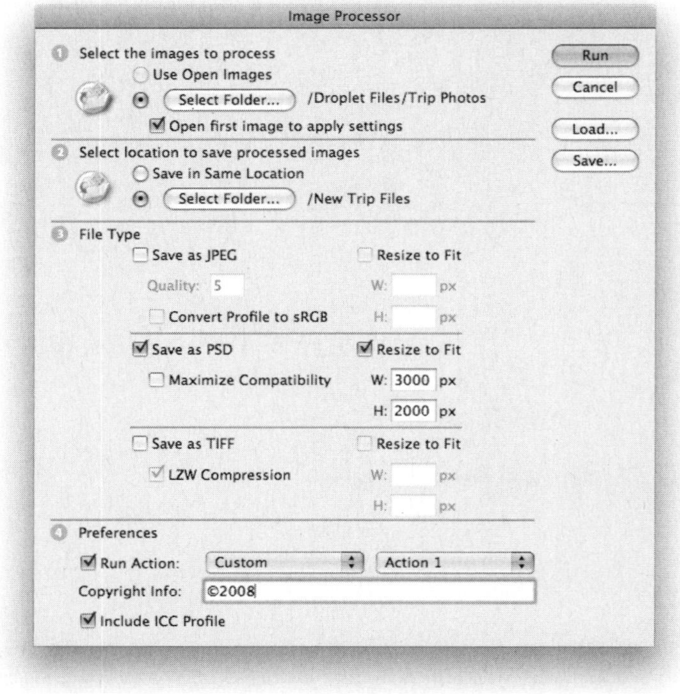

- **Select the images to process.** Section 1 allows you to select which images are processed, and whether to open the Camera Raw dialog box for the first image, in order to apply the subsequently made settings to all images that follow.

- **Select location to save processed images.** Section 2 allows you to define where to save the processed images.

- **File Type.** Section 3 provides popular options for resaving your files as JPEG, PSD, or TIFF images, including options to resize them before saving, as well as profile conversion, compatibility, and compression options, respectively.

- **Preferences.** Section 4 allows you to run a specified Action from the Commands Action Set or from a Custom Action Set, and gives you options for including a copyright in metadata and including an ICC profile.

After you've chosen your settings, click Run to begin processing the files. The beauty of the Image Processor is that it allows you to save specific combinations of settings as presets, so that you can reuse them later. The Image Processor is an invaluable tool for those who need to work with high volumes of images on a regular basis.

Export Layers To Files

This script allows users to create discrete files from the layers in a document. There can be a variety of reasons for using this dialog box, shown in Figure 25.21, but one of the more common uses is for motion graphics applications like Adobe After Effects or Apple Motion.

FIGURE 25.21

The Export Layers To Files dialog box

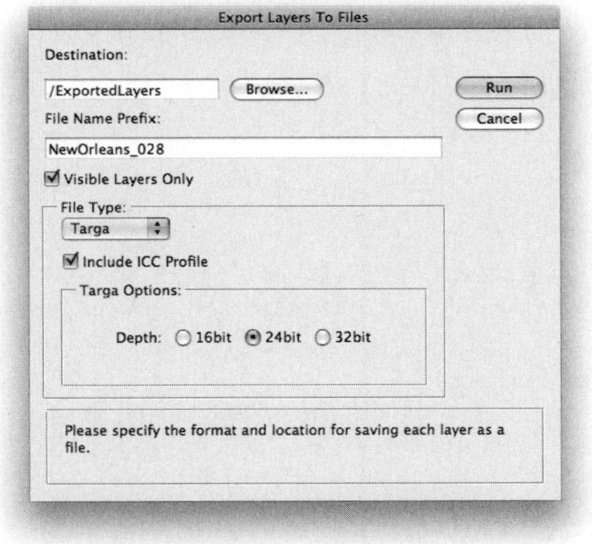

When creating compositing projects, it's sometimes helpful to be able to break files down into their component visual parts, so that those parts can be animated and manipulated individually. You can save your layers to many popular formats, including Targa, which is often used by motion graphics companies. You can also save your exported layer files to print-friendly formats like PDF or Web formats like JPEG or PNG.

Load Files into Stack

This script opens the Load Layers dialog box, shown in Figure 25.22, and is useful if you are creating HDR images or blending multiple identically composed images together for other compositing purposes.

The Load Layers dialog box

Tips for sharing images

One of the most vexing issues Photoshop professionals — especially photographers — must deal with is how to effectively organize and share images and artwork they have created without spending a lot of time setting things up.

Chapters 1 and 3 discuss the functional aspects of managing your digital assets, but sometimes staying on top of things goes beyond just your computer or a few external hard drives. Often you must work directly or indirectly with other parties who will be using your images for business or academic purposes. This means that you must not only name and save your files in ways that make sense to you and to others, but you must also consider carefully where you save things and what information you include with your saved locations and files.

File-sharing setup tips

Among the many things you can do to organize and share your images effectively (there are entire books written on Digital Asset Management), the most important is the proper application of metadata, including keywords. But even before metadata and keywords can aid your shared workflow, you must put the appropriate images within reach of the other parties involved.

Here are some tips to help ensure the right people can access and find your files when needed:

- **Use a project folder hierarchy.** Every project should have its own folder, with subfolders that can contain anything from original RAW files, to layout copy, to finished PSD files that have been retouched, color managed, and are ready for press.

- **Name your project folders with relevant information:** Include the date, project (or client), and subject.

  Consider these two folder names: "2008_Sluggers_apparel-shots" versus "Sluggers products." What if you've worked with the Sluggers Company before or intend to work with them again? Will the latter folder name mean anything to you (or them) when you've worked on several projects? Do they carry other products besides apparel? When were those shots taken? Naming your folders the right way can save time for all involved.

- **If files are to be shared from a company computer or server, make sure the proper sharing permissions or privileges are active.** Also make sure that the people using these images have the appropriate connection type and information to access your files.

  Depending on your computer hardware and which version of Mac OS X or Windows you have installed, the appropriate controls are often found under System Preferences or Control Panel, respectively. Figure 25.23 shows the Mac OS X Single User Sharing panel from version 10.5 (also called "Leopard").

FIGURE 25.23

The Mac OS X (10.5) Sharing panel, found under System Preferences

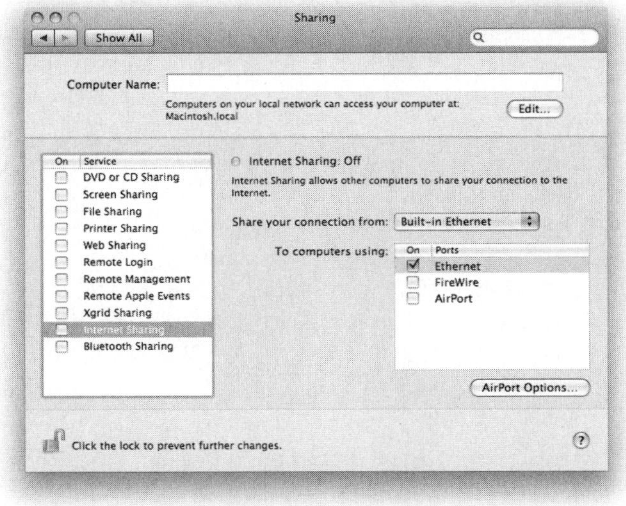

- **If you're sharing files via a Web site, the settings for creating FTP (short for File Transfer Protocol) accounts that others can access are typically found in the Site Control panel.** You can access this area by logging on from your browser with your site's primary login information. Contact your hosting provider for more details.

- **Share your naming system with the people you're working with, especially if you use any codes to identify certain types of files.** Sometimes it helps to provide others with a quick cheat sheet or key so that they can quickly familiarize themselves with your naming system.

- **Make sure everyone understands the rules when it comes to adding new files into the project folders, overwriting existing files, or deleting existing files!** Many times folders can be set up to allow or disallow certain users from performing certain activities (such as deleting files or creating them or renaming them). Consider carefully which users or categories of users should have these privileges.

- **Never put your only copy of a given file in a shared folder.** Always have backups somewhere else that are accessible only to you (assuming you are responsible for them) in case something goes wrong.

Metadata and keyword tips

Once you've set the foundation for sharing your files in whatever mediums you have chosen, it's very important that you provide additional information about your files, via their metadata and keywords, which you now know how to apply using Bridge CS4. Here are some important bits of metadata to always include with your shared files:

- **Copyright holder and applicable rights usage.** While an ill-meaning third party can circumvent metadata, it is nonetheless important to provide ownership and rights information with your images. They act as a simple reminder to others using your images, stating who the owner is, when the work was shot or designed, and what usage rights the user or viewer has, if any.

- **Subject and location.** These are helpful because subject and location are often two of the first search terms a person uses when looking for specific shots that they can't otherwise find by name in OS X Finder or Windows Explorer.

- **Name keywords.** Who is in the shot, if anyone? Names are another common search criteria, and because there is also a new keyword item in the Bridge CS4 Filter panel, having the right names associated with a file allows you to quickly show only those files when needed.

- **Events.** This is another common search criteria and a good use for keywords. "Jane's Birthday," "Labor Day 2008," "Town Hall Meeting," and "Japanese Wedding" are all good examples of descriptive event-based keywords that could make finding files within a workgroup much easier.

Using a few simple guidelines such as these can spare you and your clients (or team members) many headaches as you begin your creative projects. Yes, it may take a few extra minutes in the beginning of the process to set up your computers or Web site appropriately and tag the appropriate metadata to your shared files in Bridge CS4, but in the long run, these steps are likely to make you more efficient and productive.

Summary

The information in this chapter has provided suggestions streamlining your workflow and ultimately improving the quality of your images. Many important workflow and automation processes were covered, including the following: ACR Output Options; important Photoshop preferences including performance preferences; choosing the best file format and naming conventions for your workflow; understanding the basic sequence of edits for digital photography workflows; taking advantage of the Layers and History panels during retouching and compositing workflows; Photoshop Web output functions; steps for improving color management as part of the printing process; using Actions and Droplets to automate your repetitive workflow tasks; and ways to use metadata and system-level file sharing functions to facilitate the sharing of images in a workflow.

Part VIII

Video, 3D Images, and Technical Images

Chapter 26

Working with Video

As of version CS3, Photoshop now includes support for video in its Extended version. You could be excused for wondering exactly why you'd want to edit video in Photoshop. After all, it's supposed to be the world's premier photo- and image-editing software, right? Well, what is video but a series of images displayed rapidly one after the other? Essentially this feature simply adds another dimension to Photoshop's image-editing ability: time.

Almost anything that you can think of doing with still images — painting, compositing, masking, color-correcting, cloning — you can now do with imported video. You can also create animations in Photoshop, and export them to numerous video formats.

As covered back in Chapter 24, you can also use Photoshop to create frame-based animations, which are more along the lines of the standard Web animations you've seen in Web banners and in short animated graphics on Web pages.

Photoshop also offers the ability to preview your completed video compositions on external devices like video monitors or televisions, and to export the finished products to numerous video formats. Speaking of formats, you should be aware that Photoshop's video features require you to have at least QuickTime 7.1 installed on your machine. The latest version of QuickTime is available as a free download from Apple, Inc.'s Web site.

While by no means a comprehensive text on video editing, this chapter offers an overview of the video and animation tools offered by Photoshop.

Video and Animation in Photoshop

One of the first things you should be clear about in terms of working with video in Photoshop is the distinction between what you can and can't do. For instance, you can't re-cut existing footage, and you probably shouldn't expect to be able to edit the next *Citizen Kane* armed only with a hand-held camcorder and Photoshop. However, you can import clips of video, reposition them in relation to each other, transition between one clip and the next, overlay existing photos, add text captions or titles, and so on.

Video formats

Photoshop offers support for the following standard video formats:

- **MOV.** This is the native format for Apple's QuickTime software. The QuickTime format can act as a wrapper for other media, including video and audio tracks encoded using various different codecs. QuickTime is compatible with both Mac OS and Windows systems.

- **AVI.** Audio Video Interleave, or AVI as it's commonly known, is Microsoft's default video format for Windows systems.

- **MPEG/MPG.** This is the video format developed by the Motion Picture Experts Group. Different flavors of the MPEG format are used for varying purposes, and by default you can import MPEG-1 and MPEG-4 into Photoshop. If you have installed an MPEG encoder on your system, you can also import MPEG-2, which is the standard for broadcast-quality video.

- **FLV.** FLV stands for Flash Video, and it's the default format that much of the video on the Internet today is encoded in, due to the ubiquity of the Flash player. If you have Flash 8 or higher installed on your machine, you can import the FLV format via QuickTime.

In addition to the standard video formats that it supports, Photoshop can import image sequences and combine them sequentially to form a video clip. RGB or Grayscale images with a bit depth of 8, 16, or 32 can be imported, while CMYK and Lab images of 8 or 16 bits per channel are supported. You can import any of the following image formats for use with Photoshop's video tools:

- BMP
- DICOM
- JPEG
- OpenEXR
- PNG
- PSD
- Targa/TGA
- TIFF

CROSS-REF What, you mean you don't remember all the intricate details of all those file formats? For in-depth information, refer to Chapter 7.

Any of the document formats that support layers, including Photoshop's native format (PSD), TIFF, and PSB, will preserve your video edits and animation information so you can edit them later. Adobe software like After Effects and Premiere will also recognize these formats, but to bring your work into other video-editing software, you should export your files in one of the video formats mentioned earlier by choosing File ⇨ Export ⇨ Render Video. Exporting video is given in-depth coverage later in this chapter.

Photoshop's video tools

Following is an overview of the tools and menus available for working with video in Photoshop. When working with video, one of the first places to start is to narrow down Photoshop's sprawling menus to just the ones relevant to video-related tasks, by switching to the Video workspace. Choose Window ⇨ Workspace ⇨ Video to configure the workspace, as shown in Figure 26.1.

FIGURE 26.1

The Photoshop workspace reconfigured for working with video

The Animation panel

The Animation panel (illustrated in Figure 26.2) comes in two flavors: Timeline mode and Frame mode. Frame mode is what you would use to create animated GIF images, which you'll learn a bit more about later in this chapter. Timeline mode offers the controls necessary to work with video. Use it to arrange layers of content, set the duration that content appears within your video, apply effects that change over time, and preview specific portions of your movie. If you don't see the Animation panel on your screen, choose Windows ➪ Animation.

 **TIP** If the Animation panel opens in Frame mode, you can switch it to Timeline mode by clicking the icon at the bottom-right corner of the panel.

FIGURE 26.2

Photoshop's Animation panel in Timeline mode

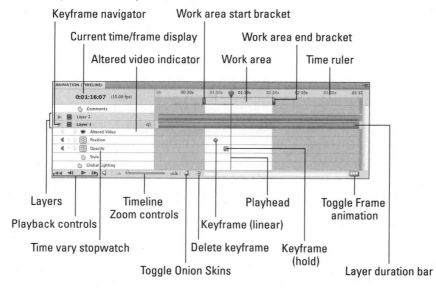

Think of the timeline as a visual representation of your document's layers over time — the layers in the Animation panel correspond to the layers over in the Layers panel. Changes you make to a layer's properties (visibility and name, for example) in either panel are reflected in the other. Repositioning the playhead, or current-time indicator, to a different point along the timeline moves to the corresponding point in your video. Changing the state of those layers at different points in time by adding *keyframes* produces animation.

Here's an overview of the main controls available in the Timeline panel:

■ **Altered frame indicator.** This indicates whether a frame has been modified in any way.

■ **Current time display.** This displays the current point in time that the current-time indicator is positioned at in either time code or frames, depending on the timeline preferences. Drag your cursor over these numbers to move the current-time indicator's position in the video. Double-click to numerically position the playhead at a specific point in the video.

■ **Delete keyframes.** Click this icon to delete the selected keyframe. Alternately, you can highlight a keyframe in the timeline and press the Delete/Backspace button on your keyboard.

■ **Enable audio playback.** This button allows you to preview audio that's embedded in the video files that you import. Video layers that include embedded audio are indicated with a little speaker icon; click that icon to toggle muting on or off for that particular video layer.

■ **Keyframe/altered video navigators.** Use these arrows to automatically position the current-time indicator on the previous or next keyframe. In the case of the altered video indicator, you can use these arrows to move the current-time indicator to the previous or next frame that has been altered.

■ **Layer duration bar.** This indicates the duration of each layer in the animation or movie. If the duration bar for a layer spans the entire duration of the movie on the timeline, the layer will be persistent throughout the movie, meaning you can animate the layer's properties at any point in the movie. If, on the other hand the duration bar only spans a portion of the movie's timeline — say, the first 10 seconds — it will only be available during that time. To change the point at which a layer becomes available, or stops being available in the movie, drag its start and end points.

■ **Playback controls.** If you've used a VCR or any type of playback device in the last 40 years or so, these controls should be at least somewhat familiar to you. Press the play button (or press the Spacebar) to see a preview of the portion of your video that's within the current work area. The other controls allow you to step forward or backward frame by frame, or rewind to the first frame of the video.

■ **Time ruler.** This measures the duration of the document in frames or in seconds, depending on your document's settings.

■ **Work area indicators.** Drag the brackets (they'll be blue on the screen, which isn't exactly obvious from the illustration in this book) to the beginning and end of the portion of video you want to work with. This also selects the portion of video that is previewed and exported.

Customizing the Animation panel

Like most panels in Photoshop, you can specify options for how the animation panel is displayed. Choose Panel Options from the fly-out menu on the top right of the panel, and specify whether layers in the panel should have thumbnail icons and how big they should be. The default is no icons. You can also specify whether the time ruler should display time in timecode (the standard for video production) or frames.

Working with Images for Video

In addition to importing existing video or image sequences into a composition, you can create documents from scratch; create or import artwork, photos, and other elements to be animated; and export your animations in the video formats mentioned earlier in this chapter. You can also move your Photoshop files with video and animation information between video applications like Adobe Premiere and After Effects. Read on to learn how to prepare images for video.

> **TIP**   Into automation? Photoshop ships with a number of actions specifically designed to automatically perform complex sets of video-related actions. To use these time-saving features, show the Actions menu by choosing it from the Window menu. Next, choose Video Actions from the Actions panel's Options menu. Specify whether to Replace or Append the actions to the currently loaded selections, and you're ready to go.

Creating images for video

To create a new document using standard video presets, choose File ➪ New, and select Film & Video from the Preset menu (see Figure 26.3). From the Size menu, you can specify the format that your video is destined for, and Photoshop applies the correct pixel dimensions, frame rate, and aspect ratio to your file.

FIGURE 26.3

The Film & Video presets automatically configure your document to the settings used for various video output formats.

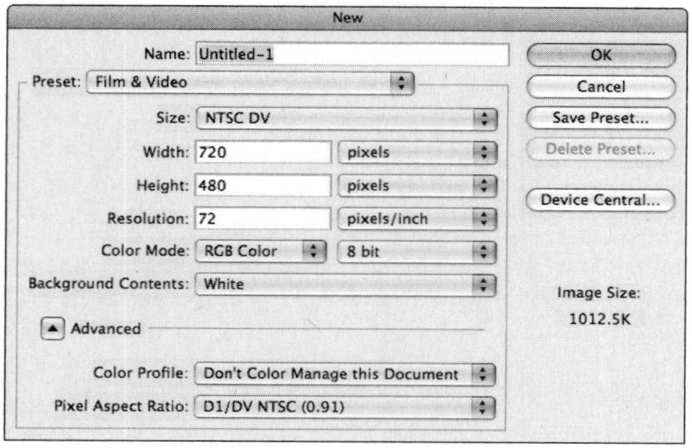

Another benefit of using the predefined video settings is that Photoshop automatically creates guides that indicate the standard safe zones used in broadcast video production, as shown in Figure 26.4. Typically, TV sets crop off the outer portions of the video that they display, so any action or text that appears on those areas can get cut off. Complicating the issue is the fact that different television models crop the picture by varying amounts. To ensure that your content is visible on most sets, keep it within the safe zones. Keep text and titles within the Title Safe areas indicated by the inner set of guides, and keep other important elements within the Action Safe region.

The guides shown in this screenshot indicate the safe zones that are commonly used in the film and video industry.

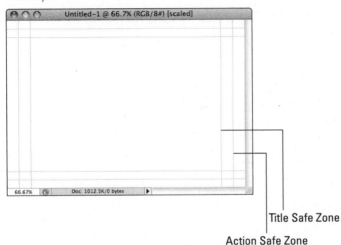

Title Safe Zone

Action Safe Zone

By default, using a video preset also turns on *Pixel Aspect Ratio Correction*, which alters the way the document is displayed to avoid distortion in images that use nonsquare pixels. Confused? Don't worry — this is all explained in greater detail later in this section.

Frame rates and duration

Animation and movies create the illusion of motion by rapidly displaying a series of still images, or frames, one after the other in quick succession. The speed at which the frames are displayed is called the *frame rate*, and it is measured in frames per second (fps). Frame rates vary depending on the format of the video:

- NTSC is the standard format used for North American video systems, and it uses a frame rate of 29.97fps.

- PAL is the default for much of the rest of the world, including parts of Europe, Asia, Africa, South America, and Australia, and it uses a frame rate of 25fps.

- Film, used for motion pictures, has a frame rate of 24fps.

- The frame rate used for most video used on the Web and on CD-ROMs varies, but for best performance on a wide variety of computers, use a setting of 10–15fps.

The default duration of documents created in Photoshop is 10 seconds, and unless you used one of the video presets, the frame rate is set to 30fps. If you forgot to specify this, don't worry — these settings aren't cast in stone. You can change the frame rate and duration settings after the fact by choosing Document Settings from the Timeline's fly-out menu. The Document Timeline Settings dialog box is shown in Figure 26.5. Keep in mind that reducing the overall duration of your document trims any animation or keyframes from the end of your video.

FIGURE 26.5

Use the Document Timeline Settings dialog box to adjust the frame rate and duration of your document.

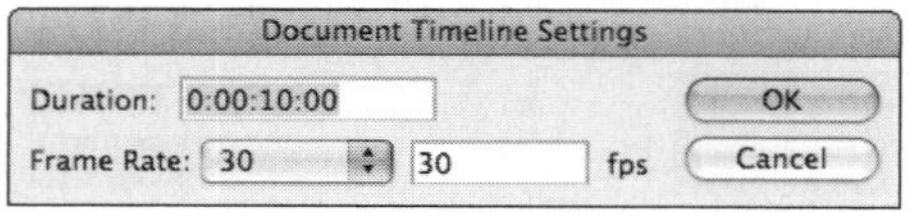

Aspect ratios

Aspect ratios can be a somewhat confusing aspect of video production. For the uninitiated, you can refer to either *frame aspect ratios* or *pixel aspect ratios*, both of which vary across devices and video standards. Frame aspect ratios define the ratio of the width to the height of a frame of video (the pixel width and height of the document). NTSC video typically has a frame aspect ratio of 4:3, while widescreen formats are typically 16:9, although some movies are filmed using even wider aspect ratios. Because most films are shot for widescreen aspect ratios, when they are displayed on broadcast television sets, they must either be cropped to fit the 4:3 format, or be scaled to the width of the format, which results in the black bars at the top and bottom of the display (also known as letterboxing).

Different devices also render pixels differently and can have varying pixel aspect ratios. Most computer monitors have square pixels, which have 1:1 aspect ratios. On the other hand, the NTSC standard uses a pixel aspect ratio of 0.9, which makes its pixels rectangular (nonsquare). Displaying documents with nonsquare pixels on a computer monitor would result in distortion, even though the image would display correctly on a TV or broadcast-quality monitor. That's where Pixel Aspect Ratio Correction comes in — Photoshop automatically alters the way the image is displayed so that the image is proportioned correctly.

Compare the two images shown in Figure 26.6. Both images show a circle in an NTSC DV document, which means it's formatted for a 4:3 display with nonsquare pixels. In the top image, Pixel Aspect Ratio Correction is turned on, simulating what the document will look like on a television screen. The bottom image shows the document with Pixel Aspect Ratio Correction disabled — you can see that the circle becomes stretched, because the pixels are rectangular. You can toggle Pixel Aspect Ratio Correction on or off by choosing that option from the View menu.

If you need to change the pixel aspect ratio of a document after the fact, you can do so using the settings located under View ⇨ Pixel Aspect Ratio. Use one of the given presets or enter a custom pixel aspect ratio, which you can save as your own preset. Generally, you'd only want to enter a custom setting if you know exactly what you're doing and are creating video for an output device that uses a nonstandard setting.

FIGURE 26.6

The top image shows an NTSC DV document with Pixel Aspect Ratio Correction enabled. In the bottom image, correction has been disabled, resulting in a distorted display. Note that this image will still display correctly on a display device that uses nonsquare pixels.

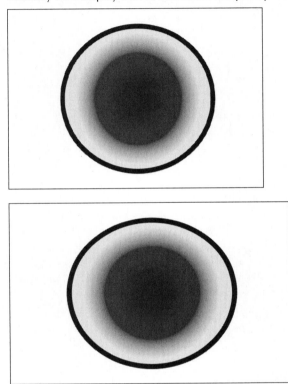

Color managing video files

When using Photoshop's painting tools with video, you'll want to be aware of color management and how it can affect your output video. If the video you imported is untagged — that is, it doesn't have an embedded color profile — edits that you make to the video frames are stored using the document's default color profile. If, on the other hand, the video has a profile that differs from that of the document, the color might not appear as you expect.

To fix this, you can change your document's color profile to match that of the imported video, and leave the imported footage unmanaged. Alternately, you can convert the imported video's color profile to that of the document using the Interpret Footage command. You can also convert all the colors to a single profile using the Edit ➪ Convert Profile or Edit ➪ Assign Profile command. In the case of the Assign Profile command, pixel edits that you've made to the video using the paintbrush, cloning stamp, or other tools aren't converted, so this is another situation where you may see color mismatches occur.

Preparing video for use in After Effects

So, you've been working on a masterpiece of a video composition in Photoshop, and it's time to bring it over to After Effects for some more compositing work. After Effects and many other video-editing programs can import native Photoshop files, preserving layers, layer styles, transparencies, masks, and just about any other edits you create in Photoshop, but there are a few things you should know before you take that step:

- **Name your layers and layer groups using unique names.** After Effects is confused by layers with duplicate names. Making things worse, if you rename layers or layer groups in Photoshop after the document has already been imported into After Effects, After Effects claims that the footage is missing.

- **Group different bits of animation into individual Smart Objects.** When brought into After Effects, those Smart Objects can then be manipulated independently of each other.

- **Check the bit depth of your images.** After Effects should be okay with 16-bit or higher images, but if your files will end up being used with other video editing software, you could face issues with compatibility.

- **Choose Always Maximize PSD/PSB compatibility.** Chose this option to embed a flattened composite of your document in the file, just in case. Enable this in the File Handling section of Photoshop's Preferences dialog box.

- **To be sure you're using the correct video settings, use the Film & Video presets found in the New dialog box (that is, the one that appears when you choose File ➪ New).** These presets are found in the File ➪ New dialog box. This ensures that you have the right pixel aspect ratio and frame rate for the format you're outputting to.

- **Do any color correction, scaling, cropping, and other edits in Photoshop.** The ensures that After Effects will not have to do any extra image processing work. Also, make sure your color management settings are specified in Photoshop prior to importing your document into After Effects.

Importing Video

When bringing video into Photoshop, it is automatically placed in a video layer, which you can manipulate in a whole host of ways. Read on for more information on importing video for use in Photoshop.

Using video layers

Photoshop allows you to treat video layers just as you would other types of layers — you can mask them, apply transformations, apply blending modes, change their layer styles, and adjust their opacity. Use the painting tools to edit the video frames, and use the selection tools to restrict your edits to certain portions of the video. You can even group video layers into folders as you would regular layers.

When a movie or image sequence is brought into Photoshop as a video layer, the original file (or files) is untouched — the video layer simply makes a reference to the source material. Photoshop generally tries to maintain the link to the referenced video even if you rename the file, but despite its best efforts, the link to a video can be broken if you either delete the video file (obviously) or move it to a different location, particularly on a Windows PC. On a Mac, the link remains unbroken unless you move the source material to a different volume. To re-associate the footage with a video layer, choose Layer ➪ Video Layers ➪ Replace Footage.

You can bring video footage into Photoshop in a few different ways. Choose File ➪ Open and navigate to a video file or image sequence to bring it into Photoshop. If you're adding video to an existing document, choose Layer ➪ Video Layers ➪ New Video Layer from File.

To work with video layers, choose Layer ➪ Video Layers to produce the menu shown in Figure 26.7.

FIGURE 26.7

The Video Layers menu offers these commands for working with video content in Photoshop.

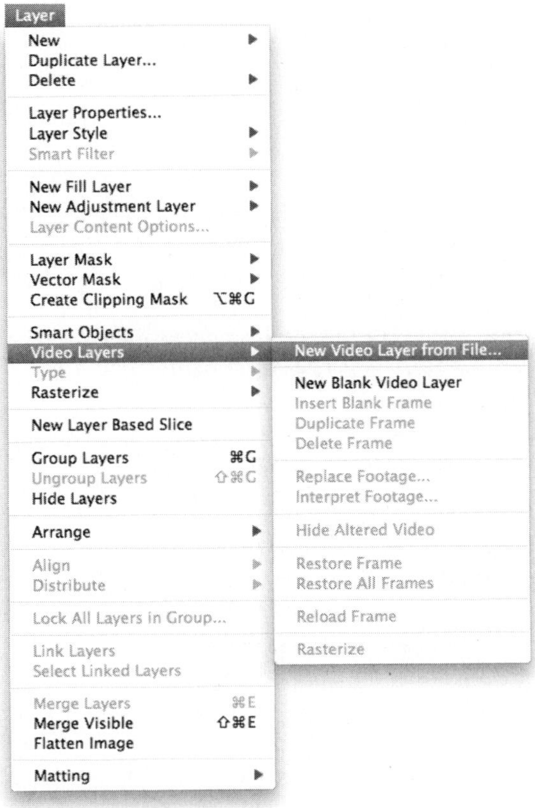

Here are the highlights:

- **New Video Layer from File.** Use this option to import a video into the current Photoshop document. You can use this to combine multiple videos in one document.

- **New Blank Video Layer.** You can optionally perform any edits, such as cloning or painting on a blank video layer. This keeps your edits separate from the actual video, and also allows you to produce hand-drawn animations. When working with a blank video layer, you can use the Insert Blank Frame, Duplicate Frame, and Delete Frame commands.

- **Replace Footage.** Use the Replace Footage command to update the link to a referenced video that you moved to a new location.

- **Interpret Footage.** This command tells Photoshop how to treat transparency, interlacing, and color management in the video or image sequences you import or open. You can also specify the frame rate of the imported footage. This command and its options are covered in more detail later in this section.

- **Show/Hide Altered Video:** This command allows you to toggle the visibility of any edits (for example, with the Brush, Cloning Stamp, Patch or other painting tools) that you've made to the video layer.

- **Restore Frame/Restore All Frames.** To get rid of any edits you've made to the current frame of a video layer, use the Restore Frame command. Restore All Frames discards all edits you've made throughout the duration of the video or animation.

- **Reload Frame.** As mentioned earlier, Photoshop does a pretty good job of keeping tabs on the external files that are referenced by a video layer. If the external content is modified by another application while the Photoshop document is open, you can force the content of the current frame to be reloaded by using the Reload Frame command. Subsequent frames are updated when you move the current-time indicator through the video.

- **Rasterize.** Use this command to create a flattened composite of the currently selected frame of your video. You can rasterize multiple video layers by Shift-selecting the layers in the Layers panel, and choosing Layer ➪ Rasterize ➪ Layers.

Importing image sequences

Importing an image sequence brings each image into Photoshop, turning it into a frame of video. Animations are often output from 3D software like Autodesk Maya or 3DStudio Max as image sequences, so that each image can be color corrected or tweaked individually. As long as your images are named consistently in alphabetical or numerical order (for example, file0001.jpg, file0002.jpg, and so on), and as long as the images are by themselves in a folder with no other file types, you can select the first image and click the Image Sequence check box and let Photoshop do the rest. Photoshop is smart enough to detect what's going on, and it brings in each image in the correct order and embeds the whole sequence in a video layer.

 Make sure all your images share the same pixel dimensions before importing them as a sequence.

Placing video

Importing video using the File ⇨ Place command brings it into your document with the familiar transform handles active. You can scale, rotate, warp, or otherwise transform your video, then commit those changes to place it in your document as a Smart Object. When video is placed inside a Smart Object, you can move through its frames using the Timeline, but you can't paint directly on its frames unless you double-click its thumbnail to open it as a PSB file. Instead, you can insert a blank video layer above the imported footage, and paint your edits there.

Using the Interpret Footage command

Use this command to tell Photoshop how to process video that you've opened or imported. The dialog box for this command is shown in Figure 26.8.

FIGURE 26.8

Use the options in the Interpret Footage window to let Photoshop know how to treat imported video.

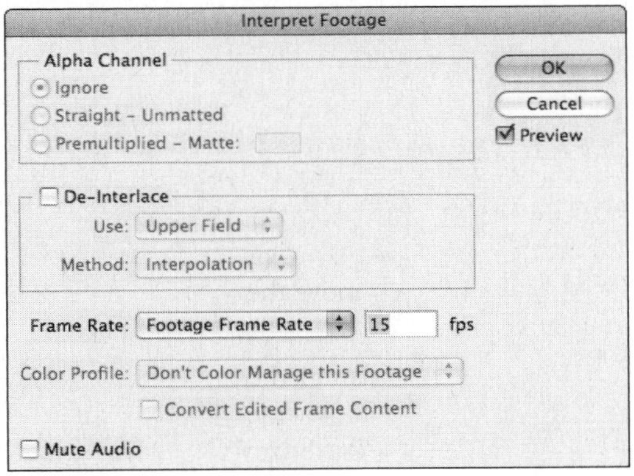

- **Alpha Channel.** The options under this section tell Photoshop how to deal with transparent areas in the video. These options are only available if the video you're importing contains an alpha channel:

  - **Ignore.** This tells Photoshop to ignore the alpha channel in the imported video.

  - **Straight — Unmatted.** If your video contains transparency information only in its alpha channel, select this option. This will depend on the application that was used to produce the video.

  - **Premultiplied – Matte.** Premultiplied alpha channels contain transparency information in all the RGB color channels, as well as the alpha channel. The image is usually premultiplied against black, white, or a custom color, which you can specify by clicking on the color swatch and choosing the appropriate color from the Color Picker. Correctly specifying the alpha type can avoid halos around the semi-transparent pixels in your video.

- **De-Interlace.** Video can be *interlaced* or *non-interlaced* depending on its destination. Most broadcast and high-definition television content is interlaced, meaning that each frame of video is divided into fields. Each field contains half of the lines that make up the image, and they're split into even- and odd-numbered lines. When interlaced video is displayed, the fields are displayed in alternating turns. In the case of NTSC video, the fields are displayed at a rate of 60fps — conveniently double the native NTSC frame rate of approximately 30fps. Non-interlaced video displays all the horizontal lines simultaneously, and is used for progressive scan monitors, which encompasses virtually all computer monitors.

  So with all of that said — if your video is destined for computer screens, enable the De-Interlace option, and choose whether to use the even- or odd-numbered field. The options in the Method menu tell Photoshop how to come up with the rest of the field information — either by duplicating the selected field, or by interpolating (that is, by averaging pixel information to produce the additional data).

- **Frame Rate.** Use this option to change the frame rate of the imported video footage.

- **Color Profile.** Manage the color profile of the imported video footage using this option. You can either leave it unmanaged or change it to match the default color profile of the document. Be aware that this can lead to color shifts, so use this option carefully.

Editing video and animation layers

So far, I've talked a lot about how you can edit video and animation layers in Photoshop just as you can other types of layers, but what does that actually mean? This section aims to clear that up with specific examples.

Transforming video layers

To use the transform tools with a video layer, simply highlight the layer in either the Timeline panel or the Layers panel, and press Ctrl+T (⌘+T on a Mac). Transforming a video layer automatically places it inside a Smart Object as soon you commit the changes. Photoshop reminds you of this when you use the command; once you've read and understood the displayed message, you can dismiss it, and opt not to show it ever again, if you like. Once you're in Transform mode, you can use any of the various transform tools, as shown in Figure 26.9.

Painting, drawing, and cloning

Using Photoshop's brush-based tools, you can create some unique effects with imported footage. For example, you can create a *rotoscoped* video by painting frame-by-frame over an imported video. Rotoscoping is an old animation technique where artists traced over live-action film movement. You could use this technique to produce an art-piece that pays tribute to a bygone era of cinema — or you could use it for more lowbrow purposes, such as putting a funny hat and monocle on a relative you don't like. Just be aware that at high frame rates, such as 30fps, you're going to find yourself with a lot of drawing to do. Figure 26.10 illustrates the latter approach, where I've drawn a decidedly unthreatening shark looming in the background of this scuba-diving footage.

To add a frame-by-frame drawing over video, choose Layer ➪ Video Layers ➪ New Blank Video Layer, and start drawing with one of the brush tools. To navigate between frames, use the arrow keys on your keyboard, or the previous/next frame buttons down at the bottom of the Timeline panel.

Using the transform tools with a video layer

To duplicate the content you've drawn on a frame on the next frame, choose Layer ➪ Video Layers ➪ Duplicate Frame. This allows you to build gradually on top of edits you've already made. To remove edits, choose Layer ➪ Video Layers ➪ Delete Frame.

Another technique you could try would be to clone areas of video from your imported video into a blank video layer, or even clone pixels from another document.

Of course, you can also paint directly on top of frames of video rather than on a blank video layer. If you go that route, remember that you can restore a frame to its original contents by choosing Layer ➪ Video Layers ➪ Restore Frame. Painting on video layers in Photoshop is nondestructive — to remove all your edits, choose Layer ➪ Video Layers ➪ Restore All Frames.

An important distinction should be made between drawing on regular layers and drawing on video layers. If you add a regular layer on top of your video, content that you draw on that layer won't be animated on a frame-by-frame basis. You can change its duration on the timeline by setting its In and Out points (covered later in this section), and you can change its position, opacity, and other attributes over time, but if you want to create an animation that changes frame-by-frame, you need to do it within a video layer — preferably a blank video layer.

The Brush tool was used to stage this rather weak shark attack.

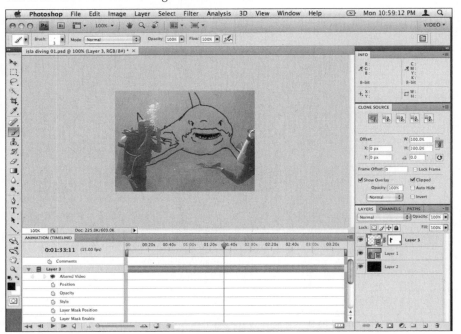

So, to animate my shark attack, I would need to make sure I draw each frame of the shark's animation in a blank video layer. If I wanted to tween (animate) my shark across the screen from left to right, I could draw it on a regular layer and animate its position over time.

Working with filters

You can also use Photoshop's filters with video layers, as you would with any other layer. Be aware that applying a filter applies it just to the current frame — the rest of the video remains untouched, unless you apply the filter to each frame in the video layer. The easy way to do this would be to group your video layer within a Smart Object (choose Layer ➪ Smart Objects ➪ Convert to Smart Object), and apply the filter as a Smart Filter. You then have the added advantage of being able to go back and edit the filter settings at any time.

Set Work Area

The Work Area defines the portion of video footage that you're working with. By default, the Work Area includes the entire duration of your timeline, but you can restrict it to any portion of that by dragging the brackets at the start and end of your Work Area bar so that they enclose the portion of the timeline you want to export or preview. A more precise alternative would be to position the current-time indicator at a point in your video and choose Set Start of Work Area or Set End of Work Area from the Timeline panel menu.

To get rid of everything outside of the work area, choose the Trim Document Duration to Work Area option from the Animation panel's Options menu.

Setting layer In and Out points

The point in the animation or movie where a layer first appears is called its In point. The layer's In point can be at the very beginning of the animation, but it doesn't have to be. For example, if you want a text layer to appear 3 seconds into the animation, you can drag the start of its duration bar to the 3-second mark. Likewise, the point at which a layer disappears from the animation is called its Out point.

You can also set In and Out points by moving the current-time indicator to a point on the timeline and choosing Trim Layer Start to Current Time or Trim Layer End to Current Time from the Timeline's fly-out menu. In the case of imported footage, setting In and Out points has the effect of hiding the video that appears outside of the layer duration bar's bounds — if you want to recover any of that video, you can simply extend the duration bar to the left or right. The video layer shown in Figure 26.11 shows a trimmed video layer whose In point has been set to appear at the 3-second mark.

FIGURE 26.11

The imported video layer has been trimmed to start at the 3-second mark, and end 12 seconds later at the 15-second mark.

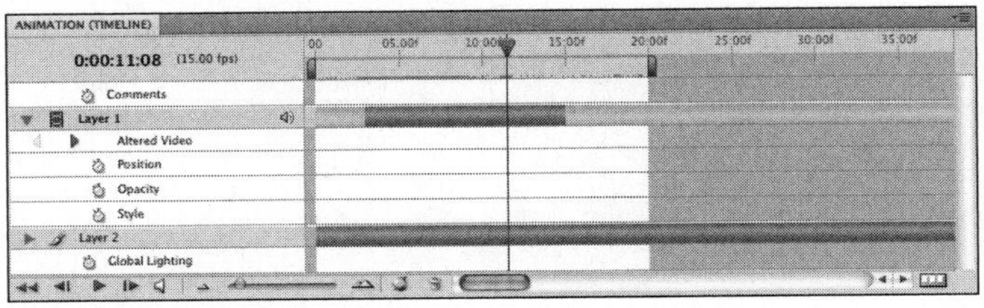

You can also change the position on the timeline of the start and end of a layer. It's a subtle distinction from the previous option. Think of it as the difference between changing the duration of the footage (trimming it), and repositioning the entire chunk of video on the timeline (moving it). Position the current-time marker at a location in the timeline and choose Move Layer In Point to Current Time or Move Layer Out Point to Current Time to reposition the start or end point of the current layer.

Lift Work Area and Extract Work Area

The Lift Work Area and Extract Work Area commands delete a specified chunk of footage from unlocked layers. The Lift Work Area command affects only the currently selected layer, while the Extract Work Area command affects all layers on the timeline.

To use the Lift Work Area command, position the Work Area around the area you want to get rid of. Select the target layer, making sure it's unlocked, and choose Lift Work Area from the Timeline fly-out menu. An area the size of the work area you defined is removed from the selected layer, leaving a gap in the timeline (see Figure 26.12). The remaining content from that layer is copied to a new layer.

FIGURE 26.12

The results of the Lift Work Area command — the selected layer has had a chunk of video the size of the work area removed.

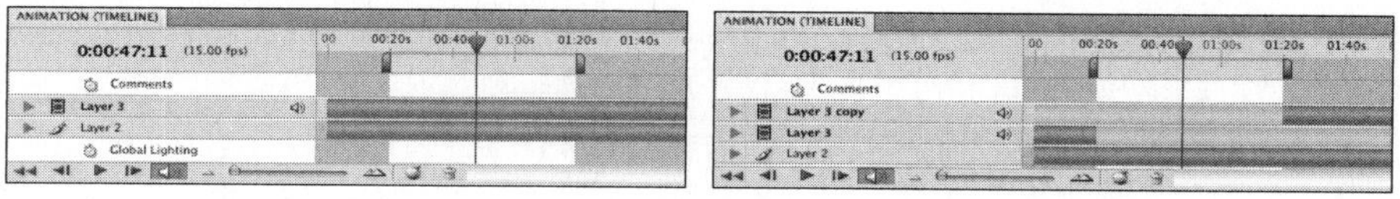

The Extract Work Area command (see Figure 26.13) works in a similar manner, except there's no gap left where the removed video used to be. Define a portion of video to remove by positioning the start and end of the Work Area, and make sure to lock any layers that should remain intact. Choose Extract Work Area from the Timeline fly-out menu, and a chunk of video the size of the Work Area is removed. The remaining content is copied to new layers.

FIGURE 26.13

The Extract Work Area command is used to remove a portion of the selected video layers. The original video is on the left, and the resulting timeline is shown on the right.

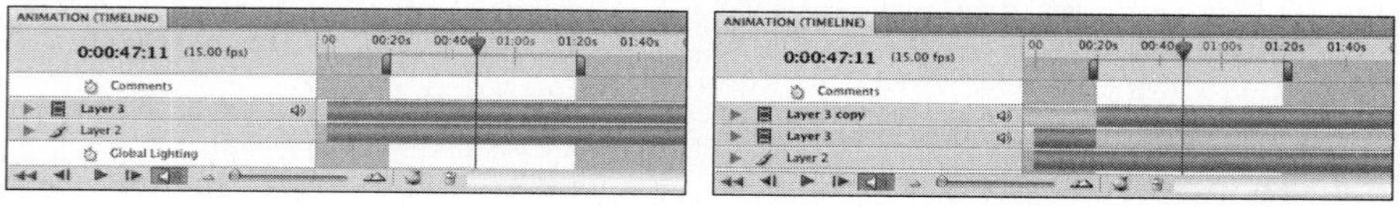

Split Layer

The Split Layer command performs the equivalent of duplicating a video layer, then repositioning the start point of one layer to match the end point of the other, as illustrated in Figure 26.14. Use this technique to reposition the resulting layers on the timeline and insert a transition between the two portions of video.

FIGURE 26.14

The original video layer shown on the left has been split into two layers using the Split Layer command.

Creating Timeline Animations

In traditional animation, a lead animator or artist draws the character on sheets of transparent *cel* paper in key poses; for example, the hand at the top, and then at the bottom of a waving motion. Other artists on the team then draw each of the in-between poses of the hand to create a complete waving motion. Applying these principles to video animation, the key poses become keyframes, and instead of a team of animators, the software figures out the in-between poses via interpolation. This process of figuring out the in-betweens is called *tweening*. Let's take a closer look at the Timeline panel to see how to use these techniques in Photoshop.

Creating keyframes in Photoshop involves setting a layer's properties (such as its position, opacity, or layer style) at one point in the timeline, and then changing those attributes at a different point in the timeline. Photoshop calculates the in-betweens. Each layer in the Timeline panel has a disclosure triangle to the left of its name (refer to Figure 26.2). Clicking the triangle reveals layer properties that can have keyframes applied to them.

Adding and removing keyframes

To create a keyframe, position the current-time indicator where you want the first state of your animation to happen, and click the time-vary stopwatch next to the property (or properties) you want to animate. This tells Photoshop that this property can be animated. Next, move the current-time indicator to another point on the timeline, and change that property. Photoshop automatically creates another keyframe, and you now have animation. Move the current-time indicator (or *scrub*, as it's also called) along the timeline between those two keyframes, or press the Spacebar to preview the animation.

There are two types of keyframes available in Photoshop, depending on how you want the tweens to be calculated:

- **Linear keyframes.** Diamond-shaped icons on the timeline indicate linear keyframes. These cause the animation to blend smoothly over time between keyframes.

- **Hold keyframes.** These keyframes switch abruptly between the states of the property being animated as soon as the current-time indicator reaches the next keyframe. You use this method for strobes or flashing effects.

By default, Photoshop creates linear keyframes. To choose an interpolation method (that is, how the tweens should be calculated), right-click (Ctrl+click, for Mac users) on a selected keyframe and choose either Linear or Hold Interpolation from the context menu.

To alter the duration of a property's animation — that is, to speed it up or slow it down — simply drag the keyframe and reposition it on the timeline.

To remove a keyframe from the timeline, highlight it and click the trashcan icon at the bottom of the Timeline panel. If you want to remove all the animation from a layer property, click the time-vary stopwatch next to that property, removing the ability of the property to be animated.

> **TIP**   You might have noticed that Global Lighting layer at the bottom of the Animation panel — this allows you to apply keyframes to and change the values of the Global Lighting setting over time. This means you can animate drop-shadows, glows, bevels, and other layer styles that use the Global Lighting attribute all at the same time. Set a keyframe on the Global Lighting layer, then choose Layer ➪ Layer Style ➪ Global Light to change its properties.

Navigating between keyframes

Once the time-vary stopwatch next to a layer property has been turned on, you'll notice two arrows and a diamond-shaped button next to that layer property. These are the keyframe navigation arrows; clicking them positions the current-time indicator at either the next or previous keyframe on the timeline. Clicking the diamond-shaped button in between the navigation arrows either adds a keyframe or removes the current keyframe from the timeline.

Using Onion Skin mode

Understanding the concept of Onion Skins goes back to the traditional animation model. *Onionskinning* refers to the animation technique where animators would draw intermediate poses of animation on thin, see-through onionskin paper placed on a light box. That way they could overlay and change each successive frame visually in relation to the ones that went before. As you would imagine, this technique is especially useful when drawing or painting frame-by-frame animations, as described earlier in this chapter.

To use this technique in Photoshop, click the Toggle Onion Skins button at the bottom of the Animation panel. In Figure 26.15, a circle is being tweened across the screen, and you can see its position on the current frame and, at a reduced opacity, on the previous and next frames as well.

Edit the Onion Skin settings via the Animation panel's options menu. Click Onion Skin settings to display the dialog box shown in Figure 26.16. The Onion Skin Count setting lets you specify how many frames before and after the current frame to display. With the Frame Spacing setting, you can specify an increment for the frames that are displayed (for example, to display every other frame, set the Frame Spacing setting to 2; for every 5 frames set it to 5, and so on).

FIGURE 26.15

With Onion Skins turned on, you can see the frames both before and after the current frame.

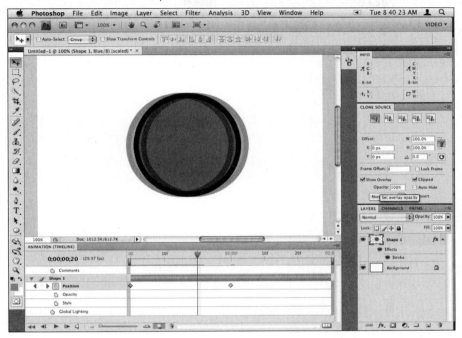

You can also set Minimum and Maximum Opacity values for the frames that are displayed. You won't really see the effect of the Minimum Opacity setting unless your Onion Skin Count values are greater than 1. Finally, setting a blending mode for the Onion Skin effect changes the way it interacts with the background, and could make the frames that are displayed easier to see.

FIGURE 26.16

Edit the settings of the Onion Skins feature using the options in this dialog box.

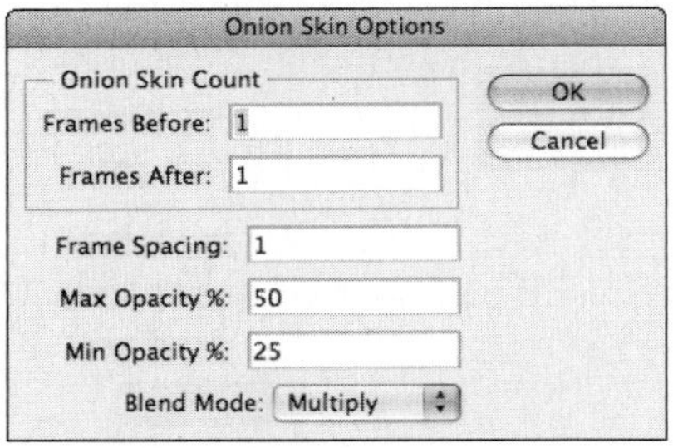

Creating Frame Animations

So far, the focus of this chapter has been on the Timeline mode of the Animation panel (available only in Photoshop CS4 Extended), which lends itself to editing and creating animations for output to video devices. In this section, you'll learn about using the Animation panel in Frames mode to create simple Web animations in either version of Photoshop CS4. Create frame-based animations by combining different layer (or layer group) configurations for each frame, and output the resulting animation in GIF format.

To switch the Animation panel to Frame mode (shown in Figure 26.17), click the little icon at the lower-right corner of the panel, or choose Convert to Frame Animation from the Animation panel's Options menu.

Most of the basics of creating frame-based animation were covered in the step-by-step walkthrough of how to create a Web banner, back in Chapter 24. Here I'll give you a quick review, as well as cover some additional fine points of frame animation.

FIGURE 26.17

The Animation panel, shown here in Frame mode, allows you to create simple animations based on enabling or disabling layers' visibility in different frames.

Frame

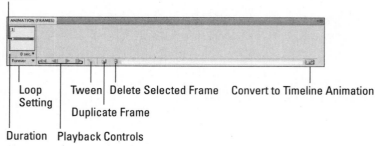

Loop Setting   Tween   Delete Selected Frame   Convert to Timeline Animation

Duplicate Frame

Duration   Playback Controls

Adding and deleting frames

When you display the Animation panel in Frames mode, one frame is automatically added, based on the current state of your document. To add more frames to the Animation panel, and thus increase the duration of your animation, select one or more frames and click the Duplicate Selected Frames button.

To remove frames from your animation, highlight them and click the trashcan icon at the bottom of the Animation panel.

Editing frame content

You can add frames until you're blue in the face and not actually create any animation if you're not changing the attributes of your layers from frame to frame. Attributes that you can animate include layer position, opacity, and layer styles. Changing a frame's visibility is another way of creating animation. Simply click on a frame, select a layer or layers, and make your modifications. Keep adding frames to gradually build your animation. Here are a few controls you can use when editing frame content:

■ **Propagate Frame 1.** Frame 1 is a special frame, because by default, any change you make to a layer while that frame is targeted is automatically carried over to the rest of the frames of your animation. This can be an extremely useful time-saver, but it can also be frustrating if you've meticulously set up your animation, and you innocently go back to Frame 1 and make a modification that you only expect to see on that frame. You can change this behavior on a layer-by-layer basis, though, by selecting a layer and toggling the Propagate Frame 1 check box found at the top of the Layers panel.

■ **Unify Position/Visibility/Layer Style.** You can maintain certain layer attributes throughout your animation with the Unify buttons found at the top of the Layers panel. You can unify the position, visibility, and layer style of the selected layer across the animation. Click the check box for the attribute you want to unify — if the corresponding attribute doesn't match up on every frame of your animation, Photoshop first asks if it should make everything consistent before proceeding. Once an attribute is unified, any changes you make are updated across the board, no matter which frame is selected.

Incidentally, by default, the Unify options appear in the Layers panel automatically if the Animation timeline is visible and in Frame mode. You can change this setting in the Animation panel's options menu.

■ **Match Layer Across Frames.** This is another way of making sure things are consistent throughout your animation. To use this option, select a layer and choose Match Layer Across Frames from the Animation panel's options menu. From the resulting dialog box, select any or all of the available options and click OK. The difference between this method and the Unify method is that future changes to the selected layer are not reflected throughout the animation.

Setting frame duration

Frame-based animations don't have a global frame-rate setting that determines how long each frame is visible; rather, you set the delay in seconds of each frame. To set the duration of a frame, click on the duration value, and from the resulting menu, select a time or choose Other to enter a custom value. If you set the delay of a frame, any frames you add subsequently will remember the last-used delay.

Creating in-between frames

You can create tweens in frame-based animations just as you can in timeline animations, although the procedure is slightly different. First, create two keyframes — that is, two frames that reflect the way your animation should look at the start and end of the tween. For example, you could have one frame where a text layer is transparent, and a second keyframe where the text layer is fully opaque. Select one of the frames and click the Tween button at the bottom of the Animation panel.

Depending on which keyframe you selected, insert the tween either before or after the selected frame by choosing the appropriate option from the Tween With menu. Choose which layers to tween — either the selected layer or all layers. If you choose Selected Layers, Photoshop literally only tweens whichever layer is currently selected, inserting new frames with only the tweened layer visible. Finally, select the parameters that you want to tween, and click OK. Figure 26.18 shows the Animation panel before and after a tween was performed.

FIGURE 26.18

The Animation panel on the top shows two frames of an animation. The bottom panel shows the result of applying a tween to update the position of the golf ball, moving it from left to right across the screen.

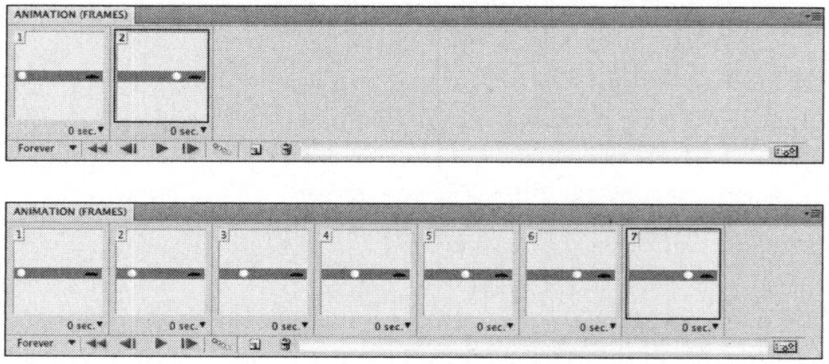

Specifying looping options

A frame-based animation can play continuously, looping around to the beginning when it reaches the end. Use the Looping option to determine how many times the animation plays. Click on the looping setting at the bottom left of the Animation panel, and choose either Forever, Once, or Other from the resulting menu.

Previewing and exporting frame-based animations

You can preview your frame-based animation by using the playback controls at the bottom of the Animation panel. This gives you a rough idea of how your movement will look, but you shouldn't rely on this method for an accurate preview of how the animation will look once it's being viewed in a Web browser. Rather, choose File ➪ Save for Web & Devices, and click the Preview button to see what the animation will look like in your default Web browser, and go back and adjust the frame delay settings if necessary.

Once you are ready to export a GIF of your animation for publishing on the Web, use the Save for Web & Devices dialog box to specify optimization settings, and then click Save. For more specifics on using the Save for Web & Devices dialog box, refer to Chapter 24.

Converting to Timeline animation

Frame-based animations can be converted to timeline animations and vice-versa by clicking the icon at the bottom right of the Animation panel, or by choosing the available conversion option from the Animation panel. Note that not all keyframed animations convert correctly when switching from timeline to frame-based animation. Also, video layers won't play in frame-based animation.

Saving Video and Animations

Creating and editing video and animations is all well and good, but at some point, you may want to get your work out of Photoshop and onto a television screen or some other output device. This section covers previewing your video on a video monitor and exporting your final work as a QuickTime file. You'll also review how to preview and optimize frame-based animations for the Web.

Previewing video on a video monitor

Before exporting your video for final output, or for use in another software package, you'll want to make sure it looks right. Using the Video Preview plug-in that ships with Photoshop, you can preview video on a monitor that's connected to your computer over a FireWire connection (also known by the less human-friendly name of IEEE 1394). The preview plug-in supports RGB, Grayscale, and Indexed Color images, and automatically converts 16-bit files to 8 bits as they are being displayed.

If you've never previewed video and specified output options, choose File ➪ Export ➪ Video Preview. This opens the Video Preview dialog box shown in Figure 26.19, which allows you to configure the preview settings for your device.

FIGURE 26.19

The Video Preview dialog box is used to specify video output settings.

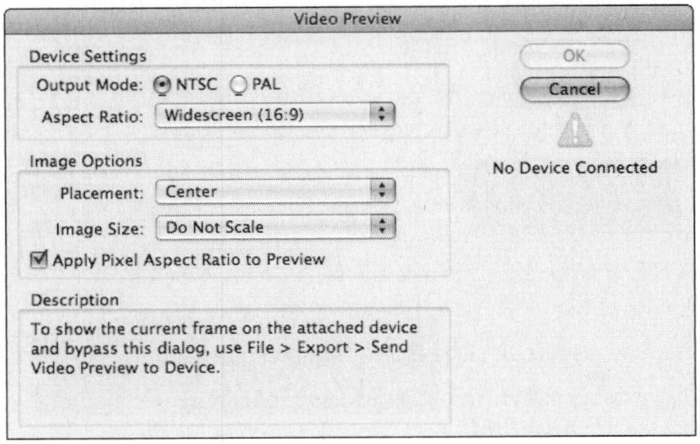

Configure the following options in the Video Preview window:

- **Under Device Settings, select an Output Mode and Aspect Ratio.** Choose from either NTSC or PAL depending on whether your video is intended for North American or international viewing. From the Aspect Ratio menu, select whether the device has a 4:3 or 16:9 aspect ratio.

- **Specify how your image should be placed within the monitor.** The available options depend on the aspect ratio of the display you chose in the Device Settings section. If you specified a 4:3 aspect ratio, you can choose to center the preview or crop it to fit it in a widescreen aspect ratio.

- **Choose a scaling option for the video preview.** Either scale the pixels to fit the display or display them at 100 percent. If you're previewing widescreen content on a 4:3 device and you select Scale to Fit Within Frame, the content shrinks to letterboxed format.

- **Click in the Apply Pixel Aspect Ratio to Preview check box to use the document's pixel aspect ratio on the connected monitor.** If you're creating content with a non-square pixel aspect ratio, you should leave this box checked.

To reuse the most recent preview settings, choose File ➪ Export ➪ Send Video Preview to Device. This automatically shows the preview on your video monitor, bypassing the setup dialog box.

Rendering video

Unless you're ready to produce final output, you should save your video work as a layered file in Photoshop's native PSD format. This allows you to maintain the greatest degree of editability possible, should you need to go back and rearrange things later. In addition, many video-editing programs, including After Effects and Final Cut, support importing layered PSD files, so there's no need to output a video format for import into one of those programs.

That said, once your work is final and you need to output the finished product, choose File ➪ Export ➪ Render Video to specify your export settings. Figure 26.20 shows the Render Video dialog box.

Here's a quick run-through of the options available in the Render Video dialog box:

- **Choose a filename and a location for your exported video files.** If necessary — for example, if you're creating an image sequence — you can opt to create a new subfolder in the process.

- **Under File Options, choose one of the export formats supported by QuickTime.** Click Settings and specify compression options based on the output format you've selected. The current compression settings are conveniently summarized in the area directly beneath the output format. The available choices are as follows:

  - **3G:** A multimedia format used by mobile devices on high-speed networks.
  - **Windows Media:** The format used by Microsoft's Windows Media Player.
  - **FLC:** Also referred to as FLI, this is an animation format used on MS-DOS systems. It doesn't support audio or video, but rather stores animation as a sequence of images.

FIGURE 26.20

Specify the export settings for your video using the Render Video dialog box.

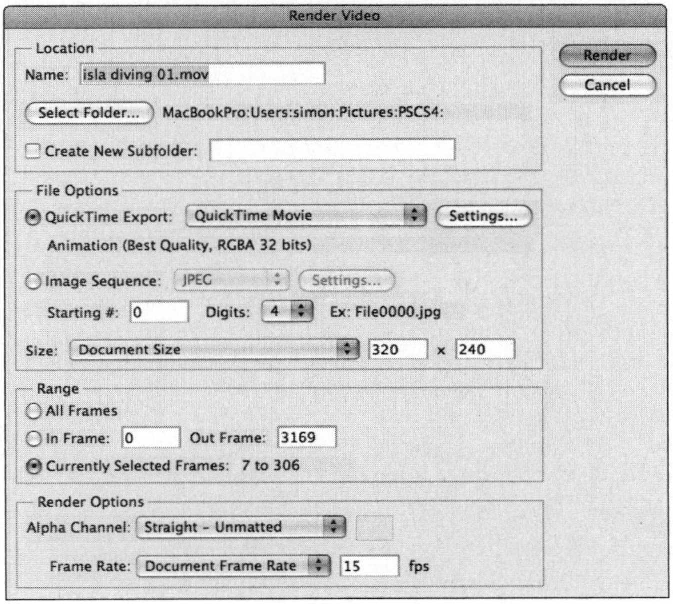

- **FLV:** The standard video format used with Adobe Flash Player. This format is available if the FLV QuickTime Export plug-in is installed on your system.

- **QuickTime Movie:** The default format for Apple's QuickTime player.

- **AVI:** The default video format for Windows-based systems.

- **DV Stream:** A high-quality video format designed for use with non-linear editing systems (like Final Cut Pro, Avid, or even iMovie on a Mac).

- **Image Sequence:** This setting allows you to output a sequence of images in various formats. The options aren't as flexible as the ones provided under the File Options section of the Video Preview dialog box, so you should use that option when exporting images.

- **MPEG-4:** A universal video format used for a wide range of purposes including broadcast, DVD, and Internet delivery.

- **Alternately, you can choose to output your video as a numbered sequence of image files.** Specify an image format and a starting number for the filenames that are given to your images. Depending on how many frames there are in your video, you can also specify the number of digits for the numerical file-naming sequence. If you have thousands of frames, choose at least four digits.

- **Enter the pixel dimensions for your exported file.** Specify custom dimensions or choose a preset from the provided popup menu.

- **Specify what portion of your animation to export.** By default, the range of frames that's contained within your Work Area in the Animation panel in Timeline mode is automatically selected. If you want, you can choose to export the entire timeline's worth of frames, or enter a custom frame range for export.

- **Alpha channel options are available only if your export file format supports it.** If your video contains transparency information, choose how the alpha information should be treated. Choose Straight — Unmatted to keep transparency information in a separate alpha channel and not in the RGB channels. Alternately, you can premultiply the alpha channel against either black, white, or a custom color if you're exporting the video for use in a program that supports it.

- **Specify a frame rate for your video.** In most cases, you'll want to leave the frame rate at your document's default settings, otherwise the video you output will be inconsistent with what you've been seeing inside of Photoshop.

Once you're happy with your choices, click Render to begin processing your file. Depending on the length of your video, the settings you've chosen, and other factors such as Smart Objects, Smart Filters, adjustment layers, and transparency, it could take a while for your video to export.

Summary

This chapter introduced you to the video capabilities of Photoshop CS4 Extended. You learned about the video and image formats that Photoshop can import or export for use with video layers. You learned other video-related information, including frame rates, aspect ratios, and output formats, and how to prepare your documents for use in other video-editing applications. You learned about working with the Animation panel in Timeline mode to manipulate video, and to create smooth, tweened keyframe animations.

You also learned about using Photoshop's painting tools, filters, blending modes, masks, and layer styles with video content. Frame-based animation was also reviewed in this chapter. Finally, you learned how to preview and export your video content in different file formats.

Chapter 27

Working with 3D Images

It was a happy day for many designers back in 2007, when Photoshop CS3 made its debut, and we learned that Adobe's crack team of engineers had introduced support for 3D objects in the Extended edition of the software. With this new functionality, we can now import 3D models directly into Photoshop for real-time compositing with our photography and designs. In the past, if you wanted to do similar things, you simply couldn't without access to 3D authoring software, which can be prohibitively expensive and often comes with a serious learning curve.

For Photoshop CS4 (Extended), Adobe has made significant improvements to the 3D engine built in to the software — in fact, so much new functionality has been added that it merited the addition of a dedicated 3D menu. The long list of new features includes support for the use of 2-D images as 3D textures, and the ability to paint interactively on the textures of an object.

By nature, the world of 3D modeling, rendering, and animation is very complex, and it is far beyond the scope of this book to give in-depth instruction on all aspects of working with 3D. Also, there are limits to what you should expect from Photoshop's 3D capabilities, expanded though they might be (for instance, you still have to perform complex modeling tasks in 3D software like AutoDesk Maya or Modo). With that said, if you're new to 3D, this chapter should show you that it's simple enough to get started with incorporating 3D objects into your Photoshop compositions. If you're an experienced 3D user, you'll also benefit from seeing how Photoshop can become an even more integral part of your 3D workflow.

3D Files in Photoshop

The two main ways to get 3D objects into Photoshop are either to import an existing 3D file in a supported format or to create an object from a layer or layers. Photoshop also ships with several shape presets that you can apply artwork or images to, as you'll see later on in this chapter.

Opening a 3D model in Photoshop brings in all that object's data as it was defined in the 3D authoring software used to create it — the vertices and polygons that define its structure, and the textures (if any) that give it its color. Once that data is in Photoshop, you can transform the object, paint or modify textures that have been applied to it, and add lighting effects to it. 3D objects also have a "camera" that you can manipulate to view the model from different vantage points. Using the keyframing techniques described in Chapter 26, you can even animate properties of 3D layers and cameras, and you can export your animations in video formats. You can't, however, alter the geometry or physical structure of the object in Photoshop — as mentioned earlier, that must be done in a 3D software package.

Supported 3D file formats

The first thing you need to know about bringing 3D objects into Photoshop is which file formats it supports. The formats differ depending on the software that was used to create the model, and can contain varying amounts of information — from basic structure and color information to full scenes with animation. Photoshop offers support for the following formats:

- **3DS.** Available only on the Windows platform, AutoDesk's 3D Studio Max is one of the most commonly used 3D applications. The 3DS format is 3D Studio Max's native format.

- **COLLADA (.DAE).** COLLADA started out as the official format for Sony's PlayStation 3 and PSP video game consoles. It was originally used as a data exchange format for passing 3D information between different graphics applications. The Khronos group, an industry consortium, has since taken joint ownership of the format along with Sony, and the format has become the standard for a growing number of game development studios. COLLADA files use the DAE (Digital Asset Exchange) file extension.

- **KMZ.** KMZ stands for Keyhole Markup Language-zipped, and was the default file format for a 3D program called Keyhole. Keyhole was eventually bought by Google, and is now available as a free download in its new incarnation as Google Sketchup. Along with COLLADA files, KMZ files are readable by Google Earth for overlaying 3D geometry of buildings and structures around the globe.

- **OBJ.** Several widely used 3D authoring tools including AutoDesk Maya, Blender, 3D Studio Max, Poser, and Lightwave use this open format to export models for use with other graphics software packages. The OBJ format only contains information about an object's geometry — where each vertex and polygon that make up the object lie. It supports materials or textures by referring to an external MTL file.

- **U3D.** Universal 3D was developed by a consortium of companies including Adobe, Intel, and HP as a standard format for the exchange of 3D information for use in business and architectural drawing applications. U3D objects can be embedded in PDF documents and viewed in Acrobat Reader.

If you haven't worked with 3D objects before, or don't have access to 3D modeling software, you might be wondering where you can get files in these formats from. Google Warehouse, along with lots of Web sites including the excellent www.turbosquid.com, offer downloadable models either for free or at varying prices.

> **CAUTION** I'll offer the usual warning here about being wary of downloading software from spurious sources, even though I'm sure that at this point, it's completely unnecessary. (Right? Right.)

Opening and placing 3D files

Opening a 3D model in Photoshop is pretty simple. If you're starting from scratch, choose File ⇨ Open, navigate to the 3D file, and click Open. If you want to add a 3D object to an existing file, you can choose 3D ⇨ New 3D Layer from File. Using either of these methods brings the 3D data into Photoshop and places it in a 3D layer. In the case of KMZ files, you must first enter dimensions for the canvas before opening the file. This number isn't necessarily set in stone, however, as you can scale 3D objects without losing resolution.

Another way to bring a 3D file into Photoshop is to use the Place command. Choose File ⇨ Place and navigate to the file. When you click the Open button, the file is brought into Photoshop with the familiar Free Transform bounding box and handles surrounding it, so that you can transform and position it. Accepting the transformations places the model on a 3D layer inside a Smart Object, which means you can take advantage of all the benefits that Smart Objects offer (Smart Filters and so on). To edit the properties of the 3D object, as with any Smart Object, double-click the layer's thumbnail, make your changes, and save the resulting PSB file to have those edits reflected in the originating document.

3D layers and the 3D panel

Like video layers, 3D layers store references to external content. Video layers reference video or image sequences, and allow you to move around frame-by-frame within that content. 3D layers, on the other hand, store data generated by 3D authoring software, such as AutoDesk's 3D Studio Max or Maya, and treat this data collectively as a *scene*.

As shown in Figure 27.1, the 3D layer includes sub-layers representing textures that were applied to the object when it was originally created. You can enable and disable these textures by clicking the eyeball icon associated with each sub-layer. As you'll learn later in this chapter, you can also edit the appearance of these textures in a new document window using any of the tools in Photoshop's arsenal, by simply double-clicking on their names in the Layers panel.

Each 3D layer is treated as an independent scene with its own lighting, materials, objects, and camera. Moving the camera associated with one 3D scene doesn't affect the camera position on other layers — unless you merge individual 3D layers into one scene by selecting the uppermost 3D layer in the Layers panel and choosing Merge down from the panel's options menu.

Double-clicking the thumbnail opens the 3D panel (see Figure 27.2), which gives you access to myriad different types of controls for the elements that make up the current scene.

FIGURE 27.1

A 3D layer shown in the Layers panel

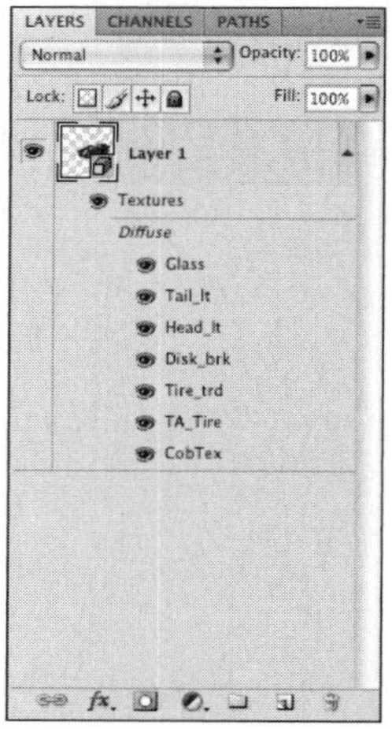

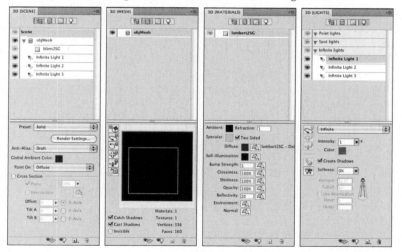

FIGURE 27.2

The 3D panel, showing Scene, Mesh, Materials, and Lights modes

The upper part of the panel is reserved for displaying the scene hierarchy for the selected layer. Click on the topmost level of the hierarchy — labeled "Scene" — to edit overall settings for the 3D layer, such as its render mode and anti-aliasing quality. Selecting any of the elements in the scene hierarchy switches the panel's mode and updates the area at the bottom of the 3D panel with information and controls that are related to the selected scene element. You'll also notice that the label on the 3D panel's tab changes to reflect the mode it's currently in. These are the different types of elements that can make up a scene:

- **Mesh.** This is the actual geometry that makes up the 3D object. The mesh is made up of polygons (or faces) and vertices, put together in the original 3D application.

- **Materials.** Textures or surfaces are what give 3D objects their color and other attributes.

- **Lights.** Without lights in the scene, the 3D object would appear as a black silhouette. Each object has three default lights associated with it, but you can either remove or add lights in Photoshop.

Clicking on any of the four icons at the top of the 3D panel filters its display to just the related scene elements and controls, which you will learn more about later in this chapter.

Creating 3D objects in Photoshop

In addition to importing models created in 3D software, you can use existing layers in Photoshop to generate 3D objects, either by applying them like decals to a 3D shape, or by actually generating geometry based on the contents of the layer or layers. The following techniques are available in the 3D menu:

- **New 3D Postcard from Layer.** This command applies the selected layer or layers to a plane that can be rotated in 3D space.

- **New Shape from Layer.** Photoshop ships with several 3D shape presets, which you can wrap the contents of a layer around, as you would a decal. With a layer or image selected, choose 3D ➪ New Shape from Layer, and select one of the shape presets. Figure 27.3 illustrates a photograph wrapped around the label of the Wine Bottle shape preset.

  These shapes are models saved in the COLLADA format — if you have your own models, you can add them to this menu by saving them in the Presets/Meshes folder, inside the Photoshop application folder.

  One of the more interesting options in this menu is Spherical Panorama. If you have a series of images shot as a panorama, you can wrap them around the inside of a sphere, and use the 3D camera positioning tools to look around the scene. Stitch the images together into a single panoramic image by choosing Edit ➪ Auto-Align Layers. Next, eliminate any seams in the composition by choosing Edit ➪ Auto-Blend Layers. Select Panorama as the Blend Method from the resulting dialog box and click OK. Finally, choose 3D ➪ New Shape from Layer ➪ Spherical Panorama. The 3D camera is placed inside the sphere, and can now be rotated and manipulated to view the scene. You can also paint and merge 2D layers into the 3D scene. Painting on 3D objects is covered later in this chapter.

FIGURE 27.3

Using the New Shape from Layer command, a photograph was wrapped around the label area of this wine bottle model.

For best results you should use a series of images shot as a 360-degree panorama, but fewer images will also work.

TIP   Quickly stitch panoramic images together by selecting them in Bridge and choosing
       Tools ⇨ Photoshop ⇨ Photomerge. Choose a layout and specify blending options,
then click OK.

- **New Mesh from Grayscale.** Use this command to create 3D geometry from the grayscale information contained in the selected layers. Similar to depth maps (or *dmaps*, covered in Chapter 21), the depth of the geometry is created based on the grayscale values. White areas are pushed out farthest from the surface of the object. Black areas are recessed, and 50-percent gray areas are even with the surface of the object.

- **New Volume from Layers.** Medical imaging machines like echocardiograms use slices saved in the DICOM format to display a thin cross-section of the human heart to cardiologists. This command allows you to recombine these slices into a 3D image of the heart.

CROSS-REF   Read more about the DICOM format in Chapter 28.

Using the 3D Camera

3D isn't called 3D just because it's a catchy name — the name refers to the three-dimensional space that 3D objects occupy. In this space, coordinates along x-, y-, and z-axes represent an object's position. The center or *origin* of the coordinate system is located at x, y, and z values of 0, 0, 0. What all of this means is that you can view the object from any angle by positioning the 3D camera in space relative to the object.

This might all sound fairly complex, but the good news is that Photoshop offers a 3D View tool that allows you to move the camera in a multitude of ways relative to the object in the scene. Figure 27.4 shows the various iterations of the View tool, which are all grouped together in the Toolbox.

These additional modes are also available in the Options Bar whenever any of the camera manipulation tools is active. To use the 3D View tools, first select a 3D layer in the Layers panel, and then click on one of the tools, or press the N key. You'll notice that when you select one of these tools and hover over the canvas, your cursor changes to give you a visual indication of what the current tool actually does.

NOTE   If the currently selected layer isn't a 3D layer, you'll see the familiar "oh-no-you-
        don't" circle with a line through it when you hover your cursor over the canvas.
Select a 3D layer and you'll be good to go.

FIGURE 27.4

Photoshop's 3D camera tools share the N key as a keyboard shortcut, and allow you to change the vantage point from which an object is viewed.

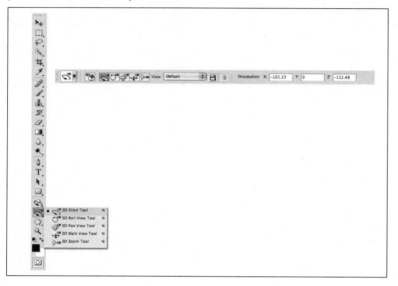

Press N or Shift-N to cycle through the following tool modes:

- **Orbit.** Select the tool, then click and drag your cursor in your document's canvas to rotate your camera in a freeform manner around the 3D object. Hold down the Shift key while dragging to constrain the camera movements in the direction you are dragging (either up and down, or left and right).

- **Roll View.** Use this tool to tilt your camera to the left or right about its z-axis. Imagine holding a video camera, pointing it at your subject, and spinning it so that your subject flips upside down.

- **Pan View.** Use this tool to move the camera to the left and right, or up and down.

- **Walk View.** With this tool, you can move the camera closer to or farther away from the 3D object.

- **Zoom.** This tool changes the focal length of the camera, allowing you to zoom in or out for a close-up or a long shot of your subject.

A useful shortcut to remember when working with the 3D camera tools is that in some cases, you can switch between related tools if you hold down the Alt or Option key; for example, the Orbit tool switches to Roll and vice-versa. Right-clicking/Ctrl+clicking while dragging with a tool also switches over to an alternate function, depending on which tool is currently active.

NOTE   Remember, each 3D object you import or create has its own independent camera, unless you merge the 3D layers.

Positioning the camera numerically

Another way of manipulating the 3D camera is available to you in the Options Bar. Selecting either the 3D Orbit or 3D Roll View tool allows you to enter the camera's rotation in degrees about its x-, y-, or z-axis in the Options Bar fields. The 3D Pan View or 3D Walk View tool allows you to specify the camera's position along any of its three axes. Finally, with the Zoom tool selected, you can set the camera's field of view vertically or horizontally, or set its focal length in millimeters.

Camera presets

There are seven preset views available for each camera: Default, Left, Right, Top, Bottom, Front, and Back. Select any of these views from the View menu in the Options Bar to position the 3D camera in relation to the object. This comes in handy if you've moved the camera around and want to get it back to the default position it was in when you first imported it, or if you want to see an object from a specific vantage point.

Perspective versus orthographic views

The Default view displays your object in perspective — that is, the way that the human eye sees things. Objects farther away from the camera are smaller than objects close to the camera, and parallel lines recede toward a common vanishing point. The other six views available in the View menu are *orthographic* views — that is, they display the object as though it were being viewed with a camera from an infinite distance away, with an infinite zoom. This results in parallel lines in the scene actually being displayed as parallel, and objects that are farther away from the camera appearing at the same size as objects that are in the foreground.

Figure 27.5 illustrates the difference between a perspective view and an orthographic view. The sides of the cube, which we know in reality are parallel to each other, actually appear to be receding toward the same vanishing point. The image on the right shows an orthographic view of the same cube — note that the sides of the cube are actually parallel to each other.

You can toggle your custom views between orthographic and perspective modes by selecting the Zoom View tool and clicking on the perspective and orthographic view icons (shown in Figure 27.6) in the Options Bar.

Saving custom views

If you've come up with a vantage point you like for the current scene, you can add it to the View menu by saving it as a preset. Click the save button in the Options Bar (it looks like a floppy disk icon) and enter a name for your custom view. You can reuse this preset with the current scene, which is useful if you've moved the scene's camera around and decide you want to return to a particular vantage point.

FIGURE 27.5

The image on the left shows a cube as seen from a perspective camera. The image on the right shows an orthographic view of the same cube — note that the sides of the cube are actually parallel to each other.

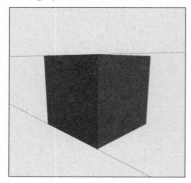 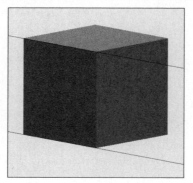

You can also apply the camera position of one 3D layer to another layer in the same document. From the View menu, select the name of the layer whose camera position you want to apply to the current scene.

FIGURE 27.6

Click the icons to toggle your camera between perspective and orthographic modes.

Orthographic view

Perspective view

Working with 3D Models

So far, you've learned how to import or create 3D objects, and how to manipulate the 3D camera around an object. Now you'll learn about setting up options for displaying the contents of a 3D layer. You'll also learn how to modify the object itself — how to transform it, change its textures or materials, and adjust its lighting properties.

Setting Scene options

The 3D panel is one of the first places to look when setting up the way your 3D scene is displayed or *rendered*. Choices range from simple wireframes to high-quality previews, and the system resources required to generate these displays varies accordingly. You may want to change your rendering preset to a low-quality setting while you're working, and then bump it up to a high-quality setting for final output. Or, your design may call for a flat, geometrically shaded version of your object — that option is available too.

Select a 3D layer and double-click its thumbnail to display the 3D panel if it's not shown (or select the panel from the View menu). Figure 27.7 shows an example of the 3D panel in Scene mode (which is reflected by the label on the panel's tab). The upper part of the 3D panel is populated with the scene hierarchy — that is, the meshes, materials, and lights that make up the selected 3D object.

FIGURE 27.7

Use the controls in the 3D panel's Scene mode to change display settings for the current 3D layer.

 To keep your scenes organized, get in the habit of giving your meshes, lights, and materials descriptive names. Double-click an item in the scene hierarchy to change its name.

Here's a description of the controls below the scene hierarchy:

- **Preset.** Select a rendering preset from the 17 choices available here. Each preset governs the way the objects in the scene are displayed. The default setting is Solid, which applies smoothing to the polygons to form curved surfaces. The Wireframe option displays the lines for each polygon that makes up the 3D objects in the scene. Shaded Wireframe combines the two methods described above. Raytraced is the highest-quality setting available, capable of producing photorealistic results with accurately calculated reflections and shadows. As you might expect, it is also the most computationally intensive choice, and will definitely put your computer's graphics hardware through its paces.

Some of the rendering presets are used to give you information about the geometry of the object. For instance, the Normals preset indicates information about which direction the polygons that make up the surface of the object are facing, and Paint Mask shows the optimal areas that can be painted on using 3D Paint Mode (covered later in this section). Figure 27.8 shows some examples of different rendering presets.

- **Render Settings.** Click on the Render Settings button to create a custom Rendering Preset. Specify options for the display of the scene's faces, edges, and vertices, and save your settings by clicking the floppy disk icon at the top of the 3D Render Settings dialog box (see Figure 27.9). Different options will be available depending on the combination of settings you choose. For instance, you can make a selection in the Texture menu only if you choose Unlit Texture from the Face Style menu, and you can choose to enable or disable Reflections, Refractions and Shadows if your Face Style is set to Ray Traced.

FIGURE 27.8

Examples of rendering presets. Top row (l-r): Solid, Solid Wireframe, Shaded Illustration. Middle row: Line Illustration, Hidden Wireframe, Shaded Vertices. Bottom row: Normals, Paint Mask, Raytraced.

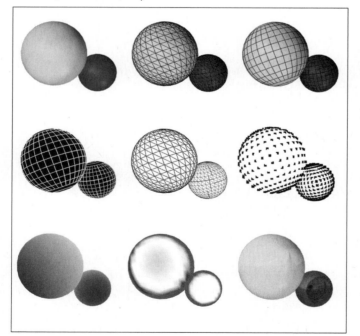

FIGURE 27.9

Create custom rendering presets with the 3D Render Settings dialog box.

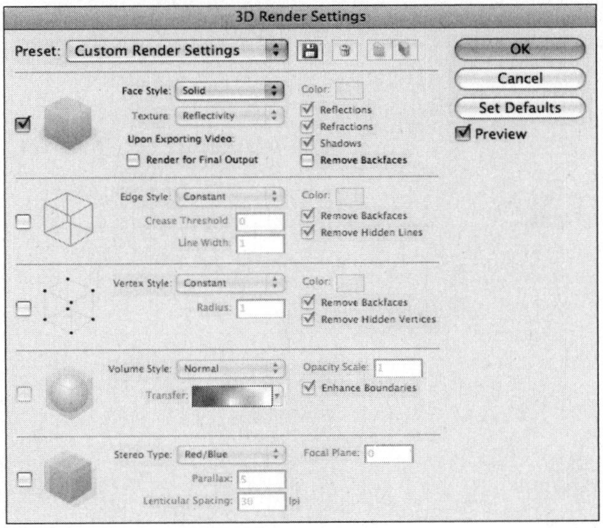

The last two sections in the 3D Render Settings dialog box provide advanced rendering options. Volume rendering allows you to control the display of volume objects created by combining DICOM slices into a 3D volume object. The Stereo Type options let you render stereo images that appear three-dimensional when viewed with 3D glasses.

- **Anti-Alias.** By now, you're no doubt familiar with the concept of anti-aliasing. Just in case you need a refresher, anti-aliasing is a technique that smoothes jagged edges in computer-generated images. Choose an Anti-Alias preset to set the strength of the smoothing that's applied to the edges of your 3D model. Setting the Anti-Alias preset to Best creates the smoothest edges, but also causes your display to refresh very slowly. I recommend using the Draft setting while you're working, and changing the setting to Best when you're ready to produce your final image.

- **Global Ambient Color.** Ambient color refers to the color that exists in the shadows, or areas lit by reflected light in a scene. You can use the Global Ambient Color swatch to specify an ambient color for your scene, giving it an overall mood or tone.

- **Paint On.** Select a texture map to paint on using 3D Paint mode. Attempting to paint on an object that doesn't have the specified type of texture map results in a warning dialog box and the opportunity to allow Photoshop to add a new texture to the object. Read more about 3D Paint mode later in this section.

- **Cross Section.** This option lets you display a cutaway view of the selected object. It doesn't actually modify the object's geometry; it just displays the object as though it were cut in two. Using the default settings, a semi-transparent plane is inserted in the scene, cutting the selected object in half. Using the options in the panel, you can choose the axis about which the object is bisected, tilt the bisection, set the opacity and color of the plane that is used to cut the object, or hide the plane entirely. Use the Offset slider to move the point on the object where the division is made, as illustrated in Figure 27.10.

FIGURE 27.10

The Cross Section tool is used to show a cutaway view of the soda can model shown on the left. In the image on the right, the Offset slider was used to reposition the point on the can where the cut was made.

Transforming 3D models

As an alternative (or in addition) to moving the 3D camera to set up the way your object is displayed, you can use the 3D Transform tools to scale, rotate, and move all the objects contained in the selected scene within three-dimensional space. The 3D Transform tools are grouped together in the Toolbox, and share the K key as a shortcut (users of previous versions of Photoshop will recognize that this keyboard shortcut once belonged to the Slice tool). As is the case with the 3D View tools, the alternate versions of the 3D Transform tools are also accessible via their icons in the Options Bar when any one of them is active. The 3D Transform tools are illustrated in Figure 27.11.

NOTE   Your cursor changes into a circle with a line through it if the currently selected layer isn't a 3D layer.

Most of the tools for transforming 3D objects function just like the tools used to manipulate the 3D camera. The Rotate and Roll tools spin the object (or objects) on the selected 3D layer around its axes; the Pan tool moves the object left and right, or up and down. The Slide tool moves the object closer to or farther away from the camera, and the Scale tool makes the object bigger or smaller.

FIGURE 27.11

The 3D Transform tools allow you to manipulate the object or objects on the selected 3D layer.

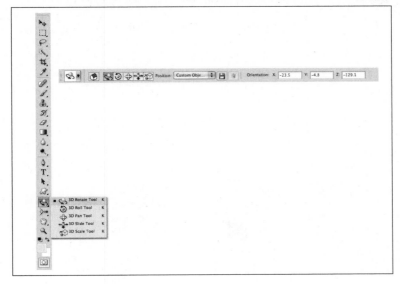

Again, you can also use the fields provided in the Options Bar to position or otherwise transform the current object numerically.

Using object position presets

The 3D Transform tools' Options Bar offers some preset object positions, just as the 3D View tools offer preset camera positions. To use the presets, select a 3D layer and choose an option from the Position menu. Default returns your object to its initial position (you can also click the Home icon on the left of the Options Bar). The remaining six icons are a convenient way of displaying your object from the front, back, top, bottom, left side, or right side.

Create a custom position preset by clicking the Save Preset icon (it looks like a floppy disk) and entering a descriptive name for the preset. Position presets are married, so to speak, to the 3D layers they were created for, but you can apply the positioning of the objects on one 3D layer to those on other layers in the same document just as you can with camera presets. Select the 3D layer whose position you'd like to change. Click the Position menu and choose the name of the 3D layer whose position you'd like to copy.

Using the 3D Axis widget

New to Photoshop CS4, Photoshop offers another way of transforming 3D objects. Selecting a 3D layer produces the red, yellow, and green 3D Axis widget shown in Figure 27.12, which gives you a visual indication of how your object is oriented.

FIGURE 27.12

The 3D Axis widget appears whenever Photoshop's 3D tools are active. Use the handles available on each axis to transform the selected object interactively.

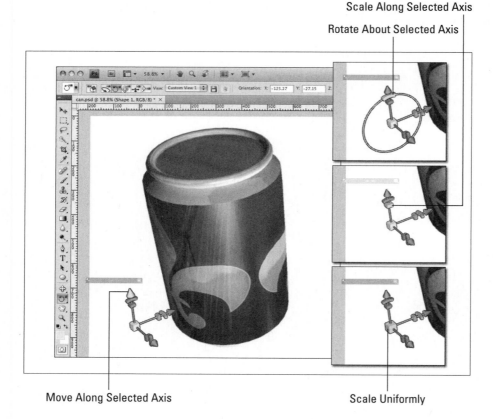

Each axis also has a scale, rotate, and position handle that you can drag to transform the object along that axis. As an added convenience, you can use this widget to transform the selected object even if one of the 3D View tools is active, saving you from having to switch back and forth between transform and camera controls as you compose your view.

Transforming meshes within a 3D layer

The 3D Transform tools in the Toolbox are used to transform all the objects contained in a scene as a unit. To manipulate individual pieces or *meshes* that make up a 3D object, you need to use the Mesh Transform tools located in the 3D panel. Select the 3D layer containing the meshes you want to manipulate, and make sure the 3D panel is visible. To restrict the contents of the 3D panel so you're only dealing with the selected object's meshes, click the Filter By: Meshes icon at the top of the panel.

Figure 27.13 shows the 3D panel in Mesh mode. As you can see, the soda can object that is currently selected is made up of two meshes: the cap, which is in fact both the top and bottom cap of the can; and the label, which is the part of the can with the artwork.

FIGURE 27.13

The Mesh Transform tools become available in the 3D panel when a mesh is selected. Use these tools to manipulate individual components of a 3D object.

When one of the meshes is selected, the lower part of the 3D panel offers six Mesh Transform tools that function in exactly the same way as the 3D Object Transform tools. You can spin, roll, pan, slide, or scale individual meshes, or click the home icon to return the mesh to its default position.

While on the subject of the 3D panel in Mesh view, there are a few other things to take note of:

- **The preview area displays a thumbnail of the object with a highlight around the currently selected mesh.** This is useful when dealing with complex objects or scenes that are made up of many meshes.

- **In the area immediately below the object preview, some information about the selected mesh is given.** The information includes the number of materials attached to the mesh, the number of textures that make up that material, and the number of vertices and faces that the object is made of. Complex objects with a high polygon count slow down Photoshop's performance, which is something to be aware of when importing 3D models from other programs.

- **Using the check boxes on the left, you can specify whether the mesh receives shadows cast by the other meshes that make up the object and whether it casts shadows on other meshes.**

Colors and textures

In the 3D world, bitmap files called *texture maps* govern the physical appearance of an object. The object's color, transparency, reflectivity, and a multitude of other attributes can all be mapped with a 2-D image to make the object appear as realistic or fantastical as you like. Photoshop supports the use of just about any file format as a texture map. This means you can use PSD files with layer styles, shape layers, adjustment layers, blending modes, editable text — virtually any of the tools available in the program to add texture to an object. Neat, huh? As an alternative, you can use a numerical value to control the strength of a particular attribute, like shininess or reflectivity, instead of using a 2-D image.

The texture maps associated with an object are listed as sub-layers in the Layers panel. Figure 27.14 demonstrates that if you hover over one of the texture maps listed under a 3D layer for a few seconds, you'll see a thumbnail of the image used for that texture, along with its filename and pixel dimensions.

FIGURE 27.14

A 3D soda can and the Layers panel showing the textures that give it its appearance

Double-clicking one of the textures associated with an object opens it in another window, allowing you to edit it to your heart's content. Any changes you made to the texture are reflected immediately on the object back in the original document. If the texture is saved in a format that supports editable layers, you can reopen the texture at any time and edit its components.

Types of textures

Several types of texture maps can be combined to make up an object's *material*. For example, the soda can used in the previous example (Figure 27.14) required two diffuse textures and an environment texture to make it look like a shiny, reflective soda can. The types of textures often found on 3D objects are as follows:

- **Diffuse.** This gives the object its base color, as it appears without any highlights or shadows.

- **Bump.** A bump map uses grayscale information to simulate the appearance of bumps, crevices, or other variations in the surface of an object without having to physically create those computationally intensive details. Black areas recede below the surface of the object, white areas appear to extend above the surface of the object, and 50-percent gray areas are flush with the surface of the object. The dimples in a golf ball or the texture of a brick wall could be generated with a bump map.

- **Glossiness.** Adding a glossy texture can give an object the appearance of slick, clear plastic, or a glossy coat of paint on a car.

- **Opacity.** An object's transparency is controlled with an opacity map. If a grayscale image is used, black areas are transparent and white areas are fully opaque, while gray values are semi-transparent. You could use an opacity map to punch holes in an object, as demonstrated in Figure 27.15.

FIGURE 27.15

The image on the right was mapped to this can's opacity texture, punching a hole straight through it.

- **Shininess.** Similar to glossiness, shininess has to do with how "shiny" an object is. The difference is in the highlights — a highly shiny surface has a very tightly focused specular highlight, while a low degree of shininess produces a broad, diffuse highlight. Think of soft plastic in comparison to hard plastic.

- **Self-illumination.** Applying a self-illumination map to an object causes it to appear to give off light. You could apply a self-illumination map to create a glowing surface, such as an LED light or a digital display. Again, grayscale information can be used to control the level of illumination an object gives off.

- **Reflectivity.** Reflectivity maps use grayscale information to control how much of its environment an object reflects. The environment includes other objects in the scene as well as an image mapped to the environment's texture (there's more on environmental textures a little later in the chapter).

Editing materials with the Layers panel

To edit the attributes of the textures applied to the selected object, make sure the 3D panel is visible, and click the Filter By: Materials icon at the top of the panel (see Figure 27.16). Click on a material to edit its properties using the fields and popup menus in the panel.

FIGURE 27.16

Editing the attributes of the selected texture using the 3D panel

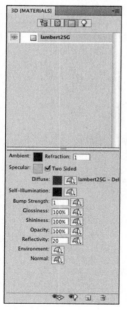

Here's what you need to know about editing textures:

■ **The Diffuse attribute controls the basic color or appearance of the selected material.** The soda can in Figure 27.17 was made by creating a shape with the Custom Shape tool and then choosing 3D ➪ New Shape from Layer ➪ Soda Can. The custom shape (a fleur-de-lis) is applied as the diffuse texture of the can's label. In this case, choosing a color from the diffuse color swatch doesn't make a difference, because I added a gradient background in the fleur-de-lis texture file, and it covers the material's base color. If, however, my fleur-de-lis had areas of transparency, the diffuse color would show through in those areas.

FIGURE 27.17

This soda can was created with a custom shape applied to its label's diffuse color attribute.

■ **For each of the texture map types described earlier, you can enter either a numerical value or attach a 2-D image as a texture.** Bump Strength takes a value from 1 to 10, while Reflectivity takes a number from 0 to 100. Otherwise, enter a percentage value to control the intensity of the selected texture.

■ **Aside from the Global Ambient Color, you can specify the ambient color of the selected texture.** Click the color swatch and select a value for the color of the areas of this texture that aren't directly lit. You can also specify a Specular color — that is, the color of the brightest highlights on the material.

■ **Each attribute that has a Texture Map popup icon next to it can have a 2-D image —
in just about any format that Photoshop supports — applied as a texture map.**
Choose one of the following:

▪ **New Texture:** Select this option to create a new document to be applied as a texture
to the selected material attribute. Enter the material's dimensions in the New file dialog box, then click OK. Double click on the newly added material in the Layers panel
to edit it, then save the document to have your changes reflected on the model. It's
recommended that when you add new textures to your model, you use the same document dimensions, color mode, and bit depth as used by existing texture files. A good
way to check this information in your existing textures is to hover over the texture
names in the Layers panel for several seconds. The resulting thumbnail texture preview includes file information.

▪ **Load Texture:** Use this option to navigate to an existing image on your hard drive
that you want to apply as a texture map.

▪ **Open Texture:** This option opens an attached texture in a new window for editing.
Save the document to update any materials that use this texture with your edits.

▪ **Edit Properties:** Select this option to change the way a texture is mapped to the
selected material. Change the texture map's scaling, or offset its positioning on the
object. For most users, leaving this option at its default settings should be just fine.

▪ **Remove Texture:** The name says it all. Use this option to remove an attached texture
from a material attribute.

▪ **Environment map:** In the 3D world, you must provide an environment for the
objects to reflect, and you can do so with an *environment map*. This gives your 3D
compositions a higher degree of realism, especially when rendered using Raytracing
mode, as demonstrated in Figure 27.18. The soda can on the left has no environment
map, while a photograph of a beach has been added as an environment map to the
materials applied to the can on the right. You can't really see any of the beach details,
but it definitely makes the can look much more realistic because of the irregular
reflections that appear on its surface.

■ **You can reuse the same images for different texture attributes.** For example, for the
soda can model used in the previous example, I used the same beach image as an environment map for the label's texture as well as for the upper and lower parts of the can's
texture. Photoshop helpfully notifies you with a dialog box if you use an image as a texture more than once; there's no downside to doing this, Photoshop's just being thorough.
Click OK to proceed.

FIGURE 27.18

This illustration shows the difference that using an environment map makes.

3D Paint Mode

Photoshop CS4 brings you a completely new, interactive way of editing an object's textures in the form of 3D Paint Mode. Using this technique, you can choose one of the texture maps assigned to the selected object and paint directly on it in the 3D view using any of Photoshop's brush-based tools.

To begin, make sure a 3D layer is selected, then choose a material attribute from the 3D ⇨ 3D Paint Mode menu. Alternatively, you can select a texture from the 3D panel's Paint On menu, which is available when the 3D panel is in Scene mode. Choose a brush-based tool and begin painting on the object (demonstrated in Figure 27.19), using the 3D View and 3D Transform tools to reposition the object as necessary. If you've selected an attribute that doesn't currently have a texture map assigned to it, Photoshop alerts you with the dialog box shown in Figure 27.20, and gives you the option of creating one.

> **NOTE** You can use just about any of Photoshop's tools to edit the currently selected texture — fills, gradients, filters, or the History Brush. Your results may vary, but experiment to your heart's content.

FIGURE 27.19

3D Paint Mode provides an interactive way to edit an object's textures.

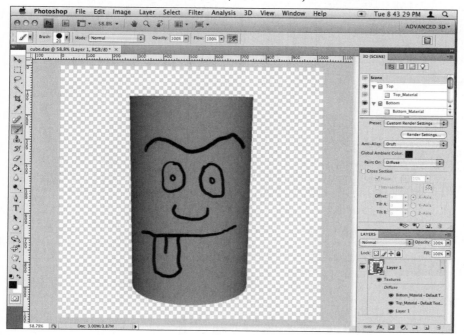

FIGURE 27.20

Attempting to paint on a texture that isn't currently assigned to the selected material produces this alert. Click OK to create the required texture, and proceed with editing.

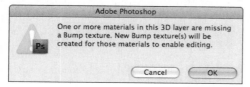

The pixels that can be painted on in 3D Paint Mode are limited to those that fall within the 3D Paint Threshold. You may want to lower this value so that you're not accidentally painting on portions of the model that you don't mean to affect. To edit the Paint Threshold limits, choose 3D Paint Threshold and enter a value for the Maximum and Minimum angles (see Figure 27.21). The highest value you can set in the Minimum angle field is 55 degrees, while you can go as high as 90 degrees in the Maximum angle field.

FIGURE 27.21

The 3D Paint Falloff dialog box allows you to specify minimum and maximum paintable angles.

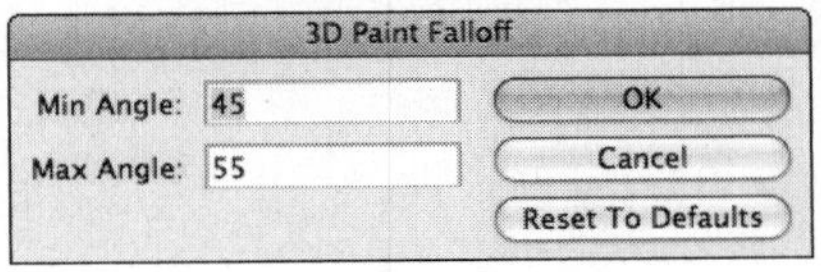

3D Paint Falloff	
Min Angle: 45	OK
Max Angle: 55	Cancel
	Reset To Defaults

To preview the paintable parts of the model, select the Paint Mask render mode from the Paint On popup menu in the 3D panel. This render mode displays paintable areas in white, while areas that can't be painted on are displayed in red.

NOTE To continue painting, you must change the render mode from Paint Mask back to one that supports painting, such as Solid, Solid Wireframe, or Raytraced.

Hiding and showing portions of a model

It can be useful at times to hide portions of a model so you can paint or edit only a certain part of it, or to get at portions of a 3D object that would otherwise be obscured. Using any of the selection tools, drag a selection around the portion of the model you want to hide and do one of the following:

■ Choose 3D ➪ Hide Nearest Surface to hide the portions of the model closed to the 3D camera, as demonstrated in Figure 27.22.

■ Choose 3D ➪ Only Hide Enclosed Polygons to hide the polygons that fall fully within your selection. A good way to see which polygons are hidden is to switch your rendering mode to Solid Wireframe. Any polygon that is partially enclosed by your selection is not hidden, as demonstrated in Figure 27.23.

■ Swap the visible portions of the model with the hidden ones by choosing 3D ➪ Invert Visible Surfaces.

■ Bring back any portions of the model that you've hidden by choosing 3D ➪ Reveal All Surfaces.

Using materials presets

What would life be without presets? It would probably involve lots of repetitive configuring of 3D materials settings, that's what. Avoid repetition by using the materials presets that ship with Photoshop. Saved as Adobe's proprietary P3M format, these files offer preconfigured attributes for such materials as brick, brushed steel, bumpy plastic, rusty metal, and pink granite. To apply one of these materials presets to your own objects, select an existing material and choose Replace Materials from the 3D panel's options menu. If necessary, navigate to the Presets/Materials folder in Photoshop's application folder.

Of course, it wouldn't be Photoshop if you couldn't save your own materials settings as presets. To do so, simply choose Save Material from the options menu and navigate to a suitable location for saving your materials files.

FIGURE 27.22

Using the Hide Nearest Surface command to temporarily hide portions of a model

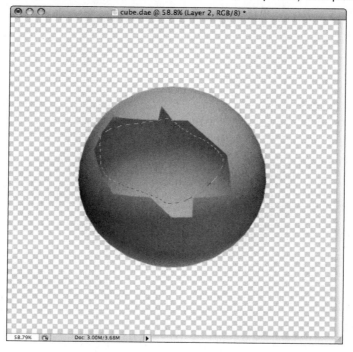

NOTE If the materials options are grayed out in the 3D panel's fly-out menu, that's probably because you don't have a material selected in the 3D panel's scene hierarchy.

Lighting

Lighting is one of the most important components of photography, film, theater, and most other visual media, and 3D visualization is no exception. Without lights in the scene, 3D objects would appear as solid black silhouettes. Usually, when you import a 3D object or create one from a layer in Photoshop, three default lights are added to the scene.

By no means are you required to stick with these three lights; in fact, in most cases, you should almost definitely change the lighting setup to one that is customized to your scene. Using the 3D panel's lighting options, you can add, delete, or reposition lights; you can adjust their color or intensity; and you can use presets to apply your favorite configurations to multiple 3D layers.

FIGURE 27.23

Polygons that fall outside of the "marching ants" selection are not hidden.

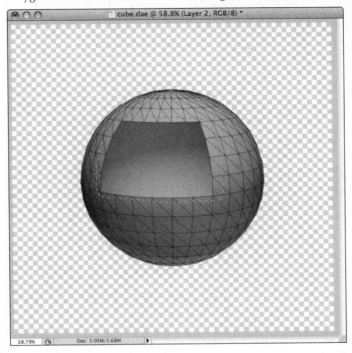

Viewing and modifying a scene's lighting setup

To view or change the existing lights in a scene, select a 3D layer and open the 3D panel. Scrolling through the scene hierarchy displays any available lights along with the materials and meshes that make up the selected object or scene.

Alternatively, you can focus on the lights by clicking the Filter By: Lights icon at the top of the panel as shown in Figure 27.24 (it's the icon that looks like a little light bulb). Lights are grouped by type in the scene hierarchy, so you can easily select them and position them. Selecting one of the available lights allows you to modify that light's settings, including its intensity, color, and light type. You can also double-click on a light's name and change it to something more descriptive of its function or position in the scene.

To place additional lights in the current scene, click the New Light button at the bottom of the 3D panel and choose a light type from the resulting popup menu. Delete an existing light by selecting it and clicking the trashcan icon. You can also temporarily disable all the lights in the scene by clicking the Toggle Lights icon.

FIGURE 27.24

The 3D panel's Lights mode allows you to configure the current 3D layer's lighting options.

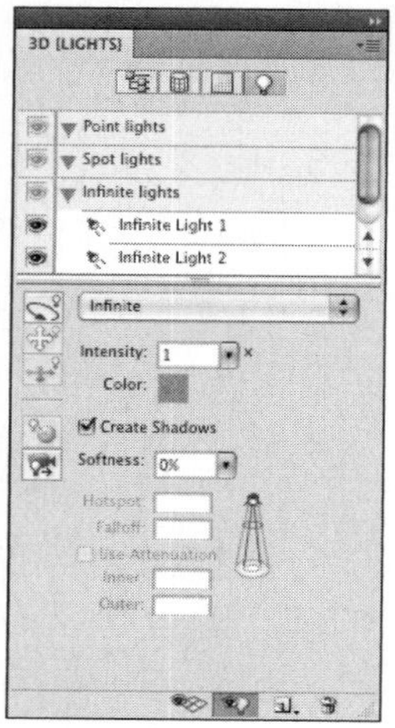

Using Light Guides

There are no physical meshes in the scene to represent lights, so although you can see their effect, you can't see the actual light sources when you render a scene, nor can you easily pick them up to move or rotate them. To help you position the lights, however, Photoshop offers Light Guides for each 3D layer.

To toggle Light Guides, make sure a light is selected in the 3D scene hierarchy, and choose Light Guides from the 3D panel's fly-out menu (see Figure 27.25). Each light in the scene is displayed using an icon that indicates what type of light it is.

Light types

There are three types of lights you can choose from in Photoshop:

- **Infinite.** The default lights that most scenes open with are infinite lights. This type of light simulates parallel rays of light coming from a given direction that maintain a consistent intensity. Photoshop doesn't let you move infinite lights, because they don't come from a single location. You can use the Rotate Light tool to change the direction the light is coming from. This option is best for simulating sunlight or the light coming into a room from a big open window.

- **Point.** Light emanates outward in all directions from a specified point in the scene. You could use a point light to simulate the light coming from a street lamp or light bulb, for example. Point lights can be moved around and placed in a specific location in a scene, but they can't be rotated. Point lights have an attenuation attribute — this is the amount by which the light's intensity decreases as you move farther away from the light source.

- **Spot.** Spotlights emanate in a conical shape from a specified source. You can point them at an object and position them anywhere in a scene.

FIGURE 27.25

Light guides help you see and position lights more accurately.

Infinite Light   Point Light   Spot Light

Setting light attributes

The controls at the bottom of the 3D panel in Lights mode allow you to perform a great deal of customization to the lights associated with a 3D layer. Here's a brief description of what's available:

- **Select an existing light and change its type by using the Light Type menu.**

- **Adjust the selected light's position and rotation with the three Transform tools available on the left of the 3D panel.** Depending on its type, you can change the angle at which the selected light hits an object using the Rotate button. Use the Drag button to move the light up and down or left and right; or Slide the light toward or away from the 3D camera.

- **Use the Point at Origin icon to orient the light so that it's pointing at the exact center of the 3D object.** If you've changed the orientation and position of the 3D camera, you can use the Move to Current View icon to bring the selected light within the current field of view.

- **You can change the selected light's color, or apply a digital "gel" to it, by clicking on the Color swatch and choosing a color from the resulting Color Picker.**

- Choose whether the selected light casts shadows using the Create Shadows check box.

- **Spot lights have hotspot and falloff attributes that work together to control the quality of the light that is cast on a surface.** The hotspot is the brightest area that's illuminated by the Spot light. The falloff refers to the angle of the outer cone of light, and it must be larger than the light's hotspot. Decreasing the size of the hotspot results in a softer-edged light, as illustrated in Figure 27.26. Increasing the size of the falloff gives the selected Spot light a bigger cone.

FIGURE 27.26

Increasing the size of the falloff produces the soft-edged light shown on the left.

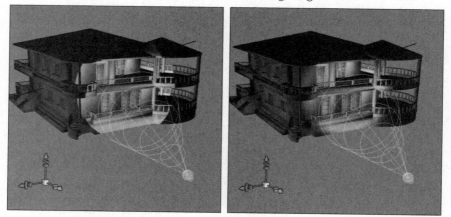

Using lighting presets

True to form, Photoshop allows you to choose from several pre-configured lighting setups by selecting Add Lights from the 3D panel's options menu, and, if necessary, navigating to the Presets/Lighting folder inside Photoshop's application folder. And, of course, you can save your own lighting configurations as a custom preset for use with different 3D layers or across Photoshop documents. Choose Save Lights Preset from the panel's options menu to save the current lights as a P3l file.

Saving 3D files

You can save your editable 3D scenes and layers in any of the file formats that support layers, including native Photoshop PSD, PSB, TIFF, and PDF. For maximum compatibility with older versions of Photoshop and other graphics software, make sure you select Always from the compatibility menu in the File Handling section of Photoshop's preferences. This at least ensures that a flattened composite version of your file is saved and can be viewed with programs that don't necessarily support Photoshop CS4's advanced 3D features.

Generating high-quality renders

When your 3D scene is ready for publishing, or to be composited with other artwork, you should generate a high-quality render of it. This produces a version of the scene with all the lights, textures, reflections, and shadows fully smoothed and anti-aliased. To generate a high-quality render of your image, choose Render for Final Output from the 3D menu. Depending on a number of factors, including your computer's processor speed, the graphics card in your machine, the complexity of the scene, the dimensions of the canvas, the number of lights in the scene, and the amount of reflections that Photoshop has to calculate, rendering the final image could take as long as an hour or more.

When the render is completed and you've given yourself a moment to appreciate your fine work, you should save a flattened version of the image and retain an editable version as your master file. Any changes to the position or camera angle of the 3D layer will erase the final render from memory, so make sure you've saved a flattened copy if you're happy with the finished product.

If you've created an animation, you have the option render each frame of the animation at the highest quality final output setting. From the Render Settings dialog box, click in the Render for Final Output checkbox.

Figure 27.27 shows the Raytraced final render of an image I put together using a model of a Ferrari I found on Google Warehouse, and a photo I took of my friend's driveway. The scene only has one infinite light, but the car is made up of over 41,000 polygons. This image took around thirty minutes to render at final output quality on my fairly recent MacBook Pro. To finish the scene, I rasterized my 3D layer to preserve the Raytraced render. The car needed a shadow under it to complete the illusion, and since I hadn't added a floor to my 3D layer, I simply created a blank layer under the car layer, and painted on it with the Brush tool.

> **NOTE** If you move or reposition something in the scene after the render has completed, you'll have to re-render it to reflect your changes.

FIGURE 27.27

A high-quality Raytraced image, complete with environment maps

Rasterize 3D layer

If you want to edit the individual pixels of a 3D layer — for example, if you want to use the Liquify tool or the Blur tool to blend portions of a 3D layer with another piece of artwork — you can flatten the 3D layer into pixels by choosing 3D ⇨ Rasterize. This removes all editability from the 3D layer, so you'll want to make sure you save a master version of your file or duplicate the 3D layer as an editable backup before applying the Rasterize command.

Exporting meshes

If you work with others in a collaborative environment, or if you want to edit your 3D objects more freely, you can export them as meshes, which can be used in 3D authoring software. Choose 3D ⇨ Export 3D Layer and make a selection from the Format menu. The available formats are the same as the ones that Photoshop can read, with the exception of 3DS, which is a closed format that software other than AutoDesk 3D Studio Max isn't allowed to write to. Give your file a name and click Save to output the file. If you've got texture maps associated with your 3D layer, Photoshop displays the dialog box shown in Figure 27.28, giving you the opportunity either to use the original file format or to specify a different format for the image files. Click OK, and Photoshop collects the object and its associated files in the selected folder.

The 3D Export Options dialog box

Summary

This chapter introduced you to some fairly advanced concepts related to 3D modeling. You learned about the 3D file formats that are supported by Photoshop CS4, and how to bring models created by 3D authoring software into Photoshop. You also learned how to create 3D objects from layered content in Photoshop. Navigating in 3D space using the View tools was covered, as was transforming and manipulating 3D objects.

You were also introduced to the concept of using texture maps to create materials for the objects in your scene. You learned about the different types of lights available in Photoshop, and about using different render modes to display your scene using differing levels of realism — from simple Wireframes to Raytraced previews with accurate reflections and shadows. Finally, you learned about different options for saving your 3D files, and you learned how to generate a full-quality image for final output.

Working with Technical Images

Photoshop's robust features make it a critical tool for professionals working in a wide range of industries. In this chapter, you'll be introduced to the advanced features that are available in the Extended version of Photoshop CS4 and that are quickly becoming indispensable to medical professionals, scientists, engineers, and architects. DICOM support makes it possible to work with images generated by medical scans. MATLAB integration allows scientists and engineers to visualize complex algorithms using Photoshop. And architects can benefit from the enhanced measuring tools that Photoshop CS4 offers.

These are complex tools, and this book is already thick enough without trying to go into detail about medical imaging or visualizing financial data, but there should be enough information here to pique the interest of casual users. Advanced users who are familiar with these concepts should also benefit, as this chapter should give you some idea as to how Photoshop can become a part of your workflow, if it isn't already.

Using DICOM Medical Scans in Photoshop

DICOM (Digital Imaging and Communications in Medicine) is a standard for storing and transmitting information generated by medical imaging devices, such as X-ray, CT, PET, magnetic resonance, and ultrasound devices. The communications part of the DICOM standard refers to its networking component: It is made for the networked hardware, such as scanners, printers, servers, and workstations with redundant backup, that form a PACS (picture archiving and communication system) used by medical facilities. A sample DICOM image is shown in Figure 28.1.

FIGURE 28.1

A DICOM scan produced by an X-ray machine

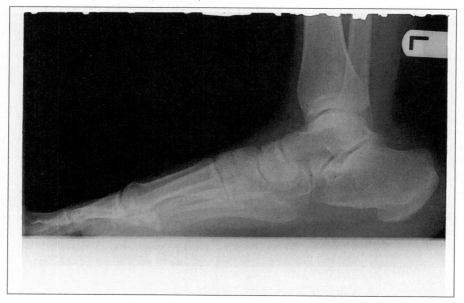

In addition to pixel data, DICOM files contain patient information, which helps to ensure that an image never gets separated from the patient it's associated with. This information is viewable in Photoshop's File Info dialog box, or in the Metadata panel in Adobe Bridge. DICOM images can also contain multiple frames, or *slices*, combining data from a multi-part scan.

Opening DICOM files in Photoshop

Using Photoshop CS4, DICOM images can be imported and edited or annotated using any of Photoshop's tools. One benefit of Photoshop's support for the format is that physicians and medical professionals are no longer tied to PACS proprietary software. Instead, they can now review, analyze, edit, and prepare images for publication using one tool.

DICOM supports 8-, 10-, 12-, or 16-bit files (though Photoshop converts 10- and 12-bit DICOM files to 16-bit images). To open a DICOM image, choose File ➪ Open. Figure 28.2 shows the resulting dialog box, which doesn't look too scary, all things considered. Here's an overview of the available options:

- **If the selected DICOM file contains multiple frames, or slices, they appear as thumbnails in the area on the left side of the dialog box.** Shift+click or Ctrl+click (⌘+click on a Mac) to select multiple frames, or click Select All to work with all the frames.

- **You can adjust the contrast of the selected frames before actually opening them.** Select the Window Level tool (the black-and-white circle in the Toolbar) and drag left or right in the preview area.

- **Choose to open multi-framed DICOM files as frames in the Animation panel, or in an N-up configuration (otherwise known as a *grid*).** Enter the number of rows and columns in which to arrange the selected frames.

  New to Photoshop CS4, you also have the option to import the selected slices as a 3-D volume, allowing you to reconstruct a scanned heart or brain, slice by slice. Use the Render Modes in the 3D panel to change the way the imported object is displayed.

- **You can quickly export the selected frame or frames as JPEG files.** Under the Export Options area, enter a prefix for the exported images' filenames, and click the Export presentation (JPEG) button. Next, navigate to a suitable location on your hard drive, and click Select.

- **You can completely remove the patient information that is contained in DICOM files before they are published.** This information is definitely there for a purpose, but if you want to remove it, place a check mark in the Anonymize box to strip out all the sensitive patient information that is included in the DICOM format's header.

FIGURE 28.2

The DICOM Import Options window

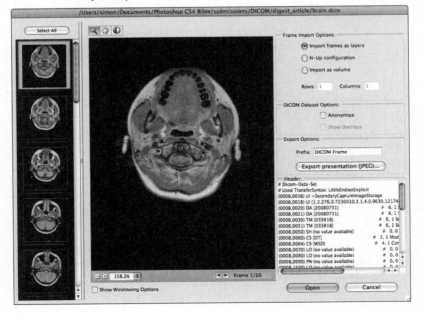

Open a DICOM image sequence

A folder full of single-frame DICOM images can also be imported as an image sequence into a video layer. This makes it possible to create an animation from a sequence of magnetic resonance scans of the heart or brain, for instance.

To open a DICOM sequence, follow these steps:

1. Choose File ⇨ Open, and navigate to a folder full of single-frame DICOM files (remember, this works best if there aren't any files that don't belong to the image sequence in the folder).

2. Select one of the files and make sure the Image Sequence check box is checked, as shown in Figure 28.3.

FIGURE 28.3

Importing single-frame DICOM files as an Image Sequence puts them into a video layer.

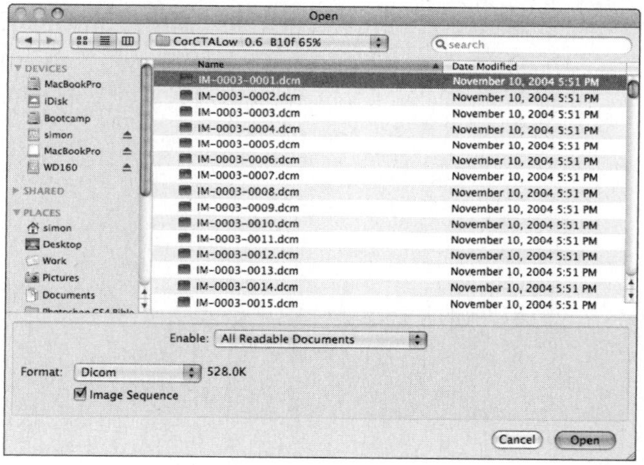

3. Enter a frame rate and click Open to place the images sequentially in a video layer, which you can then play or scrub through using the Animation panel (see Figure 28.4).

4. If the Animation panel isn't visible, choose Window ⇨ Animation to show it.

5. From there, you can use Photoshop's tools to edit or annotate individual frames, non-destructively apply filters or adjustment layers to the entire animation, and preview or export the final animation as a video file.

CROSS-REF Check out Chapter 26 for a refresher on working with video and animation in Photoshop.

FIGURE 28.4

Working with an animated DICOM image sequence

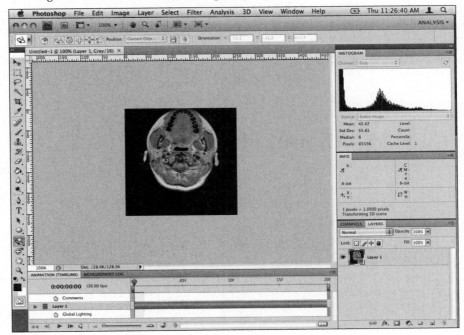

Saving DICOM files

Of course, once they've been opened in Photoshop, 8-bit DICOM files can be saved to any format that Photoshop supports. Sixteen-bit DICOM files must either be converted to 8-bit images, or saved in a format that handles high-bit-depth content, like the native Photoshop format, PSB, or TIFF — or they can simply be re-saved in the DICOM format. If you've created a file with animation, saving it in Photoshop's native format gives you the option of going back and making edits later if necessary, while final animations can be exported for video output by selecting File ➪ Export ➪ Render Video and choosing an appropriate video format.

CROSS-REF Exporting video from Photoshop is covered in Chapter 26.

When saving DICOM files, be aware that any nonstandard layers, layer effects, alpha channels, or masks will be stripped from the file, as indicated in the alert shown in Figure 28.5.

FIGURE 28.5

Any nonstandard elements will be lost when saving DICOM files that have been modified in Photoshop.

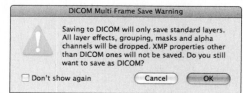

MATLAB and Photoshop

MATLAB (short for Mathematics Laboratory) is a computing environment and programming language used in engineering, scientific, and many other technical industries. MathWorks, the makers of MATLAB, describe it as follows on their Web site:

> MATLAB *is a high-level language and interactive environment that enables you to perform computationally intensive tasks faster than with traditional programming languages such as C, C++, and Fortran.*

MATLAB offers toolboxes that expand its capabilities to perform such tasks as plotting functions and algorithms, financial modeling and analysis, signal processing, technical computing, and image processing.

Photoshop integration with MATLAB was added in Photoshop CS3 Extended. This integration provides functions that allow pixels to be sent to Photoshop for manipulation, or brought into MATLAB for analysis and visualization. This capability was originally included for the benefit of professionals working in the scientific and engineering fields, but artists and designers have been taking advantage of its ability to analyze images for tasks such as generating custom color palettes.

The MATLAB software must be installed on your computer in order to take advantage of integration with Photoshop. MATLAB isn't free, and it isn't a part of the Photoshop installation, so you'd know if you had it on your computer. If you use MATLAB, most likely you're part of a workgroup or academic group, or you're a student, and you have access to the software through your educational institution.

To open the channels of communication between MATLAB and Photoshop, you must add the MATLAB folder that's in the Photoshop application folder as a path within the MATLAB environment. Follow these steps:

1. **If it's not already running, launch Photoshop CS4 Extended, and then launch MATLAB.**

2. **In MATLAB, choose File ⇨ Set Path, and from the resulting dialog box, choose Add With Subfolders.**

3. **Navigate to the Photoshop CS4/MATLAB folder on your hard drive.** This folder contains the definitions for various commands and functions that you can run from the MATLAB command line to send instructions to Photoshop.

4. **To verify that your integration of MATLAB and Photoshop is functioning correctly, from the MATLAB Desktop, set the current directory to Photoshop CS4/MATLAB/ Required/tests, and type** testall **on the command line.**

Running the command should initiate a series of 14 tests, and if everything went well, you should see a number of windows opening and closing in Photoshop. At the end of the tests, the MATLAB command line displays a message that confirms whether the tests were successfully executed.

Where do you go from here? Well, Photoshop's MATLAB folder contains several demo functions and algorithms that you can either run or view in MATLAB's script editor to get an idea of what's possible. If you're handy with scripting languages, this should be a good starting point for creating your own custom algorithms. And, MathWorks' Web site is chock-full of additional demos and examples for new users.

Enhanced Measurement and Counting

Photoshop has always provided the ability to make basic width, height, and angle measurements using the Ruler tool. With the arrival of Photoshop CS3 Extended, that measuring capability was greatly enhanced with a new suite of advanced measurement tools. Photoshop now makes it possible for professionals working with technical imagery to create a custom scale for accurate measurements of features in images, such as maps, buildings, or microscopic cells.

Select portions of an image using any of Photoshop's selection methods, and calculate the height, width, area, or perimeter of your selections. Count the number of windows in a photograph of a skyscraper, or track cellular features using the Count tool. Finally, you can record measurements and counted items using the Measurement Log panel, and export that data for use with spreadsheet programs such as Microsoft Excel.

NOTE In the spirit of sticking with a task-based workflow, you can switch to the Analysis workspace by choosing Window ⇨ Workspace menu, or click the Workspace menu at the top right of Photoshop's Application Frame.

Set measurement scale

By default, Photoshop is set to use a 1:1 scale based on pixels. When you use the Ruler tool with the Default scale, it gives you its results in pixels. This isn't particularly useful when you want to measure the length of a bridge in an aerial map or calculate the area of a cell, so the first step in recording accurate measurements is to create a measurement scale. Choose Analysis ⇨ Set Measurement Scale ⇨ Custom to produce the dialog box shown in Figure 28.6. To create a custom scale, do one of the following:

■ If you're working with a map or other image with a known scale, you can use this to set a specified number of pixels in the image equal to a known Logical Length, and then enter the name of Logical Units to work with (for example, inches, centimeters, or microns).

■ Use the overall document dimensions or a measurement from within the image to fill in the Pixel Length, Logical Length, and Logical Units. The Ruler tool automatically becomes active when you're working with the Measurement Scale dialog box, so you can take measurements from your image.

To save your custom scale as a reusable preset, click the Save Preset button in the Measurement Scale dialog box.

FIGURE 28.6

Creating a custom measurement scale

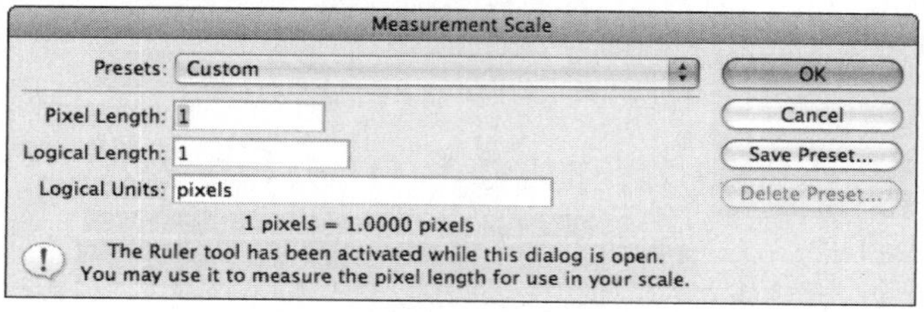

TIP   It's useful to set the Status Display at the bottom of your document window to display the current measurement scale.

The Measurement Log panel

Once you've created or selected a preset measurement scale, you can track measurements in a document, or even across multiple documents, using the Measurement Log panel (see Figure 28.7). If it isn't visible at the bottom of your document window, choose Window ➪ Measurement Log to view it. Next, either use the Ruler tool to measure a feature in the document window, or make a selection or selections with any of Photoshop's selection methods. Choose Analysis ➪ Record Measurements or click the Record Measurements button in the Measurement Log panel to add a measurement to the log. Scroll the Measurement Log to the right to view all the data points that have been recorded. Here's what you need to know about tracking measurements:

■ **Data is persistent across documents, so you can log measurements from multiple files.** The document from which the measurement was taken is included in the log.

■ **The columns of data in the Measurement Log can be customized.** Drag a column header to the left or right to rearrange its position in the panel. Ctrl+click or right-click a column header to sort its contents in ascending or descending order, or click Delete to get rid of an entire column.

- **You can export selected rows from the log to a tab-delimited text file for use with spreadsheet applications.** Select a row or rows, and then click the Export Selected Measurements icon (it's the one right next to the tiny trashcan icon) at the top of the Measurement Log. Enter a filename, and click Save.

- **Data tracked in the Measurement Log isn't saved across Photoshop sessions.** Be sure to export your logs if you need to retain that information.

FIGURE 28.7

The Measurement Log panel

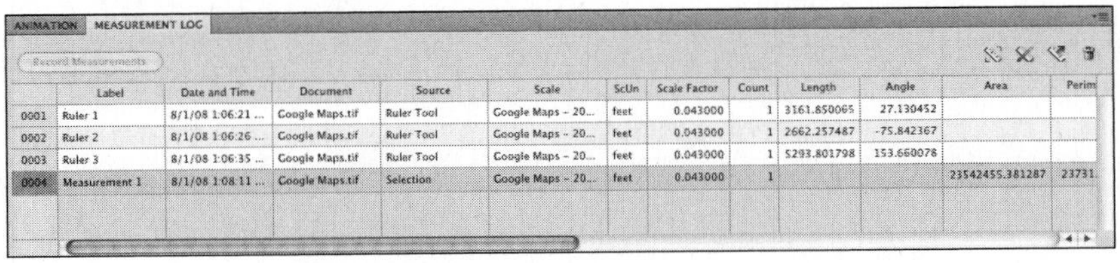

Select data points

To customize the columns of data that are recorded in the Measurement Log, choose Analysis ⇨ Select Data Points. By default, all data points are selected, as shown in Figure 28.8. However, even if all the data points are selected, the types of data that are recorded depend on the currently selected measuring tool. For instance, the Ruler tool records only length, angle, and height. On the other hand, data recorded when portions of an image are selected using one of Photoshop's various selection methods includes area, perimeter, number of pixels, and average gray value of the selection or selections.

Speaking of which, if you record a measurement from multiple selections, one entry is placed in the log containing comprehensive information for all the selected areas, and an additional entry is placed in the log for each of the individual selected areas.

> **TIP** Once you've selected a custom group of data points, you can save that group as a preset for later use.

Add a scale marker

To include a graphic indicating the scale that was used to record measurements for a document, choose Analysis ⇨ Place Scale Marker. Customize the options available in the Measurement Scale Marker window (see Figure 28.9), and click OK to place the marker in a new layer group in your document. You can then use the Move tool to reposition the scale marker as necessary.

FIGURE 28.8

Customize the data points to specify which columns of data are shown in the Measurement Log.

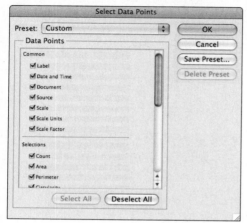

TIP   If you change your measurement scale after you place a scale marker, Photoshop is smart enough to alert you that your scale marker may have become invalid, and it offers to remove it.

FIGURE 28.9

Specify options for the font and color of your scale marker using the options shown here.

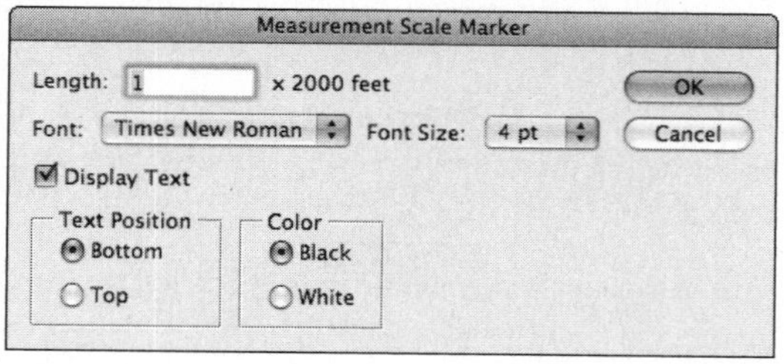

Counting

Use the Count tool to track features or objects in technical images. Clicking in an image with the Count tool overlays a numerical marker on top of each counted feature, as illustrated in Figure 28.10.

Select the Count tool from the Toolbox (it's grouped with the Eyedropper tool) or from the Analysis menu, and click on each object that you want to count. To remove a count number, Alt+click/Option+click on it. This updates the total number of counted items. Move existing count numbers by hovering your cursor over the marker until it turns into a four-way arrow, and then drag the marker to a new location. Click the Record Measurements button or press Shift+Ctrl+M/ Shift+⌘+M to add the counted items to the Measurement Log.

Be aware that count information added to the Measurement Log isn't updated if you add or delete count numbers after the fact — if you add to your current count data, you'll have to record it as a new measurement.

You can also show or hide count numbers by clicking the eyeball icon in the Options Bar, or by choosing View➪Show➪Count. You can also create multiple count groups and set the color and size of the markers and their labels.

Saving your document in a format like PSD or TIFF, which supports Photoshop's extra features, retains your count numbers or groups.

TIP Automatically count features in an image by selecting them using the Quick Select, Lasso, Marquee, or other selection methods, and then adding them to the Measurement Log, as described in the previous section.

FIGURE 28.10

The Count tool overlays a number for each counted feature in an image. Click the Record Measurements button to add counted features to the Measurement Log.

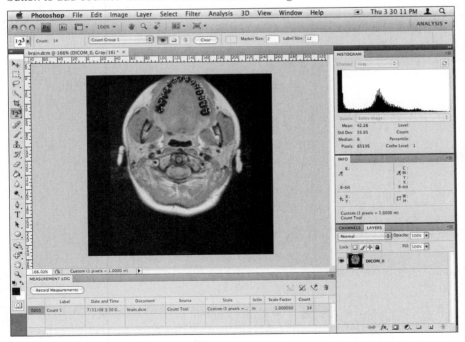

Summary

This chapter provided you with an overview of some of the advanced features geared toward the segment of Photoshop users who work in medical, technical, and scientific fields. You learned about the DICOM medical imaging format and how to work with these images in Photoshop.

You also learned about MATLAB and how this computing environment can be used to "drive" Photoshop to produce images and analyze pixels. Finally, you learned about the enhanced measurement tools that Photoshop provides for use with technical imagery.

Part IX

Appendixes

Appendix A

Charts

This section covers useful functionalities and information that can help streamline your Photoshop experience and improve your workflows. Included are commonly used keyboard shortcuts, a list of commonly used file formats, their purpose and extension, as well as information about popular color modes and color working spaces.

IN THIS APPENDIX

Popular keyboard shortcuts

Popular file formats

Color modes and working spaces

Popular Keyboard Shortcuts

While they may take a little getting used to, anyone with extensive Photoshop experience can vouch for the usefulness of knowing by heart some of the most commonly used Photoshop shortcuts. Most people find that a quick tapping of the keyboard produces more efficient results for some options than using a mouse and menu. Once you get accustomed to using shortcuts, you'll wonder why you didn't use them from the start!

Table A.1 details some of the most commonly used (default) shortcuts. Note that all Toolbar and menu shortcuts found in Photoshop CS4 Standard are also found in Photoshop CS4 Extended, while the extra tools found in the Extended edition are not found in the Standard edition (see Table A.2).

Table A.3 lists some popular menu command shortcuts.

TABLE A.1

Standard Toolbar Shortcuts

Photoshop CS4 Standard Toolbar	Mac Shortcut	PC Shortcut
Move tool	V	V
Rectangular Marquee tool	M	M
Cycle Marquee tools	Shift+M	Shift+M
Lasso tool	L	L
Cycle Lasso tools	Shift+L	Shift+L
Quick Selection tools	W	Q
Cycle Quick Selection, Magic Wand tools	Shift+W	Shift+W
Crop tool	C	C
Cycle Crop, Slice tools	Shift+C	Shift+C
Eyedropper tool	I	I
Cycle Eyedropper, Color Sampler, Ruler, Note tools	Shift+I	Shift+I
Spot Healing Brush	J	J
Cycle Spot Healing Brush, Healing Brush, Patch, and Red Eye tools	Shift+J	Shift+J
Brush tool	B	B
Cycle Brush, Pencil, and Color Replacement tools	Shift+B	Shift+B
Clone Stamp tool	S	S
Cycle Clone Stamp, Pattern Stamp tools	Shift+S	Shift+S
History Brush tool	Y	Y
Cycle History Brush, Art History Brush tools	Shift+Y	Shift+Y
Eraser tool	E	E

Photoshop CS4 Standard Toolbar	Mac Shortcut	PC Shortcut
Cycle Eraser, Background Eraser, and Magic Eraser tools	Shift+E	Shift+E
Gradient tool	G	G
Cycle Gradient, Paint Bucket tools	Shift+G	Shift+G
Blur, Smudge, Sharpen tools	No default shortcut	No default shortcut
Dodge tool	O	O
Cycle Dodge, Burn, Sponge tools	Shift+O	Shift+O
Pen tool	P	P
Cycle Pen, Freeform Pen tools	Shift+P	Shift+P
Add, Delete, Convert Anchor Point tools	No default shortcut	No default shortcut
Horizontal Type tool	T	T
Cycle Horizontal Type, Vertical Type, Horizontal Type Mask, Vertical Type Mask tools	Shift+T	Shift+T
Path Selection tool	A	A
Cycle Path Selection, Direct Selection tools	Shift+A	Shift+A
Rectangle tool	U	U
Cycle Rectangle, Rounded Rectangle, Ellipse, Polygon, Line, Custom Shape tools	Shift+U	Shift+U
Hand tool	H+spacebar	H+spacebar
Rotate tool	R	R
Zoom tool	Z	Z
Swap Foreground, Background Color	X	X
Swap Foreground, Background Colors to Black and White	D	D
Edit in Quick Mask Mode	Q	Q

TABLE A.2

Extended Toolbar Shortcuts

Photoshop CS4 Extended Tools	Mac Shortcut	PC Shortcut
Count tool	I	I
3-D Rotate tool	K	K
Cycle 3-D Rotate, 3-D Roll, 3-D Pan, 3-D Slide, 3-D Scale tools	Shift+K	Shift+K
3-D Orbit tool	N	N
Cycle 3-D Orbit, 3-D Roll View, 3-D Pan View, 3-D Walk View, 3-D Zoom tools	Shift+N	Shift+N

TABLE A.3

Popular Menu Command Shortcuts

Popular Menu Command Defaults	Mac Shortcut	PC Shortcut
New Document	⌘+N	Ctrl+N
Open Document	⌘+O	Ctrl+O
Browse in Bridge	⌘+Option+O	Ctrl+Alt+O
Close Document	⌘+W	Ctrl+W
Print Document	⌘+P	Ctrl+P
Undo	⌘+Z	Ctrl+Z
Step Forward	⌘+Shift+Z	Ctrl+Shift+Z
Step Backward	⌘+Shift+F	Ctrl+Shift+F
Fade...	⌘+Shift+F	Ctrl+Shift+F
Fill...	Shift+F5	Shift+F5
Free Transform	⌘+T	Ctrl+T
Color Settings...	⌘+Shift+K	Ctrl+Shift+K
Image Size...	⌘+Option+I	Ctrl+Alt+I
Canvas Size...	⌘+Option+C	Ctrl+Alt+C
Levels...	⌘+L	Ctrl+L
Curves...	⌘+M	Ctrl+M
Hue & Saturation...	⌘+U	Ctrl+U
Color Balance...	⌘+B	Ctrl+B
New Layer	⌘+Shift+N	Ctrl+Shift+N
New Layer via Copy	⌘+J	Ctrl+J

Popular Menu Command Defaults	Mac Shortcut	PC Shortcut
Group Layers	⌘+G	Ctrl+G
Merge Layers	⌘+E	Ctrl+E
Select All	⌘+A	Ctrl+A
Deselect All	⌘+D	Ctrl+D
Inverse (Selection)	⌘+Shift+I	Ctrl+Shift+I
Refine Edge…	⌘+Option+R	Ctrl+Alt+R
Last Filter	⌘+F	Ctrl+F
Proof Colors	⌘+Y	Ctrl+Y
Gamut Warning	⌘+Shift+Y	Ctrl+Shift+Y
Zoom in	⌘+plus(+)	Ctrl+plus(+)
Zoom out	⌘+minus(-)	Ctrl+minus(-)
Fit on Screen	⌘+0	Ctrl+0
(show) Actual Pixels	⌘+1	Ctrl+1
Show-Hide Extras	⌘+H	Ctrl+H
Rulers	⌘+R	Ctrl+R
Brushes Panel	F5	F5
Layers Panel	F7	F7
Info Panel	F8	F8
Photoshop Help	⌘+/	Ctrl+/
Increase Brush Diameter	]	]
Decrease Brush Diameter	[	[
Increase Brush Hardness	Shift+]	Shift+]
Decrease Brush Hardness	Shift+[	Shift+[

Popular File Formats

Most Photoshop users know about formats like JPEG, used as the standard image format in many cameras and also as the standard picture format for the Web, but there are other commonly used Photoshop formats that are not as obvious in their purpose.

Table A.4 lists several commonly used Photoshop file formats, their file extension, and any specialized uses that may be applicable. For most purposes, the native PSD Photoshop file format can be the most versatile and reliable, but it is a good idea to have a basic understanding of the other formats. For example, you may have a client who has requested a particular format. Knowing which formats serve which purposes can help you to provide your client with valuable advice that may save you both some time and trouble.

TABLE A.4

Commonly Used File Formats

File Type Name	Extension	Background and Usage
Photoshop	.psd	Photoshop's native, uncompressed raster image format. Useful in the following workflows: retouching, compositing, graphic design, Web design, video, 3-D.
TIFF	.tif	Tagged Image File Format. More widely compatible than .psd but not as versatile. Used mainly for retouching, compositing, and graphic design.
EPS	.eps	Encapsulated Post-Script file. Widely used vector illustration format. It's primarily used to swap design elements between Photoshop and illustration and page layout programs, such as Illustrator and InDesign.
TARGA	.tga	Specialized raster image format widely used by professionals in the video post-production and motion graphics world.
Radiance	.hdr	Specialized raster format designed for 32-bit, HDR (High Dynamic Range) imaging.
DNG	.dng	Digital Negative file. Used as an alternative to storing and processing your RAW files in a proprietary camera format. DNG is a stable-definition, open-source format and, unlike manufacturer formats, does not change in its inner-makeup often.

Color Modes and Working Spaces

It is important to not confuse color modes with color spaces. The former defines the general color model being leveraged as part of your current workflow, while the latter describes a specific set of color instructions that fall within that color model. The following sections describe some of the most common color modes and several common color spaces and their typical uses.

RGB mode

RGB stands for Red, Green, Blue. This color mode is used by all monitors, and works by combining specific amounts of red, green, and blue per pixel to create an image. It is designed for mediums that project rather than reflect light. Also called *additive color*, because the more red, green, and blue you add together, the closer the displayed value gets to pure white.

It is generally a good idea to edit raster images in RGB mode whenever possible, unless the image was provided to you in CMYK mode and is destined for press output, in which case it is better to leave the image in CMYK mode as you edit.

CMYK mode

CMYK stands for Cyan, Magenta, Yellow, Black. This is the color model used by four-color printing presses and is also the basis for inkjet printing systems. It is designed for physical mediums like paper. Its colors are created when certain components of light are absorbed (or subtracted) by the physical medium; the remaining colors that we see are those that were reflected. For this reason CMYK is often called "subtractive color."

Keep in mind that even if you are editing a file in CMYK mode, you are still looking at an RGB interpretation of those CMYK colors.

Lab mode

This is a color model designed to mimic the limits of human color perception. Unlike RGB and CMYK, which merely express instructions for reproducing a certain color, Lab mode describes — in computer terms — what a color is supposed to look like. Lab is sometimes called *device independent color*, or at least that's the goal.

This may seem like a strange distinction, and in general, using Lab color is not an intuitive process. Lab is broken into three channels: Lightness (L), Red/Green (a*), and Blue/Yellow (b*). That means, for example, that for each curve movement in the a or b channel, you are actually affecting two color variables instead of just one.

L*a*b* has its own color space, called CIELAB, that is used by Photoshop to translate images from RGB to CMYK mode and vice versa.

Adobe RGB 1998

Adobe RGB 1998 is very frequently used as an editing space by retouching and graphics pros because it contains nearly 100 percent of the popular SWOP v2 and Sheetfed Coated v2 CMYK color spaces. This means there should be fewer color clipping issues when printing the CMYK version of your original image, versus starting with smaller RGB spaces during the editing process.

High-end LCD monitors designed for graphics pros use the ability to reproduce 100 percent of the Adobe RGB color space as their benchmark. Many of these achieve between 92 and 95 percent reproduction of the Adobe RGB space.

sRGB

sRGB is the native working space for JPEG images, and in turn for photos destined for the Web. It has a much smaller gamut (or range of colors) within it than Adobe RGB.

Do not use sRGB as your editing space unless the image was originally captured as an sRGB file, only needs minor corrections and is intended for display output versus printed output.

ProPhoto RGB

This is a wide-gamut color space designed to maximize high-quality photographic prints. ProPhoto contains many colors in its gamut that are within the capabilities of expensive inkjet printing systems, but that are outside the Adobe RGB gamut.

Best used in closed-loop situations, with 16-bit images that are edited on one computer using a calibrated, high-end LCD, and subsequently printed on a high-end inkjet printer.

Because ProPhoto RGB contains many colors that fall outside the capability of four-color printing presses, ProPhoto is not a good starting point for most images destined for CMYK.

ColorMatch RGB and Apple RGB

Both of these are outdated color spaces with relatively small gamuts. They're only a good choice when you're dealing with legacy images that were originally edited in these spaces.

U.S. Web Coated (SWOP) v2

This is the de facto standard in the U.S. and Canada for images that are destined for high-volume, high-quality print runs, and it is often used by magazines with very large circulations.

U.S. Sheetfed Coated v2

This is the de facto standard for images destined for sheetfed printing presses in the U.S. and Canada that use coated paper types. It is commonly used for magazines that require high-quality photographic reproduction (such as fashion magazines).

U.S. Web Uncoated v2

This is commonly used on images that are destined for newspapers and other very high-volume projects, but that do not require coated paper for higher-quality photographic reproduction.

U.S. Sheetfed Uncoated v2

This is commonly used on image-based projects that are suited to sheetfed presses, such as newsletters, but that do not require large print runs or high-quality photo reproduction.

Appendix B

Professional Resources

Professional Organizations

- www.photoshopuser.com

  The leading organization for Photoshop professionals, the National Association of Photoshop Professionals (NAPP) offers a wealth of information, tutorials, freebies, an expert help desk, employment listings, and some so-so discounts for members. *Photoshop User* magazine is a great resource with timely Photoshop news and articles, and all members receive it bimonthly.

  NAPP's reasonably priced membership is worth the magazine alone. NAPP is the organizer of the world's top Photoshop conference: Photoshop World, www.photoshopworld.com. NAPP members receive a significant Photoshop World conference discount.

Certification

- www.adobe.com/support/certification

  Find information on becoming an Adobe Certified Associate, Expert, or Instructor; information about the Training Center is also available.

Training and Conferences

- www.photoshopworld.com

  The world's top Photoshop conference, Photoshop World, is usually held twice a year, once on the East Coast, once on the West Coast. Organizer: NAPP. NAPP members receive a significant Photoshop World conference discount.

- www.adobe.com/training

  Search for Adobe Certified Instructors and Adobe Authorized Training Centers in your area.

- www.mydamnchannel.com

  You Suck at Photoshop videos is also on YouTube.

- www.lynda.com

  Online training library, educator resources, and more.

- www.adimconference.com

  Annual Art Directors Invitational Master Class. Hands-on, multi-day instructional course for using Adobe software.

- www.andersonranch.org

  Anderson Ranch Arts Center. Art and digital media workshops, events. Snowmass Village, near Aspen, Colorado.

- www.sfworkshop.com

  Santa Fe Photographic Workshops. Santa Fe, New Mexico, and travel workshops in numerous countries.

Help

- www.adobe.com/support/photoshop

  Up-to-date help resource for Photoshop.

- www.adobe.com/designcenter/video_workshop/

  Video tutorials for Photoshop and other Adobe software.

- www.photoshopuser.com

  National Association of Photoshop Professionals (NAPP). Video tutorials, articles, help desk.

- www.photoshoptips.net

  Video tutorials, help, articles.

General Info Resources

- `www.photoshopnews.com`

  The latest news about Photoshop. Links and other professional resources.

- `www.creativepro.com`

  News, articles, reviews.

- `www.macworld.com`

  News, articles, reviews.

- `www.retouchpro.com`

  Web community for retouchers. Retouch challenges.

- `www.digitaldog.net`

  Color management, Photoshop, and digital imaging information.

- `www.colorremedies.com`

  Color management information.

- `istockphoto.com`

  Good stock photo and art service, reasonably priced. Sell your own work, too.

- `stock-photography-service-review.toptenreviews.com/`

  2008 Stock Photography Services Review.

- `www.pricegrabber.com`

  Search many stores for best prices on any kind of equipment you need to work with Photoshop.

Freebies

- `www.adobe.com/cfusion/exchange/index.cfm`

  Hundreds of extensions, time-saving functions, code, and more.

- `www.photoshopuser.com`

  Members of NAPP have access to many Photoshop freebies, such as shapes and custom brushes.

- `www.brushes.obsidiandawn.com`

  Free custom Photoshop brushes and more.

- `www.sxc.hu/`

  Stock.XCHNG, free stock photography.

- `www.versiontracker.com`

  Software including freeware and shareware.

Appendix C

What's on the CD?

This appendix provides you with information on the contents of the CD that accompanies this book. For the latest and greatest information, please refer to the ReadMe file located at the root of the CD.

System Requirements

Make sure that your computer meets the minimum system requirements listed in this section. If your computer doesn't match up to most of these requirements, you may have a problem using the contents of the CD:

- PC running Windows 98 or later or a Macintosh running Mac OS X or later
- A CD-ROM drive

Using the CD

To access the content from the CD, follow these steps:

1. **Insert the CD into your computer's CD-ROM drive.** The license agreement appears.

   Note to Windows users: The interface won't launch if you have autorun disabled. In that case, choose Start ➪ Run (for Windows Vista, Start ➪ All Programs ➪ Accessories ➪ Run). In the dialog box that appears, type **D:\Start.exe**. (Replace D with the proper letter if your CD drive uses a different letter. If you don't know the letter, see how your CD drive is listed under My Computer.) Click OK.

2. **Read through the license agreement and then click the Accept button if you want to use the CD.** The CD interface appears. The interface allows you to install the programs and run the demos with just a click of a button (or two).

What's on the CD

Many of the images used in the book are found on the CD, in folders, by chapters. You can use these images to practice the techniques covered in the book. The folders are labeled as follows:

- Ch03
- Ch04
- Ch06
- Ch07
- Ch08
- Ch13
- Ch14
- Ch15
- Ch16
- Ch17
- Ch19
- Ch20
- Ch21
- Ch23
- Ch24

The complete text of this book is also available on the CD in Adobe's Portable Document Format (PDF). You can read and search through the file with the Adobe Acrobat Reader (also included on the CD). This file cannot be printed.

Troubleshooting

If you have difficulty installing or using any of the materials on the companion CD, try the following solutions:

- **Turn off any antivirus software that you may have running.** Installers sometimes mimic virus activity and can make your computer incorrectly believe that it is being infected by a virus. (Be sure to turn the antivirus software back on later.)

- **Close all running programs.** The more programs you're running, the less memory is available to other programs. Installers also typically update files and programs; if you keep other programs running, installation may not work properly.

- **Reference the ReadMe:** Please refer to the ReadMe file located at the root of the CD-ROM for the latest product information at the time of publication.

Customer Care

If you have trouble with the CD-ROM, please call the Wiley Product Technical Support phone number at (800) 762-2974. Outside the United States, call 1(317) 572-3994. You can also contact Wiley Product Technical Support at `http://support.wiley.com`. John Wiley & Sons will provide technical support only for installation and other general quality control items. For technical support on the applications themselves, consult the program's vendor or author.

To place additional orders or to request information about other Wiley products, please call (877) 762-2974.

Index

Symbols and Numerics

A

B

Z

ZigZag filter, 709–710
ZIP compression, 198
ZIP files, loading, 29
Zipit software, 29
Zoom Clicked Point to Center, 62
Zoom Resizes Window, 62
Zoom tool, 95–96, 133, 591
Zoom with Scroll Window, 62
Zoomify plug-in, 789–790

zooming
3D camera, 876
Camera Raw, 133
centering the zoomed window, 62
image windows, 54, 62
images, 95–96
lens correction, 591
with mouse scroll wheel, 62
smoothing, 54